MW00789206

Managing to Optimize the Beneficial Outcomes of Recreation

Managing to Optimize the Beneficial Outcomes of Recreation

edited by

B. L. Driver

Venture Publishing, Inc.
State College, Pennsylvania

Venture Publishing, Inc.
1999 Cato Avenue
State College, PA 16801
Phone 814–234-4561
Fax 814–234-1651

Manuscript Editing: George W. Lauer, Richard Yocum
Production Manager: Richard Yocum
Cover Design: George W. Lauer

Library of Congress Catalogue Card Number: 2008942616
ISBN-10: 1-892132-83-4
ISBN-13: 978-1-892132-83-3

Table of Contents

Chapter 3

Chapter 4

Chapter 5

Chapter 6

Chapter 7

Chapter 8

Chapter 9

Chapter 10

Chapter 15

Chapter 16

Chapter 17

Chapter 18

Chapter 19

Chapter 20

Chapter 21

Chapter 22

Chapter 23

Chapter 24

Chapter 25

Acknowledgements

Work on this text stretched over a two-year period. During that time, thirty eight talented and dedicated people wrote the introductory endorsements and most of the chapters. Each of those contributions is greatly appreciated.

This is the fifth text on which I have worked with Venture Publishing, Inc. as a lead author or editor. It has been a positive and rewarding experience every time, and this text would not have been developed and published without Venture's continued support of the "benefits movement." Rich Yocum and his talented editorial staff have been extremely helpful and a pleasure with whom to work.

For many decades, many administrators, managers, and planners with public park and recreation agencies have supported and contributed to the "benefits movement." In addition, many leisure scientists and academics have helped advance the science-based knowledge about the benefits of leisure and helped define and refine the requirements for applying and implementing the outcomes approach in recreation policy development and management. The efforts of those many people have given the outcomes approach applied and scientific credibility, made it more understandable and acceptable. This text would not have been possible without their contributions.

Thanks also to my wife Susan for her support and understanding. B. L. D.

Author Biographies

Allen, Lawrence R. is the Dean of the College of Health, Education, and Human Development at Clemson University, where he was previously the Head of the Department of Parks, Recreation, and Tourism Management. He has written extensively on the role of parks and recreation in human and community development with a focus on benefits-based programming and management. He is a member of the Academy of Leisure Sciences and the American Academy of Park and Recreation Administration.

Anderson, Dorothy H. is Professor and Department Head of Parks Recreation and Tourism Management at North Carolina State University. Prior to joining North Carolina State University, she was Distinguished Professor of Recreation Resource Management at University of Minnesota in the Department of Forest Resources. For more than 30 years, she has been involved in research on the human dimensions of natural resource management. Her research over the last 15 years has focused on identifying visitor and community benefits resulting from public land management and relationships between the influence of community members' attachment to special places and trust in agency management and attainment of community benefits. She is a member of the International Union of Forest Research Organizations and serves as a deputy coordinator for forest recreation, landscape, and nature conservation. She is also a member of the International Association for Society and Natural Resources and the Society of American Foresters.

Arkins, John was the outdoor recreation planner for the BLM's Gunnison Gorge National Conservation Area. John started his BLM career as a River Ranger in the Gunnison Gorge in 1990. He relocated to Kremmling, Colorado for a permanent Outdoor Recreation Planner position managing the BLM's Upper Colorado River Special Recreation Management Area. In 2005, John returned to the Gunnison Gorge.

Booth, Kay is a private consultant in New Zealand, specializing in parks, recreation, and tourism research and planning. As an academic at Lincoln University for 13 years, she led the parks and recreation management program prior to which she was a social scientist with the New Zealand Department of Conservation. She has worked on several projects assessing OFM/BBM for the Department of Conservation, including its current application within the Rakiura National Park management planning process. Kay holds governmental appointments with the New Zealand Conservation Authority and the New Zealand Geographic Board.

Brown, Perry is Dean and Professor, College of Forestry and Conservation, and Director of the Montana Forest and Conservation Experiment Station, at the University of Montana-Missoula. He has widely recognized expertise in natural resource social science, policy and planning, recreation behavior, and wilderness studies. A life-long westerner, he has served on the faculties of Utah State University, Colorado State University, and Oregon State University in addition to his current assignment in Montana. He has served in formal advisory appointments with both the USDA Forest Service and the USDI Bureau of Land Management, and has served as chair or on the executive/advisory committees of many national and international organizations, such as the National Association of University Forest Resources Programs, the National Research Council's Committee on Forestry Research Capacity, the Pinchot Institute's National Panel on Wilderness Stewardship, the International Union for Forest Research Organizations, the Ecosystem Management Research Institute (a private nonprofit research institute), the National Forest Foundation, the National Forest Service Historical Museum, and the Rocky Mountains Cooperative Ecosystem Studies Unit. He has authored or coauthored over 100 scientific publications and has mentored 49 masters and 11 Ph.D. students.

Bruns, Don is the recreation program lead for the Bureau of Land Management's Colorado State Office in Lakewood, Colorado. He has been very influential in helping develop and refine BBM and document its requirements. He has played a key role in training others how to apply BBM and has been actively involved in applications of BBM in the United States and several other countries.

Davenport, Mae A. is an Assistant Professor and co-leader of the Human Dimensions Research Unit in the Department of Forestry at Southern Illinois University. Her research explores relationships residents have with nearby protected areas and natural landscapes. She is currently developing a Community Partnership Handbook for natural resource managers and community leaders in southern Illinois to promote citizen support for and engagement in ecosystem restoration initiatives. She is a member of International Union of Forest Research Organizations, serving as deputy coordinator in the Landscape Planning and Management Working Group. She is also a member of the International Association for Society and Natural Resources, Society of American Foresters, and American Planning Association.

Driver, B. L. is a retired leisure scientist and the author or coauthor of over 200 scientific and technology-transfer publications as well as the author, coauthor, editor, or co-editor of five texts prior to this one. He has held faculty appointments at The University of Michigan and Yale University, along with faculty affiliate appointments at Colorado State University and the University of Wyoming, and has chaired at least 20 doctoral and 20 master's degree committees. From 1982 until 1993, he directed the Recreation Research Project of the USDA Forest Service's Rocky Mountain Research Station, and served as a scientist on such until 1997. For over 35 years, he studied the benefits of leisure and helped develop and refine five recreation resource management systems (including OFM) that have received wide application in the U.S. and other countries. He has visited over 30 of those countries professionally and is the recipient of over a dozen rather significant awards for his research and applied efforts. But he still burps occasionally!

Edginton, Michael is the recreation manager for the New Zealand Department of Conservation, where he has been involved in recreation management since the Department was formed in 1987. His roles have included regional and strategic planning for recreation, and the development and implementation of the Department's national asset management systems for outdoor recreation sites and facilities. His work has taken him to Asian and Pacific countries where he has been involved in the development of national parks and community conservation programs.

Fulton, David C. is a U.S. Geological Survey research scientist and Assistant Unit Leader in the Minnesota Cooperative Fish & Wildlife Research Unit. He is also an adjunct associate professor in the Fisheries, Wildlife, and Conservation Biology Department at the University of Minnesota. He received a Ph.D. in the Human Dimensions of Natural Resources at Colorado State University. Prior to arriving at Minnesota he worked as a regional planner and human dimensions of wildlife researcher for Alaska Department of Fish and Game. His current research is focused largely on the recreational management of fisheries and wildlife for the benefit of hunters and anglers, as well as achieving biological objectives of resource management. He has conducted dozens of research projects with the Minnesota Department of Natural Resources, the U.S. Fish and Wildlife Service, and the National Park Service addressing both recreation management and conflict associated with managing fisheries and wildlife resources.

Hopkins, Brian is the community planner for the BLM's Glenwood Springs Field Office in Glenwood Springs, Colorado. He received a bachelor's degree in Resource Management from Slippery Rock University in Pennsylvania. He has played a key role in training others how to apply BBM, and teaches Recreation Planning: Effective Engagement in BLM's Land Use Planning Process for the BLM. He has been actively involved in several applications of BBM/OFM in the BLM.

Jaten, Allen is Director of the USDA Forest Service's Recreation and Heritage Resources Integrated Business Service Center. He is that agency's lead for the recreation facility master planning project that uses a variety of customer preference, demographic, and analysis instruments to better facilitate users' connection with desired experiences and the recreation settings on which they depend. He was a member of the team charged with designing the implementation strategy of OFM (then BBM) for the USFS. He also designed the measures needed to meet the recreation-related strategic planning objectives of the agency. Before joining the USFS, Allen worked with the Maricopa County Regional Parks system in Phoenix, AZ for nine years and was on the faculty at Arizona State University for eight years teaching courses and conducting research on outdoor recreation.

Knopf, Richard, C. is the Associate Dean for Community Initiatives and the Director of the Partnership for Community Development at Arizona State University. Much of his research has focused on the role of parks, recreation, and tourism in community development, life quality enhancement, and economic growth. His specialty areas include: strategic planning, survey research, program evaluation, public involvement, public recreation program design and management, tourism marketing and promotion, community building, and citizen involvement in public policy formation.

Leahy, Jessica E. is an Assistant Professor of Parks, Recreation, and Tourism at the University of Maine. Her research focuses on environmental and forestry communication issues related to resource-dependent communities, small woodland owners, and the general public. She serves as a deputy for the Nature Conservation and Protected Areas Working Group of the International Union of Forest Research Organizations and as a chair of the Social and Related Sciences Working Group of the New England Society of American Foresters, and she is also a member of the International Association for Society and Natural Resources and the National Association for Interpretation.

Lee, Marty is a Professor in the School of Forestry at Northern Arizona University where she teaches undergraduate and graduate classes in the human dimensions of ecosystem management including wildland recreation management and planning, multicultural perspectives of natural resource management, and wilderness management. She has more than 20 years experience conducting research on recreation use and users including their preferences for management, desired recreation settings, experiences, and benefits. She has collaborated with managers of the U.S. Forest Service, National Park Service, Bureau of Land Management, and Arizona Game and Fish on funded research projects, class projects, and as an informal consultant.

Lewis, Darrell, E. is the retired Chief, Natural Resources Management Branch, Operations Division, Civil Works Directorate, Headquarters, U.S. Army Corps of Engineers. Before then, he was Chief, Recreation and Cultural Resource Division of the USDI Bureau of Land Management. He is on the Board of Directors of the Corps of Engineers Natural Resources Education Foundation.

Manfredo, Michael J. is Head of the Departments of Human Dimensions of Natural Resources and Forest, Rangeland and Watershed Stewardship at Colorado State University. His teaching and outreach activities focus on the role of social science in natural resource management. His theoretical focus is on attitudes, values, and macro-micro models to explain shifting cognitions about natural resources. He has published over 75 peer-reviewed articles in a wide variety of natural resource journals. He was the founding co-editor of the journal *Human Dimensions of Wildlife*. He recently coedited his third book and is currently taking the lead on two other books. Mike has also has been principal investigator of over 75 research projects with funds primarily obtained from fish, wildlife, and land management agencies.

Marans, Robert W. is a registered architect, holds a doctorate in urban and regional planning, is a research professor in the University of Michigan's Institute of Social Research, and professor emeritus in the College of Architecture and Urban Planning. During the past 30 years, his research interests have included quality of community life indicators, neighborhood and housing planning, community development, recreation resource planning and management, and behavioral aspects of energy conservation. He is the author or coauthor of seven books and more than 100 technical articles and reports. He is a charter member of the Washtenaw County [Michigan] Parks and Recreation Commission and a Commissioner of the Huron-Clinton Metropolitan [Regional Parks] Authority in southeastern Michigan. He has lectured, in several countries in Europe, Asia, South America, and the Middle East as well as at many locations in the United States.

Nilsen, Per is a Special Advisor to the Chief Administrative Officer, Parks Canada Agency. Before that he was the Acting Chief of Ecosystem Protection within the Ecological Integrity Branch of the National Parks Directorate, Parks Canada Agency. After graduating from the University of Waterloo with a Master's Degree in Recreation, he began his career with Parks Canada by working closely with Grant Tayler and others in the development and implementation of the Visitor Activity Management Process. Over the last 20 years, he has been influential in advancing the understanding and application of Outcomes-Focused Management within Parks Canada through various projects, publications, and policy initiatives. He has worked closely with colleagues in Canada, and in the United States, Australia, and Argentina by sharing best practices and promoting an integrated approach to park and recreation planning and management, and with others in the development and implementation of the Visitor Activity Management Process.

O'Sullivan, Ellen L. is professor Emeritus of Southern Connecticut State University serves as principal of Leisure Lifestyle Consulting. Ellen was the lead trainer for the Hearts N' Park initiative, a successful partnership among the National Institutes of Health, the National Recreation and Park Association (NRPA), and local park and recreation departments across the country. O'Sullivan, recipient of the Sutherland Practitioner Award from the Academy of Park and Recreation Administration and the Distinguished Professional Award from NRPA, wrote two marketing textbooks for the field and two benefits-based publications for the NRPA.

Overbaugh, Bill is the Recreation Program Leader for the Bureau of Land Management in Alaska that administers 90 million acres of public lands and waters. National and international work include serving as Chair of the Bureau's Recreation & Visitor Service Advisory Team and protected area management efforts in Mexico and Russia. He received Bachelor and Master Degrees from the Universities of Michigan and New Mexico, respectively, and is currently a Ph.D. Candidate at the University of Alaska studying Recreation Benefit Outcomes for Improving Community Resilience. When not at work or school, he can be found with his family sea kayaking, rafting, biking, and skiing in the Alaska backcountry.

Peck, Paul is Manager of the McInnis Canyons National Conservation Area that is administered by the Grand Junction (Colorado) Field Office of the Bureau of Land Management. He received a bachelor's degree in Outdoor Recreation Management from Colorado State University. He has thirty years experience with the U.S. Forest Service and three years experience with the BLM with a strong emphasis in all aspects of recreation management.

Senior, John is the Manager of the Strategic Partnerships section of Parks Victoria. He was an instigator of the "Healthy Parks, Healthy People" program in Australia and has forged strategic partnerships with many of the health providers discussed in Chapter 12, as well as with universities and other park agencies. John is a member and national convener of Parks and Leisure Australia.

Spangler, Kathy J. currently serves as Executive Vice President for America's Promise Alliance, the largest multisector coalition dedicated to improving the lives of all children. She served for twenty years at the National Recreation and Park Association, where she established the national partnerships department and successfully developed nationally recognized strategic alliances and benefits-based initiatives in health, youth development, and quality sports. She is a member of the American Academy of Park and Recreation Administration.

Stafford, Bill has been the Recreation, Wilderness, and Trails Staff Officer for the Red Rock Ranger District of the Coconino National Forest for 27 years. He has worked as Assistant Recreation and Lands Staff on the Lincoln National Forest, Cloudcroft Ranger District Fire Management Officer for the "old" Crown King District of the Prescott National Forest and as an Assistant District Forester and District Forester for the New Mexico Department of State Forestry. He is a 1971 forestry graduate of Northern Arizona University and attended Clemson University for the Recreation Short Course in 1992. Bill has represented the Forest Service in numerous benefits-based management workshops.

Stein, Taylor V. is an Associate Professor in the School of Forest Resources and Conservation at the University of Florida. His research and teaching interests focus on identifying tools and techniques to plan and manage for the multiple of economic and noneconomic benefits nature-based tourism and recreation can provide to communities, visitors, and the environment. Taylor is a member of International Union of Forest Research Organizations, serving as deputy coordinator of the Landscape Planning and Management Working Group. He is also a member of the Society of American Foresters and is Chair of its Recreation Working Group.

Stynes, Daniel J. is Professor Emeritus in the Department of Community, Agriculture, Recreation and Resource Studies at Michigan State University. He has taught courses in recreation and tourism planning and research methods since 1976. For the past 15 years, his research has focused on measuring recreation and travel spending and associated economic impacts. He developed the current version of the Money Generation Model for the National Park Service in 2001 and has applied the model and variations thereof to a wide range of economic impact assessment problems.

Tucker, Karen is the manager of the BLM's Gunnison Gorge National Conservation Area (NCA) & Wilderness in Montrose, Colorado, involving 24 miles of the Gunnison River; Gunnison Gorge Wilderness commercial use allocations; a 10,000-acre Off-highway Vehicle Recreation Area. Karen collaborates with multiple public-private partners on river access, riparian and fishery enhancement, sage-grouse recovery, mancos shale research and reclamation, visitor services, and environmental education issues. She also oversees the recreation, wilderness, and cultural programs for the BLM's Uncompahgre Field Office. Karen began her natural resource career with the National Park Service, has worked with the U.S. Forest Service, and has been a managing partner of a natural resource-oriented landscaping business in southwest Colorado.

Tucker, Teresa W. is a doctoral student in the Parks, Recreation, & Tourism Department at Clemson University. Her study interests include professional development for camp staff and inclusion of people with disabilities into community based recreation programs. Prior to her arrival at Clemson, she worked in the organized camp profession for 20 years. She serves on the board of directors for the Southeastern section of the American Camp Association.

Virden, Randy J. was the former Director of the School of Community Resources and Development and has been a member of the Parks and Recreation Management faculty at Arizona State University since 1986. He is now Chair of the Department of Hospitality, Recreation, and Tourism Management at San Jose State University. He has conducted outdoor recreation and tourism research in California, Oregon, Arizona, Utah, Colorado, Nevada, and Wyoming over the past 25 years. He has advised and conducted funded research projects with the U.S. Forest Service, National Park Service, Bureau of Land Management, Bureau of Reclamation, Arizona State Parks, and Maricopa County Parks and Recreation Department.

Vogt, Christine is an associate professor in the Department of Community, Agriculture, Recreation, and Resource Studies at Michigan State University where she has been a faculty member since 2001. Her research area is marketing communications and resident attitudes on tourism, travel, and natural resource issues. She is currently working on several transportation and land use research projects in the area of trails, green and open space, and Safe Routes to School. Most of her work is in Michigan and Arizona, where she was on faculty with Randy Virden and Richard Knopf.

Weber, Delene is a senior lecturer at the University of South Australia's School of Natural and Built Environments. Her research and teaching efforts include planning, management, and interpretation of park and wilderness areas. Delene came to academia after working in natural resource management in Australia and the United States and started working with issues related to OFM while with the South Carolina State Park Service. Her current projects center on issues of place attachment and social capital. She is a member of the National Association for Interpretation, the Interpretation Association Australia, Parks and Leisure Australia, and the International Association of Society and Natural Resources.

Zanon, Dino develops and manages the visitor research program for Parks Victoria. In that capacity, his efforts have helped advance Park Victoria's modeling of important aspects of park management including its ability to monitor and improve its performance. His work has also been influential in the formation of five major parks around Melbourne.

Preface and Endorsements

This text focuses on the need for public park and recreation agencies to optimize the beneficial outcomes of recreational opportunities they provide and on how such optimization can be achieved. The introductory six chapters in Part 1 of the text explain what Outcomes-Focused Management (OFM) is, how it evolved, why it is needed, why it is credible, how it can and should be implemented by public municipal and wildland recreation park and recreation agencies, why every segment of a country's population needs to understand the existing science-based knowledge about the benefits of leisure, and why repositioning of people's currently too limited understanding and appreciation of the benefits of leisure is so badly needed.

The six chapters of Part 2 describe how OFM has been used to help guide park and recreation *policy development* by agencies in Australia, Canada, the U.S., and New Zealand. Part 3 is comprised of eight chapters that describe how OFM has been applied to guide the *development and implementation of management plans* by various public park and recreation agencies. A large proportion of the chapters in Parts 2 and 3 were authored by practitioners who were directly involved in the applications described. Those chapters are rich in their descriptions of what was learned about how to, and how not to, apply and implement OFM. The four chapters of Part 4 describe other *applications of OFM* such as to promote more attention on the benefits to residents of local communities, determine the local impacts of recreation and tourism, and guide recreation-related health initiatives and wildlife management. The summary chapter critiques the text and suggests future needed direction.

The editor of this text is not really a masochist, but the text was designed to be of interest to a very wide audience. Included are people who consider themselves to be leisure professionals as well as interested others such as lay persons, interested individuals in the political arenas, or persons in the diverse media. But, the primary hoped-for readers fall into three groups: leisure scientists, academics, and students; leisure professionals who work for municipal park and recreation agencies; and their counterparts who work for agencies that manage public wildlands on which outdoor recreation opportunities are provided.

The editor of this text is thrilled that very well-known and highly respected representatives from each of these three groups of targeted readers have enthusiastically endorsed this text by their writing the "Foreword" or offering the following endorsements of it. Thanks for reading the text, stay involved, and stay well. B. L. D.

*****

Since the early 1990s, many of us have endorsed and helped develop and promote the "benefits approach to leisure," and by now many talks and papers have been written about it. This text is particularly important because it goes beyond explaining why the benefits approach is needed and what it is. Its significant contribution is that it explains in detail how to, and not to, apply and implement the benefits approach both by municipal park and recreation agencies and agencies that manage public wildlands to provide outdoor recreation opportunities. Such detailed instruction has not been available before other than in the "fugitive literature," which by definition is not readily available.

I know from my personal experiences that the benefits approach must guide the administration, management, and planning of pubic park and recreation agencies. I know because ever since I began my career in recreation in the late 1960s with the Palm Springs, California Department of Parks and Recreation, I have realized that the users of our programs and services did in fact benefit in many ways from the programs and recreation opportunities we provide.

There was too little research to support my early observations and convictions about the benefits of recreation, but as explained in Chapter 1 of this text, much credible research now exists to document the wide variety of benefits of leisure. I am proud to state that I helped facilitate some of that research when I was Director of the Parks and Recreation Department of Portland, Oregon. That research has given needed credibility to and has significantly advanced the benefits movement.

I also feel fortunate to have been the author of a frequently cited chapter ("Parks and Recreation: More Than Fun and Games") in the text ("Benefits of Leisure") which was also published by Venture and was the first attempt to comprehensively document what was then known about the benefits of leisure and what else needed to be known. That text also helped spawn the very influential 1997 "The Benefits Catalogue" that was created, published and distributed by Canadian Parks/Recreation Association. When the chapters of that text were being reviewed in 1989 by a meeting of its authors, I and several others emphasized that we needed not only to understand the science-based knowledge about the benefits of leisure; we also needed to know how to use that knowledge more effectively. Shortly after that, I was invited to keynote the Application of Leisure Benefits Workshop which was held in Estes Park, Colorado (described in Chapter 1 of this text) at which the early concepts of Benefits-Based Management (BBM) were discussed and refined and from which BBM (renamed Outcomes-Focused Management, or OFM, in this text) emerged.

I came away from my early involvements in the benefits movement with a feeling of empowerment and excitement. I had a story to tell which I hoped would help elevate recognition of the critical personal and social values of parks and recreation. For many reasons, greater appreciation of those values has been more widely recognized within the leisure professions since the early 1990s. But, I didn't realize how difficult it would be to achieve actual implementation of BBM by municipal and wildland park and recreation agencies even though the benefits of leisure were much better understood and appreciated than before. In retrospect, probably the biggest restraint was the relative absence of clearly described guidelines about how to apply and implement BBM both in municipal areas and on public wildlands. For the first time, this text provides those detailed instructions as well as its 20 applications chapters that present very useful information about lessons learned about how to, and not to, apply and implement outcomes-focused management. And, thanks to Venture Publishing, Inc., those detailed guidelines and lessons learned are provided in a readily available source. For those reasons I strongly endorse this text.

Even though I endorse this text, I wish to emphasize, as I have in many talks, that although OFM is a vitally important approach, it should not be rejected because of its novelty and appearance of needing to cause great changes over current practices of park and recreation agencies. To emphasize that point, I have explained that the benefits approach is really not all that complex, and I have encouraged agencies to start using it incrementally to learn as they go. OFM is intuitively logical and asks you to think not only of recreation programs, activities, and the needed settings/environments needed for those activities to be realized, but also to start by asking the much more fundamental question "what do our customers" get out of it. *It is the benefits they realize that is important*, and the programs, services, activities and settings are provided only to ensure realization of those benefits.

I close with a proposition to which I have become incrementally committed to emphasize something that we in the leisure professions must attend to more than ever before. Put simply, although it is vitally important that the benefits movement focus on all citizens, I believe that it must increasingly focus on the youth in an urbanized society which do not have the choices of "creating" their own recreation opportunities as many of us older folk did. For example, when I was growing up in a segregated environment in Kilgore Texas, I never visited a park. I didn't need it. I had the great outdoors. Down there we called them "the woods," which provided food, fun, medicine, exercise and appreciation. Even if parks were available, I did not then need them for lessons I learned from the great outdoors. Now, that important "outdoors" is not readily accessible for most of the youth in the U.S. population approximately 80 percent of which live in essentially urban environments. This is also true of the populations of many other countries.

Large percentages of people in most countries now have considerable mobility that allows them to enjoy outdoor recreation opportunities and the important and significant benefits they provide. Nevertheless most societies are facing the challenge of providing *readily at-hand recreation opportunities for youth.* Here again is yet another opportunity to demonstrate that we are "more than just fun and games." We are not just nice to have but we are critical to any strategy designed to address challenge related to our youth. Every day thousands of them are in parks, pools, climbing walls, gymnasiums, etc. We pick them up, patch them up, and fill them up. The youth of every country are its future. Public parks and recreation now influence that future more than they *ever did in the past.*

Charles Jordan is the Chairperson of the Conservation Fund. He has been Director of the Parks and Recreation Departments of Austin, Texas and Portland, Oregon; Director of the Model Cities Program for Portland and a City Commissioner there for ten years; and was a very active commissioner on President Reagan's Commission on "Americans Outdoors." Among thousands of recreation practitioners, he is distinctive in that he has worked actively in both the public municipal and wildlands park and recreation arenas. He remains in demand as a highly motivating speaker.

*****

For over thirty-five years of serving in the profession of outdoor recreation management, I have witnessed many changes in the body of knowledge that supports that field. While there have been many significant changes, one stands out head and shoulders above the rest. That is the idea that participation in leisure activities generates outcomes. The idea that benefits and detriments come from leisure activities isn't that unique, but the idea of managing recreation programs based on that fact is. That concept allows all players--participants, managers, policy makers, funding decision makers--to communicate with definable terms. That is something we have not been able to do in the past. I encourage all natural resource managers to take the time to understand Outcomes Focused Management and incorporate the concepts and *requirements of it described in this text into their management activities.*

Darrell E. Lewis is the retired Chief, Natural Resources Management, Headquarters, U.S. Army Corps of Engineers and before that he was Chief, Recreation and Cultural Resources Division, Headquarters, USDI Bureau of Land Management. He is on the Board of Directors of the Corps of Engineers Natural Resources Education Foundation.

*****

During my 40-year career with the U. S. Army, one of my more important assignments was serving as the Deputy Assistant Secretary of Defense for Military Personnel and Force Management from 1979-1983. I was responsible for all policies directing the Morale, Welfare and Recreation (MWR) programs in the Armed Forces. In that position, I recognized more keenly the importance of recreational opportunities to human morale and welfare. I retained that awareness after I retired from the Army and became Executive Director of the National Recreation and Park Association in 1986. That awareness was transformed into action by the NRPA after I attended the Benefits of Leisure Applications Workshop in Estes Park, Colorado in May of 1991, which is described in Chapter 1 of this text. It was then that I started to think more seriously about the need for public park and recreation agencies to overtly center their policies and managerial actions on the benefits of leisure. Thereafter, one of my agendas for NRPA was to help promote the benefits movement.

The benefits movement has advanced significantly since the early 1990s because of the efforts of the NRPA, other organizations, and many individuals. Because I can only comment on the role of the NRPA while I was at its helm, I will mention some of its contributions to the benefits movement in outline form:

During the late 1990s and early 2000s, many articles appeared in the NRPA's "Parks and Recreation" magazine about the benefits of leisure and managing for benefits.

During the same period, many presentations related to the benefits movement were made at different sessions of the annual conventions of the NRPA.

NRPA and/or its associated National Park Foundation sponsored considerable research and many publications oriented directly to the benefits movement. Included are the works of: Geof Godbey and his associates on the benefits of local recreation and park services; John Crompton on the impact of parks and related amenities on residential property values and municipal property tax revenues, the local economic impacts of visitors to sports tournaments and special events, and community benefits and repositioning; Ellen O'Sullivan's "Setting a Course for Change: The Benefits Movement;" Larry Allen's and his associates several publications on benefits-based management and benefits programming; and grants to several universities to research the role of recreation opportunities in addressing problems associated with at-risk youth.

The "Benefits Are Endless" movement sponsored by the NRPA, although promotional with too little information provided about "how to," stimulated much awareness about the need for park and recreation agencies to devote more attention to the benefits of recreation. For example, if you enter "benefits of recreation are endless" in Google, you will get 384,000 "hits" many of which are redundant and some of which do not relate directly to that NRPA program. But, literally hundreds, if not thousands, of those hits describe greater attention being given to the benefits of recreation by municipal, regional, state and federal agencies responsible for providing recreation opportunities.

Many state and local chapters of NRPA have taken concerted efforts to promote the benefits movement in many ways, some albeit more actively than others.

In summary, I consider promotion of the benefits movement one of my most significant contributions when I was director of the NRPA.

I endorse this text because it is needed to keep the benefits movement going. It is because it fills the need for readily available and detailed instructions about how park and recreation agencies can develop policies and take managerial actions that are purposefully oriented to optimizing the beneficial outcomes of recreation. For that reason, I wholeheartedly encourage *all leisure professionals to review and study this very practical and informative text.*

Dean Tice was the Executive Director at the National Recreation and Park Association for 15 years (1986-2001), which was a remarkable period of growth in membership (from about 14,000 to over 23,000), in total net worth (from $430,000 to $9 million), and in outside respect for the NRPA. Dean traveled extensively to promote the benefits of parks and recreation. He made appearances in all 50 states, testified before Congress, met with U.S. presidents and White House officials, and established NRPA's international presence, most prominently with protocol agreements with seven nations. He retired from the U.S. Army as a lieutenant general, is the recipient of several significant awards, and in 2001 was appointed a Life Trustee to the Governing Board of the NRPA.

Foreword

This book represents a major step forward in understanding the rationale and techniques for outcomes-focused management of all public park and recreation resources and programs. The editor, Bev Driver, has been and remains a pivotal scholar of recreation behavior and the management of public park and recreation resources and programs. His contributions to that area of learning are second to none, and he has attracted a very distinguished group of authors, some of whom he served as a mentor and colleague.

In a sense, this book represents a revolution in thinking about what constitutes "success" in the management of public park and recreation resources and programs in municipal areas and on public wildlands—or private lands for that matter—in terms of how to plan, manage, and evaluate human use of those park and recreation resources and programs. In one rather sudden paradigm shift, it renders the notion of counting recreating visitors irrelevant as the primary measure of success or at least the sine qua non of management. While Congress and the American public have been taught that more visitation is always better, that distortion must now be recognized and dealt with. The imperative question is not the numeric one, How Many, but instead the existential one, What Happened?

Driver and his talented colleagues seek to answer the existential question with science—how can one measure what happened; what benefits occurred? To the extent that these questions can be answered, the discretionary use of public park and recreation areas by the American public can finally be "judged" scientifically. A basis can be formed to compare the benefits of such use to the use of other publicly-provided social services (e.g., education) and to other uses of public park and recreation resources. Indeed, this book explains how the methods of the outcomes approach should be used to help guide all policy as well as managerial decisions of public park and recreation agencies in this era of global warming, urbanization, aging, and public desires and expectations for accountable, responsive, and efficient management.

In some ways, the evolution of experience-focused to outcomes-focused management parallels the emergence of the experiential economy. That is, there is a progression of wants in the psyche of Americans, particularly middle class and above, such that memorable experiences are valued more in relation to both services and to products. The relative importance of a hotel, for example, and the services provided by the hotel staffs are comparatively less important that what experiences may be encountered near the hotel.

Historically, recreation and parks was a means to an end in terms of local government—a tool to help rural people who migrated to the cities adjust to urban life. Outcomes were not measured since it was a matter of faith that positive outcomes would result from these services. Gradually, however, attendance became the primary measure used to document success. While many urban recreation programs clearly were implemented to achieve positive changes, from declines in juvenile delinquency to improvements in physical fitness or sense of community, it was just assumed that such changes occurred. Counting heads remained critical—often the only quantitative data collected.

While federal, state, and municipal lands began to be used for recreation and parks, such use was the stepchild of other purposes. Flood control, timber, mining, ranching, preservation, housing development, economic development, and other uses dominated. Recreation began to be managed only after the public entered the government forests and lakes for recreation purposes. After enough forest fires had been set and enough people drowned, managing recreation became a function, albeit not a desired one, of government. The public was often ignorant of life outdoor and needed to be controlled. It was not apparent how the more than one-third of the landmass of the U.S. which was managed by government could or should be used in terms of recreation. Once again, measures of visitation became central.

Early management practices at the federal level were somewhat akin to British land management practices in India. Much of the early development of management of the National Park Service followed that model. The lifestyle of foresters and park rangers was critical in how forests and waters were managed. Visitors were suspect. Gradually, however, an expanded population and a larger middle class that resulted after World War Two, led to a boom in outdoor recreation interest and participation—generally to the chagrin of many of those who managed the land, were trained professionally, and were oriented to production of commodities such as timber and minerals. This burgeoning participation level was gradually assumed to be the critical variable in making sense of outdoor recreation. More is better. More is justification.

In answering questions concerning beneficial outcomes, the scholars who have written here actually provide the justification for managing public lands for recreational purposes by other means. In doing so, they contribute to a revolution in progress which concerns the extent to which public lands are merely resources to subsidize extractive industries such as logging and mining, cattle and other live "stock" grazing, or whether such lands will evolve into areas which are planned, conserved, and preserved for outdoor recreation.

Certainly global warming will transfigure such lands. Even as this is being written, warmer winters in British Columbia mean that the Mountain Pine Beetle is killing one quarter of these trees, since the winters are no longer cold enough to kill off substantial portions of this predator. Regardless of the condition of such lands and waters, however, the changing human uses of them will still need to be understood in terms of satisfying experiences and other beneficial outcomes. In a sense, the approach taken to understanding the impacts of public lands from the standpoint of recreation is impervious to global warming. While uses may change, the centrality of the satisfying experiences and other benefits to intelligent management will not. Additionally, as extractive industries continue to decline, the question of purpose in regard to public lands will reassert itself. Driver and the authors of this book are laying the groundwork to answer that question.

This is an important book, not only because it helps us arrive at the tipping point for a major paradigm shift in the management of municipal and wildland recreation resources, but, more importantly, because of the detailed instructions it provides about how to *apply and implement* outcomes–focused management to optimize the beneficial outcomes of recreation by all public park and recreation agencies. Such detailed instructions have not been published in any source before.

Driver and his colleagues have produced a text that will be relevant for a long time. Read it carefully.

Geof Godbey is the President of Next Consulting, a company concerned with repositioning leisure and tourism services for the near future as well as Professor Emeritus in the Department of Recreation, Park and Tourism Management at Penn State University. His research has been funded by many different organizations, and he has consulted widely in the U.S. and visited at least 24 other countries professionally, frequently to give keynote addresses. Geof is the recipient of several significant awards and is the author of ten books and over 100 articles concerning leisure, work, time use, aging, recreation and parks, tourism, health, and the future. He has written for or been extensively quoted by a wide variety of academic journals, popular periodicals, and the broadcast media. His poetry has appeared in numerous outlets including "The Nation." Last, but certainly not least, Geof is a cofounder and editor of Venture Publishing, Inc.

Chapter 1
Why Outcomes-Focused Management is Needed

B. L. Driver

Learning Objectives:

1. Understand the purposes of this text.
2. Be able to define what is meant by the terms "outcomes" and "outcomes-focused management."
3. Determine whether a sufficient and reliable body of knowledge exists about the benefits of recreation to give outcomes-focused management (OFM) adequate scientific credibility.
4. Explain why recreation professionals must understand and act on existing objective knowledge about the beneficial as well as the undesirable consequences of the management and use of recreation and related amenity resources and programs.
5. Understand why outcomes-focused management should be adopted more widely.

A Comment on the Title of This Text

The Beneficial Outcomes Approach to Leisure (BOAL) emerged in the early 1990s to serve as a broad paradigm within which all thought and action about leisure could be framed, whether leisure teaching/training, research, policy development, management, marketing, or repositioning the image of leisure. Within the BOAL, Benefits-Based Management (BBM) was developed to guide management of recreation resources and programs. Both concepts have gained rather wide recognition (Allen & Cooper, 2003; Allen & other, 1998; Driver & Bruns, 1999; Driver, Bruns & Booth, 2000; Moore & Driver, 2005: Chapters 12 & 13); and O'Sullivan, 1999.

The title of this text is *Managing to Optimize the Beneficial Outcomes of Recreation* for two reasons.

1. The major purpose of the BOAL and BBM was to promote more attention on all the benefits of leisure. They have been successful in doing that, but too many people (e.g., More, 2002) have inappropriately criticized the BOAL and BBM as considering only beneficial outcomes and ignoring negative/unwanted outcomes, despite concerted attempts to correct this misperception in several published papers. To help stop such misrepresentations, the editor of this text proposed to the authors invited to write chapters that the title of this text be "Outcomes-Focused Management of Recreation Resources and Programs." That title was proposed because it clearly emphasized that both beneficial and unwanted outcomes are being considered. However, many of the authors strongly insisted that the word "benefits" must be included in the title to help keep the "benefits movement" going. After much deliberation and compromise, the title *Managing to Optimize the Beneficial Outcomes of Recreation* was chosen. That title promotes attention to benefits and allows the text to focus on outcomes-focused management as originally intended, because the word "optimizing" means that both benefits and costs, or both beneficial as well as undesirable outcomes, must be considered.
2. Since the BOAL and BBM were developed, several paradigms have emerged that are nearly identical to it, but promote an outcomes orientation more *explicitly* than the BOAL and BBM did. This movement toward outcomes is reflected by: the body of literature on public administration that focuses on the growing uses of performance measures (see Chapter 4 of this text) that employ measures of outcomes and other measures of performance (especially outputs); a recent publication of the United Way of America (1996) that promotes an outcomes approach to the delivery of social services; and web sites for the Logic Models[1]. OFM is complementary to these other outcomes-oriented

models and can be more readily identified with them than BBM can.

It should be noted that, except for the name change, OFM, as considered in this text, is identical to BBM, and the Outcomes-Focused Paragon (OFP) is identical to the BOAL.

Purposes of This Text

This text focuses on explaining what OFM is, why it should be applied more widely to the management of recreation and related amenity resources and programs that are managed by public agencies, and how such management can and should be done. Specifically, the text has two major and two minor purposes.

Two Major Purposes

The first major purpose is to promote wider understanding about and use of OFM by public agencies that manage park, recreation, and related amenity resources, programs, and services. Chapters 1 and 2 attempt to do this by explaining why OFM is needed and what OFM is about.

The second major purpose of this text is to provide, *in a readily available source*, instructions about *how* public park and recreation agencies can apply OFM in policy development and management in ways that meet all the requirements of OFM. Accomplishment of this purpose is critically important, because all but one or two narrow-in-focus papers on how to apply OFM are in the "fugitive literature." By its nature, that literature is not identified in bibliographies or by search engines, is generally limited in its scope and detail, and is not integrated but is instead fragmented in different sources.

This second major purpose of this text is approached in two ways: by the detailed instructions on how to implement OFM on public wild lands and in municipalities that are provided in Chapters 3 and 4, and by the 18 chapters that describe successful real-world applications of OFM in policy development and management by different park and recreation agencies in their different countries.

Minor Purposes

The two minor purposes of this text are:

- To provide a review, in Chapter 2, of the basic concepts, principles, definitions inherent to, and advantages of OFM and contrast it with other approaches.
- To provide a review, in Chapters 5 and 6, on why all segments of a society need to better understand the benefits of leisure and why repositioning the image of leisure (Crompton, 1993 and Crompton & Witt, 1998) and knowledge about how to do it remains important and depends on knowledge about the benefits of recreation. The too commonly held image is that leisure is just "fun and games" (Jordan, 1991) or a residual after more important things are done. The correct image recognizes that recreation and related amenities add as much value to individuals and a society as any other social service, including educational and medical services, as elaborated in Moore & Driver (2005:26-33).

Terminology Used

The remainder of this chapter describes the evolution of OFM and explains why it needs to be applied more widely. But first, some definitions and distinctions must be established to help avoid confusion and facilitate the dialogue in this and other chapters.

Related Amenity Resources

As stated earlier, a major purpose of this text is to promote wider application of OFM to the management of recreation and related amenity resources, programs, and services. Related amenity resources and programs are resources and programs that are not maintained and managed solely, or even primarily, for recreational use, but receive a considerable amount of such use. Included are fishery, wildlife, and cultural resources; wilderness and other reserved or designated natural areas; public libraries, museums, concert centers, art galleries, continuing education courses, "night basketball" programs, and other publicly provided programs that promote relaxation, exercise, etc. Therefore, this text focuses on all recreation and related amenity services delivered by any public agency, whether within cities or on a remote mountain top. As a reminder of that focus, the words "recreation and related amenity resources and programs" will be used at the beginning of many of the chapters. For brevity, however, the word "recreation" will normally be used singly, but still imply related amenities.

Customers and Associated Providers

As will be emphasized in Chapters 2, 3, and other chapters, OFM requires that attention be given to all relevant customers and associated providers. *Customers* are the people served by the recreation opportunities that are provided. OFM prefers use of the word "customers" instead of visitors, because, as elaborated in Chapter 2, there are both on- and off-site customers and users. On-site customers are the people who visit the areas being managed, and the off-site customers are served by the recreation opportunities that are provided. Off-site customers do not visit the area but benefit from knowing the basic resources are being maintained, and some of them in adjoining or nearby communities realize some of the negative impacts associated with management and use of the area. *Associated providers* are the businesses, organizations, and others that provide associated or auxiliary services that (1) complement or supplement the services being provided by the managing provider, (2) affect the types, quantity, and/or quality of the recreation opportunities being provided, and/or (3) are essential to both the managing provider or the customers. As elaborated in Chapter 2, they include providers of on-site services (e.g., electric power, medical services, law enforcement, outfitter and tour guides, and concessionaires) and off-site services (e.g., lodging, dining opportunities and groceries, laundry services, and those for providing passenger vehicles). Also included are amenity providers including art galleries, museums, libraries, concert centers, etc. It is often mentioned in this text that public agencies provide recreation opportunities, but remember that the associated providers are almost always involved; there is seldom, if ever, a sole-source provider, such as a public agency.

Recreation and Tourism

Much has been written that tends to separate the topics of recreation and tourism, and several professional journals focus on each concept as somewhat distinct entities. For simplicity, when the word "recreation" is used in this text, it will include tourism and tourists unless an author makes a distinction. The view taken here is that tourists are a particular type of recreationists who reside outside the geographical area in which the recreation opportunities are being provided. Some writers prefer to add that if they own vacation homes/cabins in that area, they are not considered to be tourists. Distinctions between recreation and tourism customers are not necessary in this text, because neither change the concepts of OFM.

Managing Recreation Resources versus Managing Customer Services

This text often refers to managing recreation and related amenity resources, programs, and services. Some of the authors believe that the word "services" needed to be added to emphasize that "management of recreation resources and programs" goes considerably beyond just the protection, maintenance, and improvement of the basic resources and other necessary assets. It also includes doing all those things necessary to provide and monitor the realization of high quality recreation experiences that can be realized by on-site users, as well as reasonably accommodating the preferences of the off-site users who desire that basic resources are professionally cared for. As explained in Chapter 3, *everything* done under OFM is ultimately oriented to managing customer services. That is true whether the managerial efforts are building and maintaining trails, providing information (e.g., agency brochures, tourism marketing, interpretive opportunities), conducting focus groups or surveys with customers to determine degrees of and reasons for satisfaction and dissatisfaction, consummating agreements with associated providers for their needed services, or just custodially tending the resources. The significance of this fact is reflected by the USDI Bureau of Land Management changing the name of its Division of Recreation to Recreation and Visitor Services. Lastly, the reason that neither the word "resources" or "services'" is in the title of this text, is that some of the authors wanted both words, some wanted one of those words, and some wanted the other, so that just the word "managing" is used. As ole Abe said, the editor "tried to please all the people all the time!"

What Are Outcomes?

The word "outcomes" is used within OFM in a *highly specialized way* to refer *only* to the beneficial and nonbeneficial consequences (i.e., outcomes) of the management and use of recreation and related amenity resources and programs. As such, outcomes do not refer to "outputs" such as picnic tables, ice rinks, playgrounds, swimming pools, tennis courts, ball parks, dance or yoga programs, hiking trails, campgrounds, interpretive talks, acres of designated wilderness protected, numbers and types of large wildlife and fish available for preservation of gene pools, numbers of cultural/historic sites preserved, etc. As explained in Chapter 2, such facilitators of recreation opportunities are important because they are needed for beneficial outcomes to be realized and nonbeneficial outcomes to be avoided or reduced, but they are not outcomes the way that word is used in OFM. Specifically, OFM focuses on *why* practitioners take *any* actions to provide recreation and related amenity services. That "why" question is answered *solely* in terms of clearly defined and *overtly* managerially targeted beneficial and nonbeneficial probable outcomes of using the opportunities created by the facilitating outputs just listed. This is the most critical thing to understand about the OFP and OFM. Therefore, to implement OFM, practitioners must have a good understanding of what the probable and feasible positive and negative consequences of their policies and managerial actions will be. Put simply, practitioners cannot apply OFM properly unless they can clearly identify (with the help of relevant customer and associated provider stakeholders) probable specific beneficial outcomes to be realized and nonbeneficial outcomes to be reduced in magnitude or avoided.

Because the word "benefit" has several different definitions, practitioners who desire to apply the OFM *must* have a clear and exact understanding of how three types of benefits are defined in specialized ways by OFM. This is important, because many people still inappropriately use the limiting definition of a benefit of leisure as "an improved condition" that appeared in Driver, Brown & Peterson (1991: 4). When pilot testing OFM (then BBM) started in the early 1990s, it very soon became apparent that this definition was insufficient for reasons explained in Driver & Bruns (1999: 355), especially the need to make explicit that the improved conditions associated with many types of satisfying recreation experiences *cannot* be readily identified, but receiving those satisfactions is nevertheless beneficial. As a result, the following three types of benefits were defined to make BBM and OFM operational.

- *An improved change in a condition:* This first type draws on the definition of a benefit found in most dictionaries. It is a state that is viewed as more desirable than a previously existing condition or state; an improved condition. That beneficial change can be to individuals, groups of individuals, or to biophysical and cultural/heritage resources. Examples include improved mental or physical health, increased learning of different types, increased bonding among members of a family unit, a more economically viable local community, improvements made in natural environments, and a refurbished archeological structure. The benefits can be psychological, physiological, social, economic, and environmental in nature.
- *Maintenance of a desired condition, prevention of an undesired condition, or reduction of an undesired condition:* This second type of benefit is the maintenance of a desired condition to prevent an unwanted condition from occurring, prevention of an undesired condition from becoming worse, or reduction of the unwanted impacts of an existing undesired condition. The OFM requires recognition of the fact that practitioners do much more than just provide opportunities to realize improved conditions. Examples include maintaining and protecting existing natural and cultural/historic resources, providing opportunities for users to maintain their physical and mental health, stimulating tourism to help maintain the economic stability of local communities, helping prevent some youth from becoming "at risk" or more at risk, preventing incidences (or greater incidences) of vandalism. Another example would be taking actions to reduce adverse visitor impacts, such as erosion on trails, damage to shorelines or streams, compaction of vegetation, or wear and tear on a playground or ball field. One can note that reducing the magnitude of an undesired condition is really an improved condition and should logically be a part of the first definition. It was put here strategically to emphasize that OFM is concerned with negative impacts as well as beneficial ones. So, all aspects of reducing negative impacts were put in this definition to reduce incorrect criticism that OFM emphasizes only beneficial outcomes.
- *Realization of a satisfying recreation experience:* A special type of benefit covered by this third definition is that a person benefits when she or he realizes a satisfying experience, whether or not an actual improved condition or maintained desired condition is readily apparent. Because most, if not all, recreation and related amenity opportunities are provided so that users/customers can realize some type(s) of satisfying experience(s), it seems logical to assume that such satisfying experiences are psychologically or physiologically beneficial for at least some period of time. Nevertheless, it is frequently difficult for a practitioner to iden-

tify, define, and/or measure what improved or maintained desired conditions results from some types of satisfying experiences. For example, the improved conditions that result from experiencing psychophysiological relaxation, increased physical fitness, improved family kinship, or increased knowledge gained (say from walking an interpreted nature trail or visiting a museum) are more apparent and tractable scientifically than are any improved conditions that might be associated with experiencing nature-based spiritual renewal, enjoying a scenic vista, hearing one's children laugh as they play, marveling at the complexity and seemingly ongoing scheme of things reflected by the functioning of a natural ecosystem, or being overwhelmed by the second movement of Mozart's Clarinet Concerto (K622).

While the types of specific improved conditions (i.e., benefits) associated with some satisfying experiences are difficult to define, those experiences themselves can be identified, defined, and measured reasonably accurately (Driver, 2003). More importantly, *practitioners can and do provide opportunities for specific experiences to be realized*, which in fact constitutes a significant part of what reasonably accommodating customer preferences is about. As stated elsewhere "The realization of leisure experiences constitutes the basis of all leisure behavior" (Driver, 2003).

Lastly, on this third type of benefit, many of the benefits that accompany the realization of satisfying experiences are realized later in what has been called the "Benefit Chain of Causality" (Lee & Driver, 1992 & Driver & Bruns, 1999: pp. 358–359). That concept shows that one type of benefit (e.g., increased learning about nature, enhanced family togetherness, or temporarily reducing everyday life stresses) can lead to subsequent ("chained") benefits (i.e., greater commitments to environmental stewardship, increased family solidarity, better mental and physical health, and increased productivity at work, respectively). Put simply, satisfying experiences are a very important type of benefit regardless of whether or not the improved conditions associated with them are easily discernable.

To thoroughly understand and appreciate the usefulness of the three types of benefits, one must recognize the following characteristics.

- Together, the three types cover all of the benefits (desirable outcomes) associated with the delivery and use of leisure and related amenity services. They do, because the benefits can accrue not only to individuals, but also to groups of individuals including society at large, as well as to the biophysical and cultural/historical resources being managed.
- The aforementioned definitions are silent with respect to whether a particular changed condition, maintained condition, or satisfying recreation experience are ones that are socially acceptable, and not all people agree on what is acceptable. For example, nude bathing is socially acceptable at some locations and in some countries and not in others. Of course, managers must be concerned about the socially desirability of the benefit opportunities they target, and that is one reason why collaboration with relevant stakeholders is so important.
- The way the three types of benefits are defined is not directly related to how the word "benefit" is used in economic benefit-cost (B-C) analyses. In those analyses, benefits are defined and measured in terms of some index (e.g., monetary price) of the economic worth of the goods and services that will be provided or of the resources that are being protected.

No definitions seem necessary about the types and nature of undesirable outcomes, because practitioners generally understand them better than they do the benefits. This is because since passage of the Environmental Protection Act of 1969, practitioners have attended rather carefully to many negative impacts in the large number of environmental and social impacts assessments they have made. Many of them have also made use of recreation and related amenity resource impact management systems, such as the Limits of Acceptable Change (Stankey & others, 1985). Applications of those systems have focused mostly on environmental impacts, but have also considered some social impacts, especially those related to crowding. Nevertheless, more attention needs to be given to the personal and social impacts/outcomes, and the OFP and OFM were designed to help assure that such attention is provided.

Some outcome paradigms distinguish between outcomes and subsequent desired and undesired impacts. Many of these subsequent impacts occur within what was referred to immediately above as "the benefit chain of causality." Although OFM requires that recreation resource policy makers, planners, and managers be aware of and overtly target these subsequent impacts, OFM does not require attempting to target *all* subsequent/chained benefits in management plans simply because of the difficulty of identifying all of them and the time spans required for some of them to materialize.

Evolution of Managerially Relevant Knowledge about the Benefits of Leisure

It was just stated that application of the OFM requires a good understanding of the benefits of recreation and related amenity resources and programs. Some practitioners still question if enough objective knowledge about those benefit exists to give the OFM needed scientific credibility. Yes, it does, and greater appreciation of the credibility of OFM can be gained if one understands how knowledge about those benefits has evolved. Therefore, this section will briefly review that history and attempt to document the current state of knowledge about the benefits. It will start with a sampling of the philosophical, normative, intuitive, and experientially interpretive statements made about the benefits, and then briefly summarize the results of scientific studies of those benefits. The focus will be on the benefits and not on related important topics such as who does and does not have adequate, appropriate, and real opportunities to enjoy leisure and related amenities.

Normative and Intuitive Interpretations

Most people who write about the benefits of leisure start with Aristotle and other classical Greek thinkers of his era of about two and one-half millennia ago. The Bammels (1996:18) wrote "For Aristotle, only the man of leisure can truly be happy, for he spends his time using his highest faculty to contemplate the noblest and best truths--and what would give greater happiness?.... Aristotle's vision of leisure includes much more than just solitary contemplation. Aristotle's vision of the good life demands more than becoming a truly virtuous individual--and virtue is developed only by action in society. Hence 'civility,' that is, doing all that is necessary to be a good citizen, is an integral part of leisure." The Bammels (1992:17) wrote earlier that "the 'classical' or 'normative' perspective expressed by Aristotle...has been updated by such writers as St. Thomas Aquinas in the thirteenth century, and Joseph Pieper and Sebastian de Grazia in the twentieth."

Despite several early perspectives about the individual and social benefits of leisure, little can be found in the literature about these benefits until after the Industrial Revolution in the mid 18th and early 19th centuries. Edginton & Others (1995:66) mention that "During the Industrial Revolution, life became clock-driven; the clock regulated both work and play. Children and adults adjusted their work efforts to a schedule--not personal desires, needs, and abilities....They started to look outside of their work environment for satisfaction. Leisure became a method for compensating for dissatisfying work experiences." Since the beginning of the Industrial Revolution, and until the 1960s when some early results of scientific studies of selected benefits were published, pronouncements about those benefits remained either normative or intuitive/interpretive in nature and substance. *Normative*, in that the benefits articulated were based on the writers' judgment of what the role of leisure is in a society should be. *Intuitive/interpretive*, because the proclaimed benefits were gleaned by the proponents from what their associates and customers had told those the benefits of leisure were or from the benefits the proponents believed they had realized from their personal recreational engagements.

George Marshall (1933:465) expressed the situation in these words "The only common denominator for the recreational and commodity value of the forest is the human happiness which may be derived from each use. Unfortunately no quantitative measure of human happiness has ever been designed, and consequently it is impossible to describe accurately the contribution which forest recreation makes toward the welfare of mankind. About all one can do is to point out the purposes for which men seek the forest and let each reader make his own evaluation of their intrinsic importance."

Despite Marshall's perceptivity and influence, much progress has been made in defining and scientifically measuring different dimensions of human "happiness" (i.e., satisfaction). However, this does not mean that early and current intuitive and personal experiential interpretations and pronouncement of benefits were or are erroneous or trivial. To the contrary, they were tremendously important in stimulating the emergence of playgrounds and the park and recreation movements in many countries. Furthermore, they have been and remain influential in guiding public policy about, and management of, recreation and related amenity resources and programs. For brevity, only a few of the many influential individuals who articulated their perceptions of the benefits are mentioned.

Frederick Law Olmstead, the father of landscape architecture and the designer of many parks (e.g., Central Park in New York City) and related areas, was a prolific writer and an early proponent of the values to humans of parks, especially nature-based ones. Olmstead (1953:21) expressed his belief that natural scenery and parks should be available to all people and not just to the rich who could afford their private green estates in these words: "The establishment by government of great public grounds for the free enjoyment of the people under certain conditions, is thus justified …as a political duty." Fabos, Milde, & Weinmayr (1968:12) claimed that "Olmstead believed implicitly that a close association with natural beauty was one of three most necessary elements of human life." They continued that Olmstead stated [in a convoluted way]:

> "It is a scientific fact that the occasional contemplation of natural scenes of an impressive nature, particularly if this contemplation occurs in connection with relief from ordinary cares, change of air and change of habits, is favorable to the health and vigor on men and especially to the vigor and health of their intellect beyond any other conditions which can be offered them, that it not only gives pleasure for the time being but increases the subsequent capacity for happiness and the means of securing happiness. The want of such occasional recreation where men and women are habitually pressed by their business or household cares often results in a class of disorders the characteristic quality of which is mental disability, sometimes taking the severe forms of softening the brain, paralysis, palsy, monomania, moroseness, melancholy or irascibility, incapacitating the subject for the proper exercise of the intellectual and moral forces."

Jane Addams was another prominent articulator of the benefits of leisure and also helped spawn the parks and recreation movement in the U.S. in the late 19th century. In 1894, she established a model playground in Chicago adjacent to Hull House, which was located in a crowded urban area inhabited by immigrants and other poor people. She worked to relieve the suffering of those people in many ways and was an avid proponent of their need for readily available recreational opportunities. She had significant influence because she was a prolific writer and maintained active speaking engagements.

Many other influential people, including several holding high political positions, were strong proponents of the benefits of parks and recreation and associated amenities at the end of the 19th and beginning of the 20th centuries. That list of people is long and includes Charles Elio, Luther Gulick, Josepth Lee, Stephen Mather, John Muir, Stuart Udall, and Theodore Roosevelt.

Statements about the benefits of recreation grew in frequency in the 1950s and continue today, because from the end of World War II until about 1960, national interest and participation in urban and outdoor recreation increased rapidly (Cf Moore & Driver, 2005: Chapter 3). During that time, many studies were made of the rapidly increasing demands for recreation and related amenity opportunities and the resources available to accommodate those demands. For example, the American Academy of Political and Social Science (1957) published a volume "Recreation in the Age of Automation," but it did not focus on the benefits of recreation. That deficiency can also be found in the summary report of the Outdoor Recreation Resources Review Commission (ORRRC). That Commission was created by the U.S. Congress on June 18, 1958 by Public Law 85-470. The threefold mission of the ORRRC was to "…determine: the outdoor recreation wants and needs of the American people now and what they will want in the years 1976 and 2000; the recreation resources of the Nation available to satisfy those needs now and in the years 1976 and 2000; and what policies and programs should be recommended to ensure that the needs of the present and future generations are adequately and efficiently met?"

Despite the great influence of the summary and the other 27 reports of the ORRRC, little mention is made in its summary volume, "Outdoor Recreation for America" (ORRRC, 1962) about the benefits of outdoor recreation in particular and leisure in general. The following are the only statements about benefits found in that summary report: "Although the chief reason for providing outdoor recreation is the broad social and individual benefits it produces, it also brings about desirable economic effects. Its provision enhances community values by creating a better place to live…." (pg. 4); "From the beginning, one of the strongest currents in American thought has been that the outdoors is a *right* of Americans—not only something to be enjoyed but vital to our spirit." (pg. 13); "All in all, being in the outdoors is a good, wholesome, and healthful use of leisure that can help create a better life." (pg. 24); and "Outdoor recreation produces many benefits. It provides healthful exercise necessary for individual physical fitness. It promotes mental health. It offers spiritual values, for being in the outdoors can be a deeply moving experience. It is valuable for education in the world of nature." (pg. 75).

Despite little mention of the specific benefits of recreation in the ORRRC reports, it is relevant to mention that Laurence Rockefeller, Chairperson of the ORRRC, set up a study group to examine the mental health benefits of outdoor recreation. It was chaired by Leonard Duhl (then with the Professional Services

Branch, National Institute of Mental Health) and was comprised of well-known social and behavioral scientists, who met in Williamsburg, Virginia on June 1-3, 1961. The three questions posed to that group by Rockefeller were:

- Is there reason to believe that the out-of-doors and outdoor recreation provide conditions favorable for human activities, which activities tend in themselves to provide security and a sense of well-being leading toward mental health?
- Is the out-of-doors and outdoor recreation favorable in term of mental health values than other environments?
- Are there significant relations between outdoor recreation, physical fitness, and mental health?

Samuel T. Dana (then Dean Emeritus, School of Natural Resources, The University of Michigan) was a Presidential Commissioner of the ORRRC and a member of the study group. He gave the author of this chapter his copy of the proceeding of the three days the group met. Dana said that the ORRRC Commissioners decided not to publish the results of the deliberations of the group, because there was too little scientific documentation to back the personal opinions of the members of the group about the benefits[2].The author of this chapter was unable to locate a copy of the formal conclusions and recommendations of that task force. But, the recorded statements of the participants in the proceedings of the last day clearly indicate that they believed that outdoor recreation in particular and leisure offered many and sizable benefits. Some examples of those statements follow. One member stated, "...I don't think we could conclusively demonstrate an answer to Mr. Rockefeller's question that outdoor recreation was absolutely necessary to physical well-being and mental health, but ...I feel...that outdoor recreation is essential to human well-being...." Another member then commented, "There is ample evidence based on experience of workers in the health professions, recorded in the literature, and utilized in actual practice, that outdoor activity in general, and outdoor recreation in particular, is beneficial to the promotion and maintenance of physical and mental health...." The then-president of the American Psychological Association followed that statement with,

> "...I think there is sufficient evidence which has to be validated from time to time...and everyone has expressed it here--that man will seek the great out of doors as an expression of an innate psychobiological urge towards greater expansion and enrichment of life....He seeks the outdoors not only to get back to his old self, that is to recreate, but to go forward to a new self, that is, to create. Therefore, I would say that free and easy access to the great outdoors is essential for our wholesome growth and development ...."

A fourth member's statement captured the conclusion I drew from reading the transcripts of the proceedings: "...we need research work in order to prove ...whether these empirical experiences are definitively scientifically based... (Federal Reporting Service, 1961). As explained in the following section, a lot of research has been done on the psychological and other benefits of leisure since 1961. Given current interest in the benefits of leisure, it would have been useful if a separate volume had been added to the 27 ORRRC reports that summarized this study group's deliberations and opinions.

Many subjective proclamations about the benefits of recreation and related amenity services have been made since the reports of the ORRRC were published in 1962. As only one example, Gray and Greben (1974) expressed disillusionment with the prevailing perspectives of parks and recreation professionals stating, "They are activity centered. Definition in terms of activities is unsatisfactory" (pg. 49). They argued that this activity orientation meant the field was still focusing on supply and had a custodial mentality that its mission was to look after facilities: "For thirty or forty years or more the recreation and park movement has been deluded by a false perception of recreation. This has warped our services, given us false priorities, prevented effective evaluation of results, and inhibited our ability to interpret what we do. Worst of all, it has prevented us from developing an understanding of our goals and methods" (pg. 50). They also stated "We should have discovered long ago the nature of the business we are in, but we have not ... The critical questions are not, How many were there? or who won? The critical question is, What happened to Jose, Mary, Sam, and Joan in this experience?" (pg. 49). On January 28, 1985, President Reagan created The President's Commission on Americans Outdoors by Executive Order No.12503. Unlike the ORRRC reports, which hardly mentioned the benefits of outdoor recreation, the reports of this Commission probably presented the most thorough appraisal of those benefits made until then. Those benefits were not only extolled in the summary report for that Commission, but were detailed in the section on "Values and Benefits" of the over two-inch thick "Literature Review" done for the Commission. In fact, that section was the second largest (103 pages) of the 11 different sections in that review. More recently, Jordan (1991:368) wrote " You can lay to rest, once and for all time, the idea that parks and recreation is nothing more than fun and games. Let there be no doubt that we provide a positive, vital, and basic service. For many Americans, we can be the difference between a productive future and no future at all." Many others have also spoken and written about their perceptions of the benefits of leisure since President Reagan's Commission on American Outdoors. But space deters elaboration, because we need to move to the evolution of scientific (more objective) knowledge about the benefits of leisure.

Scientific Documentation of Benefits

The foregoing section presented an overview of many influential people's normative and intuitive/interpretive beliefs about the benefits of recreation. This section offers a brief summary of results of research about those benefits. To start, the following excerpt was taken from Moore & Driver (2005:24&25).

> ...very little scientific research was done in any of the sub-areas of leisure before 1960[3]. There were several sociological studies within the context of the broader community; a few investigations of the impacts of outdoor recreationists on the biophysical environment; several efforts to estimate the economic impacts of tourists by calculations of economic multipliers; and some research directed at estimating recreational use of dispersed recreation areas. This poverty of empirical studies was pointed out in Volume 27 of the Outdoor Recreation Resources Review Commission (1962), entitled "Bibliography and Literature Review." Over 90 percent of the literature citations there were to administrative studies that discussed increasing use rates and other factors that indicated needs to provide more opportunities to meet growing demands. Also indicative of this very recent history of science-based knowledge is the fact that the first research journal in leisure (the *Journal of Leisure Research*) was not published until the mid-1960s. Put simply, the knowledge about leisure in 1960 was primarily based on philosophical writings and administrative studies measuring trends in recreational use.
>
> Research on the benefits of leisure began even later. Few results regarding benefits were reported before the early 1980s, and they were limited mostly to the mental and physical health benefits of getting exercise during one's leisure, psychological benefits of participating in sports, and beneficial secondary economic impacts of tourists' expenditures. The notable exceptions were the considerable amount of research on people's economic willingness to pay for leisure services and on different types of beneficial satisfying experiences realized from leisure engagements. Even given these studies, there was little widespread scientific interest in the benefits of leisure before the middle to late 1980s.
>
> Since about 1985, scientific interest in leisure benefits has increased rapidly. That interest was stimulated, in part, by a growing number of publications on benefits, notably the *Benefits of Leisure* (Driver, Brown, & Peterson, 1991), *The Benefits of Recreation Research Update* (Sefton & Mummery, 1995), *The Benefits Catalogue* (Canadian Parks/Recreation Association (1997), and *Setting a Course for Change: The Benefits Movement* (O'Sullivan, 1999). Research now in progress and results of future research will continue to advance our science-based knowledge about the benefits.

Rather than review the vast number of scientific studies that have been done on the benefits, the reader is referred to a recent chapter that comprehensively reviewed what is known objectively about the benefits of leisure (Moore & Driver, 2005: Chapter 2). Table 1.1 is reproduced from page 29 of that chapter, on which it was designated as Table 2.2. It lists the different types of benefits of leisure for which at least *one* scientific study has documented there existence. Although Table 1.1 lists mostly specific types of benefits, it also includes some general categories of benefits, which subsume some of those specific types, and to that extent there is some redundancy. *The Benefits Catalogue* (Canadian Parks/Recreation Association (1997) describes many of the types of benefits listed, and it cites specific scientific reports that documented them.

I. Personal Benefits

A. Psychological

1. Mental Health and Maintenance of such:
   - Holistic sense of wellness
   - Stress management (prevention, mediation, and restoration)
   - Catharsis
   - Prevention of and reduced depression, anxiety, and/or anger
   - Positive changes in mood and emotion

2. Personal Development and Growth; Improvements in:
   - Self-esteem
   - Self-confidence
   - Self-reliance
   - Self-competence
   - Self-assurance
   - Self-affirmation
   - Value clarification
   - Learn new skills and develop and apply other skills
   - Academic/cognitive performance
   - Independence/autonomy
   - Sense of control over one's life
   - Humility
   - Leadership ability
   - Aesthetic enhancement/greater appreciation of beauty
   - Creativity enhancement
   - Spiritual growth and greater appreciation and greater tolerance of different ethnic interpretations of spirituality
   - Adaptability
   - Cognitive efficiency
   - Teamwork/cooperation
   - Problem solving
   - Nature learning
   - Cultural/historical appreciation
   - Environmental awareness/understanding
   - Tolerance
   - Balanced competitiveness
   - Balanced living
   - Willingness to take risks
   - Acceptance of one's responsibility
   - Academic and other mental performance

3. Personal Appreciation/Satisfaction from:
   - Sense of freedom
   - Self-actualization
   - Flow/absorption
   - Exhilaration
   - Stimulation
   - Sense of adventure
   - Challenge
   - Nostalgia
   - Perceived quality of life/life satisfaction
   - Creative expression
   - Aesthetic appreciation
   - Nature appreciation
   - Spirituality
   - Positive change in mood/emotion
   - Environmental stewardship
   - Identification with special places/feeling of geographical belonging or physical grounding
   - Transcendent experiences

B. Psychophysiological

- Improved perceived quality of life
- Cardiovascular benefits, including prevention of strokes
- Reduced or prevented hypertension
- Reduced serum cholesterol and triglycerides
- Rehabilitation of patients with heart problems
- Improved control and prevention of diabetes
- Reduced risk of lung and colon cancer
- Better muscle strength and joint functioning
- Reduced spinal problems
- Decreased body fat/obesity/weight control
- Improved neuropsychological functioning
- Increased bone mass and strength in children
- Promotion of better balance
- Increased muscle strength and better connective tissue
- Respiratory benefits (increased lung capacity, benefits to people with asthma)
- Improved response time
- Reduced incidence of disease
- Improved bladder control in the elderly
- Increased life expectancy
- Reduced anxiety and somatic complaints
- Management of menstrual cycles
- Management of arthritis
- Improved functioning of the immune system (resistance to illness)
- Reduced depression and improved mood
- Reduced consumption of alcohol, tobacco and other drugs
- Reduced need for some medications

II. Social/Cultural Benefits and Improvements

- Community satisfaction and morale
- Community identity
- Pride in community/nation (pride in place/patriotism)
- Cultural/historical awareness and appreciation
- Reduced social alienation
- Reduced illness and social impacts of such
- Community/political involvement
- Increased productivity and job satisfaction
- Ethnic social integration
- Social bonding/cohesion/cooperation
- Reduced social alienation
- Conflict resolution/harmony
- Reduced crime
- Greater community involvement in environmental decision making
- Social support
- Support for democratic ideal of freedom
- Family bonding/better family life
- Keeping children engaged and away from less desirable activities
- Higher class attendance
- Lower dropout rates
- Increased trust in others
- Increased compassion for others
- Reduced loneliness
- Reciprocity/sharing
- Social mobility
- Improved image of public agencies
- Community integration
- Promotion of voluntary community efforts
- Nurturing of others
- Understanding and tolerance of others
- Environmental awareness, sensitivity
- Enhanced world view
- Nurture new community leaders
- Socialization/acculturation
- Cultural identity
- Cultural continuity
- Prevention of social problems by at-risk youth
- Developmental benefits in children
- Increased independence of older people
- Networking by seniors
- Increased longevity and perceived quality of life

III. Economic Benefits

- Reduced health costs
- Increased productivity
- Less work absenteeism
- Reduced on-the-job accidents
- Amenity use of hazard areas
- Decreased job turn-over
- International balance of payments (from tourism)
- Local and regional economic growth
- Local amenities help attract industry
- Employment opportunities
- Contributions to net national economic development
- Promotion of places to retire and associated economic growth
- Increased property values

IV. Environmental Benefits

- Maintenance of physical facilities
- Stewardship/preservation of options
- Improved air quality through urban forestry
- Husbandry/improved relationships with natural world
- Increases in "leave no trace" use
- Understanding of human dependency on the natural world
- Environmental ethic
- Public involvement in environmental issues
- Environmental protection
- Ecosystem sustainability
- Species biodiversity
- Maintenance of natural scientific laboratories
- Preservation of particular natural sites and areas
- Preservation of cultural/heritage/historic sites and areas
- Promotion of ecotourism

Sources: Table 1.1 was first published in Driver (1990), updated in Driver & Bruns (1999), and updated considerably in Moore & Driver (2005: 19).

Table 1.1. Specific types and general categories of benefits that have been attributed to leisure by one or more scientific studies

When reviewing the large number of benefits listed in Table 1.1, it is important to remember that much more research has been done on some of the benefits than on others. For example, much more research has been done on the health-related benefits of physical exercise, the psychological experiences realized, and the economic benefits of tourism on local communities than on spiritual benefits and the role of leisure in building social networks and support systems which are especially important for many elderly people. Thus, more research on the benefits of leisure is needed.

Moore & Driver (2005:28) made the following comments about Table 1.1

> ...a close inspection shows that the listed benefits pervade all aspects of human behavior and performance including mental and physical health; family and community relations; self-concept; personal value clarification; perceived personal freedom; sense of fitting in; understanding local, community and national historical events and cultural characteristics; pride in one's community and nation; learning of many types; performance in school and at work; sharing; ethnic identity; identities formed with sports and sports teams; formation of close friendships and systems of social support; spiritual definition, renewal, and facilitation; involvement in community affairs; local community cohesion and stability; environmental understanding and stewardship; and economic development, growth, and stability. It should also be noticed that many of the benefits listed in Table 2.2 [Table 1.1 in this text] are experiential in nature and are based on psychological studies of perceived benefits. The results of those psychological studies provide very useful information, but they are sometimes viewed as less reliable than studies using "hard" measures, such as the physiological studies measuring the cardiovascular benefits of activity during leisure. That view is now antiquated, because the states of the art in psychological and social-psychological research have advanced greatly in the past two decades and now have considerable validity and reliability.

The reader will gain a better understanding of the breadth and scope of these experiential benefits if he or she reflects on a few of his or her favorite recreation activities, looks down the list and answers the questions:

- Do I ever receive that type of benefit from my recreation?
- Do I believe other individuals probably do so?
- Do groups of people (from members of a family, through local communities, to the society as a whole) receive the types of social benefits listed?
- Do natural and cultural/historic resources benefit in the ways listed?

Through this simple exercise, one can become more aware of the great number of benefits of leisure that research has identified.

In ending this section about the evolution of scientific knowledge of the benefits of leisure, perhaps the most important thing to recognize is how far we have come in a relatively short period of time. It is difficult to think of but a few other professions for which the science-based body of knowledge has advanced as much as it has for leisure during the past four decades. Communication sciences, space engineering, and some fields of medicine have done so. But, 40 years is an extremely short period of time for any profession to advance from practically no science-based knowledge to where the leisure professions are today. All leisure and related amenity professionals should be proud of this remarkable achievement.

Conclusions about the State of Knowledge

Some people still question whether enough objective knowledge about the benefits of leisure now exists to give OFM needed scientific credibility. The above review indicates the answer is *yes*. It showed that the knowledge about those benefits was derived from two supplemental sources: (1) the results of systematic research that documented the many types of benefits listed in Table 1.1 and (2) the intuitive, reflective, and experiential judgments of practitioners and others who had observed and talked to the people who received these benefits and who had also reflected on the benefits they received from their personal recreational engagements. Those judgments by practitioners and other interested in leisure and related amenities have strongly influenced the policies, planning, and management for which those practitioners have been and remain responsible. Thus, it is erroneous and arrogant to claim that outcomes-oriented policies and management have been based solely on the results of scientific research. However, it is not erroneous to state that intuitive judgments of practitioners and other promoters of the values of leisure did too little to overcome the still pervasive image of leisure as not being as significant as other services, such as educational and medical services. More relevant is the fact the OFP and OFM could not have been developed without the scientific knowledge about the benefits.

OFM as a Science-Based Approach

Moore & Driver (2005: Chapters 12 & 13) described the OFP (i.e., the BOAL) as a "science-based" paradigm and OFM (i.e., BBM) as a "science-based" management system. "Science-based" means that the OFP and OFM are empirically supported by the results of scientific research. In addition, the OFP also incorporates widely accepted concepts about leisure and relevant theories from other pertinent professional bodies of knowledge, such as modern management science, marketing, conflict management (i.e., how to establish and maintain meaning collaborative partnerships with stakeholders), psychology, sociology, economics, the resource management disciplines, and public policy development. If the OFP and OFM did not have empirical support and integrate relevant concepts and principles from other disciplines, they would and should be suspect. Without that scientific integrity, practitioners managing recreation and related resources, agency administrators, members of legislators who partially fund recreation and related programs, people in other relevant agencies, stakeholders, and the public at large could and would question the credibility and reliability of the OFP and OFM.

To iterate, subjective beliefs about the nature and scope of some of the benefits of recreation and related amenities might well be correct, and they most certainly have been of great influence in park and recreation policy development and management. Nevertheless, an empirically supported (i.e., professional) body of knowledge cannot be based on subjective impressions and opinions and neither can the extremely important efforts to "reposition the image" of leisure within the leisure professions as elaborated in Chapter 5. Certainly, there must be art in any profession, but there must also be science. That is why much time and effort has been spent to assure that the OFP and OFM have scientific credibility. This brings us to the questions: What is a profession, and are there leisure professions?

Are We Professionals? If so, What Does That Imply?

It seems that most people who work in any of the subspecializations of leisure and related amenities (i.e., teaching, research, extension services, therapeutic recreation, policy development and implementation, planning, and management) now view themselves as professionals. But, what does that mean; what is a professional? Moore & Driver, 2005: 22) defined a profession as follows:

> A profession is commonly defined as an area of expertise that is founded on an empirically supported body of knowledge. Some writers also like to add that most professions have one or more professional organizations (e.g., the National Recreation and Park Association, the America Medical Association, and the Society of American Foresters) that exist to (1) advance professional knowledge and promote and publicize professional activities; (2) determine subject areas (normally defined as courses and curricula of formal education) in which a person must demonstrate satisfactory training before admittance to the professional organization is granted; (3) set up licensing procedures, including tests of professional knowledge; and (4) establish codes of ethics for the profession, such as the Hippocratic creed in the medical professions. Of these, the most important professional requirement is that of understanding the professional body of empirically supported, or science-based, knowledge....

From the above definition, it is apparent that widely accepted subjective and informed judgments about benefits, while enhancing the "art" of any profession (e.g., "the practice and *art* of medicine") cannot be accepted as a credible source of science-based professional knowledge. Of course, many people other than those normally considered to be scientists conduct small "scientific" studies. As a simple example, a recreation resource manager might believe (i.e., hypothesize) that visitors from certain subcultures desire to picnic with larger groups than most members of other subcultures do. The manager might then observe whether a higher proportion of visitors from that subculture select group picnicking areas more frequently than visitors representing other subcultures (i.e., systematically). A manager may also collect data to test his or her hypothesis, replicate that study several times to see if there is a consistent pattern, analyze the results, obverse supporting patterns of behavior across the several replications, and draw the conclusion that is supportable by the results. Or, while grocery shopping, a person might question whether the bigger, flashier, and more expensive box of cereal is really a better buy than the smaller, less expensive one, then determine that the bigger box has fewer net ounces than the smaller one, and reach the conclusion that it would be imprudent to pay more for the flashy advertising and empty space in the larger box. Such systematic "small scale research" is done frequently by people, including recreation practitioners, to answer specific questions, which basically is what research is about. While useful, such small-scale research cannot build the science-based knowledge required by any profession.

If a profession *must* be based on a body of scientifically-supported knowledge, then for a person to merit professional status, he or she must not only learn that body of knowledge and continually stay abreast of new additions to that knowledge, but also be able to apply that knowledge. Members of a profession cannot perform effectively if they do not keep up with the states of knowledge within their respective professions. This is true for teachers, scientists, doctors, lawyers, engineers, architects, or members of other professions. People would have little confidence in anyone who claimed to be a professional if they left the impression they did not possess the professional knowledge expected of them. For example, few of us would seek the services of a medical doctor if we thought he or she did not apply the most recent and accepted medical knowledge. Nor would we opt to take any elective courses from professors who left the impression they did not know the concepts and principles we wanted to learn. Incidentally, if someone is truly professional, he or she has have already taken a big first step toward being able to apply OFM, because it requires a good understanding of the benefits of leisure and what leisure is really about (more on that in Chapters 2 and 3).

Given this discussion, the question then arises: Does a sufficient empirically supported body of knowledge now exist so a person can gain that knowledge to entitle him or her to be called a leisure or related amenity professional? The answer is a definite yes, despite the need for additional scientific documentation of the benefits of leisure and related amenities. That need is common to all professions, but they act on their knowledge just as recreation and related amenity professionals must.

Albeit gently, the question must now be raised: Do too many park and recreation so-called professionals still have inadequate understanding of the beneficial and negative outcomes of leisure? If so, can practitioners lacking that knowledge really know what they are doing? Raising this question might seem a little harsh because practically all practitioners are dedicated, conscientious, and have contributed greatly by their provision of recreation and related amenity opportunities. However, if practitioners do not have adequate understanding of the science-based knowledge about the benefits of recreation, they must rely mostly on their personal judgments and intuitions, which are necessary but not sufficient for professionalism. This questioning is not meant to imply that each professional person must be aware of and understand each and every benefit listed in Table1.1. It *does* suggest that they must have an adequate understanding of the types of benefits relevant to their particular area of specialization. It also means that they must work closely with relevant stakeholders to obtain information from them about the beneficial outcomes they desire to be realized and the negative outcomes they wish to avoid. Many applications of OFM have shown that those stakeholders have a good idea of what these outcomes are[4].

To put the aforementioned questions in a different context, few, if any, medical professionals are accused of quackery today. Instead, all medical professionals are now expected to understand and apply the science-based knowledge that is relevant to their particular specialization. In fact, many of them have to periodically pass qualifying examinations to maintain their licenses to practice. While licensing of recreation professionals is not being advocated here, it is advocated they must stay abreast of the professional knowledge that is relevant to them.

The following two questions now seem relevant:

- Is there any way to achieve the degree of professional standing advocated here for recreation professionals other than to adopt and apply OFM to guide policy development and management? The central question asked by OFM is *why provide any recreation and related amenity service?* The answer requires that practitioners answer that question in terms of likely positive outcomes that will be realized and negative outcomes that will be avoided or reduced in magnitude.
- Is there any other way to reposition the widely held, incorrect, and misleading images about leisure and related amenity resources and services other than promoting the resulting benefits? How can we more convincingly lead others to understand the tremendous values that these

resources and services add to peoples' lives and to any society unless we recreational professionals first understand and then articulate the benefits of leisure and promote management that attempts to optimize those benefits?

Current Status of OFM

Applications are Increasing

Perceptive practitioners have been applying part of the basic logic of OFM for decades on a piecemeal basis. This has occurred when: group picnicking opportunities are provided for people to affiliate and enjoy camaraderie; scenic vistas are maintained for scenic enjoyment; gates at campgrounds are closed after 10:00 p.m. to help assure a sense of security; interpretive nature trails are provided for environmental learning; water bars are placed on trails to prevent erosion; tourism is supported to help the economic vitality of nearby communities; yoga classes are offered to help cope with everyday life stresses and to realize other beneficial outcomes; and on and on. While commendable, these piecemeal and sporadic actions, that generally focused on only one type of benefit, do not constitute implementation of the OFM as described in detail in Chapters 2 and 3. For example, those past efforts may or may not have: (1) started the management planning process with evaluations of what *outcomes* could be targeted given existing and likely attainable resources and other assets instead of focusing mostly on what recreation activity opportunities could be produced and (2) included collaboration with relevant stakeholders to determine what outcomes should be targeted managerially. Each is a fundamental requirement of OFM.

Slowly but surely, OFM is receiving wider application by public agencies that offer recreation and related amenity opportunities. That progress is documented by the 18 chapters of this text that describe applications of OFM to guide policy development and management of many different public park and recreation agencies in the U.S., Australia, Canada, and New Zealand. Progress was shown also when the Executive Leadership Team of the USDI Bureau of Land Management issued a directive on January 5, 2006 that requires use of the OFM throughout that agency (see Chapter 8 of this text). Key words in that directive state "...Field Managers will assess and evaluate effects of proposed projects in Special Recreation Management Areas on activities, *experiences, beneficial outcomes* and recreation setting character to ensure consistency with benefits-based management [OFM] concepts." [emphasis added]

In this section on applications of OFM, the rather wide adoption of Experience-Focused Management (EFM) should be mentioned. Remember, the third definition of a benefit of leisure given early in this chapter was the realization of a satisfying recreation experience. Thus, since satisfying experiences are benefits, EFM is a limited application of OFM. It is limited because it considers only experiential benefits, and not the other two types of benefits of leisure (defined earlier) that are covered by OFM. EFM is practiced when opportunities to realize specific types of satisfying experiences are overtly targeted by practitioners and when management is directed toward providing those opportunities, which is not uncommon. It happens frequently by agencies managing both municipal and wild land recreation and related amenity resources and programs. For example, Manfredo (2002) edited a text that focused on applying EFM to wildlife management, and a summary of that perspective is given in Chapter 21 of this text. Perhaps the best known application of EFM is accomplished by use of the Recreation Opportunity Spectrum (ROS) system which was brought on line in the early 1980s (see Chapter 9 of this text).

Success with applying the ROS was a major stimulus for developing OFM to consider not only experiential benefits, but all the benefits of leisure. In one sense, the ROS is a *macro* application of EFM, because the ROS system was designed to inventory and manage relatively large wild land areas according to six or seven broad classes of recreation opportunity that afforded opportunities to realize different recreation activities and experiences. Inventory and managerial criteria for each ROS class establish guidelines for what managerial actions *can and cannot* be taken in each area managerially designated as a particular ROS zone. Therefore, the ROS is not a project or site, or *micro-level* management system, but the managerial guidelines it sets for the larger area in which projects and sites are located both constrain and facilitate what types and amounts of recreation opportunities can be produced. An academic description of the ROS can be found in Driver, Brown, & Gregoire (1987), a comprehensive review of it is given in Moore & Driver (2005:168-175), and a practical guide to it is presented in the "ROS User Guide" (USDA Forest Service, 1982). The ROS has been applied nationwide by the USDA Forest Service (see Chapter 9 of this text), used widely by the USDI Bureau of Land Management, is a central recreation management system of the New Zealand's Department of Conservation, and has been used in several states in the U.S., providences of Canada, and quite a few other countries including Australia, Norway, Denmark, and Thailand. Practitioners report that if they are familiar with the ROS system, that makes OFM easier for them to understand and apply, and many of them have incorporated concepts from the ROS system into applications of OFM especially to help define logical recreation management zones and develop setting condition prescriptions as discussed in Chapter 3.

Current Restraints and Misinterpretations

In spite of increasing applications of the OFM, at least the following major problems still exist.

1. Too few lead administrators and managers of park and recreation agencies understand OFM and therefore have not issued directives to apply it, as the Executive Leadership Team of the BLM did.
2. Too many practitioners do not understand the benefits of leisure.
3. It is not uncommon for agencies to believe they are implementing OFM when in fact they are not. They believe that piece-meal and sporadic management for specific benefits is OFM, but they do not understand what is really involved with implementing OFM. This seems to occur because most people working for a public park or recreation agency believe, at least philosophically, that they are providing opportunities to realize benefits and reduce unwanted impacts. However, thinking and talking about desirable and undesirable outcomes is only a necessary, not sufficient, step toward adopting OFM; sufficiency is attained by implementing all *of the requirements* of OFM described in Chapters 3 and 4.
4. Too often the direction of park and recreation management is too strongly influenced by (caters to) powerful interest groups and/or "partners." This limits the freedom of the managers to respond to other stakeholders and thereby results in developments that serve a limited number of people. As a result, it reduces the total value that could be added to the larger number of users that are ignored.
5. Many practitioners believe they do not have time to implement OFM[5]. The author of this chapter and other supporters of OFM do not believe that this often heard argument reflects sound professional judgment. Is it sound professional behavior to reject a scientifically credible, relevant, and useful management system that other practitioners have adopted and approved? Would medical or other professionals ever give the reason that they do not have time to adopt a proven innovation? In addition, many other professionals have to understand a far larger and more complex amount of technical knowledge than is required by understanding the benefits of leisure and how to implement OFM. Put simply, OFM will not be implemented unless professionalism carries the day.

Literature Cited

Allen, L. & Cooper, N. (2003). *Benefits based programming curriculum manual.* Ashburn, VA: The National Recreation and Park Association.

Allen, L., Stevens, B., Hurtes, K., & Harwell, R. (1998). *Benefits-based programming of recreation services training manual.* Ashburn, VA: The National Recreation and Park Association.

American Academy of Political and Social Sciences. (1957). *Recreation in the age of automation.* The Annuals. Vol. 313. Sept. Philadelphia. PA.

Bammel, G. & Bammel, L. (1992). *Leisure and human behavior.* 2nd Ed. Dubuque, IA: Wm. C. Brown Publishers.

Bammel, G. & Burrus-Bammel, L. (1996). *Leisure and human behavior.* 3rd. ed. Dubuque, IA: Brown & Benchmark Publisher.

Canadian Parks/Recreation Association. (1997). *The Benefits Catalogue.* Gloucester, ON, Canada: Canadian Parks/Recreation Association.

Crompton, J. (1993). Repositioning recreation and park services: An overview. *Trends,* 30 (4) 2–5.

Crompton, J. & Witt, P. (1996). Repositioning: The key to building community support. *Parks and Recreation.* October, 80–90.

Driver, B. L. (2003). Leisure experiences. In J. Jenkins and J. Program (Eds.). *Encyclopedia of Leisure and Outdoor Recreation.* London. Routledge (an imprint of Taylor & Francis Books Ltd.).

Driver, B. L. (1990). The North American experience in measuring the benefits of leisure. In Elery Hamilton-Smith (Compiler), *Proceeding, National workshop on the measurement of_recreation benefits.* Bandoora, Victoria, Australia: Phillips Institute of Technology

Driver, B. L., Brown, P., Stankey, G. & Gregorie, T. (1987). The ROS planning system: Evolution, basic concepts, and research needed. *Leisure Sciences*. 9: 201–212.

Driver, B. L., Brown, P., & Peterson, G. (Eds.). (1991). *Benefits of leisure*. State College, PA: Venture Publishing, Inc.

Driver, B. L. & Bruns, D. (1999). Concepts and uses of the Benefits Approach to Leisure. In E. Jackson and T. Burton (Eds.), *Leisure studies: prospects for the twenty-first century*. State College, PA: Venture Publishing, Inc.: 349–368.

Driver, B. L., Bruns, D., & Booth, K. (2001). Status and common misunderstandings of the net benefits approach to leisure. In *Trends 2000: Shaping the future. Contributed Papers for the 5th Outdoor Recreation & Tourism Trends Conference* (pp. 245–263). East Lansing, MI: Michigan State University, Department of Park, Recreation, and Tourism Resources.

de Grazia, G. (1992). *Of time, work, and leisure*. Glencoe, IL: The Free Press.

Edginton, C., Jordan, D., DeGraft, D., & Edginton, S. (1995). *Leisure and life satisfaction: Fundamental principles*. Dubuque, Iowa: Brown & Benchmark Publishers.

Fabos, J., Milde, G., & Weinmayr, V. (1968). *Frederick Law Olmstead*. Amherst, MA: The University of Massachusetts Press.

Gray, D. E. & Greben, S. (1974). Future Perspectives. *Parks and Recreation*. July, 26–33, 47–56

Federal Reporting Service (1961). Transcript of Proceedings: Conference on Leisure-Outdoor Recreation and Mental Health. Williamsburg, VA: June 1–3, 1961. For the Outdoor Recreation Resources Review Commision. Washington, D.C.

Jordon, C. (1991). Parks and Recreation: More than Fun and Games. In. B. L. Driver, P. Brown, and G. Peterson, (Eds.), *Benefits of leisure*. (pp. 365–368) State College, PA: Venture Publishing, Inc.

Lee, M. E. & Driver, B. L. (1992). Benefits-Based Management: A New Paradigm for Managing Amenity Resources. Paper presented at The Second Canada/US Workshop on Visitor Management in Parks, Forests, and Protected Areas. May 13-16, 1992. University of Wisconsin-Madison, Madison, WI.

Manfredo, M. (2002). *Wildlife viewing: A management handbook*. Corvallis, OR: Oregon State University Press. Marshall, G. (1933). *The forest for recreation and a program for forest recreation*. From: A National Plan for American Forests. Report Prepared by the Forest Service, U. S. Department of Agriculture in Response to Senate Resolution 175 (72d Congress). Senate Document No. 12, Separate No. 6. Washington, D.C.: U. S. Government Printing Office.

Moore, D. & Driver, B. L. (2005). *Introduction to outdoor recreation: Providing and manageing natural resource based opportunites*. State College, PA: Venture Publishing, Inc.

More, T. (2002). "The parks are being loved to death" and other fraud and deceits in recreation management. *Journal of leisure research*, *34*(1), 52–78.

Olmstead, F. (1953). *The Yosemite Valley and the Mariposa Big Trees*. A preliminary report as reconstructed by .L. W. Roper. Landscape Architecture. 44:12–25.

O'Sullivan, E. (1999). *Setting a course for change: The benefits movement*. Ashborn, VA. National Recreation and Parks Association.

Outdoor Recreation Resources Review Commission. (1962). *Outdoor recreation for America*. Summary Volume. Washington, D.C.: U. S. Government Printing Office.

Pieper, J. (1972). *Leisure, the basis of culture*. NY: Random House. Inc.

Sefton, J. & Mummery, W. (1995). *Benefits of recreation research update*. State College, PA: Venture Publishing, Inc.

Stankey, D, Cole, D., Lucas, R., Peterson, M., & Frissell, S. Others. (1985). *The limits of acceptable change (LAC) system for wilderness planning*. Gen. Tech. Report INT-176. Logan, Utah: Intermountain Forest and Range Experiment Station. USDA Forest Service.

USDA Forest Service. (1982). *ROS User Guide*. Washington, D.C.

United Way of America. (1996). *Measuring program outcomes: A practical approach*. Item No. 0989. Washington, D.C.

The President's Commission on Americans Outdoors. (1986). *A literature review*. Section on Values and Benefits. Washington, D.C.: U.S. Government Printing Office.

Footnotes

1. See for example http://www.uwex.edu/ces/pdande/evaluation/evallogicmodel.html and http://www.wkkf.org/Pubs/Tools/Evaluation/Pub3669.pdf.
2. An overview of the deliberations of the Rockefeller study group is included here, because over the past 40 years, the author of this chap-

ter has not met any person, except Dean Dana, who knew about it. I desired to see something published about it for posterity. BLD

3. The summary volume of the ORRRC (1962) stated "As outdoor recreation increases in importance, it will need more land....Yet, there is little research to provide basic information on its relative importance. More needs to be established factually about the values of outdoor recreation to our society...." (pg. 5)
4. If one accepts the above reasoning, is it illogical to propose that those who claim to be recreation and related amenity professionals are in fact professionally irresponsible if their professional actions are not guided by best available scientific knowledge? It will be left to the reader to decide the degree to which he or she believes that situation exists in the management of public park and recreation resources and programs. But, if someone is truly professional, he or she has already taken a big first step toward being able to apply OFM, because it requires a good understanding of the benefits of leisure and what leisure is really about (more on that in Chapters 2 and 3).
5. As one example of this impediment to wider implementation of OFM, the author of this text was asked in 1997 by the then head of the recreation staff of a large public wild land management agency to work with two members of his staff to assure that OFM (i.e., BBM) would be implemented within that agency. After meeting with those staff members, along with four other professionals familiar with that agency's purposes and operations and with OFM, and after the author prepared several documents that group wanted, he was told by the staff member in charge of getting BBM implemented in that agency that the agency was already applying BBM and that it could not take on an effort to apply it incrementally (as was planned) because of other demands on that staff group! Little progress has been made to implement OFM fully in that agency as explained in Chapter 9 of this text.

Chapter 2
What is Outcomes-Focused Management?

B. L. Driver

Learning Objectives

1. Understand the reasons for and evolution of the Outcomes Focused Paragon (OFP[1]) and Outcomes-Focused Management (OFM).
2. Appreciate how OFM became an important application of the OFP.
3. Understand the basic concepts, principles, requirements, and advantages of the OFP and OFM.
4. Understand how OFM differs from other approaches to the management of recreation and related amenity resources and programs.

To repeat from Chapter 1, Outcomes-Focused Management (OFM) is an important application of its umbrella Outcomes-Focused Paragon (OFP). Unlike its predecessor, the Beneficial Outcomes Approach to Leisure (BOAL), the OFP does not focus just on so-called recreation resources and programs, but also includes related amenity resources and programs, which for brevity are hereafter referred to when recreation resources are mentioned. Chapter 1 also explained that the major purpose of this text was to promote wider understanding and application of OFM in recreation policy development and management of public agencies. This chapter sets the stage for accomplishing that purpose by describing what OFM is; why it was developed; its evolution; its basic concepts, principles, requirements, and advantages; and how OFM contrasts with other management systems, especially supply-oriented Activity-Focused Management (AFM). A more comprehensive review can be found of BBM in Chapters 12 and 13 of Moore & Driver (2005). Other useful references include Allen & McGovern (1997), Canadian Parks/Recreation Association (1997), O'Sullivan (1999), Driver & Bruns (1999), Driver, Bruns & Booth (2002), and Crompton, Jackson, & Witt (2005).

Reasons Why OFM Was Developed

The four related reasons the OFP and OFM were developed are:

1. Changing public values and demands required new approaches, and public recreation and park agencies needed to respond.
2. Perceptive professionals have long argued that greater attention needed be given to the benefits of recreation.
3. Increased scientific knowledge about the benefits of leisure and related amenity services permitted development of the OFP and OFM with scientific credibility.
4. Alternative acceptable management systems were not available.

For greater elaboration of these reasons and public agency responses to them than is given below, see Moore & Driver (2005:188–196).

Changing Public Values, Required Development, and Use of OFM

On April 8, 1997, Mike Dombeck (1997) the Chief of the USDA Forest Service (USFS), stated: "Today, society's priorities are shifting. Our management priorities must keep pace with…society's values." Those shifting public values have been particularly relevant to the management of recreation resources and programs because during the past several decades, there has been increasing and widespread concern by many people about the perceived quality of their lives. Most evidential is the fact that many people have increasingly become more concerned about better nutrition and weight management, stress management, physical activity, reduced smoking, moderation in the use of alcohol, adoption of conventional and alternative religious/spiritual orientations, and choices of leisure opportunities to realize specific desired benefits. These shifting societal priorities and behaviors are particularly relevant because users of recreation resources have become quite aware of what does and does not contribute to their perceived quality of their life. Consequently, many, if not most, users are now able to clearly articulate their desires for specific types of opportunities and, more importantly, what benefits they anticipate realizing from using those opportunities as well as the undesirable outcomes they wish to avoid. Put simply, most customers now know what characteristics of those opportunities are important to them and why. As a result, providers of outdoor recreation opportunities are now serving more introspective and astute customers who can articulate their preferences clearly.

In addition, the public has increasingly demanded that public agencies managing recreation and related amenity resources and programs be more efficient, cost-effective, fair/equitable, responsive, accountable, and able to sustain the biophysical and cultural/heritage resources they manage. Also, since the passage of the Environmental Protection Act of 1969 and failures of public resource management agencies to adequately meet its requirements for public involvement, members of the public have articulated their demands that all managerially-relevant stakeholders not just be in involved occasionally, but also be partners with planners and managers in environmental decision making--and often in the actual implementation of resource management plans. These demands for more systematic involvement of relevant stakeholders is central to the public demand that agencies become more responsive, but it is listed separately for emphasis because it is a critical requirement of the OFP and thus of OFM. In large part, the OFP and OFM were developed to help meet all the public demands reviewed in this paragraph.

In addition to the demand for change by the public, Chapter 1 briefly documented the fact that for decades many prominent spokespersons and writers have been promoting the argument that greater attention needs to be paid to the personal and social benefits of recreation. That too was an important reason the OFP and OFM were developed. Another reason was that there were no other cost-effective and scientifically creditable recreation resource planning and management systems available to meet the just-described demands.

Advancements in the States of Knowledge Have Facilitated Better Management Practice[2]

Chapter 1 documented that there have been great increases in scientific knowledge about the benefits of recreation and related amenities since the early 1960s. As that knowledge has improved, so has the delivery of recreation opportunities. An excellent example of such relationships between research and management is the incremental improvement in knowledge about public demands for recreation opportunities and the accompanying development of new managerial approaches to accommodate those demands. Those demands can be envisioned as existing within a "recreation and related amenity demand hierarchy." That hierarchy is illustrated in Figure 2.1 which is Figure 12.1 in Moore & Driver (2005:161). It shows three related types, or levels, of demand for different types of recreation and related amenity opportunities identified as opportunities to engage in desired activities, to realize satisfying experiences, and to realize benefits other than those experiences. Those demands are hierarchical because of the increasing complexity that is associated with attempts to define and understand, research, and managerially accommodate each type (or level) of demand as one moves from the less complex Level 1 demands (for activities) to the Level 2 demands (to realize satisfying experiences) to the much more complex Level 3 demands (to have opportunities to realize all types of benefits including the Level 2 demands to realize satisfying psychological experiences).

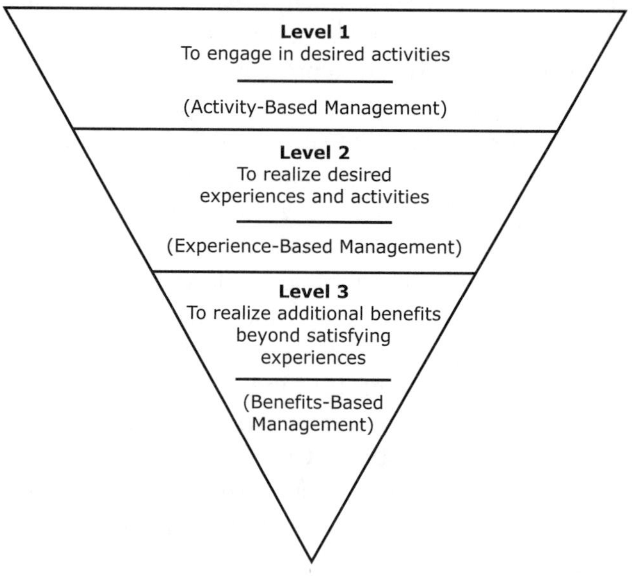

Figure 2.1 Hierarchy of demands for recreation and related amenity opportunities

Too many practitioners still focus primarily on the Level 1 demands, to a lesser extent on the Level 2 demands, and much less on the Level 3 demands. This was understandable in the past, because, as explained in Chapter 1, most scientific understanding of the Level 2 demands for satisfying experiences had not been gained until about the middle to late 1970s, and sufficient scientific knowledge about the other benefits has been gained only since about 1985. Consequently, managers could not understand and accommodate the Level 2 and Level 3 demands as well as they could the Level 1 demands. Therefore, they mostly practiced Activity-Based Management (or ABM, which is called Activity-Focused Management or AFM in this text), which incrementally has been supplemented, but not replaced, first by Experienced-Based Management (or EBM, which in this text is called Experience Management or EFM) and is now being supplemented by OFM (which replaced BBM in this text for the reasons given in Chapter 1). The characteristics of each will now be outlined so that OFM can be contrasted with AFM and EFM to show how OFM does not replace AFM or EFM, but instead supplements them.

Activity-Focused Management (AFM)

- AFM is required in all recreation resource management to meet customers' demand for activities in which they can participate.
- While necessary, AFM is much less complex than EFM and OFM, because it defines recreation only as the human behavior of participating in a recreation activity, just as eating and sleeping are human behaviors.
- AFM is supply oriented and focuses on the facilities or resources. It gives little attention to the demand side of management other than the demands for specific activity opportunities (i.e., the Level 1 demands).
- By just describing and documenting different types of activities provided and counts of people using different types of recreation and related amenity opportunities, AFM says nothing about how those customers are affected or impacted by the provision of those opportunities.
- AFM defines the user inputs to the recreation and related amenity opportunity production process in the same terms as it does the outputs of that process. Specifically, user inputs (other than their demands for activity opportunities and for facilitating attributes of the managed settings) are defined as users coming, and user outputs are defined as users going. Therefore, the inputs are the same as the outputs, and we do not know what the positive and negative impacts of participation are. By analogy, hospitals need better measures of their social contributions than just counts of the patients coming and leaving. They also need to know what happened to the patients while they were in and before they left the hospital.
- Given its focus on the biophysical and cultural/heritage resources, AFM provides too little opportunity to consider the quality of the recreation and related amenity activity opportunities provided or used. It does require consideration of the specific attributes of the recreation settings that are necessary for activity opportunities to be created. But it does not explicitly require professional understanding of why those attributes are needed and desired.
- Under AFM, management objectives, prescriptions, guidelines, and actions are oriented only to the provision of recreation and related amenity activity opportunities.
- The research support for AFM focused on types of recreation and related amenity activity opportunities people desired, how much they used the opportunities provided, the features/attributes of the physical and social settings needed for particular activity opportunities to be provided, how best to design attractive and cost-effective settings to encourage and accommodate use, how to reduce hazards to the users and prevent damage to the resources and facilities, and administrative concerns dealing with needed support services (e.g., law enforcement and medical assistance) and users' willingness to pay entrance and use fees.

Until recently, it is fair to say that probably 90 percent of most recreation and related amenity resource management was *primarily* AFM. And it is professionally embarrassing to say that too much of such management still remains primarily AFM.

Experienced-Focused Management (EFM)

EFM supplements, *but does not replace AFM*, so AFM is necessary but not sufficient. The essential characteristics of EBM follow:

- It is more complex than AFM, because it defines recreation as a psychological state in experiential terms and not just the behavior of participating in a recreation activity. See Moore & Driver (2005: Chapter 1) for an elaboration of this concept and definitions of leisure and recreation).
- It requires understanding of both supply and demand factors, including information from the customers about the types of experience opportunities they desire to be provided.
- It focuses on the types of psychological experiences that the customers desire to realize, so it is customer driven. This contrasts with AFM, which provides little focus on the customers' demand and expectations other than for activity opportunities and the attributes of the recreation settings necessary for them to be created.
- EFM provides a better basis for understanding and improving the quality of recreation and related amenity opportunities provided and the experiences actually realized from using those opportunities. It does because it requires analyses and evaluations of user satisfaction in experiential terms. It also requires relating preferences for experiences both to activity opportunities and the attributes/features of the recreation settings necessary for those activities and experiences to take place. Therefore, it requires very specific delineation of setting attributes that both add to and detract from the quality of specific types of experiences demanded, such as realizing solitude or applying and testing one's skills.
- Under EFM, management objectives explicitly state the types of experience opportunities that will be provided when, where, for whom, and in what amount. Then management prescriptions, guidelines, and standards are written to help assure that those targeted experience opportunities will be delivered within the time frame proposed by the plan for which the experience opportunity management objectives have been written.
- Until recently, applications of EFM focused on the on-site visitors/customers, but now EFM refers to all customers who realize satisfying psychological experiences from either the management or use of recreation and related amenity resources. Thus, EFM covers the visitors to the facilities, sites, and areas being managed; the residents of local communities who take pride in nearby amenities; and also the tax-paying owners of the public outdoor recreation resources who live more remotely than residents of local communities, even in distant large cities, and who receive psychological stewardship-related satisfactions from just knowing that the resources are being protected and maintained and pursue learning about those resources from many sources such as television programs, movies, coffee-table atlas, and other publications from many media including news bulletins and magazines from environmental organizations.
- EFM is an important but limited type of OFM, as outlined below because Chapter 1 defined the third type of benefit of recreation as the realization of satisfying recreation experiences. Thus, since EFM addresses satisfying experiences, EFM is a limited type of OFM because OFM covers all types of benefits and not just the experiential benefit.
- All of the types of research needed to support AFM are also needed to support EFM, because as stated, EFM supplements but does not replace AFM. In addition, research was needed on the on- and off-site users' expected and realized/attained desired (positive/beneficial) and undesired (negative/unwanted) psychological experiences, their relationships to characteristics of the settings being managed, and experience-based conflicts between users and how to avoid and reduce them. This additional research and the additional managerial requirements show why EFM is more complex than AFM and could not be implemented fully until results of the research just mentioned were available.

A good example of EFM is the use of the Recreation Opportunity Spectrum (ROS) system as explained in Chapter 1 and elaborated in Moore & Driver (2005:168–175).

Outcomes-Focused Management (OFM)

OFM supplements *but does not replace AFM and EFM.* The remainder of this chapter and Chapters 4 and 5 (that explain how to implement OFM) describe the other characteristics of OFM that are not outlined below in its comparison to AFM and EFM.

- OFM considers not only psychological experiences but also psychophysiological, physiological outcomes, and all other types of benefits of the management and use of recreation and related amenity resources, including benefits to individuals, groups of individuals (extending from the family and other smaller groups, through communities to the nation at large), and to the biophysical and cultural/heritage resources.
- It considers not only immediate benefits but also long-term benefits.
- It requires consideration of negative as well as positive outcomes.
- It requires that planners and managers collaborate with all affecting and affected stakeholders about the types of benefit opportunities that should be provided and negative outcomes that should be reduced or avoided.
- It requires that planners and managers work collaboratively with relevant associated providers who provide needed supplemental and/or auxiliary services.
- It requires that recreation and related amenity professionals understand how to capture the positive and avoid the negative effects of their management and use of the resources they manage and then, with this understanding, manage accordingly.
- It requires that management plans overtly target well-defined positive and negative outcomes and that the means for attaining those outcome goals defined by time-bound, realistic/achievable, and cost-effective management objectives (as elaborated in Chapters 4 and 5).
- It could not be developed and implemented fully until sufficient research had been done on the benefits of leisure (other than experiential) that were available, which demonstrates its greater complexity than AFM and EFM.

As a caution, it should be mentioned that some practitioners who apply OFM confusingly think that they must also practice EBM *separately*. That thinking is a carry over from the time that EBM was evolving into OFM as additional scientific knowledge about the other benefits of recreation was emerging to facilitate early applications of OFM. To iterate, OFM focuses on *all* relevant positive and negative outcomes, so it encompassed the satisfying psychological experiential benefits (that define EBM) as well as all other relevant benefits.

To be fair, it should be mentioned that the above three approaches to the management of recreation resources and programs have not been as discretely different in practice as the above comparisons suggests. Many managers have intentionally provided opportunities for the realization of satisfying psychological experiences and other benefits while they primarily practiced AFM. Nevertheless, until EFM and OFM were developed as science-based management systems, these earlier applications of EFM and OFM were mostly intuitive and not as systematic as required by OFM. In a nutshell, EFM evolved and supplemented, but did not replace AFM, and OFM did the same for EFM.

Evolution of the OFP and OFM

From the above, it is seen that science-based EFM evolved from AFM, and science-based OFM evolved from EFM incrementally over time since the late 1970s. An important dimension of that evolution was the successful implementation of the Recreation Opportunity Spectrum (ROS) system in the early 1980s, which was a significant application of EFM as explained in more detail in Moore & Driver (2005:168-175). About the same time other managerial applications of EFM were being proposed (cf. Manfredo, Driver, & Brown, 1983). Starting around the mid 1980s, many leisure scientists and practitioners argued that OMF needed to go beyond the experiential benefits considered by EFM. This led to accelerated support for more research on those other benefits that would give OFM reasonable scientific credibility. Those efforts resulted in several publications that revealed and promoted wider attention to science-based knowledge about the benefits of recreation and related amenities. Included were *Benefits of Leisure* (Driver, Brown, & Peterson, 1991), *The Benefits of Recreation Research Update* (Sefton & Mummery, 1995), and *The Benefits Catalogue* (Canadian Parks/Recreation Association, 1997). These publications in turn attracted the attention of other recreation and related amenity professionals, especially forward-thinking practitioners.

Particularly significant in the evolution of OFM and the OFP were the comments of several authors and coauthors of the text *Benefits of Leisure* who met at Snowbird, Utah in 1989 to preview near-final drafts of that text. Those authors, including recreation and related amenity agency administrators and agency staff members, expressed strong interest in their need to consider more credible the beneficial outcomes of their policy and managerial decisions. They wanted more information about how they could do that. Their concerns led to a Benefits of Leisure Application Workshop, held in Estes Park, Colorado, in May of 1991. Thirty-five leaders and managers of federal, state, regional, and municipal recreation agencies or staff groups attended that workshop, as did another 35 leisure scientists and educators interested in the benefits of leisure who wanted to see more of the results of leisure research applied in recreation and related amenity policy development and management. The participants were from the United States and Canada, and the Canadian participants were involved in drafting the first and shorter edition of *The Benefits Catalogue* referenced above and cited in the "Literature Cited" section at the end of this chapter.

The ideas, purposes, and advantages of the OFM were developed at the Estes Park, Colorado Benefits Application Workshop, and it was then called Benefits-Based Management (BBM). At first, BBM focused only on the management of recreation resources. But very soon, heads of recreation agencies/staff groups recognized the advantages to them of the logic and requirements of BBM in policy development (especially in better justifying their budget requests). In addition, leisure educators and scientists recognized the merits of BBM as an overriding normative paragon for their efforts too. So, BBM was expanded into the Beneficial Outcomes Approach to Leisure (BOAL) as an umbrella paradigm that encompassed all aspects of leisure. The reasons the participants in the workshop desired to see BBM (OFM) and the BOAL (OFP) developed were reviewed in Moore & Driver (2005:188) as follows.

> ...top administrators of public P&R agencies needed better information about the social and other benefits of recreation so they could more accurately describe them with enhanced credibility to elected officials responsible for funding the delivery of publicly provided leisure services. Put simply, recreation was then still generally viewed by the legislators as merely "fun and games" (cf. Jordan, 1991) and as providing few benefits to society as a whole. Therefore, legislators believed that the users, not the taxpayers, should bear most of the costs of providing leisure opportunities. This erroneous perception that leisure was relatively trivial for society created regular funding crunches for top-level administrators of public P&R agencies. When proposing and justifying budget requests, they badly needed a scientifically credible benefits-oriented paradigm to provide better documentation that significant benefits of leisure to a society include but go beyond the benefits realized by individuals (e.g., the role of leisure in helping to prevent/reduce the rapidly increasing public costs of health care). Second, the field-level planners and managers present at the workshop, while believing that conventional social, economic, and environmental impact assessments were useful, found those assessments were typically too general and provided inadequate specific guidance for managerial actions once the results of these assessments had been used to help guide basic resource allocation decisions. Also, although they understood the need to practice both ABM and EBM, they also realized the time was ripe to move into BBM to supplement ABM and EBM, and they needed guidelines on how to do so. In short, they wanted to know how to optimize the net benefits that would accrue from their planning and managerial actions. In particular, the field-level managers wanted to predictably know which types of positive outcomes their managerial actions could most effectively and responsibly provide and which negative outcomes or impacts of management could be minimized in cost-effective ways, while sustaining the basic biophysical and cultural/heritage resources they managed. Third, the leisure scientists and university educators at the workshop desired to better understand the positive and negative consequences of leisure behavior, how the net benefits of such could be enhanced, and how they could work more closely with practitioners to facilitate better management. They were also all committed to creating a more accurate perception and understanding of the social values of leisure (i.e., reposition the image) in the minds of other people outside the leisure professions. They believed strongly that understanding and then articulating the benefits was the best way to do this. (p. 188)

The original concepts, principles, and requirements of BBM (or OFM in this text) have changed considerably since 1991 as it has been applied to help guide policy development and management of recreation resources and programs. The characteristics of the evolved OFM will now be described.

Essential Characteristics of the OFM[3]

The four most distinguishing characteristics of OFM are described below:

1. It focuses on positive and negative outcomes.
2. OFM requires collaborative involvement with relevant stakeholders.
3. It describes cause and effect relationships within the recreation opportunity production system (or production process).
4. OFM requires development of outcomes-oriented management objectives that specific, overtly targeted outcome goals will be attained by implementing specific management actions.

OFM Focuses on Positive and Negative Outcomes

Two fundamental premises of OFM are that when recreation and related amenities are conceived broadly: (1) the value they add to most societies equals or exceeds the value added by any other social service and (2) they comprise one of the largest economic sectors of many nations in the world, again when considered comprehensively. See Chapter 1 of Moore & Driver (2005) for justifications of these two perhaps bold statements. The OFM also recognizes that too few people realize these tremendous personal, social, economic, and environmental benefits. More relevant to this text, the many benefits of recreation are not given sufficient attention in recreation policy development and management. For that reason, the basic question raised by OFM is: *Why* should any recreation and related amenity opportunities be provided? The answer to that question includes consideration of what has been done in the past. But the OFM does not accept past actions, in and of themselves, as sufficient basis for continuing those actions. Instead, the "why" question must be answered in terms of positive outcomes to be realized and negative outcomes to be avoided or reduced for identified targeted markets or customers within the context of what the public agencies are legislatively mandated to do and what it can do feasibly within the constraints of its budget allocation and other available resources. As emphasized in Chapter 1, the only way this "why" question can be addressed properly is for policy makers and managers to understand what benefits should be provided and what unwanted likely negative effects can be avoided or reduced in magnitude.

OFM Requires Establishing and Maintaining Collaborative Partnerships with Relevant Stakeholders

The second important requirement of OFM is to build and maintain collaborative partnerships with all relevant stakeholders. OFM adopts a much broader than normal definition of the word *stakeholder* to include any person or group that affects, is affected by, or is just seriously interested to *a managerially relevant degree*, and it believes that such relevance must be determined by the practitioners concerned. Under OFM, there are two important types of stakeholders: the customers and the associated providers.

Customer Stakeholders

OFM recognizes two types of customers/users--the on-site visitors and the off-site users. The *on-site* customers are those who visit and use the recreation areas and sites being managed. There are *two types of off-site users*, local and remote ones. The local customers are those people who live *near* the recreation/amenity resources being managed, such as in local host/gateway communities or just down the street from a park or open space in a city. However, they do not use the area or site for recreational purposes. The *remote* off-site customers live farther away from the recreation areas or sites being managed but still realize stewardship and other appreciative (vicarious) benefits from learning about the protection and management of those resources from television, movies, books, and other publications and media.

Research on the nearby off-site users has shown that whether or not they ever visit the areas or sites being managed, the residents of local communities and neighborhoods realize beneficial and negative outcomes from the management of those areas or sites (cf. Allen, 1991; Campbell, 1981; Harper, Neider, Godbey, & Lamont, 1997; Marans & Mohai, 1991; Stein, Anderson & Thompson, 1999). That research documents that nearby amenities help maintain a local sense of place, contribute to local residents' overall perceived quality of life, and increase their property values (Crompton, 2004). In addition, scores of studies have documented that tourism contributes significantly to the economic stability and growth of many local communities, which benefit both the on-site and off-site users residing there (cf. Chapter 21 this text). On the other hand, members of local communities have also expressed concerns about how nearby public recreation/tourism developments and the associated influx of new visitors and residents and the ensuing community growth have negatively impacted local communities. Such changes can cause greater traffic congestion, increased crime, reduced neighborhood safety, and related problems. In some areas, local communities have deteriorated, as have adjoining natural landscapes, because of poorly and insensitively planned large-scale, unsightly, or otherwise incongruent tourism-related structures and uses. Weakened community capability to protect local property rights and to maintain distinctive main streets and residential architecture has also been experienced, which has eroded the character, quality, and sense of place of many small-town rural landscapes. These negative consequences of development and use of nearby recreation/amenity resources have frequently complicated the task of nurturing or maintaining good relationships between the communities, the managers, and the users of those resources.

The significance of both the near and more remote off-site users has been documented by several regional household surveys and at least one national study that established the economic willingness of these off-site users to pay taxes for responsible public land management is sizable and exceeds the on-site users' willingness to pay for such management (Loomis & Walsh, 1997: 366–367). Furthermore, the number of off-site users equals or exceeds the number of on-site users. Basic principles of consumer economics state that if people have a willingness to pay, or expend their scarce personal resources, they must be receiving some type of utility or benefit. Given the large number of such off-site users and their expressed willingness to pay for protection of recreation and other amenity resources, it is reasonable to believe that the total benefits realized by these off-site customers probably exceed the total benefits realized by the relatively much smaller number of on-site users, to whom the greatest policy and managerial attention is usually given.

OFM recognizes that the off-site financial supporters of managing public resources are as *much* "owners" of those resources as are the on-site users. Put simply, they are relevant (albeit too frequently forgotten) customer stakeholders, who should be involved in helping answer the basic *why* question. Therefore, both the on- and off-site customer stakeholders must be involved collaboratively in allocation decisions, because they are the best source of information about the primary outputs (i.e., recreation/amenity opportunities) and the positive and negative outcomes toward which recreation and related amenity policy and managerial decisions should be directed. In addition, local off-site users have often volunteered their time and have also been helpful in implementing approved plans, especially the monitoring of such.

Frequently, too little attention is given to the off-site users who do not visit the structures, sites, or areas being managed, because those off-site users are difficult to identify and involve in recreation and related amenity policy and managerial decisions. Nevertheless, they should and can be involved more by obtaining demand information from nearby residents and relying on results of existing relevant public surveys.

Associated Provider Stakeholders

OFM not only requires a broader than normal definition of "stakeholder" to include the off-site users but also expands the traditional concepts of *service provider* beyond that of the providing organization responsible for managing the resources on which recreation and related amenity opportunities are provided. It does this because of the very significant influences that *associated providers* have on the types, amounts, and quality of the total package of opportunities made available. They provide necessary services that are supplemental or auxiliary to the services provided by the managing agency. Such associated providers include the following:

- Businesses that provide medical, laundry, and dry-cleaning services; sell groceries; sell hunting and fishing licenses; etc.
- Hospitality industries that provide lodging, places to eat, transportation (rental cars), etc.
- Owners and mangers of local automotive service stations.
- Tourism organizations that provide information as well as other services.
- Services offered by outfitters and guides, concessionaires, and tour operators.
- Private tourism business destinations/attractions.
- Cultural establishments such as museums, art galleries, theatres, etc.
- Local private landowners.

- Providers that offer complementary, supplemental, and even competing recreation and related amenity opportunities, such as art galleries, museum, movie theatres, etc.
- Public agencies, such as local sheriff and police departments, which frequently assist in law enforcement at recreation/amenity facilities and areas.
- Local public and private organizations that provide needed services such as electric power and RV waste disposal options.

Without the assistance of these associated providers, most recreation and related amenity opportunities would have an altogether different character, and many would not exist at all. This is particularly true of outdoor recreation and related amenity opportunities, which rely heavily on local host/gateway communities. Put simply, all recreation/related amenity providers that affect the character or availability of opportunities produced must be involved collaboratively, simply because of their profound influence. In addition, it is important to remember that the total recreation experiences realized by on-site users are multiphasic, encompassing trip planning, travel to the site, on-site engagements, travel back, and recollection (Clawson & Knetsch, 1966: pp. 33–36). Associated providers frequently affect several of these phases more than the responsible providing organization does. Furthermore, associated providers play an important role in communicating various messages about recreation/amenity area management and protection. They have an impact on the images the customers have about the providing organization, influence customer expectations and preferences, and promote a positive understanding of the social importance of recreation and related amenities.

In short, OFM recognizes the impossibility of attempting to produce opportunities for desired outcomes and minimizing undesired outcomes without the collaboration of associated providers. Therefore, all relevant associate providers must be involved collaboratively. Their influence and importance is the major reason why the recreation opportunity production system defined by OFM must be conceptualized as much broader than just a physically defined area, site, or structure--as it too typically is when the managing agency is viewed as the sole source provider. Just as environmental factors (rain, hail, sun, wind, etc.) outside a farmer's cornfield affect that system, the associated providers normally operate off-site, or away from, a physically defined recreation or related amenity facility, site, or area; but operatively, the system must be defined to include those important "environmental" influences.

Movement toward establishing and maintaining collaborative partnerships with relevant stakeholders is probably the greatest advance in recreation and related amenity resource management made recently.

True Collaboration is not Technocratic

Lastly on collaboration, it should be apparent that OFM rejects a technocratic approach by practitioners. Under such an approach, trained professionals behave as if they technically know what all stakeholder values and preferences are and what managerial decisions are the right ones to make. With these all-knowing attitudes, they fail to solicit information from the stakeholders that will be affected by, or can usefully affect, managerial decisions. Yes, professionally trained recreation and amenity resource managers do have needed expertise on how to protect and maintain the basic resources and other matters. Nevertheless, they do not always know what the best decision is to make for the customers they serve. This fact was emphasized by Jack Ward Thomas (1996), when he was Chief of the USDA Forest Service. He stated, "...each [decision] reflects a set of 'value mixes,' including judgments about what is fair for future [and current] generations. Thus, these decisions are in the realm of ethics whether we recognize it or not." (p. xxiv). Similar sentiments were also reflected by Wondolleck (1996), whose research has concentrated on establishing collaborative partnerships. She wrote, "...there is simply no [one]...right answer that systematic technical analysis will uncover." (p. 257). Put simply, while the OFP recognizes the need for technical expertise and is based on professional understanding of science-based knowledge, it rejects a technocratic approach.

Contrasting True Collaboration with the Common Practice of Establishing Partnerships

Many public and related amenity public agencies have established what they call partnerships with different organizations and individuals. While these partnerships are important for the provision of opportunities, most are actually implementing partnerships that facilitate on-site program operations (i.e., they implement decisions the provider has made). Hence, the following list outlines what constitutes true collaboration:

- It is more than just involving "partners" who will gain from working part-time with the managing public agencies. Instead it requires collaborative involvement in all aspects of all the planning and plan implementation processes.
- It engages all relevant customer and associated provider stakeholders in an ongoing and active basis.
- It includes representatives of local governments and of the nearby communities.
- It does not leverage a large part of the attention of a public recreation and related amenity agency away from its primary missions toward meeting the demands, financial commitments, and other support of special interest groups who want to partner with a particular agency of administrative subunit of such. Partnerships are useful, but they should not be controlling of what any public agency can or cannot do. This has become problematic and is in conflict with the basis tenets of OFM!

The topic of collaboration is too important to try to summarize it here in a few paragraphs. For further elaboration, the reader is referred to several excellent publications that explain why collaboration with relevant stakeholders is so important, what its characteristics are, and how it can be achieved. Especially recommended are Wondolleck & Yaffee (2000) and USDA Forest Service (1993). A good synopsis of that literature is found in Chapter 17 of Moore & Driver (2005).

There are No Sole-Source Providers

From the foregoing discussion, it should be apparent that OFM recognizes and requires that public park and recreation agencies coordinate management planning and plan implementation with relevant customer and associated provider stakeholders who play important roles in the production of recreation opportunities. Thus, while most agencies claim to be the producers of recreation opportunities, the fact is that they are not "sole-source" providers of the opportunities produced simply because the opportunities can seldom, if ever, be provided without the assistance of the associated providers. For that reason, OFM strongly prefers use of the words "provider actions" instead of just agency actions. Therefore, when the word "provider" is used in this text, it will generally refer both to the managing agency and all associated providers.

The OFP and OFM View the Delivery of Recreation and Related Amenity Opportunities as an Opportunity Production System

Under OFM, the provision of recreation opportunities is viewed as "a recreation opportunity production system." Unless one understands how and why OFM is based on the concept of a recreation opportunity production system (or process), she or he cannot appreciate what OFM is about, because that concept integrates the cause and effect relationships and systems perspectives necessary for proper and successful implementation of OFM. That process, which is explained in this section, is based on earlier similar works (Driver & Brown, 1975; Driver & Rosenthal, 1982; Brown, 1984; and Moore and Driver, 2005).

To enhance understanding, a few comments must be made about some of the words just used. First, the word *system* is important, because a system is defined as a whole that functions as a whole because of the *interdependencies of its parts* (Buckley, 1968). Understanding these interdependencies of the parts of the system involved in producing recreation opportunities is what is meant by the critical need to understand the many cause and effect relationships involved. Second, note that the concept of *producing* opportunities contrasts with the normal concept of *providing* opportunities. The word production is emphasized, simply because the concept of provision does not explicitly denote the need to understand *all the cause and effect relationships* that go into providing those opportunities. In contrast, the concept of *producing* anything requires a clear and comprehensive understanding of the production function involved (a very useful economic concept) whereas provision does not.

To describe the recreation opportunity production system of the OFM, the basic system model will first be described and then expanded into the model proposed by the OFM. That basic model is illustrated in Figure 2.2, which is Figure 13.1 in Moore & Driver (2005: 191). For more details about the characteristics of systems, see pages 191–195 of the text.

An example of this simple systems model was given by Driver and Bruns (1999: 356) of a farmer managing a corn-producing system. The farmer *inputs* knowledge (e.g., what to do, such as what type of seed corn to use and the proper time to plant), labor (e.g., tilling the soil), seed, fertilizer, and perhaps irrigation and chemicals to control weeds or the corn

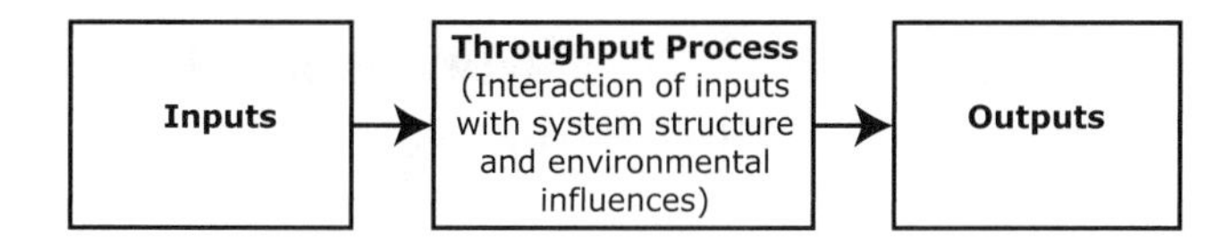

Figure 2.2 Basic systems model

borer insect. The physical structure of the system is the cornfield and includes the soil as well as any weed seeds and corn borer larva. But, the system also has surrounding "*environmental inputs*," such as rain, hail, wind, and sunshine. Through interaction of the rain or irrigation water, soil, temperature, seed, fertilizer, tilling, and any chemicals used during the *throughput process*, outputs are produced. Those *outputs* are corn kernels, corn cobs, corn stalks, weeds, and perhaps soil erosion--with the weeds and erosion showing that not all outputs are desirable. Similar simple conceptualizations can be made for many other types of systems (e.g., a stereo system, the human circulatory system, a car production system, etc.).

Too many recreation and related amenity resource management agencies still define their management systems pretty much as illustrated in Figure 2.2. That model is problematic for the production of recreation opportunities and explicit consideration of outcomes, simply because it does not consider outcomes, only outputs. The problem centers on the fact that the word "output" is normally used to refer *only* to the physically defined things that are produced by managerial actions. Examples include numbers of campgrounds or picnic areas installed and/or maintained, acres of critical winter or summer habitat maintained for a species of game, watchable wildlife viewing platforms installed and maintained, huts installed or maintained along a trail, miles or kilometers of trail installed and/or maintained, numbers of interpretative talks given, and so on. Traditionally, these types of outputs were the ones that field-level managers received operating budgets to produce. In addition, annual performance evaluations were based primarily on the degree to which the managers produced the outputs budgeted for and targeted in annual work plans. For these two reasons, those outputs were called *hard targets* by some public agencies. The big problem is that, while these types of outputs *must be produced*, they say absolutely nothing about resultant outcomes, which makes the Figure 2.2 inadequate for the purposes of OFM!

Given the current state of scientific knowledge about the benefits (as reviewed in Chapter 1), it is no longer professionally adequate to consider only inputs and outputs. In addition to protecting and improving the basic resources, the *primary* purpose of management is to optimize the realization of net benefits (positive outcomes minus negative ones) by capturing all possible positive outcomes and reducing and avoiding negative outcomes. To help correct current practices (i.e., deficiencies of the Figure 2.2 model), the OFM built upon and made very significant changes in the Figure 2.2 model of the recreation opportunity production system. Those changes are illustrated by Figure 2.3, which is a refinement of Figure 13.2 in Moore & Driver (2005: p. 193). Because the terms used in Figure 2.3 must be understood to properly apply OFM, they will now be described in detail.

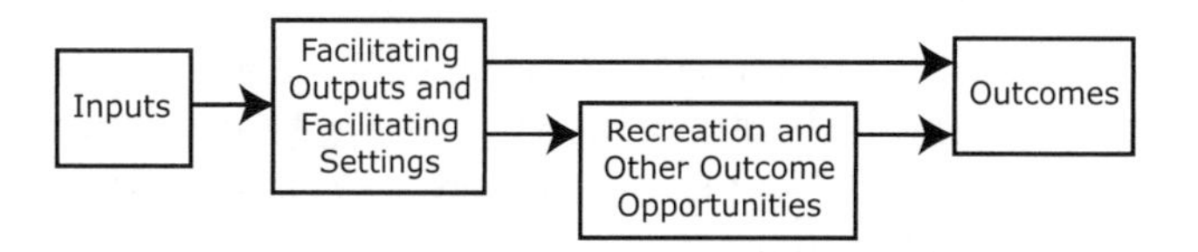

Figure 2.3 Expanded OFP and OFM model of the recreation and related amenity opportunity production process

Inputs

Inputs are things put into recreation and related amenity systems that are defined by their physical, biological, administrative, and social/cultural components. They include time/labor/effort, professional knowledge and skills, on-site presence of agency personnel, recreation capital investments, information on customer and other stakeholder preferences, social norms and mores, regulations, fees or lack of fees, administrative vehicles, materials for informational brochures and maps, reductions of hazards, on-site interpretive programs and guided tours, stocking of fish, materials to construct infrastructure (e.g., roads, parking lots, picnic tables, exhibits), sanitation and potable water systems, and so on. The customers and other stakeholders input their expectations, preferences, knowledge, past experiences, numbers of users (who contribute to on-site density), and the pets and other trappings the customers bring, including vehicles, equipment, radios, musical instruments, dance costumes, and electrical generators. The associated providers (defined in the next major section) also input their services, prices, and regulations (e.g., use of easements across private lands). Inputs from the natural environment include climatic influences, floods, infestations of unwanted plants, etc. From these examples, it can be seen that many of the inputs are the services that are provided to create the recreation opportunities. Provision of these services is frequently viewed as a service delivery system, which can be viewed as a subsystem (necessary part) of the OFP's and OFM's larger recreation opportunity production system.

Facilitating Outputs and Facilitating Settings

Facilitating Outputs: Under OFM, facilitating outputs are human-contributed components of the recreation opportunity production system that help produce opportunities for benefits to be realized and negative outcomes to be avoided/reduced. Some of the facilitating outputs of the Figure 2.3 model are identical to the conventional outputs shown in the right-hand box of the Figure 2.2 model, where they are acknowledged to represent facilitators of recreation opportunities but not generally outcome opportunities as they do under OFM. They are called facilitating outputs to emphasize that provisions of these outputs is not the ends of recreation and related amenity resource management, but that these facilitating outputs are produced only to *facilitate* the realization of positive outcomes and prevention of unwanted outcomes, which are the actual objectives of management. Unfortunately, other approaches to the management of recreation and related amenity resources still commonly view the production of facilitating outputs, in and of themselves, as the ends of management, which is why traditional performance evaluations of managers tend to consider them solely (i.e., without proper attention to outcomes), as considered more fully at the end of Chapter 3 under the section "Performance Evaluations."

Facilitating Settings: All recreation takes place within settings that facilitate the realization of different types of outcomes, such as satisfying experiences. For example, remote settings facilitate enjoyment of solitude and testing of outdoor skills, interpreted nature trails facilitate learning about nature, group camping areas facilitate camaraderie and social bonding, and so on. Some settings (e.g., beaches, vast landscapes, etc.) constitute part of the "environment" of the production system being managed, and other setting components (e.g., density of use allowed, regulations regarding pets, litter, and noise) are more under direct control of the providers of the recreation opportunities being produced. As will be emphasized in Chapter 3, managing requiring the attributes of desired settings is an extremely important requirement of OFM. That chapter describes three components of a recreation setting that affect the types and quality of recreation opportunities that can be produced. These are elaborated in Chapter 3 as the biophysical, social, and managerial/administrative components.

Recreation and Outcome Opportunities

Recreation Opportunities: These are opportunities to engage in particular recreation activities within particular settings to realize a satisfying experience and additional personal benefits, and to avoid undesired ones. Under OFM, most provider actions are oriented toward producing opportunities for beneficial outcomes to be realized and preventing or reducing negative outcomes. Those opportunities are produced by the facilitating outputs interacting with features of the facilitating physical, social, and managerial/administrative settings.

Other Outcome Opportunities: Included are the opportunities made available to realize economic, social, and environmental benefits. Most of these outcome opportunities are closely linked to the use of the recreation opportunities produced while others are produced directly by the providers' actions of recreation opportunities and services, as explained in the following paragraph. Under BBM, the nature and magnitudes of feasible beneficial and negative outcomes must be understood clearly before they can be targeted managerially and overtly managed for. This point will be elaborated in Chapter 3.

Outcomes Realized

As explained in Chapter 1, OFM defines outcomes *only* as beneficial (desirable) and nonbeneficial (undesirable) consequences of the management and use of recreation and related amenity resources and programs. Those outcomes are produced in three ways: by the on- and off-site customers, directly by managerial actions, and as chained/subsequent benefits. The critical point to understand is that the managers and associated providers do not produce most of the outcomes. Some outcomes result *directly* from managerial actions regardless of whether or not the recreation opportunities produced are ever used. They are indicated by the arrow in Figure 2.2 that goes directly from "Facilitating Outputs and Facilitating Settings" directly to "Outcomes." Examples include increased salaries of agency employees, revenues gained by contractors with agencies, the local economic multiplier effects of provider expenditures, resource protection activities, benefits of future generations from such protection, and any negative outcomes caused directly by managerial actions. Nevertheless, most of the positive and negative outcomes result from the use of the provided recreation opportunities by on-site and off-site customers. Those customers use those opportunities to produce satisfying experiences and other benefits for themselves and for other people who receive spin-off benefits. The critical point is that the managers and associated providers do not produce most of the outcomes. Some authors (More, 2002) have argued erroneously that OFM advocates "engineering of experiences." In fact, the OFP only "engineers" recreation opportunities, not experiences; the customers engineer or produce the experiences and other benefits for themselves through the ways they use the opportunities provided.

Another important point is that the on-site customers can significantly influence the nature of the recreation and outcome opportunities by their on-site numbers and behaviors and the things (dogs, boom boxes, etc.) they bring with them. As such, the on-site visitors represent a part of the structure of the recreation production system described earlier. The users don't just use the opportunities provided; they help mold them.

In review, the recreation opportunity production system inherent to OFM requires clear distinctions between inputs, facilitating outputs and facilitating settings, recreation and outcomes, and actual outcomes realized. To iterate, those distinctions cannot be appreciated unless the cause and effect relationships inherent to the Figure 2.2 recreation opportunity production process are understood.

Planning from Right to Left and Implementing from Left to Right

The expanded recreation opportunity production model is central to OFM, because it requires that policy makers and managers: (1) be able to answer not only the question *why* but also what, how, for whom, in what amount, and when the opportunities will be delivered and (2) understand the cause and effect relationships that exist within the expanded model of the recreation opportunity production system shown in Figure 2.3. That model makes those cause and effect relationships explicit, not implicit. The need to understand those relationships is just as much a requirement of professional recreation practitioners as it is for professionals who deliver medical, educational, welfare assistance, communication, transportation, and other social services must ask and answer the same questions.

In flow diagram terms, it is easier to understand the cause and effect relationships if one views *planning* of a recreation service delivery system as going from the right to the left side of the opportunity production process shown in Figure 2.3. That planning process *starts* with decisions about what beneficial *outcomes* will be targeted and which negative *outcomes* will be avoided or reduced in impact. Put simply, the desired outcomes determine what will be done and why; that is why it is called *Outcomes-*Focused Management! Once the targeted outcomes have been determined, they directly determine what facilitating outputs and facilitating settings need to be provided and created and/or maintained. But, from a plan implementation perspective, one moves from the left of Figure 2.3 to the right—provider inputs needed to attain targeted outcomes to attainment of those outcomes. These left-to-right plan implementation and right-to-left plan development processes contrast sharply with conventional approaches as well as with how performance is generally evaluated by public-sector park, recreation, and related amenity providers. Under OFM, managerial performance must be evaluated primarily in terms of the positive outcomes facilitated and the negative outcomes prevented. In the past, and continuing in most instances today, performance has been and still is evaluated primarily in terms of numbers and types of facilitating outputs produced and numbers of users/visitors, but not in terms of the net benefits realized. That emphasis on facilitating outputs instead of on outcomes has occurred for three reasons:

- Too many providers of outdoor recreation/amenity opportunities do not understand adequately the cause and effect relationships explained by the recreation opportunity production process and/or they have difficulty revising their old mindsets.
- Production of the facilitating outputs represents the largest part of the costs of producing outdoor recreation/amenity opportunities. They therefore receive inordinate attention, and are viewed as the ends of management.
- Headquarters of practically all public agencies require that subunits report their performance primarily in terms of the types and numbers of facilitating outputs (e.g., campsites) produced or maintained. The obvious problem from the

perspective of OFM is that such reporting in the past, and too frequently today, does not report what outcomes will be facilitated by production of those facilitating outputs and why.

These reasons reflect the view that producing the facilitating outputs is the goal of management. That errant viewpoint reflects the lack, or acceptance, of understanding of the logic and requirements of OFM. To reiterate, OFM views management of inputs and the production of facilitating outputs within facilitating settings *only* as necessary means to the production of primary outputs (i.e., opportunities to realize beneficial outcomes and avoid undesirable ones) necessary for the attainment of the explicitly defined and clearly articulated real ends of management, which are to capture the targeted beneficial outcomes and reduce and prevent unwanted outcomes.

OFM Requires Developing Outcomes-Oriented Management Objectives, Prescribed Setting Conditions, and Implementing Actions

The fourth fundamental and rather comprehensive requirement of OFM is the development of outcomes-oriented management objectives that specify overtly targeted outcome goals to be attained by explicit implementing actions to assure that prescribed setting conditions are being maintained, as elaborated in Chapter 3.

Additional Requirements of OFM

The four most fundamental requirements of OFM have just been reviewed. They and other requirements of OFM are detailed in Chapter 3. But as a preview the following overview is offered of some of the other things that must be done under OFM: (1) Do demand and supply analyses to determine the primary recreation-tourism market or customers that will be served and if they can be served, (2) Define logical recreation management zones and their corresponding recreation market niches, (3) Overtly specify feasible outcomes to target, (4) Develop management objectives to be implemented, (5) Develop setting condition prescriptions necessary to maintain the essential setting characteristics needed to produce, sustain, and facilitate attainment of outcomes targeted in the plan, (6) Collaboratively determine how to sustain the delivery of necessary inputs with the help of all affecting, affected, and interested providers, (7) Develop a marketing plan, (8) Develop an implementation and monitoring plan to *carefully* monitor plan implementation, (9) Assign responsibilities to responsible parties, (10) Revise the plan as needed, and (11) Assure that performance evaluations give adequate attention to the degree to which targeted outcomes have been attained. These determinations must address all that needs to be done, by whom, when, where, and how much. They also include monitoring for the attainment of approved management objectives and setting prescriptions.

In partial review, to make OFM work, one must decide what the *primary recreation market* will be for a particular facility, site, or logical management unit or zone of a larger recreation area; in other words, one needs to decide what particular and number of customers will be served where and when. Responsive and successful management cannot be accomplished for undefined customers. Next, *management objectives* must be developed that specify targeted outcomes for specific facilities, sites, management units, and even definable recreation "niches" within management units, with these outcomes focused on the targeted customer market(s). Then, *setting condition prescriptions* must be written that define and specify the characteristics of particular facilities, sites, management units, and recreation niches that must be created and/or maintained. In essence, they determine the planned recreational capacities of those facilities, sites, management units, and niches and when implemented, those prescriptions help create, enhance and sustain the recreational opportunities planned for the settings. For that reason, those prescriptions must not be compromised during plan implementation and monitoring. Last but certainly not least, for each management objective, a set of implementing actions must be written to assure the management objective will be met. This means the Figure 2.3 (pg. 29) inputs (i.e., provider actions or inputs) must be related to facilitating outputs and facilitating settings, and targeted outcomes in a way that maintains the productive capacity of recreation settings and facilities. In addition, quantitative but certainly objective standards must be developed to provide benchmarks against which monitoring occurs.

Uses of OFM

This chapter will be closed with a review of how OFM has been used in different ways to accomplish different, but related, purposes as follows.

- To assure an array of benefit opportunities are being provided by a particular provider of recreation opportunities, with different organizations deciding how wide that array should be, given their own resources and responsibilities.
- To target and facilitate the realization of one or more, but only a few, specific types of benefits desired, such as to promote physical fitness, to increase understanding of the natural environment, or to increase understanding and appreciation of a particular cultural/ heritage site or event. One example of this second type of use of the OFM is to prevent or resolve the social problems associated with at-risk youth, defined as young people who have problems with accepting social authority, are delinquent, abuse substances such as alcohol or other drugs, are doing poorly in school, have poor patterns of social interaction, and display social alienation or related issues. In the United States, about 70% of municipal park and recreation departments have programs targeted to at-risk youth, and they attempt to prevent those youth from becoming greater problems to themselves and/or to society. In most of these applications, public park and recreation agencies are cooperating closely with the justice, education, public welfare, and other relevant public agencies through recreation programming as an intervention strategy to help targeted youth.

It should also be mentioned that the above two uses of OFM are sometimes combined so that an array of benefit opportunities is targeted, of which particular subsets are emphasized. This might happen when a provider has special skills in providing certain benefit opportunities and/or because some types of benefits are deemed more important than others.

Lastly on uses of OFM, we should raise the difficult but very important question of to what degree a public recreation or related amenity agency should purposefully extend its reach beyond its normal interpretation of its administrative jurisdictions and responsibilities to consider how the services it provides can better serve the general welfare in particular ways. Deciding whether particular social benefits should be given special emphasis for that reason is an example. Each agency must determine individually. Examples of such targeting include:

- Promoting and maintaining physical and mental health and thereby reducing the rapidly rising cost of health care.
- Reducing social alienation and antisocial behaviors, such as crime, and the high social costs associated with such behaviors.
- Promoting a nonradical environmental ethic related to sustainable development and management of a nation's natural resources.
- Increasing understanding of the history of local, regional, and national places and events to promote, nurture, and maintain cultural mores/values; pride in communities, regions, and nations; and better citizenship.

Certainly each of these social benefits of recreation and related amenities now gets some attention, but each could, and perhaps should be given a lot more attention. Naturally, that is an issue for each reader to decide.

Summary

This chapter described the following essential requirements of the OFP and OFM.

- The "why" question is central.
- The recreation opportunity production system must be understood, as must the cause and effect relationships among the components of that model.
- The providing organization, especially public-sector agencies, must collaborate with all managerially relevant affecting and affected customer and associated provider stakeholders; a technocratic approach must be avoided.
- Relevant outcomes to both on-site and off-site customers must be considered.
- Specific management objectives must be written that overtly and explicitly specify the types of opportunities for positive outcomes that will be provided, the negative effects that will be minimized, and where and when the outcomes will be realized and in what amounts. Then, management and setting prescriptions, guidelines, and standards must be written and implemented during monitoring of plan implementation to assure attainment of outcome goals.

In addition, the chapter emphasized that the boundaries of the recreation opportunity production system extend beyond the physical boundaries of the area, site or structure being managed to include (1) "environmental influences, such as the interests and preferences of the off-site users and the significant roles of associated providers and (2) not only be constrained to conventional recreation resources but also include related amenity resources.

Literature Cited

Allen, L. (1991). Benefits of leisure services to community satisfaction. In B. Driver, P. Brown, and G. Peterson (Eds.), *Benefits of leisure* (pp. 331–350). State College, PA: Venture Publishing, Inc.

Brown, P. (1984). Benefits of outdoor recreation and some ideas for valuing recreation opportunities. In. G. Peterson and A. Randall (Eds.), *Valuation of wildland resource benefits*. (pp. 209–220). Boulder, CO. Westview Press, Inc.

Buckley, W. (1968). *Modern systems research for the behavioral scientist*. Chicago, IL: Aldine.

Campbell, A. (1981). *The sense of well-being in America: Recent patterns and trends*. New York, NY: McGraw-Hill.

Canadian Parks/Recreation Association. (1997). *The benefits catalogue*. Gloucester, Ontario, Canada.

Clawson, M. & Knetsch, J. (1966). *Economics of outdoor planning*. Baltimore, MD: The Johns Hopkins University Press.

Crompton, J. (1993). Repositioning recreation and park services: An overview. *Trends, 30*(4) 2–5.

Crompton, J. & Witt, P. (1998, October). Repositioning: The key to building community support. *Parks and Recreation*, 80–90.

Crompton, J., Jackson, E., & Witt, P. (2005). Integrating benefits to leisure with constraints to leisure. In E. Jackson (Ed.), *Constraints to leisure*. Chapter 16. State College, PA: Venture Publishing, Inc.

Dombeck, M. (1997, June 24). Presentation to Public Lands Forum of Outdoor Writers' Association of America. Grenefee, FL.

Driver, B. L. & Brown, P. (1975). A social-psychological definition of recreation demand, with implications for recreation resource planning. In *Assessing demand for outdoor recreation*. The Committee on Assessment of Demand for Outdoor Recreation Resources, by the Assembly of Behavioral and Social Sciences of the National Research Council of the National Academy of Science. Appendix A (pp. 63–88). Washington, D.C. Bureau of Outdoor Recreation, U.S. Department of the Interior.

Driver, B. L. & Rosenthal, D. (1982). Measuring and improving effectiveness of public outdoor recreation programs (p. 40). Washington, D. C. George Washington University, Department of Human Kinetics and Leisure Studies.

Driver, B. L., Brown, P., & Peterson, G. (Eds.). (1991). *Benefits of leisure*. State College, PA: Venture Publishing, Inc.

Driver, B. L. & Bruns, D. (1999). Concepts and uses of the beneficial approach to leisure. In. E. Jackson and T. Burton (Eds.), *Leisure studies: Prospects for the twenty-first century* (pp. 349–368). State College, PA: Venture Publishing, Inc.

Driver, B. L., Bruns, D., & Booth, K. (2001). Status and common misunderstandings of the net benefits approach to leisure. In *Trends 2000: Shaping the future*. Contributed Papers for the 5th Outdoor Recreation & Tourism Trends Conference (pp. 245–263). East Lansing, MI: Michigan State University, Department of Park, Recreation, and Tourism Resources.

Harper, J., Neider, D., Godbey, G., & Lamont, D. (1997). *The use and benenfits of local government parks and recreation services: A Canadian perspective*. Winnepeg, Manitoba, Canada: Health, Leisure, ands Human Dimensions Researcgh Institute. University of Manatoba.

Lee, M. E. & Driver, B. L. (1992). Benefits-Based Management: A New Paradigm for Managing Amenity Resources. Paper presented at The Second Canada/US Workshop on Visitor Management in Parks, Forests, and Protected Areas. May 13–16, 1992. University of Wisconsin-Madison, Madison, WI.

Loomis, J. & Walsh, R, (1997). *Recreation economic decisions* (2nd ed.). State College, PA: Venture Publishing, Inc.

Manfredo, M. (Ed.). (2002). *Wildlife viewing: A management handbook*. Corvallis, OR: Oregon State University Press.

Marans, R. & Mohai, P. (1991). Leisure resources, recreation activity, and the quality of life. In B. L. Driver, P. Brown, and G. Peterson (Eds.), *Benefits of leisure*. (pp. 351–363). State College, PA: Venture Publishing, Inc.

More, T. (2002). "The parks are being loved to death and other frauds and deceits in recreation management." *Journal of Leisure Research, 34*(1), 52–78.

More, T. & Kuentzel, W. (1999). Five Reasons to Have Reservations about Benefits-Based Management. In G. Kyle (Ed.), *Proceedings of the 1999 northeastern recreation research symposium*.

PP.295-303. Gen. Tech. Report.NE-269. Newton Square, PA. USDA Forest Service. Northeastern Research Station.

Stein, T., Anderson, A., & Thompson,D. (1999). Identifying and managing for community benefits in Minnesota state parks. *Journal of Park and Recreation Administration 17*(4), 1–19.

Thomas, J. (1996). Foreword. In B. L. Driver, D. Dustin, T. Baltic, G. Elsner, & G. Peterson (Eds.), *Nature and the human spirit: Toward an expanded land management ethic* (pp. xxiii–xxv). State College, PA: Venture Publishing, Inc.

United Way of America. (1996). *Measuring program outcomes: A practical approach* (Item No. 0989). Washington, D.C.

Marans, R. & Mohai, P. (1991). Leisure resources, recreation activity, and the quality of life. In B. Driver, P. Brown, and G. Peterson (Eds.), *Benefits of leisure* (pp. 351–363). State College, PA: Venture Publishing, Inc.

Moore, R. & Driver, B. (2005). *Introduction to outdoor recreation: Providing and managing natural resource based opportunities.* State College, PA: Venture Publishing, Inc.

O'Sullivan, E. (1999). *Setting a course for change: The benefits movement.* Ashborn, VA. National Recreation and Parks Association.

Wondolleck, J. (1996). Incorporating hard-to-define values into public lands decision making: A conflict management perspective. In B. L. Driver, D. Dustin, T. Baltic, G. Elsner, and G. Peterson (Eds.), *Nature and the human spirit: Toward an expanded land management ethic* (pp. 257–262). State College, PA: Venture Publishing, Inc.

Appendix to Chapter 2: Advantages of the OFP and OFM

The following advantages of the OFP and OFM are taken directly from Moore & Driver (2005: 204–205).

Promotes greater public understanding and appreciation of the social significance of recreation and related amenities. Although leisure is one of the most important economic sectors and the most beneficial social service, it is not publicly recognized as such. A major reason for this paradox is that professionals in all the sub-disciplines of leisure have not successfully or effectively articulated the social importance of leisure. One of the purposes of the OFP is to provide a systematically integrated and scientifically and conceptually sound (i.e., creditable) framework for promoting more widespread understanding of the important contributions of recreation and related amenities to improving humans' welfare. That knowledge helps to correct (i.e., reposition) the too frequent misperception that recreation is trivial and helps advance greater recognition of the real contributions of recreation to human happiness and productivity. Widespread understanding of the benefits of recreation will increase public support for recreation. Such support is necessary to any profession that delivers a social service that is highly dependent on public funding. In addition, this increased public understanding will facilitate more effective working relationships not only among the customers served and recreation professionals but also between leisure and other professionals.

Justifies allocations of public funds to recreation and related amenities in the policy arena. Policymakers need to compare the benefits and costs of alternative uses of public resources. These comparisons, which include but go beyond economic measures of benefits, have grown in importance as demands on public resources have increased and broadened in the face of increasingly stringent agency budgets. As a consequence, public officials, including those in recreation and related amenity agencies, are being held more accountable. They must explain more explicitly how the public goods and services they provide relate to specific social needs, why those goods and services are being provided, and the likely desirable and undesirable consequences of the production and use of those goods and services. The OFP objectively defines those social needs and orients delivery of recreation opportunities explicitly to them. As such, it makes policy decisions less subjective and public policymakers more responsive, accountable, and efficient.

Helps planners and managers to develop clearer management objectives. Once public policy decisions have allocated public resources to a particular type of recreation or related amenities, information on benefits improves the ability of recreation and related amenity planners and managers to define clear management objectives and prescriptions and then to establish more explicit standards and guidelines for meeting those objectives. Provision of exercise trails, opportunities for challenge, quiet places, sites for socialization (e.g., enhancing family kinship), and options to be free from specific everyday pressures are examples of the results of discrete management actions that can assure opportunities to realize specific types of benefits. Understanding of the outcomes of the leisure recreation opportunity production system by the OFP and OFM helps to clarify the management actions needed. The OFP and OFM require such understanding.

Facilitates social interventions. Increasingly recreation and related amenity agencies are being given social mandates to promote particular benefits—for example, environmental learning, increased physical fitness, and the many benefits associated with the use of leisure programs to prevent a specific social problem, such as reduction in crime or substance abuse through various recreation programs, such as midnight basketball. While the OFP itself is silent with regard to such social engineering, it provides guidance on how to meet social agendas.

Facilitates more meaningful recreation/amenity demand analyses. By focusing on ends rather than means (i.e., outcomes instead of just inputs and outputs), the OFP and OFM make explicit the different types of recreation demands (i.e., demands for activity, experience, and other benefit opportunities, as explained in Chapter 12). Thus, under the OFP and OFM, the on-site and off-site customers can now better communicate their recreation and related amenity demands to managers than they could when their demands were managerially interpreted only in terms of demands for activity opportunities.

Facilitates a collaborative style of management. More public recreation and park agencies are adopting a collaborative/participatory style of policymaking and management that actively involves a wide array of partners and stakeholders in the planning and delivery of recreation opportunities. The OFP and OFM reject the common idea that a recreation or related amenity agency is a sole provider, and it requires a collaborative style of decision making that necessitates forming partnerships with other providers who affect provision of recreation opportunities and with all other affecting or affected, or just interested, stakeholders. The OFP provides a useful and effective framework for facilitating such a style of management.

Provides flexibility to managers. Practitioners appreciate the flexibility the OFP and OFM afford them. It can be implemented incrementally, and it can be practiced at different degrees of comprehensiveness. For example, one agency and its collaborating partners might decide to focus on only one key benefit (e.g., improved physical fitness) or a selected group of the most significant and widespread benefits, while another agency and its partners might decide to look more comprehensively at a wider number of benefits (i.e., optimize an array of benefit opportunities).

Better identifies conflict and substitutes. Different customers desiring different types of benefits cause most conflicts among customers. The OFP and OFM make conflicting demands more explicit. It also facilitates better identification of complementary or noncompetitive demands and therefore affords better understanding of which recreation/amenity activities and settings are and are not substitutes one for the other.

Enhances the customers' choice processes and consumer sovereignty. The OFP and OFM assume that the individual generally knows best what does and does not improve his or her personal welfare. Much of this knowing is derived from experiential learning by trial-and-error. Certainly each individual's personal knowledge is highly subjective and is mediated by social norms, mores, personal values, beliefs, and conditioning. Nevertheless, a considerable amount of each individual's personal knowledge comes from the factual sources of information outside the individual. Examples include research-derived information on the probable effects on an individual's personal welfare of the use of seat belts, the avoidance of excessive low density lipid cholesterol in one's bloodstream, hypertension, overexposure to the sun, substance abuse (including tobacco and alcohol), failure to manage stress, physical inactivity, and poor nutrition. In a similar vein, the information on the likely beneficial (and detrimental) consequences of specific leisure activities required by the OFP helps create more informed choices of leisure opportunities by citizens. In this way, human welfare is promoted, and the role of leisure opportunities in doing so is better understood and appreciated.

Facilities marketing. Because the OFP and OFM make the products of recreation and related amenity management explicit, the managing agencies can use this information to develop more explicit informational packages and recreation/amenity opportunity guides orientated to the specified types of activity, experience, and other benefit opportunities being made available where, when, in what amount, and of what relative quality. The OFP also facilitates promotion of specific benefit opportunities if the agency has the social mandate/consensus to do so.

Enhances the rationality of recreation and related amenity fee programs. Most, if not all, public recreation/amenity agencies must now consider implementing or increasing the entrance and use fees they charge. This is an emotion-laden issue in which the two-sided sword of equity cuts in both directions. One side says don't constrain access by charging fees, and the other says it is unfair for the nonuser to subsidize the costs of provision and maintenance of recreation opportunities for users. Some people argue that the users should pay their fair share of these costs, while other people expand this reasoning and say the beneficiaries and not just the users should pay. Their logic is that since recreation is a "merit good" (i.e., one that provides spin-off benefits from users to nonusers), it is only fair that those who receive these social benefits (e.g., enhanced local physical amenities) help to pay the costs of providing opportunities to realize those benefits. The OFP helps to implement this beneficiaries-should-pay rationale because it requires identification and, to the extent possible, quantification of all benefits to all beneficiaries. Therefore, the OFP helps to identify those beneficiaries to whom the costs can most fairly be apportioned, either as user fees or as tax levies.

Advances knowledge. The scientific community is interested in knowledge about the benefits of recreation and related amenities, because scientists and educators want to understand better what recreation is and how it contributes to human welfare. The OFP motivates scientists and educators to attain this understanding. That understanding advances basic knowledge about recreation and related amenities and thereby promotes better professional practice.

Facilitates additional research. Given that research is a building process, an understanding of the beneficial and negative consequences of all leisure-related behavior nurtures additional hypotheses and research about the positive and negative outcomes of the management and use of recreation and related amenity resources.

Promotes better education. Better understanding of the benefits of recreation/amenities facilitates better formal training of students and on-the-job training of practitioners because of that improved knowledge base.

Increases pride in the professions. Lastly, and of subtle but vital importance, these advantages serve to increase the pride of recreation and related amenity professionals in their fields and careers. This helps to make leisure professionals less defensive and allows them to take more pride in their socially important roles. It also causes more highly talented people to enter the leisure professions, a trend clearly apparent during the past 20 years, as the systematic body of knowledge about leisure behavior has increased.

Footnotes

1. Many people helped develop and refine the OFP and OFM described in this chapter. Particularly notable are Larry Allen, Dorothy Anderson, Kay Booth (New Zealand), Brian Hopkins, Chris Jenkins (New Zealand), Marty Lee, and especially Don Bruns.
2. It should be noted that except for the name change, Outcomes-Focused Management (OFM), as considered in this text, is identical to BBM, and the Outcome-Focused Paragon (OFP) is identical to the BOAL.
3. This section and the following one were taken almost verbatim from parts of Chapters 12 and 13 Moore & Driver (2005) with the permission of Venture Publishing, Inc. Many explanatory passages are omitted for brevity, because as explained in Chapter 1, reviewing the OFP and OFM is a minor purpose of this text.

Chapter 3
Implementing OFM on Public Nature-Based Recreation and Related Amenity Resources

B. L. Driver and Don Bruns

Learning Objectives:

1. Understand why Outcomes-Focused Management (OFM) cannot be successfully implemented by any public park and recreation agencies if the lead administrators of that agency do not support and promote OFM.
2. Understand relationships and differences between implementing OFM on public wild lands in contrast to implementing it within municipalities.
3. Understand the requirements of the comprehensive normative model of how to implement and apply OFM on publicly administered wild lands. In particular, grasp the significance and necessity of incorporating outcomes-oriented management objectives and setting prescriptions into management plans.

Introduction

This chapter on how to apply and implement OFM on public nature-based recreation and related amenity resources and the following one (on how to implement OFM in municipal areas) are particularly important, actually central, to this text. This is because the major purpose of the text is to promote better understanding and wider use of OFM (previously called Benefits-Based Management, or BBM), and such understanding cannot be attained before the detailed instructions on how to implement OFM provided in this chapter and Chapter 4 have been published in this more readily available source. All other such instructions remain in the "fugitive" literature. The other chapters of this text are equally significant in complementary ways. Chapters 5 and 6 focus on changing incorrect perceptions about the social significance of leisure services how that can be accomplished. Eighteen additional "applications" chapters provide practical information about how OFM has been used by documenting OFM-related things that were done well, other things not done as well as they should have been, and things that should not have been done. Chapters 14, 17, and 18 use the OFM model described in this chapter to evaluate the application and implementation of OFM on three wildland areas administered by the USDI Bureau of Land Management (BLM). Those chapters provide additional practical information about the OFM model than could be offered in this chapter.

This chapter builds on Chapters 1 and 2, so familiarity with the content of those chapters will significantly enhance comprehension of the discussion of how to apply and implement the OFM model presented in this chapter. In fact, it is assumed the reader of this chapter understands the definitions and terminology established in those two chapters.

Evolution of the Normative Model Described in This Chapter

The model for applying and implementing OFM described in this chapter evolved over several decades of considerable thought about why people engage in leisure activities, what they obtain from such engagements; what park and recreation administrators, managers, and planners need to understand about the production of recreation opportunities and about the positive and negative outcomes associated with the production and use of those opportunities; and what actions they need to take or not take to optimize the beneficial outcomes of recreation. As mentioned in Chapter 1 of this text, such thinking about leisure began as early as Aristotle, over two millennia ago, but it was not until the 1960s that many scientists researched the benefits of leisure and began to present social-psychological models of leisure behavior. An overview of those early efforts is given in Manfredo, Driver, & Brown (1983: 263–264) as follows:

> A frequently cited goal of recreation management—to provide opportunities for a wide range of satisfying recreation experiences appropriate for a given area—has been emphasized with slight variation by many researchers. Wagar (1964; 1974) suggested managing recreation areas to meet a range of human needs; Driver & Tocher (1970) to provide opportunities for the "package" of highly desired experiences; Brown, Dyer, & Whaley (1973) to satisfy recreation motives; Lucas & Stankey (1974) to maximize user satisfactions; and Hendee (1974) to provide multiple satisfactions. In a similar fashion Driver and Brown (1975; 1978) have called for planning that delineates the opportunities for experiences offered to users. In addition, they have offered a model of the recreation decision process useful in guiding behavioral research which will aid managers in meeting their goals (Driver & Brown, 1975; 1978; Hass, Driver, & Brown 1981).

The publications cited above focused primarily on needs for additional research. Concurrent with and as a part of some of those writings, publications were also appearing that had a more practical orientation, and models were described which focused on what recreation practitioners needed to understand to help them provide quality recreation opportunities, satisfying experiences, other beneficial outcomes, and the reduction of negative outcomes (cf. Brown, 1984: 211–214; Brown, 1984; Brown, Driver, & McConnell, 1978:74–76; Crompton, 1977; Driver & Rosenthal, 1982:6–7; Driver & Brown, 1975:71–76). Those models built on the same concepts (e.g., inputs, throughputs and outputs, etc.) of General Systems Theory (Buckley, I968) on which the model shown as Figure 2.3 in Chapter 2 of this text (and repeated as Figure 3,.1 in this chapter) was based. Over time those earlier models were refined and integrated (cf. :356–359; Allen, 1996; Allen, Stevens, Hurtes, & Harwell, 1998; Driver & Bruns, 1999:356–359; O'Sullivan, 1999) and became the basis for the OFM model described in this chapter.

In summary, much past thought stimulated the development of the OFM model described in this chapter. What value it will have to park and recreation practitioners and to others in the leisure professions in the future will be founded on earlier versions being incrementally refined by results of the applications of it described in Chapters 7 through 24 of this text. The model evolved over several decades and is still evolving.

Use of the Outcomes Approach in Policy Development

As indicated by its title, this text focuses on the application of OFM to the planning and *management* of recreation and related amenity resources, programs, and services. But, as emphasized in Chapters 1 and 2 of this text, the outcomes approach should be used not only to guide management planning and managerial decisions, but also *policy* decisions. Therefore, this section gives an overview of the importance of using the outcomes approach in policy decisions.

To begin, it is important to remember that policy, administrative, planning, and managerial decisions serve different purposes within any organization as explained in Chapter 11 of Moore & Driver (2005). That chapter pointed out that public policy decisions are established by elected public officials and heads (and to a lesser extent by regional directors and field-level officers) of public agencies, with some policy directions established by judicial authorities. Those policies generally establish broad guidelines to govern how a public agency operates except that many policies related to fiscal, procurement, and personnel matters can be quite specific. Most policy directives are not time bound and stay in effect for years, even decades. Those policies affect how management plans will be developed and implemented. In contrast, management planning and managerial decisions establish specific, explicit, exacting, and time-bound guidelines for actions that must be taken to assure that policy guidelines will be met. Examples of such directions are those dictated by the management objectives, setting prescriptions, and implementing actions. Therefore, policy decisions, while distinct from management planning and managerial decisions, guide all managerial decisions, as well as set the boundaries (legal, fiscal, personnel, procurement, accountability, etc.) within which managerial decisions can be made and implemented[1]. This holds true for all public agencies that operate at any level of government. Therefore, it is of *paramount importance* that heads of public recreation and related amenity resource management agencies fully support the adoption and use of the outcomes approach to guide policy development and management within their respective agencies.

Since passage of the Federal Performance and Results Act of 1993, public agencies at all levels of government have been giving increasing attention to performance measures to evaluate their performance and help guide administration and management. That trend is documented by the growing number of articles about performance measures in the journals on public administration. That literature points out that a variety of measures are being used, especially those of outputs and outcomes. Chapter 4 of this text discusses movement toward use of outcomes-oriented performance measure by some municipal park and recreation agencies. Despite increasing use of performance measures, most park and recreation agencies still measure performance in terms of facilitating outputs instead of recreation opportunities and outcomes as explained in Chapter 2 (see explanation of Figure 2.2 in that chapter which is repeated as Figure 3.1 in this chapter). This situation exists primarily because too few directors or leadership teams of the many federal, provincial, state, regional, county, and municipal public agencies that provide recreation and related amenity opportunities have yet to formally issue directives that require adoption of *outcomes-focused* performance measures in their agencies. The last section of this chapter considers relationships between performance evaluations and OFM. The conclusion is that OFM will never be implemented as widely as it can and should be until performance evaluations/reports explicitly consider management results in terms of the attainment of targeted outcomes.

Marketing/promotional material that is distributed by most public park and recreation agencies extol the benefits produced by their agencies. For example, if one enters "benefits are endless+leisure" in Google, over 700,000 hits will appear. Among them are a very large number of web sites of park and recreation agencies that promote the benefits they produce. Chapter 2 of this text emphasized that such statements reflect outcomes-oriented mindsets and movements in the right direction, but they fall far short of explicit endorsement, promotion, and implementation of an outcomes approach. Put simply, authentic OFM will not be applied more widely until agency policymakers go beyond just mentioning benefits in mission statements. They must adopt an expanded model for recreation management that addresses *all components* of the production of recreation opportunities and their attainment.

Although this chapter does not provide details about how to apply the outcomes approach in policy development, it is pertinent to mention that the following five critical actions are ones that leaders of public park and recreation agencies can take to remove the current major constraints on implementing the outcomes approach more widely in their policymaking arenas:

- Recognize that while mentioning positive and negative outcomes in their agency mission statements and other promotional literature is fitting, proper, and expected by the publics served, such "spin" is far removed from adopting an outcomes approached as defined in Chapters 1 and 2 and this chapter.
- Adopt and apply the outcomes approach formally, explicitly, and overtly in policy development.
- Promote and support the use of OFM by field-level mangers and planners.
- Realize and understand why that, although producing and maintaining facilitating outputs (e.g., trails, interpretive exhibits, campsites, etc.) is a necessary part of park and recreation resource management, those outputs are not the *ends* of management. Instead, as emphasized in Chapter 2 and later in this chapter, producing those outputs are only *means* to the real *ends* of facilitating the realization of beneficial outcomes and minimizing negative outcomes.
- Stop measuring success primarily in terms of programs advanced or projects completed, but also include measures of the degree to which desired outcomes are being attained and negative outcomes are being reduced. Formally establish and then implement outcomes-directed criteria for making performance evaluations, and reward performance accordingly.

Because of the authority and influence lead officers have within their agencies, much can happen if they take these five actions. Those of us who have worked to help get OFM implemented have witnessed many instances where OFM was being implemented by a particular agency or subunit of such primarily because of the strong support of OFM by its leader. Their sustained commitment is of paramount importance, especially for use of a new technology such as OFM.

Contrasting Uses of OFM on Public Wildlands and in Municipal Areas

As implied by its title, this chapter presents and describes a normative model of how OFM should be applied to the management of wildland recreation and related amenity resources. As such, this chapter is written to help guide the management of such areas that are administered by public land management agencies at all levels of government, whether federal, provincial, state, regional, county, and even municipal, when large natural areas are managed at least in part by cities. Thus, the recreation areas relevant to this chapter are usually large in scale, but OFM is often applied to only a part or several subparts of those areas as elaborated later in this chapter. Chapter 4 provides details on how to implement OFM in municipalities. While there is overlap between this chapter and Chapter 4, both chapters are needed because of the following differences between implementing OFM on wild land recreation resources and in municipalities.

- Although many municipalities manage large nature areas primarily or in part to provide recreation and related amenity opportunities, most recreation/amenity opportunities in municipalities are not provided on relatively large natural areas. Instead, they are provided at specific sites or structures that provide opportunities to engage in one or more specific recreation activities, whether tennis; golf; swimming; ice skating and hockey; basketball; baseball, softball; volleyball; horseback riding, walking, jogging, and hiking; cycling; skateboarding; attending concerts, plays, and commemorative events; visiting museums, art galleries, and historic sites; taking yoga, meditation, cooking, sewing, and physical fitness classes, etc. In contrast, public land management agencies focus mostly on outdoor recreation activities that require larger units of land or contiguous natural landscapes. Although public land management agencies do offer recreation-related programs (interpretive talks, moonlight walks, demonstrations, etc.), programmatic and facility-dependent recreation opportunities are generally more pervasive within municipal recreation programs.
- An important and rather difficult task for recreation managers of large wildland areas is to address how their management both positively and negatively affects residents (and associated providers) who live in (and operate from) nearby communities, commonly called "gateway" communities. Chapter 2 emphasized that these residents and associated providers not only significantly affect the type, number, and quality of the opportunities that can be provided, but they also benefit and realize negative impacts from the management and use of the nearby public recreation and related amenity resources. Of course, municipal park and recreation agencies must also be attentive to the effects of their actions on the residents of their cities and their associated providers. But, their situation sometimes differs because of the physical distances and patterns of land ownership that generally, but not always, separate the public wild lands being managed from relevant residents and associate providers in adjoining and nearby communities.
- The types of relevant customer and associated provider stakeholders of municipal and public wildland recreation agencies, and their interests and motivations, usually differ to varying degrees.
- Lastly, the laws and directives governing these two types of providers tend to be considerably different (e.g., needs to conform to federal laws and practice sustainable ecosystems management, authority to levy and charge user fees, etc.).

The Cause and Effect Relationships that Describe OFM's Recreation Opportunity Production Process Must be Understood

Most of this chapter describes how OFM should be applied and implemented on public wildlands. That discussion centers on the logic of the recreation opportunity production process described in detail in Chapter 9. Therefore, before a person can properly implement and apply OFM on nature-based areas or in municipalities areas, she or he *must understand and accept* the logic behind that process. Such cannot be happen if relationships between and among inputs, facilitating outputs, facilitating settings, recreation opportunities, and outcomes are not understood clearly. Because those relationships are so fundamental to understanding OFM, they will be reviewed to set the stage for development of the model of how OFM should be implemented. Those relationships were illustrated by Figure 2.3 of Chapter 2, which is reproduced in Figure 3.1.

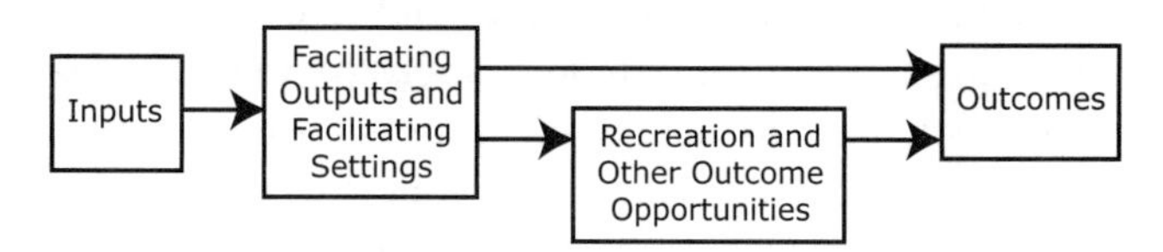

Figure 3.1: Expanded OFM Model of the Recreation Opportunity Production Process

Figure 3.1 reflects two important perspectives about the production of recreation opportunities. One relates to planning, and the other relates to plan implementation. From a recreation resource *management planning* perspective, the actions of the planner(s) should move from the right to the left of Figure 3.1; from outcomes to inputs. The reason is that one must decide what outcome opportunities are to be produced before the conditions and actions necessary to produce them are addressed. To explain, the OFM *management planning* process *starts* with decisions about what beneficial outcomes will be overtly targeted and which negative outcomes will be avoided or reduced in magnitude. Remember that those decisions will determine what recreation and other outcome opportunities, facilitating outputs (e.g., picnics tables, hiking trails, nature interpretive talks, campgrounds, marinas, etc.) and inputs will be required to meet the outcome goals established. Then, from a *plan implementation* perspective, movement should be from left to right; from inputs to facilitating outputs though facilitating recreation settings to recreation and outcome opportunities to actual outcomes realized (some of which might not have been targeted in the management plan). Under this left-to-right plan implementation perspective, only provider actions that facilitate the realization of desired high quality recreation opportunities and attainment of targeted outcomes are appropriate. Put simply, both in planning and plan implementation, the desired outcomes determine what provider actions are appropriate and what are not appropriate and why. And, that sentence captures the essence of OFM.

These right-to-left plan development and left-to-right plan implementation processes contrast sharply with conventional approaches to planning and management as well as to how managerial performance is generally evaluated by public sector recreation and related amenity providers. In the past, and in most instances today, performance has been evaluated primarily in terms of numbers and types of facilitating outputs produced and numbers of users/visitors, but not in terms of outcome attainment. Therefore, the more traditional planning processes still start with focusing on what facilitating outputs to produce instead of on outcomes. That misplaced emphasis on facilitating outputs instead of on outcomes has occurred for the following reasons.

- Providers (i.e., public agencies and their associated providers) of outdoor recreation and related amenity opportunities have been and remain focused primarily on providing recreation activity opportunities and on the things they can see (picnic tables, camp sites, etc.) and count (miles of trail created and/or maintained and numbers of on site users) instead of on what benefits can be optimized given budget and other constraints. Yes, it is comparatively easier to focus on rather discrete things, but OFM demands much more as this chapter hopes to show.
- The more influential and well-organized activity-specific user and interest groups, focused on projects and programs that serve their wants, continue to drive project-centered management. OFM requires taking a broader view that guides and constrains projects and programs so that only those which facilitate the attainment of targeted outcomes are approved.
- Restructuring provider inputs to produce only essential facilitating outputs and protecting and improving the basic resources being managed still comprise the largest parts of the costs of producing outdoor recreation and related amenity opportunities. That helps explain why most planning and managerial activities have focused on those facilitating outputs, but only to facilitate recreation activity opportunities. Under OFM, additional considerations are required to produce outcome opportunities. That distinction is extremely important.
- Public recreation and related amenity agencies are committed to many special programs and initiatives, and each initiative requires some types of facilitating outputs. Examples include trail programs, on-site environmental education programs and outreach initiatives, orienteering programs, watchable wildlife publications and facilities, catch-and-release fishing events, and junior ranger programs. Each require facilitating outputs, but the problem is that the required facilitating outputs rather, than the outcomes of those initiatives, tend to drive managerial actions. Yes, we should build facilities to watch wildlife, but why? Remember that OFM requires that all actions be conditioned upon their demonstrated ability to achieve targeted outcomes.
- The operations and orientations of too many recreation and related amenity agencies have become excessively leveraged, and in too many instances co-opted, by organized and special groups and "partners," which provide funding and political support to make what they want happen. Again, the facilitating outputs required by those programs become the dominant focus

of those activities. Negative newspaper articles, professional journals, and even street corner conversations provide ample evidence that this practice runs roughshod over the desires and interests of other potential off- and on-site customers who have other outcomes in mind.

- As elaborated at the end of this chapter, headquarters of practically all public park and recreation agencies and their field units report performance primarily in terms of types and numbers of facilitating outputs (e.g., campsites, picnic areas, hiking trails, wildlife viewing sites, numbers of game animals available) produced or maintained and numbers of users of the areas and facilities managed. To repeat for emphasis, the obvious problem from the perspective of OFM is that such reporting does not include documentation of outcomes that have been facilitated or realized. The performance of any agency wanting to adopt OFM must include reporting of outcome attainment as well as output attainment.

The Comprehensive Normative Model for Implementing OFM

Some Introductory Comments

The term "normative model" is used to emphasize that the OFM model described in the rest of this chapter is one that shows how OFM *should be applied and implemented* if the intention is to implement OFM completely. It details the requirements for doing so. That model will be described in detail, because (a) it has been refined as a result of what was learned for the applications of OFM described in Chapters 7–24 of this text and (b) it has not been published in a readily available source. Before those details are provided, the following introductory comments are made.

- Although a challenging task, this chapter was written for readers who have widely different levels of understanding of how recreation resource management plans should be made for public wild lands--from students who have little such knowledge to practitioners with considerable experience except for applying and implementing OFM. Therefore, the amount of detail provided in this chapter will probably seem excessive to readers who want little more than an overview of what is involved in applying and implementing OFM. For such readers, it is strongly recommended that they focus mostly of the bold print that designates the eight phases of planning activity (and the steps within each phase) required to implement the model.
- OFM can be implemented at different levels of completeness depending on resources available and whether a particular manager or an administrative subunit of an agency desires to adopt OFM incrementally and then move toward fuller implementation as experience with OFM is gained. These small mistakes help avoid making big ones! Whatever scale of implementing OFM is adopted, it is important that the planner(s) and manager(s) move *immediately* beyond practicing activity-focused management (AFM) and experience-focused management (EFM) to OFM.
- Recognize that although OFM is a different approach, it adopts many of the requirements and terminology of conventional approaches, which should facilitate easier understanding of the model.

Steps for Implementing Outcomes-Focused Management

It was stated earlier in this chapter that the reader familiar with land use planning will notice that much of planning for OFM follows the conventional land use planning process. Because it has additional requirements, the steps of OFM planning will now be explained in detail. Those steps are divided into eight sequential phases. The following description of each phase and step will show that OFM planning, like all planning endeavors, is iterative, because what is done at each step should be viewed as tentative. Determinations made at subsequent steps can change what was done at previous steps. Furthermore, it must be understood that several of the required planning actions (e.g., making supply and demand analyses) can be undertaken simultaneously, which is not indicated by the linear/sequential model described below. Lastly, the terminology used in this text, as described at the beginning of Chapter 1 of this text and requirements of OFM described in Chapter 2, are used in the following discussion.

Phase 1: Preparatory Actions.

- **Ensure that Relevant Supervisor(s) and Managers Approve and Support Adoption of OFM.** Experience has shown that it is virtually impossible to implement and apply OFM properly if relevant supervisor(s) of the affected planners and managers do not approve of using OFM or do so only weakly. Therefore, if a planner or manager who wants to implement OFM does not have the approval of his or her immediate supervisor(s), it is unlikely that the effort will be successful. Therefore, the first step is to secure such administrative commitment.
- **Organize the Planning Team.** Planning teams for land-use planning vary considerably by types of plan and the scope and complexity of the planning efforts. On very small recreation projects (e.g., planning a campground), there might only be one or two planners on multiple-use land management planning efforts, multidisciplinary teams of a dozen or more people might comprise the team. In any event, the planning team is the individual or group of individuals who will develop a recommended management plan for a particular outdoor recreation facility, site, or area. The OFM requires that relevant on- and off-site customer and associated provider stakeholders *are involved in all phases* of the management planning and plan implementation processes—they either serve as members of the planning team or at least are *regularly* consult with it. On- and off-site customer and associated provider stakeholders are defined in Chapter 2, which also explains why ongoing meaningful collaboration with these stakeholders is a fundamental requirement of OFM.
- **Ensure that All Members of the Planning Team Understand OFM.** It is *vitally* important that each member of the planning team and stakeholders collaborating with them have a reasonably good understanding of what OFM is, why it is being applied, and what it requires. This is particularly important if some members of the planning team do not have that understanding, because they are probably not accustomed to focusing on outcomes as required by OFM. In those instances, a brainstorming exercise is proposed that has proven to be invaluable in past applications of OFM. It does not need to take much time and only requires that all members of the planning team *as a group* try to identify and list the most readily apparent types of beneficial and negative outcomes that are being realized by current management of the area or facility for which the plan will be developed. The purpose is *not* to determine what outcomes goals *will be* established, but instead just to brainstorm (i.e., list without critique or criticism) those outcomes that appear to be important and are probably being realized now by different clientele (i.e., visitors, local residents, affecting providers, etc.), as well as which outcome opportunities currently being produced are not important and which ones not being produced perhaps should be. In this OFM training exercise, it is important to adopt the definitions of benefits that are used by OFM that were explained in detail in Chapter 1 of this text and reviewed in the sole appendix of this chapter. Lastly, outcomes checklists, such as the one in that appendix, have helped members of several planning teams to better understand both the many diverse types of outcomes and the fundamental importance of maintaining an outcomes orientation when attempting to develop plans using the outcomes approach. To iterate, this brief exercise is to enhance one's thinking in terms of outcomes!
- **Understand Responsibilities and Constraints.** Roles and responsibilities that have been identified as appropriate (and what is not considered appropriate) for the field unit that is taking the lead on implementing OFM and existing and likely constraints must be understood clearly to establish boundaries on what can and cannot be done. The roles and responsibilities are established by legislation, agency rules and regulations, and field-level managerial directives that govern the operations of the leading providing agency and that of all collaborating providers. So, all members of the planning team must understand the agency's relevant mission, goals, and current policy and managerial directives, as well as those of all collaborating providers to help ensure efficient, effective, and responsible management planning. Possible constraints include, but are not limited to, number and skills of existing personnel, limited fiscal resources, insufficient collaborative involvement of potential associated providers and local government, and internal staff/managerial resistance or outright opposition to adopting OFM. These

constraints must be recognized and contingency measures developed to address them. Such deliberations and actions are necessary for the planning team to succeed.

- **Consider Essential Needs for Collaborative Management and Related Public Involvement Efforts.** Decide, at least on a preliminary basis, what public involvement/collaborative efforts will be made and what other customer and associated provider stakeholders will be involved *in addition to* the ones already selected to serve on the planning team and/or to work very closely with it. Remember from Chapter 2 that OFM requires close collaboration with all relevant customer and associated provider stakeholders.
- **Identify Critical Issues and Concerns.** The planning team should review past planning and managerial efforts for the planning unit to familiarize themselves with issues and concerns that have previously surfaced to determine if they are relevant. Pressing issues and concerns that beg to be addressed in the plan are equally important and must be considered. This identification of critical issues and concerns should trigger recreation planners' thoughts to immediately begin strategizing how the plan and ensuring recreation operations can resolve problems, issues, and concerns. This is commonly done in planning as a part that is called "scoping."

Phase 2: Gather, Analyze, Interpret, and Integrate Supply and Demand Information.

Supply and demand analyses accomplish several things. They ensure that recreation opportunities targeted in plans are indeed desired by relevant identifiable customers. At the same time, they prevent providers from redundantly producing recreation opportunities already provided by other providers. More importantly, they ensure that planned actions are geared to produce what is most desired. Under activity-focused planning frameworks, supply and demand analyses were simply a matter of considering which recreation activities to accommodate. But, that activity-focused approach left important recreation components unaddressed. In contrast, OFM requires analyzing supply and demand not only for opportunities to engage in specific activities, but also to realize desired satisfying experiences and other benefits, and to avoid unwanted outcomes, as well as the characteristics of settings within which they occur and upon which their sustained attainment depends.

- **Assess Recreation Preferences of the Most Relevant Recreation Participants and Affected Residents of Local Communities.** Demand studies must be conducted to determine which types of recreation activities, experiences, and other benefits are most desired and which types of negative outcomes should be avoided or reduced in impact by probable on- and off-site customers. Remember from Chapter 2 that OFM addresses both types of customers.

  Many texts and articles have been published about the advantages and shortcomings of, and how to implement, the many different methods of estimating these demands both in economic and other terms. So, each possible technique of demand assessment is beyond the scope of this text. Those methods include use of focus groups, informal interviews, and both personally administered and mail-back questionnaires, as well as analyses of the results of other comparable demand studies, measures of past and current use by the remote time-lapse cameras, traffic counters, and infrared beams; and completed visitor registration forms. Each technique has its comparative advantages and disadvantages, including costs, burdens on the respondents, technical expertise required, and utility of the results. Available secondary sources of data, such as economic, social, and environmental impact assessments should be reviewed and used if applicable.

  When making the demand analyses of probable on- and off-site customers, it should be remembered from Chapter 1 that preferences for recreation activities have guided most past recreation demand assessments. In sharp contrast, OFM planning demands restructuring of the entire process for assessing preferences of on- and off-site customers for satisfying experiences and other benefits or undesirable outcomes they seek to avoid. Assessments must address both recreation participants as well as nonparticipants (both affected citizens and affecting recreation service and infrastructure providers, such as businesses and local governments). Information about their preferences for the setting conditions is essential to facilitate the production and realization of their desired outcome opportunities and for the associated recreation activities. For an increasingly large off-site customer clientele, however, personal on-site participation is irrelevant, and most highly-valued outcomes are directly related to sustaining the distinctive setting character of public land adjoining the communities where they live, work, or visit.

Many methods used to estimate demand require the development of special instruments such as information schedules (i.e., questionnaires). They should be pilot-tested and revised as needed before they are administered. Under OFM, the focus should be on the beneficial outcomes desired, the unwanted negative outcomes to be avoided or reduced in magnitude, and the desired and undesired attributes of relevant recreation settings.

The checklists of different positive and negative outcomes, given in the appendix of this chapter, can serve as a reminder of particular outcomes to consider in this step and thereby help prevent the omission of possibly relevant outcomes in demand studies. Those checklists are to be used only to identify the feasible and appropriate beneficial outcomes for selected markets and niches. Contrary to uninformed published opinion (e.g., Moore, 2002), those lists were never intended to *dictate* what beneficial outcomes *should be* targeted. The managers and the collaborating customer and associated provider stakeholders make those determinations, not arbitrarily by a checklist.

Some specific guidelines for conducting demand analyses follow:

1. Care should be taken not to generate information that will never be used and not to excessively burden the people being contacted.
2. Be aware of the regional, national, and international user clienteles that you share with other outdoor recreation and related amenity agencies and recreation-tourism providers. Talk to them whenever there is overlap.
3. Remember that many customer visitors might have more definitive information about some specific types of recreation and related amenity opportunities than you do.
4. It is useful to know the origins of your customers, which can be obtained from zip codes. In the same vein, it is instructive to know how many of your potential customers are residents of nearby communities and how many will be visitors from outside areas.

Some of the methods are easily employed by land-use planners, while others should *only* be applied with the assistance and guidance of professionals technically trained to do so. There are many qualified people in universities and research institutions who are willing to provide such assistance, sometimes at little or no cost.

- **Inventory or Update Inventories of Key Recreation-Tourism Resource Attractions and Services.** There are two distinct parts to this step. The first is to inventory attractions. The title reads "recreation-tourism resource attractions" because while these supply inventories involve natural resources, they are far more inclusive. Specifically, they need to address (1) significant natural attractions such as outstanding natural features involving mountaineering and spelunking, cultural and heritage appreciation, and paleontology or other geologic studies; (2) developed campgrounds, interpretive exhibits, and visitor centers within the service area; (3) nearby outdoor academies, youth camps, campgrounds, dude ranches, and hunting/fishing cabins; and (4) adjoining destination resorts and related summer and winter attractions such as ski areas, Nordic ski trails, groomed snowmobile trails, and hot springs. The second part is to inventory services. They include services provided by the managing agency as well as both complementary and competing services provided by other agencies, local communities, and private sector businesses. These must include both on-site services (e.g., tours and outfitted trips) and off-site support services (e.g., equipment rentals, transportation, retails services, motel and resort accommodations, and restaurants).

These inventories should go beyond simply documenting the existence of such facilities and services to also identify both facility and service capacity. The rationale is that there is a need to define a baseline capacity against which the adequacy of facility and service demand associated with plan alternatives may be assessed. The key to completing a useable and functional inventory of facilities and services is arriving at an appropriate balance between having an inventory that is sufficiently detailed to describe and quantify the available supply, yet concise enough to make the task eminently doable.

- **Analyze Recreation Opportunity Supply by Possible Recreation Management Zones and Corresponding Customer Market Demand.** This step is essential to ensure that the types of recreation outcome opportunities being targeted complement and do not duplicate the available supply of similar recreation activity and outcome opportunities (and the character of settings in which they occur) provided elsewhere in the market area. It is equally necessary to ensure that the outcome opportunities being considered as management objectives are indeed highly valued by identifiable relevant markets segments (i.e., niches). Recreation planners must be able to identify who their customers are and where they live if managers are to be afforded a reasonable opportunity to do follow-up marketing, monitoring, and evaluation of desired outcome attainment. Because both recreation supply and demand varies by logically defined recreation management units or Recreation Management Zones (RMZs), and often widely so, these analyses need also to be completed by RMZs. The task appears daunting, but can be made far less so by employing a simplified matrix to facilitate comparing what exists and what is desired for each RMZ. Graphically sketching out the supply of recreation opportunities that can meet demands of relevant market niches helps recreation planners decide which recreation opportunities to target in which kinds of recreation settings. Certainly, under OFM, the parameters for analyzing supply and demand must be more inclusive that merely considering desired recreation activities.
- **Select Relevant Recreation-Tourism Markets and Market Segments.** To make OFM work, it is necessary to select the *relevant recreation market(s)* from the many markets that desire benefits from the recreation area for which the plan is being made. This must happen, because no one management area can simultaneously be managed to be all things to all people. So, in this step, you will first need to identify all of the recreation markets that have used the area in the past and are likely to use it in the future. To define those markets, try to get a good idea of who your competing suppliers are for the kinds of recreation provided within the area and what kinds of similar recreation-tourism opportunities they are providing for those relevant markets and market segments. Several public agencies devote a lot of attention to determining these markets and market segments and use a variety of methods to identify them, including informal interviews, focus groups, and surveys. To get started, here are some useful hints: (a) contact other agency personnel, visitor center personnel, outfitters, tour operators, tourism industry officials, chambers of commerce, visitor and convention bureaus, local government officials, and known recreation-tourism enthusiasts; (b) find out who have been going where, what they are doing, and what they want; and (c) where are they from and where else do they go? But, do not limit your focus just to recreation participants: (a) talk to real estate developers and county planners; (b) find out how the local populace feels about what is going on and about what is being planned; and finally (c) ask the local residents.
- **Identify the Most Logical Recreation Management Zones and Corresponding Niches within the Primary Market(s).** Unless the area being planned and managed is quite small, it will be necessary to define and delineate physically on maps the boundaries of logical RMZs in which recreation opportunities will be provided for the relevant market segment or segments (i.e., niches) to be served (i.e., wherein the demands of relevant market segments/niches will be planned to be met). It is important to understand that when planning recreation and related amenity resources and services under the OFM, each RMZ and its associated niche(s) is (are) essentially defined by synergistic supply and market demand parameters. In some instances, it will be necessary to make a RMZ large enough to meet the demands of more than one, *but always compatible*, market niche.

The number of RMZs you will have will be determined by the commonality of visitor use patterns, the distinctiveness of setting characteristics, and both the nature and diversity of your recreation area's natural, cultural, and heritage resources and analyses of demand. The RMZ boundaries define logical management units, hence the term Recreation Management Zone. Therefore, delineation of the boundaries of RMZs is significant managerially. Just as human physiology cannot be described in terms of the entire human body, neither can the characteristics and management of a large wild land be described and managed in terms of that entire area. Specifically, the RMZs:

1. Facilitate analyses of recreation demand and facilitate supply analyses.
2. Help determine what types of recreation activity and outcome opportunities can be provided and where.
3. Facilitate meshing of relevant demands with available resources that can meet that demand.
4. Facilitate the identification and protection of recreation settings that must be maintained to accommodate the customer demands identified for each zone.
5. Enable the development of clear and specific management objectives, implementing actions, and monitoring actions within those specific zones.
6. Enhance the marketing of the types, amounts, and locations of the recreation and outcome opportunities provided.
7. Are necessary for assigning and scheduling plan implementation field operations to fulfill all affecting provider responsibilities.

After completing subsequent steps of OFM planning, it is probable that the boundaries of the RMZs might have to be refined somewhat.

Phase 3: Develop the Management Plan

This phase describes the steps required to develop the proposed plan offered for public review. Phase 4 discusses implementation planning.

- **Determine which Outcomes Can Feasibly, and Should be, Targeted within Each Recreation Management Zone and to Determine Feasible Alternatives (When Necessary).** As elaborated in a subsequent section, several feasible alternatives must be considered in most wildland management plans. Under OFM, development of feasible recreation alternatives depends on determining what combinations of outcomes can feasibly be targeted in each of the RMZs. Three types of beneficial outcomes of recreation were defined in Chapter 1 and are summarized in the appendix to this chapter. When appraising beneficial outcomes in this and other steps of management planning, frequently reference needs to be made to a specific benefit (i.e., preventing erosion on a trail or promoting environmental or cultural learning from an interpretive talk). In addition, several outcomes operating *synergistically as gestalts* must be considered. So must the few *most highly preferred benefits* within each benefit gestalt. In addition, the planner must consider the associated benefits that will occur after participation in what has been called the "benefits chain of causality." Considerable research has documented each of these three characteristics of the benefits of leisure. Because OFM requires that each of these three characteristics be understood, a brief description will be provided:

1. **Recreation Benefit Gestalts:** This concept was described as a "recreation experience/benefit gestalt" in Moore & Driver (2005: 33–35) as follows:

   The experience/other benefit gestalt relates to the qualitative dimensions of leisure preferences and refers to the fact that many dozens of research studies have disclosed that a group (package) of generally three to six *very specific* satisfying experiences represent those experiences that are most highly valued by participants in a particular recreation activity within a particular setting. In combination, this group of most satisfying or gratifying beneficial experiences represents the gestalt. The word gestalt is used purposefully to denote a *synergistic/holistic* total experience that is greater than the sum of its parts, with each component experience representing a very specific dimension of that total experience. For example, a person hiking in a remote nature area might seek and value most highly the experience/benefit gestalt formed from realizing the specific satisfying experiences of getting physical exercise, enjoying nature, enjoying solitude, and releasing some everyday tensions. Alternatively, another person visiting the Anasazi cliff dwellings in Mesa Verde National Park with a spouse and their young children might realize the satisfying experience/benefit gestalt created synergistically from the interplay between learning about the Anasazi culture, experiencing family bonding, and getting some mild physical exercise. So, just as the separate instruments of a symphony orchestra combine with sound waves from one instrument affecting the sounds produced by other instruments to produce a gestalt melody, so do the limited number of most highly valued specific satisfying experiences, just mentioned for the hiker and visitor to the cliff dwelling, synergistically produce a holistic recreation experience/benefit gestalt.

2. **Most Salient Experiences:** Much research has also shown that within a particular gestalt, one or a few of the most highly desired experiences that form that gestalt are more highly valued than are the others in that gestalt. They therefore have a dominating influence on the type of recreation activity and setting that will be chosen to experience a particular gestalt. For example, in the above cliff dwelling example, learning about the Anasazi culture will be a dominant desired experience.
3. **Benefits Chain of Causality:** Research has also documented that many benefits result later from other previously realized benefits within what has been called the benefit chain of causality (Lee & Driver, 1992 & Driver & Bruns, 1999: pp. 358–359). Put simply, that concept recognizes that one type of benefit can lead to later benefits. Some chained outcomes are transmitted socially (enjoying being with one's family can lead to later increased family bonding and solidarity), others are chained psychophysiologically (releasing/reducing some built-up tensions can be translated into later improved mental and physical health as well as increased improved work performance and productivity), and still others are transferred cognitively (on-site learning about nature can lead to later commitments to the conservation of natural resources). In addition, although many chained benefits accrue to the recreation participants who realize the initial beneficial outcome, others flow to nonparticipants. For example, since recreation participation helps keep people healthy, the social costs of health care are reduced for everyone.

- **Relevance of These Three Concepts:** Under OFM, the concept of a benefit gestalt is important, because (despite what one will find in the literature) when: (a) *each benefit is taken singly*, they do not depend on *one* specific type of setting but instead can be realized in many different facilitating settings; (b) when more than one type of experience interacts synergistically to form a recreation experience *gestalt*, then indeed setting dependency increases proportionally to the number of experiences that comprise that gestalt and/or how highly desired or valued those experiences are relative to other available experience opportunities; and (c) the most salient or *most preferred* experiences in the gestalt do influence the type of recreation setting preferred. The subsequent chained benefits must be considered simply because people do recreate to realize them (e.g., they exercise for physical fitness), and even when they do not, those subsequent benefits must be considered when delivering any public service. The same holds true for any chained negative outcomes. Thus, the recreation planner and manager must be able to identify the specific types of benefits that form the gestalts, which benefits are preferred most highly within a gestalt, and recognize logically chained benefits and negative outcomes. These needs will be elaborated in subsequent steps of the comprehensive normative model for implementing OFM being described in this chapter.

The feasible positive outcomes (i.e., conditions improved, maintained, and satisfying experiences) to be realized and negative outcomes (i.e., worsened conditions) to be avoided must be explicitly stated in this step of planning under OFM. Decisions about which outcomes can be feasibly targeted should not be subjective. Proceed with insights gained from the supply and demand analyses completed above. And remember to consider the relationships between setting-dependent outcomes and what setting conditions are realistically achievable and sustainable, which is considered in a subsequent step. Part of this objectivity about the cause-and-effect relationships between settings and outcomes has been documented by research, while another part is derived from the professional experiences and consensus practitioners, but some of the very best comes from conversations with visitor and resident customers as well as with other affecting recreation-tourism providers (see customer preference assessments above).

- **Develop Management Objectives.** A fundamental premise of OFM is that objectives will determine the character of recreation settings and which provider actions will be planned and implemented as day-to-day field operations. Stating this in reverse helps underscore its importance; OFM subjects all provider actions and all required recreation setting characteristics to explicitly stated OFM management objectives. To develop those objectives, you must determine which specific recreation opportunities are to provided and facilitated and what associated outcomes will be targeted. This means you must develop management objectives for each of the recreation management zones. To do that, you must choose among all the outcomes desired by relevant customers by considering the characteristics of the recreation settings and the recreation services on which those outcomes depend. Put simply, practicing OFM involves managing all components of the recreation opportunity production process illustrated by Figure 3.1. To iterate, that cannot be done unless the cause and effect relationships among those components are understood. For example, when planners select the outcomes around which all future recreation programs, initiatives, projects, and actions are to be structured (or restructured), they must bear in mind the dependencies attaining those targeted outcomes have on the other components of recreation opportunity production.

  Under OFM, recreation management objectives are written, not as projects to be completed nor as programs to be implemented, but as *specific* outcome opportunities to be provided for identified and selected recreation-tourism markets and niches, including off-site customers in nearby communities. This most basic requirement of OFM prevents the too-common fuzzy thinking about what management objectives are and what purpose they serve. Here the aforementioned concept of a recreation benefit gestalt becomes particularly important when selecting and targeting specific outcomes in management objectives. For example, it is relatively easy to identify broadly-defined outcome gestalts such as experiencing a remote, undisturbed natural environment or enjoying driving off-road vehicles on undeveloped roads in the backcountry with friends or members of one's family. But, these gestalts are not comprised on only one desired benefit. Therefore, as OFM requires, it is quite another thing to actually define each beneficial component of each gestalt. In planning, OFM focuses on outcomes *first*, then activities and facilitating settings and outputs. It also requires consideration of the chained benefits that flow through the benefit chain of causality.

  If the supply and demand analyses described in previous steps have been thorough, you will already know what your relevant recreation markets are and you will have a good idea of how the products of each particular RMZ compare with the available recreation opportunities provided elsewhere, both within the planning area and in the larger market area. This step requires trying to find the best match between the capabilities of each RMZ to provide desired benefit outcomes with one of the more relevant recreation markets which reflect the greatest desire or need for those outcomes. Begin by asking some strategic questions about supply and customer demand that you have already analyzed above:

  1. Which of all recreation setting characteristics represented within this RMZ and the associated recreation opportunities being produced, or capable of being produced, are (a) highly valued and (b) distinctive/scarce/unique?
  2. Are those opportunities being provided anywhere else in the market area? If so, then why provide them here?
  3. Is there something about those opportunities that makes them distinctive? If so, is that distinctiveness significant enough to make a relevant recreation-tourism market niche?

  There are logical reasons for selecting certain outcomes over others, and that is not at all a subjective process of picking what looks good. The following ideas have been found helpful in making these determinations, and planners must be thinking about all of these things as they select the outcomes that will guide the development of management objectives under OFM:

1. Before selecting any outcome, be sure you know what it will take to produce and sustain it.
2. Not all outcomes are produced and attained as a direct result of having the proper provider services or as the indirect result of having the right setting conditions. Many outcomes flow from other outcomes that have already been attained, through the benefit causality chain which recognizes that one type of outcome (e.g., enjoying being with ones family) can lead to later outcomes (e.g., increased family bonding and solidarity).
3. Having reasoned through all of the above considerations, it is often all too easy to arrive at an extraordinarily large and tentative list of outcomes for each alternative being considered or as final management objectives. Nevertheless, you must select only those which are most distinctive for each RMZ (resource attractions, character of the settings in which they occur, and necessary services) and relevant market niches.
4. Each set of targeted outcomes, along with corresponding recreation activity opportunities being targeted, in effect become the management objectives that guide plans for realizing those outcomes.
5. Lastly, the management objectives should meet the following requirements drawn in part from Schomaker (1984):
    - Specific in that they require the manager who implements the plan to know exactly what is to be done and what will happen.
    - Outcomes oriented, which is what OFM is.
    - Focused on what is to be accomplished instead of how to accomplish it.
    - Measurable, including the use of quantifiable monitoring standards and guidelines.
    - Time-bound in that you must specify time horizons by which the objectives will be met.
    - Realistically attainable given available and likely needed resources.

- **Identify and Prescribe the Essential Setting Characteristics.** After the outcomes have been targeted for the relevant markets segment(s) for each RMZ and for relevant off-site customers, the next task is to prescribe the essential setting conditions that *must* be present or created and maintained to produce targeted recreation opportunities and facilitate realization of targeted outcomes. This step is vitally important to ensure that setting-dependent recreation opportunities are in fact produced and that the associated outcomes are realized.

To identify which sets of outcomes are setting-dependent and the essential setting conditions upon which the sustained production and attainment of those outcome opportunities depends, it is necessary to understand the previously-described concept of a recreation benefit/experience gestalt. It will not work to oversimplify OFM by just targeting outcome gestalts and giving them generic labels that erroneously denote that only one beneficial outcome is being realized instead of identifying the more precise component benefits of which each gestalt is comprised. The reason why this is necessary is bound up in the definition of the gestalt itself given above. If one is to be serious (and responsible) about managing for outcomes, he or she must ascertain precisely what each of those outcomes are. Sure, one can philosophize about the setting dependency that exists for any number of outcome gestalts as if they are isolated, solitary outcomes. However, one can neither plan nor manage that way, because the gestalt lacks adequate definition. That lack of definition prevents linking up the gestalt with the *essential setting characteristics* upon which its realization or attainment depends. This can only be done by isolating the individual outcome components of which each outcome gestalt is comprised. For example, if a setting-dependent gestalt, such as "realizing solitude, isolation, and being independent," has been targeted, the setting conditions necessary to produce those experiences and facilitate their attainment must be specified, prescribed, even created, and maintained. Under OFM, those essential setting conditions must be made explicit in the plan, and they must prescriptively guide and constrain all implementing actions by the providers.

To accomplish this objective, it is important to understand that most, if not all, recreation settings have three components that affect the types and nature of recreation activities that can be provided and the experiences and other outcomes that can be realized. They are the physical, social, and managerial components of recreation settings. OFM recognizes that *specific attributes/characteristics* of those three setting components determine whether setting-dependent recreation and outcome opportunities can be produced. The most distinguishing attributes of each of the three setting components are listed below. More detail is given about the attributes and influence of the *three components of recreation settings* in the USDA Forest Service's ROS Users' Guide (1982) and Moore & Driver (2005).

- Biophysical Components of Recreation Settings: Defined in terms of proximity of roads bearing different amounts and types of vehicular traffic, degree of naturalness, types and characteristics of fauna and flora, size of area, and amount and types of development. These attributes define the character of geophysical features and all physical infrastructure provided by management (e.g., bulletin boards, signs, bridges, interpretative centers, amphitheatres, picnic tables, camping pads, roads, boat launch ramps, entrance stations, registration boxes)[2].
- Social Components of Recreation Settings: Defined in terms of numbers of on-site customers/users, sizes of individual groups, evidence of other users, proximity to other people and groups. These attributes define the character of user behavior and the types of things they bring with them (RVs, stereos, pets, generators, etc.).
- Managerial Components of Recreation Settings: Defined by the attributes of both agency and associated providers, including the on-site presence or absence of managerial personnel (including volunteers and maintenance workers), the behavior and demeanor of the managers (i.e., authoritative or more participative), managerially imposed rules and regulations, and the services offered[3].

Specific attributes of the biophysical, social, and managerial components of recreation settings interact synergistically to create the overall on-site recreation/related amenity environment. For example, increased numbers of visitors (a social attribute) often requires stepped up visitor services by providers (a managerial attribute). Or, increased facility developments will not only change the physical setting but also become a magnet for higher user densities, which in turn will require that different regulations and visitor services by providers become essential attributes of the managerial settings. To iterate, the attributes of the three setting components interact synergistically to impart a distinctive character to each setting, which ends up producing and facilitating equally distinctive recreation opportunities and outcomes. For this reason, the Recreation Opportunity Spectrum (ROS) system recognizes that setting characteristics influence both the kinds and quality of recreation opportunities produced as well as the kinds of outcomes that can be can be realized.

So it can be seen, that the specific attributes that comprise each of the three setting components can be used to comprehensively describe the character of any recreation place. Those descriptions lend objectivity to some of the loosely-defined notions of places. The question therefore arises, "Do I need to prescribe conditions for each of these components?" The answer is quite simple: "Only the ones you intend to manage!" Therefore, setting prescriptions must be written with enough descriptive precision to ensure the sustained production and attainment of the recreation opportunities and outcomes targeted by management objectives. They must be, because customers have preferences for specific attributes of the settings in which they recreate (or live, in the case of residents of nearby or adjoining communities) and they know they cannot achieve the outcomes they desire if those attributes are not present. This helps explain why facilitating settings are the most tangible of all the recreation production components illustrated by Figure 3.1.

Much detail is provided here on recreation settings, because their importance cannot be overstated; they are *essential.* They are, because the setting prescriptions developed in this step and refined as you move on through the planning process determine the area's productive capacity and condition all land management and recreation-tourism provider actions. To be more specific, the plan's prescribed setting conditions determine the capacity of each RMZ to produce targeted recreation opportunities and facilitate consequent attainment of targeted outcomes. At the same time, prescribed settings also guide and constrain all recreation management, marketing, monitoring, and supporting administrative actions. As you can see, when done right, setting prescriptions demonstrate professional understanding of what needs to be done and understanding of the cause and effect relations inherent among all components of recreation opportunity production, and they bring the recreation profession back to its roots by ensuring that the application of OFM really does benefit many lives, communities, and the environment itself. In addition, setting prescriptions opens what is needed and why to all providers. They thereby help facilitate the collaborative actions of all key affecting providers as managing partners, which is essential for OFM applications to succeed. This also helps ensure managerial responsiveness, accountability, effectiveness, and efficiency (or cost-effectiveness), which, as mentioned at the beginning of Chapter 2, OFM was purposefully designed to help ensure.

While the need to consider outcome preferences of the off-site customers is emphasized above and in Chapter 2, it is iterated here to emphasize that the plan needs to be responsive to the effect that recreation setting characteristics have on the quality of life of affected local residents of nearby and adjoining gateway communities as well as the more remote off-site users described in Chapter 2. The news is replete with accounts of how recreation-tourism development and use, done wrong, produces a variety of worsened conditions to the social, economic and physical environments of local communities. For example, as mentioned in Chapter 2, changes in tourism caused by the plan can have both beneficial and deleterious affects on local communities. That is why the boundaries of the recreation and related amenity production system were defined in Chapter 2 to include such "environmental effects" on local communities. By forging viable collaborative managerial efforts with elected officials and the business community within these communities, land managers have been able facilitate the management of setting conditions on public lands and within the communities to achieve desired, positive outcomes.

Define the Essential Recreation-Tourism Service Environment. This step outlines both the composition and breadth of the necessary recreation-tourism service delivery system upon which your agency customers depend for achievement and realization of outcomes targeted for your particular area. That information establishes the operative framework within which the recreation plan is to be implemented by defining the service delivery system's geographic bounds and its key players. It will provide a good idea of who the competing suppliers are for the kinds of recreation opportunities desired within your recreation market area. Such market areas will vary is size in terms of the size of the area for which the plan is being made, the variety and types of recreation opportunities that can be provided by your agency and your associate providers and by other providers such as other public park and recreation agencies (including both on-site service providers such as tour operators and guides, and off-site retail services and equipment rentals), local governments (providing essential transportation infrastructure), private-sector organizations, and not-for-profit providers (such as the Nature Conservancy). Simply stated, the purpose of this step is to identify all of the key providers who materially affect the character of recreation settings within which this occurs, the kinds of recreation being produced, as well as what outcomes are realized and to what extent. Secondly, it outlines the framework required for the successful and sustained collaborative engagement of these providers as managing partners with the principle managing agency, unit of government, or other organization.

One of the most interesting phenomena of present-day professional recreation practice is the survival of activity-based management despite ample evidence that customers care as much or more about the character of the settings in which those activities take place as well as the kinds of outcomes these activities yield. There are many reasons this outmoded practice persists, but one of the most obvious is that is much easier for any recreation provider to single-handedly continue developing supporting on-site infrastructure (e.g., facilities, programs, information, events) required to accommodate ever greater levels of activity-based recreation demand. And, when it cannot, there are plenty of organized user and interest groups who have the resources necessary to fuel this type of "industrial" recreation development.

OFM, however, takes a broader view. As detailed in Chapter 2, it requires looking beyond simple recreation activity participation to its effects upon the character of recreation settings; it considers not just visitors, but affected households and communities, economies, and the environment. And, of course, this requires the principal recreation managing agency or organization to reexamine its long-established partnerships with activity-based user groups and advocates. Instead, OFM demands redefining partnerships to include the collaborative involvement of associated providers. As emphasized in Chapter 2, those affecting providers, sometimes individually but certainly collectively, significantly influence a recreation area's capacity to sustain production and the types, amounts, and quality of recreation services provided, as well as influence the quality of the lives of members of nearby communities.

To implement this step, look at the targeted outcomes and prescribed settings for each alternative, then think about what recreation-tourism providers the managing provider must involve not only to review the plan, but far more importantly, to implement it as managing partners. This includes managing, marketing, monitoring, and administering the recreation area efficiently and effectively (i.e., to minimize investments and to maximize achievement of management objectives and setting prescriptions). Then decide when and how to ensure their sustained engagement as collaborating providers. Remember that the following implementation plan will specify the minimum essential actions that these providers will have to agree to do if the management objectives and setting prescriptions are to be achieved.

Which recreation providers must be engaged as partners to provide what services? The ones who can be expected to contribute either positively or negatively to implementation of the plan design. In other words, some provide essential services without which plan objectives will not be achieved; and the actions of others, if not brought into harmony with the plan design, will produce undesirable, value-subtracting, worsened conditions. And how are they to be engaged as collaborating providers to implement the plan design? It will take an effective strategy for involving them as managing partners. There must be something in it for each of them. You must be sure to identify or provide whatever that is! Be aware of the regional, national, and international user clienteles that you share with other outdoor recreation and related amenity agencies and recreation-tourism providers. The following is a list of questions that can help you complete this step:

1. For service-providing businesses and industry:
    a. Could the actions of outfitters or tour guides change setting character? Which ones?
    b. Do adequate on-site services exist for the use and enjoyment of the recreation area? Or are new vendors, equipment liveries, or outfitter services needed?
    c. How are visitors to acquire the knowledge and skills required for responsible use and enjoyment of the area?
    d. How will the diverse recreation opportunity and outcome offerings, the distinctive character of recreation settings in which they occur, and available services be communicated to prospective visitors so they can make informed outing choices—among this and other venues—and not end up in the wrong place for the outcomes they desire?
    e. Will tourism industry promotional message content change numbers of types of visitors to the area and influence setting character? What industry organizations are positioned to promote the area, or already are promoting the area?
    f. What kinds of support services will visitors be dependent upon for use and enjoyment of the recreation area? Which retail businesses and hospitality industries are they dependent on?
    g. Are there real-estate developers whose developments are in close enough proximity to public lands to change recreation setting character and its capacity to facilitate desired outcome attainment?

2. For local governments:
   a. Are visitors dependent upon the road and transportation infrastructure provided by local governments? What will it take to ensure that these developments remain consistent with essential setting conditions prescribed?
   b. Have any outcomes been targeted which require the involvement of local school districts, social services, or other units of government (e.g., increased access to hands-on environmental learning, greater community involvement in land-use decisions, reduced exposure to at-risk youth)?
   c. Have other outcomes been targeted which require working more closely with county planners and offices of economic development (e.g., improved local economic stability, maintenance of the community's small-town character, increased desirability as a place to live or retire).
   d. Is the principal recreation managing agency or organization able to provide for search and rescue and other emergency services, or is it dependent upon units of local government to provide these services?

- Evaluate Alternatives and Select the Preferred Alternative. The extent to which alternatives (in plans for nature-based areas) need to be evaluated and displayed for public review in a proposed plan depends on the following factors.
  1. Multiple-use resource management plans for large tracts of public wildlands, of which recreation use and values have become increasingly significant, practically always evaluate feasible alternative approaches to management. In fact, federal natural resource management agencies are legally responsible for reasonably evaluating alternatives, and many interest groups have legally contested plans which they believed erred in doing so properly. Typically, the proposed multiple-use plan that is distributed for review will offer a preferred alternative and compare it with other feasible alternatives, which vary from plan to plan. Some might select a preferred alternative that economically focuses on commodity production, ecosystems sustainability, recreational values, or some combination of several of these. In such multiple-use plans, recreation will never be the only use or value considered.
  2. If the plan is being made for recreation only (i.e., not within a multiple-use context), for an area that has a variety of recreation settings and for which diverse preferences by potential customers have been identified for different recreation activities, experiences, and other benefits, then alternatives must be considered. A preferred alternative should be recommended and compared with other feasible alternatives in a proposed plan submitted for public review.
  3. If there are few identified conflicting recreation demands, then fewer alternatives need to be considered.
  4. At the other, perhaps unlikely, extreme, if no conflicting preferences are identified, one alternative can accommodate them, and no other alternative is feasible, then alternatives need not be proposed.

Any proposed alternative must be feasible, clearly stated, evaluated, and justified. It must also meet the legal and other established guidelines that govern the planning agency, and conform to established planning criteria, such as ensure collaborative planning and following approved criteria for evaluating alternatives. All recreation production components comprising each alternative must be addressed. This requires use of information acquired in previous steps of the planning process on: demand (by relevant primary market segments and resident customers); the outcome-based management objectives that are particularly important to the planning agency and its collaborating partners; the existing setting conditions; and especially what is feasible and within the agency's policy guidelines.

Experienced planners and managers have learned that the amount of work required to assemble a final plan following public review and comment is inversely proportional to the effort that is expended to put this kind of definitive content into draft plans. This is what encourages the kinds of review comments that contribute most to the development of an effective final management plan.

There are different yet equally defensible ways of managing recreation within most recreation areas. But each alternative yields different arrays of outcome opportunities and produces different effects. This means that managing for varying sets of outcome opportunities for different market segments requires different setting prescriptions and involves notable changes in the service environment (i.e., the service communities and providers within each who would need to be engaged in implementing the alternative).

At the time of this writing, completed OFM planning has demonstrated that all of this can become inordinately complex and make alternative descriptions difficult to understand. Indeed, a common objective to managing for outcomes is that it is too difficult to grasp. It has been the authors' experience that while OFM does require recreation professionals to address components of recreation production which has heretofore often been largely ignored, the only thing that is really inordinately complex have been planners' efforts to portray the content of required alternatives using only narrative descriptions. The challenge therefore is portraying alternatives and the components of each in such a way that their content, including important similarities and differences among them, can be easily grasped. First, this needs to be clear to the recreation planners who write them. This need for clarity is critically important for the field practitioners who ultimately shoulder responsibility for implementing them in approved management plans. Such clarity is also essential if the proposed plan and alternatives are to be understood by reviewers well enough to enable them to provide comments useful for helping planners prepare the best final management plan possible. Experience has shown that it is unrealistic to expect managers or reviewers to read or understand the content of a plan if it consists only of narrative text descriptions without more definitive accompanying summary tables and supporting map graphics.

One of the easiest and most digestible ways of displaying OFM management plan alternatives is to outline the content of key plan components for each alternative side-by-side using a tabular matrix display format and develop accompanying maps (i.e., defining RMZs, prescribed recreation setting character classes, and so forth). Such summary displays make it very easy to determine, for each alternative, the spatial configuration of relevant recreation areas and RMZs or other recreation management units, the composition of corresponding primary market niches, OFM objectives, necessary setting conditions upon which the sustained production and attainment of those outcomes depend, and the identification of key communities and associated providers comprising the relevant service environment.

Because one alterative must be designed as the preferred alternative in the proposed plan that is submitted for public review, the proposed plan should explain why it was selected instead of the other alternatives.

Phase 4: Develop an Implementation Plan

It is all too easy to underestimate the importance of this phase. In review, among other things, OFM insists that many critical actions must be taken, including: relevant market segments must be identified, the recreation activities and beneficial outcomes targeted for customers must be identified as management objectives, essential setting conditions required to produce and attain those outcome opportunities must be identified and prescribed, and the framework within which essential services are to be delivered must be specified. While these actions are critically important, the perception exists that they are the most important of all because they set everything else in motion. However, that motion or momentum will be lost if necessary implementing actions are not planned carefully, specified clearly, and followed through on diligently.

The following five steps comprise this phase of developing an implementation plan, which is a most important part of the overall plan. They are listed in the cause-and-effect order in which they must be addressed to help assure that actions identified under each ensuing step are fully supplementary and complementary of the previous ones. Remember that a different set of implementation actions is required for each RMZ because each one has its distinctive market-define customers, management objectives, setting prescriptions, and service delivery environment.

- **Identify Management Actions to be Implemented.** In the simplest of terms, this step outlines *all* recreation management actions required to achieve prescribed biophysical, social setting, and managerial conditions, and produce the targeted recreation opportunities and targeted outcomes. Among other things, they include recreation and transportation networks (motorized, mechanized, and pedestrian) facilities needed to facilitate use and enjoyment and rehabilitative actions to achieve setting character prescriptions. One of the most noticeable departures from activity-focused management shows up in this step. Recreation management is no longer a matter of just building more facilities and implementing more programs to accommodate more use, disregarding what this does to the character of recreation settings and the ability of other customers to achieve what they presently enjoy from those settings. OFM goes beyond this to ask why those settings are desirable; it focuses on outcomes, not recreation activities.

- **Identify Marketing Actions to be Implemented.** The term "marketing" is used here as an umbrella concept that covers all information, outreach, education, interpretation, and promotional activities required to maintain prescribed setting characteristics and to facilitate the attainment of targeted outcomes by identified primary visitors and resident customers. It should be observed that while this is not a classic application of "marketing" per se (i.e., "product, price, place, and promotion"), OFM nonetheless insists that customers be informed about what kinds of recreation opportunities are being provided. Marketing, in this sense, is not simply a matter of promoting more use, because social setting character matters for certain outcomes. Nor is this a matter of building more interpretive exhibits to advance the interpretive program. Instead, marketing means providing the right kinds of information by whatever means is appropriate to maintain prescribed setting conditions, produce targeted opportunities, and facilitate targeted outcome attainment. Thus, interpretation (along with its sister marketing tools of visitor information, education, and promotion) needs to be balanced and measured with other marketing tools to select the one that best achieves planned ends.

    To accomplish this step, determine whether or not the marketing information and the way it is presented will: (a) help achieve targeted outcomes, (b) conform to the setting prescriptions, (c) tell the same story as managers have already told themselves (in the preceding step), and (d) be faithful to the supporting administrative actions (outlined in the following fourth). As such, marketing actions should complement management actions. Management actions tell the providing agencies or organizations what they must do, and marketing actions inform customers what opportunities the providers have agreed to produce, what setting conditions they have agreed to maintain, and what services they intend to provide.
- **Identify Monitoring Actions.** When done right, the preceding planning steps already outline the appropriate monitoring indicators and standards. All that remains is to identify appropriate monitoring methods, actions, and schedules. Specifically, the standards used to monitor the desired social settings are defined by the social setting prescriptions. So, that monitoring requires determining if those targeted outcomes are being realized. It requires asking visitors and resident customers to what degree the targeted outcomes are being attained from the targeted recreation activities. Similarly, the standards for monitoring the achievement or maintenance of biophysical and managerial setting conditions are defined by setting prescriptions already included for them in the plan.
- **Identify Supporting Administrative Actions.** This is the caboose to all planned recreation actions. The biggest challenge of this step is to prevent these actions from becoming the engine that drives what gets done, rather than being the final car on the planning train. Include in this step whatever administrative actions are required to support the management, marketing, and monitoring actions identified above. Address the following kinds of actions: funding, collaborative management agreements, assistance agreements, user fees and fund-raising, external funding grants, and development of outcomes-directed criteria for making performance evaluations of those responsible for implementing OFM (a critical requirement discussed in the last section of this chapter). A noteworthy condition that may need to be applied is that some collaborative management agreements may need to be executed early in order to facilitate the full participation of those providers upon whom sustained delivery of targeted outcome opportunities depends on as managing partners in development of the plan (which will not happen if this necessity is not

addressed until this phase and step of plan development). The positioning of all supporting administrative actions to the role that is truly supportive of management is absolutely essential.

In sum, standards for monitoring to ensure that the management, marketing, monitoring, and supporting administrative actions are being implemented as planned come from this implementation plan section of the overall plan. Problems disclosed by monitoring will suggest ways to adaptively shift implementation actions to ensure that approved management objectives are being achieved (e.g., that targeted outcomes are being realized) and that setting character conditions are being achieved and maintained. These adaptations might require minor or major changes to the plan being implemented. Under an OFM framework, adaptive changes to the implementing actions phase of the plan typically do not require plan revisions. Such changes are simply a part of agile plan implementation. Changes in relevant market niches, management objectives, and/or setting prescriptions, however, normally require a plan revision.

- **Provide Ample Opportunities and Time-Frames for Review of the Proposed Plan.** As mentioned, the proposed plan (with a summary of why the preferred alternative was selected) should be submitted for public review, so that it can be finalized and become the approved plan to be implemented. While plan reviews are customary, it is doubly important that all collaborating providers identified in the above steps are not only given the opportunity to review the proposed plan, but are engaged as partners in responding to review comments. This will require providing adequate time frames for review of the proposed plan.

Phase 5: Adjust Management/ Implementation Plan as Needed and Approve Final Plan

Public review comments have a way of helping planners and managers reconfigure elements of the proposed plan. Therefore, useful comments about the proposed plan enable recreation planners and managers to be more objective in assembling the content of the plan that will be approved for implementation. For example, elements of one or more well-written alternatives will end up stimulating more substantive review comments than the recommended preferred alternative does. Also, in some instances, creative but realistic new alternatives may even end up being selected for the approved plan. In other instances, elements from the proposed plan end up being pieced together with a preferred alternative to come up with the most responsive final management plan possible.

The same kind of tabular format used to portray alternatives can also be used to help planners to contrast and compare which, if any, of the alternatives best responds to substantive review comments. The implications of any suggested change to any element of the final plan design on other plan elements is thereby made more apparent. Planners and managers can more readily grasp what those implications are, compare similarities and differences, weigh the advantages and disadvantages of each, and make needed changes accordingly. For example, recommended changes in relevant market segments or even slight shifts therein will have implications for how corresponding RMZs must be configured or reconfigured. Needed shifts in targeted outcome opportunities reveal themselves more readily. Necessary changes in the service environment and changes to the mix of key providers that need to be engaged as managing partners also become more obvious.

The process of responding to public review comments has implications for finalizing implementation plans as well as management plans. Here too, graphic summaries of alternatives help planners spot which elements of the alternatives are most responsive to public comments. Changes in relevant market niches, targeted outcome opportunities, setting prescriptions, and the service environment all may require changing the types of management, marketing, monitoring, and supporting actions required to achieve the plan design. Graphic summaries helps planners more readily make the changes needed. They also aid planners in more completely integrating provider actions into each of the aforementioned four components of the implementation plan. In sum, the recommended graphic portrayals following public reviews helps attain a more complete synthesis of the revised plan and thereby promotes more responsive management.

Phase 6: Implement the Plan and Adjust Field Operations Accordingly

Incorporate implementing actions into all field operations. In a sense, the most difficult part of adopting OFM is plan implementation. Restructuring traditional field operations to make the shift from activity-focused programs and project-centered management to OFM is no easy task. Actually managing recreation setting character for the production and attainment of targeted recreation opportunities and outcomes targeted for selected market niches in every RMZ requires a good deal of introspective and innovative work. This might require additional training of existing staff or the hiring of new staff that are committed to OFM. It might also involve cost-sharing and other cooperative arrangements with the agency's partners. Before implementation is commenced, it is necessary to assure that needed administrative and managerial support is or will be available for efficient and successful plan implementation. Another operational necessity is the incorporation of all actions into annual operating plans. Those plans should define clearly who will do what and when. Each responsible party, including relevant customers and associated providers, should have a clear understanding of its responsibilities and agree to follow through on schedule and in the manner agreed to. Collaborative management agreements with associate providers and other partners should be written with language that clearly addresses these requirements.

This moves recreation management beyond its more customary "do it yourself" mode in which dozens of independent partners work in isolation for their own activity-oriented ends. Instead, it ensures that no partnership is allowed to proceed without being operationally integrated with all other pending actions. Making this an operational reality requires an unprecedented level of teamwork and program constraint. Both the necessity for and consequences of every action and partnership are constantly evaluated in terms of its effect on all others. This requires managing recreation field operations through an ongoing project lifecycle that is continuously adjusted with the goal of ensuring that only those actions needed to achieve prescribed setting character conditions and facilitate realization of targeted outcomes are allowed to proceed.

The need for restructuring field operations in accordance with the plan design can hardly be overstated. When any OFM is implemented, the need for and appropriateness of each and every implementing action must be weighed along four essential dimensions. First, is the action necessary to produce one or more of the outcome opportunities targeted in management objectives and to facilitate actual attainment of those outcomes as realized experiences and other benefits by targeted niche markets? Second, is the action sufficiently integrated across otherwise piecemeal programs (e.g., rivers, trails, ATVs, mountain bikes, interpretation, etc.)? Third, is the action balanced and complementary with the other remaining functional inputs (i.e., management, marketing, monitoring, and administrative support)? Fourth, does the action appropriately guide and constrain existing field operations to eliminate all needless and counterproductive programs and initiatives?

Phase 7: Revise the Plan as Needed or Required by Agency Directives

Normally, under OFM, adaptive changes to the plan will be made during monitoring. Those changes typically do not require plan revisions and are part of agile and adaptive plan implementation. Changes in primary recreation markets, management objectives, and/or setting prescriptions, however, normally require a plan revision. They can occur for many reasons, such as the implementation of alternative land management uses such as extensive mineral developments or the creation of major transportation systems through the area. In addition, some public wildland management agencies require periodic revisions, which generally involve starting a new planning process for the area.

Phase 8: Ensure that Performance Reports and Evaluations Document and Recognize the Sustained Production and Attainment of Targeted Outcome Opportunities to the Extent Feasible

The need for implementing these actions is so important it is considered separately as the last major section of this chapter.

Synopsis of Why OFM Planning Is Different

Some wildland recreation management plans dispense with much of the analyses and definition required by OFM planning. For example, the management objectives ignore adequate consideration of the desired and required setting conditions and the development of setting prescriptions that facilitate explicitly defined outcomes. Others do not give adequate, if any, attention to associated providers or actively involve members of adjoining or nearby communities in the planning process. More problematic, many recreation plans still focus on accommodating activity-focused recreation demands. Within that context, management actions are taken primarily from cues provided by the most well-organized and influential activity-oriented users and special interest groups. Understandably, these actions tend to simply perpetuate status quo recreation program management (e.g., management of rivers and trails, interpretation, off-highway vehicles, wilderness, recreation facilities, accessibility, permits and fees). This focus also nicely accommodates and advances special initiatives (e.g., scenic byways, watchable wildlife, heritage tourism), which is fine, but too many of them do not consider outcomes or not do so comprehensively enough.

A major deficiency of such activity-focused project and program-focused recreation planning and management is that it provides no balanced, integrative conceptual framework for ensuring both effective and efficient investments. Each program is recognized as having its own merit (regardless of what is actually achieved by customers and the environment), and recreation professionals define success in terms of numbers of on-site visitors, projects completed, or programs implemented and sustained. Despite the reality that many such programs have long operated cross purposes with one another, each survives because it is supported by established activity-focused partnerships. So, accomplishments are measured in terms of how those partnerships' activity-oriented desires stimulate further project development and program advocacy.

In sharp contrast to the above, OFM regards all provider actions as only the means to accomplishment of the real ends of recreation management (i.e., outcome attainment). That is why they are called implementing actions. Within this context, it is critically important that planners shift from advancing well-established programs and projects to instead ensuring that each and every action be tailored to (a) fit within prescribed setting prescriptions, (b) facilitate production of targeted recreation opportunities, (c) facilitate attainment of satisfying experiences and other improved conditions, and (d) reduce the magnitudes of unwanted outcomes. Only in those ways can management be realized that optimizes the beneficial outcomes of recreation.

Rather than addressing provider actions as projects, programs, or other initiatives, OFM requires ensuring that they do indeed facilitate the attainment of targeted outcomes. Under OFM, the simple advancement of programs and special initiatives and the completion of projects are in and of themselves immaterial. The most straightforward way to stop driving programs, projects, and special initiatives as ends unto themselves is to adopt OFM planning. Under OFM, it is incumbent upon managers and planners to demonstrate that each and every planned action is really a required means of achieving outcome attainment.

OFM Is a Different Approach, But You Can Do It!

A lot of detail has been presented about the comprehensive normative model for applying and implementing OFM just described. While it might seem overwhelming, it is really not that difficult once the basic logic is understood and accepted. Nevertheless, experience has shown that people who have attended workshops on how to implement OFM seem to appreciate and grasp the concepts and requirements then surprisingly ask "Now how do I implement it?" Some of us who have helped conduct those workshops believe those responses are caused not so much by perceptions of any complexities involved, but instead for the following three reasons: (1) the trainees have a difficult time changing their mindsets away from the notion that planning starts with consideration of what resources and other assets are available and what should be done with them instead of what feasible array of outcomes can be targeted by the management of those resources; (2) most recreation planners and managers remain locked into the idea that their primary responsibility is providing recreation activity opportunities (i.e., do activity-focused planning as described in Chapter 2); and (3) there is a desire to see what facilitating outputs have been produced (i.e., hiking trail, picnic tables, campgrounds) without sufficiently questioning *why* they are produced in terms off resulting outcomes. The following simple example should demonstrate that OFM, while a somewhat different way of thinking, is really not that complex, nor is it difficult to implement.

Assume that your demand studies have shown that your customers desire to have opportunities to learn more about nature and the functioning of natural ecosystems while recreating in a natural area. As such, OFM would require targeting such learning as an outcome opportunity. Then what would you have to do? First, you would need to write specific management objectives detailing the specific outcomes you intend to target, identifying all relevant outcome opportunities and where they are to be provided, and to whom. But you would want to ensure that the outcomes being targeted could actually be produced and realized. Next, you would need to identify whether you either have or can achieve the setting conditions necessary for producing the activity as well as other beneficial or experiential opportunities targeted in your management objectives. These would become your setting prescriptions. Then you would need to identify the minimum essential implementing actions required to achieve these ends. For example, you would need to identify all management actions required to ensure the desired setting characteristics will be maintained and the outcome opportunities targeted in your management objectives are produced and realized. To do that, you would need to know whether you could facilitate your targeted results by nature trails without such facilities; with or without interpretive signs, through presentations by interpretive naturalists, audio-video presentations, exhibits, or through self-discovery; facilitated by presenting appropriate observation, focus, synthesis, and summary questions; or what?

You would also need to identify the essential marketing actions required to adequately inform your targeted customers about the kinds of recreation opportunities being provided, where to find them, and how to responsibly use and enjoy them. What key informational, promotional, and educational/interpretive messages do your customers need? What do you need to facilitate efficient and effective management? You must then identify your monitoring standards to ensure that all of the above conditions are being met as planned (i.e., outcomes attained, setting characteristics maintained, and both management and marketing actions implemented). In addition, you would need to determine if relevant customer and associated providers need to be involved in helping produce the outcome opportunities and in doing so ensure that the prescribed essential setting conditions are achieved and maintained. You would then need to identify the essential collaborative management agreements required to ensure that all affecting providers are working together and towards the same ends.

From this simple example, it should be apparent that while OFM represents a different way of thinking, it is not all that difficult to implement once it is understood. It does, however, require paying attention to all components of the recreation opportunity production process depicted by Figure 3.1 and explained in Chapter 2. In a nutshell, the *first* decisions are *what outcomes* are desired by your customers and whether opportunities to realize them be provided, and if so, where and by whom (the agency or the agency in cooperation with relevant stakeholders, especially associated providers)? Then you must identify the essential setting characteristics required to produce those opportunities. Finally, you must identify what provider actions are required to ensure that both those setting conditions and the outcome opportunities are being produced as planned. As emphasized earlier in this chapter, OFM planning goes from the right to the left in Figure 3.1, and plan implementation goes in the opposite direction, from left to right. However, in both processes, the focus is on *why* any leisure service should be provided and under *what* conditions. That is the required mindset, and once that mindset is adopted, you can do it!

OFM Performance Reporting and Evaluations

The institutionalized systems of rewarding the performance of agencies and their personnel are not only recognized and understood, they are the *primary* determinants of the actions of agencies and the behavior of their employees. Therefore, it is of fundamental importance that agencies, subunits of such, and the professional personnel responsible for adopting OFM be rewarded for attainment of targeted outcomes. That will only be accomplished if formal outcomes-focused performance reporting and evaluation criteria are developed and used to guide the performance of professional personnel and park and recreation agencies. Unless this happens, OFM will not be implemented as widely as it should be regardless of any arguments made in this text about the merits of OFM! That is true simply because the actions of agencies, their subunits, and employees are closely related not only to what they are asked to do, but especially to what they are rewarded to do. For that reason, this chapter will end with a discussion of two types of performance evaluations. One type comprises the periodic (usually annual) evaluations of a public agency and of an administrative subunit that document what it has accomplished during the reporting period. The other comprises the periodic (usually at least annually) performance evaluations of the field-level professional personnel (as well as their supervisors) in administrative subunits that are responsible for the development and implementation of recreation resource management plans. Each type will be discussed with emphasis on the need to more fully report on outcome attainment.

Evaluating the Performance of Public Agencies and Their Administrative Subunits

The performance of every public park, recreation, and related amenity agency is evaluated in many ways and at all of its administrative levels. This holds true for the top levels--whether the office of the Chief of the USDA Forest Service (USFS) or of the Director of the USDI Bureau of Land Management (BLM)--down to the lower administrative subunits (e.g., a Ranger District of the USFS or a Field Office of the BLM). It also holds true for higher levels of government, whether federal or municipal. For example, the performance of all federal agencies is always under review by oversight committees of the House and Senate of the U. S. Congress. In addition, other units (e.g., the Office of Management and Budget in the Office of the President as well as the General Accounting Office) also maintain a close watch of the performance of federal agencies. Further review is offered by a large number of social, economic, and environmental interest groups that represent diverse and often conflicting interests (e.g., the Natural Resource Defense Council and the Heritage Foundation). Affected gateway communities and their residents also exercise a different kind of evaluation of agency performance, especially in terms of impacts on their quality of life, local economic stability, and maintenance of environmental quality. Such oversight and critique that extends from the top to lower administrative levels exists not only for federal agencies, but also for public agencies that exist at other levels of government whether state, county, or municipal. As just explained, this oversight is exercised both internally within government and externally by many affected and concerned entities. Each of these evaluations of agency performance significantly affects budgetary allocations and an agency's ability to work efficiently and effectively with the collaborating providers upon whom they depend, and it ultimately affects the discretion given to an agency and its managers.

Since passage of the federal Government Performance and Results Act of 1993 (GPRA), use of performance measures has increased at all levels of government. Concomitant with that growth has been an increase in the number of articles on performance measures in relevant journals (especially *Public Administration Review*) and other publications. Those papers show that different measures are being used by public agencies, with some attention given to outcomes by those agencies (see Chapter 4 of this text), but most attention is given to outputs. That is understandable, because the outcomes movement is relatively new, and it is generally easier to measure and document production of facilitating outputs than outcomes, irrespective of whether these outputs actually facilitate the results desired by customers for themselves, their communities, and the environment. Therefore, when allocating funds and making rewards, most legislatures, budget offices, and agency administrators have focused (and still focus) mostly on production of facilitating outputs. This situation exists for agencies at all levels of government, but it needs to change before OFM will be implemented as widely as it should be to facilitate realization of the beneficial outcomes that matter most to the publics served. But, effecting such change at the federal level has been difficult because of the requirements of the GPRA discussed below.

GPRA and OFM

Because this chapter focuses on use of OFM by agencies that manage wildlands, comments are made in this section about the influence of the GPRA on their use of OFM. That act was created to help prevent "waste and inefficiency in Federal programs" and to "improve federal program effectiveness and public accountability" by promoting "a new focus on *results, service quality, and customer satisfaction*." The act requires that each federal agency shall submit to the Director of the Office of Management and Budget (OMB) a strategic plan that among other things shall contain a statement of the "general goals and objectives, *including outcome related goals and objectives*, for the major functions and operations of the agency." In addition, the act requires that each agency shall "...establish performance indicators to be used in measuring or assessing the relevant outputs, service levels, *and outcomes* of each program activity." In turn, the act established necessary definitions including "'outcome *measure*' means the assessment of the *results* of a program activity'" and "'output *measure*' means the tabulation, calculation, or recording of activity or effort and can be expressed in a quantitative or qualitative manner."

Italicized type was added to selected portions of the above quotations from the GPRA to show that it clearly requires attention be given to outcomes as well as outputs. In particular, notice that the act defines outcomes in terms of results. The good news is that some agency guidance now directs recreation programs to manage for beneficial outcomes. Nevertheless, in the applications of OFM conducted so far, it does not appear that *any* federal recreation providing agency making those applications has yet come close to reporting the attainment of outcome goals to the extent the GPRA requires. Instead, their evaluations of performance have focused on facilitating outputs (e.g., picnic tables, hiking trails, campgrounds, marinas) that have been created and/or maintained, with too little attention given to beneficial outcomes realized although some negative outcomes avoided or reduced in impact are reported and deal mostly with environmental protection.

The disclaimer must be made here that the editor of this text has not been required to make public agency performance evaluations other than as a research scientist, which is an entirely different ball game. However, his personal discussions with quite a few administrators and managers who work for federal wildland agencies have revealed that the current approach of focusing on outputs is guided by the way the federal agencies interpret Section 4 of the act. That section describes how the annual "Performance Plans and Reports" required by the act shall be prepared, and there are two requirements that (1) they must include "performance goals," which are defined by the act as "a target level of performance expressed as a *tangible, measurable, and objective, against which actual achievement can be compared, including a goal expressed as a quantitative standard, value, or rate*" and (2) performance goals must be expressed (and reported on) in an "objective, quantifiable, and measurable form unless authorized to be in an alternative form." We will return to the italicized emphasis shortly, because the GPRA does not require that all outcome measures need to meet the just-stated "tangible, measurable, and objective" criteria even though getting those less tangible measures accepted by the OMB has reportedly been problematic.

It is understood that the reporting of agency performance primarily in terms of facilitating outputs occurs because many outcome measures cannot be expressed in the required "tangible, objective, and/or measurable" terms. Also, many outcomes are not realized within an annual accounting time period. Given those problems, agencies "justify" their current practice of mostly reporting facilitating outputs, under the rationale that their performance related to producing and maintaining facilitating outputs serves as a *proxy* evaluation of their performance toward the attainment of the overtly targeted outcome goals. As such, they are relying on the logic of the recreation opportunity production process illustrated by Figure 3.1 and Figure 2.3 of Chapter 2, which describes that process. To review, the basic logic of that recreation opportunity production process is that the right kinds of managerial outputs and settings will directly facilitate the production of targeted outcome opportunities. This logic is understandable to some degree given the difficulty of evaluating all outcome goal attainment in tangible, objective, and measurable terms. But, it is only partially accurate, can be self-deceiving and misleading, and certainly nurtures other than OFM-guided planning and management. That common approach to what attainment reporting does is deficient for two related reasons. First, even when attainment of outcomes is presumed to happen if the necessary outputs are being produced, those outcomes are seldom described in the performance reports. Second, outcomes should be reported and *not just* assumed. If specific outcomes are not defined and targeted overtly, how can the reporting agencies know for sure that the outputs they are reporting are the ones *actually needed* for the realization of the unspecified and presumed outcomes? Considerable restructuring of reported outputs might well be needed for the assumed outcome opportunities to be realized.

It *must be* understood that under OFM the outcomes determine the outputs and *not* vice versa! By analogy, it would be inadequate for medical professionals to evaluate the effectiveness of their performance by reporting only their facilitating outputs (e.g., numbers of beds provided/occupied, shots given, operations conducted, etc.) or for transportation engineers to report their outputs (e.g., traffic lights installed, miles of highway built and/or maintained, etc.) and just presume that the outcomes of their efforts will be attained and recognized. To iterate, the outcomes determine what outputs need to be created by the medical professionals and transportation engineers--and by recreation professionals. Yes, outputs *must* be measured and reported, but reporting just outputs is inadequate without further considering end results. Remember that the GPRA calls for reporting performance in terms of both outputs and outcomes. It calls for assessments "of the *results* of a program activity." The word "results" is in the title name of the act, and the act defines the word "results" as "outcomes."

Despite current practices, personal communication with strong supporters of OFM who have occupied head and other positions in federal wildland management agencies have convinced the editor of this text that at lease two institutional constraints deter use of outcomes-oriented measures in federal agency reporting of performance and in personnel evaluations. First, too few agency administrators have tried to exercise the discretion they already have under the GRPA and tried to use more real outcome measures. Second, the OMB and/or agency budgetary officials have not been receptive to the use of those outcome measures.

A workable solution might lie somewhere between the exercise of greater agency leadership and the U.S. Congress passing amendments to the GPRA that authorize more use of outcome measures without the agencies having to contend with the constraints outlined in Section 4 (b) of that act. It states "If an agency, in consultation with the Director of the Office of Management and Budget, determines that it is not feasible to express the performance goals for a particular program activity in an objective, quantifiable, and measurable form, the Director of the Office of Management and Budget may authorize an alternative form." The act then states "Such alternative form shall [among other things]...include separate descriptive statements of...a successful program." It would be very helpful if the U.S. Congress gave authorization *directly to the agencies* to use outcome measures without needing special and prior approval by the OMB (as the GPRA now requires), so long as information measuring output performance also continues to be provided to OMB. This does not seem unreasonable, because a growing number of outcome measures can now be written in tangible and objectively measurable terms. Examples include the following:

1. The executive branch of the U. S. government, as well as the executive and legislative governments of states, provinces, and municipalities in the U. S. and other countries are increasingly concerned about the continually growing social coats of health care. For example, the U. S. Department of Health and Human Services is pursuing programs to advance a healthier nation (see Chapters 12 and 22 of this text for related programs). Fortunately, the very significant contributions of recreation to health and fitness are being documented much better every year and can be documented objectively in performance reports at least at the agency level because of difficulties of allocating those benefits to specific administrative units.
2. Members of the U.S. Congress have responded to credible information about the economic impacts of tourism within their jurisdictions to the maintenance and enhancement of the economic viability of nearby communities (see Chapter 21 of this text). In addition, many countries now quantify the contributions of tourism to balance of payment accounts.
3. Research has identified and quantified other recreation-related benefits, such as those related to youth development (see Chapter 23 of this text), better health of senior citizens, family solidarity, pride and commitment to places where people live, and the positive contributions of such to overall perceived quality of life, etc. (see Chapter 20). Benefits related to the conservation, preservation, protection, and/or improvement of natural landscapes and historic sites can also be quantified objectively.

In addition to the aforementioned types of rather tangible outcome measures, performance reports can document the degree to which opportunities to realize beneficial outcomes and avoid/reduce negative outcomes are created and maintained. Some of that documentation might only be descriptive, but that is preferable to not addressing outcomes at all. Of course, some outcomes-related measures require obtaining periodic feedback from relevant customer and associated provider stakeholders, including visitors and local residents. In this day and age, that information can be obtained at relatively low costs through the use of surveys, unstructured interviews, and focus groups. Other useful information can be obtained from standing citizens' advisory groups.

Evaluating the Performance of Field-Level Personnel

As stated at the beginning of this major section, annual performance evaluations of the field-level professional personnel responsible for the planning, implementation, and revision of plans, and of their immediate supervisors, are required by most, if not all, public recreation and related amenity agencies. The current practice for making those performance evaluations is the same as for evaluating the performance of a public recreation and related amenity agency and its administrative subunits. They are, because most of them focus on facilitating outputs and give outcomes inadequate consideration. This is problematic from the perspective of OFM, because professional people understand what the reward structures are of the organization for which they work. If attaining targeted outcomes is not included in the evaluative criteria used to guide periodic performance evaluations of those professionals, they will naturally direct their attention to satisfying the managerial output criteria that exist. Therefore, as for evaluations of agencies and their subunits, outcomes can and should be given more attention in performance evaluations of agency personnel.

Despite the constraining effects of the GPRA and OMB on using outcomes-oriented measures to document the performances of federal and (perhaps other recreation and related amenity) agencies, there appears to be no constraints to the use of outcome measures and related evaluative criteria to evaluate the performance of individuals. Logically, the best situation would be for the agency and its employees to be evaluated using the same performance measures. But, as explained above, that would mean continuation of the practice of focusing on output attainment. Nevertheless, each agency currently has discretion to evaluate it employees at least *in part* by outcome attainment. Of course, such evaluations must be limited to outcome attainment over which the employee has control.

Brief Summary of OFM Performance Reporting and Evaluations

Outputs *must be* considered in the performance evaluations of agencies, their administrative subunits, and professional personnel, but *so must* outcomes. Because OFM is a relatively new approach, incorporating outcome attainment in performance evaluations is a new wrinkle. Not only is it new, it has been made even more difficult, because, while the GPRA calls for outcome performance measures, the way it is being implemented appears to be constraining use of such measures. Despite these problems, unless outcome attainment is reflected in performance reporting and evaluations, the fundamental objectives of outcomes-focused policy development and management cannot be implemented as widely as it can and should be.

Information used to make outcomes-focused performance evaluations of agencies and responsible professional personnel must include information obtained from relevant on-site and resident customers. Yes, that might require surveying visitors and resident customers, but that is now already being done by many wild land managing agencies to measure customer satisfaction.

Recap of this Chapter

Because of the amount of detail presented in this chapter, it is impossible to summarize it briefly. So, here in outline form is a short summary of the requirements for applying and implementing OFM:

- Understand what OFM is about and why its adoption and practice facilitates more efficient and effective recreation management.
- Establish ongoing collaborative involvement of relevant customers and associated providers in key aspects of planning and plan implementation processes.
- Identify relevant recreation market segments or customers (including visitors, communities, and/or residents) for each recreation area.
- Identify managerially coherent and logical recreation management zones within the planning area and identify corresponding recreation niches.
- Do necessary recreation supply and demand analyses and apply them to development of the management objectives and prescribed setting conditions.
- Identify outcomes that can be targeted in each management zone to meet the desires of the principal recreation market selected that zone.
- Describe the essential recreation setting conditions necessary to produce the recreation opportunities and to realize the outcomes targeted in the preferred alternative.
- Rank feasible alternatives and select the preferred alternative.
- Develop implementing, marketing, monitoring, and supportive administrative actions to monitor implementation of the approved plan.
- Distribute the proposed plan for public review and prepare the plan to be implemented.
- Assure that administrative and managerial support necessary for successful and efficient plan implementation is available.
- Schedule and assign responsibilities for plan implementation to responsible parties, including all management, marketing, monitoring, and administrative actions.
- Implement and monitor the plan to assure that the management objectives and prescribed recreation setting characteristics are being achieved and that management, marketing, monitoring, and administrative support actions are being implemented.
- Revise the plan as needed.
- Develop and apply formally distributed performance evaluation criteria that reward attainment of targeted outcomes.

Again, if you are just beginning to implement OFM, do not be reluctant to apply it incrementally. Learn as you go, and contact and learn from others experienced with OFM, including the many authors and coauthors of the applications chapters of this text. We are confident that you will understand it better and appreciate it more each time you apply it, just as others have.

Literature Cited in the Text and the Appendix

Allen, L. (1996). A primer: Benefits-based management of recreation services. *Parks and Recreation*. March: 64–76.

Allen, L., Stevens, B., Hurtes, K., & Harwell, R. (1998). *Benefits-based programming of recreation services training manual*. Ashburn, VA: The National Recreation and Park Association.

Brown, P. (1984). Benefits of outdoor recreation and some ideas for valuing recreation opportunities. In G. Peterson & A. Randall (Eds.), *Valuation of wildland resource benefits* (pp. 209–220). Boulder, CO: Westview Press.

Brown, P., Dyer, A. & Whaley. R. (1973). Recreation research-so what? *Journal of Leisure Research*. 5(1):16–24.

Brown, P., Driver, B., & McConnell, C. (1978). The opportunity spectrum concept and behavioral information in outdoor recreation resource supply inventories: Background and application. In *Proceedings of the integrated renewable resources inventories workshop* (pp. 73-84). Washington, D.C. USDA Forest Service General Technical Report RM-55.

Buckley, W. (1968). *Modern systems research for the behavioral scientist*. Aldine Chicago, IL: Publishing Company.

Crompton, J. (1977). A recreation system model. *Leisure Sciences 1*(1):53–65

Driver, B. L. (1990). The North American experience in measuring the benefits of leisure. In E. Hamilton-Smith (Compiler), *Proceeding, National workshop on the measurement of_recreation benefits*. Bandoora, Victoria, Australia: Phillips Institute of Technology.

Driver, B. L. & Tocher, S. (1970). Toward a behavioral interpretation of recreation with implications for planning. In B. L. Driver (Ed.), *Elements of Outdoor Recreation Planning* (pp. 9–31). Ann Arbor, MI: The University of Michigan Press.

Driver, B. L. & Brown, P. (1975). A sociopsychological definition of recreation demand, with implications for recreation resource planning. In *Assessing Demand for Outdoor Recreation*. Washington, D.C.: National Academy of Sciences.

Driver, B. L. & Brown, P. (1978). The opportunity spectrum concept in outdoor recreation supply inventories; a rationale. Pages 24–31. In *Proceedings of the integrated renewable resources inventories workshop* (pp. 24–31). Washington, D.C. USDA Forest Service General Technical Report RM-55.

Driver, B. L. & Rosenthal, D. (Compilers,1982). Measuring and improving the effectiveness of public outdoor recreation programs. Washington, D.C.: George Washington University

Driver, B. L., Tinsley, H., & Manfredo, M. (1991). The paragraphs about leisure and recreation experience scales: Results from two inventories designed to assess the breadth of the perceived benefits of leisure. In. B. Driver, P. Brown, & G. Peterson (Eds.), *Benefits of leisure* (pp. 263–286). State College, PA: Venture Publishing, Inc.

Driver, B, L. & Bruns, D. (1999). Concepts and uses of the Benefits Approach to Leisure. In E. Jackson and T, Burton (Eds.), *Leisure studies: Prospects for the twenty-first century* (pp. 349–368). State College, PA: Venture Publishing, Inc.

Hass, G., Driver, B. L., & Brown, P. (1981). Measuring wilderness recreation experiences. In L. Cannon (Ed.), *Proceedings of the wilderness psychology group annual conference* (pp. 25–30). Durham, NH. University of New Hampshire, Department of Psychology.

Hendee, J. (1974). A multiple-satisfactions approach to game management. *Wildlife Society Bulletin* 2(3):104–113.

Jordon, C. (1991). Parks and recreation: More than fun and games. In. B. L. Driver, P. Brown, and G. Peterson (Eds.), *Benefits of leisure* (pp. 365–368). State College, PA. Venture Publishing, Inc.

Lee, M. & Driver, B. L. (1992). Benefits-Based Management: A new paradigm for managing amenity resources. Paper presented at The Second Canada/US Workshop on Visitor Management in Parks, Forests, and Protected Areas. May 13–16, 1992. Madison, WI: University of Wisconsin-Madison.

Lucas, R, & Stankey, G. (1974). Social carrying capacity for backcountry recreation. In *Outdoor recreation research: Applying the results* (pp. 14–23). St. Paul, MN.USDA Forest Service. North Central Forest Experiment Station. Gen. Tech. Rep. NC-9.

Manfredo, M., Driver, B. L., & Brown, P. (1983). A test of concepts inherent in experience-based setting management of outdoor recreation areas. *Journal of Leisure Research, 15*(3), 263–283.

Moore, R. & Driver, B. (2005). *Introduction to outdoor recreation: Providing and managing natural resource-based opportunities*. State College, PA: Venture Publishing, Inc.

More, T. (2002). The parks are being loved to death: Fraud and deceits in recreation management. *Journal of Leisure Research, 34*(1), 52–78.

O'Sullivan, E. (1999). *Setting a course for change: The benefits movement.* Ashborn, VA. National Recreation and Parks Association.

Schomaker, J. (1984). Writing quantifiable river management objectives. In. J. Popadiac, D. Butterfield, D. Anderson, and M. Popiadic (Eds.), *1984 National River Recreation Symposium Proceedings* (pp. 249–253). St. Paul, MN: University of Minnesota.

Stankey, G. (1974). Criteria for the determination of recreational carrying capacity in the Colorado River basin. In A. Crawford and D. Peterson (Eds.), *Environmental management in the Colorado River basin.* Logan, Utah: Utah State University Press.

USDA Forest Service. (1982). *The ROS User Guide.* Washington, D.C.

USDA Forest Service. (1993). *The power of collaborative planning: The report of a national workshop.* FS-553. Washington, D.C.

Wagar, J. (1964). The social carrying capacity of wildlands for recreation. Washington, D.C. Society of Foresters. Monograph 7.

Wagar, J. (1974) Recreational carrying capacity reconsidered. *Journal of Forestry, 72*(5):274–278.

Wondolleck, J. & Yaffee, S. (2000). *Making collaboration work: Lessons from innovation in natural resources.* Washington, D.C.: Island Press.

Appendix to Chapter 3 Positive and Negative Outcomes Checklists

The following checklists have been used to help analyze past demands; guide studies of present and future demands; define recreation niches and their corresponding recreation management zones; develop outcomes-focused management objectives; and finally, to formulate management and marketing actions, monitoring actions and corresponding standards and guidelines; and supporting administrative actions. The checklists have also proven helpful in enabling recreation planners and managers to better understand and appreciate the breadth and magnitude of the many significant benefits of recreation and related amenities. There are two major components of the list, or actually two checklists. The first checklist lists examples of *beneficial outcomes,* and the second lists examples of *undesirable or negative outcomes.* Beneficial and unwanted outcomes are shown for on-site recreating customers, as well as for residents of nearby communities and their households.

When using these checklists, remember that BBM adopts and incorporates definitions of three related but different types of benefits that can be realized from the management and use of recreation and related amenity resources. The definitions of these three types of benefits (and the reasons for each) are given in Chapter 1 of this text and are summarized as follows: (1) creation of an improved condition; (2) maintenance of a desired condition, prevention of an unwanted condition, or reduction of an unwanted condition; and (3) realization of a satisfying experience. For this reason, and to help assure comprehensiveness of the checklists of beneficial outcomes, two broad types of beneficial outcomes are shown. One is identified as "experiential benefits" and all others are "other benefits."

For some of the experiential benefits, the accompanying improved conditions are obvious, but for others it is less discrete and many of them are realized later in the "benefit chain of causality" described earlier in this chapter. Too frequently, practitioners forget about these "chained benefits" and inappropriately concentrate only on those satisfying experiences for which the improved conditions are readily apparent. In addition to the "chained benefits," it is important to remember that not all positive and negative outcomes are created directly by the on- and off-site customers using the recreation opportunities and services provided, but instead accrue directly from provider actions. Examples include improvement and protection of the basic natural and heritage resources and economic benefits resulting from salaries paid to local agency employees and funds allocated to local contractors and cooperators.

The checklists were developed by expanding two published lists of the benefits of leisure. One was of items for the Recreation Experience Preference (REP) scales (Driver, Tinsley, and Manfredo, 1991; and Moore and Driver, 2005). The REP scales were developed to "tap" many different types of recreation experiences. The other published list of benefits (Moore & Driver, 2005) is repeated as Table 1.1 of Chapter 1 of this text and shows all known benefits of leisure for which at least one (and generally more than one) scientific study supported the existence of each type of benefits listed. The first version of that list (Driver, 1990) was used to help develop "The Benefits Catalogue" (Canadian Parks/Recreation Association, 1997). It expanded that 1990 list of benefits and referenced the research publications that documented their existence and magnitudes. Later still, the second author of this case study report and his colleagues in the

BLM expanded the Moore and Driver list of benefits, adapted the list of Benefits to Community Residents from work done for the BLM by Marty Lee of Northern Arizona University, and created the Negative Outcomes Checklist.

Because many of the experiential benefits identified by the REP scales are repeated in the Moore and Driver (2005) list and also in the list of "Benefits to Community Residents, there is considerable redundancy among the lists. No attempt was made to reduce that redundancy in order the show the content of the two original lists.

Beneficial Outcomes Checklist From which to Select or Craft Items for Visitor/Resident Customer Preference Studies and for Benefits-Based Recreation Management Objectives

Condensed list of Experiential Benefits to Recreation Participants.

Defined by the Recreation Experience Preference Scales

A: Achievement/Stimulation
- Developing your skills and abilities
- Having others think highly of you for doing this
- Testing your endurance
- Gaining a greater sense of self-confidence
- Being able to tell others about the trip

B: Autonomy/Leadership
- Experiencing a greater sense of independence
- Enjoying going exploring on my/our own
- Being in control of things that happen

C: Risk-Taking
- Enjoying risk-taking adventure

D: Equipment
- Talking to others about your equipment

E/F/G: Family Togetherness/Similar People/New People
- Enjoying the closeness of friends and family
- Relishing group affiliation and togetherness
- Enjoying meeting new people with similar interests
- Enjoying participating in group outdoor events

H: Learning
- Learning more about things here
- Enjoying having access to hands-on
- environmental learning
- Enjoying learning outdoor social skills

I: Enjoy nature
- Savoring the total sensory--sight, sound, and
- smell--experience of a natural landscape
- Enjoying having easy access to natural landscapes

J: Introspection
- Enjoying being more contemplative
- Reflecting on my own character and personal values
- Thinking about and shaping my own spiritual values
- Contemplating man's relationship with the land

K: Creativity
- Doing something creative
- Enjoying artistic expression of nature

L: Nostalgia
- Bringing back pleasant memories

M: Exercise-Physical Fitness
- Enjoying getting some needed physical exercise
- Enjoying strenuous physical exercise
- Enjoying having a wide variety of environments
- within a single park or recreation area
- Enjoying having access to close-to-home
- outdoor amenities
- Enjoying being able to frequently participate in desired activities in the settings I like

N: Physical Rest
- Enjoying getting some needed physical rest

O: Escape Personal-Social Pressures
- Releasing or reducing some built-up mental tensions
- Escaping everyday responsibilities for awhile

P: Escape Physical Pressure
- Feeling good about solitude
- isolation, and being independent
- Enjoying an escape from crowds of people

Q: Social Security
- Being near more considerate people

R: Escape Family
- Getting away from family for awhile

S: Teaching-Leading Others
- Enjoying teaching others about the outdoors

T: Risk Reduction
- Having others nearby who could help you if needed
- Having a greater understanding about what will happen while I am here

Benefits to Community Residents
(Adapted by Bruns and colleagues from work done for the BLM by Marty Lee, Northern Arizona University)

A: Lifestyle
- Enjoying the hustle and bustle of having new people in town
- Enjoying the peace and quiet of this small-town community
- Enjoying maintaining out-of-town country solitude
- Living a slower pace of life
- Avoiding compromising the quality of life here

B: Sense of Place
- Feeling like I belong to this community and liking it
- Avoiding having outsiders make me feel alienated from my own community
- Observing visitors treat our community with respect
- Feeling that this community is a special place to live
- Just knowing this attraction is here, in or near my community

C: Personal/Character
- Nurturing my own spiritual values and growth
- Developing a greater understanding of outsiders

D: Interacting with People
- Appreciating personal interaction with visitors
- Enjoying telling visitors what makes this community a special place to live and work
- Encouraging visitors to help safeguard our lifestyle and quality of life
- Sharing our cultural heritage with new people
- Seeing visitors get excited about this area
- Communicating our cultural heritage with those already living here

E: Change
- Liking change and new growth here
- Knowing that things are not going to change too much

F: Stewardship and Hospitality
- Feeling good about the way our cultural heritage is being protected
- Feeling good about how visitors are being managed
- Feeling good about how natural resources and facilities are being managed
- Feeling good about how this attraction is being used and enjoyed

Other and Related Benefits (From Moore & Driver, 2005)

I. To Individuals

A. Psychological

1. Better mental health and health maintenance
- A more holistic sense of wellness
- Restored mind from unwanted stress
- Diminished mental anxiety
- Improved mental well-being
- More committed to close-to-home recreation or consistent health improvement
- Greater commitment to pay more to re-create now to avoid paying more for health care later

2. Personal development and growth
- Greater self-reliance
- Confirmation/development of my own values
- Improved academic and cognitive performance
- Improved sense of control over one's life
- Improved skills for outdoor enjoyment
- Improved skills for enjoying the outdoors alone
- Improved skills for outdoor enjoyment with others
- Improved leadership abilities
- Improved teamwork and cooperation

- Improved outdoor knowledge and self-confidence
- Improved outdoor recreation skills
- Deeper sense of personal humility
- More balanced competitive spirit
- Improved competence from being challenged
- Greater sensitivity to/awareness of outdoor aesthetics, nature's art and its elegance
- Enlarged sense of wonder
- Greater spiritual growth
- Greater cognitive efficiency
- Increased capacity for artistic expression
- Improved ability to think things through and solve problems
- Increased adaptability
- Stronger ties with my family and friends
- Greater sensitivity to/respect for other visitors
- Increased understanding and tolerance of others
- Greater respect for my cultural heritage
- Enhanced awareness and understanding of nature
- Improved sensitivity and know-how to use and enjoy without adverse impact
- Greater understanding of the importance of recreation and tourism to our community
- Better sense of my place within my community
- Improved ability to relate to local cultures
- More well-informed and responsible visitor
- Greater sense of responsibility for my own quality of life
- Improved balance of work and play in my life
- Greater personal accountability and know-how in avoiding or causing conflict with others
- Enlarged understanding of my responsibility to help care for community and keep it clean
- Improved sense of personal accountability for control of domestic pets and livestock

3. Personal appreciation and satisfaction
- Closer relationship with the natural world
- A more outdoor-oriented lifestyle
- Improved reconnection to my rural roots
- Enhanced sense of personal freedom
- Greater sense of personal security
- Greater sense of adventure
- Improved appreciation of nature's splendor
- Improved opportunity to view wildlife close-up
- Greater appreciation of the arts
- Better understanding of wildlife's contribution to my own quality of life
- Greater freedom from urban living
- Greater appreciation for my wildland and park heritage and how managers care for it
- Greater personal enrichment through involvement with other people
- Improved personal awareness, learning and appreciation of others' cultural values
- Increased acceptance of others who are different
- Greater cultivation of natural resource stewardship ethic
- Increased appreciation of area's cultural history
- Greater awareness that this community is a special place
- Better understanding of my community's cultural identity
- Greater respect for private property and local lifestyles
- An improved stewardship ethic towards adjoining/host communities
- Improved understanding of how this community's rural-urban interface impacts its quality of life
- Improved understanding of this/our community's dependence and impact on public lands

B. Psychophysiological
- Improved physical fitness and health maintenance
- Restored body from fatigue
- Improved cardiovascular health
- Reduced hypertension
- Improved capacity for outdoor physical activity
- Improved physical capacity to do my favorite recreation activities
- Greater opportunity for people with different skills to exercise in the same place
- Decreased body fat and obesity
- Improved muscle strength and connective tissue
- Increased lung capacity
- Reduced incidence of disease

II. To Households and Communities

- Heightened sense of community satisfaction
- Increased community sense of place
- Greater household awareness of and appreciation for our cultural heritage
- More informed citizenry about where to go for different kinds of recreation experiences and benefits
- Reduced social isolation

- Improved community integration
- Improved functioning of individuals in family and community
- Greater family bonding
- Improved parenting skills
- More well-rounded childhood development
- Improved group cooperation
- Greater community involvement in recreation and other land use decisions
- Increased community involvement reducing erosion of our community's small-town, rural character
- Reduced numbers of at-risk youth
- Less juvenile delinquency
- Higher school class attendance
- Lower school drop-out rates
- More highly motivated students/improved scholarship
- Reduced social alienation
- Increased compassion for others
- Lifestyle improvement or maintenance
- Enhanced lifestyle
- Enlarged sense of community dependency on public lands
- Increased nurturance/tolerance of others
- Increased independence/autonomy among seniors
- Increased community interdependence and friendliness
- Greater interaction with visitors from different cultures
- Greater community valuation of its ethnic diversity

III. Economic Benefits

- Reduced health maintenance costs
- Increased work productivity
- Reduced absenteeism from work
- Decreased job turnover
- Improved local economic stability
- More positive contributions to local-regional economy
- Increased local tax revenue from visitors
- Increased local job opportunities
- Greater value-added local services/industry
- Increased desirability as a place to live or retire
- Enhanced ability for visitors to find areas providing wanted recreation experiences and benefits
- Maintenance of community's distinctive recreation-tourism market niche or character
- Increased local tourism revenue
- Greater diversification of local job offerings
- Increased property values
- Greater fiscal capacity to maintain essential infrastructure and services

IV. Environmental Benefits

- Greater retention of community's distinctive architecture and structures
- Maintenance of distinctive small-town atmosphere
- Maintenance of distinctive recreation setting character
- Improved maintenance of physical facilities
- Reduced looting and vandalism of historic/prehistoric sites
- Greater community ownership and stewardship of park, recreation, and natural resources
- Greater retention of distinctive natural landscape features
- Reduced wildlife harassment by recreation users
- Reduced wildlife disturbance from recreation facility development
- Reduced wildlife predation by domestic pets
- Greater protection of area historic structures and archaeological sites
- Sustainability of community's cultural heritage
- Improved respect for privately-owned lands
- Improved care for community aesthetics
- Improved soil, water, and air quality
- Greater protection of fish, wildlife, and plant habitat from growth, development, and public use impacts
- Increased awareness and protection of natural landscapes
- Reduced negative human impacts such as litter, vegetative trampling, and unplanned trails
- Increased ecologically friendly tourism operations
- Reduced spread of invasive species such as plants, insects, and aquatic organisms
- Greater recycling
- Conservation of entire sustainable ecosystems
- Improved maintenance of distinctive community character and identity

Negative Outcomes Checklist
From which to Select or Craft Additional Items for Resident Customer Preference Studies
(Adapted by Bruns and colleagues)

I. Personal Negative Outcomes

A. Psychological
- Increased personal stress
- Loss of an important sense of place
- Loss of control over one's desired future
- Loss of control over my way of life

B. Personal development and growth
- Reduced ability to cultivate outdoor-oriented lifestyle
- Greater sense of residents being alienated from one's own community

II. Social and Cultural Negative Outcomes
- Decreased family solidarity
- Reduced ability to cultivate outdoor-oriented lifestyle
- Increased exposure of at-risk youth to delinquency
- Increased erosion of community's small-town atmosphere
- Increased erosion of our sense of community
- Diminished sense of community cohesion/friendliness
- Increased crime
- Greater conflict with outsider attitudes towards community
- Greater sense of resignation among local residents towards continued growth and development
- Increased personal disregard for local residents
- Increased personal disregard for other visitors
- Increased conflict with a new residents whose culture conflicts with our lifestyles

III. Economic Negative Outcomes

- Higher cost of living
- Increased property taxes
- Loss of economic productivity
- Loss of family legacy (e.g., family ranch or other business)
- Loss of recreation-tourism product character and our community's market share
- Decreased tourism revenue
- Inability to cover costs of basic household necessities

IV. Environmental Negative Outcomes

- More rapid loss of distinctive community architecture
- Loss of environmental quality within the recreation area
- Increased disregard for natural resources
- Increased visitor disregard for stewardship of community infrastructure
- Increased urbanization of the natural landscape
- Loss of community's defining, distinctive character
- Increased pollution, litter, and traffic noise
- Transformation of community by growth, development, and modernization

Footnotes

1. See Chapter 11 of Moore & Driver (2005) for an elaboration of the different decision processes.
2. The term "physical," instead of "biophysical" is used in the "ROS User Guide" (USDA Forest Service, 1982), with which many readers are familiar, but "biophysical" seems more appropriate.
3. The USDI Bureau of Land Management uses the word "administrative" instead of "managerial" as reflected by use of that word in Chapters 14, 17, and 18 of this text. The first author of this chapter prefers use of the word "managerial" to remain consistent with that usage in the 1982 "ROS User Guide" and to clearly differentiate the four decision processes (including administrative) he described in Chapter 11 of Moore & Driver (2005). Both authors believe that "operational" is more definitive than "administrative."

Chapter 4
Implementing OFM in Municipal Parks and Recreation Departments

Teresa W. Tucker and Lawrence R. Allen

Learning Objectives

1. Understand the role of outcome performance measures in public administration and their influence on the implementation of outcomes-focused management (OFM) in municipal parks and recreation departments.
2. Understand the unique issues of implementing OFM in municipalities.
3. Understand the process of implementing an OFM model in municipal parks and recreation programs.
4. Recognize that there is flexibility in implementing OFM to accommodate particular situations and managerial objectives for municipalities.

Introduction

This chapter focuses on the implementation of OFM in municipal parks and recreation departments. As emphasized in Chapter 1 and the "Introduction" section of Chapter 3, the major purpose of this text is not only to promote the use of OFM, but to provide agencies with the knowledge, instructions, and insights on how to implement such a model. In relation to municipal parks and recreation departments, OFM will be defined as "*a systematic approach to program development through the process of:*

- *establishing strategic outcomes*
- *measuring those outcomes*
- *collecting, analyzing, reviewing, and reporting on the outcomes*
- *using the data to drive further program development*"

(Artley, Ellison, & Kennedy, 2001: p. 5)

Because the process of implementing OFM in municipal parks and recreation departments is somewhat similar to the process for nature-based recreation and related amenity areas as discussed in Chapter 3, the overlapping of some concepts will be inevitable. However, this chapter differs in that it specifically addresses the unique issues of implementing OFM for municipal parks and recreation departments. In order to understand these unique issues, this chapter will examine the role of outcome measurements for municipalities, the steps for implementing OFM, and the impact of OFM on program development and outcome-focused programming (OFP). Additionally, "real world" examples will be infused throughout this chapter to highlight concepts. Future chapters will look at different "real world" examples in greater detail so that agencies, whether they are municipal parks and recreation departments or nature-based areas, can learn, modify, and adapt OFM to best suit their purpose.

Role of Outcome Performance Measures in Public Administration

To facilitate the implementation of OFM in municipal parks and recreation departments, it is important to gain some perspective on the evolution of outcome-based performance measures in public administration in general and how it has impacted local government in particular. In other words, sometimes one has to look to the past to create the future.

The use of outcome-focused performance measurements is not a new concept. Since the 1990s, there has been a marked increase in the use of outcome-focused performance measures at all levels of government (Nicholson-Crotty, Theobald, Nicholson-Crotty, 2002). Shifts in politics, economics, society, and government are the major factors for this increase (Page, 2005). Specifically, voters and elected officials are demanding more responsive services that are also cost effective. Therefore, a primary purpose of outcome measurements is to foster effective government (Page, 2005). Additionally, the public is no longer satisfied with the utilization of performance measures primarily for examining internal government accountability (Heinrich, 2002). Public accountability and public funding are increasingly tied to organizational performance (Nicholson-Crotty et al., 2002). In addressing public accountability and government effectiveness, outcome-focused performance measures are used to (Behn, 2003):

- evaluate different policies and approaches to managing and delivering government services
- monitor program process and document management and program changes simultaneously
- make budget decisions and requests
- motivate employees
- promote organization to stakeholders and political principals
- celebrate accomplishments
- learn about program efficacy
- improve performance

At the federal level, there are examples that exemplify a gradual shift to a more outcomes-focused performance measurement system. The Government Performance and Results Act of 1993 (GPRA), as amended, holds agencies accountable to improve performance by measuring outcomes and to report results within a performance budget process (Melkers & Wiloughby, 2005). One of the unique aspects of this Act is that administrators are allowed flexibility and discretion in developing the operational processes. The emergence of Performance Based Organizations (PBO), such as the Office of Student Finance Assistance in the Department of Education, is another example of the shift to a more outcome-focused system within the federal government. The essential characteristics of PBOs include: a clear mission, measurable services, a performance measurement system with top management support, a focus on external customers, operations separate from policy making, and funding levels that correspond to business operations (Kamensky, 2002). Similarly, the National Partnership for Reinventing Government (1999) emphasized that agencies should translate strategic direction into a set of specific outcomes that can be tracked and monitored (Edwards & Thomas, 2005). Even as recently as the Bush administration, attention has been given to the integration of outcome-focused performance measurement into budgetary decisions. There has been some criticism regarding the extent to which performance measurements not only impact decision making and budgeting (Gilmour & Lewis, 2006), but also to the extent that these agencies are actually measuring outcomes rather than outputs as described in the previous chapters of this text. Despite this criticism the examples above illustrate a growing trend of the federal government toward the intention of developing a more outcome-focused approach.

Role of Outcome-Focused Measures in Local Government

Does the shift to a more outcome focused performance system at the federal level translate to a similar shift at the local government level? The answer is *yes*. Although the government structure at the local level can vary greatly among cities and counties, administrators continue to be optimistic about the benefits and impact of performance measurement adoption and use (Melkers & Wiloughby, 2005). In a research study conducted by Melkers & Wiloughby (2005), 71% of the 277 city and county administrators who responded to the survey agreed that performance measurements enhanced program management in those departments that utilized them. Additionally, in the same study, 68% of the respondents agreed and 15% strongly agreed that local government is "better off" since using performance measurements. With respect specifically to outcome measures, the majority of respondents indicated that at least half of their departments used them. Melkers & Wiloughby states that the results of this study "attests to the evolution in the use of performance measures, from easy-to-measure output measures to more meaningful measures of impacts" (p. 184). Within local government, a performance measurement system should (Wang, 2002; Ho, 2005):

- impact decision making
- go beyond just reporting information
- complement or be linked with changes in strategic planning, goal setting, and governance (*this is critical*)
- address the achievement of outcome or organizational goals directly
- not only reflect voters' expectations and demands, but also be used in determining and meeting their expectations and demands

Knowing the purpose of a performance measurement system is one thing. Knowing how to successfully implement such a system for sustainability in municipalities is quite another. Listed below are some criteria needed to implement a performance measurement system (Julnes & Holzer, 2001; Wang, 2002; Ho, 2005):

- proper accounting and management information systems
- sufficient funding
- ability to interpret data

- "readiness" in terms of knowledge and support
- identification and involvement of internal and external interest groups
- ability of managers to work with elected officials and the citizenry
- development of "performance improvement" culture

Although this list is not necessarily all-inclusive, it is important to note that these themes are prevalent throughout the research done on implementing a performance measurement system. Additionally, city and county administrators should be aware that there are many ways to measure the same outcome. Therefore, the choice of measurement can have a significant impact on outcome evaluations (Nicholson-Crotty et al., 2002). The match of organizational characteristics and types of outcome measurements will contribute to the usefulness of information to administrators (Nicholson-Crotty et al., 2002). To better understand how a outcome performance measurement system can be implemented, a case study of the Atlanta Dashboard will be presented.

Atlanta: A Case Study

The Atlanta Dashboard, established under Mayor Shirley Frank, illustrates steps utilized by a municipality to implement a performance measurement system (Edwards & Thomas, 2005). Prior to Shirley Frank's election as mayor, the citizens of Atlanta were distrustful of their local government. This distrust grew out of allegations of corruption among city officials. Additionally, a lack of "performance culture," as illustrated through the scarcity of performance data, perpetuated ineffective and insufficient public services. Once in office, Shirley Frank charged her staff to the following principals:

- "We serve citizens, and we care about outcomes as experienced by citizens."
- "We will be open and transparent."
- "We will be effective and efficient."

One of the first steps to implement this system was to build consensus around this vision among top management. Another important first step was to communicate this vision at all levels and within all departments. Efficiency and effectiveness (scope and quality of services) were the two major concerns of Atlanta's citizens. Establishing a performance measurement system would serve as the centerpiece of how Mayor Frank would turn around the city government of Atlanta. Mayor Frank wanted a performance management system to provide:

- accurate and timely updates of public services
- managers of departments with outcomes based on target issues and a means to track progress to increase management accountability
- a way for citizens to witness the city's operating environment to increase public trust

Along with improving efficiency and effectiveness, the outcomes to be measured were directly tied to Mayor Frank's other strategic priorities, which were to improve public safety, to improve public infrastructure, and to create stability.

Managers of each department were not only responsible for linking their efforts to the strategic priorities outlined by the mayor, but also for advancement of these priorities. Additionally, they were also held accountable for the citizens' perception of their departments' effectiveness and efficiencies. Each department had to reconsider the services they were providing to reflect the strategic outcomes. To maximize the impact of their department's efforts to meet the targeted outcomes, they would need to cooperate with others outside their department (i.e., partners, public, other departments). In an effort to regain public trust, department mangers would also need to market their services to reflect both effectiveness and efficiency. While managers were given latitude in establishing their operational philosophy, they were ultimately held accountable to the strategic outcomes. Weekly meetings were used as a forum to review performance progress, to collaborate and problem solve with other departments, and to reevaluate performance goals if necessary.

To date, the Atlanta Dashboard, a performance measurement system, continues to evolve. It exemplifies the growing trend among municipalities toward an outcomes-focused system, which in turn will directly impact municipal parks and recreation departments. The next section will outline the specific steps municipal park and recreation departments can take to implement outcomes-focused management.

Outcome-Focused Management for Municipal Parks and Recreation Departments

The development of OFM for municipal parks and recreation departments has many similarities but also some distinct differences from establishing OFM for nature-based recreation agencies and related amenity resources as discussed in the previous chapter. The key difference is that the "heart" of municipal park and recreation departments is the offering of programs and services to the public. Directing and developing programs are a significant part of what these departments do. Therefore, implementing outcome-focused management for municipal parks and recreation programs is more than just utilizing a new management system; it is about adopting a new programming philosophy. With OFM, the focus now becomes the delivery of purposeful programs and the provision of effective services that have a demonstrable impact on the individual and the community. Municipal parks and recreation agencies have always promoted positive experiences for its users and participants, but now the focus is on very directed and specific outcomes of participation in a specific program. For example, rather than a general goal or objective related to improved health, outcome-focused programs would identify a specific outcome such as weight loss, increased fitness, changed eating habits, etc. Thus, OFP for municipal parks and recreation departments becomes a dominant philosophy and strategy within the framework of an agency-wide OFM system.

In writing this chapter, a survey was conducted utilizing a small sample of municipal parks and recreation agencies throughout the country that had indicated a focus on outcome measures through various NRPA publications in order to gain their perspective on OFM. Their results, examples, and comments will appear throughout the remainder of the chapter in the outlined boxes. The results of the survey help describe what agencies are doing that purport a performance-based management system: the results should not be construed to suggest the extent to which the total profession is adopting a more outcome-focused performance system and they cannot be generalized to all municipal parts and recreation agencies.

In order to facilitate a comprehensive outcome-focused management strategy, several agency-wide changes need to take place. Some of the agency-wide changes that will occur in support of OFM and the outcome-focused programs that result include:

- Mission and agency goals
- Staffing
- Budgeting process
- Marketing strategies

Analyze the Mission

What, as a municipal parks and recreation department, do we want to accomplish? How does our mission, goals, and management practices relate specifically to the recreation opportunities and programs we offer to the public? Critical analysis of these key questions is a good starting point. With OFM, municipal parks and recreation departments would concentrate on utilizing programs, services, and other formally structured experiences to address desired outcomes. Possible desired outcomes can come from any of the seven major areas of outcomes identified earlier in the text: physical health, mental health, personal growth, personal satisfaction, sociocultural benefits, economic benefits, and environmental benefits. Part of the leadership's responsibility would be to narrow down the list of targeted outcomes to ones that can be feasibly addressed through programs the department offers.

Modify Mission and Goals

The next step in this process is to gather input from stakeholders and to conduct a comprehensive analysis of the department's mission, goals, and management plan in order to modify the department's mission and goals. Under the modified version, the department's mission and goals should reflect targeted outcomes. An illustration of the modification of a mission statement is below.

An actual mission statement for a municipality in the United States was as follows:

> "To provide a comprehensive system of leisure service delivery in the greater (Name of City) area which assists people in the development of leisure skills, attitudes, and awareness and promotes their personal and community leisure participation."

After the process of analysis with an orientation toward outcomes focused management, the Mission Statement could be revised to the following:

> "To provide preventive, developmental, and rehabilitative leisure services in the greater (Name of City) area which assist citizens in the acquisition and enhancement of skills, attitudes, and behaviors that improve their leisure well-being and enhance their overall individual and community well-being. Through leisure and recreation programs, facilities and areas, measurable benefits will be realized to the individual, the community, the economy, and the environment."

Oftentimes, the mission and goals of parks and recreation departments reflect those of the entire municipality; therefore, the parks and recreation department may not have the discretion to modify their goals and mission. However, as pointed out earlier in this chapter, there is a shift among municipalities to identify desired outcomes in their goals. As with municipalities, parks and recreation departments need to design performance measures that are tied directly to targeted outcomes. Once the mission is identified, and modified if necessary, the stage is set for the foundation of department wide outcome goals.

Examples of department wide outcome goals might be:

- The Department of Parks and Recreation aspires to provide recreation programs, facilities and areas that enhance the sense of collegiality among the citizens of (Name of City).
- The Department of Parks and Recreation aspires to provide recreation programs, facilities and areas that reduce the level of stress among the citizens of (Name of City).
- The Department of Parks and Recreation aspires to provide recreation programs, facilities and areas that build a sense of community and pride among the citizens of (Name of City).
- The Department of Parks and Recreation aspires to provide recreation programs, facilities and areas that improve the physical health among the citizens of (Name of City).

Staffing

Staffing is another area that will need to be addressed with the implementation of outcome-focused management and programming. Staff will need to be adequately trained in the outcome-focused philosophy and procedures, in general, and specifically, the identification of outcomes addressed through the programs they offer, so that they can confidentially convey the benefits and/or positive outcomes of their programs to the public. Staff need to know why they are doing (i.e., the purpose of the program) what they are doing. This will, in turn, assist in the development of an outcome-focused culture.

Besides being trained in identifying and addressing important outcomes, staff will also need to be trained about the systematic evaluation process and the role it plays for programs and the department. In the initial stages, an agency might have to hire a consultant who has expertise in the development of effective evaluation tools and procedures. Once a system is in place, staff will need to be trained in their role within that system. For the majority of staff, their role will revolve around administering the designated evaluation process and/or tools for a particular program.

With OFM, departments might need to hire personnel whose sole responsibility within the agency is to conduct program and department-wide evaluation, including the development of reports that interpret the data in a manner that is clear and understandable by community leaders and the general public.

Budget Process

Traditionally within municipal parks and recreation departments, outputs (i.e., number of people served, number of programs offered, number of parks) drive the budgetary process. Knowing outputs are still a vital part of the budget process, but with OFM, the budget process changes slightly. Not only will the department look at the outputs, but it will now also determine whether or not the program met their outcomes when making budgetary decisions. Basically, departments will not only look at whether or not a program is cost-efficient, but also whether or not the program is effective. Therefore, budgets will be based upon both how many people participated and on the positive outcomes the program or service had on the participants.

Additionally by documenting clear outcomes of a program, opportunities for additional funding might become available thus impacting a department's budget. Communities fund what they understand and value. There will be more discussion about funding later in this chapter.

Marketing Strategies

Recreation professionals know the value of recreation and their programs. By implementing an OFM system, municipal parks and recreation departments will actually be able to prove recreation's value. However, what's the good of proving it if no one else knows about it? With OFM, communicating the outcomes and the results become an integral part of a department's marketing strategy. It permeates every piece of information and promotion the department presents to the public. Every program description, every news release, every brochure, etc. will communicate outcomes to put the value of recreation and each program and service in the forefront. Thus, the marketing strategy changes from what the agency does to what difference agency programs and services made in the lives of the citizens it serves. It basically lets everyone know, "We have a valuable and positive impact on individuals and the community and this is how we impact individuals and the community." In Step 4 of OFP, there will be more specific marketing strategies discussed.

Outcomes-Focused Programming

The remainder of this chapter outlines a process for implementation of OFP within municipal parks and recreation departments. As previously stated, some concepts of implementation overlap those discussed in Chapter 3. This chapter is based on the culmination of the exploratory work and numerous trainings conducted on benefits-based programming and management within the last ten years conducted by the faculty and staff at Clemson University, municipal research projects conducted by various state recreation and park associations, the NRPA's, *Benefits Based Programming Curriculum Manual* (Allen & Cooper, 2003), and the fine examples of outcome-focused recreation programming being offered by a few parks and recreation agencies across the United States.

Previous chapters discuss OFM in great detail; this chapter will discuss OFP within the framework of OFM. Put simply, OFM is the management system that supports OFP (see Appendix A). Basically, outcomes are the driving force for every decision, every program, and every little and big thing an agency does. Intentionally going beyond a focus on just outputs (i.e., how many people signed up for a program) to a focus on specific outcomes is the essence of OFP. So how does an agency implement OFP?

In today's world, where city departments compete for a piece of the budget and there is an increasing call for accountability, recreation departments have to go beyond diversionary programming. More and more recreation departments are being challenged to devise programs that contribute and perpetuate the well-being of the individual and the community. Generally, the outcomes of recreation fall into the following categories:

- developmental
- prevention
- rehabilitation
- diversion

These categories reflect that outcomes are not just about benefits or positive results, but also how they curtail and minimize negative influences on individuals and communities. Although OFP may not directly address social issues, its purpose is to address some of the underlying characteristics and conditions associated with social issues.

The Benefits-Based Programming Model (Allen, Stevens, Hurtes, & Harwell, 1998) serves as the basis for implementation of OFP. The steps of this model are as follows:

- Step 1: Identify Target Issues & Outcomes
- Step 2: Develop Programs to Specifically Address Outcomes
- Step 3: Measure Program Goals & Outcomes
- Step 4: Realize Impacts & Communicate Successes

Step 1: Identify Target Issues & Outcomes

As stated earlier, outcomes are central to the implementation of OFP. Identifying the target issues and outcomes to be addressed by a department and/or program are critical in OFP. It can't be emphasized enough that whatever outcomes an agency chooses to address will serve as the driving force of every program, every service, and every decision that an agency makes. How does a recreation department identify its outcomes?

1.1 Identify Stakeholders' Needs

An essential step in identifying target issues and outcomes is the inclusion of a cross section of constituents in this process. The agency would conduct its normal assessment of community needs and issues with its various stakeholders including, but not limited to the: city council, neighborhood leaders, mayor, other human service professionals, and of course, the citizens of the municipality. These groups can provide insight and expertise on the complexity of issues that the community may want to address. With the general public, surveys and needs assessments could be designed to include clarification of issues that they deem critical for the community; thus, the assessment goes well beyond the identification of recreation interests and needs. All of these stakeholders can assist in narrowing down and prioritizing desired outcomes to a manageable number. It is necessary to note that programs offered by municipal parks and recreation departments may not directly address a social issue such as youth violence, but they can address the underlying characteristics, causes and/or conditions associated with a social issue or problem. Also, while it is not the sole responsibility of municipal parks and recreation departments to address social issues facing the community, but they should be an active partner in the process. Pointing out to stakeholders that municipal parks and recreation departments are partners in addressing social issues serves to further solidify the position of recreation as an essential service for the community.

1.2 Identify Target Issues

Once the comprehensive community assessment is complete, the recreation planner with other professionals or members of a planning committee would analyze the results to determine dominant community issues and/or concerns. Most communities face many of the same concerns (potential target issues) as other communities: nationwide-substance abuse, violence, homelessness, ethnic conflict, unemployment, lack of open space, crime, traffic, senior citizen issues, education issues, etc. Once the dominant issues and/or concerns have been identified, the planner must then determine which issues could be most effectively addressed through the recreation department. Obviously, some issues are outside the realm of responsibility of a municipal recreation agency. One way of prioritizing issues is simply to ask a series of questions related to each identified issue. For example:

- Can recreation programs feasibly have a role in resolving and/or addressing any of these issues?
- Does the agency have the resources and expertise to respond to the issue?
- Are any of the identified issues politically important to address?
- Are there known ways to assess the recreation program's impact on the issues?

1.3 Identify Targeted Program Goals

Once the target issues have been prioritized and the agency has selected those issues it wishes to address, general programmatic goals need to be established. These goals would state the proposed outcomes to be accomplished through the specific recreation programs to be developed. For example, assume that the recreation planner and the staff have selected a target issue related to teenage substance abuse. Certainly, recreation professionals are not substance counselors or mental health specialists, but there are ways that recreation professionals, through their programs, can have an impact on issues of this nature by identifying underlying conditions and/or circumstances.

Although there are many etiologies associated with substance abuse, some circumstances that have led young people into drug and alcohol use have been feelings of isolation, boredom, lack of acceptance, the need for excitement or challenge, and low self-esteem. Therefore, program goals could be related to developing the youths' social networks, providing outlets for challenging and exciting experiences, or building their sense of self-esteem. Examples of program goals relating to these behaviors are as follows:

- As a result of participating in (*program to be determined in Step 2*), the youths will establish high adventure recreation interests to channel their need for thrill, excitement and sense of accomplishment.
- As a result of participation in (*program to be determined in Step 2*), the youths will establish a network of three friends who have common interests and motivations.
- As a result of participation in (*program to be determined in Step 2*), the youths will increase their sense of self-esteem by 20%.
- At a six month follow-up, the youth participating in (*program to be determined in Step 2*), will be continuing their participation in the high adventure recreation programs.

Although the specific program has not been identified at this time, certainly the general direction and type of program has begun to evolve.

1.4 Develop Collaborative Partnerships

With so many of the target issues, the recreation agency should be partnering with other human service agencies and resources to provide a comprehensive and effective program. Certainly with the example of addressing teenage drug and alcohol use, working with any local public or nonprofit agencies directly equipped to address these behaviors would be valuable. Many municipalities have health departments, youth services agencies, and mental health groups that would provide important expertise, resources, and credibility to the program.

Regardless of the target issue being addressed, collaborative partnerships hold great value and should be encouraged because of the many advantages and benefits that can accrue from these relationships. Benefits that can be derived from collaborative partnerships include (Allen & Cooper, 2003):

- Shared expertise
- Shared programming ideas
- Shared staff

- Shared facilities
- Shared labor and effort
- Shared expenses
- Synergistic programming (the program result is greater than what could be accomplished independently)

There are many advantages to collaborative programming; however, many times agencies choose to go it alone because collaboration is difficult and time-consuming. In order to create successful collaborative partnerships that minimize the effort and time, five key components must be present:

- *Trust.* Trust is the component upon which the other four components are based. All individuals and agencies must practice a professional trust, respecting each other's efforts and interests.
- *Buy In.* The agency and its representatives must understand the program and why it is being conducted. Further, they must buy in to the program goals.
- *Benefits.* All agencies involved must understand not only how the program will benefit them and the individuals they serve, but also how it can reduce negative outcomes.
- *Ownership.* All agency participants must feel a sense of ownership, carry their share of the load and understand their role in offering the program.
- *Recognition.* All individuals and organizations involved must be recognized for the part they play in the success of the program.

Step 2: Develop Programs to Specifically Address Targeted Goals

Programs are the backbone of most municipal parks and recreation departments. Although the general perception is that recreation programs are good, as a profession we can't assume that all recreation programs are inherently beneficial to the individual and the community. Under OFP, programs are designed and developed specifically to address the identified targeted outcome goals. Recreation programs become effective tools for personal and community development, and recreational programming becomes intentional and purposeful, yet maintains levels of fun and enjoyment.

In developing outcome-focused programs, it is essential to understand the following:

- Recreation Programming Fundamental Guidelines
- Outcome-Based Programming Concepts
- Program Identification and Activity Analysis
- Program Structure and Daily Outcome Objectives
- Processing the Recreation Experience
- Monitoring of Programs

Each of these topics will be discussed briefly. For more detail, please refer to Section 7 of *Benefits-Based Programming Curriculum Manual* by Allen and Cooper (2003).

2.1 Recreation Programming Fundamental Guidelines

These are the key ingredients for planning any recreation program:

- *Program structure must be unique to specific communities, participants, and situations.* No program has universal appeal; it must be tailored to the local circumstances based upon the comprehensive community assessment that is periodically undertaken. Further, it should reflect the mission, vision and goals of the agency.
- *Program structure and content must be developed to directly address target issues and outcomes.* Developing structure and content of programs without direct consideration of program goals and/or outcome objectives results in programs with little direction and impact. One cannot assume that any program structure and content will accomplish the intended outcomes.
- *Program must be multifaceted.* Because outcome-focused programs place a heavy emphasis on individual and community change, most programs must include expertise, resources, and ideas from other human service professionals. By creating multifaceted programs, they can address the complexity of the issues, concerns, or circumstances for which they are intended to address.
- *Processing should be a component of all programs.*

All experiences should include an effort to help the participants describe, reflect, analyze and communicate what they have experienced. Athletic coaches do this frequently in analyzing the results of a game. This same strategy should be employed with many outcome-focused recreation programs.

- *Strategies for assessing outcomes must be established.* For OFP to be successful, there must be a plan for conducting the assessment of the intended outcomes. This is an element of the planning process that is frequently neglected because it is perceived as time-consuming and difficult. However, after establishing consistent procedures and support systems, assessment can become a routine part of the planning process.
- *Evaluation must be an active part of the programming process.* Creating the assessment process is not enough. It must be carried out. Recreation planners and programmers must conduct an evaluation, using the assessment plan, to document the impact of the programs offered.

2.2 Outcome-Based Programming Concepts

Under Outcome-Focused Management, the concepts listed below should be incorporated into *every recreation experience*:

- *Accomplishment.* Every program or experience should be structured to give the participant a sense of accomplishment during every session, regardless of how small.
- *Encouragement.* All participants need encouragement. This is a universal need and should never be compromised.
- *High Expectations.* Participants rise to a leader's expectations. By promoting high expectations, the leader communicates a sense of support and confidence in the abilities of the participants.
- *Recognition.* Again, all participants desire recognition for their accomplishments regardless of how small. A pat on the back or a brief word of encouragement can be very meaningful to most participants.
- *Support System.* Universal support for all participants is essential. Especially when dealing with high risk participants, they need to know that the leaders will be there for them. This does not mean that rules, procedures or safety are ever compromised; however, it does mean that the leaders must use sensitivity and discretional in communicating with participants.

These concepts were originally designed to address programming for at-risk youth. However, they can be generalized to all programming groups.

2.3 Program Identification, Structure and Daily Outcomes

With the OFP strategy, the general targeted outcome goals are identified before the program is determined. However, in reality, these two things, desired targeted outcome goals and program identification, are done simultaneously. In our example with teenage substance abuse, we first identified the general targeted outcome goals. We alluded to some types of programs, but the specific program was not identified. Now it would be appropriate to identify a specific program with its many parts or facets. Continuing with our example, we may establish an outdoor adventure program involving various challenge experiences such as white-water rafting, rock climbing, rappelling, spelunking, and general outdoor skills development. The program would include a series of instructional sessions with several local trips throughout the course of the program. This program may have already existed within the agency, but now it is redesigned to specifically address the four targeted outcome goals that were established.

We specifically chose a program that had the key elements or ingredients to allow us to fulfill the overall targeted outcome goals. In some cases the recreation planner may undertake an activity analysis to examine the structure of various recreation experiences to determine if the experiences have the right component parts. Basically, activity analysis is taking an activity and breaking it down into its structural elements. These considerations could include: skill level of participants, environmental setting, physical characteristics of the activity, and constraints.

Adhering to an outcome-focused programming strategy does not mean you must create totally new programs. Many existing programs may be adapted to promote outcomes! Under OFP, these programs should be assessed to determine if they already address targeted outcome goals. If the program doesn't address targeted goals, why is it operating? What is the purpose of the program? In trying to allocate funds, a department must be able to justify why they operate the programs they do. With existing programs, it might be necessary to modify the program so that it incorporates targeted outcome goals.

To ensure there is a direct connection between the designed recreational experience and the program's targeted outcome goals, the recreation planner must also consider the daily structure and objectives of the program. Daily or session objectives are a way to map out how the program will achieve the overall program goals (outcomes). Daily objectives will also gauge the program's progress in meeting the targeted goals. The process is similar to how teachers develop lesson plans for a class. It is imperative that the daily objectives (all objectives, for that matter) are SMART (Specific, Measurable, Achievable, Relevant, Time connected). In other words, objectives should be based on clear, specific, and behavior-based or observable criteria. Furthermore, the criteria of all objectives should be related to the targeted outcome goals that also examine the cumulative impact of the program on the individual and/or the community.

2.4 Processing the Recreation Experience

Processing is an opportunity that encourages the individual to reflect, describe, analyze, and communicate feelings and thoughts about situations that happened during an activity (Luckner & Nadler, 1997). For facilitators of experiential education, group initiatives, and ropes courses, processing is an integral and essential part of every activity. Processing is a way for the recreation professional to assist the participant in linking recreation programs and activities to real world situations. It has been identified as one of the most successful strategies for facilitating change and development in program participants.

Processing can be either informal or formal. The role of the recreation profession is that of a facilitator. Listed below are examples of different ways processing can be utilized:

- teachable moments
- one-on-one conversations
- group discussions
- journaling

Ways recreational professionals can enhance processing:

- Listen actively and allow the participants to direct the flow of ideas.
- Refrain from judgment and do not allow participants to become judgmental of each other.
- Use open-ended questions to encourage participation.
- Avoid asking "Why?"
- Use a circle arrangement whenever possible.
- Assure participants and enforce the policy that what is said in the group remains in the group.
- Encourage participants to focus on their own individual feelings rather than generalizing the sentiments of the entire group.

In its most simple form, processing addresses these questions:

1. *What?* (What actually happened during the experience?)
2. *So what?* (What does it mean to the participants?)
3. *Now what?* (What can participants take away or learn from the experience?)

2.5 Monitoring Programs

A key (and often overlooked) aspect of effective programming is continuous monitoring. Monitoring involves constant review and feedback of a program and is considered a type of formative evaluation. This information can be obtained through daily objective sheets. Monitoring is a means through which one can ascertain the effectiveness of a program while remaining focused and sensitive to the program's outcomes and objectives. If things are not working, adjustments can be made while the program is in operation.

Several advantages to continuous program monitoring are:

- Achievement of daily outcome objectives is documented.
- Staff can deal with problems as they arise.
- Solutions to problems can be noted for future references.
- Progress toward goals can be continually assessed.
- Direction can be adjusted when needed.
- Programs can be offered more effectively in the future.
- Planning new programs for the future is facilitated. (i.e., We know what works or what doesn't work.).
- Staff takes pride in knowing they have been successful.

Before concluding this section on program development, the importance of staff training cannot be emphasized enough. Program staff are the ones who serve on the front lines of recreation program delivery. It is imperative that all, including part-time and seasonal, staff are trained on the outcome-focused approach to programming. In order for effective and purposeful programming and services to exist, staff need to be knowledgeable about why they do what they do. Training staff about outcomes not only facilitates their ability to provide intentional programming, but also to articulate the programs' merit to the participants, the public, and themselves. The training of staff should encompass targeted goals and outcomes at the department and program levels, outcomes-based programming, and the evaluation process.

Step 3: Measure Program Goals, Including Outcomes

What happens in programs and how do we know it happens? The answer: systematic evaluation process. This is not a new concept to recreation and leisure professionals. Part of the accreditation process for the National Recreation & Parks Association (NRPA) calls for departments and programs to have a systematic evaluation process in place. With OFP, this process focuses on the assessment of targeted outcome goals and daily outcome (objectives) as they relate to the target issues. The evaluation of the goals, including targeted outcomes, is essential in the program planning process.

3.1 Why Evaluate

Evaluation is a "systematic collection and analysis of data to address criteria as to make judgments about the worth or improvement of something; making decisions based on identified criteria and supporting evidence" (Henderson, 2006). A systematic evaluation process can:

- *Determine accountability.* Results can justify expenditures and serve to solicit future funding.
- *Assess goals and objectives.* It can determine if goals and objectives are being accomplished. It also assists with improving programming effectiveness.
- *Ascertain outcomes and impacts.* It can identify the level of impact a program has made on participants that in turn can enhance the credibility of the program.
- *Explain keys to the program's success/failure.*
- *Improve or set future directions for the program.*
- *Be used in periodic evaluations of personnel responsible for the program.*

Figure 4.1 is an example of a statement of purpose regarding evaluation from the Leisure Services Department of Canton, MI:

The key to evaluation is knowing what one is evaluating. If we have developed our targeted goals properly, we have already determined what we want to happen as a result of participation in our program. We may ask the following questions to be sure we have clearly stated our targeted goals:

- What do we expect to happen to participants through this program?
- What do we want participants to gain, learn, or do as a result of this program?

3.2 Assessment Techniques

There are many methods that can be used to evaluate programs. These methods include:

- Questionnaires/Surveys
- Interviews (Individual and Focus Groups)

"PURPOSE: To provide a systematic evaluation program and strategic use of department resources for Leisure Services programs, facilities, and services that guide the department to a healthy future.

The program will define performance goals, conduct assessments and provide unbiased valid data that will be analyzed and interpreted to help identify trends, safety issues, necessary improvements and community expectations. This information will then be disseminated to the appropriate divisions to ensure effective delivery of service and compliance with department goals."

Figure 4.1 Statement of Purpose

- Journals
- Systematic Observations

It is important to keep the following in mind for deciding the method to use:

- Purpose of the evaluation
- Resources available
- Who has the information
- How the data will be analyzed and used

Questionnaires and surveys are instruments that most municipal parks and recreation departments currently use. In developing and/or utilizing questionnaires and surveys, consider the following questions:

- Is the questionnaire/survey reliable and valid? Does it measure what you want it to measure? When using an existing questionnaire/survey, make sure that it has proven levels of validity. If you are developing your own questionnaire/survey, consult with an individual who is knowledgeable about instrument construction and testing.
- Is the questionnaire/survey appropriate for the participants? If the participants are minors, it is important to get permission from the appropriate parties before the questionnaire/survey is administered.
- Is the questionnaire/survey reasonable to administer and affordable? Although initially the prospect of the systematic evaluation process seems overwhelming and cost prohibitive, the reality is that once a system is in place, it is ultimately cost-effective. Questionnaires/surveys do not need to be long, intense, and time-consuming to get the information one needs to ensure effective programming.

- Are directions on the questionnaire/survey clear, concise, and unambiguous? If a participant cannot read or understand the directions, assistance should be made available to that participant.
- Is the questionnaire/survey easy to score (with directions on how to)? There are computer programs available that will actually score and analyze the data. Identification numbers are used for the assessment process.
- Is this questionnaire/survey the best way to measure the targeted outcome? Remember that there are many methods available to measure targeted outcomes. It is important to choose one or a combination of several methods that will provide the necessary information about the effectiveness of the program to address the targeted outcomes.

3.3 Levels of Evaluation

The rigor and extensiveness of the evaluation process is influenced by purpose, time, money, or other resource constraints. The level of evaluation chosen will depend upon how much information the department desires and/or requires to justify the resources committed to the program. The simplest form of evaluation may involve a *post-program assessment* of the participants' perceptions of the quality and/or positive affect of the program. For example, the participants may be asked to indicate whether there has been a change in their attitude related to a particular targeted goal of the program (e.g., attitude toward the environment, exercise and physical fitness).

If a higher level of evaluation is necessary to justify the resources for a program, the approach might involve conducting a *pre- and post-test* of participants' behavior, attitudes, or satisfactions, again as they relate to the identified targeted program goals. This would allow for an assessment of the actual change in the participants that might be related to their participation in the program. However, you cannot confirm that this change was due specifically to the program because other factors may have actually caused the change.

A slightly more comprehensive level of evaluation contains both the pre- and post-test evaluation with the inclusion of a control group. A control group would involve individuals with similar demographics to the program participants but who have not had access to the actual program. In this manner, the change in the participants is compared against the change in the members of the control group. In this circumstance, the change can be more confidently attributed to the program.

There are several other levels of evaluation available to recreation professionals; however, the time, cost, and expertise necessary to implement these procedures must be weighed in comparison to the added value to the department. It is beyond the scope of this chapter to discuss these higher levels of evaluation.

Figure 4.3 provides an example of a draft of the operations policy regarding program evaluation/surveys from the Leisure Services Department of Canton, MI. Each of the three levels involves a somewhat more rigorous approach to the evaluation. The higher the level of evaluation used, the more confidence one can have in the results of the program.

This is just one example of the way a parks and recreation department can implement a systematic evaluation process. It is important to keep in mind that there are many ways to develop this process utilizing the guidelines outlined in this section. Since there are no two municipal parks and recreation departments that are exactly alike, recreation professionals should develop a system that will best fit their department. The basic premise with OFM is that structured, purposeful recreational activities with clear outcome-oriented goals and comprehensive assessment procedures will ensure significant positive results.

Step 4: Realize Impacts and Communicate Successes

Realizing the impacts of recreation programs and communicating successes is an important final step in the implementation of outcome-focused management. Creative marketing procedures need to be developed to articulate, both within the department and outside the department, the impact and the success stories that recreation programs have on the individual and the community. Failure to do so can result in the loss of opportunity to share the positive impacts of programs and services parks and recreation departments' offer. It might even diminish a recreation department's ability to continue providing these programs and services. It is essential to get the word out about what recreation programs do and why they are essential, coupled with the documentation to back it up. Communities fund what they understand and value.

Canton Leisure Services
Program Evaluation Tool Sample
B.L.O.C.K. Youth and Teen Center

Thank you for taking the time to complete this questionnaire. Please, keep your child in mind when providing us with the following:

1. Since the start of this program, I believe my child has: (please check all that apply)

_____ Increased Social Skills
_____ Increased Self Confidence
_____ Feels accepted by others
_____ Felt the staff cared for him/her

2. Please rate the staff for this program in the following areas, on a scale of 1 to 5, with 5 being the highest:

Organization..	1	2	3	4	5
Friendliness...	1	2	3	4	5
Professionalism..	1	2	3	4	5
A caring AND safe environment for the child.....	1	2	3	4	5

3. Due to your participation in the B.L.O.C.K. Youth and Teen Center, have you registered for any additional programs or services than you traditionally have in the past as a direct result of the new facility being opened? (Examples of additional programs or services could be the Canton Express Transportation program, a membership, Friday night Teen Night Out activities, etc.)

_____ No _____ Yes If so, please identify the programs and services:

4. Do you believe that Canton Leisure Services offers participants and the community the following benefits: (please check all that apply)

_____ Safe environments within the community for youth
_____ Opportunities that keep youth positively engaged during after school hours
_____ Opportunities that keep youth positively engaged during evenings and weekends
_____ Opportunities that increase connectivity with the Canton community

5. To ensure we continue providing quality programs, please share with us any other thoughts about this or any other leisure programs you may wish to participate in.

- -

This section of the survey asks for descriptive information of your household. This information will help Canton Leisure Services provide quality programs/facilities to all of the community residents. This information will be kept in the strictest confidence and used for statistical purposes only.

What is the participant's gender? ________ Male ________ Female

What school does the participant attend? ______________________________

What are the ages of adults and children in your household? (fill in for each person who resides in your household)

Adult ages: _____ _____ Children ages: _____ _____ _____ _____ _____ _____

Figure 4.2 Example of Questionnaire

4.1 Communicating Outcomes

Not only is it important for a parks and recreation department to communicate the value of a program, but the means by which they communicate it is as equally important. What is the most effective method? Pictures, stories, charts, and statistics are just a few examples. More examples include:

- Press releases
- Program descriptions
- All marketing pieces (i.e., banners, flyers, local cable ads)
- Reports to stakeholders and grant funders
- Board reports
- Annual reports
- Annual budget
- Newsletters
- Quarterly and/or monthly reports to county/city managers
- Individual conversations with community members and parents

4.2 Internal Audiences

It is important to communicate impacts and success stories with internal audiences because these audiences are intimately involved in the success of recreation programs. They should be constantly aware of the importance and impact that programs have on individuals and the community.

These key internal audiences include:

Level I Goal or outcome directed post-test evaluation only (may also include specifically selected mid-point survey)

1. Surveys shall be formatted using the Level One Survey Template which includes:
   a. Question #1- Program Specific
   b. Question #2- Programmer/Instructor choice
   c. Question #3- Economic Impact
   d. Question #4- Community Benefits
   e. Question #5- Marketing
   f. Other Comments
2. Surveys shall be conducted for all programs.
3. For programs that run year-round with results consistent for two consecutive surveys, the survey may be reduced to once annually. If there is a change in the program (new instructor, new format, new day, etc.) then the **Level I** survey shall be conducted again until results are consistent for two consecutive results.

Expanded Surveys

Level II A simplified pre-test and post-test evaluation.

Level III Mini study- A pre-test and post-test evaluation with an expanded questionnaire and expanded data analysis.

Full study-A pre-test and post-test evaluation with a control group. An expanded questionnaire and expanded data analysis will be performed as required in order to secure funding sources and/or demonstrate need for budget allocation.

Processing of Surveys

1. Completed surveys will be immediately provided to the designated personnel to be inputted into SPSS (a statistical analysis program).
2. Survey results will be provided to the programmer, market specialist, and division supervisor within 30 days.
3. The survey results will be analyzed and if necessary provided to consultant for additional analysis.
4. Marketing Specialist will ensure that the contact information (e-mail address, phone number, etc.) is place in centralized database.
5. Based on analysis, programmer and division supervisor make appropriate changes to the program.

Figure 4.3 Draft of Canton Leisure Services' Evaluation Policy

- Department's Staff- It is a means to validate their week. In turn, this can create a sense of pride and motivate to continue doing the good work that they do.
- Department's Board- Because they believe and support the value of recreation with their time and talents, they should know about programs' successes as well.
- Program's participants- There would be no programs without participants. It goes without saying that they should be aware of the value of recreation programs.
- Program's partners- With OFP, the development of partnerships with other organizations, such as churches or school districts, is a part of the process. Since they are invested in our programs, they should know about our successes.

4.3 External Audiences

Communicating impacts and success stories to key external audiences enables recreation departments to spread the value of their programs to a much wider audience, including:

- Press- The inclusion of documented outcomes when utilizing the press on a regular basis will make a strong impact on the value of recreation.
- Funders- People support what they value. Sharing documented outcomes that recreation departments produce through their programs can enhance fundraising, grant opportunities, and governmental funding.
- General Public- This will increase the public's awareness for the necessity of municipal parks and recreation departments and how they can positively impact the entire community.
- Other agencies (partners and competitors)- The success of the program reflects the success of the partnering agencies since they play a role in the development and implementation of the program. For competing agencies, communicating impacts can raise expectations in the quality of services and programs they provide.

As noted earlier, the public, communities, governments, boards, and foundations fund what they understand and value. Therefore, an essential responsibility of a municipal parks and recreation department is to communicate consistently and persistently the values and impacts of its programs in the positive development of individuals and communities.

In summary, OFP is a four stage process, where each stage is essential to the overall success of the program and the entire department. However, because this programming strategy may be seen as a significant change from current operating procedures it is recommended that the process be implemented in stages. Each department must choose where they can best begin. Actually, one could start at any stage except the evaluation stage. If a department feels it cannot start with stage one, it is the recommendation of these authors to start with stage two by implementing the five key programming principles. This will steer the programming staff towards looking at direct outcomes and benefits of the programs they offer. Once they approach their programming from this perspective, they will quickly begin to determine direct outcomes of the programs they offer (See Appendix B & C for examples of programs based on OFP). In this manner, a department can gradually move into an OFM/OFP culture and philosophy without overwhelming the staff.

Conclusion

The implementation of OFM is a significant cultural change for some parks and recreation departments. However, its benefits far outweigh its costs or consternation. Just as with OFP, OFM can be implemented in steps or stages. It is important that parks and recreation departments realize that this not an overnight process. Small, incremental steps will have a positive effect on the department and it will minimize the stress among the staff. To illustrate this point and to conclude this chapter, a case study of the Leisure Services Department of Canton, Michigan's implementation of outcomes-focused management is presented.

The Leisure Services Department of Canton, MI: A Case Study

Canton Leisure Services, under director Ann Conklin is an example of a municipal parks and recreation department that has successfully implemented outcome-focused management. The purpose of this case study is to illustrate the process this organization experienced in the implementation of OFM.

In June of 2000, Ann Conklin became the director of Canton Leisure Services in Canton, MI. Prior to her arrival to Canton, MI, Ms. Conklin had attended several trainings on benefits-based programming and benefits-based management as part of NRPA's "Benefits are Endless" movement. She became an advocate of this approach for the development and delivering of recreation programs and services. Her intention was to incorporate the benefits approach into Canton Leisure Services. Coincidentally, the township of Canton was undergoing a reexamination through focus groups and township study sessions of their mission and goals to reflect an outcome-focused system. Through this analysis, the mission and goals of the township as well as for Canton Leisure Services became:

"We shall be pro-active in our approach, creative in our thinking, innovative in our solutions, fair and honest in our actions, and committed to a quality work environment that fosters pride, partnerships, and a high quality of life for our community."

Goals:

- Create a sense of community and belonging
- Provide premier facilities
- Develop and cultivate partnerships
- Effectively utilize resources and demonstrate fiscal responsibility
- Create a healthy community
- Provide excellent customer service
- Develop and empower staff

"'Creating community through people, parks and programs' is Canton Leisure Services' vision. This vision cannot be met without a quality measurable plan that is based on the values and aspirations of the community." (Canton Leisure Services Strategic Plan: An Initiative for the Future, 2003)

Ms. Conklin viewed the adoption of OFM as a means to create an identity for Canton Leisure Services, thereby contributing to the survival of the department and the continuous support of the local government. Because the board understood the importance of what recreation can "bring to the table" and the importance of Ms. Conklin's view of the benefits approach, they allocated support for Canton Leisure Services to contract for the consultative services of Dr. Alicia Eckhart. Dr. Eckhart had been involved in the training and research of the Benefits Movement.

In the first year, Dr. Eckhart met once a month with the recreation administration team that consisted of nine programmers and coordinators. During these sessions, training was conducted about benefits-based programming. A key concept of these trainings was getting these programmers and coordinators to examine their programs and to analyze why they do them. What outcomes do these programs address? What purpose do they serve? How do our programs reflect the mission statement and goals of the township? The ultimate goal was to have every program reflect outcomes. Additionally, marketing and program descriptions were reworked to reflect an outcomes-focused language. Initially, this new mindset of using outcomes supported by statistics was not wholly embraced by all members of the administration team, particularly by those who had been with the department for a long time. Part of the resistance was due to perception that this approach was too overwhelming, too time consuming, and too costly to implement.

Concurrently, Canton Leisure Services decided to develop a program utilizing the Benefits-Based Programming Model that would serve as a case study. Since teen issues were a "hotspot" for the recreation department and the township as a whole, they decided to start with the development of a teen outreach program. To develop this outreach program, Jon LaFever, the program's director, met with Dr. Eckhart and other key department personnel to develop program specific outcomes as well as to brainstorm on how to measure these outcomes. A systematic evaluation process was developed. The training of program staff about outcomes and the evaluation process was conducted. This program would serve as an example of how worthwhile a benefits approach was for the department. It would contribute greatly to the buy-in of benefits-based programming for those within and outside the department who were skeptical of its value.

Over the next several years, existing programs were reworked to reflect outcomes. All marketing and program description used the language of outcomes. All staff throughout the department (including seasonal and part-time) were trained on outcomes and evaluation. New programs were developed to reflect outcomes and policies and procedures were gradually modified to reflect outcomes. A template and procedure were developed for a systematic evaluation process (found in previous section of this chapter). Utilizing SPSS, a statistical analysis program, data from evaluation forms were analyzed. In collaboration with Michigan State, graduate students operated this program for Canton Leisure Services. Because the department started growing so quickly, they were able to hire a part time statistician. Eventually internal staff (primarily program administrators) were trained to run SPSS.

Further in the budgeting process, the achievement of a program's goals and outcomes were placed on a point system grid to determine cost measures. Programs were continually examined, altered, and reexamined based on results of outcomes. Staff reported that they were more committed and more passionate about their jobs and programs because they could now more clearly articulate a sense of purpose. Even those who initially voiced resistance to this approach turned out to be the biggest advocates.

The following lists some of the keys to Canton Leisure Services' success for the implementation of OFM:

- Commitment and support from the top: Department Board, Government of Council, and Director of Canton Leisure Services
- Consultation with expert in systematic evaluation development and benefits-based programming
- Training of all staff
- Gradual implementation: start small (one program at time if need be)
- Buy In: "talk the talk" and "walk the walk"

Literature Cited

Allen, L. & Cooper, N. L. (2003). *Benefits based programming curriculum manual.* Ashburn, VA: The National Recreation and Park Association.

Allen, L., Stevens, B., Hurtes, K., & Harwell, R. (1998). *Benefits-based programming of recreation services training manual.* Ashburn, VA: The National Recreation and Park Association.

Artley, W., Ellison, D. J., & Kennedy, B. (2001). Establishing and maintaining a performance-based management program. *The performance-based management handbook: Vol 1. A six-volume compilation of techniques and tools for implementing the government Performance and Results Act of 1993.* Washington, D.C.: Performance–Based Management Special Interest Group.

Behn, R. (2003). Why measure performance? Different purposes require different measures. *Public Administration Review 63*(5). 586–604.

Edwards, D. & Thomas, J. C. (2005). Developing a municipal performance-measurement system: Reflections on the Atlanta Dashboard. *Public Administration Review 65*(3). 369–376.

Gilmour J. B. & Lewis D. E. (2006). Assessing performance budgeting at OMB: The influence of politics, performance, and program size. *Journal of Public Administration Research and Theory 16*(2), 169–186.

Heinrich, C. J. (2002). Outcomes-based performance management in the public sector: Implications for government accountability and effectiveness. *Public Administration Review 62*(6), 712–725.

Henderson, K. A. (2006, September). *Basics of Camp Evaluation: Purposeful and Systematic.* Presented at the Southeastern American Camp Association Conference, Charlotte, NC.

Ho, A. T. (2005). Accounting for the value of performance measurement from the perspective of Midwestern mayors. *Journal of Public Administration Research and Theory 16*, 217–237.

Julnes, P. D. & Holzer, M. (2001). Promoting the utilization of performance measures in public organizations: An empirical study of factors affecting adoption and implementation. *Public Administration Review 61*(6), 693–709.

Kamensky, J. (2002). Performance-based organizations: What strategies can leaders pursuer to make government more citizen-centered and public accountable? *The Public Manager 31*(1), 13.

Luckner, J. L. & Nadler, R. S. (1997). *Processing the experience: Strategies to enhance and generalize learning*. Dubuque, IA: Kendall/Hunt Publishing Company.

Melkers, J. & Willoughby, K. (2005). Models of performance-measurement use in local governments: Understanding budgeting, communication, and lasting effects. *Public Administration Review 65*(2), 180–190.

Nicholson-Crotty, S., Theobald, N. A, & Nicholson-Crotty, J. (2006). Disparate measures: Public managers and performance –measurement strategies. *Public Administration Review 66*(1), 101–113.

Page, S. (2005). What's new about the new public management? Administrative change in human service. *Public Administration Review 65*(6), 713–727.

Wang, X. H. (2002). Perception and reality in developing an outcome performance measurement system. *International Journal of Public Administration 25*(6), 805–830.

Appendix A

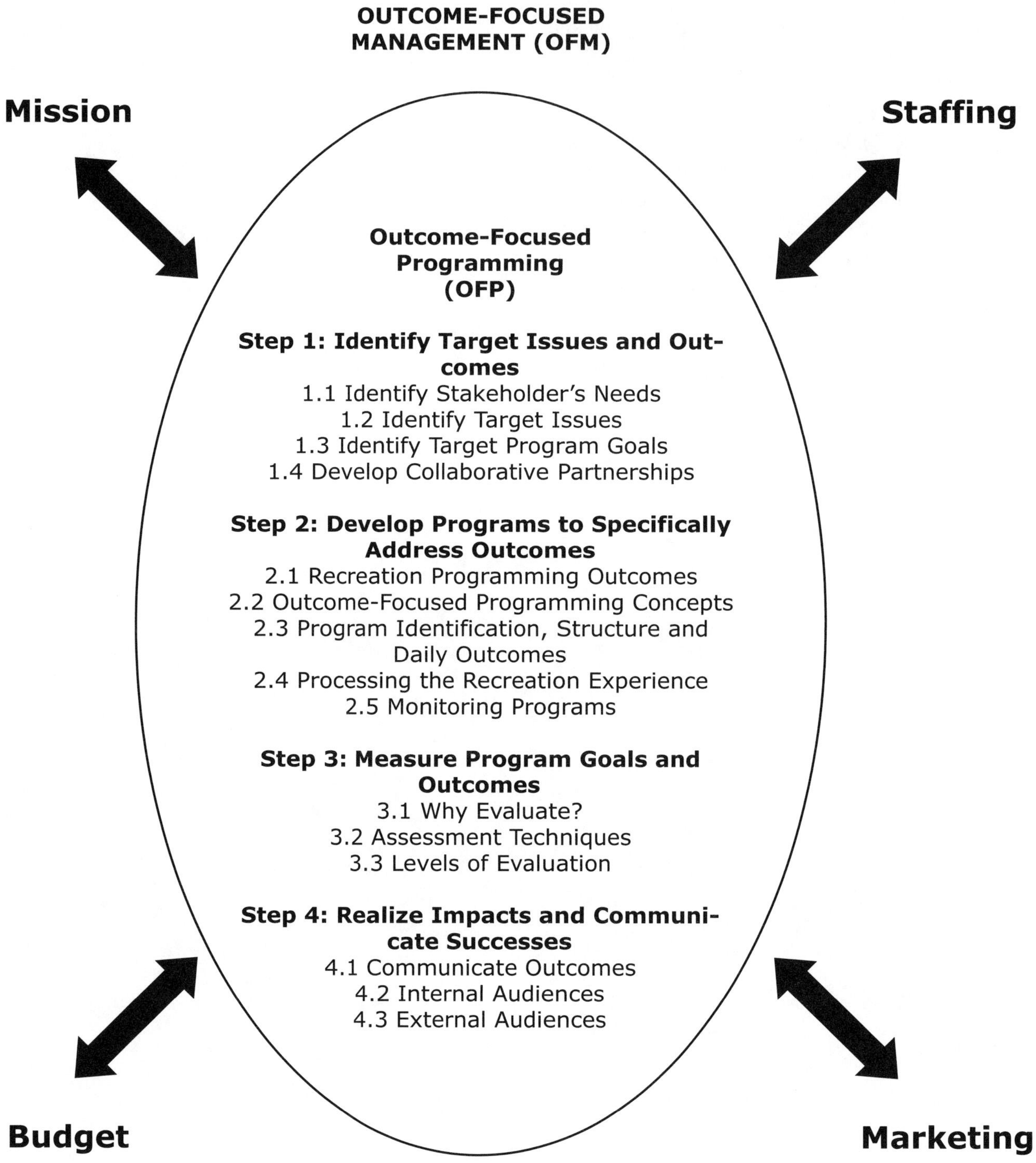

OUTCOME-FOCUSED MANAGEMENT (OFM)

Mission

Staffing

Outcome-Focused Programming (OFP)

Step 1: Identify Target Issues and Outcomes
1.1 Identify Stakeholder's Needs
1.2 Identify Target Issues
1.3 Identify Target Program Goals
1.4 Develop Collaborative Partnerships

Step 2: Develop Programs to Specifically Address Outcomes
2.1 Recreation Programming Outcomes
2.2 Outcome-Focused Programming Concepts
2.3 Program Identification, Structure and Daily Outcomes
2.4 Processing the Recreation Experience
2.5 Monitoring Programs

Step 3: Measure Program Goals and Outcomes
3.1 Why Evaluate?
3.2 Assessment Techniques
3.3 Levels of Evaluation

Step 4: Realize Impacts and Communicate Successes
4.1 Communicate Outcomes
4.2 Internal Audiences
4.3 External Audiences

Budget

Marketing

Appendix B

Outcome-Focused Program Profile
City of Fort Lauderdale Parks & Recreation Department, FL

Program Title: Club Carter Reach Our Kids Now (ROK'N) Program

Target Group: (45 youth) ages 10-18 in the General Population who are not currently participating/enrolled in M.O.S.T., Bridges, New Day, and Family Strengthening programs who meet at least two (2) of the following risk factors: 1. Have family members involved in the criminal justice system (includes siblings of DJJ youth) 2. Identified as habitually truant 3. Exhibit documented disciplinary problems in school / performing below grade level 4. Have a history of delinquency 5. Have a history of child abuse/neglect 6. Have a history of substance abuse or mental health problems 7. Reside in a high crime area 8. Receive public assistance, such as TANF, or are from a low-income family (200% of poverty level) 9. Have dropped out of school or been placed in an alternative school setting.

Partnership: Alliance for Community Transformation (ACT) Kids In Distress

Target Issue: Delinquency prevention.

Program Goal:

- To increase pro-social peer interactions.
- To promote academic success and consistent school attendance.
- To improve family communication.
- To increase positive interactions with the community.
- To reduce incidents of delinquency.

The Program: This year-round program offers low-income, at-risk youth a safe place to spend out-of-school time, both afterschool and during the summer. Youth are initially assessed for risk factors and develop an individualized service plan to help meet their needs. Program components include case management, family counseling, individualized tutoring and homework assistance, physical fitness activities, cultural arts instruction, technology instruction, family activities, and community service/service learning activities.

Evaluation Procedures: 1. "Interpersonal Assessment Scale" shall be administered to youth upon enrollment into program, at the end of each semester, and upon completion of program. 2. Using the Goal Attainment Scale Method, outcome shall be measured per semester using School Progress Reports. 3. "Family Assessment Device" administered to youth and caregiver(s) upon enrollment into program, at the end of each semester, and upon completion of program. 4. Community service log 5. Measured for all youth by obtaining DJJ face sheets each semester during program participation. This is reported on a semester basis in a format provided by the Council with face sheets of reoffenders attached.

Results: 80% improved interactions with peers/adults; 96% improved school grades/attendance; 100% participated in a minimum of three community service activities; 96% reported improved family functioning

Keys to Success: *Use of holistic strategies to address risk and protective factors; culturally competent programming; youth culturally competent incentive system; strong partnership with local school & behavioral/mental health provider; access to technology.*

Appendix C

Outcome-Focused Program Profile
City of Jackson Parks & Recreation Department, OH

Program Title: Catch Kid Club

Target Group: (30 youth) ages 6-9. This site used typical registration process as a means to get their sample.

Control Group: (30 youth) ages 6-9. To match the typical registration sample in terms of demographic characteristics, the control sample was randomly drawn from the remaining student population after the program participation group was identified.

Partnership: Jackson City Schools, Holzer Clinic, Adeana Health Systems, Jackson County Health Department, & Holzer Hospital

Target Issue: Health protection and improvement

Program Goal:
- To increase the knowledge of the dangers of tobacco use.
- To increase the knowledge of a healthy lifestyle through nutrition.
- To increase the knowledge of the importance of lifelong fitness
- To increase the knowledge of neighborhood resources.
- To increase the value on personal achievement.
- To increase the self perception of physical health.

The Program: Catch Kids Club, an afterschool program, was developed to teach children the importance of living a healthy lifestyle. Partners with this program offered health-related educational activities. Along with the many health activities, children also learned the benefits of an anti-tobacco lifestyle. Staff also followed the "Physical Best" curriculum throughout the program, which involved many forms of physical activity. Throughout the program, children learned the benefits of physical activity by keeping track of their progress.

Evaluation Procedures: The research arm of this project was two fold, assessment of physical fitness and self perception; and was conducted within the scientific approach of a pre-post control group design. 1. FITNESSGRAM ® Assessment was administered to both groups. It is the only health-related fitness assessment to use criterion-reference standards, called Healthy Fitness Zones (HFZ). For this program only two of the three components were measures: aerobic capacity and muscular strength, fitness, and flexibility. 2. "Perception Factor Assessment", a pre-post test survey to assess an individual's self perception regarding the six program goals listed above.

Results: With regards to the perception factor survey results, there was a tremendous shift in all six areas (neighborhood resources, value on achievement, life long fitness, physical health, knowledge of nutrition, dangers of tobacco). The most significant positive change was in the area of "increased knowledge of nutrition." Demonstrating the opposite effect, the control group decreased in all six areas significantly. As for results demonstrating improvement in physical activity and health, the participant group had a HFZ score of 84%, while the control group's HFZ score reached 35%.

Keys to Success: *Incorporation of education programming; strong partnership with local school & behavioral/mental health provider.*

*****Note: This program is one of nine such programs developed throughout the state of Ohio as part of the 2005-2006 Healthy Ohioans Youth Pilot Project (HOYPP). The Department of Health, Healthy Ohioans, and the Ohio Parks and Recreation Association partnered to develop a state-wide project that allowed nine cities across geographical and demographical diverse areas to participate in improving and protecting the health of youth in Ohio.**

Chapter 5
OFM and Needs for Many Segments of a Society to Better the Benefits of Leisure

B. L. Driver

Learning Objectives:

1. To better understand why practically everyone needs to have a reasonably good understanding of the benefits of leisure before OFM can be applied and implemented properly and more widely.
2. Appreciate why such a broad understanding is necessary before the contributions of publicly-provided leisure services to individual and social welfare will attain the same or even greater degree of recognition and appreciation by the general public than is now attributed by it to other public social services.

Purpose

Chapter 1 of this text emphasized that leisure professionals have the pivotal role in promoting wider adoption of OFM and that they must have a reasonably good understanding of the benefits of leisure before they can do that. The major purpose of this chapter is to expand on that theme by explaining why advancement of OFM depends on such understanding by members of other segments of society in addition to leisure professionals. Two minor purposes are to (1) explain the reasons why an understanding of benefits by leisure professionals has lagged, and (2) link broader understanding of the benefits of leisure to the long existing need for members of a society to recognize and appreciate the fact that leisure services contribute as much or more to individual and social welfare as other public services.

To pursue the major purpose of this chapter, we first need to identify all the segments of society whose members need to understand the benefits before they can more appropriately appreciate, support, promote, and advance OFM. Obviously, all leisure professionals must be mentioned first, whether teachers, scientists, extension service specialists, or practitioners. The list continues with the following: elected and appointed officials who determine public budgetary and other policies related to publicly-provided leisure services (including executive offices at all levels of government, appointed heads of public park and recreation agencies and their key staff members, budget analysts, and members of legislative bodies at all levels of government); customer and associated provider stakeholders; other constituents that affect or are affected by leisure services; and members of the general public.

Reasons Why That Understanding is Needed

There are several very specific, varying reasons why a broad understanding of the benefits is needed and how each one relates to promotion, application, and implementation of OFM. Each will be explained in the remainder of this chapter in terms of the needs to:

- Increase understanding by leisure professionals.
- Achieve wider understanding of the merit good nature of leisure.
- Attain and sustain funding for public park and recreation agencies.
- Promote wider public support of public park and recreation agencies, especially greater articulation of the benefits of leisure in various political arenas.
- Enhance collaboration with relevant customer and associated provider stakeholders.
- Enhance marketing and promotion of park, recreation, and related amenity programs, services, and opportunities to include beneficial outcomes and the avoidance of negative ones.

Increase the Understanding of Leisure Professionals

Although significant progress has been made in adopting OFM since the early 1990s, the question now is why hasn't more progress been made? The following four reasons help answer that question:

1. The science-based knowledge about those benefits is of relatively recent origin.
2. Many leisure "professionals" still rely mostly on intuition and personal experience to guide most of their thinking about the benefits.
3. Most public recreation and park policy makers, planners, and managers have not had sufficient academic or on-the-job training related specifically to understanding the science-based knowledge about the benefits of leisure; their training has focused instead on planning and managing recreation programs and events, recreation activities and settings, and on producing facilitating outputs instead of questioning *why* those services are offered in terms of their beneficial and unwanted outcomes, as required by OFM.
4. Without such training there has been little motivation or requirement to understand the benefits.

These problems will take some time to overcome, but two particular existing problems could be corrected rather easily. First, although considerable research has been done, few leisure scientists are now doing research or writing papers on benefits and/or on how to apply that knowledge so that leisure professions can be further advanced. Second, the two means of certifying professionalism in leisure do *not* now require adequate understanding of the current scientific knowledge about the benefits of leisure or how to use it. Those two means of certification are (1) the NRPA's program to help someone become a "Certified Park and Recreation Professional" (or CPRP) and (2) NRPA and the American Association for Physical Activity and Recreation's (AAPAR's) joint program for accrediting baccalaureate "programs in colleges and universities that prepare new professionals to enter the broad field of parks, recreation and leisure services."

One can review the requirements of these two certification programs on the Internet. On the NRPA's web page describing CPRP certification, there is *no* direct reference to needs to understand knowledge about the benefits of leisure and how to use it when reviewing the subject areas tested in the required CPRP examination. Specifically, if one reviews the "Test Content Outline" in the online "Candidate Handbook," no content relating to benefits can be found, and none of the many "Recommended Texts" have adequate coverage of the current knowledge about those benefits or how to use it. The same holds true for accreditation requirements of the NRPA/AAPAR. That web page shows learning/instructional requirements in several major subject areas and their many sub-topics. Considerable emphasis is given in those accreditation and certification requirements for efficient management of park and recreation resources and services. But practically no attention is given to requirements related to accountability and responsiveness of such management in terms of benefits desired and negative outcomes to be avoided, which are the central thrusts of OFM. For example, Section 8.14:02 of the "Program and Event Planning" subject displays the sole reference that is given to benefits at that site. Only there can the very few words that refer to "outcome-oriented goals and objectives" be found; no other reference is given to benefits in the other subject areas such as Delivery Systems, Administration, or Management.[1]

The unfortunate conclusion is that current certification and accreditation procedures do not require that professionally certified people who work in leisure, or the academic programs that guide their professional training, understand the very important science-based knowledge on which that professionalism should be established. If they do not understand that science-based knowledge, they certainly will not know how to apply it when attempting to implement OFM. In sum, while considerable progress has been made by leisure professionals in understanding the benefits of leisure, considerably more progress is needed.

Understand the Merit Good Nature of Leisure

The concept that leisure services are meritorious is important not only for leisure professionals to understand, but also for the public at large as well as elected and appointed officials for reasons elaborated in following sections. That concept will now be defined and supported by the results of selected research.

Definition of a Merit Good

In a competitive market economy, all or most of the goods and services provided by public agencies are provided because the private sector is not motivated to provide them and/or a society has judged that those goods and services best be provided by the public sector. There are several rationale for such, and they are reviewed in Moore & Driver (2005: 280–282) under the section entitled "Public, Merit, and Nonmarketed Goods and Services." The focus of this section is on merit goods, and particularly the merit good aspects of leisure services.

The term "merit good" is used to refer to a good or service that is considered to be meritorious socially because the creation and use of it provides benefits to others besides the direct users of the good or service. Put simply, a merit good or service benefits people other than those who use it. The classic example is education, where the pervasive belief has been that an educated populace is more civil, productive, and comprised of better citizens than an uneducated one. That is why children in the United States must remain in school until the age of 14 or 16 (it varies by state) and why there is partial subsidization of that education at the federal and state levels. The education example is similar in most industrialized countries. Similarly, most societies recognize that use of recreational services also results in benefits to others than the direct uses of those services. A few examples include: improved health of recreationists that reduces the total health care costs of a society; enhanced understanding of natural and cultural/historic structures (e.g., Mesa Verde Cliff Dwellings) and environments (e.g., Gettysburg National Battlefield) that nurtures pride in one's region and nation, thereby promoting better citizenship and greater commitment to conservation efforts and protection of these structures and sites; increased skills and productivity from use of public libraries and continuing education courses; and enhanced social networking such as family togetherness and social interaction at senior citizen centers). In fact, the major reason that public park and recreation agencies exist is because of the recognition that leisure services are good for society as a whole as well as for the individuals that comprise it. Nevertheless, inadequate and unsustained funding for public park and recreation agencies still exists, because some elected and appointed public officials responsible for allocating those funds do not adequately understand and appreciate the nature and magnitude of those wider benefits to society beyond the individual users of the recreation opportunities provided.

Merit Goods Redefined as External Economies

Following the passage of the Environmental Policy Act of 1969, there was rapid growth of the sub-specializations of micro-economics called environmental, resource, and recreation economics. Economists working in those areas expanded the concept of a merit good into the concept of external economies and the associated concept of external diseconomies.[2] The word "external" denotes the impacts associated with the production and/or consumption of a good and service are *external to* the decision entity (i.e., a person, a private firm, or any organization) that causes the impacts. As such, external economies designate good or desirable impacts, and external diseconomies designate bad or undesirable impacts. Thus, an external economy is exactly equivalent to the concept of a merit good, but it is more precise and recognizes that external economies also result from the *production*, as well as the use, of many merit goods (e.g., improving and sustaining the basic resources necessary to provide recreation opportunities). Examples of external economies that accrue from leisure services were given above. Examples of external diseconomies include air and water pollution caused by a private firm, an outdoor recreationist causing a significant wild fire, and unwanted impacts of tourism on communities near public recreation areas.

Scientific Evidence That Supports the Merit Good Aspects of Leisure Services

Despite what appears to be inadequate understanding of the externalities associated with the production and use of leisure services, there is a growing body of scientific evidence that the external economies (merit good aspect) associated with leisure are quite significant socially. That evidence comes from the results of considerable research, with selected examples reviewed here.

- Godbey, Graefe, and James (1992) conducted a study of perceived benefits in the U. S. of a national representative sample of 1,305 individuals, aged 15 and over. A practically identical survey by Harper, Neider, Godbey, and Lamond (1997) was done in Canada. Among other things, the respondents were asked to register *to whom* did the benefits of local recreation and park services accrue, and the allowable responses were "To Individuals,"

"To Households," or "To the Community at Large."[3] Respondents were asked to register their perceptions of the magnitudes of the benefits as "No Benefit," "Some Benefit," or "Great Benefit." The responses given here are *only* for benefits reported as accruing to the "Community at Large," and they are given as percentages of the respondents making each response. The results from the study in the U.S. are given first with the corresponding results from the Canadian study shown in parentheses. By *percentages of respondents*, the perception of the magnitude of the benefits of local recreation park services to the community at large were: No Benefit=5.6% (4.0%), Some Benefit=33.1% (36.0%), and Great Benefit=61.3% (58.0%). It can be observed that while less than 6% of the respondents replied that there was No Benefit to the Community at Large, roughly 60% in both countries responded that there was Great Benefit. Interestingly, that sizable response of Great Benefit To the Community at Large was much higher than are percentage responses of Great Benefit To Individuals or To Households, which were 36.7% (40%) and 31.3% (45%), respectively. In other words, it is extremely relevant that respondents perceived almost twice as many Great Benefits to the Community at Large as they did to themselves. Lastly in these studies, both users and *nonusers* were asked about the benefits they perceived, and again surprisingly 71% of the *nonusers* reported perceived benefits to themselves, their household, or their local community.

These two studies are particularly revealing by showing that 61.3% (and 58%) of the using respondents perceived Great Benefit to their local communities, and 71% of the nonusers reported receiving benefits to themselves, their household, or their local community despite their nonuse. Why would the respondents to both of these national representative surveys perceive those very rather significant *external economies* if they do not exist?

- A periodic national household surveys of outdoor recreation in America is done by Roper Starch Worldwide, Inc. for the Recreation Roundtable. The Recreation Roundtable is a group of influential individuals, including CEOs of recreational equipment manufacturing companies, who work with the American Recreation Coalition to promote political and other interests in outdoor recreation. In 2000, the survey interviewed a representative sample of 1,986 Americans. Some of the many findings of that study (Roper Starch, 2000: 3–5) documented a significant merit good aspects of recreation as follows:
    1. Close to 8 in 10 Americans (79%) believed that outdoor recreation can improve education.
    2. 98% responded that participation in outdoor physical activities create health-related benefits.
    3. 95% believed that outdoor recreation is a good way to increase people's appreciation for nature and the environment, and 90% believed it would increase understanding of the importance of environmental protection.
- Campbell (1981), Marans and Mohai (1991), and Allen (1991) documented that the existence of nearby amenities are one of the top five most important contributors to people's perceived quality of life. Although many of those beneficiaries never visit or use the nearby amenities, they are recipients of external economies created simply by the presence of those amenities. Stein, Anderson, and Thompson (1999) also documented those types of benefits to residents of local communities and the significance of such.
- Other studies have also documented the external economies perceived by significant numbers of even more remote (and non-participating on site) beneficiaries in addition to the forgoing ones residing in nearby communities. For example, several studies, one national and two regional representative studies showed that a relatively small percentage (less than 15%) of respondents to those surveys had even visited a "wilderness" area or even planned to do so. Yet, 60 to 75% responded they were very willing to have their tax dollars to go toward sustaining and protecting such areas. A related study (Loomis & Walsh, 1997: 366–367) in Colorado showed a surprisingly high "willingness to pay" taxes by large percentages of the *public at large* for several specified environmental protections, including protection of outdoor recreation resources opportunities. It is important to remember here that most of the respondents to the several studies noted were not on-site

recreationists, but they still perceived the merit good benefits to themselves and to others.

- Crompton (2004) convincingly documented that increases in property values attributable to homes being proximate to park and recreation areas contributed significantly to a local unit of government's property tax base, which in turn benefits all the citizens of that unit. Obviously, those benefits are significant external economies.
- Studies have also documented that the secondary economic impacts of tourism contribute significantly to the economic growth and vitality of local communities and regions (see Chapter 20 of this text).
- Lastly, many informed leisure professionals believe that when leisure is considered broadly, the leisure economic sector is one of the *largest economic sectors* of most industrialized societies. That bold proclamation should be explained because most people think of the economic contributions of recreation primarily in terms of opportunities provided by public park and recreation agencies. That limited perception is uninformed, because when viewed from a broader and more realistic perspective, the leisure sector of an economy is considerably larger than just the services provided by public park and recreation agencies. Economically, the leisure sector of most industrialized countries includes the costs and expenditures--though hard to track empirically--of *all* of the following: the cost and economic returns accrued that are directly attributable to the salaries, training, coaching, administration, physical infrastructure (stadiums, arenas, etc.) equipment, travel, costs of tickets, etc. of *all* professional sports and the summer and winter Olympics; domestic and international travel that in part or in whole is for recreational purposes, including costs of food, lodging, rental vehicles, and all other associated travel costs related to recreation; recreation-related expenditures on vacation homes, airplanes, boats, and other equipment needed to engage in all leisure activities such as costs of hunting and fishing licenses and of guides and tour operators; recreation-related costs of stereo equipment, radios, computers, DVDs, television sets, personal vehicles (used in part or in whole for recreational purposes which a high percentage are); recreation-related costs of constructing and maintaining the infrastructure required for and use of public libraries, museums, concert halls, movie theatres, tennis courts, swimming pools, exercise centers, and places to take yoga and dance lessons, etc.; and the costs of all recreation-related hosting and entertaining of friends; and so on. The logical conclusion is that, when the leisure economic sector of an economy is defined more appropriately than it has been in the past, the leisure economic sector is probably as large as or larger than the other economic sectors in most industrialized societies. Therefore, those yet-to-be-quantified economic benefits of leisure indicate very large external economies. It must be emphasized that most of those economic externalities are not created by the functions of public park and recreation agencies. Nevertheless, many off those externalities do accrue because of the functions of those agencies and the synergistic options they create.

It should be emphasized that the aforementioned examples are only a sample of the many documentations of the significant merit good aspects of leisure. Nevertheless, it can be stated with confidence that there is incontrovertible evidence that leisure services provide many varied significant benefits to people other than to the direct users of the recreation opportunities provided by public park and recreation agencies.

Internalizing the External Economies

Resource/environmental economists propose that practically all externalities should be internalized to the extent feasible. The logic is that the decision entities that create external economies *should not* inequitably bear all the costs of doing so and that those who create the external diseconomies *should* bear their fair share of the costs of preventing or reducing the negative impacts.

Regarding the merit good aspects of leisure services, the *only* way those external economies can be internalized by those who created them (i.e., the public agency that created the recreation opportunities and/or the customers who used those opportunities) is *for all of the people* who realize those beneficial "external" (meritorious spin-off) effects, to bear their fair share of the costs of providing those opportunities through their tax dollars and other ways that Crompton (2004) describes, including allocating state lottery funds to recreation, increasing general taxation with ear marks for park and recreation agencies, and using a variety of special ballot issues related to funding (increases in sales taxes with revenues dedicated to parks and recreation, obligation and revenue bonds for recreation programs). Likewise, damages from the example external diseconomies mentioned above should be internalized to the decision entity that causes them by requiring that (1) polluting firms to pay the necessary cost of reducing or eliminating pollution or compensating those damaged by the pollution; (2) careless recreationists who cause wildfires pay the costs of such; and (3) local communities work with providers of opportunities for the tourist to reduce and mitigate the unwanted effects of tourism in their communities.

There is a fourth reason why the concept of externalities is important. It is that when attempting to optimize the beneficial outcomes of recreation (the title of this text), OFM requires that both positive and negative outcomes (including external economies and external diseconomies) be considered. Conventional approaches to the planning and management of recreation resources and services have tended to focus mostly or entirely on the on-site users and have not considered all the impacts on all the customers on-site or off-site.

Secure and Sustain Adequate Funding

Before elected and appointed officials, who fund public park and recreation agencies, can become convinced that there are significant external economies associated with leisure, they must "reposition" their concept of the social good of leisure. As stated succinctly by Crompton and Witt (1997: 81), "Positioning refers to the place that parks and recreation occupies *in the minds of elected officials and the general public*, relative to their perceptions of other services that are the field's competitors for tax dollars (and sometimes for foundation and other private source funding). The term "position" differs from the term "image" in that it implies a frame of reference; that is, perceptions of the field are compared to those of other public services in which public officials may invest." This, and other papers on repositioning by Crompton and his associates, have recognized the pervasive needs for repositioning concepts about leisure. Earlier, Crompton (1993: 2) wrote "The present position of parks and recreation services which has been established in the minds of decision makers for the past few decades is that they are relatively discretionary, nonessential, governmental services. They are nice to have if they can be afforded. The need is to reposition recreation and park services so they are perceived to be a central contributor to alleviating the major problems identified by residents and decision makers."

Although Crompton and his associates have led the charge to promote more appropriate and sustained funding for public park and recreation agencies, how to obtain that funding, and how to manage it, others have chimed in with agreement. For example, Driver & Burns (1999: 351) wrote the following:

> Elected officials in the United States and Canada tend to hold the erroneous belief that most of all the benefits of leisure accrue to the individuals who use leisure services and that there are few to any spin-off benefits from this use to society in general. This contrasts sharply with their views about the social benefits of other public services (e.g., education, health services, police and fire protection, transportation) for which these elected officials acknowledge large benefits to society beyond those that accrue to the direct users of those services. Therefore, these officials have *improperly* adopted for leisure services the principle of public finance which dictates that limited public funds should not be allocated to a social service which does not promote the general welfare.

Progress has been and is incrementally still being made to convince the unconvinced elected and appointed officials about the social significance of these benefits. Crompton and his associates have suggested in considerable detail how to do that (cf. Kaczynski & Crompton, 2004). Hopefully, those officials will soon agree with Jordan (1991: 368) that "You can lay to rest, once and for all times, the idea that parks and recreation is nothing but fun and games. Let there be no doubt that we provide a positive, vital, and basic service." Nevertheless, "repositioning" those officials' knowledge about the sizable and significant external economies of leisure services remains one of the greatest challenges facing the leisure professions. Obtaining and maintaining adequate funding depends on it. However, such repositioning will not be enough. There also needs to be "pressure" exerted in the various political arenas by people concerned about inadequate funding. The saying that "the squeaky wheel gets the grease," is particularly germane regarding the politics for attaining adequate and sustained funding for public park and recreation agencies.

Chapter 1 of this text emphasized that OFM can be applied incrementally in an attempt to move toward full implementation. Whether partial or full application of OFM is attempted, plans need to be implemented, and OFM might require more funding than less complete approaches do. Given ever-present budget constraints, this can mean the difference between implementing and not implementing those OFM plans properly. Several chapters of the "applications" sections of this text describe situations in which OFM was applied reasonably properly as it has evolved since 1991. Those chapters did not emphasize that insufficient funding has in some applications impeded successful implementation of OFM as planned. Therefore, the rather extensive foregoing discussion about obtaining and sustaining adequate funding applies to implementing OFM as much or more as to planning under OFM.

Increase OFM-Oriented Public Involvement In Various Political Arenas

Members of the general public generally understand the characteristics and benefits to society of most social services such as education, medical care, fire and police protection, and other service professions. In contrast, they do not demonstrate nearly as much understanding of the societal contributions of various publicly provided leisure opportunities. To emphasize this problem, Moore and Driver (2005: 22) stated that:

> .... those of us who study or work in some area of leisure or recreation have frequently been asked by our parents, friends, or other associates, "how can anyone study or work in leisure?" Sometimes, this question teasingly plays on the semantics of "*work* in leisure" or "*work* in recreation." In other instances, the question reflects some understanding of the philosophy of leisure that promotes the concept of leisure as a state of being, and the person asking the question wonders either why anyone would not study philosophy instead of leisure, or how anyone could have a career in leisure so defined. But, most often, the question *reflects widespread lack of understanding* of the nature, scope, and benefits of leisure.

Moore and Driver went on to propose that a major reason why the benefits of leisure are not more widely understood by the general public is that most of the scientific knowledge about most of those benefits has emerged only relatively recently. This is true, but that knowledge has been disseminated rather rapidly, especially since publication and rather wide distribution of the Canadian "Benefits Catalogue" by the Canadian Parks and Recreation Association (1997) and promotion of the benefits in other ways, such as by the NRPA's "The Benefits are Endless" program.

The problem centers not as much on the newness of the science-based knowledge about the benefits as it does on the fact that knowledge has been disseminated only within the leisure professions. As emphasized above, increased dissemination is vitally important to enhancing leisure professionalism. We need to do much more than "preach to the choir!" Put simply, the task of repositioning the knowledge of the general public about the science-based benefits of leisure falls *squarely* on the shoulders of leisure professionals; who else can do it? It is a major professional responsibility that is not being met. Only through pervasive public understanding and appreciation of those benefits can leisure gain the social and political support it needs to gain equal footing with other public social services. In particular, such public support is of fundamental importance in achieving and sustaining proper funding of public park and recreation agencies in the political arenas within which there is great competition for allocation of limited funds. In addition, such understanding should promote greater support for and understanding of the use of the outcomes approach to guide park and recreation policy development, planning, and management.

Enhancement of Collaborative Efforts

Chapters 2 and 3 of this text emphasized that OFM requires close collaboration with managerially relevant on- and off-site customers and associated provider stakeholders. Chapter 1 emphasized that these stakeholders can help facilitate OFM better if they have a fairly good idea of the types of satisfying experiences and other benefits that are desired and should be targeted in management plans. Some customers now have that understanding and others do not. It is unknown the degree to which associated providers have that understanding and apply it to guide the provision of the supplemental and complementary services they need to offer both on-site and off-site in nearby communities. Certainly, their operations mesh better with OFM if they have good information. It is clear, however, that customer preference and related market analyses, as well as studies of user satisfaction, are facilitated and made more accurate and useful if actual and potential customers have a good understanding of the different types of benefit opportunities they desire and that can be provided. The same holds true when cooperating with the associated providers.

Experience with applying and implementing OFM has shown that the degree to which understanding of the benefits needs to be increased (i.e., repositioned toward greater awareness) among recreation planners and managers who work with relevant customers and associated providers. Those applications have also demonstrated that the task of applying and implementing OFM is much more difficult and generally less successful if adequate awareness of the benefits is lacking. Fortunately, those applications have also proven that attaining such understanding is not a difficult or time-consuming task.

Enhancing Marketing of Outcome Opportunities

One requirement of the comprehensive normative model for implementing OFM, detailed in Chapter 3 of this text, is to prepare and implement a marketing plan. Specifically, the model requires that customers be informed about what kinds of recreation and outcome opportunities will be produced when the OFM plan is implemented. That normally consists of providing the right kinds of information by whatever means is appropriate to inform potential and actual customers about the locations, types, and nature of the recreation activity, setting, and outcome opportunities that are available. It also consists of what resources, knowledge, and skills the customers should have to enjoy those opportunities and realize the outcomes targeted for the area. Many recreation opportunity guides also provide additional information about what fees are charged, when the opportunities will and will not be available, and any constraints that might exist such as the need to keep pets on leashes. The opportunity guides also typically include photographs of the area and descriptive information such as on the history of the area, length of trails, potential hazards, and so on. Such information should be readily available, inexpensive, and supported by more in-depth information such as maps and special guides.

Because OFM focuses on outcomes, information about them must be an important part of any opportunity guides. If the customers have sufficient awareness of the benefits of leisure, those guides will be much more useful in enhancing to overall quality of their recreation experiences realized on the areas for which the opportunity guides relate.

Lastly, as outcomes are specified and defined in marketing media, the users of those opportunities will become more consciously outcomes-oriented, which will supplement their demands for conventional desired recreation activities and settings orientations. As an incremental result of that learning process, they will become more supportive of OFM and of the importance of the benefits to themselves and other members of their society. It is a synergistic and iterative positive feed-backing and feed-forwarding process.

Summary

This chapter considered the needs to increase practically everyone's understanding of the considerable science-based body of knowledge about the benefits of leisure. Particular groups of people needing that repositioning were described and included: leisure professionals who work in all the different specializations of leisure (whether teachers, scientists, extension service specialists, or practitioners); elected and appointed officials who determine public budgetary and other policies related to the provision of leisure services and members of legislative bodies and executive offices at all levels of government, including budget analysts; most customer and associated provider stakeholders; other constituents that affect or are affected by leisure services; and members of the general public. The reasons why each of these groups needs enhanced understanding of the benefits of leisure were explained with emphasis on the needs to secure additional and sustained funding of Public Park and recreational agencies. Relationships between needed increased understanding of the benefits and application and implementation of OFM were described.

Literature Cited

Allen, L. (1991) Benefits of leisure services to community satisfaction. In. B. Driver, P. Brown, & G. Peterson (Eds.), *Benefits of leisure.* (pp. 331–350). State College, PA: Venture Publishing, Inc.

Campbell, A. (1981). The sense of well-being in America: Recent patterns and trends. New York, NY: McGraw Hill.

Canadian Parks/Recreation Association. (1997). *The Benefits Catalogue.* Gloucester, ON, Canada: Canadian Parks/Recreation Association.

Crompton, J. (1993). Repositioning recreation and park services: An overview. *Trends,* 30(4) 2–5.

Crompton, J. (2000). Repositioning leisure services. *Managing Leisure* 5, 65–75.

Crompton, J. (2004). *The Proximate Principle: The Impact of Parks, Open Space and Water Features on Residential Property Values and the Property Tax Base* (Second Edition). Ashburn, VA: National Recreation and Park Association.

Crompton, J. & Witt, P. 1997. Repositioning: The key to building community support. *Parks and Recreation.* October, 80–90.

Driver, B. L., Brown, P., & Peterson, G. (Eds.). (1991). *Benefits of leisure* (pp. 331–350). State College, PA: Venture Publishing, Inc.

Driver, B. L. & Bruns, D. (1999). Concepts and uses of the Benefits Approach to Leisure. In E. Jackson & T. Burton (Eds.). *Leisure studies: prospects for the twenty-first century* (pp. 349–368). State College, PA: Venture Publishing, Inc.

Godbey, G., Graefe, A., & James, S. (1992). *The benefits of local recreation and park services: A nationwide study of the perceptions of the American public.* State College, PA: The Pennsylvania State University, School of Hotel, Restaurant and Recreation Management.

Harper, J., Neider, D., Godbey, G., & Lamont, D. (1997). *The use and benefits of local government parks and recreation services: A Canadian perspective.* Winnipeg, Manitoba, Canada: Health, Leisure, and Human Dimensions Research Institute. University of Manitoba.

Jordon, C. (1991). Parks and Recreation: More than Fun and Games. In. B. L. Driver, P. Brown, & G. Peterson, G. (Eds.), *Benefits of leisure* (pp. 365–368). State College, PA: Venture Publishing, Inc.

Kaczynski, A. & Crompton, J. (2004). An operational tool for determining the optimum repositioning strategy for leisure service departments. *Managing Leisure, 9* 127–144.

Marans, R. & Mohai, P. (1991). Leisure resources, recreation activity, and the quality of life. In B. Driver, P. Brown, & G. Peterson (Eds.) *Benefits of leisure* (pp. 351–363). State College, PA: Venture Publishing, Inc.

Moore, D. & Driver, B, L. (2005). *Introduction to outdoor recreation: Providing and managing natural resource based opportunities.* State College, PA: Venure Publishing, Inc.

O'Sullivan, E. (1999). *Setting a course for change: The benefits movement.* Ashborn, VA. National Recreation and Parks Association.

Sefton, J. & Mummery, W. (1995). *Benefits of recreation research update.* State College, PA: Venture Publishing, Inc.

Stein, T., Anderson, A., & Thompson, D. (1999). Identifying and managing for community benefits in Minnesota state parks. *Journal of Park and Recreation Administration, 17*(4) 1–19.

Roper Starch. (2000). *Outdoor recreation in America 2000: Addressing Key Issues.* Prepared for the Recreation Round Table. Washington, D.C.: Roper Starch Worldwide, Inc.

Footnotes

1. To wit, a well-known professional associate, who reviewed this chapter, commented that "Both certification and accreditation are more concerned with the management of systems rather than the impacts of what we do; consequently there is very little emphasis placed on outcomes."
2. Those concepts have been a small part of micro economic theory for several decades, but were promoted by economists concerned about efficient and equitable allocations of environmental, including recreation, resources.
3. These response alternatives are not mutually exclusive, because many of the benefits can accrue to every alternative.

Chapter 6
Axioms and Strategies for Repositioning Park and Recreation Agencies Based on OFM[1]

J. L. Crompton

Learning Objectives:

1. Understand the concepts of positioning and repositioning.
2. Understand the needs for and benefits of repositioning
3. Understand strategies that have proven successful in attaining and maintaining repositioning.

In their seminal 1974 treatise Gray and Greben lamented, "We are not identified with the major problems which confront our total American Society" which they characterized as a "deep concern and disappointment" (p. 33). They went on to recommend that the field should "focus park and recreation services on the great social problems of our time and develop programs designed to contribute to the amelioration of those problems" (p. 52). Fifteen years later in 1989, this failing was again recognized when it was noted that advocating the provision of park and recreation opportunities for their own sake lacked political clout (Glyptis, 1989). In 2004, a major research study on "the language of conservation" designed to identify terminology that resonates positively with voters concluded:

> DO NOT *focus on creating new parks for their own sake* [the study's italics]. Instead, connect parks to a broader goal. While the focus groups demonstrated that "neighborhood parks" is better than the generic term "parks" (neighborhood parks resonates because it implies access and public use), the concept of new parks suffers in the abstract. For example, just 22% say a lack of neighborhood parks is an extremely or very serious problem. However, positioning parks in relation to children improves the concept. Fully 59% say that creating "parks and other places where children can play safely" is a very important reason for their state or local community to buy and protect land (Fairbank et al., 2004).

Linking parks to children's safety reiterates the plea articulated by Gray and Greben thirty years earlier, and reasserts the contention that OFM is a key to the field's future viability. Park and recreation services have to be shown to contribute to solving community problems before elected officials will see them as being a priority at budget time.

Among other things, OFM requires that an agency think in terms of how its actions can contribute to alleviating, and aligning with; a politically important concern. When managers do this, they are embracing a concept termed "positioning." Positioning entered the lexicon of the business world in the early 1970s (Ries & Trout, 1972) and has become established as one of the most central and powerful ideas in the marketing field. Indeed, an agency's position is more important to its future viability than what the agency actually does. Understanding and implementing positioning is *the* key to park and recreation agencies securing resources from legislative bodies.

This chapter builds on the call for better understanding of the benefits of leisure by all segments of a society described in the immediately preceding chapter of this text. Its focus is narrower in that it describes how public park and recreation agencies can, and should, orchestrate a shift in their strategic direction by using community benefits that are potential outcomes of park and recreation services to sustain or acquire additional budget allocations. The process is summarized in Figure 6-1 (on the following page) and it frames the structure and context of this chapter.

The starting point is to identify an agency's stakeholders' perceptions of park and recreation services. It is likely that they will be perceived as having social merit, which is nice to have if they can be afforded, but as being relatively discretionary when compared to other services for which the jurisdiction is responsible. To change this, an agency has to identify issues that are of paramount concern in the community and select a subset of community benefits (outcomes) that parks and

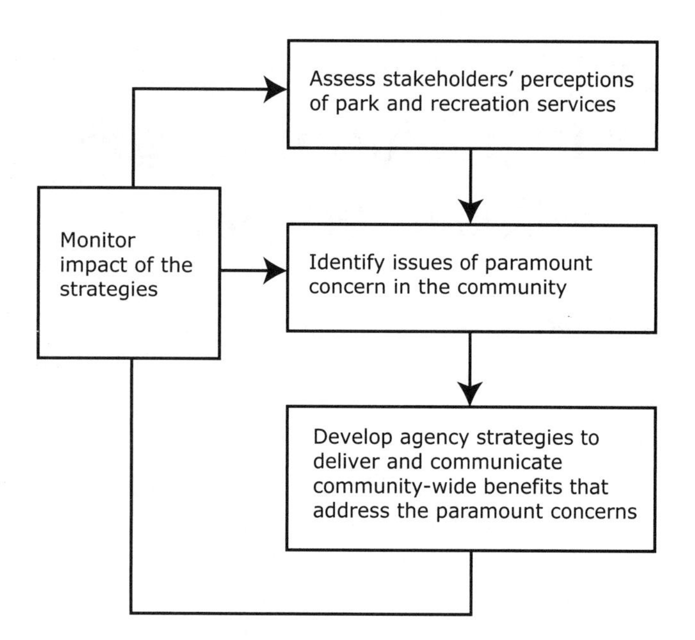

Figure 6.1 The process of orchestrating a shift in an agency's strategic direction

recreation can deliver to address those issues. The challenge then is to use four interrelated strategies to both deliver those benefits and to communicate to stakeholders that they are being effectively and efficiently delivered. The four strategies are real, associative, psychological, and competitive repositioning (These are defined and discussed later in this chapter). Periodically there needs to be a monitoring of the extent to which both stakeholders' existing perceptions and key community issues have changed, and adjustments made to the strategies accordingly.

What is Repositioning?

A *position* refers to the place that parks and recreation occupies in the minds of elected officials and the general public, relative to their perception of other services that are competing for public tax dollars. *Positioning* is the process of establishing and maintaining a distinctive and valued place in the minds of the general public and elected officials for parks and recreation relative to other services, while *repositioning* is a deliberate set of actions designed to change an agency's existing position. The originators of the positioning concept observe: "Positioning is thinking in reverse. Instead of starting with yourself, you start with the mind of the prospect. Instead of asking what you are, you ask what position you already own in the mind of the prospect" (Ries & Trout, 2001: 219).

The present position of park and recreation services that has existed in the minds of most stakeholders for several decades is that they are relatively discretionary, nonessential services. They are nice to have if they can be afforded after the important essential services have been funded. Their perceived lack of relevance among elected officials and taxpayers for addressing important issues is manifested in the absence of the field from the political platforms of people contesting elected offices at local, state, and federal levels.

Some of the services which recreation and park agencies offer will always be discretionary and nonessential. Their outcomes have social merit and a tradition of being offered in communities, but they will continue to struggle for budget allocations. For example, recreation centers, ice rinks, and senior centers may fall into this category in many communities in that their outcomes are likely to offer benefits which are confined to a relatively small group of individual users, rather than community-wide benefits.

The key to sustaining or increasing investments in park and recreation services is for them to be repositioned so they are perceived to contribute to alleviating problems which constitute the prevailing political concerns of policymakers who are responsible for allocating tax funds. Only when they are so positioned will park and recreation services be perceived positively as part of the solution to a jurisdiction's problems, rather than as peripheral services that are "nice to have" but which are a drain on a community's tax resources.

Positioning is about connecting an agency's services and their outcomes with a cause that is important to taxpayers and elected officials. Elected officials want to make improvements, so the agency's focus has to be upon what it can contribute to help elected officials accomplish their goals. One indicator of an agency's success in accomplishing this is to observe how central park and recreation services are in the narrative of elected officials. Are they frequently quoted or discussed as solutions to issues in "stump speeches"?

The "big idea" associated with repositioning is that funds are *invested in solutions* to a community's most pressing problems. The term "investing" suggests a positive, forward-looking agenda with a return on the investments. Elected officials usually have no mandate to fund programs; their mandate is to invest resources into solutions.

At this time, parks and recreation services typically are not an integral element in the repertoire of strategies used by government entities to address issues of concern, but the field has the potential to attain this status. The challenge for the next decade will be for the field to attain it. The key question is: "What outcomes can parks and recreation deliver more effectively and efficiently than other agencies or organizations which contribute to resolving important community problems?"

Recreation and park agencies will always have a need for substantial support from tax dollars. There is widespread adoption of the many non-tax supported funding and acquisition techniques that are available, but their use will not change the reality of the need for a core tax budget for much of what the field does. Money is not the field's problem because government entities have substantial budgets at their disposal. Justifying that park and recreation should receive a greater proportion of their budgets is the problem. The challenge for advocates is not to persuade elected officials to raise general fund taxes to enhance park and recreation services, because in most contexts that is an improbable scenario. Rather, the task is to raise the field's prioritization in the competition for existing tax funds. Thus, repositioning recognizes that the challenge is not economic *per se*; rather, it is political.

Members of legislative bodies who are responsible for an agency's budget decisions are elected on the basis of political platforms comprised of issues they perceive to be of concern to community residents. Thus, their mandate and moral obligation is to direct resources to address those issues. Unless elected officials are aroused by the agency's potential to do this, resources will not be forthcoming. If the outcomes from park and recreation services are not perceived to be addressing those issues, then agencies should expect their budgets to be reallocated to other services that do address them. This represents a logical and honorable action by elected officials.

In a private sector context, repositioning a product or service frequently receives urgent attention when sales are declining or stagnant, which is analogous to park and recreation agencies whose tax support is waning. The goal of repositioning is to create a long-term sustainable position(s) that will enable an agency to compete for public resources in the future with confidence. In many contexts, it is likely to be the only available inoculation against serious budgetary illness.

Other public agencies such as those responsible for education, police, fire, roads, tourism, economic development, and health, already have established positions. When residents are asked to describe the community benefits these agencies deliver, most are likely to be able to do it. Recognition of how their position(s) influences all (or a large majority of) residents' lives, results in these agencies receiving priority budgetary treatment. If parks and recreation fails to attain a similarly relevant position in its publics' minds, the field is likely to be marginalized.

Axioms of Positioning

There are four fundamental axioms of positioning: (1) formulating a position statement; (2) agencies do not position services, stakeholders do; (3) position is a relative concept rather than an absolute concept; and (4) focus. Each of these is discussed in this section.

Axiom #1: Formulate a Position Statement

There has to be consensus among residents, elected officials, and agency personnel on a position statement that articulates the agency's desired position. The selected desired position(s) will sit at the heart of the agency, driving its strategy and its direction. It represents the agency's core "truth" or purpose; its "personality"; its future *raison d'être*; how the agency is going to be identified in the public eye; and reflects its future desired reputation in the community. It should be expressed in a single line or slogan that is intended to define the agency's most salient outcomes in the minds of its stakeholders. Simplicity is the ultimate sophistication and an agency must have sufficient confidence in the position to articulate it clearly, emphatically, and without qualification. The position statement should:

- describe the problem/issue that will be ameliorated;
- be worded in terms of outcome benefits to community residents;
- be very simple, instantly understandable, and resonate with stakeholders;
- be supported by staff within the agency because they will be implementing it; and
- be honest in that its claims are scientifically sustainable and the agency has the capacity to deliver the promised benefits.

Identifying and establishing a strong desired position is the most important strategic decision that park and recreation managers make. It is likely to determine the agency's future. Once it has been made, all subsequent actions should be geared to implementing it. The goal should be to reinforce the desired position by integrating as many of the agency's actions as possible, so each component action fulfills a role in helping to establish the position in the minds of stakeholders. An established position that reflects responsiveness to a community's central concerns is key to an agency developing and nurturing a broader constituency, securing additional resources, guiding programmatic and facility priorities made by staff and stakeholders, and improving the morale of staff by raising their perceived status in the community.

Effective positioning requires an understanding of which benefits are important to stakeholders, and then a focus on delivering those benefits and communicating the effectiveness of their impacts to stakeholders. This is consistent with the political aphorism that the politics of seduction (via repositioning) are more effective than the politics of confrontation (constituent groups lobbying or harassing elected officials). It has been emphasized that, "You have to select the material that has the best chance of getting through...concentrate on the perceptions of the prospect" (Ries & Trout, 2001: 8).

A position statement is a long-term objective of what the agency is striving to become in about five or ten years time. It articulates what makes the agency's outcome contributions valuable and answers the questions, "What is our business?" and "What should it be?" (i.e., "What business do our residents and elected officials want us to be in?"). It should be sufficiently specific to give guidance to the agency in determining what strategies and actions need to be taken to achieve the desired position. It becomes a powerful organizing principle for the agency. In effect, it becomes the agency's brand. It has to provide a compelling vision of a desired position to which all stakeholders--residents, elected officials, and employees--can commit to and get excited about.

Generic position statements such as "The Benefits are Endless," "Discover the Benefits," "We are the fun experts," or "We provide the good things in life" may sound terrific, but they are not likely to be effective in repositioning parks and recreation because (1) the benefits and their role in alleviating a community's problems are not specified, and (2) if they were all specified, there would be no focus and this is needed to create the "mental fix" of what the contribution is in the minds of residents and elected officials. The Benefits are Endless, for example, could easily be adopted by those advocating transportation, education, health, or public works.

"The Benefits are Endless" and "Discover the Benefits" position statements were developed to promote the field nationally, which explains why they had to be so vague and generic. While the intent is laudatory, the rationale undergirding such an effort is muddled. It is widely recognized that in the U.S., "All politics are local." The primary concerns of communities are different. Thus, any position which the field attempts to launch nationally that is specific enough to be useful is likely to be irrelevant to a large number of communities.

Compare those generic position statements to the following, more specific position statements:

- Economic Prosperity
- Lifelong Learning
- Investing in Youth: Our Greatest Asset
- Step Up to Health: Healthy Communities Start in Parks
- Healthy by Nature
- Greener, Cleaner, Safer, Stronger
- Healthy Lifestyles, Liveable Communities: It Starts in Parks

Consider the position established by the State of Victoria parks agency in Australia "Healthy Parks, Healthy People." Their position statement is described in Figure 6.2. It clearly communicates and connects two principal health themes: environmental health and residents' physical and mental health. The message is obvious. The position statement embraces a variety of constituencies who all can identify with the slogan and say "yes, that's me" (e.g., dog owners, joggers/walkers, biophiliacs and advocates of stress relief, tree and environmental protection advocates, those concerned with air and water quality, community garden supporters).

The position statement is used on all Parks Victoria literature, a sample of which is shown in Figures 6.3a and 6.3b. The position statement is a cognitive

"Healthy Parks, Healthy People" is the position statement developed by Parks Victoria in Australia. The state park agency's starting point was: "A sustainable future for Parks Victoria is dependent on the organization's relevance to community needs and expectations." The position statement's intent was to establish a link between a healthy park system and a healthy community, and by doing so heighten people's sense of the value of parks. The position communicates two principal health themes:

- The role of Parks Victoria in keeping the environment healthy by addressing such core public concerns as enhancing air quality, enhancing water quality, and alleviating flooding.
- The physical and mental health benefits accuring to state residents using the parks.

To strengthen the position, the agency's "associative strategy" has resulted in partnerships with respected health organizations in the state including:

- Royal Australian College of General Practitioners
- Asthma Victoria
- Arthritis Victoria
- National Heart Foundation

The endorsement, active involvement, and cooperation of these organizations have enhanced the health linkage in people's minds. The "Healthy Parks, Healthy People" position appears on all the agency's literature, notepaper, signs, vehicles, etc.

Source: John Senior and Mardie Townsend (2004). "Healthy Parks, Healthy People" and other social capital initiatives of Parks Victoria, Australia. In the Urban Imperative, ed., Ted Trzyna. California Institute of Public Affairs, Sacramento, California.

Figure 6.2 The Parks Victoria position statement

Figure 6.3a Parks Victoria literature featuring its position statement

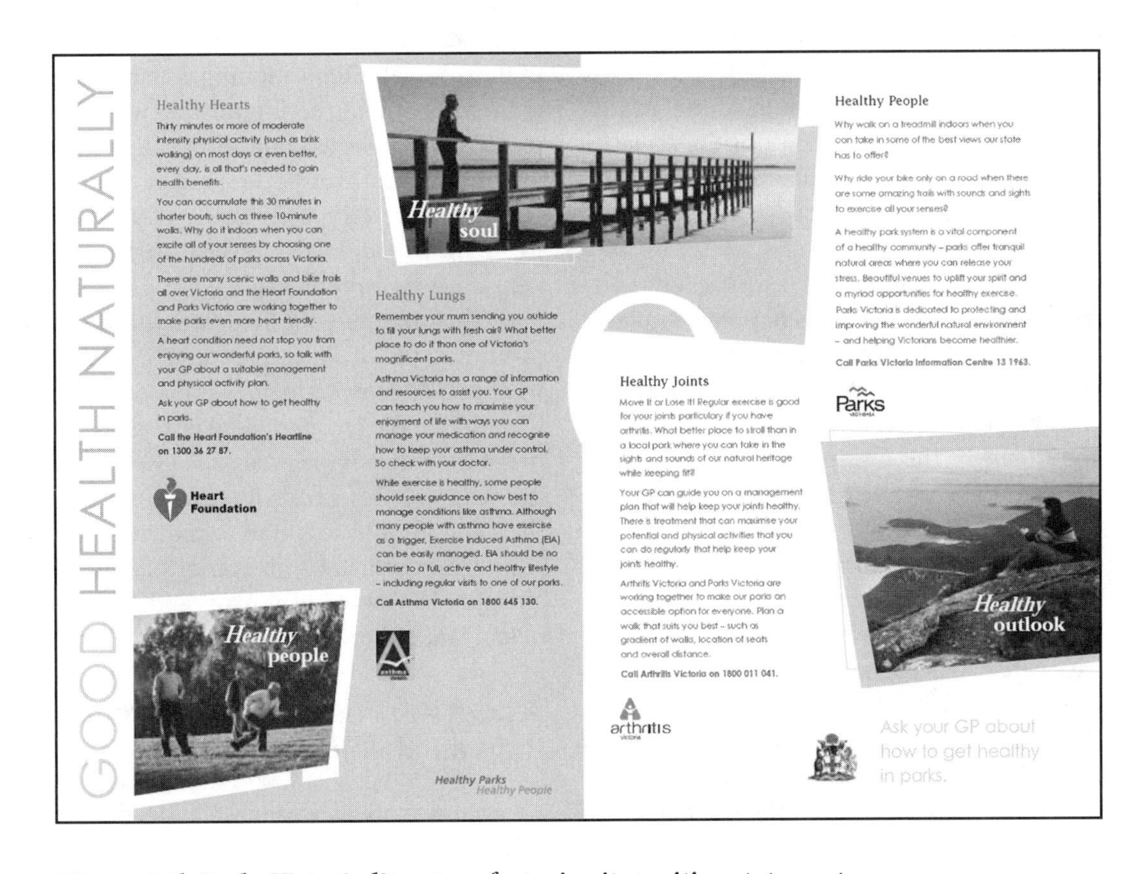

Figure 6.3b Parks Victoria literature featuring its position statement

message which relies on verbal logic to illustrate how an agency's outcomes are addressing a community issue. However, the cognitive message is reinforced if it is complemented by visual images, such as those shown in Figures 6.3a and 6.3b, which introduce emotions and feelings associated with the position. An emotional connection is stronger than a cognitive connection. This is why, for example, benefits relating to clean water and clean air resonate so effectively.

There are multiple community issues with which parks and recreation could align. However, even if elected officials care about and are impressed by park and recreation's potential outcomes to address, for example, six of them, they won't prioritize budget decisions based on all six. Hence, the challenge is to identify those benefits which resonate as being *determinate* in a community, i.e., those which determine elected officials' and residents' decisions when prioritizing public expenditures. The selected positions should be the optimum "selling ideas" for motivating residents and elected officials to allocate resources to parks and recreation.

In addition to aligning with determinate community issues, an agency has to be confident it can develop the capacity to deliver the benefits it promises, and that the benefits resonate and connect with stakeholders. It is futile to waste time and energy developing a position when the agency cannot realistically deliver those outcomes to the community.

Managers should be realistic from the outset as to what can and cannot be changed. If a position is superficial and not reasonable or credible in the eyes of employees or stakeholders, it will not survive and will adversely impact the agency. To test the robustness of a potential position statement before it is officially adopted, it may be prudent to invite agency staff to play the role of taxpayers and elected officials who are skeptical and cynical about claims implied by the position, by attacking its vulnerabilities, identifying weaknesses, and trying to ridicule it. This may provide insights into how to strengthen it and enable the agency to develop thoughtful rebuttals to future skeptics.

The average mind is likely to reject benefits and positions with which it is not familiar or which are counter-intuitive. Thus, it is often obvious, or long-standing, beliefs that resonate with stakeholders. If a selected position leads some to exclaim, "Why didn't we think of that sooner?" or "It is obvious," then it is likely to connect with stakeholders and be a viable position. In such cases, since they already believe in it, the challenge is to reinforce those dormant beliefs. This is much easier than having to establish a belief to which stakeholders do not have any positive predisposition.

Many community benefits are outcomes that have long been accepted. Indeed, some of them were the basis for communities investing in park and recreation services in past decades. Resurrecting some of these in support of a new position adds the powerful force of precedent when establishing the position. "Look what people of vision achieved in the past. What will your legacy be to future generations? Will it match the legacy we have been bequeathed by previous generations?" These are powerful enhancers which are likely to accelerate the timetable needed to reposition an agency.

Axiom #2: Agencies do not position services, stakeholders do

This axiom is consistent with the marketing aphorism, "To sell Jack Jones what Jack Jones buys, you have to see Jack Jones through Jack Jones' eyes." The agency cannot develop its position on its own terms, it has to construct it on its stakeholders' terms. Positions are not determined by the benefits or image that an agency seeks to convey, but rather by how these outcomes are perceived in the minds of its stakeholders. In the terms of one of the field's leaders it is "less important how we define ourselves and more important we begin allowing ourselves to be defined or redefined by the *community's* expectations of why we exist" (Jarvi, 1993: 62). [italics in the original]. Repositioning is about parks and recreation reconnecting their outcomes with the priorities of residents and elected officials. It means becoming "bilingual," which involves thinking, speaking, and dealing with constituents' perceptions, and using *their* language to tell the agency's story. It means asking, "How can we help solve your problems?"

The authors who first introduced the concept of positioning in the late 1970s stated, "Positioning is not what you do to a product. Positioning is what you do to the mind of the prospect. That is, you position the product in the mind of the prospect" (Ries & Trout, 2001: 3). This axiom follows from a realization that people make their decisions based on their individual perceptions of reality, rather than on an agency's definition of that reality. It means looking at parks and recreation from the outside in, rather than from the inside out.

Axiom #3: Positioning is a relative rather than an absolute concept

An agency is not viewed in isolation, but rather it is perceived within a framework that contains competitors. This comparative framework is the key difference between the concepts of image and positioning.

Most park and recreation agencies have a positive image in their communities. Surveys invariably report an overwhelming percentage of residents as being "satisfied" or "very satisfied" with an agency's performance. However, such responses for the most part do not reflect a high level of affection, care for, or identification with the agency's services; rather they reflect a lack of dissatisfaction. Many residents do not use the services and are indifferent to them. It is only when something is conspicuously bad that negative satisfaction rankings are likely to emerge.

A strong positive image is a necessary, but not a sufficient condition, for having a strong position. Even if high image or satisfaction scores genuinely reflect widespread emotional attachment and commitment to parks and recreation, it is still unlikely this would suffice to attract resources. This is because image rankings say nothing about how *important* the agency's services are to residents in the community vis-à-vis other services. Relative importance reflects an agency's position. Image measures evaluate an agency in isolation without the context or comparative framework necessary to relate the importance and performance of its outcomes to those of other agencies with which it is competing for funds. Thinking in terms of position rather than image is more useful, because it embraces comparison with competitors. It compares elected officials' and taxpayers' perceptions of the park and recreation agency's outcomes with those they hold of other public services in which they may invest.

This comparative framework may be conceptualized as a ladder such as that shown in Figure 6-4. (The arrows marked "Competitive Repositioning" and "Real, Associative and Psychological Repositioning" are discussed later in the chapter). The connotations associated with the ladder analogy indicate that the term "positioning" is a *double entendre,* meaning both a niche in a person's mind that reflects his or her perceptions of a service *and* its ranking vis-à-vis other public services. The other public services with which parks and recreation is in competition are represented on each rung of the ladder.

Their positions shown in Figure 6.4 reflect the aggregate annual public expenditures on each of them by local jurisdictions in the U.S. showing, for example, that education receives the largest investment of public funds while libraries receive the smallest. Those services shown above the vertical serrated line in Figure 6.4 are widely perceived to be "core" services, while those below it often are perceived to be relatively "discretionary."

When asked why he robbed banks for a living, the legendary bank robber Willie Sutton replied, "That's where the money is." The challenge for park and recreation advocates is to identify where the money is in their communities and then to align their services and outcomes with the issues which that money is intended

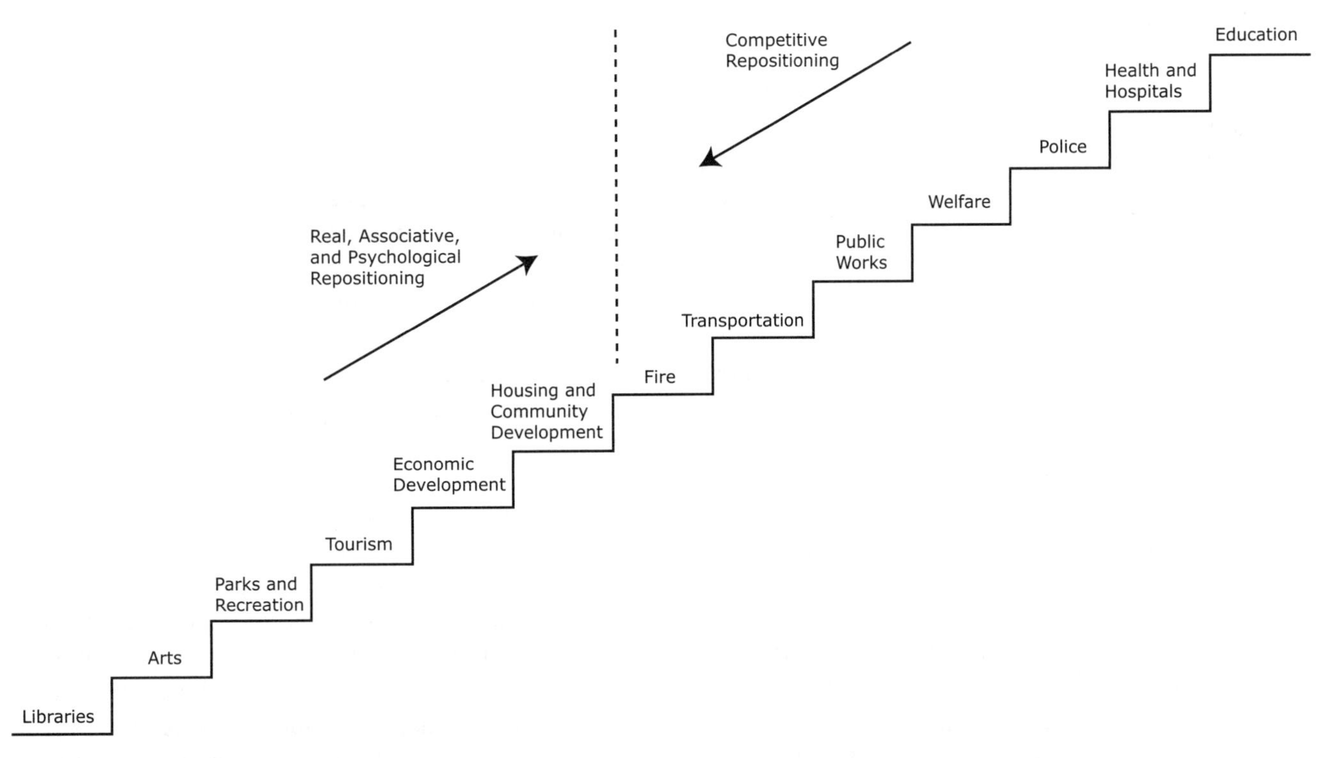

Figure 6.4 Residents' perceptions of the relative importance of alternate public services in local jurisdictions in the U.S.

to address. The exhibit suggests that at local government level the largest potential increases in park and recreation budgets are likely to come from addressing education, health, and crime issues. Figure 6.4 assumes that the aggregate expenditure rankings reflect the public's perceptions of the relative priority of these services but, obviously, this will vary among jurisdictions. An objective way for an agency to identify its contemporary position on the ladder is to check changes in the level of tax support it has received in the past five years vis-à-vis the community's other public service departments.

Focusing on positioning rather than image moves the field beyond seeking resources based on exhorting the "wonderfulness" of parks and recreation, and forces advocates to address such questions as "What is the case for allocating resources to parks and recreation rather than putting more police officers on the streets, or providing more temporary residences for the homeless?"

Parks and recreation differs from most of the public services in Figure 6.4 in that their output is tangible and highly visible. People cannot touch, feel, smell, see, or hear many of the outputs associated with such services as education, health, police, welfare, but these senses are exposed to parks, urban forestry, and public landscaping everyday. These services are a city's "canary in the coal mine." They are barometers that convey a visible impression of the city's economic and social health and viability. They are its signatures from which generalizable inferences are drawn. If the city's green infrastructure is "tired," dilapidated, dispirited, and run-down, then the inference is likely to be that these adjectives characterize the whole city or neighborhood. In contrast, if these amenities are beautiful, captivating, and vibrant, it is likely that many will express their impressions of the city in these terms. In short, parks have the potential to be a city's "wow" factor!

Axiom #4: Focus

Focus has two manifestations: (1) the number of positions sought should be small; and (2) communications describing them should be succinct and persistent. The goal is to ensure that stakeholders have a "mental fix" on the business the agency is in and how its outcomes contribute to accomplishing priority community goals.

The first manifestation of focus is that *only a small number of positions should be contemplated*--at the most three, and preferably one or two. It is tempting to adopt multiple positions because parks and recreation services have the potential to alleviate many different types of community problems. It may be frustrating to ignore some of these potential opportunities, but if many positions are adopted it is likely that the agency's message will be perceived as overpromising, unbelievable, and having connotations of hucksterism. Further, diversity and expansion lead to confusion, so multiple positions would result in parks and recreation retaining its existing fuzzy, nebulous, amorphous status, rather than attaining the distinctive position which it seeks. The key is not to tell the entire story, but rather to focus on one or two key positions and drive them into stakeholders' minds.

Those who are experienced in establishing positions for products and services in the private sector frequently recommend that only a single position should be selected. However, the wide and eclectic array of services and outcomes that park and recreation agencies can potentially deliver suggest there is scope to develop more than one position. In some respects, park and recreation agencies are analogous to companies which adopt independent positions for each of their products, rather than a single position for all a company's offerings. A single position, such as enhancing economic development, may not resonate with all residents, nor may it be possible for some of an agency's services to align with it (for example, those concerned with youth development). Selecting more than one position is, in essence, a segmentation approach. Indeed, positioning shares the microeconomic roots of segmentation in that after ascertaining the issues that are important in a community, an agency has to select which of them to focus upon.

The second manifestation of focus after a small number of positions have been selected is to *communicate them with messages that are consistent, persistent, and tightly focused*. The major benefits or associations must be repeatedly emphasized and reiterated so they become salient in the minds of elected officials and residents. They are only likely to grasp the headlines (i.e., the essence of the position, not the details). This is because in order to manage the cacophony of information to which they are exposed, individuals limit their intake to the minimum they need to get by. Hence, they tend to know a small amount about many things, but they don't know much about anything. This applies to the outcomes of a park and recreation agency equally as well as it does to those of any other public agency, private organization, or commercial business.

To residents, perceptions are truth. Their perceptions may not be correct, especially those of nonusers who have little contact with a park and recreation agency, but it is what they know and they have no reason to make an effort to know more. Thus, most taxpayers are unlikely to pay much attention to the details, subtleties, and complexities of a park and recreation agency's position. In the age of the sound bite, focus is everything. The message has to be pervasive. The best an agency can hope for is that an occasional piece of information may penetrate to reinforce or amend residents' existing perceptions. Hence, the value of consistency in maintaining a position over time and in communication messages cannot be overemphasized.

Without focusing and concentrating resources to support the selected position(s), repositioning will not succeed. Aligning with multiple issues and communicating multiple messages may be tempting, but such efforts are unlikely to be successful. The probable outcome of such diffusion is that no clear identity will be established, and that a fuzzy, confused position similar to that which currently exists will persist.

Time Frame for Repositioning

The need for focus stems from a recognition that a position reflects people's beliefs, attitudes, and value systems which are resistant to change. Thus, repositioning is difficult to accomplish because it involves shifting widely held, long established, entrenched perceptions about the field. This means it may take years before a strong position is solidified in stakeholders' minds. Repositioning is the proverbial supertanker which takes five miles to slow down and ten miles to turn in another direction. Patience and persistence are needed.

The long time horizon likely to be required to establish a new position in stakeholders' minds is also a function of the pragmatic difficulties confronting agencies in shifting to this position. The difficulties are of two types: resource reallocations and realigning staffing expertise.

The first type of difficulty recognizes the need for focusing implies that services and facilities which do not contribute to strengthening a selected position will be de-emphasized. In a private sector context, products or services can be concentrated on the most responsive and profitable target markets with minimal repercussions, so it is feasible to demarket or terminate services that don't fit the established position. In the short term, it is unlikely this strategy will be feasible for park and recreation agencies because they are required to consider the implications of their actions both on equity and on politically influential user groups, which means that repositioning actions must be careful not to preclude servicing certain citizen groups.

Thus, an agency cannot immediately abandon many of its current tasks and switch those resources to facilitate outcomes that strengthen its repositioning efforts. If this was done, there would probably be a loud outcry from those existing clienteles whose services would be retrenched. Such shifts can only be implemented over time. A "rule of thumb" adopted by some agencies is that it is practical to think in terms of moving approximately 20% of an agency's resources to support new strategic positions over a five year period.

A second internal difficulty confronting agencies when they reposition is the challenge of realigning employee expertise. For example, if an agency traditionally had a strong focus on youth development and has decided to reposition to align with economic development, a period of years will be needed to change the prevailing culture; reorganize its service offerings; and retrain or replace personnel so they have the skills, aptitude, and interest needed to attain the new position; and to plan the repositioning strategy.

A change of this nature induces anxiety within the organization. The "comfort zone" of an agency usually reflects a knowledge base of what it has done in the past. Future actions tend to incrementally build on what has gone before. A commitment to repositioning means surmounting the inertia associated with an entrenched logic and mind-set. This is likely to be a slow process accomplished only if a sense of urgency is engendered possibly by the threat of budget retrenchments. There will need to be substantial investment in educating employees as to what business the agency is getting into, how it is going to get there, and each person's role in accomplishing the new position.

Given these factors, agencies should think in terms of a ten-year, rather than a one-year, time horizon to accomplish repositioning. By way of comparison, this is probably the minimum time period for which stakeholders have held their existing position of park and recreation as a peripheral, discretionary service.

The Set of Repositioning Strategies

There are four strategies agencies can pursue to attain a revised position. They are summarized in Figure 6.5.

- *Real repositioning.* Development of new services or restructuring existing services so they better contribute to addressing the issue expressed in the desired position.
- *Associative repositioning.* Aligning with other organizations that already possess the desired position, and acquiring some of this position from the association.

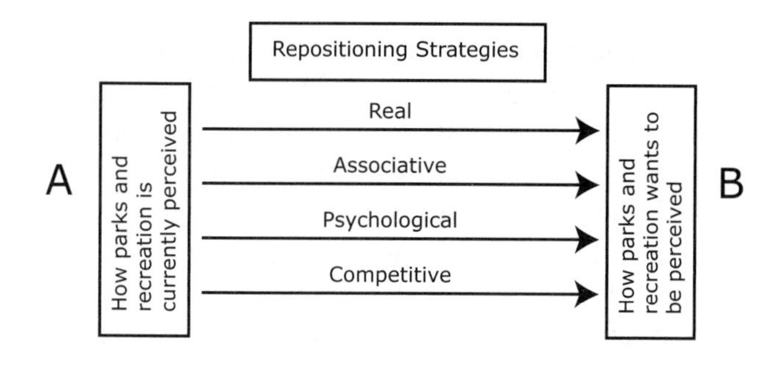

Figure 6.5 How to get from position A to position B

- *Psychological repositioning.* Changing stakeholders' beliefs about the outcomes which emanate from the services an agency offers, so they better align with the desired position.
- *Competitive repositioning.* Altering stakeholders' beliefs about what an agency's competitors do.

These four strategies are complementary, not mutually exclusive. To accomplish a revised position, all four of them should be considered and it is likely that some combination of them will be pursued simultaneously.

Real Repositioning

Real repositioning means an agency makes changes in the services that it offers. This requires starting with the desired position and identifying existing services that could be restructured or new services that could be developed which would contribute to accomplishing the position. Thus, if the position is "Enhancing Community Prosperity" or "Reducing Crime and Disorder Among Young People," then the real repositioning task is to offer a set of programs specifically designed to produce outcomes that will contribute to these goals.

The extent to which a proposed new service will contribute to accomplishing an agency's desired position should be the primary criterion in evaluating whether agency resources should be invested in it. Real services are the bedrock upon which all repositioning actions rest. The position must exemplify and amplify what is actually offered and not be a hollow fabrication. There must be substance so the communicated benefits are rooted in reality and the promised outcomes are delivered. To fabricate a false promise and pretend that a service delivers something that it doesn't simply defeats the goal of establishing credibility for the field among a wider spectrum of the community.

Sometimes there is a tendency to ignore real repositioning and to focus exclusively on psychological repositioning because the latter can be interpreted to mean only that existing services be communicated differently, which is much easier than changing the existing set of services being offered. However, such an approach is generally too limiting to be effective and invariably there needs to be some real repositioning.

Associative Repositioning

This strategy recognizes that by associating with organizations which have a firm, well-crystallized position in stakeholders' minds as leaders in addressing a given community issue, it may be possible to "transfer" that position to the agency. Associating with this established position, may provide an agency with an explicit or implicit frame of reference which can be used to frame its own contribution to an issue. It can serve as a bridging point whereby at some cognitive level stakeholders believe the agency also contributes to that issue. In essence, an agency is seeking to enhance the believability, trust, and credibility of its role in delivering a given benefit by acquiring some of the associative organization's established position in that context.

Figures 6.2 and 6.3 illustrated Parks Victoria's approach to repositioning. The credibility of their position statement, "Healthy Parks, Healthy People" was enhanced by partnering with respected health organizations in the state: Royal Australian College of General Practitioners, Asthma Victoria, Arthritis Victoria, and National Heart Foundation. The endorsement, active involvement, and cooperation of these organizations are likely to enhance the health contributions of parks in people's minds. The inference is that if they are prepared to endorse and partner with parks, then parks must be part of the solution to physical and mental health issues.

The following examples further illustrate associative repositioning:

- Alleviating juvenile crime was a primary community issue. Instead of developing its own set of programs to address this, the park and recreation agency contracted with the community's Boys and Girls Club to deliver programs in the city's recreation centers. The Club had a high profile in the community; its board was comprised of respected business, philanthropic, and civic leaders; and it was perceived to be effective in addressing this issue. Because the programs were funded by the park and recreation agency and took place in its facilities, it is likely that in many people's minds the agency was positioned as contributing to alleviating the problem.

- If economic prosperity is a primary community issue, then linking with the community tourism organization may help a park and recreation agency establish a position relating to this issue. This may be done by partnering with the tourism organization to create new events designed to attract outside visitors to stay in the jurisdiction for multiple days. Such linkages make pragmatic sense because the two organizations often have complementary assets. Tourism agencies typically have funds available for promotion, but rarely become involved in directly producing programs and services. Thus, for example, a parks and recreation agency may join with a tourism organization to jointly fund special-event coordinators who are responsible for organizing and soliciting sponsorship for special events in the community. In doing this, the tourism organization recognizes that park and recreation agencies have the expertise and a mandate to organize special events, but frequently lack the funds to launch and promote them.

This associative strategy is likely to be most effective when there is no obvious linkage between an agency's outcomes and its desired position in stakeholders' minds when the repositioning effort is launched. For example, if the desired position is "Contributes to Economic Development," the link between it and parks and recreation may not be intuitively apparent to many. Partnerships with the community's economic development or tourism agency may expedite establishment of the connection. If there is already a strong connection, then the goal of the associative strategy is to reinforce it.

In addition to associating directly with organizations, credibility and trust can be enhanced indirectly by associating with "best practice," "benchmark measures," or reference to scientific evidence relating to the outcomes being delivered. This indirect associative strategy offers an alternative approach for repositioning the impact of community benefits to stakeholders which can be used by the majority of park and recreation agencies that do not have the resources to develop their own sophisticated analysis.

Once a park and recreation agency commits to repositioning to address selected community issues, there will be a quick realization that these issues can only be resolved by working with others. Partnerships have become the foundation stones upon which park and recreation agencies build and develop their services. A holistic approach is inherent in addressing neighborhood rejuvenation, economic prosperity, lifelong learning, alleviating juvenile crime, or whatever other issue with which an agency seeks to align. The "joined-up thinking" this requires is likely to expedite repositioning because elected officials increasingly seek to encourage holistic solutions that transcend departmental boundaries.

Psychological Repositioning

This strategy is intended to alter stakeholders' beliefs about what an agency currently does. It has been suggested that park and recreation agencies have a labeling problem (Godbey, 1993) in that agencies are evaluated based on the means used (i.e., parks and recreation services), rather than on the outcomes that they deliver (i.e., the benefits espoused in their desired position). Psychological repositioning focuses on bringing the desired end outcomes to the forefront.

The methods for accomplishing psychological repositioning are summarized in Figure 6.6. The exhibit suggests that people's perceptions of an issue are molded by their personal past experiences and instincts, and by their exposure to the collective conventional wisdom of others. These two sources of information establish an individual's residual beliefs about parks and recreation. There are four potential intervention strategies that can be used to change those residual beliefs: provide scientific information which demonstrates the beliefs are ill-considered; offer testimonial evidence by individuals whose views are often from credible experts or opinion leaders in the field; offer evidence of value in benefit/cost terms which the individual has not previously considered; and change the nomenclature and semantic context used to frame the issue.

It was noted earlier in this chapter that residual beliefs are resistant to change and that repositioning

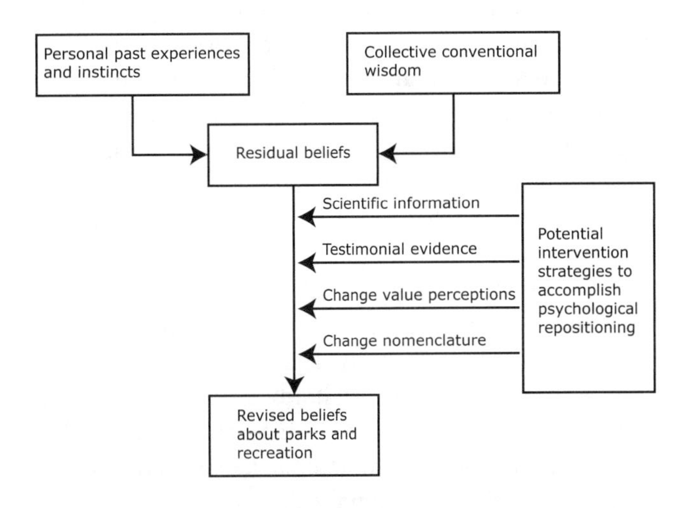

Figure 6.6 The process of psychological repositioning

them is likely to take a relatively long period of time. The effectiveness of these four strategies in changing residual beliefs will be a function of: (1) the susceptibility of individuals to be influenced by them, (2) the power of each strategy, and (3) how many of the four strategies can be implemented.

Scientific Evidence. The primary strategy for changing residual beliefs is scientific evidence which is sufficiently convincing to individuals that they are prepared to amend these entrenched beliefs. Accordingly, park and recreation agencies have demonstrated a willingness to engage in such evaluative activities as undertaking economic impact studies (Crompton, 1999), measuring the positive impact of parks on the property tax base (Crompton, 2004), assessing the impact of recreation programs on alleviating undesirable youth behavior (Witt & Crompton, 2002), calculating the economic value of trees in alleviating pollution (U.S. Forest Service, n.d.), and reducing energy costs (Heisler, 1986).

The credibility of psychological repositioning is dependent on this body of evaluation research. The effectiveness of these research findings is enhanced in communities where there is widespread general support for the field so the community is predisposed to be receptive to the findings.

In addition to changing residual beliefs, credible scientific evidence also serves to reassure stakeholders that the outcomes expressed in a position are not merely "spin," that is, twisted and misleading claims. This is why they have to be *measured and documented.* Even in situations where elected officials intuitively and emotionally believe in park and recreation's contributions, they need credible supportive data and evidence to protect them from political attacks by skeptics.

Testimonial Evidence. Repositioning is expedited if there is an emotional as well as a rational dimension to it. Elected officials and taxpayers respond to passion, excitement, and enthusiasm. They value commitment, intensity, and conviction. This emotional dimension emerges from testimonial evidence. This is different from scientific evidence in that it is anecdotal and not necessarily science based.

Testimonials may emanate from three sources. First, they may be offered by influential opinion leaders from within the community. Their influence may stem from a formal position they hold or from their widely respected reputation. But they may also be individuals who are passionate about a particular issue and the strength of their conviction is sufficient to influence the views of others.

A second source is leaders from other communities relating their experiences. These may be direct testimonials given in the community by those individuals, or they may be vicariously delivered by the media through news stories, interviews, etc. Testimony regarding the effectiveness of parks and recreation services elsewhere in addressing an issue may resonate with decision makers.

Independent experts are a third source of testimonials. They resemble expert witnesses in a court case in that their views are solicited based on perceived expertise and insight. Such consultants may, or may not, use good science in their testimony. Independent experts are valued because they are perceived to offer a knowledgeable and impartial perspective.

Change Value Perceptions. The third strategy for psychological repositioning is to change perceptions of value by using benefit/cost frameworks which the individual had not previously considered. By changing the context and conceptualizing the notion of value differently, it may then lead to the issue being perceived differently.

The framing in Figures 6.7, 6.8, 6.9, 6.10, and 6.11 illustrates ways of changing the context in which budget information is presented. It is intended to reduce perspectives of the cost of park and recreation services and, thus, to enhance the position that they are good value for money.

Figure 6.7 uses the frameworks of "net budget," "per resident investment," and "per week" to change value perceptions. The data used in the exhibit to calculate the ratio of capital, operating and self-generated revenues, and the net per resident investment are average proportions for local park and recreation agencies in the U.S. (Crompton & Kaczynski, 2003). The term *net budget* focuses on the primary concern of elected officials in that it refers to the proportion of the budget subsidized by local taxpayers and omits self-generated revenue, which typically approximates one-third of an

Total annual budget for parks and recreation	$20.989 million
Capital budget	5.872
Operating budget	15.117
Self-generated revenue	5.142
Annual **net** operating budget	9.975 million
Number of residents in the community	281.382
Net **per resident** investment	$35.45
OR **68 cents per week**	

Figure 6.7 Psychologically repositioning the budget by changing the perceived cost

agency's operating budget (Crompton & Kaczynski, 2003). A net operating budget of $9.975 million may be perceived as being substantially smaller than a budget of $20.989 million. However, once the principle of net budget has been successfully positioned as the central budget issue, the real payoff may be in future self-generated revenue being disregarded in the political decision calculus. Thus, if revenue in the following year increases by $1 million and the budget request is for $21.989 million, the agency director is able to declare the department "is seeking no increase in the net budget."

The intent of reframing the budget in terms of *per resident* investment and *per week* is to position the expenditure as a nominal, relatively inconsequential amount. Thus, it is anticipated that a position of "68 cents per resident, per week" will be perceived more favorably than a budget of $20.989 million per year.

The per capita framework is used again in Figure 6.8, but it is augmented with a framework that compares the costs and benefits of the park district with those of a local club. In this illustration, all the opportunities created by the $2.00 per week investment are listed. Most residents will not be aware of many of the opportunities listed. Their perception of value for money presumably is based on their existing knowledge of available opportunities. Expanding this awareness set may change the context in which they make judgments on value for money and lead to a more favorable position.

Any local club is unlikely to have the capacity to offer more than 10 percent (for example) of the opportunities listed by the park district in Figure 6.8, but it is

What would you do if for less than $2.00 per week you could get a membership to a local club which makes available to its members the following recreation facilities and activities?

- Over 300 acres of well-designed open space for both organized and spontaneous recreational pursuits
- Two Olympic size swimming facilities, including bathhouse, sundeck areas, and snack areas
- 24 outdoor tennis courts, located throughout the community. For your convenience, 12 courts are supervised and operated on a reservation system with the remaining 12 courts available on the rack-up system.
- An 18-hole championship golf course, driving range, putting green, and pro shop
- A recreation center housing recreation activities in art, performing arts, crafts, and a variety of programs for preschoolers through adults
- A Senior Citizens Center designed to meet the specialized leisure and social needs for those 55 years and older
- Sports Center including 2 major indoor artificial ice surfaces, pro shop, dressing areas, snack shops, instructional staff, and recreation programs for the entire family
- Opportunity to participate in over 200 recreation figure skating lessons, hockey, speed skating, and over 170 recreation programs operated under professional leadership
- A variety of playground equipment available to youngsters located in neighborhood parks through out the community
- Lighted softball, baseball, football, and soccer fields, 23 unlighted baseball/softball diamonds, 14 soccer fields, and 3 football fields for organized play
- A 30-acre lake available for fishing, paddle craft, sailboats, and canoes
- Two natural ice rinks, 2 sled hills, and two natural outdoor hockey rinks available for free use
- 15 miles of hike and bike trails
- 12 outdoor basketball courts

And what if this membership would increase the value and marketability of your home? And what if the $2.00 paid in membership fees was deductible from your federal income tax?

WOULD YOU JOIN?

The Park District offers you all of this and much more for the dollars you invest in it.

Figure 6.8 A high return on your park district tax dollar investment

The median home value in the community:	$150,000
Construction cost of the natatorium:	$2 million
Annual property tax payment by an average homeowner:	$12
Annual operation and maintenance cost:	$100,000
Annual property tax payment by an average homeowner:	$6
Total annual property tax payment by an average homeowner:	$18
which is **$1.50 per month**	

In most years, there are heartbreaking stories in the local news media of children from this community who have drowned in area lakes. An agreement with the ISD means that every fourth grader in the community will be taught to swim, so lives will be saved.

Invest $1.50 a month and save a child's life!

Figure 6.9 Psychologically repositioning a bond proposal for a new natatorium

likely to be much more expensive than $2.00 per week. Again, framing the agency's offerings in this context is likely to result in a more favorable position.

The framework in Figure 6.9 uses "annual investment for an average homeowner" and an affective appeal aimed at the emotions (but based on reality) to position the cost of a new natatorium to be a sound community investment. It seems likely that there will be a better community response when the proposal is positioned as "Invest $1.50 a month and save a child's life," than if it is baldly presented as a request to support a new natatorium at a capital cost of $2 million and an annual operating subsidy of $100,000.

There is a substantial body of scientific evidence suggesting that people are more likely to respond positively to communications which are framed to emphasize that an investment will prevent loss and a lowering of existing service expectations than those suggesting that the investment will create additional increments of benefits (Tverskey & Kahneman, 1981; Rothman & Salovey, 1997). Thus, in addition to using per capita and net budget, Figure 6.10 frames the funding issue in terms of the budget losses sustained by the Texas state parks system from 1990 to 2002 and the state's low ranking among all the other states. The data are intended to communicate the message that Texas state parks are grossly underfunded, and the associated implication that they are being allowed to deteriorate. Data reporting expenditures on parks and recreation, and all other public services, by all local and state governmental jurisdictions in the U.S. are published annually by the Census Bureau, so the types of contexts or frameworks exemplified in Figure 6.10 are relatively easy for park and recreation agencies to construct (U.S. Census Bureau, 2007).

- Texans' per capita annual investment in state parks was $2.43, which ranked Texas 49th among the 50 states. The comparative figures for Texas' neighbors were Arkansas $11.00, Louisiana $3.40, New Mexico $10.59, and Oklahoma $11.89.
- In 1990, Texas investment in state parks was 0.31% of the state's total budget; in 2002 it was 0.08%. The percentage declined every year from 1990 to 2002.
- If the 0.31% share of the budget in FY 1990 had been retained in FY 2002, then the state's investment in parks and recreation would have been $217.85 million, rather than its actual budget of $53.2 million.
- In FY 2002, Texas state parks generated $32.6 million from their operations. This represented 61.25% of total operating expenses and ranked Texas #6 among all states on this ratio.
- If the self-generating revenue is deducted from the total operating expenses then the state's net investment in operating its park and recreation facilities is 0.03% (three hundredths of one percent) of the state's total annual budget and less than $1 per state resident per year.

Figure 6.10 Seeking enhanced financial support for Texas State Parks by psychological repositioning

Parks 2001 was a coalition of parks advocates from over 700 community organizations and groups in New York City whose goal was to arrest the long-term and ongoing decline in the budget of the city's Department of Parks and Recreation (DPR). The DPR budget had declined from 0.8% to 0.4% of the city's budget between 1986 and 2000. Its status vis-à-vis the budgets of other city departments over the past three decades is shown in Figure 6.11. Parks 2001's goal was for DPR to receive 1% of the city's budget.

Instead of focusing on the budget numbers per se, which are arcane and boring to most people, the parks' losses were framed in terms of specific consequences emanating from the reduced budget. A series of graphics, each accompanied by an arresting statistic, was developed and they were effective in psychologically repositioning parks as a pressing issue in the public's mind. Samples of these graphics are shown in Figure 6.12.

Almost every print and broadcast medium in New York City provided editorial support for the 1% campaign. It culminated in the months preceding city elections with all city council and mayoral candidates being asked in public forums to sign a written pledge which asked "If elected would you work to commit 1% of the city's annual budget to maintaining city parks?" Their

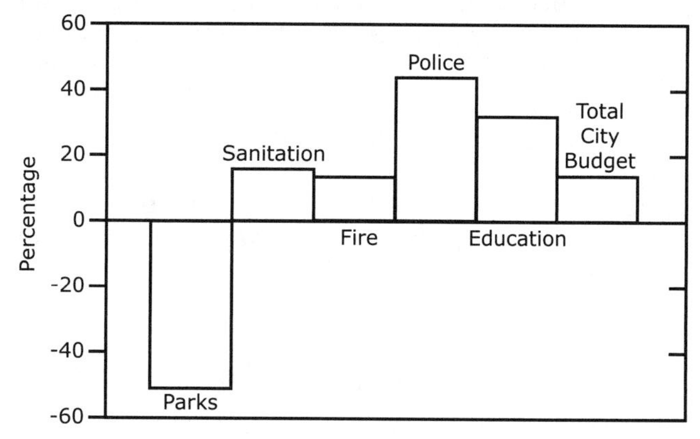

Figure 6.11 Decline in the NYC parks and recreation budget relative to budget changes in other departments

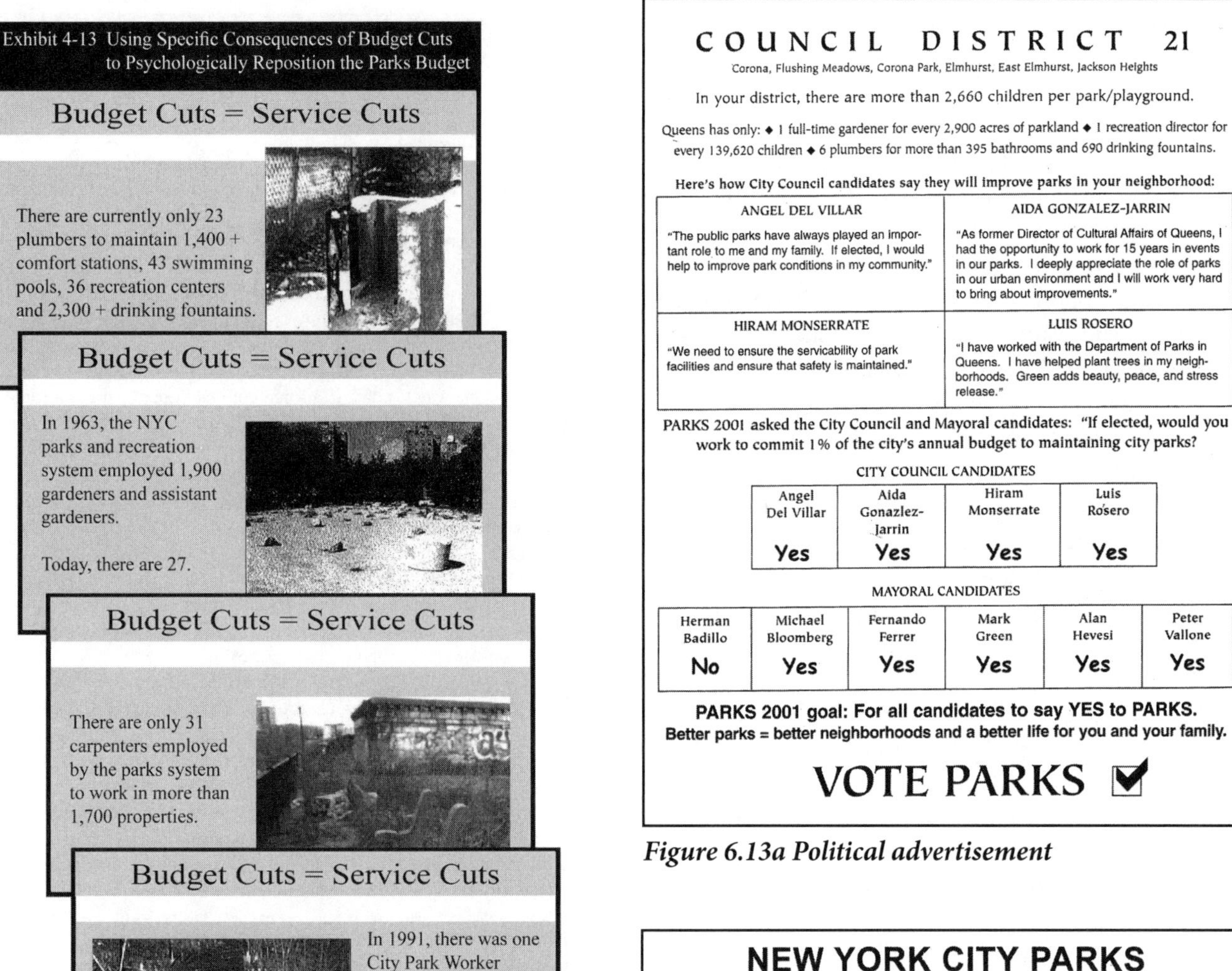

Figure 6.12 Using specific consequences of budget cuts to psychologically reposition the parks budget

COUNCIL DISTRICT 21

Corona, Flushing Meadows, Corona Park, Elmhurst, East Elmhurst, Jackson Heights

In your district, there are more than 2,660 children per park/playground.

Queens has only: ◆ 1 full-time gardener for every 2,900 acres of parkland ◆ 1 recreation director for every 139,620 children ◆ 6 plumbers for more than 395 bathrooms and 690 drinking fountains.

Here's how City Council candidates say they will improve parks in your neighborhood:

ANGEL DEL VILLAR	AIDA GONZALEZ-JARRIN
"The public parks have always played an important role to me and my family. If elected, I would help to improve park conditions in my community."	"As former Director of Cultural Affairs of Queens, I had the opportunity to work for 15 years in events in our parks. I deeply appreciate the role of parks in our urban environment and I will work very hard to bring about improvements."
HIRAM MONSERRATE	**LUIS ROSERO**
"We need to ensure the servicability of park facilities and ensure that safety is maintained."	"I have worked with the Department of Parks in Queens. I have helped plant trees in my neighborhoods. Green adds beauty, peace, and stress release."

PARKS 2001 asked the City Council and Mayoral candidates: "If elected, would you work to commit 1% of the city's annual budget to maintaining city parks?

CITY COUNCIL CANDIDATES

Angel Del Villar	Aida Gonazlez-Jarrin	Hiram Monserrate	Luis Rosero
Yes	Yes	Yes	Yes

MAYORAL CANDIDATES

Herman Badillo	Michael Bloomberg	Fernando Ferrer	Mark Green	Alan Hevesi	Peter Vallone
No	Yes	Yes	Yes	Yes	Yes

PARKS 2001 goal: For all candidates to say YES to PARKS.
Better parks = better neighborhoods and a better life for you and your family.

VOTE PARKS ☑

Figure 6.13a Political advertisement

responses were then widely disseminated by Parks 2001. Samples of the political advertisements produced are shown in Figures 6.13a and 6.13b.

Change Nomenclature

A fourth psychological repositioning strategy which may effectively complement the strategies of using scientific evidence to document the benefits, soliciting testimonial evidence, and changing perceptions of value is to change stakeholders' contexts and, hence, their perceptions by using different terminology and nomenclature. This strategy recognizes that names are important because they are the hooks that position an idea in

NEW YORK CITY PARKS ARE IN CRISIS

- NYC ranks 21st out of the largest 25 U.S. cities in terms of parks spending;
- Maintenance budget cut by 40% over the last 15 years;
- Staff cut by 70% over the last 30 years;

Deplorable conditions! Unacceptable for our children and families!

Say NO to locked bathrooms, dusty ballfields, broken water fountains and benches.

PARKS 2001 wants 1% of NYC's budget to maintain our parks.

Say YES to 1%. Say YES to PARKS.

PARKS 2001 Endorsed By:

The New York Times, Daily News, Queens Tribune, Bronx Times, Riverdale Press and *Staten Island Advance*;

Over 1 million gardeners, runners, little leaguers, businesspeople, parents, teachers, bird-watchers;

Over 1,000 community, civic and environmental organizations;

and 85% of all candidates for City Council.

Tell your City Council candidates that you want cleaner, safer and better parks in your neighborhood.

Tell them to pledge 1%.

A citywide campaign to restore, reform and revitalize parks and recreation services in New York City
Visit www.parks2001.org or call 212-490-0010 to learn what the candidates will do for your neighborhood parks.

Figure 6.13b Political advertisement

stakeholders' minds. The originators of the positioning concept stated:

> The name is the hook that hangs the brand on the product ladder in the prospects' minds...the single most important marketing decision you can make is what to name the product. Shakespeare was wrong. A rose by any other name would not smell as sweet. Not only do you see what you want to see, you also smell what you want to smell...And Hog Island in the Caribbean was going nowhere until they changed its name to Paradise Island (Ries & Trout, 2001: 66).

For example, a key rule when seeking the support of business groups for park issues is to use their language. Examples include:

- Refer to "investments" in park and recreation amenities, not "tax subsidy."
- Not "greenways" or "trails", but "dual purpose (or "green") infrastructure." The implications of using the term "green infrastructure" are elaborated upon in Figure 6.14.
- Refer to "amenities that will be attractive to knowledge workers," not "park and recreation facilities."
- Not encouraging "natural areas," but "low maintenance areas."
- Not "environmentalism," but "creating a sustainable economy," so the message resonates with the need to have a viable economy.

When you fish, you use the bait that the fish are biting on. The business mind is familiar and comfortable with phrases such as investment, infrastructure, knowledge worker amenities, and low maintenance. Park and recreation advocates have to fit their case within that existing schemata to be effective in repositioning.

One of the prevention programs targeted at at-risk-youth in the early 1990s was "Midnight Basketball" which was designed to keep youth off the streets. Most of these programs incorporated an educational/tutorial component as well as basketball games scheduled on weekend evenings. However, the position created by the name was unfortunate since it implied that recreation agencies were acting irresponsibly in encouraging youth to stay up and be out of the home so late. This resulted in some political criticism from uninformed elected officials. This probably could have been avoided if they had been termed "Youth Enrichment" programs, in recognition of their educational component.

The author is in the Department of Recreation, Park, and Tourism Sciences at Texas A&M University (RPTS). Alternate "humorous" interpretations of the

Exhibit 4-15 The Use of "Green Infrastructure" in Psychological Positioning

Some people think of parks and open space as an amenity, something nice to have but cannot be afforded in difficult economic times. However, often the same people understand that infrastructure is a necessity, not an amenity (i.e., something that communities must have, not just something that is nice to have). They view infrastructure as a primary public investment, not something they pay for with leftover money. Likewise, public officials understand that infrastructure must be constantly upgraded and maintained. It is not something they just buy and forget. Finally, they all know that infrastructure must be developed as a system, not as isolated parts.

One way to change this perception of open space as an amenity is to change the nomenclature. *Webster's New World Dictionary* defines infrastructure as "the substructure or underlying foundation, especially the basic installations or facilities upon which the continuance and growth of a community depends." People understand the need to invest in infrastructure - even in an era of deficits. Next to national defense, funding for roads, bridges, sewers, airports, and other forms of capital infrastructure are always at the top of the list. However, just as we must carefully plan for and invest in our capital infrastructure, so too must we invest in our environmental or green infrastructure.

Green infrastructure is the ecological framework needed for environmental, social, and economic sustainability. It is our nation's natural life support system. Green infrastructure is an interconnected network of green space that conserves natural ecosystem values and functions and provides a wide array of benefits to people, wildlife, and communities. For example, green infrastructure reduces a community's susceptibility to floods, fires, and other natural disasters. Documenting these public benefits is a key step toward securing adequate funding.

Words matter. A shift in nomenclature from talking about open space to talking about green infrastructure will help communities understand that green space is a basic necessity that should be planned and developed as an integrated system. A popular bumper sticker says "If you think education is expensive, try ignorance." Well, if you think green space is expensive, just imagine the future costs for clean air, clean water, and healthy natural systems if we don't invest in green infrastructure today.

Source: Edward McMahon, vice president for land use programs at The Conservation Fund. *Common Ground* 14(i) 2003, p. 2.

Figure 6.14 The use of "Green Infrastructure" in psychological positioning

RPTS acronym by uninformed students in other fields (e.g., rather play/party than study) become tiresome, irritating, and psychologically demoralizing to our own students. Indeed, the labeling problem occasionally extends to some uninformed faculty colleagues from other departments who assume that this is a "fun and games" department which attracts students who are academically weak. They are skeptical that a major research-oriented land grant university should be indulging such trivial pursuits. All members of the department attempt to address this directly by pointing out that recreation addresses youth and community development; parks is concerned with conservation and ecodiversity; while tourism is involved with sustainable economic develop-

Exhibit 4-16 Repositioning an Athletic Complex by Framing It to Fit with an Existing Successful Position

The city had plenty of money for economic development, but the council could not be persuaded to commit $15 million for a 150-acre youth athletic field complex for which there was a clearly demonstrated need. The proposed site was adjacent to two major highways and would be well suited for tournaments in such sports as soccer, rugby, baseball, softball, tennis, and lacrosse. Hence, after an initial rejection by the council, the project's supporters regrouped and repositioned the project as an "outdoor special-events center." This terminology resonated with the council and taxpayers because the city had an existing indoor special-events center, which was recognized widely to be a good investment in economic development because of the nonresident visitors it attracted.

Representatives of the hotel-motel association, restaurant association, convention and visitors bureau, and chamber of commerce came to a council meeting to lobby for the athletic complex because its supporters pointed out that the city could hold tournaments bringing 300 to 1000 people to the community each weekend from out of town. Once it was repositioned into this economic development context and viewed as an outdoor special-events center, the council approved resources to acquire the site and initiate development of the athletic field complex.

Figure 6.15 Repositioning an athletic complex by framing it to fit with an existing successful position

ment. It becomes apparent to uninformed colleagues that a department that deals with these sets of issues is doing important work, and repositions it in their minds.

Those responsible for providing resources don't "get it" the way that recreation and park advocates "get it." They don't think in the social merit outcomes frame of reference which frequently reflects the values system of those in parks and recreation, rather they think exclusively in their frame of reference which invariably is economic. To acquire resources the field has to adapt to their frame of reference; they are unlikely to adapt to the park and recreation advocates' frame of reference.

Figure 6.15 demonstrates the key role of nomenclature in the development of a large 150 acre complex of youth athletic fields. The council's primary concern was economic development. Given this frame of reference, "youth soccer fields" were not an important priority in their minds but "outdoor special events center" resonated well with that issue. Thus, the project came to fruition only when it was presented using terminology that made it compatible with an existing economic development framework. A similar example illustrating the role of names in psychological repositioning occurred in St. Charles Parish, near New Orleans:

> The recreation and parks department had long identified the need for a new gym, but no funds were available for such a discretionary activity. The agency repositioned its request as a hurricane shelter, which was designed to accommodate three full-size basketball courts or serve as an indoor football arena. Since two hurricanes had hit the area in the previous year, the facility was funded.

Figure 6.16 summarizes the findings of research commissioned to identify words that established a positive position for conservation among the general public. These may be regarded as "rules" for communication. The researchers noted, "While there can certainly be unique circumstances, we found few exceptions to these broad rules in terms of geography or key demographic groups" (Fairbank et al., 2004: n.p.).

Competitive Repositioning

Whenever resources are allocated to one service rather than another, there is an opportunity cost associated with that decision. This cost consists of the benefits that would have accrued from investing those resources in alternative service options. Hence, in this context, other public agencies such as the police, health, transportation, or economic development departments (Figure 6.4) are viewed as competitors. Many of them have much larger budgets which dwarf those available to parks and recreation, and successful repositioning is likely to offer agencies access to these large pools of funds. Competitive repositioning means altering stakeholders' beliefs about the outcomes claimed by other public service agencies, so elected officials recognize that resources allocated to them would yield a superior return in alleviating a

- DO talk about water, voters prioritize water as a critical reason to purchase and protect land, no matter how it is expressed. Voters closely link land conservation with protecting water.
- DO link land conservation to preservation of "working farms and ranches." "Working" is important.
  - "Agricultural land" and "farmland and ranchland" are less effective.
- DO evoke protecting wildlife and wildlife habitat. "Wildlife" is interpreted to fit the locale—urbanites regard rabbits and birds on their lawn as "wildlife."
- DO NOT use "endangered species"; it is more polarizing than "wildlife" with connotations of environmental regulations holding up important projects.
- DO NOT use "openspace"; it could mean empty land or abandoned lots.
  - DO use "natural areas" instead; it brings to mind positive images of trees, mountains and streams, and a pristine state.
- DO NOT just say "trails"—say "hiking, biking and walking trails"; attach meaning to them.
- DO talk about repair and maintenance of parks or preventing the closure of parks; they resonate more than creating new parks.
- DO NOT use "undeveloped land"; it has connotations that it may be developed in the future.
- DO use "poorly planned growth" rather than "unplanned growth" or "sprawl."
- DO use growth messages in local context with specific statistics (e.g. one million more people in the next 20 years).
- DO stress planning; voters want well-thought-out and responsible planning for growth (e.g., "We must plan carefully for growth and reduce its negative impacts by preserving clean air, clean water and natural areas").
- DO talk about "conservationists" and NOT "environmentalists." The latter are viewed as more radical; it is a more polarizing term.
- DO NOT needlessly politicize an issue (e.g., talking about federal government cut-backs is polarizing to those who approve).
- DO NOT say "conservation easement." The word "easement" evokes connotations of being forced into doing (or not doing) something with part of a landowner's property.
  - DO say "land preservation agreements" or "land protection agreements" instead.
- DO NOT say "purchase of development rights"; it implies someone wants to develop the land!
- DO stress the voluntary nature of land preservation agreements.

Source: Fairbank, Maslin, Maulin & Associates (2004).

Figure 6.16 Psychological positioning: The language of conservation

given community concern if they were invested in particular park and recreation services.

Competitive repositioning may be conceptualized as "depositioning" another agency since it is challenging the legitimacy or authenticity of that agency's positioning claims and trying to demote them. An irony of this strategy is that if it is successful, then it is likely that associative repositioning will follow since addressing a given problem holistically probably means that park and recreation's contributions will complement those of the other agency. Thus, the park and recreation agency will be required to associate with the agency from which resources have been reassigned. Hence, competitive repositioning has to be undertaken with caution, sensitivity, and subtlety to avoid a backlash of resentment from those in the other agency. For this reason, challenging the outcome claims of others is usually undertaken by advocates from outside the parks and recreation agency, so the personal chemistry and relationships of managers in the two agencies is not poisoned.

After a park and recreation agency has selected its preferred position(s), then other public services which contribute to that issue should be identified with the intent of pursuing associative and/or competitive repositioning strategies. This involves asking two questions: (1) To what niche(s) can parks and recreation contribute that complements what other services are doing (associative repositioning)? and (2) What outcomes claimed by others can parks and recreation deliver more effectively and/or more efficiently (competitive repositioning)?

The following paragraphs offer examples as to how positions claimed by others may be challenged by advocates making the case that resources would yield a better return if they were reallocated to parks and recreation.

In the context of at-risk youth programs, Figure 6.17 illustrates the cost-efficiency of prevention

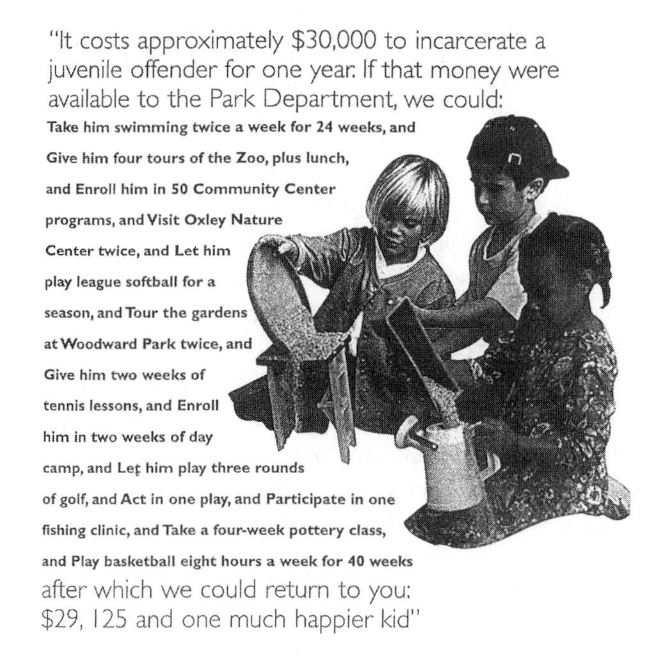

Figure 6.17 Positioning investments in youth development programs as viable alternatives to incarceration

strategies compared to the costs of incarceration. There are multiple other ways to reinforce the competitive repositioning effort in this context. Consider the following:

- During the past decade, the clearance rates reported annually by law enforcement agencies nationwide for major offenses by juveniles who were less than 18 years of age have been remarkably stable at 20% to 21%. An offense is declared cleared or solved when at least one person is arrested and charged with its commission. The major crimes to which these statistics relate are murder and non-negligent manslaughter, forcible rape, robbery, aggravated assault, burglary, larceny theft, motor vehicle theft, and arson. However, the 20% to 21% clearance rate overestimates the proportion of crimes cleared because data from the Federal Bureau of Investigation indicates that many major crimes are not reported to the police. The level of underreporting includes 50% of all violent crimes, 30% of personal thefts, 41% of household crimes, and 75% of motor vehicle thefts. Hence, for the purposes of this discussion, it has been assumed that 14%, rather than 20% to 21%, of youth crimes are solved. Of these, approximately a third are acquitted or dismissed. Of the 9% to 10% of juveniles who are convicted, approximately half receive sentences that do not involve incarceration.

Type	Year Before the Initiative	Year 2 of the Initiative	% of Change
Murder	37	29	-22
Aggravated Sexual Assault	3	10	+233
Robbery	116	83	-28
Aggravated Assault	421	319	-26
Burglary	43	27	-37
Theft	35	35	---
Auto Theft	25	25	---
TOTALS	680	528	-22

Figure 6.18 Changes in the number of serious gang-related offences committed

Obviously, incarceration is an essential component in alleviating juvenile crime. However, from a competitive repositioning perspective the point to be made is that if only 5% of the juveniles committing crimes are incarcerated and 95% of them remain available to engage in more crime, then a strategy focused predominantly on incarceration cannot solve the problem.

While the police provide crime *resolution* services these have to be supplemented with effective *preventive* services which the police are not equipped to provide. If this is pointed out and repeatedly reiterated to stakeholders, especially elected officials, then there is likely to be a realization that for major progress to be made, resources have to be allocated to prevention programs that target the overwhelming majority who are not arrested and incarcerated. Further, the evidence clearly indicates that early and consistent prevention efforts have the best chance of diminishing the need for more costly measures later.

Figure 6.18 illustrates the complementary role of recreation prevention programs. The city of Fort Worth used a holistic approach involving coordinated action from a number of city departments to address the problem of serious gang-related crime. The Fort Worth Parks and Community Services Department (which includes recreation) played a central role in the effort. Figure 6.18 shows data that compares the number of serious offenses the year before the program was launched with the number at the end of the year after the initiative was implemented.

The 22% improvement, reflecting 152 fewer offenses, was dramatic. If they had been committed by 100 young people, and if all of these individuals had been arrested and incarcerated, then using Texas Youth Commission's data which report the annual cost of incarcerating a youth is $43,000 per year, the cost of incarcerating all 100 of them for one year would have been more than $4.3 million. Given the gravity of the offenses, it appears reasonable to hypothesize that each of the individuals could have been incarcerated for an average of 10 years. With this assumption, the costs then escalate to $43 million (ignoring the time value of money). The total investment of city funds in this at-risk youth initiative was $430,000 and $678,000 in years one and two of the program, respectively. This was supplemented with $156,000 and $278,000 in the respective years from private sources. Thus, the return on each dollar invested by the city was $39 ($43 million ÷ $1.108 million). These calculations do not take into account cost savings that are also likely to have accrued from at-risk youth not engaging in other, less serious crimes not considered in Figure 6.18. This level of return made the investment unbeatable! Certainly the level of return makes it easy for elected officials to justify to their constituents the use of tax money to retain and expand their investment in this program.

From a competitive repositioning perspective, exactness of the numbers is not important. It does not matter if in some jurisdictions juvenile incarceration costs are lower, if city investment is greater, or if the magnitude of crime reduction is lower. The magnitude of the return on investment is so large that even quite major changes in the variables are unlikely to affect the principle.

If park and recreation's desired position relates to economic prosperity, then the competitive resources targeted are likely to be those allocated to tourism or economic development agencies. Tourism agencies have been effective in positioning themselves in the minds of stakeholders as important contributors to economic prosperity, and they receive resources commensurate with that favorable position.

However, when they undertake economic impact studies that show the spending of tourists in the community, this substantially overstates their contribution because many visitors would come even if there was no tourism agency, while others are there because of the park and recreation department's efforts rather than those of the tourism agency. If the discrepancies between the established position of the tourism agency and reality are subtly pointed out, then resources that would otherwise be appropriated to it may instead be allocated to parks and recreation to develop additional events or facilities that will attract visitors.

Responsibility for business recruitment in most communities has been assigned to an economic development agency. Competitive repositioning could involve subtly challenging the myth that these organizations have created about their high level of influence on company location decisions. Frequently, they claim credit for bringing XYZ company to town. The reality is that they rarely influence the company's initial decisions that result in it narrowing its list of prospective communities to a small set of between two and five communities. Narrowing the list usually occurs before community economic development organizations are contacted or have any awareness that a particular company may be planning to relocate.

Typically, they become involved only in the final stage in a company's decision progress. At that stage, their role is to serve as a conduit through which companies conveniently can request specific information from those communities that they are considering; to host and coordinate visits to the community by company officials; to coordinate company requests for easements and planning permissions; and to coordinate the negotiation of incentive packages that their community is prepared to offer (Decker & Crompton, 1993). If this more limited role becomes recognized as the real function of economic development organizations, then the scope of their operations may be scaled back and more funds released for providing amenities that companies seek.

The challenge for parks and recreation is to convince stakeholders to adopt a market-oriented rather than a product-oriented approach to business relocation. The common product oriented approach focuses on selling the community as it is, whereas a market orientation adapts a community to meet the changing needs of relocating companies which means "If small business constitutes the engine of the job generation process, then places should promote things that facilitate small business growth" (Kotler, Haider & Rein, 1993: 12). One of these things is likely to be investment in improved park and recreation amenities (Crompton, Love & More, 1997).

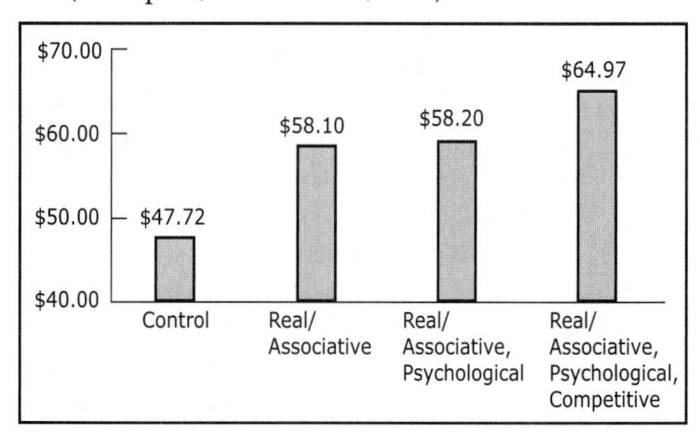

Figure 6.19 Results of an experiment showing the impact of repositioning strategies

The Impact of Repositioning Strategies

The newness of the concept of repositioning in the parks and recreation field, and the relatively long period of time needed for repositioning strategies to be effective, means that no field studies have been reported which evaluate the effectiveness of repositioning strategies. However, results of an experiment designed to measure this are summarized in Figure 6.19 (Kaczynski, Havitz, & McCarville, 2005). A sample of people in a community were given an article to read that was related to youth crime. It was designed to appear as though it had been published in a local newspaper. Four different versions of the article were produced. Each of them added information to that included in the previous version:

- A control version containing no repositioning information.
- A real/associative repositioning version reported a large number of youth programs offered by the agency and a large number of qualified staff to run them. It also incorporated associative information relating to other organizations with which the agency partnered.
- A real/associative and psychological version referenced positive outcomes to youth and the community that emanated from the programs.
- A real/associative, psychological, and competitive version added information on how funds allocated to the police department could be better used by the park and recreation agency.

After reading their version of the article, respondents were asked to divide $100 between the police department and the park and recreation agency. The control group allocated an average of $47.72 to the parks and recreation agency. When the real/associative repositioning information was added, this increased by 22% to $58.10. Adding psychological outcome information increased this only marginally to $58.20, but when competitive information was added, there was a quantum leap to $64.97, which represented a 36% increase compared to using no repositioning strategy at all. This equates to $1.8 million on a $5 million operating budget for youth development programs. This study demonstrated both the effectiveness of repositioning strategies, and that they are most effective when the four repositioning strategies are used cumulatively rather than if only one or two of them are used.

Relationship to OFM

This chapter has provided an in-depth and focused analysis to show why a particular type and application of understanding of knowledge about the benefits of leisure called for in the proceeding chapter is central to achieving the goals of OFM. Repositioning cannot be attained and sustained without that knowledge and the strategies for using that knowledge explained in this chapter. Likewise, OFM cannot be successfully applied and implemented without the repositioning called for in this chapter.

Literature Cited

Crompton, J. L. (1999). *Measuring the economic impact of visitors to sports tournaments and special events.* Ashburn, VA: National Recreation and Park Association.

Crompton, J. L. (2004). *The proximate principle: The impact of parks, open space and water features on residential property values and the property tax base.* Ashburn, VA: National Recreation and Park Association.

Crompton, J. L. & Kaczynski, A. T. (2003). Trends in local park and recreation department finances and staffing from 1964-65 to 1999-2000. *Journal of Park and Recreation Administration,* 21(4), 124–144.

Crompton, J. L., Love, L. L., & More, T. A. (1997). Characteristics of companies that considered recreation/parks/open space to be important in (re)location decisions. *Journal of Park and Recreation Administration, 15*(1), 37–58.

Decker, J. M. & Crompton, J. L. (1993). Attracting footloose companies: An investigation of the business location decision process. *Journal of Professional Services Marketing, 9*(1), 69–94.

Fairbank, Maslin, Maulin, & Associates (2004). *Lessons learned regarding the "language of conservation" from the national research program.* San Francisco, CA: Trust for Public Land.

Glyptis, S. (1989). *Leisure and unemployment.* Milton Keynes, UK: Open University.

Godbey, G. (1993). The contribution of recreation and parks to reducing health care costs: From theory to practice. *Trends, 30*(4), 37–41.

Gray, D. E. & Greben, S. (1974, July). Future perspectives. *Parks and Recreation,* 26–33, 47–56.

Heisler, G. M. (1986). Energy saving with trees. *Journal of Arboriculture, 12*(5), 113–125.

Jarvi, C. K. (1993, March). Leaders who meet today's changing needs. *Parks and Recreation,* 60–64, 162–163.

Kaczynski, A. T. & Crompton, J. L. (2004). An operational tool for determining an optimum repositioning strategy for leisure services departments. *Managing Leisure, 9*(3), 127–144.

Kaczynski, A. T. & Crompton, J. L. (2004). Development of a multi-dimensional scale for implementing positioning in public park and recreation agencies. *Journal of Park and Recreation Administration, 22*(2), 1–27.

Kaczynski, A. T., Havitz, M. E., & McCarville, R. E. (2005). Altering perceptions through repositioning: An exercise in framing. *Leisure Sciences, 27*(3), 241–261.

Kotler, P., Haider, D. H., & Rein, I. (1993). *Marketing places: Attracting investment, industry and tourism to cities, states and nations.* New York: Free Press.

Ries, A. & Trout, J. (1972, April 24, May 1, and May 8). Positioning. *Advertising Age.*

Ries, A. & Trout, J. (2001). *Positioning: The battle for your mind. Twentieth anniversary edition.* New York: McGraw-Hill.

Rothman, A. J. & Salovey, P. (1997). Shaping perceptions to motivate healthy behavior: The role of message framing. *Psychological Bulletin, 121*(1), 3–19.

Tverskey, A. & Kahneman, D. (1981, January). The framing of decisions and the psychology of choice. *Science, 211*, 453–458.

U.S. Census Bureau (2007). www.census.gov/govs/www/estimate.html. U.S. Census Bureau. State and Local Government Finances.

U.S. Forest Service (nd.) *Pollution removal calculator* www.fs.fed.us/ne/syracuse.

Witt, P. A. & Crompton, J. L. (2002). *Best practices in youth development in public park and recreation settings.* Ashburn, VA: National Recreation and Park Association.

Chapter 7
Use of the Outcomes Approach by the U. S. Army Corps of Engineers

Darrell E. Lewis

Learning Objectives:

- Understand the nature and scope of the recreation program of the U.S. Army Corps of Engineers (COE).
- Understand adoption of the outcomes approach within the COE.

Purpose and Background

The purpose of this chapter is to describe the introduction of the outcomes approach to help guide policy, planning, and management decisions of the Natural Resources Management section of the U.S. Army Corps of Engineers (COE).

The COE is one of the oldest federal land management agencies. It is located in the U.S. Department of the Army and has both a civil works and military divisions. The Corps' history began in 1775 when the Continental Congress organized the Continental Army with a Chief Engineer. A separate Corps of Engineers for the United States was authorized by the Congress on March 11, 1779, and that Corps served in the Continential Army under George Washington primarily to build battlements, fortifications, and roads for military purposes. At the end of the Revolutionary War in 1783, the engineers mustered out of service, and the Corps of Engineers as it is known today came into being on March 16, 1802. According to Dennis (2001:102) "During peacetime in 1824, Congress assigned the first civil works functions to the Corps, which was removel of sandbars and snags from the major *navigable rivers* of the East and in the Mississippi watershed. Comprehensive river basin resource development was planned in 1890, and in 1936 the Corps was given responsibility for *nationwide flood control* [that evolved into other Corps "missions" of producing hydroelectricity and supplying water for domestic use]....The authority to develop and manage outdoor recreation sites was granted by the 1944 Flood Control Act [Public Law 78-534 of December 22, 1944]. Since that time, *economic values* of water-based recreation have come to be included in *cost-benefits analyses* used in justifying water project expenses."[1] That act gave the Corps responsibility for providing safe recreation opportunities on the reservoirs and surrounding lands of the projects built for other purposes. That additional responsibility was in response to the high levels of recreation use occurring on the lands and waters administered by the Corps, especially concern for the safety of those increasing number of visitors.

The Recreation Program of the COE

Nature and Scope of the Program

The Corps' recreation program began with a focus on providing safe recreation facilities to accommodate existing informal uses of the water resource reservoirs. As new water resource projects were planned, management of new recreation areas was needed to accommodate growing demand and future likely recreation demand predicted by Corps recreation planners. It is important to note that the construction of new water resource projects to be managed by the Corps was virtually completed by the mid 1970s. Therefore, the Corps' development of new recreation areas was winding down by that time as well. After that, construction activities focused on replacement and repair of the large inventory of existing recreation facilities, with little attention devoted to changing recreation demand. By and large, new recreational activities like sailboarding and the use of personal watercraft were accommodated within the confines of existing recreational facilities. The relatively few new recreation facilities that were built were primarily to prevent and solve user conflicts.

The current overall mission of the COE recreation program is to provide quality outdoor public recreation experiences to serve the needs of present and future generations and to contribute to the quality of American life, while managing and conserving natural resources consistent with ecosystem management principles. In 2006, the goal of the COE recreation program was to ensure that projects perform to meet authorized purposes and evolving conditions. There were three performance objectives to support that goal:[2]

1. Provide justified outdoor recreation opportunities in an effective and efficient manner at all Corps-operated water resources projects.
2. Provide continued outdoor recreation opportunities to meet the needs of present and future generations.
3. Provide a safe and healthful outdoor recreation environment for Corps customers.

The Corps' nationwide, primarily water-based outdoor makes the COE a major provider of outdoor recreation opportunities in the U.S. Specifically, the COE has 456 water resource projects located in 43 states that cover over 11.6 million acres of land and water administered by the Corps. The lakes have approximately 53,000 miles of shoreline and host roughly 33 percent of all freshwater lake fishing in the U. S. There are 4,330 formal recreation areas at these reservoirs. Over 2,600 are managed by the COE while the rest are managed by state, local, nonprofit, or for-profit entities. There are over 100,000 campsites, over 55,000 picnic sites, 488 commercial marinas, 3,800 boat launch ramps, 5,000 miles of trails, and a variety of other facilities. The COE reported 348 million visitors to these facilities in fiscal year 2006, which is the largest documented use rate of any of the federal outdoor recreation resource management agencies. Those visitors participated in a wide range of activities with the bulk being boating, fishing, camping, picnicking, sightseeing, waterskiing, and sailing.

The first staff of the recreation program of the COE consisted of a small number of rangers. In 2007, the staff was comprised of 2,265 full- and part-time employees, many of whom have academic degrees in such fields as forestry, fisheries management, wildlife management, recreation, and related fields. This capability was supplemented by the contributions of almost 50,000 volunteers which were valued at approximately $21 million in 2005.

Outcomes-Focused Policies and Management[3]

Focus on Experiential Benefits

As a graduate student majoring in forest recreation, I became more aware of the importance of leisure to individuals, communities, and ultimately the nation. I realized that an understanding of recreationists' desires for satisfying experiences, as well as their desires for recreation activities and the characteristics of the recreation settings on which those activities and experiences depended, was necessary for managers to understand before those values of leisure could be realized optimally. Nevertheless, the relationships between desired activities, experiences, and settings did not become well integrated into my thinking until the late 1970s when I was Chief of the USDI Bureau of Land Management's (BLM's) Recreation and Cultural Resources Division. I recognized the need for, and supported the development of the Recreation Opportunity Spectrum (ROS) system, and worked closely with the USDA Forest Service (USFS) and several leisure scientists to develop The ROS system before it was adopted by the BLM and the USFS in the early 1980s. In retrospect, development and application of the ROS system for managing recreation resources was my first exposure to OFM. It was, because the types of outcomes the ROS focused on were the desired and undesired experiences (one of the types of outcome considered by OFM) that could be realized from participation in different recreation activities in different recreation settings that vary from urban to primitive in nature.[4]

I mentioned this background because I carried appreciation of the concepts of the ROS with me when I became Chief of Natural Resources Management in the headquarters of the COE in 1981. Nevertheless, I made the decision not to incorporate the ROS system into Corps' recreation management procedures for two reasons: (1) the ROS system was developed to guide recreation inventories and management of relatively large tracts of wildlands, such as those administered by the BLM and the USFS, that would offer opportunities along the ROS spectrum from urban to primitive, which was not a characteristic of the land and water resources administered by the COE and (2) by 1982, the COE was managing areas already developed for recreation for which the recreation-related goals and objectives had already been established and had considered customer demands for experiences as well as for activities.

Economic Impacts

The economic benefits of the Corps' recreation program are significant, especially since visitor spending on trip expenses represents a sizable component of the economy of many communities around Corps' projects. For example, the money spent by visitors to COE projects contributes significantly to local and higher economies by supporting jobs and generating income. To illustrate, in 1999, visitor spending with multiplier effects was estimated to result in $5,962,000 visitor spending within 30 miles of Corps projects. The local economies captured 66% of these expenditures as direct sales effects. Nationwide, with multiplier effects, these annual visits resulted in $6,481,000 total sales which in turn generated $3,415,000 in total income. Over 165,000 jobs in local communities were supported by this economic activity (See U.S. Army Corps of Engineers, Natural Resources Management Gateway at www.corpslakes.us).

When attempting to justify budgets for the Corps programs with the U.S. Office of Management and Budget (OMB), I used all of the accepted economic measures of the times. However, it was apparent that measures I had accepted (i.e., travel cost method) were considered irrelevant by the tough-minded OMB budget examiners. Body language told it all, and those measures were totally ineffective in convincing the OMB of the worth of the Corps' recreation program. Nevertheless, I did recognize at least some interest in how many jobs the Corps' recreation program created and sustained. So, in the late 1980s, the Corps supported studies of the economic impacts of its recreation program. They resulted in the development of the capability to define economic impacts of the Corps' recreation activities by state, lake, or best of all, Congressional Districts. The process was developed at the Corps Environmental Research and Development Center (ERDC) in Vicksburg, Mississippi in cooperation with leisure scientists at Michigan State University. Results of that conservative and economically sound process have served the Corps well over the years. But, from a professional viewpoint, it is obvious that economic impacts are not the only measure of the worth of leisure activities.

In 1989, I was invited to participate in an event that changed my professional life. It was a symposium at the Snowbird Resort in Utah, sponsored by the USDA Forest Service's Rocky Mountain Forest and Range Experiment Station and coordinated by the editor of this text. The purpose was to critique preliminary drafts of chapters of the text *Benefits of Leisure* (Driver, Brown, & Peterson, 1991), and most of the authors of chapters of that text were present. There, I learned that many professional fields had documented what was then known scientifically about many of the benefits of leisure. Those papers by top scholars from around the world validated time and again my personal belief that leisure activities are a significant part of human life. Much interest in the benefits of leisure was spawned by that text, and it also served as a stimulus for development of the *The Benefits Catalogue* (Canadian Parks and Recreation Association, 1997) which further increased interest in the benefits. The Snowbird Symposium also stimulated a follow-up Benefits of Leisure Applications Workshop which was held in May of 1991 in Estes Park, Colorado? At this workshop, about 70 others and I discussed and firmed up the preliminary concepts of BBM, as detailed in Chapter 1 of this text.

In 1998, I also attended the first training workshop on BBM in Albuquerque, NM.[5] The course was a success because over 30 individuals from a variety of agencies and private firms confirmed that BBM was a viable, credible, and needed approach. From that success, I invited the instructors of that workshop to present a shortened version of the course to the Corps' Recreation Leadership Advisory Team, a group of talented leaders in the Corps' recreation program. Having modest expectations, I introduced the session to the team as an opportunity to learn about some leading edge concepts and begged the group's indulgence. Instead, it was an amazing session. The team not only "got it," but afterward started a programmatic strategy that incorporated the concepts of OFM. It was one of the most successful work sessions with which I have ever been involved in all my years of government service.

Because of its increasing emphasis on outcomes, the Corps published the well-received, undated brochure "Values to the Nation: Individuals, Communities, Economy, and Environment." It reviewed the many benefits of the Corps' recreation program, and over 175,000 copies have been printed in response to high public demand. Since then, the Corps has made an effort to develop performance-based budgets and is documenting the full range of inputs and outputs as well as some outcomes. To enhance its understanding of OFM, the Corps has worked closely with members of the faculty in the Department of Forest Resources of the University of Minnesota in St. Paul for several years. That association has involved the Corps supporting several studies of the benefits realized by visitors to Corps projects, of the benefits realized by residents of proximate communities, and of those residents' opinions and preferences regarding nearby Corps' activities (see Chapter 20 of this text; Anderson, Schneider, Wilhelm, & Leahy (in press); and Schneider, Wilhelm, & Heisey, 2006). Those studies have helped the Corps gain a better understanding of how to more effectively serve the recreational visitors to its projects and to nurture mutually satisfactory relations with the local residents. In addition, when this chapter was written, the Corps was cooperating with those faculty members to develop guidelines on how to better apply and implement OFM. This collaboration has helped to better integrate the benefits concept better into the Corps management decision processes. In the future, the Corps' recreation program will continue to be founded on solid professional knowledge, which now includes many of the concepts on which the OFM was built.

Literature Cited

Anderson, D. H., Schneider, I. E., Wilhelm, S., & Leahy, J. (in press). Proximate and distant visitors: Differences in importance ratings of beneficial experiences. Journal of Park & Recreation Administration.

Canadian Parks/Recreation Association. (1997). *The Benefits Catalogue.* Gloucester, Ontario, Canada.

Dennis, S. (2001). *Natural resources and the informed citizen.* Champaign, IL. Sagamore Publishing.

Driver, B. L., Brown, P., & Peterson, G. (Eds.). (1991). *The benefits of leisure.* State College, PA: Venture Publishing, Inc.

Schneider, I. E., Wilhem S., & Heisey J. (2006). *Visitor benefits, crowding, and values: Cumulative visitor report 2003-2004 Lake Shelbyville and Carlyle Lake.* (Staff Paper no. 188). St. Paul, MN: University of Minnesota, Department of Forest Resources.

Footnotes

1. The Corps often refers to their dams and reservoirs and other activities as "projects."
2. Personal communication with personnel in the headquarters of the COE.
3. Note from the editor of this text: Contrary to tradition, I wanted the last section of this chapter to be expressed in the first person singular, because it is a significant endorsement of OFM from a person who has held two important and relevant administrative/policymaking positions, first as Chief, Recreation, and Cultural Resources Division in the headquarters of the USDI Bureau of Land Management and later as Chief, Natural Resources Management Branch in the headquarters of the COE.
4. Note from the editor of this text: Remember from Chapter 1 that OFM considers three types of benefits of leisure with the realization of satisfying experiences being one of them. Therefore, the ROS, which focuses on experiential outcomes, is a limited type of OFM--limited because it does not consider the two other types of benefits. As an opportunistic aside, it should also be noted that success with applying the ROS system in several agencies was a major stimulus for development of OFM.
5. Conducted by Bruns, Hopkins, and Driver, who are authors or coauthors of several chapters of this text.

Chapter 8
Bureau of Land Management: Managing for Beneficial Outcomes

Bill Overbaugh and Don Bruns

Learning Objectives:

1. Understand the Recreation and Visitor Services Program direction and strategy for the U.S. Bureau of Land Management (BLM) as it transitions from activity-focused management to outcome-focused management, or Benefits-Based Management (BBM) as it appears in the agency's program guidance.
2. Understand how the BLM's adoption of OFM was achieved through its integration within:
   - Recreation program policy outlined in *A Unified Strategy to Implement The BLM's Priorities for Recreation and Visitor Services,* and
   - Recreation planning and management policy outlined in the BLM's *Land Use Planning Handbook.*

Introduction

This chapter aims to describe the transition of the Bureau of Land Management's (BLM) Recreation and Visitor Services program to OFM. First, the agency's OFM approach is described as being recommended by the twelve BLM State Recreation Leaders and its Executive Leadership Team and other Washington Office Advisors who comprise the Recreation and Visitor Services Advisory Team (RVSAT). Then it proceeds to describe the application of OFM to program direction including the BLM's *Unified Strategy, The BLM's Priorities for Recreation and Visitor Services,* its *Land Use Planning Handbook,* interim management policy, and training. It concludes with a discussion on future steps.

OFM in the BLM

The BLM recently adopted the expanded conceptual framework of OFM as both its strategic and operational framework for managing public lands recreation-tourism. OFM now guides recreation and visitor services planning and management within a collaborative, community-based, and business-oriented context.

This represents a departure from previous recreation management methodologies. Including the management of recreation activities, the agency now also manages for targeted experience and other benefit opportunities, and sustains essential setting characteristics required to do so. They do this by working with service delivery systems larger than the BLM, such as engaging affecting local governments and private sector business providers. Because BLM is seldom, if ever, the sole source provider of recreation opportunities on public lands, its recreation plans must be developed and implemented within a community-based regional context, extending beyond boundaries of public lands to include adjoining service communities.

Adoption of OFM initiates a shift away from managing a myriad of individual competing, and sometimes conflicting, activity-based recreation programs and initiatives. Instead, all recreation programs and their actions are now subject to a hierarchy of management objectives that are functionally interrelated. This sustains the distinctive character and productive capacity of public lands recreation settings and refocuses the program on the production targeted experience and other benefit outcomes desired by identified recreation-tourism markets and niches. It also increases the program's efficiency and its effectiveness in improving the quality of life for recreation participants and affected local residents, strengthening community life, stabilizing local economies, and sustaining the integrity of both natural resource and affected community environments.

OFM's interdisciplinary systems approach redirects the management of recreation to address the transforming, emergent, self-organizing, and increasingly complexly coupled social and ecological system. This focus fits with OFM's two principal applications: to diversify recreation opportunities and to address identified problems, both in response to customer desires. Although not necessarily in these terms, the whole systems approach is enabling the BLM to effectively address concepts such as community resilience, adaptive capacity, and resource sustainability.[1] As the application of OFM is vertically integrated within the BLM organization, recreation-tourism use and enjoyment of the public lands will maintain the distinctive and productive capacity of public lands recreation settings, build community capacity, redirect the program to be more responsive to its customers and the environment, and thereby maintain social, economic, and environmental resiliency. Further understanding of the interactions and linkage mechanisms through which outcome opportunities are both produced and attained within well-defined service delivery systems, larger than the BLM or the public lands, will facilitate greater managerial agility, flexibility, and an ability to adaptively manage for beneficial outcomes, all of which will enhance greater institutional learning.

Recreation and Visitor Services Advisory Team (RVSAT)

Recreation Program Leaders within each of the BLM State Offices bridge the divide between the policy and budget arm of the Headquarters Office and on-ground implementation arm of Districts and Field Offices. The RVSAT is charged with developing advice and strategies for improving the BLM's Recreation and Visitor Services Program.

It all began with a Department of Interior strategic plan that identified recreation as one of four key missions. That strategy, coupled with ever increasing public lands recreation--both in volume and importance--led BLM's Director to request in March 2002 that the agency's Executive Leadership Team (ELT) formulate a set of national priorities for the program. Substantial in-migration to the eleven western states and increased tourism promotion and use, had fueled the growing dependence of affected rural communities on public lands to enhance their quality of life. This also demonstrated that BLM's recreation program could no longer afford to concern itself only with traditional outdoor recreation constituents. Both factors underscored the need for action. BLM California's State Director assumed ELT leadership for this effort, and BLM California engaged senior staff leadership from BLM Washington to develop a draft priorities document.

In January of 2003, the BLM's various State Office and Washington Office recreation, wilderness, and travel management leaders met in Redding, California to review the draft and finalize the *BLM's Priorities for Recreation and Visitor Services* (Workplan Fiscal Years 2003–2007). Two momentous things happened at this meeting. One was the adoption of the objective to "Manage public lands and waters for enhanced recreation experiences and quality of life" in direct response to one of the principal Departmental goals. The other was that the document (*The BLM's Priorities for Recreation and Visitor Services)* was transmitted to the field on February 27, 2004 (re. BLM Information Bulletin No. 2004-072) as a Work Plan. The seven objectives within that work plan tier off two current BLM goals, to "Ensure Quality Experiences and Enjoyment of Natural and Cultural Resources" and to "Provide for and Receive Fair Value in Recreation." It has given renewed impetus and direction to the management recreation on the public lands administered by the BLM.

While the priorities Work Plan outlined the BLM's commitment to shift the BLM's recreation program from an activity-based approach to one which focuses on recreation experience and other benefit outcomes, direction was not conveyed to the field as policy until January 10, 2006. The Washington Office transmitted to the field Instruction Memorandum No. 2006-060 entitled "Incorporating Benefits-Based Management within Recreation and Visitor Services Program Policy Changes." This directive of January 5, 2006 affirmed the BLM Executive Leadership Team's (ELT) commitment to change the conceptual framework within which public lands recreation is managed. An important part of that directive stated "... Field Managers will assess and evaluate effects of proposed projects in Special Recreation Management Areas on activities, experiences, beneficial outcomes and recreation setting character to ensure consistency with benefits-based management concepts."

For Special Recreation Management Areas, this changed historic activity-based management practice to the expanded benefits-based conceptual framework, as outlined in the BLM's *Land Use Planning Handbook*. It also requires the application of BBM principles to the interim management of Special Recreation Management Areas: "This IM affirms BLM's corporate commitment to change its framework and emphasis to benefits-based recreation management. All new and ongoing LUPs shall incorporate and implement policy contained in Appendices C and D of the LUP Handbook." Redding participants also recommended that BLM pursue formal establishment of an Advisory Team. The California State Director enthusiastically supported its creation, and on March 1, 2004, Information Bulletin No. 2004-073, formally announced its establishment to provide advice to the BLM's ELT regarding recreation and visitor services priorities, policies, programs, and budget direction to implement the new Workplan. Chartered under the Washington Office Assistant Director, Renewable Resources and Planning (WO-200), the RVSAT serves solely in an advisory capacity, and has been given wide latitude in how to formulate and provide advice. The Team's primary goals are to:

1. determine efficient and cost-effective means for improving the BLM's recreation and visitor services programs and provide recommendations to management for strengthening and advancing program capabilities and coordination;
2. identify recreation- and visitor services-related issues affecting the BLM public lands and coordinate development of issue resolution strategies and national policy recommendations for management consideration;
3. provide periodic review of the May 2003 document titled *The BLM's Priorities for Recreation and Visitor Services (Workplan Fiscal Years 2003–2007)* and to make recommendations for Workplan implementation through an annual action plan; and
4. report annually on recreation program accomplishments.

The central theme in each of RVSAT's annual meetings and monthly teleconference calls has been the integration of all recreation programs and initiatives within the OFM's expanded conceptual framework. This involves identifying where recreation-tourism markets desire for structured recreation opportunities (i.e., experience and benefit outcomes and the maintenance of recreation setting character upon which their attainment depends), managing to meet targeted market demand, and limiting program investments to custodial actions wherever structured recreation desires have not been identified.

Recreation Program Background

Among the factors which pushed the BLM to adopt OFM as the integrative conceptual framework for its Recreation and Visitor Services program, two stand out as being particularly prominent beyond the emphasis given to recreation experiences and other outcomes by the DOI strategic plan. One was a growing awareness of how central recreation experiences and enjoyment are to the quality of life of an increasing number of Americans and to the fulfillment of BLM's primary dispersed recreation role. In addition, as noted above, this also shows up as one of two key goal statements in the Department of Interior's recreation mission statement of its Strategic Plan.

The other motivating factor was a growing awareness of the importance and need to maintain the distinctive character of public lands recreation settings. For the sustained production and attainment of opportunities for many of those experience and other beneficial outcomes depends on those settings. Setting character is becoming an ever more important factor, not only to visiting recreation-tourism participants, but also to those whose lives are enriched by living nearby the open space character of public lands in the West. In a January 2004 National Recreation Forum, initiated by the BLM's Director, the agency received confirmation of this refocused direction for managing public lands direction. The BLM heard clear affirmation from a diverse spectrum of national and state constituents of the importance of maintaining setting character to sustain the capacity of public lands to provide the equally distinctive kinds of experience and other benefit opportunities for which the public lands are known. In 2005, the Western States Tourism Policy Council held its own recreation forum and also affirmed that the BLM's Workplan priorities are appropriate for the BLM's Recreation and Visitor Services program.

Neither of these factors, however, figured prominently in the historic development and structure of the BLM's recreation program. Instead, it grew out of the agency's need to reckon with rapidly growing outdoor recreation participation on public lands. The most vocal demands were those of recreation users and interest groups discovering that these "lands that nobody wanted"[2] provided some of the nation's last remaining undeveloped and untamed dispersed recreation. Quite naturally, that management response was structured around the activity-based demands of the most well-organized groups such as the Western River Guides Association/American Rivers, the American Motorcycle Association, the National Off-Highway Vehicle Coordinating Council, the International Mountain Biking Association, the American Recreation Coalition, the American Hiking Society, and the Access Fund. Because these voices were organized around specific kinds of recreation activities, the BLM's recreation program assumed the same activity-based structure.

Recreation was first recognized as being important in management of public lands in the *Classification and Multiple Use Act of 1974*. But it was not until passage of *The Federal Land Policy and Management Act of* 1976 that recreation was recognized as a major program. The current BLM recreation program then continued to evolve. In 1989, *Recreation 2000: Strategic Plan* effectively spawned numerous programs, facilities, and initiatives. These garnered new funding appropriations and increased facility infrastructure development. But this initiative lacked focus and was not sustainable. Its emphasis on short-term development neglected looking at long-term outcomes, and it soon became apparent that the BLM could not sustain either the new programs nor maintain facilities infrastructure. Moreover, the resulting program development emphasis compromised the BLM's most significant heritage, the distinctive open-space character of public lands recreation settings.

In 1995, a *Recreation 2000 Update* was published. This niche-based strategy allowed Field Offices to manage a bottom-up approach tailored more to local resource settings and customer needs. Further, it allowed the implementation of only those national initiatives that matched resource capability and sustainability. But despite this niche-based shift, continued program and facility development became the "end game" to accommodate rapidly increasing recreation activity participation. Facility development driven by organized user groups continued to compromise the BLM's most distinctive dispersed recreation role. The program continued to lack focus on anything larger than the programs and the special interests they served.

Thus, public lands recreation management emerged as numerous independent sub-programs, each vying for its own "piece of the pie." These programs were often at odds with one another and sometimes worked towards mutually incompatible ends. For example, some sub-programs worked hard to develop additional roads and trails to accommodate growing mechanized and motorized recreation use, while others worked equally hard to preserve places for dispersed and quiet recreation. And some worked equally hard to try to emulate the practice of other agencies (e.g., the National Park Service or the U.S. Forest Service), while others realized that public lands recreation should be managed differently to provide different kinds of recreation opportunities. And while the agency sought to obtain additional funding to effectively respond to this growing recreation demand, there was no unifying program direction.

It was within this overall context of amorphous program direction and a rapidly changing west that the BLM was hearing increasing concerns from constituents about the erosion of opportunities for visitors to realize the experiences and other improved conditions for which the public lands were so well-known. Constituents emphasized that the loss of desired recreation opportunities was directly tied to continued erosion of the distinctive character of public lands recreation settings, and expressed further concern that the recreation program itself was contributing to it. Some commented that the agency seemed to have an industrialized approach to recreation and was increasingly neglecting public demand for quiet recreation. Concerns about the integrity of considerable cultural and historic treasures on the public lands and associated growing heritage tourism demand only heightened those concerns. These are some of the external pressures that led the agency to reconsider the adequacy of its recreation program policy, and it was in this context that current program policy was articulated.

OFM in BLM's Recreation Program Strategy

Public lands recreation settings are now valued by an ever growing clientele of recreation-tourism participants and nonparticipating but affected community residents as well as national citizens and international visitors. Visitor profiles now include not only traditional outdoor recreation participants, but other important recreation-tourism markets including touring, winter and summer resorts, small-town community/village visits, special events, and visiting friends and relatives. Tremendous in-migration to gateway communities and metropolitan base-camp communities, along with the further development of resorts throughout the Rocky Mountain and Intermountain West within the past decade, has forced the BLM to respond to other clienteles of competing nonparticipating residents who nonetheless value public lands recreation settings for important family and community benefits. Thus, the BLM's recreation program is having to respond not only to a far more diverse clientele of recreation-tourism visitors than ever before, but also to a growing and increasingly astute clientele of affected community residents--both in addition to its more traditional activity-based user groups. Each of the resulting recreation-tourism markets value public lands settings for different sets of household and community, economic, and environmental benefits. It has therefore become increasingly difficult to satisfy these ever-growing and competing demands using the BLM's traditional project-centered and activity-based outdoor recreation management model.

This absence of an integrative framework larger than the activity-based projects around which the program was historically structured led the BLM to advance recreation program goals such as reducing user conflict, promoting visitor safety, and protecting resources. But those custodial, caretaking principles proved inadequate for proactively accommodating the continued growth of an increasingly sophisticated and discriminating public lands recreation-tourism clientele. The BLM continued its attempts to justify additional funding to more effectively manage its growing recreation-tourism demand, but with only marginal success. Finally the House Appropriations Committee, realizing that the BLM needed additional funding but lacking the necessary strategic direction to get there, called for development of a unified strategy for the management of public lands recreation:

> "The Committee recognizes that the Bureau faces increasing demands on the public lands from recreational users, and was pleased to see a request for additional funding in the 2004 budget justification. However, the request does not outline a clear long-term strategy for managing recreation on the public lands. The Bureau should report to the Committee by March 1, 2004, on efforts to develop a unified strategy for recreation management, including dispersed recreation."[3]

The first step in meeting this requirement was developing *The BLM's Priorities for Recreation and Visitor Services*. A *Unified Strategy to Implement The BLM's Priorities for Recreation and Visitor Services* has since been developed and approved, responding to the above-referenced House of Representatives' appropriations committee direction. It was transmitted to the field on January 26, 2007 and both integrates and structures interrelationships among the seven Workplan objectives (Figure 8.1) outlined within the BLM's recreation work plan (re. Instruction Memorandum No. 2007-043). The policy action transmitted by that memorandum states, significantly:

> "This IM affirms the BLM's corporate commitment to implementing a Unified Strategy that delivers a collaborative recreation and visitor services planning and management framework. The Unified Strategy provides overall guidance implementing the seven Workplan program objectives and institutionalizes them into the BLM's recreation programs, policies, guidance, and budget formulation. This IM is critical to ongoing and future land use planning efforts because it provides a logical, structured framework for analyzing recreation-tourism market demand for recreational activities, experiences, and services and the infrastructure that support them. In addition, both resource management planning and implementation planning should incorporate the concepts outlined in the Unified Strategy."

Objective 1
Manage public lands and waters for enhanced recreation experiences and quality of life.

▼

Objective 2
Encourage sustainable travel and tourism development with gateway communities, and provide community-based conservation support for visitor services.

▼

Objective 3
Provide fair value and return for recreation through fee collection and commercial services.

▼

Objective 4	*Objective 5*
Establish a comprehensive approach to travel planning and management.	Ensure public health and safety, and improve the condition and accessibility of recreation sites and facilities.

▼

Objective 6
Enhance and expand visitor services, including interpretation, information, and education.

▼

Objective 7
Encourage and sustain collaborative partnerships, volunteers, and citizen-centered public service.

Figure 8.1 Hierarchy of Seven Workplan Objectives

The Unified Strategy itself describes considerations for how and in what priority the program objectives (vs. specific management plan objectives) and actions contained in the Workplan should be implemented. It aligns the seven program objectives beginning with the primary objective of managing public lands and related waters for enhanced recreation experiences and quality-of-life outcomes. The remaining six objectives are listed in a descending, cause-and-effect hierarchy. As stated in the Unified Strategy:

> "The first three objectives *are the program's primary unifiers and should be addressed in this respective order*, as each of these unifying program objectives affect, and in fact determine, how actions that implement objectives further down in the hierarchy are addressed. These unifying objectives provide direction, integration, and ensure balance among all seven objectives and offer a planning and management framework that will ensure consistency and compatibility of actions."

"The chart illustrates the functional relationships between the seven primary Purple Book [i.e., *The BLM's Priorities for Recreation and Visitor Services*] objectives. All are essential components but not all are functional equals. The successful achievement of some is conditioned or predicated upon how others are addressed. There are cause-and-effect relationships among the seven objectives which must be observed if BLM is to avoid having disjointed, incompatible, or unsustainable recreation program components. Applying this hierarchical relationship to proposed recreation and visitor services actions is critical to achieving logical and integrated program plans and implementing actions in day-to-day recreation and visitor services operations." (Attachments 1–6 and 1–7, BLM Instruction Memorandum No. 2007–043).

"Application of the Unified Strategy helps ensure that management actions for one objective do not conflict with or preclude attainment of other individual objectives. The Unified Strategy describes the dynamic inter-relationships [sic] between objectives and shows what has to happen to ensure that none of the seven Purple Book objectives inadvertently impact or negatively affect the primary objective of attaining satisfying experiences and quality of life outcomes/benefits." (Attachment 1–11, BLM Instruction Memorandum No. 2007–043).

Practical application of the strategy may be illustrated in simplified form as follows:

- Determine which of the seven strategic objectives is most closely aligned with any proposed action or initiative.
  - e.g., Objective 5 addresses actions such as building a mountain bike trail.
- Consider implications which each of the four objectives preceding this one have for this action--how they guide and constrain it.
  - Objective 1 subjects such trail building to the approved management objectives that targeted experience and benefit outcome opportunities for the selected market niches--and that the trail fits the accompanying recreation setting prescriptions--all as essential conditions of proactive recreational trail building.
  - Objective 2 specifies ensuring that essential collaborative travel-tourism arrangements with gateway community recreation-tourism providers are in place before such trails are built.
  - Objective 3 specifies that essential considerations for ensuring that fair value-fair return principles are met have been addressed.
  - Objective 4 specifies that this trail fits within the comprehensive travel management plan guidelines and accompanying route designations.
- Adjust the proposed trail accordingly. This may mean postponing it until the above essential conditions are met, perhaps modifying it, and either narrowing or expanding its scope to incorporate elements that achieve these conditions.
- Proceed with building the trail only after all the above conditions have been met.

In this way, BLM program policy outlined in its Unified Strategy ensures that all recreation-tourism sub-programs and initiatives are subjected to the central purpose for which they exist, to: "Manage public and waters for enhanced recreation experiences and quality of life." In other words, they are managed for desired and targeted outcomes.

Further content is added to this objective by its component milestones set forth in *The BLM's Priorities for Recreation and Visitor Services* document. Those which further illustrate the BLM's commitment to OFM are as follows:

- Milestone 1: Shift the management emphasis of the recreation program from an activity-based approach to one which focuses on recreation experiences and [other] benefits.
- Milestone 3: Assess visitor and community resident preferences for recreation experiences and

quality of life outcomes such as public health and fitness and physical education.
- Milestone 4: Identify and map essential landscape settings to meet public preferences and recreation-related experience expectations.
- Milestone 5: Integrate management functions to provide opportunities for the public to obtain their desired experiences and quality of life.

To ensure adoption of OFM in actual practice, the BLM needed to further insert BBM direction within the agency's policy guidance for the development of Land Use Plans (LUPs) and Implementation Plans. This was achieved through revision of the program-specific planning guidance set forth in Appendix C of the BLM's *Land Use Planning Handbook* (H-1601-1). That amended guidance was transmitted to the field on March 11, 2005 (Release 1-1693). This transmittal preceded that for the Unified Strategy simply because the latter took longer to clear the agency's policy directives approval process.

OFM in Implementation of BLM's Recreation Strategy

It was within the context of both the *Unified Strategy* and *The BLM's Priorities for Recreation and Visitor Services Workplan* that the BLM restructured its recreation planning guidance for the development of both Land Use Plans and Recreation Implementation Plans. Ongoing land use planning efforts made urgent the need to update recreation planning guidance; and although the Unified Strategy had not yet cleared directives, the draft prepared by RVSAT provided a sufficient basis to proceed. The updated guidance now requires restructuring both plan content and ensuring field operations, subject to the Unified Strategy, the Workplan's seven program objectives, and ultimately the Department of Interior's Strategic Plan recreation mission goals.

Land Use Planning

The initial recreation Land Use Planning decision--really a management decision--now facing all public lands managers and their recreation planners is that of deciding whether there is significant, identifiable structured recreation-tourism market demand[4] for each unit of public lands. Managers subsequently must decide whether or not to commit to making the intensive management investments required to accommodate that demand. All such areas are managed as Special Recreation Management Areas (SRMAs). Conversely, all remaining lands where both of these conditions are not satisfied (i.e., either specific markets having structured recreation-tourism demands cannot be identified and a commitment to responsively accommodate it) are only managed custodially to take care of but not accommodate new recreation demands. All such areas are managed as Extensive Recreation Management Areas (ERMAs).

SRMAs

Land Use Plan Decisions

Intent: To respond to identified market demand for structured recreation (i.e., experience and other benefit outcomes and the maintenance of recreation setting character).

Context: Here the BLM has been able to identify both specific recreation-tourism markets and their differing but explicit recreation experience and other benefit outcomes and the maintenance of setting character upon which sustained attainment of those outcomes depends.

Content:

1. Identify markets/niches.
2. Write management objectives for experiences and other benefit outcomes.
3. Prescribe essential recreation setting conditions.
4. Outline implementation framework.

Land Use Implementation Decisions

a. Management actions.
b. Marketing actions.
c. Monitoring actions.
d. Administrative support actions.

ERMAs

Land Use Plan Decisions

Intent: To only take care of identified issues

Resulting from recreation activity participation, but neither to accommodate nor facilitate increased recreation activity or activities.

Context: Here the BLM has identified only custodial recreation management issues related to existing recreation activity participation (such as user conflicts, visitor safety, or resource protection). Specific recreation-tourism markets and their desires for structured outcomes are unknown.

Content:

1. Write management objectives for custodial outcomes.
2. Identify implementing actions
   a. Management
   b. Marketing
   c. Monitoring
   d. Administrative support

Post-Land Use Plan Implementation Decisions

None—generally addressed in the Land Use Plan

The significance of that policy is that the BLM authorizes more than custodial recreation management only, where managers are both able to identify structured recreation markets and their demands and willing to proactively accommodate it for selected target market niches. Thus recreation management objectives for SRMAs are written in terms of explicitly stated BBM outcomes (i.e., targeted to selected recreation-tourism markets and niches), whereas management objectives for ERMAs are written in terms in terms of custodial outcomes (i.e., targeted to identified care-taking issues). Increased recreation activity participation is therefore accommodated only where managers can associate that demand with identifiable markets and specific desired outcomes.

This is illustrated in the foregoing graphic representation of these two most basic recreation management options follows. It is noteworthy that, for SRMAs, detailed management, marketing, monitoring, and supporting administrative actions are not Land Use Allocation Decisions, but are instead Implementation decisions. As such, they may be adaptively adjusted at any phase of plan implementation as necessary to achieve management objectives and setting prescriptions. In contrast, for ERMAs, decisions regarding these same kinds of actions are generally written into Land Use Allocation plans to enable managers to begin addressing identified custodial recreation management issues without delay.

The practical outworking of this strategy has significant implications for on-the-ground recreation field operations. Under the BLM's previous activity-based management model, field operations were subject to only to getting projects done to accommodate various recreation activities. Now, all programs and projects are both guided and constrained by the relevant outcome-based management objectives. For SRMAs, all actions must be tailored to produce opportunities to achieve the explicitly stated experience and other benefit outcomes—to individuals, households, communities, economies, and the environment. In addition, SRMAs require that all actions fit within prescribed setting conditions to ensure that their capacity to sustain production of the targeted outcome opportunities is maintained. For ERMAs, all actions must be tailored to achieve the identified custodial outcomes—to provide appropriate levels of visitor safety, reduction of user conflicts, and resource protection. However, actions may only take care of recreation activities under custodial ERMA guidance. To accommodate increased recreation activity requires an SRMA managerial commitment to provide explicit experience and other benefit outcome opportunities for selected visitor and/or resident market niches.

Implementation Planning and Field Operations

For agencies like the BLM, which are transitioning from activity-based to OFM—or Benefits-Based Management as it is called within BLM, implementation planning is where the proverbial "rubber meets the road." That is because if all ongoing activity-based programs and projects within Special Recreation Management Areas are not restructured (i.e., guided, constrained, and functionally integrated) to be held accountable to outcome-focused management objectives and setting prescriptions within approved Land Use Plans, nothing will change. At the same time, if activity-based programs and projects within Extensive Recreation Management Areas—where outcome-focused markets and demands have neither been identified nor planned for—are not constrained to address only identified custodial needs, significant investments will be made for which desired outcomes have not been identified. This, of course, has implications for not only BLM's Field Offices, but for every level of the BLM organization. Increased internal program efficiency in the expenditure of limited human and fiscal resources, and greater external program effectiveness in responding to demonstrated recreation-tourism demand, is the promise of OFM. But that promise will not be realized without the application of

OFM to both the development and execution of Implementation Plans in day-to-day field operations.

Were it possible for Land Use Plans to be written well enough to win Pulitzers, without adequately well-integrated Implementation Plans, their management objectives and setting prescriptions cannot be achieved. This is because the whole point of adopting OFM's expanded conceptual framework is to align all recreation management systems, initiatives, and staffing beyond merely getting activity-based projects and programs completed or implemented. We say "beyond," because OFM requires managers to ensure that no action is implemented unless it is necessary to produce targeted outcome opportunities and facilitate their attainment, and that it sustains the character of recreation settings upon those outcomes depend. Thus, implementation plans select only actions that are both guided and constrained by approved recreation management objectives and setting prescriptions. Indeed, only those actions which are appropriately guided and constrained to actually facilitate production and attainment of targeted experience and other benefit outcome opportunities deserve to be called "facilitating outputs" (re. Chapter 3's normative application processes). This is why the BLM's *Land Use Planning Handbook* guidance requires integration of the agency's multiple and otherwise competing, and sometimes disjointed, recreation components within four basic functional inputs: 1) *management*, 2) *marketing*, 3) *monitoring*, and 4) *administrative support*. Implementation Decisions outlined in the BLM's *Land Use Planning Handbook* call for substantially greater integration and cohesion among the BLM's many "stove piped" recreation sub-programs (the metaphor is an apt illustration of programs, initiatives, and projects which are independent, unrelated, and sometimes cross each another).

Through this new *Land Use Planning Handbook* guidance, the BLM is beginning to hold all recreation resource and facility management, marketing, and administrative actions accountable to produce opportunities for the attainment of desired and targeted experiences and beneficial outcomes. When applying OFM, all program actions are made subject to outcome oriented tests of need. Because targeted outcome opportunities are both produced and attained either directly through provider actions or indirectly through the maintenance of dependent setting characteristics, all implementing actions are subject to two most basic tests:

1. Do they sustain the distinctive and highly-valued character of public lands recreation settings?
2. Do they facilitate production and attainment of desired and targeted experience and benefit outcome opportunities?

This is the kind of program integration called for by the BLM's Land Use Planning Handbook for Implementation Planning decisions:

"For all SRMAs, address four basic but broad types of recreation actions:

1. Recreation management (of resources, visitors, and facilities [i.e., developed recreation sites, roads and trails, recreation concessions]);
2. recreation marketing (including outreach, information and education, promotion, interpretation, environmental education, and other visitor services);
3. recreation monitoring (including social, environmental, and administrative indicators and standards); and
4. recreation administration (regulatory; permits and fees, including use restrictions where necessary and appropriate; recreation concessions; fiscal; data management; and customer liaison)."

Stated most simply, management actions outline how natural and cultural resource attractions, facilities, and the distinctive character of the public lands recreation settings in which they occur are to be managed. In the broadest sense of the term, marketing actions are the counterpart of management actions. They outline the informational, educational, interpretive, and promotional messages needed to provocatively (i.e., using interpreters' language) inform customers about the specific kinds of recreation opportunities being provided. In this regard, management and marketing are actually opposite sides of the job of recreation-tourism management. For the BLM, marketing is essential, both as a management tool and to facilitate the attainment of targeted experiences and other benefits by targeted recreation-tourism markets and the environment itself. Thirdly, monitoring is where the BLM holds itself accountable, both to ensure that its management and marketing actions are consistent and complementary, and that they both are being directed towards the achievement of management objectives and setting prescriptions. Finally, administrative actions outline the supporting organizational infrastructure required to achieve the first three types of actions. Here the challenge is keeping administrative actions in their supporting "caboose" position; they must not be allowed to drive management, marketing, or monitoring actions.

A couple of observations from research illustrate the necessity of sufficiently integrating implementing actions across all programs within these most basic functional inputs and, at the same time, holding them accountable to approved Land Use Plan management objectives and setting prescriptions. Regarding management and marketing, the findings of Zeithaml and her colleagues are particularly helpful (Zeithaml, Parasuraman, & Barry, 1990). They discovered several reasons for the "service quality gap" between customers' service expectations and perceptions. Among those reasons were observed inconsistencies in organizational marketing message content and actual management performance. Implementation planning has an obligation to prevent this gap from developing by ensuring that all recreation program inputs are sufficiently integrated within and balanced across BLM's most basic management and marketing outputs. Definitive marketing information is critically important to enable customers to find and responsibly use and enjoy recreation opportunities that match up with their own desires, but also to facilitate efficient and effective visitor management. Descriptive content about the opportunities provided needs to inform customers about the kinds of services provided and controls exercised, as well as how to responsibly use and enjoy public lands recreation opportunities.

Additional industry analysis by Plog encouraged his development of a tourism development and use growth curve model, through which recreation-tourism destination attractions tend to progress over time (Plog, 1991). He observed that promotion and development fuel increased use, which in turn engenders further promotion and development. Eventually, as the process of growth and development tends to shift the character of attractions from authentic to synthetic, it ends up displacing customers who first valued its authentic setting character and its associated experience and other benefit opportunities. In like manner, the desired experiences and benefit outcome opportunities targeted by LUP management objectives will be eroded and eventually lost if implementation actions are not carefully orchestrated to ensure maintenance of the prescribed setting conditions, and equally distinctive visitor services, upon which they depend. Done wrong, implementation planning not only erodes setting character and the customers' ability to achieve desired experience and other benefit outcomes. It also displaces targeted recreation-tourism market niches, and produces a descending chain of adverse outcomes to affected communities, economies, and the environment. Inappropriate setting stewardship and facility development compromises product integrity, and yet inadequate dispersed recreation investments fail to produce targeted outcome opportunities and maintain the productive capacity of recreation settings. Carefully structured and balanced management, marketing, monitoring, and supporting administrative actions are vital.

For the BLM, the shift from managing dozens of activity-based recreation programs to the restructuring of all disparate program complexity around these four functional inputs stands to make program investments substantially more efficient and cost-effective. This is because it limits program actions to only those required to achieve planned results (i.e., outcome opportunities targeted by management objectives and prescribed recreation setting character conditions). It also facilitates, if not forces, the integration of competing programs (e.g., off-highway vehicle, mountain bike, and quiet recreation; interpretation, visitor information, and tourism promotion). Finally, it curbs unnecessary spending for projects and program actions which are unrelated to approved plan outcome objectives and setting prescriptions (irrespective of however much they may advance individual programs and initiatives).

Implementation Challenges: Making this happen is not as easy as it might at first appear. Among challenges posed, one of the greatest is integrating subprograms (e.g., Accessibility, Interpretation, Permits and Fees), activity-based initiatives (e.g., Off-Highway Vehicles, Scenic Byways, Rivers), and related staffing around within these four more basic functions. Under the BLM's previous activity-based conceptual framework, the program was oriented more towards getting project developments done to accommodate desires of activity-based clienteles for increased recreation participation. Under that premise, "more is better" made sense. But BBM's expanded operating framework now requires first considering desired effects and then holding all actions accountable to targeted outcomes. Now, in the first place, all implementing actions are subject to the most basic requirement of ensuring they actually will add value to the lives of visitors and resident customers, to communities, and to the environment. In addition, for an agency like the BLM, whose primary role is dispersed recreation (and not the development of facility-dependent attractions), recreation management is more about sustaining the distinctive and productive character of recreation settings than it is about facility development. Wherever facilities are needed, the outcome-focused approach insists that they be designed and placed to indeed facilitate desired and targeted recreation outcomes--and that they maintain the essential setting characteristics upon which attainment of those improved conditions depends.

So why is making that happen so difficult? There are several reasons. Most of the BLM's staffing structure, and its workload performance measures as well, are still geared only towards getting projects done. Most existing partnerships are likewise structured to help the agency do this. Most existing management objectives formulated under an activity-based paradigm were written to get things done, not to produce desired experience and other benefit opportunities, nor to facilitate their attainment as realized outcomes. Much staffing remains structured around individual programs (e.g., off-highway vehicle management, river management, wilderness management, etc.). And most of the training has been geared towards the same ends. In the end, there is no implication in any of this that anyone is to be faulted for doing a good job of advancing greater recreation activity participation. The bottom line is that this was only the logical result of addressing recreation activities only and what strategy and policy directed at the time.

This long-standing activity-based, project and program development focus also encouraged and facilitated development of extremely strong program-specific advocacy. The resulting "stove-piped" professional perspectives produced extremely strong professional allegiances for certain activities than for others. It was within this context that each of several dozen discrete programs sought, and sometimes fought for its own turf, and in fact for its own activity-based strategies (e.g., OHV Management, Mountain Bike Management, River Management, Interpretation, Back Country Byways, Cave Management, etc.). It is, however, extremely difficult if not impossible to integrate such "stove-piped" programs, or to hold them accountable for the achievement of mutually compatible ends larger than themselves. It does not work to continue developing piecemeal, activity-based management strategies (e.g., for interpretation, environmental education, user ethics, and promotional outreach efforts) because each such initiative fails to focus beyond its own program outputs as its desired ends. The challenge is maintaining activity-based program constituent liaison while facilitating intra-activity teamwork that integrates or synthesizes program concerns to formulate appropriate sets of management, marketing, monitoring, and supportive administrative actions that respond, not to every activity-based customer clientele, but to selected primary recreation-tourism markets and niches that best fit each situation.

Operational Necessities for Implementation Planning: First of all then, two priority conditions must be observed for implementation planning within the BLM. BLM's Land Use Planning Handbook requires that implementing actions be both guided and constrained by approved management objectives. For SRMAs, implementing actions must be geared towards addressing recreation-tourism demand from identified primary recreation-tourism markets (see Appendix C, *Land Use Planning Handbook*). This requires moving away from simply accommodating the desires of activity-based project proponents. At the same time, field offices need to identify the markets they share in common with other field offices (and with other recreation-tourism providers as well) to further inter-office cooperation (and community-based collaboration) across administrative boundaries. Both conditions are essential to the elimination of waste, counter-productive program investments, and nonconstructive inter-office rivalry.

Secondly, for implementation planning, OFM calls for an unprecedented level of iterative, two-way dialogue within the BLM that is responsive to the various primary recreation-tourism customer markets targeted by management objectives. Those management objectives now require BLM's recreation planners and managers to formulate implementation actions that are responsive to targeted visitor and resident customers--and also to the affecting private sector business and local government service and infrastructure providers upon which the BLM and its customers are reliant (wherever the BLM is not a sole-source provider, which is practically everywhere). This embraces strategies for the development of functional implementation actions that end up guiding and constraining field operations (vs. program-specific strategies that advance specific recreation activities or programs).

The integrative, operational teamwork is essential for the formulation of minimum implementation actions within each of recreation's four most basic functional recreation inputs: management, monitoring, marketing, and administrative support. Integration of traditional programs into more cohesive functional inputs, for example, involves having wilderness proponents and off-highway vehicle proponents within the agency working together to determine which kinds of actions are needed, neither to advance their individual programs nor their respective constituent groups, but within each RMZ. It also requires subjecting all activity-based and program-specific initiatives to, and making their proposals conditioned upon, producing the outcome-based experience and other benefit opportunities targeted by management objectives and approved recreation setting character conditions. Unless recreation planners make these functional shifts both in implementation plans and ensuring field operations, useable plans will neither be developed, nor implemented.

A third and related challenge is ensuring, as implementing actions are integrated within these most basic management, marketing, monitoring, and administrative functions--that they consider the cause-and-effect production process interrelationships. These are reflected in the hierarchical ordering of the BLM's seven program objectives within the Unified Strategy. Properly applied, this requires conditioning all administrative partnership authorizations (program objective number 7) upon the more basic management (e.g., recreation and travel facilities, objective numbers 4 and 5), marketing (e.g., visitor information, tourism promotion, and interpretation—objective No. 6), and administrative (e.g., collaborative management agreements with affecting providers or user fees, objective numbers 2 and 3) actions which they are supposed to implement. This is a decided move away from authorizing partnerships to do the kinds of projects which advance the needs of activity-based project proponents. It further requires evaluating the appropriateness of actions proposed on the degree to which each demonstrates is explicit contribution to the achievement of outcomes-based management objectives and setting prescriptions (i.e., program objective number 1).

These are not simply ordinal implementation planning policy requirements (i.e., that actions be implemented in the right order). Both the planning and execution of implementation actions need to consider layered, cause-and-effect implications as the appropriateness of each implementing is considered down the program objective hierarchy outlined in BLM's Unified Strategy. Some actions are conditioned by multiple other precursor actions. Visitor information, for example, is first accountable to the three unifying program objectives, each in their respective cause-and-effect order (i.e., objective No. 1, provide recreation experiences and quality of life benefits [i.e., those targeted by management objectives and setting prescriptions]; objective number 2, collaboratively manage with community-based recreation-tourism providers; and objective number 3, ensure fair value and fair return). Visitor information needs also to be further integrated with other marketing actions (and its companion visitor information, interpretation, and promotion/marketing functions). Finally, these integrated and balanced marketing inputs must be held accountable to monitoring feedback and supported by appropriate administrative inputs and monitored accordingly.

Interim Management

For many BLM managers, interim management is an even larger question than the development of LUPs or Implementation Plans. That is due to the large acreage for which updated LUPs have not yet been completed, and for which scheduled plan updates are yet several years out. Meanwhile, a variety of different kinds of developments proceed, and managers therefore asked for some kind of interim recreation guidance. BLM Instruction Memorandum No. 2006-060, referenced above, entitled "Incorporating Benefits-Based Management within Recreation and Visitor Services Program Policy Changes," not only affirmed the BLM Executive Leadership Team's (ELT) commitment to apply the expanded benefits-based conceptual framework for planning and managing public lands recreation. It also requires the application of BBM principles to the interim management of Special Recreation Management Areas:

> "Until LUPs incorporating Appendices C and D policies have been approved--and for completed LUPs which do not incorporate Appendices C and D policies, Field Managers will assess and evaluate effects of proposed projects in Special Recreation Management Areas on activities, experiences, beneficial outcomes and recreation setting character to ensure consistency with benefits-based management concepts."

That implies assessing projects' affects on key recreation-tourism markets and their ability to achieve desired structured recreation experience and benefit outcomes. It also implies assessing projects' affects on maintenance of the distinctive and productive capacity of recreation setting characteristics upon which the attainment of those desired outcomes depends.

Recreation Training

The BLM's RVSAT proposed a comprehensive training curriculum supported by a suite of training courses. To move the agency forward in a timely manner given its accelerated Land Use Planning Schedule and fully implement new Land Use Planning Handbook requirements, an 8300-11 Course was developed by the BLM's National Training Center (NTC). It is being taught by a rotating cadre of Field Office and State Office recreation planners. As this chapter is being written, NTC is engaged in preplanning for an Implementation Planning training session. Completion and delivery of that training module, however, may be contingent upon the completed update of a more detailed recreation planning manual and handbook which is not yet underway.

In addition, the RVSAT advised Headquarters to implement a benefits-based curriculum or academy to guide the professional development of entry level, journeyman, and senior level BLM recreation staff. The purpose was to provide basic background as to the state of BLM's Recreation Training suite of courses, provide a compelling reason for the development of a professional level curriculum for BLM staff, and to recommend the basic parameters and guiding principals that a recreation curriculum would include.

Rationale for the recommended increased training includes prominence of recreation as one of four key Department of Interior mission statements, adoption of the expanded BBM conceptual framework, growing awareness of public recreation-tourism attractions and consequent increases in demand, and increased interest in and commitment to the program by the BLM's Executive Leadership Team. Underscoring the need for accelerated recreation planning training rationale comes from the changing composition of BLM's recreation workforce.

No longer is core recreation staffing coming to the agency having traditional resource-based university training or from within the BLM itself. This cultural change is positive, but it requires a correspondingly greater training commitment on top of that necessitated by the shift to OFM.

Consequences

Early on in the process of doing staff work for the BLM's adoption of the outcome-focused BBM framework, the RVSAT detailed some of the more important consequences to be considered, positive and negative. These figured prominently in the agency's shift to OFM and are summarized here.

Positive Consequences of Applying and Implementing OFM:

1. *Integrated service delivery for the production and attainment of outcome opportunities.* From its inception, BLM's recreation program has been comprised of a series of different, competing programs. The OFM shifts the focus away from managing programs and advancing projects produce opportunities for the attainment of satisfying experiences and other benefits to visitors, adjoining gateway communities and their residents, their economies, and the land itself.
2. *Sustaining the distinctive, productive character of public lands recreation settings.* Program and project-driven recreation management fostered facility-dependent recreation. But for BLM public lands, the agency's dispersed recreation role requires maintaining the setting characteristics upon which desired outcome attainment depends. All facility development therefore must facilitate dispersed recreation use and enjoyment rather than build facility-dependent attractions.
3. *Engagement of Key Affecting Recreation-Tourism Providers as Managing Partners.* The BLM is not a sole-source recreation-tourism provider. That is because public lands are so closely juxtaposed with hundreds of gateway communities that provide essential private sector business services and essential local government infrastructure support. BLM will therefore collaboratively engage these other recreation-tourism providers as managing partners to first decide what specific kinds of recreation opportunities are to be provided and agree on the essential setting characteristics that need to be maintained to produce these opportunities. Only then will on-site implementation partnership project work be considered.
4. *Expanding Implementing Partnerships to Include all Relevant Stakeholders.* Recreation user and interest group partnerships have extended the reach of BLM's recreation funding appropriations for years. While such partnerships have been necessary to get projects done, they have sometimes prevailed over the wider interests of a less well-organized but larger public lands recreation constituency. That constituency includes not only traditional outdoor recreation participants, but an increasingly diverse tourism clientele, affected residents within adjoining gateway, resort, and metropolitan-base camp communities. OFM also expands implementing partnership

actions to include a network of recreation service providers and managing partners.

Negative Consequences of Failing to Apply and Implement OFM:

1. *Loss of the productive capacity of public lands to enrich customers' quality of life.* More importantly than producing generally dissatisfied customers, failure to implement an outcome approach will continue producing unwanted and unintended dissatisfying experiences, negative outcomes, and will continue eroding the distinctive character of public lands recreation settings. Among those dissatisfying outcomes would be the displacement of visitors from public lands settings, and an accompanying loss of quality of life outcomes to community residents, and reduced resource stewardship.
2. *Loss of what makes public lands recreation settings distinctive and productive.* The continued transformation of desired public lands recreation setting character sometimes stems from the BLM's own recreation program investments as well as from poorly executed growth and development. It is often irreversible and irretrievable. BLM manages public lands carved out of the original frontier, and much of this acreage retains along with the small-town character of adjoining communities, its original rural character and charm. Recreation setting character is the "golden goose" which yields the desired experiences and other quality of life outcomes so important to visitors, affected communities and their residents, and to the land itself.
3. *Loss of a fair value and return to the public for the commercial use of its land.* Failure to implement OFM will shortchange the American public by providing undesirable recreation settings and outcomes and less than the fair value required. It therefore results in obtaining less than a fair return for the commercial use of the public lands. Those impacts would lead to secondary, spin-off negative consequences in the form of reduced capacity among all three key recreation-tourism provider sectors: BLM, local governments, and service-providing businesses and industry.
4. *Inability of visitors and residents to obtain desired recreation outcomes.* The inability of both existing and prospective visitors to--and for an ever growing local resident clientele--to have and find areas providing the kinds of outcome opportunities they seek would not be inconsequential. Continued accommodation of growing recreation activity demand (absent managing outcome opportunities) and undifferentiated marketing to "sell" what is presently provided (without regard for customers' specific recreation experience and benefit preferences) leads to homogenized and industrialized recreation development.
5. *Reduced visitor satisfaction and support.* While studies often focus on satisfaction as an end unto itself, ultimate impacts are experienced in lack of public support for the missing, desired responsive recreation management, should the agency fail to apply and implement OFM.
6. *Increased litigation and plan implementation delays.* As if to add insult to injury, increased litigation would even further reduce the BLM's response capacity.
7. *Reduced effectiveness and efficiency.* Should the BLM be unable to refocus its Recreation and Visitor Services program beyond simply implementing its own projects and initiatives, to instead address what matters most to its customers, both program effectiveness and efficiency would remain compromised. Attendant failure to facilitate the sustainable production and attainment of those experience and benefits most highly valued by public lands customers would also be a disincentive for affecting local governments and recreation-tourism business and industry to collaborate with the BLM as full-fledged managing partners.

Summary

There is significant enthusiasm for the BLM's adoption of BBM, or OFM. This expanded conceptual framework is a whole systems approach to the management of all components of recreation production. It directs the agency to carefully identify recreation-tourism markets and their desires for experience and benefit outcome opportunities. In this way, OFM broadens the agency's definition of customer beyond traditional outdoor recreation participants to include affected community residents and other key touring, resort, special event, and city/village markets, as well as those who come to visit friends and relatives in hundreds of gateway communities. OFM calls the agency to recognize and manage the distinctive character pubic lands recreation settings and their important contribution to the sustained production of structured recreation demand for life-enriching experiences and other benefit opportunities. It recognizes the existence of recreation-tourism service delivery systems larger than the BLM and public lands, and encourages the engagement of key service-providing businesses and local governments as managing partners with the BLM. In this way, it helps the agency meet the fair value-fair return goals of the Department of the Interior as it meets its goal to provide quality experiences and other quality of life outcomes. Last but not least, OFM requires the more efficient and effective consolidation and integration of dozens of BLM recreation program actions and initiatives into recreation's most basic functional inputs: management, marketing, monitoring, and administrative support. OFM is transforming not only the development of Land Use Plans and Implementation Plans, but implementing field operations as well. OFM is beginning to reposition the BLM as one of the nation's most innovative providers of dispersed recreation and allows the agency to relate its mission to the complex social-economic-ecological systems of which it is an integral part.

Literature Cited

Plog, S. (1991). *Leisure Travel: Making it a Growth Market...Again!* (pp. 59–84). New York: John Wiley & Sons, Inc.

Conservation Ecology 4(2):5. [online] URL: http://www.consecol.org/vol4/iss2/art5/

Hollin, C., Berkes, F. & Folke, C. (1998). Science, sustainability, and resource management. In F. Berkes & C. Folke (Eds.), *Linking Social and Ecological Systems: Management Practices and Social Mechanisms for Building Resilience.* New York: Cambridge University Press.

USDI Bureau of Land Management. (2003). *Land Use Planning Handbook* (H-1601-1, Release 1–1693, March 11, 2005). Washington D.C.

USDI Bureau of Land Management. (2006). Information Bulletin No. 2004–072, February 27, 2004, "The BLM's Priorities for Recreation and Visitor Services Workplan 2003–2007". Washington D.C.

USDI Bureau of Land Management. (2003). *The BLM's Priorities for Recreation and Visitor Services*, BLM Workplan Fiscal years 2003–2007, May 2003. Washington D.C.

USDI Bureau of Land Management. (2004). Information Bulletin No. 2004–073, March 1, 2004, "Establishment of a Recreation and Visitor Services Advisory Team (RVSAT). Washington D.C.

USDI Bureau of Land Management. (2003). The Recreation and Visitor Services Team (RVSAT) Charter, as amended, July 29, 2003. Washington D.C.

USDI Bureau of Land Management. (2006). Instruction Memorandum No. 2006-060, January 10, 2006, "Incorporating Benefits-Based Management within Recreation and Visitor Services Program Policy Changes". Washington D.C.

USDI Bureau of Land Management. (2006). Instruction Memorandum No. 2007–043, January 26, 2007, "A Unified Strategy to Implement 'BLM's Priorities for Recreation and Visitor Services' Workplan" (Purple Book). Washington D.C.

Zeithaml, V., Parasuraman, A., & Berry. L. (1990). *Delivering Quality Service* (pp. 35–49). New York: The Free Press.

Footnotes

1. The concepts of resilience, adaptive capacity, and sustainability are adapted from the works of Holling, Berkes, & Folke, 1998.
2. This phrase, "the land that nobody wanted," became an apt description of the remaining public domain which was found desirable for homesteading, mining claim entry, National Parks and Monuments, National Forests, and other reserves.
3. House of Representatives Report 108–195 (Department of the Interior and Related Agencies Appropriations Bill, 2004) under Title I—Department of the Interior, Bureau of Land Management, required the preparation of this Report to the Committee.
4. "Structured recreation-tourism market demand" describes desires for specific experiences and other benefits and accompanying maintenance of recreation setting characteristics upon which attainment of those desired outcomes depends. For recreation participants, this includes recreation activities; but in the case of resident customers, it may only include preferences for setting characteristics upon which those outcomes depend (re. BLM's Land Use Planning Handbook).

Chapter 9

Managing Recreation Opportunities for a Spectrum of Experiential Benefits by the USDA Forest Service

Allen Jaten

Learning Objectives:

1. Understand ROS as EFM, which is a limited type of OFM.
2. Understand that the USFS, while practicing limited OFM through the application of the ROS, does not fully implement OFM.

Recreation on the National Forests and Needs for Better Recreation Resource Management Systems

The nation's forests have a long and rich history of providing outdoor recreation opportunities for visitors to the varieties of landscapes managed by the USFS. A significant part of that history is the development and application of methods, including management systems, to manage the public wildlands under agency administration to provide a variety of quality recreation opportunities. Those managerial approaches have been supported by recreation researchers, managers, planners, and field-level recreation technicians, all with the focus on each visitor enjoying their respective experiences and taking with them memories of a valuable interaction with this treasured outdoor wonderland.

In a speech in 2004, then Chief Dale Bosworth stated, "For the last 40 years, the Multiple Use Sustained Yield Act of 1960 has been the foundation for much of our mission. Recreation is specifically named in the Act." He went on to say that the reason people keep coming to the national forests for their recreation is the "memories." "Most people will always remember catching their first fish, making their first climb, or seeing their first bear. People are coming for memories like these. They come for memories of wildlife, outdoor adventure, wilderness, or splendid scenery and natural landscapes which consistently rank among the highest values in our visitor surveys." Earlier, Chief Mike Dombeck (1997) acknowledged that "recreation is now the dominant use of the National Forests."

Despite the USFS's emphasis on outdoor recreation, particularly since the 1960s, an explicit outcomes-oriented managerial focus was lacking, as chronicled elsewhere (Moore & Driver 2005:157). To be sure, there were forward-thinking employees of the USFS and National Park Service (NPS) who recognized the social significance of recreational uses of the national forests and parks before then (e.g., Albright, Carhart, Marshall, and Mather). Nevertheless, recreation was not recognized as one of the primary uses of the national forests until the early 1960s. The passage of the Multiple Use and Sustained Yield Act (MUSYA, 1960) and the publishing of the Outdoor Recreation Resources Review Commission (ORRRC, 1962) findings resulted in a growing focus on a more professional approach to managing recreation opportunities on the national forests and by other similar providers. The change to this approach stimulated the incremental development of science-based methods and systems to guide the management of outdoor recreation resources and services. Prior to the early 1970s, these methods and approaches did not exist (see Chapter 12 of Moore & Driver, 2005). Indeed, the reports of the ORRRC can be viewed as the watershed event in the emergence of a professional managerial perspective about the management of outdoor recreation resources. One of the first science-based recreation-related management systems developed and applied by the USFS was its Visual Resource Management System (USDA Forest Service, 1974). Work started on the Recreation Opportunity Spectrum (ROS) System, the focus of this chapter, soon thereafter in 1978.

Evolution of the ROS

Lead Efforts by the USFS

During the active period of the ORRRC, from 1958 to 1962, Congress passed the MUSYA 1960 which mandated that the USFS give full and equal consideration to *all uses* of the public lands for which it had stewardship responsibilities; not solely the harvesting of timber by the USFS for example. Coincidentally, shortly after enacting the MUSYA 1960, Congress passed similar, but much more limited legislation, the Classification and Multiple Use Act (CMUA, 1964), applicable specifically to the US Bureau of Land Management (BLM), which had primarily focused its management on mining and grazing with much less attention given to recreation. Unfortunately, neither agency responded to these two legislative acts either in the manner, or with the results, for which Congress intended. This led to more definitive and prescriptive legislation in the National Forest Management Act (NFMA, 1976) for the USFS and the Federal Land Management and Policy Act (FLMPA, 1976) for the BLM. It took this type of attention-capturing legislation to motivate these agencies to sincerely focus on implementing management that considered the economic and social values of all the uses of public lands, including uses for outdoor recreation opportunities.

For the USFS, this was the genesis of what became known as "land management planning." Because of this nearly radical change in direction, it took time, trials, and several experiments for forest personnel to determine how to best meet the requirements of the legislation. The real underlying intent of the legislation was for agencies to work collaboratively with their various constituents in planning how the lands and resources would be allocated and used. It must be noted at this point that Congress was petitioned by constituents of both agencies to pass more stringent and specific legislation because neither agency had responded to the needs of outdoor recreation interests of both the national forests and other public lands as a result of the previous legislation. Neither agency really understood that the American public was serious about environmental concerns, including better accommodation of demands for outdoor recreation opportunities and being included in the decision-making process that led to land allocation.

For the USFS recreation managers, without a framework to systematically inventory, categorize, and quantify elements of the recreation resource in a way that would enable communication with forest users and constituents, it was a daunting task to find the tools (management systems) to meet the public desires and expectations to participate in the planning process and meet the requirements of the legislation. One of the results of the ORRRC work was the development of a classification system, the Area Classification Plan (ACP). The ACP used general characteristics of different types of lands to classify them (Moore & Driver, 2005) in the following structure:

- Class I: High-Density Recreation Areas
- Class II: General Outdoor Recreation Areas
- Class III: Natural Environment Areas
- Class IV: Unique Natural Areas
- Class V: Primitive Areas
- Class VI: Historic and Cultural Sites

As evidenced in this classification scheme, the land, or "setting" was viewed early on as a critical element for capturing, classifying, or categorizing outdoor recreation activities. Because there was no applicable science-based outdoor recreation research available at the time, this approach was not based on anything more than what seemed a logical, and intuitively identifiable, place to begin. This system was used in one form or another until the multidimensional ROS replaced its use in a number, although not a majority, of agencies and outdoor recreation providers. Many agencies yet employ the ACP.

Even after these legislative actions passed, the USFS did *not* have a tested or proven cost-effective system or method for inventorying and managing recreation resources. There were less than a half-dozen tools in use, none of which were satisfactorily effective for the USFS (even though a few other agencies have continued to use some of them). In fact, a primary result of the legislation served only to reveal that there were more basic needs in the area of recreation resources management requiring resolution than merely passing laws mandating certain actions be taken or results attained by managing agencies. For example, there was no:

- widely agreed upon definition for "recreation";
- clarification of the objects of planning and management;
- clarification of the role of management in the provision/production of what is commonly known today as recreation opportunities; and
- description of either a procedure or how recreation management might be applied as a "production system" (Driver, Brown, Stankey, and Gregoire, 1987: 202).

To help fill this void and give better theoretical standing to the concept of recreation, Driver and Tocher (1968: 9–31) introduced concepts of a "psychological interpretation" of the experiential nature of leisure behavior and its relevance to management to many leisure professionals[1]. That led Driver, while at The University of Michigan, to focus his early research on the types of psychological experiences that were both most and least valued by recreationists engaging in a wide variety of recreation activities in different settings. This research, conducted with several associates over a period of some 12 years, resulted in the development of a measurement tool, the Recreation Experience Preference (REP) scales, after exhaustive testing of their psychometric properties such as their reliability and validity. The scales are described in Appendix A of Moore & Driver (2005: 315–320). Research work and application testing of the REP scales continued on after Driver moved to take the position of Recreation Research Project Leader with the USFS Rocky Mountain Forest and Range Experiment Station. His research there was partially funded by the Recreation Directors of Regions 2, 3, and 5 of the USFS, who saw its relevance to recreation resource planning and management particularly after passage of the 1976 National Forest Management Act and its explicit mandate that recreational uses be given commensurate consideration with all other resource allocations in planning and managerial decisions.

After the NFMA was passed and the formally authorized land management planning process for the USFS was approved (i.e., characterized by several iterations of such published in the *Federal Register*, as required by law), the USFS authorized "lead" or "pilot" forests in each of its nine administrative regions to determine if any of the then available systems for inventorying, planning, and managing outdoor recreation resources and services would successfully meet the requirements of the NFMA. The Southwest region of the USFS found that none of the systems it had tried to apply were adequate systems, including the RII system then prescribed in the USFS's recreation management manual of directives (USDA FSM 1977). The demonstrated deficiencies of the systems tested paired with the mandates of the 1976 NFMA increased the urgency to develop a capable system.

That urgency led to agency managers turning to "applied research" for answers and assistance. Because the Recreation Directors and their staff members of the USFS's Rocky Mountain Region (R2), Southwest Region (R3), and Pacific Southwest Regions (R5) were familiar with and had helped to financially support the developmental work on the REP scales, Driver was invited to a meeting in R3 in 1977 at which application of the four different inadequate systems tested in R3 was discussed. The question to be deliberated was: Could a new system be developed that would meet the requirements of the NFMA, and that would consider and functionally integrate *all* the USFS values and uses, including recreation, into their land management plans? Those deliberations resulted in Driver being asked to consider working with USFS recreation planners and managers to develop a new system that would be based on inventorying and managing lands administered by the USFS not only for recreation activities, but also for the relevant psychological experiences that Driver and his associates had been researching. Driver accepted the challenge and invited an associate, Perry Brown, to help with that effort. Brown, then a professor at Colorado State University, was actively helping Driver refine the REP scales and concurrently, several of the doctoral students who worked with Brown and Driver were examining relationships between desired recreation experiences and attributes of the recreation settings on which those experiences depended. Together, and with the assistance of several USFS recreation planners, they developed and published the early concepts of what was to become the ROS system (Driver and Brown, 1978: 24–31; and Brown, Driver, & McConnell, 1978: 73–84). At the fall 1978 meeting of the USFS Director of Recreation, along with his key staff and the Regional Directors of Recreation, Wilderness, and Cultural Resources, Brown presented the concepts, applications, and results of their preliminary work on the ROS system. The presentation was well accepted and the Directors decided to adopt the ROS approach. A task force was established, with Driver as a member, to refine the ROS system and prepare it to be brought on line for a national application on all forests to meet the NFMA requirements: that all values and uses be considered and be functionally integrated in plans (land management planning) for the national forests and grasslands. Several forests moved forward in implementing and applying the ROS. One result of these applications was Driver writing an integrative ROS paper that later helped the development of the "ROS Users Guide" (USFS, 1982)[2], an effort that was led by Dave Harmer.

Not without some risk of breaking the continuity of this exposition on the evolution of the ROS at this point, it seems appropriate from an historical perspective to mention that as far back as the 1960s, several authors had proposed a spectrum of outdoor recreation opportunities. Therefore, the concept of a spectrum of recreation settings, activities, experiences, and even other benefits recognized by OFM was not novel, albeit yet undefined, when the ROS was being developed. But, what had neither been identified nor clarified were the bases for defining the different classes of recreation opportunities or resources that could be characterized along a proposed spectrum. There was practically no research supporting the concept of a specific proposed spectrum of experiences or what it was that supposedly defined what that spectrum was or how to inventory and manage such. That specificity, backed by research investigations and accepted theories of leisure behavior, was the most important among other ROS contributions that was needed to meet requirement of the 1976 NFM because of the aforementioned deficiencies of the other systems. For example, one result of the increasing focus on a more professional approach to outdoor recreation management in the 1960s by the USFS was development and use of the Recreation Inventory Instructions (RII) system (USDA FSM, 1977) for inventorying recreation opportunities on the wildlands administered by the USFS. Even though well intended and founded on a solid approach to recreation resources inventory, this system had field application problems and yielded poor results. Not the least of these was that it was single dimensional and constructed without the foundation of an empirical research base (Brown, Driver, and McConnell, 1978). The RII system was developed to be applied as an attempt to satisfy the requirements of the MUSYA 1960, but it did not produce the desired results. The major problems with it were it was (1) too costly to apply system-wide; (2) not based on credible research or theory; and (3) built on the concept of "recreation experience levels," which, in this model, emphasized "primitive" experiences over all other types with no justification for doing so.

The BLM and Development of the ROS

Shortly after the ROS task force was created, Darrell Lewis, then Director of the Recreation and Wilderness Resources of the BLM, contacted Driver and Brown because the 1976 FLMPA for the BLM mandated that the BLM meet the *same* requirements that the 1976 NFMA mandated the USFS meet. Put simply, the BLM needed a recreation resource planning and management system for the identical reasons the USFS did. Therefore, Lewis quickly became an advocate of the ROS, supporting the work of Driver and Brown through some funding from BLM to enable them to work with Lewis' staff. At the same time, Lewis worked closely with his USFS counterpart, Roy Feuchter (then Director of Recreation for the USFS). Specifically, Lewis provided some funds to Driver and Brown to help get the ROS systems tested and applied in the BLM. He and Feuchter also helped Driver prepare a videotape on the ROS at Colorado State University. The video addressed the purpose, scope, and application of the ROS. The following quote from that script provides some contextual background that the ROS was developed to meet both a long-standing management need and the requirements of the 1976 NFMA and the FLMPA.

> In the past it was difficult to integrate all resource information into a comprehensive plan. For example, until the ROS was developed, no system existed which adequately integrated outdoor recreation values into multiple-use land management planning. Now, however, the ROS system provides the land manager with a useful framework for thinking about recreation resources and their values during all stages of planning and management. Instead of being a set of hard fixed rules and requirements, the ROS is a conceptual scaffold on which management direction can be built.

The operative phrase here for the future applications was "conceptual scaffold on which management direction can be built." Pilot applications of the ROS were established in both the USFS and the BLM to refine the ROS system before the guidelines for applying it were published as the "ROS Users Guide" (USFS, 1981 and 1882). The essential elements and structure of the ROS are summarized in Chapter 12 of Moore & Driver (2005: 169-175).

The BLM adopted the same version of the ROS as the USFS did. Lewis strongly believed and understood the value of the ROS not only for fulfilling the mandates of the 1976 NFMA and the FLMPA, but also that inherent in the design of the ROS was a system that was capable of not only providing recreation resource management tools beyond simply "managing for activities," but also "managing for experiences." In Lewis' words, "In retrospect, development and application of the ROS system for managing recreation resources was my first exposure to Outcomes-Focused Management. It was, because the types of outcomes the ROS focused on were both the desired and the undesired experiences (one of the types of outcomes considered by OFM) that could be realized from participation in different recreation activities in different recreation settings that vary from urban to primitive in nature" (Chapter 7 of this text).

Particularly significant to the wide scale adoption and implementation of the ROS system wide in the USFS and the BLM were the efforts undertaken in support of those ends by Warren Bacon, then the Regional Landscape Architect, Northwest Region (R6) of the USFS.[3] Among other things, he led the preparation and development of:

- a videotape on the ROS;
- a very effective, and subsequently popular, poster-sized wall chart that illustrated by color photographs what managerial actions could and could not be permitted in the different ROS zones and for particular setting attributes, such as roads, access, density of use, etc.; and
- a valuable ROS brochure, "ROS Primer and Field Guide (R6, USDA Forest Service, April 1990). This brochure also incorporated aspects of the ROS system developed by Clark and Stankey (1979). The Clark and Stankey system was being developed during the same time frame the Driver and Brown ROS system was being developed. However, Driver and Brown had the agency lead for developing what became the ROS for both the USFS and the BLM, so the Clark and Stankey system was not formally adopted by either the USFS or the BLM.

Application of the ROS in the Forest Service

In 1982, the headquarters office of the USFS directed its field offices to use "...the Recreation Opportunity Spectrum as the basic framework for inventorying, planning, and managing the recreation resource in accordance with the Forest and Rangeland Renewable Resources Planning Act of 1974 (RPA), as amended by the National Forest Management Act of 1976 (NFMA)." As such, planning for a spectrum of recreation opportunities using the ROS was directed to be a central part of Land and Resource Management Planning. The recreation input included factors such as supply and demand, related issues, and identification of alternative responses to those issues which the planner was required to assess in order to develop management area prescriptions designed to assure the appropriate recreation experience through setting and activity management on the Forest.

The adoption of the ROS was not easy and a few problems developed within the agency on the way to full implementation. When the ROS was being brought on line in the early 1980s, the then Chief of the USFS did not fully grasp the nuances of applying an inventory system to recreation resources versus the then long-standing practice of applying an inventory system to other agency programs such as timber management. He believed that an inventory application should consist of the potential of recreation to produce opportunities; but for several reasons he did not understand the logic and purposes of the ROS system. Because of these misunderstandings, he instructed the Director of Recreation to not employ the ROS. The Director's response was that the USFS was already using ROS for recreation resource inventorying in National Forest Planning and would continue so to do. The Chief then instructed the Director to not put any information or guidance regarding the ROS out to the field, however, the "cat was already out of the bag" so to speak.

Many recreation managers in the field recognized the value of and were familiar with the ROS, or at least the principles and the need for it. One of those perceptive managers and widely respected national leaders mentioned previously, Warren Bacon, developed what became widely known in recreation practitioner circles as the "7-sheet" slide program in which he presented, simultaneously by seven slide projectors literally projecting onto seven bedsheets (before the days of PowerPoint), fading from one to another, the seven ROS classes or zones with photographic examples of the appropriate facility development levels, construction materials, settings, appropriate recreation opportunities, etc. It produced the classic "a picture is worth a thousand words" result. Bacon was invited to present his creation at a great number of locations where USFS recreation personnel were keenly interested in the ROS—from recreation conferences, to seminars, to interested university classes--while continually educating recreation practitioners to the values of the ROS system. He also produced a video dealing with the ROS as well as an influential and widely distributed brochure (see preceding BLM section).

In the 1986 edition of the USFS ROS book, Feuchter wrote:

> "A key ROS concept is that it provides a framework which allows administrators to manage for, and users to enjoy, a variety of recreation environments. This variety will more and more become the cornerstone of the National Forest System. ROS is *not* a land classification system; it is a management objective, a way of describing and providing a variety of recreation opportunities, a critical initiative if we are to excel and be viewed as balanced land managers." (1986 ROS Book).

The ROS system was firmly entrenched in USFS recreation resource management. Implementation of it would lead to the development of what today are "benefits" management systems. However, there were some problems in application of the ROS in forest-planning efforts. While recreation planners in many forests immediately recognized the value of the ROS in supporting recreation resource planning for Forest Land Management Planning in the early 1980s, it was frequently misapplied. The paradox was the ROS was an excellent tool, but it was the only tool nationally available that was capable of inventorying and classifying settings to establish zone type prescriptions for opportunity types, facility construction, and experience expectations, essentially describing the relationships among those settings, activities, facilities, and experiences and how they are affected by both recreationists and managers. But the application was designed for a large scale, "broad brush" application--prescriptions for land allocation; and not micro-design or site and project scale decisions. A vacuum of the need for a project-level analysis tool caused many planners to try to apply the ROS in a manner for which it was never intended. The ROS can be used for a variety of purposes and at many planning and management levels (Driver and Brown, 1978; Brown et al., 1978; Clark, 1980; Clark and Stankey, 1979a), but it was designed for application to relatively large tracts of land and not for project- or site-level planning. This misapplication in the void of a management system existing for project-level planning caused confusion among several critics of the ROS (see Moore & Driver, 2005: 174–175).

The ROS is not a prescriptive handbook with a set-in-concrete list of rules and formulas, but rather it is a flexible *framework* to help make judgments--the art of management--and set guideposts from which to make allocation decisions (Clark, 1982). By the time of the second round of forest planning in the 1990s, most recreation planners understood the capability of the ROS and applied it appropriately.

The aforementioned misapplication of the ROS by USFS field managers in the early rounds of forest land management planning demonstrated the need for a project and site-level management system. The research and findings related to the principles of OFM was continuing push the understanding of field-level managers. These understandings combined with the USFS site and project-level management tool, Meaningful Measures (MM), which was being developed and brought on line, pioneered by Driver's research (Jaten and Driver, 1998), during this time period enabled planners and managers to apply this more appropriate management tool for inventory and analysis purposes at the project and site level scale which worked in concert with the ROS being applied at larger land management planning and allocation scales.

The Recreation Opportunity System as an Experience-Focused Management System and therefore a Limited Application of OFM

To relate the ROS to OFM, the theme of this chapter, it is necessary to understand that the ROS is an Experience-Focused Management (EFM) application, which is a *limited type of OFM*, as explained in Chapter 1 of this text. Specifically, application of the ROS considers the experiential benefits but not the other two types of benefits of leisure defined in Chapter 1 of this text that must be considered under OFM planning and management. The USFS is demonstrating concern about some of these other types of benefits, but neither in a systematical nor integrated way under the requirements of OFM. To explain, OFM defines one benefit of leisure as the realization of a satisfying recreation experience. Since satisfying experiences are only *one* of the three types of benefits of leisure adopted by OFM, EFM, as practiced by use of the ROS, is a limited application of OFM. To reiterate, it is limited because it considers only experiential benefits and not the other two types of benefits of leisure that are included in a full application of OFM. To review from Chapter 2 of this text, EFM is practiced when opportunities to realize specific types of satisfying experiences are overtly targeted by practitioners and when management is directed toward providing those opportunities, which is precisely what is targeted by the USFS's use of the ROS. As such, the best known and most widely practiced application of EFM is the use of the ROS system. The ROS system was brought on line in the early 1980s, led by the USFS and significantly supported by the BLM, and has been implemented in many countries in addition to the U.S.

It should be noted that success with applying the ROS led to developing a recreation resource and services planning and management system that was first called BBM and in this text is called OFM for the reasons given in chapter 1. Specifically, OFM built on to the foundational structure of the ROS to consider not only experiential benefits but *all* the benefits of leisure.

In addition to the national application of the ROS by the USFS and the BLM, it has become a primary recreation management system of the Department of Conservation in New Zealand; has been applied by the state parks agencies in a number of states in the U.S.; in several provinces of Canada; and a number of other countries including Australia, Norway, Denmark, and Thailand. Internationally, recreation managers report the principles of OFM are much easier for them to understand and apply because of their initial introduction to those concepts through the structure of the ROS system, which has led to many of them incorporating concepts from the ROS system into applications of OFM especially to help define logical recreation management zones and develop setting condition prescriptions.

The US Forest Service and OFM

As explained in Chapter 2 of this text, science-based EFM evolved from Activities-Focused Management (AFM), and science-based OFM evolved incrementally from EFM over time beginning in the late 1970s. An important dimension of that evolution was the successful implementation of the ROS system in the early 1980s, which was a significant application of EFM as explained earlier. This chapter on use of the ROS illustrates that the USFS is making progress in implementing at least some elements of OFM in recreation resources management, albeit somewhat limited; limited in that it only considers satisfying recreation experiences and in many if not most applications they are not explicitly articulated, because the focus is on the ROS zones (which connect those experiential outcomes) rather than on giving the experiences a more explicit focus in specific management objectives as required by OFM. To reiterate, the ROS is a limited type of OFM because it clearly promotes managing for the psychological benefits realizable in the different ROS zones even though it does *not* consider other types of benefits that is required by full implementation of OFM. Therefore, although there are some managerial elements of OFM that have been mandated for all federal agencies to implement which will be discussed later, the USFS has not developed a process, system, or strategy for fully implementing OFM as a recreation resource management system in any of its programmatic areas (with some limited exceptions of "pilot forests" testing OFM applications). In addition to application of the ROS, there are other recreation-related benefits and negative outcomes on which the USFS does focus through other program management activities such as various environmental (wildlife habitat protection, erosion prevention, clean drinking water sources, tourism to local communities), scenic resources, and preservation of cultural/historic sites.

In 1993, Congress passed the Government Performance and Results Act (GPRA) which mandated every federal agency to develop a strategic plan that must contain, among other things, (a) a comprehensive agency mission statement and (b) goals and objectives that are "*outcome-related*" for the major functions and operation. The GPRA further requires the establishment of measurable performance indicators and articulated "*outcomes*" for each program activity; and that means be established to verify and validate the measurements. The performance measures for the goals and objectives were to be expressed in a "benefit" form and format. The USFS began developing a management structure to respond to the GPRA in 1997 and one of the goals of the USFS Strategic Plan for 2000 was "Multiple Benefits to People: Provide a variety of uses, values, products, and services for present and future generations (p. 11)." The objective relating this goal to recreation resources management states, "Improve the capability of the Nation's forests and grasslands to provide diverse, high-quality outdoor recreation opportunities." However, the link to complete the OFM system is missing both between the goal and the objective, and between the objective and the "strategy to achieve the objective." For example, of the four strategies outlined to achieve the objective of improving the capability to provide high-quality recreation opportunities (which is one of the foundations of meeting the goal of providing multiple benefits to people), all of the four strategies ask "what" will be done, but not one addresses the "why" question, which is the most critical requirement of OFM. OFM insists that the "why" question be answered *only* in terms of beneficial outcomes to be promoted and negative outcomes to be avoided or reduced as a result of managerial actions (see Chapter 2 of this text). Even though the USFS has begun to change its management toward the direction of an OFM system, there are yet critical elements of OFM that need to be addressed.

The USFS recreation program leadership began developing an OFM system strategy for recreation resources during the period when Lyle Laverty was the national Director of Recreation, Wilderness, and Cultural Resources of the USFS.[4] He was a strong supporter of OFM and for several years partially funded Driver's work on it at the Rocky Mountain Forest and Range Experiment Station. In 1997, Laverty formed a task force (of which Driver and the author of this chapter were members) to develop a strategy for implementing OFM into recreation resources planning and management in the USFS. For several reasons, that strategy was not implemented, and unfortunately the momentum to fully apply OFM in the USFS was lost.

Nevertheless, during this same period, the USFS developed a National Recreation Agenda with the intent of tiering it to the agency Strategic Plan. However, a careful reading of the Recreation Agenda illustrates that, for the most part, USFS recreation resource management was still focused on AFM despite its full use of the ROS. For example, rather than stating that the benefits to be provided to the American people are the result of various management actions, the Recreation Agenda enumerates the inventory of recreation facilities the agency manages (miles of trails, roads, and numbers of heritage sites, campgrounds, etc.) as the subject on which the agency focuses, implying that recreation management is maintaining and operating resources to facilitate the conventional production of opportunities to participate in activities rather than articulating the specific beneficial outcomes (benefits) to be promoted (and negative outcomes to be avoided or reduced by some measure). The Recreation Agenda does speak to EFM in areas where it links settings, experiences, and opportunities; and where it speaks to protecting the natural character of the landscapes. However, even in those areas, the Agenda falls short of completing the link when it states in part, "As we strive for correct limits of use and balance, we will manage recreation *activities*" demonstrating that rather than focusing on benefits and negative outcomes as the primary managerial targets and using activities as the currency to achieve the benefits, the focus remains on managing activities. The Agenda does finish with correct concepts such as promoting stakeholder collaboration, although it is not nearly strong enough. For example, it states in part, "We will prioritize projects based on *feedback* from our partners and local communities," which misses the point of true collaboration where the provider "sits at the table" as an equal partner with all other stakeholders to determine which benefits to target, how to target them, and how to measure the success of delivering the targeted opportunities for the realization of benefits. Put simply, management objectives in forest plans do not overtly target specific recreation-related benefits as required by OFM, which is being done widely in the BLM. Thus, even though the recreation management program of the USFS has begun to change management toward the direction of an OFM system, there are yet elements of OFM that need to be addressed.

Results of the USFS Implementation of the ROS

The USFS has fully implemented the ROS system on all national forests, thereby embracing at least a partial form of OFM (i.e., EFM). So the original application intended by the development of the ROS has been realized. Further, the ROS has influenced later USFS recreation management efforts such as the Meaningful Measures in 1999 and 2001's Built Environment Image Guide (BEIG). The BEIG integrates the principles and guidance from the ROS into its recommendations and prescriptions for not only the recreation constructed facilities, but also the administrative or office facilities as well. Because the ROS is based on the premise that people expect certain levels of development related to the character of a recreation setting and the type of recreation opportunities they seek, the BEIG stipulates that a facility intended to create a safe, controlled environment for large numbers of people should be highly developed using modern materials and providing ample conveniences. Conversely, again following the structure of the ROS, the BEIG states that consistent with visitor expectations, a more primitive "backwoods" area should have far fewer constructed elements and those constructed features should generally be small in scale and made of natural materials. The BEIG is intended to improve the image, aesthetics, sustainability, and overall quality of FS facilities consistent with the agency's role as leaders in land stewardship. As much as the natural environment does, the built environment influences the visitor experience and the identity of the agency as a provider of high-quality outdoor recreation opportunities, and it conveys impressions regarding how the agency is fulfilling its stewardship mission. The ROS, brought on line in the early 1980s continues to influence, as it should, recreation managerial direction for the USFS into the current century.

Another valuable study, conducted by Anderson and Snedeger (1993), documented that the ROS has been well received in the USFS and by related researchers and academicians. In their study, they used the Delphi method to ascertain from 126 USFS managers and 24 university and USFS scientists what they believed was the most significant development to date in outdoor recreation resource management. The response was a resounding and unequivocal "the ROS." Their research also revealed that the respondents rated the ROS system the highest (over all other systems) of any of the innovations made in the past 20 years to improve outdoor recreation management. The first round of the study employed a "voluntary response" section and the

ROS ranked first by number of respondents listing it. The ROS also ranked high in terms of its contributions among all the other innovations that were considered, many of which were process oriented. The ROS has been recognized as one of the most valuable innovations in the field of outdoor recreation management in the past quarter century.

Conclusion

Despite the myriad outdoor recreation resources available on forest lands from the beginning of the agency in 1905, the USFS's management emphasis or focus on outdoor recreation was lacking, particularly in comparison to the other resources under its stewardship. A marked beginning of that changing was the 1962 ORRRC reports and the subsequent federal legislation that created an environment which forced the agency to give more attention to the outdoor recreation resources in aspects of its management. This focus led to greater activity from applied research resulting in the development of recreation management systems whose primary focus was, in the beginning, providing quality outdoor recreation opportunities. Research then demonstrated that there was more to managing recreation resources than just the activities--and that the experiences users sought were directly related to the settings or environment. This research led to the development, adoption, and application of the ROS. The USFS has fully implemented the ROS system on all national forests, thereby embracing at least a partial, but only a partial, form of OFM (i.e., EFM). So the original application intended by the development of the ROS has been realized. And while research building on the results of the application of the ROS led to further knowledge and insight in outdoor recreation resources management and the development and application of OFM, the USFS has not brought most of the principles and application of OFM on line.

Literature Cited

Anderson, D. & Snedeger, I. (1993). Using the Delphi process to identify significant recreation research based innovations. *Journal of Parks & Recreation Administration II, 1,* 25–36 .

Brown, P. J., Driver, B. L., & McConnell, C. (1978). The opportunity spectrum concept in outdoor recreation supply inventories; background and application. Pages 73–84. In *Proceedings of the integrated renewable resources inventories workshop.* USDA Forest Service General Technical Report RM-55.

Clark, R. N. & Stankey. G. H. (1979). *The recreation opportunity spectrum: A framework for planning, management and research.* USDA Forest Service Research Paper PNW-98, 32 pp.

Dombeck, M. (1997). Remarks at the Public Lands Forum of the Outdoor Writers'Association of America. June 24, 1997. Grenefee, FL.

Driver, B. L., & Brown, P. J. (1978). The opportunity spectrum concept in outdoor recreation supply inventories; a rationale. Pages 24–31. In *Proceedings of the integrated renewable resources inventories workshop.* USDA Forest Service General Technical Report RM-55.

Driver, B. L., & Tocher, S. R. (1970). Toward a behavioral interpretation of recreational engagements, with implications for planning Pages 9–13. In B. L. Driver (ed.), *Elements of outdoor recreation planning.* Ann Arbor, MI: University of Michigan Press.

Driver, B. L., Brown, P. J., Stankey, G. H., & Gregoire, T. G. (1987). The ROS planning system: Evolution, basic concepts and research needed. *Journal of Leisure Sciences, 9,* 201–212.

Jaten, A. & Driver, B. L. (1998). Meaningful Measures for Quality Recreation Management. Pages 43–57 in *Journal of Park and Recreation Administration, 16,* No. 3.

Moore, D. & Driver, B. L. (2005). *Introduction to outdoor recreation: Providing and manageing natural resource based opportunites.* State College, PA: Venure Publishing, Inc.

Outdoor Recreation Resources Review Commission. (1962). *Outdoor recreation for America.* Summary Volume. Washington, D.C.: U. S. Government Printing Office.

USDA Forest Service. (1974). *National forest landscape management.* Volume 1 (Agriculture Handbook 434). USGPO. Washington, D.C.

USDA Forest Service. (1977). *Forest Service Manual.* 2302.1 and 2331.11c. Washington, D.C.

USDA Forest Service. (1982). *ROS User Guide.* Washington, D.C.

USDA Forest Service. (1986). *1986 ROS Book.* Washington, D.C.

USDA Forest Service (2000). *USDA Forest Service Service Strategic Plan* (2000 Revision). Washington D.C.

USDA Forest Service. (2001). *Built Environment Image Guide (BEIG).* Washington D.C.

Footnotes

1. A few other leisure scientists had written about the experiential nature of leisure, but the referenced work of Driver and Tocher received wide attention.
2. The first and limited version of the "Guide" was printed in 1981 and was undated, but most copies now available are dated 1982.
3. Earlier, Bacon was the leader in developing the USFS's Visual Resource Management System and later modifying it into the Scenery Management System.
4. Laverty served as Director of Colorado State Parks after retiring from the USDA Forest Service, and on October 5, 2007 was appointed Assistant Secretary of Interior for Fish, Wildlife, and Parks.

Chapter 10
Challenges of Adopting the Outcomes Approach: New Zealand's Department of Conservation

Kay Booth and Michael Edginton

Learning Objectives:

1. Understand the incremental adoption of the outcomes approach by the New Zealand Department of Conservation.
2. Appreciate more fully from this chapter and the following one that the outcomes approach is being used in several different countries.

New Zealand's Department of Conservation (DOC) is increasingly taking an outcomes-focused approach to its management of protected areas and recreation resources. The examination of outcomes-focused management (OFM) in the DOC in this chapter offers a unique perspective on the implementation of the approach, because key characteristics of that New Zealand agency contrast with park and recreation agencies in North America.

New Zealand's Protected Area System and the Department of Conservation

The DOC is a national agency which administers one third of New Zealand's landmass within a country equivalent in size to Colorado. The Department fills the niche of a combined federal and state/provincial park agency.

New Zealand's protected areas are managed for natural and/or historic heritage protection alongside (to varying degrees) provision for recreation. Some extractive uses (such as mining) are accommodated but are not a purpose of these areas; productive public lands are managed separately by commercially motivated agencies of state. Indeed, the strong protection mandate of the Conservation Act of 1987 places extractive uses uncomfortably alongside protection and recreation. However, public conservation lands continue to play a key role in New Zealand's burgeoning international tourism industry, an industry now critical to the New Zealand economy.

New Zealand's generous endowment of park land (30 percent) exceeds the 20 percent global average for high-income countries (World Bank, 2004). These parks are largely remote to the New Zealand populace (86 percent of New Zealanders live in urban areas) and encompass large areas of mountainous temperate rain forest.

As manager of these lands and waters, the DOC is the primary outdoor recreation resource provider in New Zealand. Recreation facilities and services administered or commissioned by the DOC are extensive and account for over NZ$500 million in infrastructural assets. A large track and hut (backcountry cabin) network facilitates hiking and other foot-based activities. This backcountry provision is matched with a substantial investment in road-end facilities, like short walks and viewpoints.

Factors Influencing Adopting OFM

The Department's adoption of OFM, discussed in the next major section, has been influenced by several key factors. These include institutional restructuring, directions from the New Zealand Government, prevailing socioeconomic conditions, and a Departmental recreation facility failure. they are identified here as the public policy, socioeconomic, and recreation provision contexts.

Public Policy Context

Environmental administrative reforms during the 1980s, led to the passing of the Conservation Act 1987. This drew together most conservation functions under a single agency, the DOC. Former multiple-use agencies, such as the New Zealand Forest Service, were disbanded. The DOC was forced to create a new policy framework, owing to substantially different statutory obligations from predecessor agencies. Slow to develop policy, the policy emphasis that has occurred in the past 10 years has coincided with the adoption of an outcomes focus. The outcomes approach within policy statements is reviewed in the next section.

In 2002, the New Zealand Government introduced a "whole of government" approach to public agency management. This was articulated as a set of overarching themes, currently represented by three priority areas and described in terms of societal outcomes:

1. Economic transformation: Working to progress our economic transformation to a high-income, knowledge-based market economy, which is both innovative and creative, and provides a unique quality of life to all New Zealanders. This theme will be achieved though the subthemes of: growing globally competitive firms; world class infrastructure; innovative and productive workplaces, underpinned by high standards in education, skills and research; an internationally competitive city--Auckland; and environmental sustainability.
2. Families, young and old: All families have the support and choices they need to be secure and able to reach their full potential within our knowledge-based economy. This theme will be achieved through the subthemes of: creating strong families; healthy confident kids; safe communities; better health for all; and positive ageing.
3. National identity: All New Zealanders can take pride in who and what we are, through our arts, culture, film, sports, and music; our appreciation of our natural environment; our understanding of our history and our stance on international issues. This theme will be achieved through the subthemes of: who we are, what we do, where we live, and how we are seen by the world.

All government departments are instructed to take these themes into account in their planning processes and consider how their core business can be aligned to support them. The DOC has input into delivering on each of these themes and specifies how this is achieved in detailed form in the Department's Statement of Intent (SOI). This three-year strategic document (prepared annually) is the Department's contract with the Government. Following the Government's lead, the SOI has increasingly shifted towards outcomes measure-

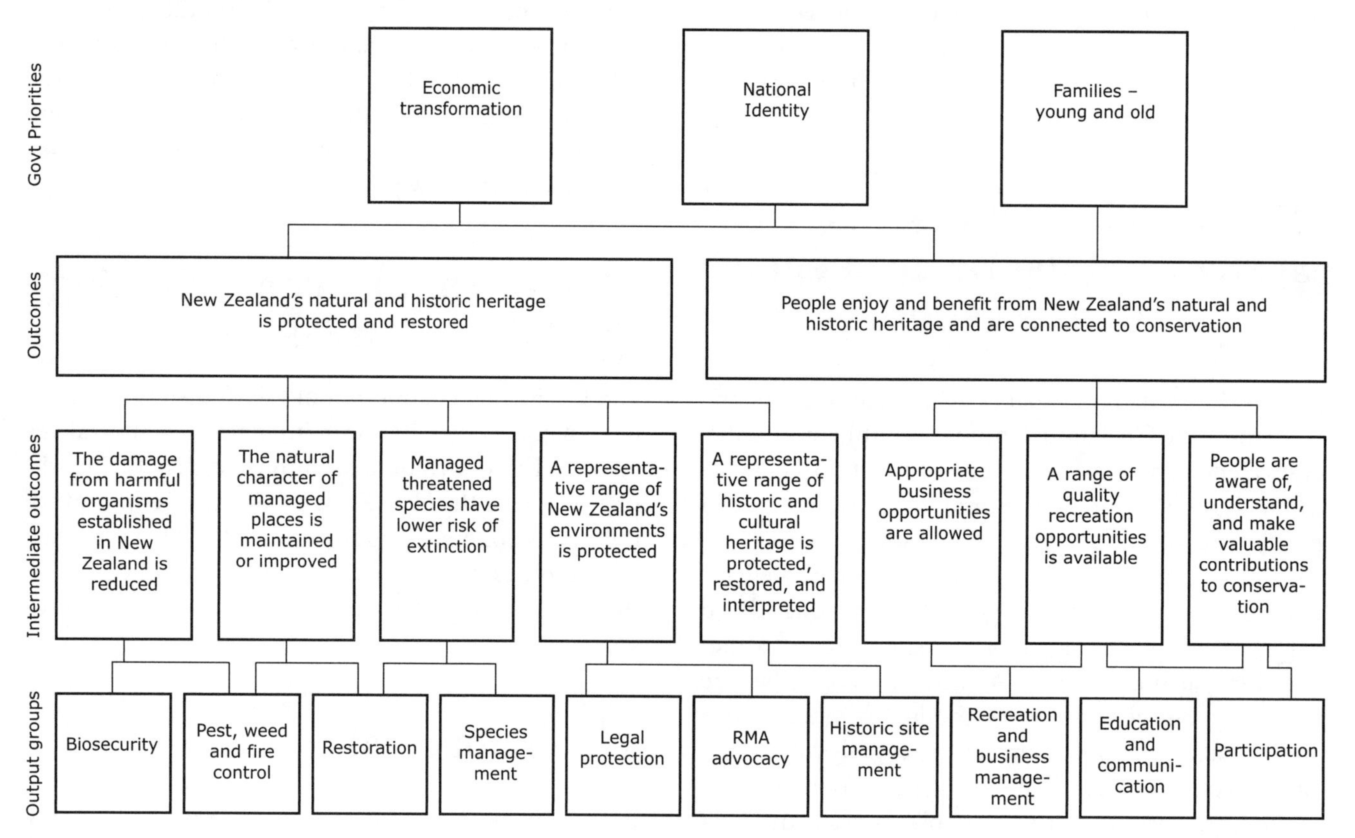

Figure 10.1: Relationship between Governmental themes, and DOC outcomes and outputs (DOC, 2006a:17)

ment (discussed in the next section). Figure 10.1 shows the relationship between the Government's themes, the Department's overarching outcome statements, and the output work areas.

Socioeconomic Context

The restructuring of environmental agencies in the 1980s was undertaken within a period that has been called "the great New Zealand experiment" (Kelsey, 1997). Widely acknowledged as taking economic reform further than other countries, New Zealand's economic reforms saw: (1) A more clear definition of the role of government with commercial aspects seen to be the preserve of the private sector, leaving the public sector to provide public goods; (2) A user-pays philosophy – beneficiaries of public goods and services should pay for these benefits; and (3) Public agencies adopting greater transparency and accountability. As a result, government agencies have had to ensure that their efforts are focused upon delivering the outcomes required by the government.

Recreation Provision Context

While the DOC and predecessor agencies have a long history in producing recreation outputs, it took a tragedy in 1995 to create an administrative culture with a strong focus on recreational asset management. A DOC viewing platform collapsed at Cave Creek, Paparoa National Park, sending 14 people to their deaths and seriously injuring several others. In response, the Department introduced an output-focused approach to recreation management (discussed in the next section) and became very risk conscious about its role in visitor management.

The Department ran a safety audit of all its visitor structures (bridges, platforms, etc.) and in 1998-1999 spent NZ$30 million upgrading, replacing or closing substandard facilities. This work drew criticism from the recreation community and was highly controversial. The specter of "Cave Creek," as it was simply called, overruled many objections to facility closures. This incident remains significant in the social history of New Zealand and has influenced the rest of its government through major changes to legislation, making government officials criminally liable for failure to meet the necessary requirements of the Health and Safety in Employment Act 1992 and the Building Act 2004.

Outcomes-Focused Management in DOC

The DOC has incorporated an outcomes focus at a strategic policy level. Therefore, many policy statements indicate a shift towards OFM within the DOC. While philosophically, the DOC is "thinking outcomes," the agency has not made the shift to *apply* the OFM process at a specific place, or used the approach to address a specific issue or operate a program. This section reviews key Departmental policy and planning documents; the Department's recreation output management; and the involvement of the public in the DOC's work.

Policies with an Outcomes Orientation

The Department's planning framework is outlined in Figure 10.2. Then, key documents are reviewed with respect to their adoption of an outcomes approach.

Strategic Direction Statement

In 2006, the Director-General released a one-page overarching strategic document to provide general direction for DOC staff (DOC, 2006b). Despite its internal focus, the document has gained wide external distribution. The so-called "Strategic Direction" is outcomes oriented and acknowledges the human dimensions of conservation management.

It is headed by the outcomes-related statement that "New Zealanders want their natural and historical

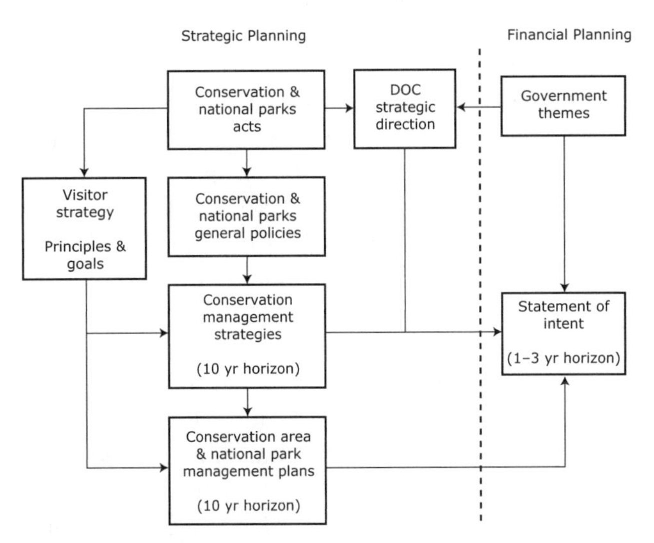

Figure 10.2: Planning framework of the Department of Conservation

heritage conserved" and describes DOC's purpose as "to increase the value of conservation to New Zealanders." Five objectives are listed to achieve this goal, including that "the Department will seek to entrench conservation as an essential part of the sustainable social and economic future of New Zealand" and "the Department will actively promote outdoor recreation for New Zealanders, especially through fostering recreation, use, and enjoyment on conservation land" (DOC, 2006b:1).

The Strategic Direction makes plain the *public* outcomes of DOC's work. While the document identifies the DOC's recreation provision mandate, it is much broader in its definition of the human dimensions of conservation management than simply the recreation-related benefits. In this respect, it is a significant step forward from the Department's previous preoccupation with users and has embraced the OFM model of a broad definition of social outcomes.

Statement of Intent

In 1998, the Department prepared the first of its long-term strategic business plans, which later became known as Statements of Intent (SOI). It was called *Restoring the Dawn Chorus*, a reference to a biodiversity recovery plan to bring endangered wildlife (especially native birds) back from the brink of extinction. In the 1998-2002 (4-year) plan, the Department's recreation goal was to: "Manage a range of recreational opportunities and provide or manage the provision of a range of recreational and educational facilities and services that enable visitors to enjoy the natural and historic values of areas and species managed by the Department" (DOC, 1998: 43). This goal was a combination of outcomes and outputs, and it set the tone for the Statement of Intent (SOI) that followed.

A SOI is a key document for all government agencies in New Zealand. Despite their title, the content of each SOI is focused upon a one-year timeframe. Analysis of the DOC's SOIs between 2001 and 2006 indicates a subtle shift in thinking each year. Cumulatively, this amounts to a significant reframing of recreation management strategy from outputs to outcomes management. Concomitant with this development has been a simplification of language. Put simply, readers did not understand the message of early documents.

The first appearance of an outcomes-related statement occurred in the 2001–2004 SOI (DOC, 2001). These statements were called "National Priority Outcomes" and included a combination of outputs and outcomes. It is in this year that we first see the term "benefits" referenced (DOC, 2001: 30, italics added to denote outcomes):

1. More New Zealanders enjoy protected areas and receive in full measure the *inspiration, enjoyment, recreation, and other benefits* that may be derived from them, consistent with the protection of their conservation values.
2. The Department's facilities and services are located, designed, constructed, and maintained and operated in accordance with all relevant legislation and best practice, to meet user needs to appropriate standards.
3. *Visitor impacts* on natural and historic heritage values are minimal.

The next year, the SOI outcome statement was called "Recreational enjoyment" and combined the protection values and the enjoyment/benefits: "More New Zealanders enjoy protected areas and receive in full measure the *inspiration, enjoyment, recreation and other benefits* that may be derived from them, consistent with the protection of their conservation values" (DOC, 2002: 32).

In the SOI for 2003–06, the outcome statement changed to include a range of opportunities from which people could derive benefits: "A range of quality recreation opportunities, consistent with the protection of conservation values, is provided in areas managed by the Department, and promoted so that all New Zealanders have the opportunity to *derive benefits* from them" (DOC, 2003: 37).

The 2004-07 outcome statement changed subtly again under the heading of "Appreciation," this time identifying what benefits there were and stressing a community connection to conservation:

> "People have opportunities to appreciate and *benefit** from their natural and historic heritage and are involved and connected with conservation.*Benefits may include: *enjoyment, education, health, inspiration, recreation and economic* (within the constraints of the legislation)" (DOC, 2004: 32).

The outcome statement for the 2005–08 and 2006–09 SOIs remained consistent with the 2004–07 document, stressing benefits and connection with conservation in more simplified language: "People enjoy and *benefit* from New Zealand's natural and historic heritage and are connected with conservation" (DOC, 2005a: 68; DOC, 2006a: 71)

"Benefits" are defined within these two documents: "Benefits means to enhance or improve social conditions (such as *community health*) or to receive some personal or individual advantage, gain or profit through passive or active involvement with New Zealand's indigenous *biodiversity* for a range of reasons, including recreation, education, tourism and business at places managed by the Department of Conservation" (ibid). Benefits are explained as encompassing "household and community benefits, personal benefits (such as *better mental health, physical health, personal development and growth, personal appreciation and satisfaction, and physical fitness), economic benefits and environmental benefits*" (ibid).

Visitor Strategy

The development of the Department's recreation policy, the *Visitor Strategy* (DOC, 1996), heralded the beginning of outcomes thinking in the DOC. The Visitor Strategy established the direction for outdoor recreation and defined the Department's role in natural and heritage tourism based activities. It also identified seven key visitor (customer) groups[1], the level of service (outputs) to be provided for each group, and general guidance on the types of outcomes sought by visitors to each recreation opportunity. The document is structured around five key goals. Two example goals are:

- Goal 1: Protection: To ensure that the intrinsic natural and historic values of areas managed by the department are not compromised by the impacts of visitor activities and related facilities and services.
- Goal 4: Informing and Educating Visitors: To share knowledge about our natural and historic heritage with visitors, to satisfy their requirement for information, deepen their understanding of this heritage and develop an awareness of the need for its conservation.

These goals articulate outcomes sought by the Department in its recreation/tourism management. Each goal is supported by a discussion of the outputs that the DOC will provide to achieve each goal. For example, for Goal 4: Informing and educating visitors, the *Visitor Strategy* outlines where it will communicate with visitors, what different visitors group require, and the information/education techniques the DOC will use.

General Policy

In 2005, two general policy statements were published. One covered national parks (NZCA, 2005), while the other encompassed all other types of protected area (DOC, 2005b). These documents provide "guidance for consistent management planning for the wide range of places and resources administered or managed by the Department" (DOC, 2005b: 9). This guidance is constructed around the notion of "outcomes at place." In doing so, these documents establish an outcomes orientation for the DOC's statutory planning framework, although the general policies stop short of presenting outcome statements *per se*.

"Outcomes" are defined as "a goal or *end result* of conservation action or a series of actions" (DOC, 2005b: 59, emphasis added) and are integral to management planning, in that "The starting point for determining the management objectives for a place is to identify the values of the place... which need to be preserved and protected. Management objectives can then be formulated to achieve planned outcomes that are consistent with the intrinsic values" (DOC, 2005b: 12). Through the policies they express, these documents cement outcomes-focused planning. For example:

- Each national park management plan will identify the outcomes planned for places within the national park consistent with the values of those places identified in the planning process (*General Policy for National Parks*, policy 8.1a).
- Recreation opportunities will be provided on public conservation lands and waters. Where provided, they should be consistent with the values and outcomes planned for places (*Conservation General Policy*, policy 9.1a).
- People and organizations interested in national parks will be consulted when statutory planning documents for national parks are developed, including outcomes sought for places within national parks (*General Policy for National Parks*, policy 3d).

Given their "high level" strategic role, the importance of the general policies relates to the direction they provide for the management planning documents which sit "underneath" them. They are discussed next.

Conservation Management Strategies

Conservation management in each of the 13 conservancies that comprise the DOC's regional structure is guided by a document which expresses strategic management direction for the conservancy. These documents are called Conservation Management Strategies

(CMS). In 2006 a template for the preparation of these documents was prepared (DOC, 2006c), structured around "outcomes at place." The template specifies what a CMS will cover and includes:

- National statements (that apply to all CMS).
- A framework for statements about particular conservation issues, such as pest animals/plants.
- Standard outcome statements: A "pick and mix" selection will be made from a list of outcomes.
- Recreation opportunity specification: A simplified recreational opportunity experience classification system will be used as the foundation for describing the range of opportunities available.

The operative components of CMS will be: (1) Management objectives and policies (general direction across/among places or for resources not included in specified places); and (2) Place objectives, outcomes and policies. For each "place" identified within a CMS, the strategy will identify:

1. An outcome statement: "Word pictures" of a future desired state as it will be experienced by visitors to that place. This may be broadly similar to, or better than, the present state. The language of the outcome will be written in an appealing or inspiring manner.
2. An objectives statement: The actions required to achieve the desired outcome(s). "Objectives" are statements of a future desired state of a place, which may not necessarily relate to the experience of a visitor, that are clear and specific about the end result sought in terms of its nature, extent, or scale. Place objectives in a CMS may be time bound but this is not a requirement.
3. Policy statements: "Policies" for places establish principles or courses for action and can be decision-making tools that help achieve the outcomes or objectives.

Because CMSs are about the management of places, "place" outcomes are restricted to user-specific benefits within the CMS template (see (1) above). In order to achieve all facets of the broad social outcomes mandate established by the DOC's *Strategic* Direction, including recreation-related benefits that accrue off-site (such as health benefits), the DOC will need to pursue nonplace outcomes via other mechanisms. This may include, for example, enhanced societal attitudes toward conservation/recreation.

Management Plans

A draft management plan for Abel Tasman National Park was released in January 2006 and provides an example of how park management plans are being written to execute the outcomes approach required by the General Policies. The plan opens with a vision statement and a list of outcomes. It states (DOC, 2006d:11):

The long-term vision for Abel Tasman National Park is a coastal park where:

- Indigenous vegetation has fully regenerated;
- Indigenous flora and fauna have been restored and are not threatened by introduced plants or animals;
- Scenic and geological values have been preserved;
- The cultural and historic heritage of the park has been protected and preserved;
- People come to experience the unique and accessible coastal setting and the beauty and tranquillity of the park, in harmony with nature and each other; and
- The adjacent coastal environment is managed in a way that is integrated with the management of the park.

The purpose of this plan is to advance toward this Vision.

Each section of the management plan (such as Indigenous Species and Ecosystems, and Visitor Management) discusses issues, states policies, lists implementations ("how to" statements), and identifies outcomes at place. This is presented for the park as a whole and then for the three "places" identified within the plan: The Coast, The Interior, and The Islands. The following recreation outcome statements illustrate the manner in which this management plan conceptualizes outcomes (emphasis added):

- Visitors experience a traditional, self-reliant, basic New Zealand family beach holiday camp in a national park setting (Visitor Management section: The Coast, p. 89).
- Self-reliant, experienced, adventurous visitors enjoy nature, quiet, and solitude in the remote untracked parts of the Interior (Visitor Facilities section: The Interior, p. 112).
- No open fires are lit, except in the fireplaces provided, and visitors are aware of the risks posed by fire (Visitor Facilities section: The Coast, p. 110).
- Facilities are provided and maintained to a basic level, consistent with the recreational settings and the natural, self-reliant character of the park (Visitor Facilities section: Whole park, p. 103).

The outcome statements vary in style. Some adhere to the general policy definition of an "outcome at place" (a future desired state as it will be experienced by visitors to that place), while others represent output statements that contribute to the desired state.

Other Work

Three research projects are pertinent to this discussion. In 2000–01, a process was developed by which the DOC could identify and prioritise positive and negative social outcomes of conservation and recreation management (Booth, Driver, Espiner & Kappelle, 2002). The process adapted the OFM for New Zealand, and for the DOC context specifically. This assessment identified factors that inhibited the successful implementation of an outcomes approach within the Department. These included legislative and Departmental ambiguity over the DOC's role in visitor management, confusion over the lengths to which the DOC should go to achieve desired management outcomes, narrow perceptions of the DOC's social mandate, and emphasis on satisfying site-based users rather than the wider public (Booth et al., 2002). A recommendation of the 2002 report was the incremental adoption of OFM. In response to this call, a project was underway at the time of writing this chapter, with the purpose of testing the applicability of OFM to New Zealand's statutory conservation management planning process. OFM will be implemented using a case study of the Rakiura National Park management plan.

Finally, in order to support its Strategic Direction (increasing the value of conservation to New Zealanders), at the time this chapter was written, the DOC was commissioning research into the values and benefits the public associates with conservation. The two primary intended uses for the research results are to provide a benchmark survey to measure changes over time in people's understanding and appreciation of conservation, and to help inform the Department's organizational development and operations.

Summary of Policy Analysis

Since the early 2000s, the DOC has shifted to a strong social outcomes focus within its strategic documents. This is beginning to filter down into management planning documents. To date, the written specification of outcomes is a mixture of output and outcome statements. The DOC has moved from a narrow definition of social outcomes and a strong emphasis upon satisfying site-based users, to recognition of a full spectrum of outcomes for the public.

Output Management

The Department and its predecessor agencies have a long history of managing recreational facilities such as tracks and huts. This is critical to the adoption of OFM, as sound facility (output) management is required in order to achieve outcomes.

The network of recreation facilities managed by the DOC grew out of the need for facilities to support ground-based hunters who helped to control introduced wild animals (deer, pigs, goats, tahr, and chamois). Many thousands of kilometers of track, thousands of bridges, and hundreds of huts were established to enable hunters to access the remote backcountry areas where these animals threatened forests and grasslands. This network of facilities was quickly adopted by recreation visitors (hikers, climbers, hunters), and it now forms the basis of many of the recreation opportunities managed by the DOC.

In 1995, after the tragedy at Cave Creek, the Department began a program to assess the condition and status of all the assets that it managed. This assessment indicated that many of the facilities were at the end of their useful lives and that the loss of these assets would impact on the range of recreation opportunities that the Department could provide. The Government responded by providing the Department with an additional NZ$349 million over 10 years (2002–2012) to replace or upgrade the facilities.

The Department recognized that to be able to manage recreation opportunities effectively, it is essential to have an intimate understanding of the users and the assets that contribute to these opportunities. To achieve this, the DOC implemented a national system to describe the opportunities, the users of these places, and the assets it owned. This information was combined into a purpose-built recreation management system (VAMS–Visitor Asset Management System) that is now used for strategic, business, and operational planning and reporting, and which forms a basic building block for recreation management.

The DOC is influenced by public policy developed by other agencies of the state, some of which affects DOC recreation outputs. For example, the Building Act of 2004 specifies minimum standards for buildings irrespective of their location, and the Health Act 1956 specifies standards for campgrounds. This legislation impacts on the Department's ability to set minimum service standards for places like campsites and other accommodations in the backcountry, often requiring a much higher level of service than might be expected (or wanted) by the users of those facilities.

To better understand the recreation opportunities offered by the Department, a review of the Recreation Opportunity Spectrum (ROS) framework was undertaken. Having adapted the ROS to New Zealand conditions in the 1980s (Taylor, 1993), the Department revisited the New Zealand opportunity classes and now uses it nationally to enable those involved in planning for recreation opportunities (statutory land managers, communities, user groups and the public at large) to compare and quantify the recreation setting values. As pointed out in Chapters 2 and 8 of this text, the ROS system is a limited type of OFM because it focuses on the provision of opportunities to realize satisfying recreation experiences. And, as mentioned in Chapter 1, satisfying experiences are one of the three types of benefits of leisure defined and adopted by OFM. The ROS is therefore a limited type of OFM because it does not consider the other two types of benefits as required by full application and implementation of OFM.

Within the DOC's adaptation of the ROS system, the key setting attributes (biophysical, social and managerial) have been applied across six classes appropriate to the New Zealand outdoor recreation context: Urban, Rural, Front Country, Back Country, Remote and Wilderness (DOC, 2007). The factors used by the DOC to define each opportunity class are: access (difficulty), remoteness from the sights and sounds of human activity and other nonrecreational uses, onsite management (extent of facilities/services and regimentation), and size of the area. The ROS is used to describe the distribution and abundance of recreation settings in conjunction with the New Zealand Landscape Classification (Brabyn, 2007), a national inventory of landscape character. Based within a Geographic Information System database, information on landscapes can be combined with the ROS setting parameters to identify the abundance and rarity (expressed as hectares or percentage of land) of recreation opportunities by landscape class. Using this information, it has been possible to assess the relative "value" (and therefore potential benefit) of recreation opportunities on a range of scales based on the location of the opportunity relative to population centers. There are two key assumptions in this analysis:

The lower the percentage of a ROS class in a specific landscape type, the higher the recreation value of that ROS-landscape class. The rarest ROS-landscape classes have the highest value. The value of each ROS-landscape class will be highest (in actual use terms) for those living closest to that recreation/landscape opportunity.

Collaboration with Stakeholders

Chapter 2 emphasized that involvement of stakeholders is critical to the successful implementation of OFM. Similar to other public agencies, the Department encourages public participation. This effort is driven by attempts to pursue sound management practices, rather than legislative requirement. Other than an overarching reference to the Treaty of Waitangi[2] (and thus a requirement for a relationship with Maori), public participation clauses in conservation legislation are weak. Primarily they relate to the preparation and approval of management planning documents. Illustrative of this approach is the process laid out in the National Parks Act 1980 (section 47) for the preparation/review of national park management plans:

- Consult with the Conservation Board.
- Through notices in newspapers, notify the public of the intention to prepare/review the management plan, and invite written suggestions.
- Prepare the draft management plan in consultation with the Conservation Board.
- Through notices in newspapers, invite written submissions from the public on the draft management plan.
- Write to those people who provided written suggestions earlier in the process, inviting written submissions on the draft management plan.
- Provide free inspection copies of the draft management plan.
- Hear oral submissions from submitters who request this opportunity.
- Amend the draft plan as appropriate.
- Send revised plan to the New Zealand Conservation Authority for their approval.
- The Authority is to consult with the Minister of Conservation in their deliberations.

In their design of an outcomes framework for the DOC, Booth et al. (2002, p. 31) concluded that "the Department's work with stakeholders places emphasis on site-based users... off-site consumers do not receive the level of consultation equivalent to the magnitude and significance of this group." Furthermore, the same authors noted that community involvement appeared to be viewed by the Department as a prerequisite for achieving conservation goals, rather than with any view of promoting the benefits to stakeholders from their participation.

The Department concentrates its consultation upon two stakeholder groups: Maori and recreationists. Recent consultation processes with these groups are discussed next.

Engagement with Maori

An increasing number of statutes refer to the Treaty of Waitangi, including the Conservation Act 1987, which states, "This Act shall be so interpreted and administered as to give effect to the principles of the Treaty of Waitangi" (section 4, Conservation Act 1987). King (2003), a prominent New Zealand historian, observed that ratification of the Treaty in this way represented acknowledgment by Parliament that "now recognised [the Treaty] as providing a framework for the present and future relationship of Maori and the Crown, the two Treaty partners." (p. 501). While the Treaty does not have the force of law, it is accepted by the courts that legislation will be made and interpreted in a way that is consistent with the principles of the Treaty wherever possible (McDowell & Webb, 1998).

Section 4 of the Conservation Act 1987 represents strong legal wording within New Zealand statute law with respect to the Treaty--no doubt a reflection of the Department's direct land management role. It places the DOC at the forefront of public agencies in acknowledging and involving Maori in government activities. To fulfill this obligation, the Department has implemented several key actions, such as guaranteeing the Maori representation on the local Conservation Boards and the New Zealand Conservation Authority as advisors to regional managers (Conservators), the Director-General of Conservation, and the Minister of Conservation.

Specific positions exist within the Department, at several levels, dedicated to Maori liaison. All positions are held by Maori. A parallel situation occurs for all Conservation Boards and the New Zealand Conservation Authority. The *New Zealand Conservation Authority* and the 14 regional *Conservation Boards*, established under the Conservation Law Reform Act in 1990, advise the DOC on conservation policy and planning. The Authority operates at a national level and has a particular role in approving conservation management strategies and national park management plans. The Boards operate at a regional level and prepare, in conjunction with the Department, national park management plans and conservation management strategies. Board members are appointed by the Minister of Conservation. Authority members are also appointed by the Minister, but he or she draws from a pool of nominees from particular organizations, such as Federated Mountain Clubs, the Minister of Local Government, and Te Runanga o Ngai Tahu (a South Island Maori tribe), as well as four public members.

Collaboration and Consultation with Recreationists

The Department also works with recreation groups. Initiatives range from nation-wide consultation processes, to joint management committees for recreation facilities. In some areas, local recreation clubs contribute to the management of recreation facilities. The Tararua Aorangi Hut Committee is an example. Comprising representatives from a group of recreational clubs, it meets regularly with the Department to plan the maintenance of 40 huts in the Tararua and Aorangi Forest Parks near Wellington. This model has been operating successfully since 1989.

A substantial consultation process was associated with a major recreation program, the Recreation Opportunities Review, in 2003. As already noted, the Government provided considerable extra funding for recreation facilities from 2002, but choices about what facilities were to be retained or retired were required. To do this, the Department consulted extensively with local recreation groups and the wider public throughout New Zealand. The DOC found a very high level of interest, with several thousand submissions received about facilities and the opportunities they provided. The main messages were: New Zealanders are passionate about their recreation inheritance and want a say in how it is managed; they want most of the huts and tracks maintained; and they want more access to the frontcountry.

It has been estimated that around 12 percent of outdoor recreationists in New Zealand belong to a recreation or conservation organization (Shultis, 1991). Clearly, the majority of recreationists remain outside such participatory systems. These "unstructured" recreationists present the greatest challenge to agencies and remain difficult to engage.

Evaluating Community Consultation

The success of the DOC's community consultation remains largely untested. In one of the few evaluations of this aspect of the DOC's work, consultation issues were identified by stakeholders. These included the lack of consultation feedback from the DOC, undervaluing community knowledge and conservation ethics, and the need for enhanced relationship building (CRESA, 1998). Questions remain about the community's satisfaction with the DOC's consultation processes, the scope of who is being engaged (and who is not), and whether the consultation results in better outcomes.

Lessons and Challenges

The DOC's attempts to shift to an outcomes approach provide several lessons.

- First, the "outcomes at place" notion that is integral to DOC's planning framework was borne out of a lack of resources to manage all places intensively. The identification of "places" (that is, the important parts) in CMS documents and management plans, provides a lesson about the need to be strategic and put resources into the places that matter most. By preparing strong strategic documents (general policies and CMS), the need for detailed park management plans is reduced, and planning resources are used more effectively.
- Second, the DOC approach allows for the identification of a standard national set of outcomes–the "pick and mix" approach identified in the CMS template. Use of a national typology of benefit/outcome statements will minimize "reinventing the wheel" behavior. This has obvious resource savings.
- Third, the initiative for adopting OFM into the DOC was strongly influenced by the New Zealand Government's "whole of government" focus on outcomes. This set the stage for DOC to follow suit. When it did so, recreation management was a key driver, based on the Visitor Strategy (DOC, 1996) which specified goals and defined outcomes for different visitor (customer) group experiences. This indicates that recreation can lead other facets of park agencies' work.
- Fourth, a shift in the DOC's focus from on-site visitors to the wider public of New Zealand has been highlighted in the Department's Strategic Vision ("New Zealanders want their natural and historical heritage conserved") and in the SOI documents which now describe benefits from, and connection with, conservation. This fits with the OFM approach. The Department is now setting out to collect relevant data on public values to inform this approach.

Despite progress made, the DOC faces some challenges in further integrating OFM into its work.

- Prior experience with adopting recreation planning tools (such as the Recreation Opportunity Spectrum), suggests that the uptake of OFM may be slow and initially inconsistent in its application. The institutional culture has been one of output management, and it will take several years to change this through the implementation of "place-based outcomes" in the Conservation Management Strategies.
- The written specification of outcomes requires refinement, as illustrated by the Abel Tasman National Park draft management plan, which suffers from a hybrid approach (outputs and outcomes) within its outcome statements.
- It cannot be assumed that outcomes will be achieved, and the DOC must do more than simply measure output achievement. Output measurement is important and can indicate a certain level of outcome achievement, but it is critical to also directly measure outcomes. A corollary is that before outcomes can be measured, there must be well-written outcomes statements.
- The Department is faced with the issue of measuring outcomes outside of "place," specifically: (1) How to incorporate benefits from recreation to the national health bill when the DOC's mandate is restricted to managing protected areas; and (2) How to measure outcomes at place–what do you measure and how do you judge success? The best means to achieve such measurement remains unclear, but it is apparent that the Department is not resourced to measure all potential outcomes and that it will take a multiagency approach to achieve this.

Where to from Here?

The DOC has embraced the outcomes philosophy but not its practice. Key management documents formulate outcomes statements; however, these have yet to be tested through implementation, such as via management plans. The development of CMS planning documents about outcomes-focused measurement is encouraging, together with the evaluation of OFM within the Rakiura National Park management planning process. Given the recent adoption of the outcomes approachby the DOC, the jury is still out on its success within this New Zealand agency.

Literature Cited

Booth, K. L., Driver, B. L., Espiner, S. R., & Kappelle, R. J. (2002). Managing Public Conservation Lands by the Beneficial Outcomes Approach with Emphasis on Social Outcomes. *Department of Conservation Science Internal Series 52*. Wellington, New Zealand: Department of Conservation.

Brabyn, L. (2007). *New Zealand Landscape Classification (Version II): A Classification of Visual Landscape Character*. Unpublished. Available from http://www.waikato.ac.nz/wfass/subjects/geography/staff/lars/landscape/index.shtml

Centre for Research, Evaluation and Social Assessment, 1998. *Community Consultation by the Department of Conservation: An Independent Review.* Wellington, New Zealand: Department of Conservation.

Department of Conservation. (1996). *Visitor Strategy*. Wellington, New Zealand: Department of Conservation.

Department of Conservation. (1998). *Restoring the Dawn Chorus: Department of Conservation Strategic Business Plan 1998–2002*. Wellington, New Zealand: Department of Conservation.

Department of Conservation. (2001). *Restoring the Dawn Chorus 2001–2004 [Statement of Intent]*. Wellington, New Zealand: Department of Conservation.

Department of Conservation. (2002). *Restoring the Dawn Chorus 2002–2005 [Statement of Intent]*. Wellington, New Zealand: Department of Conservation.

Department of Conservation. (2003). *Statement of Intent 2003–2006*. Wellington, New Zealand: Department of Conservation.

Department of Conservation. (2004). *Statement of Intent 2004–2007*. Wellington, New Zealand: Department of Conservation.

Department of Conservation. (2005a). *Department of Conservation Statement of Intent 2005–2008*. Wellington, New Zealand: Department of Conservation.

Department of Conservation (2005b). *Conservation General Policy.* Wellington, New Zealand: Department of Conservation.

Department of Conservation. (2006a). *Department of Conservation Statement of Intent 2006–2009*. Wellington, New Zealand: Department of Conservation.

Department of Conservation. (2006b). *Strategic Direction*. Wellington, New Zealand: Department of Conservation.

Department of Conservation. (2006c). *Conservation Management Strategies–Structure and Content Guidance*. Unpublished document dated 1 September 2006. Wellington, New Zealand: Department of Conservation.

Department of Conservation. (2006d). *Abel Tasman National Park Draft Management Plan*. Nelson, New Zealand: Department of Conservation.

Department of Conservation. (2007). *The Recreation Opportunity Spectrum: Application in the Department of Conservation*. Unpublished report dated 23 May 2007. Wellington, New Zealand: Research, Development and Improvement Division, Department of Conservation.

Kelsey, J. (1997). *The New Zealand Experiment: A World Model for Structural Adjustment?* Auckland, New Zealand: Auckland University Press/ Bridget Williams Books.

King, M. (2003). *The Penguin History of New Zealand*. Auckland, New Zealand: Penguin Books.

McDowell, M. & Webb, D. (1998). *The New Zealand Legal System: Structures, processes and legal theory*. Wellington, New Zealand: Butterworths.

New Zealand Conservation Authority. (2005). *General Policy for National Parks*. Wellington, New Zealand: Department of Conservation for the New Zealand Conservation Authority.

Shultis, J. D. (1991). Natural environments, wilderness and protected areas: An analysis of historical Western attitudes and utilisation, and their expression in contemporary New Zealand. PhD thesis. Dunedin, New Zealand: Department of Geography, University of Otago.

Taylor, P. C. (1993). *The NZ Recreation Opportunity Spectrum – Guidelines for Users.* Wellington, New Zealand: Department of Conservation and the Hillary Commission.

World Bank. (2004). *The Little Green Data Book 2004*, Washington D.C.: World Bank.

Footnotes

1. Short Stop Travelers, Day Visitors, Overnighters, Backcountry Comfort Seekers, Backcountry Adventurers, Remoteness Seekers, and Thrill Seekers.
2. Te Tiriti O Waitangi/the Treaty of Waitangi was signed in 1840 between Britain and more than 500 Maori chiefs, establishing New Zealand as a British colony. The Treaty has an important and increasingly recognized role within New Zealand's legal, social, and economic fabric; however, its interpretation remains contested.

Chapter 11
Adopting the Outcomes-Focused Approach in Parks Canada

Per Nilsen

Learning Objectives:

1. Understand the role of Parks Canada as a protected areas agency.
2. Appreciate the evolution and extent to which outcomes-focused management (OFM) has been adopted in a Canadian parks and recreation context.
3. Understand, through examples, how the outcomes-focused paragon (OFP) and OFM have been used for planning, management, and evaluation purposes in Parks Canada.

Introduction

Parks and recreation professionals in Canada, including those who work for the Parks Canada Agency, have followed and used the concepts and principles of the OFP and OFM for more than twenty years. This chapter provides examples of how both the OFP and the OFM approach have contributed to improved planning, management, and evaluation and, more recently, program renewal within Parks Canada. Much of the early work in Parks Canada was ahead of its time, and acceptance proved challenging. Adoption of a results-based management approach by the federal government as a whole and Parks Canada in particular is now creating a more conducive environment for the acceptance of OFM.

Background

Parks Canada derives its mandate from several pieces of legislation, most notably the *Parks Canada Agency Act,* as well as the *Historic Sites and Monuments Act*, the *Canada Natonal Parks Act,* and the *Canada National Marine Conservation Areas Act*. Parks Canada is a special operating agency within the Government of Canada. As a federal agency it administers 153 of the 912 sites designated as being of national significance in Canada as well as 42 national parks (264,730 square km) and 2 national marine conservation areas. The parks, marine conservation areas, and sites managed by Parks Canada receive over 22 million visitors per year. The *Parks Canada Agency Corporate Plan 2006/07–2010/11* states that the Agency's strategic outcome is to "protect and present nationally significant examples of Canada's natural and cultural heritage, and foster public understanding appreciation and enjoyment in ways that ensure the ecological and commemorative integrity of these places for present and future generations" (PCA, 2006).

Results for Canadians

To understand the journey of Parks Canada Agency towards adopting OFM, it is important to situate the Agency within the broader Canadian context. The mid-1990s saw the beginning of significant public sector reform in many jurisdictions such as the Government of Canada, where there was a move away from management by rules and procedures towards a focus on demonstrating that results that matter to citizens were being achieved with tax dollars being spent (Mayne, 2001). *Results for Canadians: A Management Framework for the Government of Canada* (Treasury Board of Canada Secretariat, 2001) established a framework for management and an agenda for changes in the way federal departments and agencies manage and deliver their programs and services.

The framework and associated agenda emphasized:

- a citizen focus built into all programs and services delivered by the government;
- the importance of sound public service values;
- achievement of results for Canadians; and
- promotion of discipline, due diligence and value for money in the use of public funds.

More specifically *Results for Canadians* states that public service managers are expected to define anticipated results, continually focus attention toward results achievement, measure performance regularly and objectively, learn from this information, and adjust to improve efficiency and effectiveness. This in turn led to government-wide implementation of a Modern Controllership Initiative, which places requirements on all federal departments and agencies to adopt and implement Planning, Reporting and Accountability Structures (PRAS), performance reporting, and Reports on Plans and Priorities (RPPs) using a common results-based management approach and language. While Treasury Board direction has been in place since 2001, many departments and agencies are still wrestling with the concepts of results-based management and reporting, and what it means for the diversity of programs and services delivered by the Government of Canada.

OFM in Parks and Recreation in Canada

One might be surprised to learn that, in Canada, there has been considerable interest and work undertaken by parks and recreation practitioners to understand and promote the principles and application of OFM.

In the late 1980s, the competition for increasingly scarce public funds, and a preoccupation with inputs and activities caused politicians, some administrators, and members of the public to lose sight of the benefits of parks and recreation. Inspired by the work of Bev Driver and his colleagues, as well as the text *Benefits of Leisure,* the Parks and Recreation Federation of Ontario and the Ontario Ministry of Tourism and Recreation, with assistance from THE RETHINK GROUP and participACTION, produced the first edition of *The Benefits of Parks and Recreation: A Catalogue* (Canadian Parks and Recreation Association, 1992).

The first catalogue was distributed by the Canadian Parks and Recreation Association (CPRA), which later worked with provincial and territorial partners to create a National Benefits Network to produce *The Benefits Catalogue* (CPRA, 1997) in both English and French. The publication of the second catalogue enabled additional recent research to be included to support the benefits statements. The second edition also saw the introduction of an emphasis on outcomes, the inclusion of marketing message statements, and an increase in the number of benefit or outcome statements from 27 to 44. Now, nearly 10 years later, the CPRA is involved in another initiative to update the catalogue.

Benefits Based Recreation: Awareness into Action - A Guide Book (1996), produced by the Alberta Parks and Recreation, also complemented the second benefits catalogue. It was developed as a resource for practitioners and not only presents concepts and principles but includes exercises and examples of applications to help people move from awareness to action.

Another recent initiative, developed by the Canada Parks Council (CPC), called *Heathy by Nature* (CPC, 2006), also incorporates the concepts of OFM Building on the *Healthy Parks, Healthy People* program developed by Australia's Parks Victoria. Making linkages to Canada's federal and provincial Health Minister's Healthy Living Strategy, a CPC working group developed the *Healthy by Nature* brand and related key messages to capitalize upon and extend the connections between the environment, parks and population health more directly. The very popular Parks Ontario (Ministry of Natural Resources, Ontario) and the Canada Parks Council web site illustrate how the *Healthy by Nature* brand and key messages are being used in day-to-day operations.

OFM in Parks Canada

For many people the adoption of a simplified results-based management or OFP within Parks Canada generally correlates with the period following the establishment of the Parks Canada Agency (1988) and the introduction of the *Results for Canadians: A Management Framework* in 2001. Annual corporate plans and performance reports illustrate the emphasis on outcomes or results at the corporate level. These plans and reports are reviewed annually by the Office of the Auditor General (OAG) of Canada. Using the OAG's feedback, the Agency continues to refine its plans and reports using "planned results and performance expectations statements."

While this may represent a more generic adoption of the OFP, there was considerable work already underway, starting in the mid 1970s with subsequent peaks and valleys of activity in the intervening years. The origins of this work can be linked to Grant Tayler, a long-term specialist in interpretation and planning. Tayler was instrumental in identifying the need for a decision-making framework that would better integrate consideration of humans into protected area planning and management as described in the *Federal Provincial Task Force Report on Interpretation* (1975). He later developed the *Visitor Activity Management Process* (1985), or VAMP as it became more commonly known, working in close collaboration with Scott Meis, a social scientist at Parks Canada at the time.

While the name of the planning process suggests an emphasis on Activity-Focused Management (AFM), when one looks at the basic VAMP Model (Tayler, 1990) one can see that elements of the OFP and OFM were built into the model. Although it was not presented as a logic model, looking back, it is evident that the elements of such a model are present. Inputs are identified as natural resource features and values, as well as the public's own needs and expectations. Facilitating outputs are park facilities (e.g., roads, campgrounds, interpretation centers) and on-site presence of managers and staff providing guidance and services. Primary outputs include the provision of recreation and learning opportunities that in turn lead to personal, social, physical and environmental benefits.

While developing the VAMP, Grant Tayler and Scott Meis sought advice and assistance from many practitioners and researchers within Canada. They also followed the work of Bev Driver and Richard Schreyer as well as those who were working on planning and decision-making frameworks including Roger Clark, and George Stankey (Recreation Opportunity Spectrum Methodology) , Stephen McCool and Dave Cole (Limits of Acceptable Change), and Alan Graefe (Visitor Impact Management Framework). This later culminated in two important Canada-US workshops on Visitor Management (see *Towards Serving Visitors and Managing Our Resources* (1990) and *For the Record - Second Canada - US Workshop on Visitor Management in Parks, Forests and Protected Areas* (1993)).

One of the rationales for holding these workshops was to gain further appreciation and acceptance of these types of decision-making frameworks as well as the overall concepts of OFM. When the VAMP was being developed, Grant Tayler had considerable difficulty in introducing and then sustaining interest in the systems-based model. While he knew and sought to convince others of the important relationships between inputs, facilitating outputs, primary outputs and outcomes or what has been called the "benefits chain of causality," the only concept that managers and practitioners could relate to beyond the basic inputs and facilitating outputs was activities. Recognizing this difficulty, Tayler worked closely with a team of recognized leaders within Parks Canada to engage managers and staff, using this vocabulary as a starting point.

The subsequent handbooks and training courses resulted in multidisciplinary teams of managers and staff having conversations about the connections between inputs (by Parks Canada and the clients), the facilitating outputs (visitor centers campgrounds, trails), and the activities. More importantly this dialogue led staff and managers, indirectly, to important conversations about the kinds of recreation and learning opportunities provided to realize benefits and/or to reduce negative outcomes.

Since the most pressing need in the late 1980s was to evaluate and then improve the delivery of existing services to current visitors, thereby improving the quality of opportunities available and the subsequent benefits derived, efforts were focused at the park delivery level. The OFP that was the true basis of the VAMP created both challenges and opportunities. Initially the process was considered to be data and information intensive. Experience gained through practical applications demonstrated that there was no shortage of data and information available. The systems approach enabled staff to organize data, understand the relationships between resulting information and refocus future studies to start filling gaps.

A second challenge was that the VAMP required planners, managers and staff to look at the regional context in which the park or site was operating and to understand the larger systems model in which parks and sites were operating. Consideration of the regional context was important in each of the different planning contexts ranging from park establishment to development of management plans, and finally to the development of service and operations plans. The VAMP was ahead of its time but fit well with Parks Canada's adoption of an ecosystem-based approach to management, which gained traction in the late 1990s and is standard operating practice today. This kind of broader systems thinking was also important as it set the stage for planning and managing in cooperation with regional residents, partners, and stakeholders.

Another challenge was that the focus on operational planning and the use of the OFP forced Parks Canada staff to think about the kinds of outcomes that a given park or site was to provide for both existing and future visitors. Normally the desired outcomes or range of opportunities to be provided would be reflected in the park or site management plan. It soon became evident that the definition of the desired outcomes, given the park or sites mandate and the associated "benefits chain of causality," had not been fully understood or linked in many management plans.

These challenges in turn created an opportunity to provide a new policy direction within the *Guiding Principles and Operating Policies* (Parks Canada, 1994). The *Policies* required managers to better define outcomes both from an ecosystem management/cultural resource management perspective and from a recreation and learning opportunity perspective, in consultation with the public, through the management planning process. This emphasis on outcomes was also incorporated into a revised guide to management planning and a complementary guide called the *Visitor Activity Concept Handbook* (Parks Canada, 1992). As stated in Chapter 2, "the expanded recreation opportunity production model enabled managers to be able to answer questions about why but also what, how, for whom, in what amount and when..."

Another initiative, undertaken in the late 1990s, was the pilot application of the ROS Methodology. This initiative provides an additional example of the application of the expanded recreation opportunity production model in Parks Canada. When Grant Tayler developed the VAMP, he and others recognized that a key element of the overall framework should be a method of assessing and then defining the range of recreation opportunities available in a national park. Given the other challenges being faced in developing and implementing the VAMP within a large, highly decentralized organization like Parks Canada, combined with the knowledge that the ROS was being applied in the U.S. and elsewhere, a decision was made to focus on gaining acceptance of the larger decision-making framework first and then seeking acceptance of the ROS methodology later. With Grant's retirement in the early 1990s, I continued to work on advancing OFM within Parks Canada for recreation planning and management purposes.

Working in collaboration with Lakehead University, pilot applications of the ROS at Pukaskwa and Yoho National Parks (Payne et al., 1997) were completed. These applications supplied the managers of these parks with a better understanding of the range of opportunities that they were offering. It also provided guidance on how previous and future decisions related to the management of these opportunity areas can significantly influence the kinds of benefits and outcomes that are offered by the parks. At Yoho National Park, the analysis showed that recent decisions to reduce vehicular access in certain areas of the park (facilitating inputs) had increased the availability of nature-based opportunities in an ecologically sensitive area of the park. In the case of Pukaskwa National Park, the application demonstrated the influence of forestry activities outside the park on the wilderness character of the park.

A final example of the use of OFM for recreation planning and management is the *Spectrum of Appropriate National Park Opportunities Handbook* (Nilsen and Tayler, 1999). The latter part of the 1990s resulted in yet another round of program reviews within the federal government that challenged managers once again to be more efficient and effective in the delivery of programs to achieve desired results. There was also an increasing emphasis on maintaining and/or restoring ecological integrity, enhancing heritage presentation, and improving opportunities for visitor experience. This was occurring at a time when there was also emphasis on streamlining processes and taking a more integrated, interdisciplinary approach to planning and management.

The handbook was developed for managers and staff and sought to bring together much of the experience that had been gained over the previous 20 years. The key message that the handbook conveys is that there is a hierarchy of decision making (or recreation production process) and that one needs to understand the inputs, facilitating outputs, primary outputs and outcomes. By describing this production process, the handbook also stresses the importance of planning from the right to left (particularly when dealing with new park establishment) and implementing the plan by moving from left to right. The reality for many of national parks and sites is that they have been operating for many years with management plans that have yet to truly address the question of the outcomes that are to be delivered both from an ecological integrity perspective as well as a visitor experience perspective. The handbook is another tool which enables managers to be able to answer questions not only about why they are providing opportunities or protecting resources but also what, how, for whom, in what amount and when, in an integrated manner.

Related Applications

The OFP and the OFM basis of the VAMP decision-making framework significantly influenced several other initiatives in Parks Canada in the mid to late 1990s. The first initiative was the revision of Parks Canada's approach to public safety management. For many years the agency had focused simply on identifying hazards and developing mitigation measures where appropriate. It also ensured that appropriate search and rescue response services were available. Using the thinking and outcomes-based concepts of the VAMP and the principles of risk management, Parks Canada developed and began implementing the *Visitor Risk Management Handbook* (Parks Canada, 1996).

The purpose of this decision-making and planning framework is to use an integrated, multidisciplinary approach and the recreation opportunity production process to better understand the inputs, including hazards and visitors, and facilitating outputs and primary outputs (e.g., opportunities and risks). As stated in Chapter

2, "Of particular significance is the fact that the nature and magnitudes of probable beneficial and negative outcomes must be understood before one can understand the character of and manage for the primary outputs that are needed to facilitate the realization of those benefits and the reduction of negative effects."

The Visitor Risk Management process developed and implemented by Parks Canada enabled the Agency to refocus its public safety program to proactively manage risk where appropriate, improve the quality of opportunities for experiences being offered, and place a greater emphasis on prevention of public safety incidents, while at the same time offering more efficient and effective public safety services.

More recently, a Performance Evaluation and Management Framework for public safety was developed based upon the Agency's previous work (Table 11.1, p. 174) This framework was used to complete a national evaluation of the public safety program and led to recommendations for further program enhancements including an updated policy framework and continued implementation of the Parks Canada Occurrence Tracking System.

Renewed Focus on Outcomes

As you read this chapter and followed the citations, you probably noted that there was a lot of work completed between the mid-1980s through to the latter part of the 1990s. During this period there was a concentrated effort to introduce the OFP and OFM way of thinking. There was a systematic progression from use of thinking from activity-based management to experience-based management using the recreation production process model as the basis for program development and implementation. Through the mid-1990s concerns about the amount of time and effort being spent on planning, combined with program reviews and budget reductions across the federal government, resulted in the dismantling of what was then known as the Visitor Activities Branch in Parks Canada at the national office and in the regional offices. While much of the early work produced many positive results it was, in fact, ahead of its time and could not withstand the winds of change.

As we all know, the winds of change can blow from different directions over time. The establishment of the Parks Canada Agency in 1998, the Panel on the Ecological Integrity of Canada's National Parks in 2000, the OAG and Commissioner of the Environment and Sustainable Development 2005 audit report on *Ecological Integrity in Canada's National Parks*, and the Minister's Roundtable 2005 contributed to the realization that it was time to refocus on the outcomes that are described in the Agency's legislation. These three outcomes are simply: protection, education, and opportunities for visitor experiences. The Minster's Round Table and the OAG/Commissioner of the Environment and Sustainable Development called for Parks Canada to take a more integrated approach to public education and visitor experience. The relationship between these three elements is illustrated in Figure 11.1.

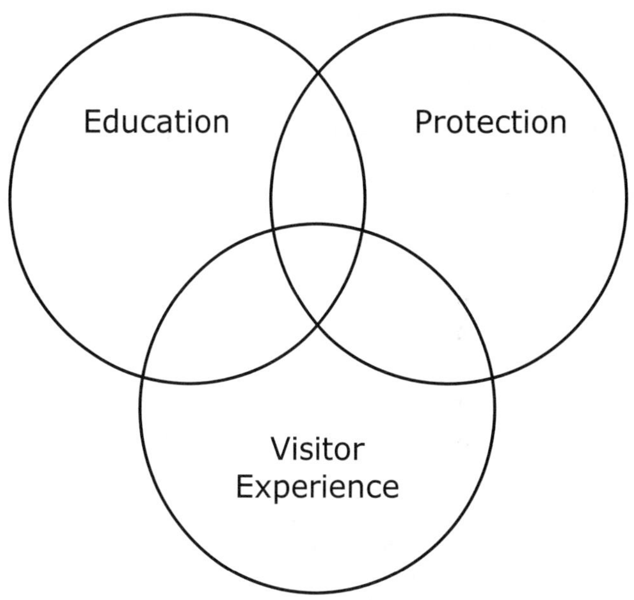

***Figure 11.1** The relationship between protection, education, and visitor experience*

Parks Canada has responded organizationally by creating, at the national office level, a new External Relations and Visitor Experience Directorate that is now providing national leadership, policy direction, and support to field staff in the outcome areas of education and visitor experience. More importantly all program areas are being directed to work on the horizontal integration of inputs, facilitating outputs, and primary outputs to achieve the broader program outcomes. This integrated approach is essential to ensuring that the Parks Canada Agency continues to be representative of Canada and relevant to Canadians as we deliver our legislated requirements.

Summary

Since the late-1990s there has been an increasing emphasis on results-based management within the federal government of Canada. This relatively recent emphasis was in fact preceded by many years of effort by parks and recreation professionals throughout Canada to

How		Who		Why	
Resources/ Inputs	Activities	Outputs	Reach	Intermediate Outcomes	Long-Term Outcomes
Operations and salary budget, 2001–02 FY: $4,929K including 67 FTEs (based on 1997–98 estimate); these figures include National Office resources: 1 GT-5, one third of a PM-6	Planning and risk management nationally and at sites Policy development/ horizontal coordination Prevention programming nationally and at sites Maintain search and rescue readiness Provide search and rescue response Undertake activities to reduce the Crown's potential for liability Data collection, analysis, and reporting Emergency response planning Represent Parks Canada at National Search and Rescue Secretariat	Risk to visitors and public reduced Policies and directives Prevention activities delivered Staff is equipped and trained to provide effective Search and Rescue Search and Rescue carried out Public Safety Program for reducing the Crown's potential for liabillity Local and national reporting on incidents and expenditure Emergency response plans and procedures Participation in NSS for planning and coordination of Agency SAR Program with the federal SAR plan	**Clients** Clients/Beneficiaries • Visitors and potential visitors at Protected Heritage Areas (PHAs) • Parks residents and businesses • Federal agencies • Provincial and municipal governments **Co-Delivery Agents** • SAR Secretariat • NGOs, examples: Canadian Avalanche Association, SMARTRISK cable stations (PSAs) • Canadian Coast Guard • Weather services • Provincial police forces • Ground SAR organizations	Self-reliant visitors undertaking activities consistent with their level of knowledge and skill Visitors aware of and knowledgeable about risks and risk management Client satisfaction with public safety services Effective search and rescue response Effective search and rescue response Reduction in Crown's potential for liability Satisfaction of partners Agency SAR program working in a coordinated fashion with other federal SAR programs	Number and severity of incidents in National Parks and National Historic Sites reduced Safer visitor experience at National Parks and National Historic Sites and canals

Table 11.1 Performance Evaluation and Management Framework for public safety

adopt and implement the OFP, building upon the work that was initiated by Bev Driver and others in the United States. The need to focus on the beneficial outcomes of parks and recreation became imperative as parks and recreation programs fought for survival in the 1990s during a period of severe restraint. There has been yet another renewal of interest in this work as a result of the Parks Victoria "*Healthy Parks and Health People*" initiative and the CPC "*Healthy by Nature*" program.

Under the leadership of Grant Tayler, members of the staff of Parks Canada were early adopters of the OFP through work on the VAMP decision-making framework. During the late-1980s and early-1990s, Tayler and his team worked closely with U.S. counterparts to gain further understanding and acceptance of the OFP approach. Operational realities, however, required the adoption of an activity and opportunities for experience management vocabulary to gain initial acceptance. Implementation of the VAMP presented both challenges and opportunities, and it has led to policy change and new policy development. Much of the thinking subsequently migrated into other program areas, including the development and implementation of Parks Canada's approach to Visitor Risk Management. Numerous studies and reports between 2000 and 2005 called for a renewed emphasis on OFM, and Parks Canada has begun to look, once again, at what its true program delivery outcomes are (plan from the right to left) so it can achieve improved integrated program delivery (implementation from the left to the right).

Literature Cited

Alberta Parks and Recreation. (1996). *Benefits Based Recreation: Awareness into Action - A Guide Book.* Edmonton, Alberta: Alberta Parks and Recreation. 51 pages.

Canada Parks Council. (2006). *Healthy by Nature.* Canada Parks Council.

Federal-Provincial Parks Conference. (1975). Report of the Federal Provincial Task Force on Interpretation. Ottawa. Parks Canada.

Graham. R. (1990). Visitor Management in Canada's National Parks. In R. Graham and R. Lawrence (Eds.), *Towards serving visitors and managing our resources.* (pp. 271–296). University of Waterloo: Tourism Research Centre.

Mayne, J. (2001) Addressing Attribution through Contribution Analysis: Using Performance Measures Sensibly. *The Canadian Journal of Program Evaluation, 16*(1) 1–24.

Nilsen, P. & Tayler, G. E. *Parks Canada's Spectrum of Appropriate National Park Opportunities Handbook.* Ottawa. Parks Canada.

Officer of the Auditor General and the Commissioner of the Environment and Sustainable Development. 2005. Chapter 2—Ecological Integrity in Canada's National Parks. Ottawa: Ministry of Public Works and Government Services.

Parks Canada. (1996). *Visitor Risk Management Handbook.* Ottawa. Parks Canada.

Parks Canada. (1994). *Guiding Principles and Operating Policies.* Ottawa. Parks Canada.

Parks Canada. (1992). *Visitor Activity Concept Handbook.* Ottawa. Parks Canada.

Parks Canada. (1988). *Getting Started - A Guide to Service Planning.* Ottawa. Parks Canada.

Parks Canada. (1985). *Management Process for Visitor Activities.* Ottawa. Parks Canada.

Parks Canada Agency. (2006). *Parks Canada Agency Corporate Plan 2006/07–2010/11.* PCA.

Payne, R. J., Carr, A., & Cline, E. (1997). *Applying the Recreation Opportunity Spectrum (ROS) for Visitor Opportunity Assessment in Two Canadian National Parks: A Demonstration Project.* Ottawa, Parks Canada.

Tayler. G. E. 1990. The Visitor Management Process. In R. Graham and R. Lawrence (Eds.). *Towards serving visitors and managing our resources.* (pp. 235–247). University of Waterloo: Tourism Research Centre.

Treasury Board of Canada Secretariat (2001). *Results for Canadians: A Management Framework for the Government of Canada.* Government of Canada.

Chapter 12
Healthy Parks, Healthy People: Assessing the Benefits Gained by Australian Park Visitors

Delene L. Weber, John Senior, Dino Zanon, and Dorothy Anderson

Learning Objectives:

1. Describe a study that reflects the commitment of Australia's park and recreation agencies to outcomes-focused management (OFM).
2. Offer recommendations to administrators, managers, and planners of parks and other areas that provide outdoor recreation opportunities in Australia and elsewhere to help them apply OFM.

Purpose

This chapter briefly describes how OFM is being used to help guide policy, managerial, and planning decisions about the recreational use of public lands in Australia. Following a general introduction about the interest in OFM in Australia, an overview of an OFM study conducted in southeastern Australia between 2003 and 2005 is described, findings relevant to ODFM are discussed, and recommendations are made. That study identified the types of benefits most important to visitors to developed metropolitan parks and larger, less developed, nonurban, nature-based parks and then investigated the influence of activities and settings on the attainment of those benefits.[1] After presenting an overview of the study, recommendations are made for integrating the findings into the strategic management of parks.

Introduction

In Chapter 6, Crompton explains why park and recreation agencies need to reposition themselves to demonstrate that they are addressing relevant community concerns and making positive contributions to important relevant community problems. He argues that to avoid being perceived as providers of relatively unimportant discretionary services (when compared to other government departments), park and recreation agencies must identify issues of paramount concern to the community and select a group of outcomes that parks can deliver to address those issues. He contends that agencies should be "perceived to contribute to alleviating problems which constitute the prevailing political concerns of policy makers who are responsible for allocating tax funds." In Australia, as well as most other countries, public health is an issue of substantial political and social concern to which several park and recreation agencies are aligning themselves (see Chapter 22 of this text). Similar to the United States, Australia is recording unprecedented rates of childhood obesity, cardiovascular disease, and stress-related illnesses. Political and media focus is centered on this issue, with increasing sedentary lifestyles, social isolation, increased traffic, and lack of ready access to parks and green space being depicted as the key culprits. Park and recreation agencies can play an important role in addressing these issues. For example, growing evidence shows that contact with nature affects individual health and community well-being, and that access to park and recreation areas and services can foster greater physical activity, promote healing, increase immunity, decrease stress, and help fulfill psychological, emotional, and spiritual needs (Kaczynski & Henderson, 2007; Maller, Townsend, Brown & St. Leger, 2002).

A notable example of how park and recreation agencies are positioning themselves as providers of important health outcomes is the Healthy Parks, Healthy People (HPHP) program (see Chapter 6 of this text).[2] The program aims to promote the mental and physical benefits of spending time in park and recreation areas. The program was initiated by Parks Victoria and has been adopted by several of Australia's other major park and recreation agencies, including the Department of Environment and Heritage (South Australia), the Department of Conservation and Land Management (Western Australia), and the Sydney Parks Group. A national coordination group has been established to promote collaboration on future events and to create leverage in terms of media coverage and public awareness. Park and recreation agencies have also used the campaign to attract partnerships from other health providers, again providing a means of increasing awareness of the campaign. For example, in Victoria, partnerships have been forged with various universities, Arthritis Victoria, Asthma Victoria, Osteoporosis Victoria, the National Heart Foundation, and the Royal Australasian College of General Practitioners.

The HPHP program has actively promoted the benefits of outdoor recreation through various media and special events designed to get people outdoors and participating in physical activity. These events have included walks targeting nontraditional park users such as the "World's Greatest Pram Stroll" and the "Million Paws Walk;" innovative health programs such as "Feel Blue, Touch Green" that link depression sufferers with park volunteer opportunities; festivals; and a variety of activities designed to get people outdoors and enjoying themselves.

But does everyone receive the plethora of benefits espoused by the program? And if not, why? Understanding the precursors to benefit attainment is vital information for park managers interested in knowing if there are specific things they can do to help facilitate benefits. In the State of Victoria, a research program aimed at better understanding benefit (outcome) attainment commenced in 2002. It began with a review of literature on the benefits of contact with nature (Maller et al., 2002) and now focuses on primary research into benefits, social values, community participation and equity. This work has been conducted through multiple university partners and Collaborative Research Centres (CRC). This research has shaped the marketing campaigns of the state by providing more precise information on the types of benefits visitors desire and attain. Policy has also been affected by this research, particularly in terms of equity decisions concerning underrepresented community groups (primarily ethnic minorities, women, and the elderly). New metropolitan parks and recreation areas have been established, and park and recreation facilities have been modified (e.g., the addition of flatter, wider trails, more drinking fountains, and increased seating along trails to better serve the elderly and sufferers of arthritis). Some parks have marketed these health-related opportunities more than others. In addition, this attention on visitor outcomes is apparent in corporate plans for all parks and related areas. A similar pattern has been experienced in the state of South Australia. Therefore, this chapter reports on an OFM study comparing visitor outcomes in parks in Australia's states of Victoria and South Australia.

Managers of the parks in this study were interested in expanding the HPHP program beyond the realms of marketing to learning more about the underlying reasons "why" (the central question raised by OFM as explained in Chapter 1) people visit parks, and in particular about the wide variety of benefits they desire and attain as a result of those visits. Specifically, they wanted to know how they could manage developed metropolitan parks and related recreation areas as well as larger less-developed national parks in a way that would optimize the benefits visitors desired without compromising the protection of the resources entrusted to them. They hoped that OFM might be a tool to achieve that goal because it focuses on the reasons for participation in outdoor recreation, such as management conditions and activities that facilitate the attainment of desired outcomes as well as reducing negative impacts. This chapter provides an overview of the OFM approach that was taken to provide Australian park and recreation area managers with the information they desired and needed.

Purpose of the Research and Design of The Study

Because most of the research on the recreational benefits of natural areas has been conducted in the U.S., much of what is known about such benefits is based on U.S. populations and the values and perspectives of U.S. citizens. Although U.S. citizens and Australian citizens share many similar interests and engage in many of the same outdoor recreation pursuits, their reasons for engaging in those activities and the outcomes of their engagement in those activities may differ. The study aimed to determine the benefits Australian visitors associate with their parklands and to investigate the type of relationship that existed between levels of development and beneficial outcomes.

To accomplish the purpose of the study a mixed-methods approach was used. After initial consultation with park managers, a pre-study was conducted and this was followed by two focus group discussions. That information shaped the survey questions that were used to interview 1479 visitors across four parks, and also to design the mail-back questionnaires that were mailed later to those willing to participate further in the study. The on-site interviews collected information about visitors' use of the park, favorite places, activities, primary motivations for visiting, and basic demographic information. The mail-back questionnaires were designed to solicit information pertaining to the types of benefits that were viewed to be most important to the visitors as well as other types of information not reported here.

Study Sites

The study was conducted in four parks in southeastern Australia. Southeastern Australia is a relatively densely populated region of Australia comprising a diversity of ecosystems and a rich network of protected areas that experience high levels of visitation. For the purpose of the study, two large national parks located in nonurban areas (Wilsons Promontory and Innes National Parks) and two smaller, more developed metropolitan parks (Jells Park and Belair National Park) were selected. Wilsons Promontory National Park is located at the southernmost point of the Australian mainland, approximately three hours from the Victorian capital city of Melbourne. The park is renowned for its spectacular coastline and for hiking opportunities amidst granite mountains, heathland, and patches of rainforest. Innes National Park lies at the foot of the Yorke Peninsula, approximately a three and a half hour drive from the South Australian capital city of Adelaide. The weathered cliffs and beaches backed by sand dunes, salt lake flats, and mallee scrub have given Innes a reputation as having one of the most outstanding coastlines in the country. Jells Park, the most highly visited of the four parks, is located in eastern Melbourne and is part of a 10 kilometer corridor or greenway of parklands. Jells Lake provides a scenic backdrop for the park, which includes large picnic areas, trails, adventure playgrounds, and a popular tea-house. Belair National Park is nestled in the Adelaide Hills. The park includes extensive walking trails, horse-riding trails, cricket ovals, and tennis courts. As one of the world's oldest national parks, it comprises an eclectic mix of native and European vegetation, reflecting its colonial history. All parks have distinct conservation and recreation management zones, and in consultation with managers, recreation opportunity spectrum classes were defined for the study.

Methods Used

The multi-methods approach employed had three parts, a qualitative phase, an on-site survey, and use of mail-back questionnaires.

The qualitative phase of research preceded the collection of quantitative data. This consisted of discussions with managers, a pre-study using protocol analysis where respondents were asked to verbalize everything they were thinking as they considered and formulated answers, and two focus groups. This data, although not necessarily representative of the views held by park visitors in general, provided information which was used to develop a conceptual model to test using more traditional surveys with random sampling. The key findings that emerged from this preliminary stage were:

- Both managers and visitors intuitively understood the concept of OFM.
- It appeared the benefits visitors desired and attained at metropolitan parks were a sub-set of a more diverse range of benefits sought at larger parks. A core group of benefits including enjoying nature, escaping personal and physical pressures and spending time with family were important to visitors at both types of parks.
- Some participants believed positive memories led to repeat visitation and a sense of attachment to the parks, which may lead to greater attainment of benefits and a desire to engage in conservation/civic actions.

On-Site Survey

An on-site interview survey consisting of 32 base questions was conducted at each park. This method allowed for the collection of a random sample of park visitors on weekdays and weekends during both peak and non-peak periods. The interviews were designed to collect basic use and demographic information from visitors to allow differentiation among visitors based on activity and setting preferences. The interviews were intentionally designed to require minimal time (less than 10 minutes) in an effort to reduce refusals and to maximize the number of visitors who could be interviewed in a survey period. A target of 400 visitor contacts per park was based on expected response rates and the desire to obtain a sample of 250 returned mail-back questionnaires for each park (i.e., 1,000 total). Resource limitations meant surveying could not be done simultaneously at each park, but quotas were established to ensure consistency among the parks in terms of the number of survey periods conducted on weekdays, weekends, peak-periods, pubic holidays, and non-peak periods.

At the conclusion of the interview, participants were asked if they were willing to participate in further components of the study and offered an enticement of a small gift in addition to being entered into a drawing for an annual parks pass. Over 90 percent of respondents interviewed at each park agreed to participate in the mail survey and provided their names and addresses.

Mail-Back Questionnaires

Self-administered questionnaires were sent to those participants interviewed on-site who agreed to participate in a more comprehensive study of the benefits of parks. The six-page questionnaires were designed to collect information on five main topics:

1. the relative importance of various benefits when they chose to visit the park on the day they were interviewed;
2. their satisfaction in obtaining a range of benefits following their park experience on the day they were interviewed;
3. the emotional and functional attachment they associate with the parks;
4. their level of engagement in conservation actions; and
5. their preferences in terms of environmental, social, and managerial conditions.

The questionnaire included several psychometric scales, some of which had previously been extensively tested for reliability and validity. Specifically, the Recreation Experience Preference (REP) scales developed by Driver and associates (Driver, Tinsley, & Manfredo, 1991) were used to examine the experiential benefits desired and attained by the respondents. The place attachment scales developed and tested by Dan Williams and his colleagues (Williams & Vaske, 2003) were used to measure place attachment.

Engagement in conservation actions was measured by asking respondents to indicate the level of frequency with which they participated in various conservation actions over the past two years. The list was modified from statements used in previous studies (Anderson, Schertz, Thompson, & Thompson, 2006). Development preferences was measured via a series of statements adapted from other studies, the basis of which was the widely used Recreation Opportunity Spectrum system developed by leisure researchers in close cooperation with recreation planners in the USDA Forest Service and the USDI Bureau of Land Management (USDA Forest Service, 1982 and summarized in Moore & Driver, 2005: 168–175)

If the mail survey had not been returned after two weeks from the date of the on-site interview, participants had a reminder letter, another survey with a postage-paid envelope, and an embossed pen forwarded to their address. A second wave of reminders occurred at week four.

Results

A total of 1479 park visitors were interviewed on-site across the four parks. Response rates are reported in Table 12.1.

Lower than expected use of Jells Park during weekdays, and a greater than expected population who felt their English was not sufficiently proficient to be interviewed resulted in a low overall response rate for Jells Park. The response rate was also smaller than expected at Wilsons Promontory because of a large fire that resulted in closure of the park during one survey period. The sociodemographic profiles of visitors to each park was similar. The majority (52%) of the study participants at all parks except Innes were female. Almost one third of the respondents for the metropolitan parks were in the age bracket 30-39 years, whereas the younger age bracket of 20-29 years was represented most strongly at the nonurban parks. Over a quarter of participants at the metropolitan sites identified themselves as young to middle-aged family groups. While these groups were still well-represented at regional parks, young singles, and young couples without children were represented in higher numbers. Most respondents had completed tertiary or high school education. The most common group size was two for all parks and the median group size was between 4–11, reflecting a substantial number of multi-family and organized groups using the parks, particularly at the metropolitan sites. Approximately half of the respondents at each park considered themselves regular visitors. Most visitors tended to visit the park where they were surveyed between one and three times a year, with visitation to the metropolitan parks more frequent but for shorter periods of time.

Walking and rest/relaxation were important activities at all four parks. Other activities that respondents attributed to their greatest satisfaction varied between the metropolitan and nonurban parks. At the metropolitan

	Belair	Jells	Innes	Wilsons Promon-tory	Overall
On-site surveys	400	261	497	321	1479
Benefits mail-back surveys	273	119	265	227	884
Returned to sender	4	8	5	4	21
Response rate (%)	68.9	47.0	53.9	71.6	60.6

Table 12.1 Number of surveys completed and returned at each park

Rank	Important Benefits at Each Park	N	Av. Importance[a]	SD	Av. Importance[b]	SD
	Belair National Park					
1	Enjoy the natural scenery	268	4.62	0.66	4.49	0.62
2	Enjoy the sounds and smells of nature	267	4.50	0.74	4.43	0.68
3	Get away from the usual demands of life	268	4.47	0.76	4.30	0.74
4	Escape the noise of everyday life	266	4.26	0.88	4.11	0.86
5	Experience the outdoor climate	263	4.24	0.88	4.35	0.77
6	Spend time with friends	267	4.23	1.01	4.36	0.87
7	Get away from crowds	268	4.21	0.91	3.97	0.91
8	Feel healthier	267	4.16	0.84	4.17	0.78
9	Experience tranquility /solitude	267	4.14	0.97	3.99	0.93
10	Slow down mentally	266	4.10	0.96	4.11	0.84
11	Escape the overload of work	264	4.10	1.01	4.09	0.95
12	Bring my family closer together	264	4.07	1.18	4.15	0.99
13	Help release or reduce built up tension	266	4.00	0.94	4.07	0.88
	Jells Park					
1	Get away from usual demands of life	103	4.50	0.65	4.16	0.80
2	Enjoy the natural scenery	115	4.43	0.75	4.38	0.68
3	Spend time with friends	114	4.31	1.01	4.41	0.81
4	Feel healthier	115	4.30	0.74	4.21	0.74
5	Enjoy sounds and smells of nature	115	4.29	0.80	4.27	0.82
6	Escape the noise of everyday life	103	4.23	0.89	3.89	0.95
7	Slow down mentally	103	4.13	0.88	4.05	0.90
8	Get away from crowds	115	4.13	0.89	3.72	1.06
9	Experience tranquility /solitude	115	4.13	0.99	3.82	1.01
10	Experience the outdoor climate	113	4.11	0.91	4.22	0.92
11	Bring my family closer together	112	4.10	1.19	4.28	0.88
12	Escape the overload of work	102	4.07	0.99	3.86	1.02
13	Help release / reduce built up tension	114	4.01	0.92	4.05	0.83
	Innes National Park					
1	Enjoy the natural scenery	257	4.74	0.52	4.66	0.58
2	Get away from the usual demands of life	172	4.67	0.66	4.34	0.83
3	Escape the noise of everyday life	172	4.56	0.71	4.24	0.91
4	Experience tranquility /solitude	257	4.49	0.77	4.11	0.98
5	Enjoy the sounds and smells of nature	257	4.45	0.78	4.48	0.74
6	Get away from crowds	258	4.45	0.83	3.95	1.05
7	Escape the overload of work	171	4.37	1.00	4.22	0.92
8	Experience the outdoor climate	255	4.34	0.76	4.49	0.69
9	Slow down mentally	172	4.22	0.91	4.13	0.88
10	Enjoy privacy	172	4.18	0.88	3.88	1.06
11	Feel healthier	257	4.14	0.88	4.08	0.84
12	Explore a new area	258	4.13	0.96	4.24	0.97
13	Help release or reduce built up tension	258	4.11	1.00	4.12	0.89
	Wilsons Promontory National Park					
1	Enjoy the natural scenery	227	4.86	0.45	4.75	0.57
2	Get away from the usual demands of life	227	4.67	0.60	4.41	0.79
3	Enjoy the sounds and smells of nature	227	4.63	0.67	4.60	0.67
4	Escape the noise of everyday life	226	4.43	0.77	4.17	0.95
5	Experience tranquility /solitude	226	4.41	0.84	4.11	0.97
6	Escape the overload of work	224	4.36	0.89	4.32	0.86
7	Experience the outdoor climate	227	4.34	0.81	4.38	0.72
8	Get away from crowds	227	4.30	0.84	3.84	1.09
9	Feel healthier	227	4.30	0.81	4.25	0.78
10	Slow down mentally	227	4.15	0.99	4.16	0.89
11	Help release or reduce built up tension	226	4.12	0.94	4.15	0.83
12	Enjoy privacy	226	4.00	0.92	3.66	1.04

[a]Importance was calculated using on a 5-point response format scale where 1=completely unimportant/not relevant; 2=relatively unimportant; 3=neither important nor unimportant; 4=relatively important; and 5=very important.

[b]Attainment was calculated using a 5-point response format on which 1=completely nsatisfied;=relatively unsatisfied; 3=neither satisfied nor unsatisfied; 4=relatively satisfied; and 5=totally satisfied.

Table 12. 2: Important experiential benefits at each park and level of attainment

parks, respondents were most likely to cite socializing, attending a planned event, or participating in activities for children, whereas important activities for visitors to the regional parks included hiking, surfing, fishing, and other beach-related activities. The existence of a greater range of ROS classes at the other two parks meant there were relatively smaller percentages of visitors to those parks citing developed zones as the setting where their best experience occurred.

In terms of the benefits that were most important to visitors at each park, a core group of benefits, similar to those found in U.S. studies (Anderson, Nickerson, Stein, & Lee, 2000) was identified. Respondents rated the importance of 43 benefits on a 1-5 response format, on which 1 indicated the benefit was completely unimportant to the visitor and 5 indicated it was very important. Table 12.2 shows only those benefits that averaged above 4. Of the experiential benefits rated as important, a total of eleven were rated such across the four parks: enjoy the natural scenery; enjoy the sounds and smells of nature; get away from the usual demands of life; experience the outdoor climate; escape the noise of everyday life; get away from crowds; feel healthier; experience tranquility/solitude; slow down mentally; escape the overload of work; and help release/reduce built-up tension. "Spend time with friends" and "bring my family closer together" were reported as important benefits at both metropolitan parks, but not at either nonurban park. "Enjoy privacy" was considered as an important benefit at both nonurban parks, but not at the metropolitan parks. "Explore a new area" was rated as an important benefit for Innes participants, but not at any other park.

The types of experiential benefits listed in Table 12.2 were drawn from seven benefit "domains" into related REP scales (experiences 0 were grouped (see Moore & Driver, 2005: Appendix A: 316). The selected domains were: *enjoy nature; escape personal/social pressure; escape physical pressure; temperature; similar people; family togetherness;* and *learning.* When comparing the importance at this larger domain level, there is consistency among the parks in terms of those benefits identified as being most important and those identified as being least important. Table 12.3 shows this pattern, demonstrating that the "top ten benefit domains" and the "bottom ten benefit domains" are common across the four parks. Enjoying nature is unilaterally perceived to be the most important domain to park visitors. *Temperature (experiencing the outdoor climate)* was the second most important domain at Belair and Wilsons Promontory National Parks, whereas *similar people* is the second most important domain at Jells Park and *escaping physical pressure* is the second most important domain at Innes National Park. *Escaping personal or social pressure* is ranked as the third or fourth most important benefit at each park. At an aggregate level, benefits such as *risk taking, meeting new people, risk reduction,* and *escaping the family*, are not important to the participants in this study.

The analyses showed that selected recreation activity was a key predictor of the attainment of benefits and concluded that people engaged in more active pursuits such as hiking, were more likely to attain several important benefits domains (e.g., enjoying nature, physical fitness, learning, teaching/leading others, autonomy/leadership, and achievement/stimulation) than were people participating in more passive pursuits, such as picnicking. In this study, the park type (i.e., metropolitan or nonurban) was a better predictor of benefit attainment than the ROS class in which the respondents had their best experience. Market segments based on the centrality of recreation in the participant's lifestyle, various demographic characteristics, use characteristics, and experience mode were also evaluated in terms of their affect on benefit attainment. They were found to have a negligible affect compared to either setting or activity characteristics.

More specific recommendations based on the findings are provided in the following section. The information about benefits and its links to experience preferences supports our conceptual understanding of OFM. Regional and metropolitan parks have much in common, but noticeable differences were found in the attainment of the domains *family togetherness* and *similar people*, which were significantly greater at the metropolitan parks. Attainment was significantly greater at the regional parks than the metropolitan parks for the benefits *enjoy nature, physical rest, learning, nostalgia, creativity,* and *achievement/stimulation*. The relationships found between place attachment and benefit attainment contribute to the theory of OFM, while the relationship between development preferences and conservation action support previous findings concerning the antecedent conditions of responsible environmental actions (Hartig, Kaiser, & Bowler, 2001).

Recommendations

This study provided managers with tangible data about the outcomes desired and attained by visitors. This can be used as a basis for strategic planning and marketing decisions. The most expensive component of this study was the on-site survey. However, the value of

	Belair		Jells		Innes		Wilsons Promontory	
Benefit Domains	Mean	Rank	Mean	Rank	Mean	Rank	Mean	Rank
Most Important Domains								
Enjoy Nature	4.55	1	4.36	1	4.59	1	4.75	1
Temperature	4.24	2	4.11	4	4.34	3	4.34	2
Escape Personal/Social Pressures	4.16	4	4.20	3	4.25	4	4.32	3
Escape Physical Pressure	4.10	5	4.07	6	4.44	2	4.28	4
Similar People	4.23	3	4.31	2	3.90	6	3.94	5
Family Togetherness	4.07	6	4.10	5	3.77	7	3.72	9
Physical Fitness	3.70	7	3.91	7	3.49	11	3.84	6
Physical Rest	3.57	9	3.83	8	3.69	8	3.76	8
Learning	3.47	10	3.40	10	3.92	5	3.78	7
Social Security	3.60	8	3.59	9	3.51	9	3.66	10
Less Important Domains								
Introspection	3.45	11	3.25	11	3.30	12	3.49	13
Creativity	2.92	14	3.03	14	3.51	10	3.57	11
Nostalgia	3.16	13	3.05	12	3.28	14	3.53	12
Teaching/Leading Others	3.17	12	3.04	13	3.30	13	3.22	14
Autonomy/Leadership	2.92	15	2.86	16	3.10	16	3.15	15
Achievement/Stimulation	2.89	16	2.85	17	3.19	15	3.15	16
New People	2.89	17	2.96	15	3.08	17	2.99	17
Risk Taking	2.71	18	2.48	19	2.96	18	2.94	18
Risk Reduction	2.52	19	2.52	18	2.42	20	2.55	19
Escape Family	2.22	20	2.29	20	2.43	19	2.20	20

Importance was calculated using a 5-point response format on whiche 1=completely unimportant/not relevant; 2=relatively unimportant; 3=neither important nor unimportant; 4=relatively important; and 5=very important.

Table 12.3: Relative importance of experiential benefit domains at each park

this component lay not only as a means to identify a random sample, but also in the unsolicited comments provided by participants. Issues not identified by either managers or through the focus groups arose during the interviews and many comments provided insights that could not be collected adequately using traditional mail surveys. To defray costs associated with research, rather than eliminate expensive interviews, we would instead recommend shorter survey periods and possibly decreasing the number of benefit domains considered. This study was conducted over a longer period than traditional benefit studies that only collect data over a summer period. However, we found little difference in terms of those benefits considered important by visitors at different times of the year, and only minor differences in terms of attainment. Similar to previous U.S. studies, we found overwhelming support that a core group of benefits important to all visitors exists. If dealing with similar types of parks, it may therefore be prudent to spend more time on those benefits rather than spend excessive amounts of time dealing with those benefits perceived to be less important.

The strengths of OFM include allowing managers and policy makers to understand how their actions and decisions affect their actual and potential customers through making more explicit links between inputs and outcomes (as explained in Chapter 2 of this text); helping planners and managers to develop clearer management objectives; creating improved visitor experience opportunities as a result of more meaningful recreation demand analyses and giving careful attention to recreation settings conditions on which the desired experiences depend; better understanding the needs of residents of nearby communities; promoting greater understanding and appreciation of the social significance of protected areas; assisting managers in developing more competitive marketing strategies; facilitating a collaborative style of management; improving documentation of results; and providing succinct meaningful information to legislators to assist in the development of intelligent policy positions as explained in the four introductory chapters to this text. These broad strengths formed the basis of the following recommendations about how park and recreation administrators, managers, and planners in Australia and elsewhere can integrate and use the findings from this study:

- Develop vision statements, goals, and objectives that recognize the benefits people desire

Variables	Related variables	Important management considerations for developed parks (e.g., metropolitan parks)	Important management considerations for natural parks (e.g., regional parks)
Benefit Domains	Benefit desire and attainment was affected by setting characteristics, activity and place attachment. There was minor influence exerted by visitor clusters.	Restorative benefits such as slowing down mentally, escaping the noise of everyday life and experiencing tranquility were important to visitors at both regional and metropolitan parks. The domains that were significantly more important to visitors at metropolitan parks were family togetherness and similar people, suggesting managers should maintain sufficient infrastructure to support such benefit attainment. Attainment of the benefits similar people and physical fitness were higher for participants in metropolitan parks with lower levels of place identity, compared to their regional park counterparts. This may suggest an opportunity to build attachment with transitory groups such as runners, cyclists and friends invited to events, perhaps through special events catering for their interests, or interpretation highlighting the uniqueness of the park.	Importance and attainment of the domains enjoy nature, learning, and creativity were significantly greater at regional parks compared to metropolitan parks. In addition to maintaining/developing strong interpretive offerings, there may be value in exploring opportunities for artist-in-resident programs, or creative workshops that may appeal to not only existing constituents but attract new visitors. Employing strategies to build place attachment may also enhance benefit attainment. Regional park visitors with high levels of place attachment exhibited higher levels of benefit attainment than their metropolitan park counterparts for the following benefits: enjoy nature, temperature, physical rest, learning, teaching/leading others, nostalgia, creativity autonomy/leadership and achievement/stimulation.
Experience Preferences	Both setting and activity preferences affected the type of benefits that were important to people and the benefits they attained. The desire for less developed settings also significantly predicted place attachment and conservation action.	Socialising, attending planned events, picnicking and engaging in activities with children were all more important to metropolitan park visitors than regional park visitors. Providing the infrastructure to facilitate such activities is important but it should be done in a way that still allows fellow visitors to gain benefits such as experiencing tranquility and getting away from crowds. Zoning the park and making visitors at developed hubs aware of alternate opportunities in other parts of the park is recommended. The variability in the level of intensity of physical activity people were engaged in was more pronounced at metropolitan parks, with some people using the parks exclusively as a setting to engage in high intensity activities such as running, while many others engaged in low intensity activities such as sitting, talking and eating. Methods to enhance physical activity should be considered. These may include guided walks, less discrete information about walking opportunities, and psychological design that encourages exploration.	There were several benefits that were significantly more important to people who preferred less developed areas. For example, enjoy nature, escape personal pressure, escape physical pressure, physical fitness, physical rest, learning, achievement/stimulation and risk-taking. Providing opportunities to facilitate privacy and a sense of tranquility is therefore important, as are opportunities that allow visitors to challenge themselves. The range of activities people engage in at regional parks were greater than those at metropolitan parks and most people seemed to participate in some form of moderate intensity physical activity daily. Managers should work with interest groups to best facilitate appropriate recreation opportunities whilst maintaining strategies that provide privacy for those seeking escapism (e.g., through screening and zoning).
Conservation Action	The probability of an individual being involved in conservation action is positively affected by preference for less developed setting characteristics, networks with park staff and the community, and trust in the moral competence of staff. It is negatively influenced by trust in staff technical competence. Conservation action is also linked to place dependence and hence may be more likely to develop if repeat visitation is encouraged so people feel a greater sense of ownership of the park, and view it as the best place for participating in particular activities.	Interpretation and psychological design may play a key part in instilling a conservation ethic among visitors to developed parks. Encouraging people to explore less developed areas of the park may improve conservation outcomes. This may be done either through design that make trails leading to, or passing through, less developed areas more noticeable and appealing, or through guided interpretive trails that may provide an improved perception of safety and interest in less developed areas. Interpretation opportunities may also play important roles in helping to develop improved networks amongst constituents and park staff and build trust in the moral competence of staff.	People visiting less developed parks are more likely to be engaged in conservation. However, providing opportunities for staff to interact with visitors and community members is likely to enhance conservation engagement. Providing knowledge of opportunities to help out are also essential. Building rapport with constituents may help enhance trust in the moral competence of staff. Better communication with constituents will also provide opportunities to demonstrate that technical competence of staff is insufficient to address larger goals of conservation.

Table 12.4: Overview of variables investigated, relationships, and implications

and the negative impacts they wish to avoid. Knowledge of the setting and activity conditions likely to facilitate particular benefits can provide managers with the necessary direction to articulate clear, achievable objectives. Using vision statements, goals, and objectives to drive an outcomes approach is a very effective way of keeping desired outcomes clear in the mind of all stakeholders and makes it more likely that changes to optimize benefit attainment will be made.

- Plan for "green areas" with low levels of development. The strong association between preferences for low development and the attainment of various experiential benefits stresses the importance of areas. It is recommended that planners and managers maintain or expand existing low-development areas and that new parks be planned to ensure adequate green space. Managers are encouraged to use interpretation and marketing tools to promote greater exploration of less developed areas within parks, and to promote less-developed parks as tourist destinations. Guided walks and hikes could provide visitors with the necessary confidence, in terms of security and safety, to explore less developed areas of a park, while also affording an opportunity to educate visitors about broader park-based recreation options within the respective systems. Use of nature-based tourism operators could help facilitate this goal. Managers should also consider other creative ways in which to encourage interactions with nature.
- Design parks with the intention of facilitating social interactions yet encouraging exploration of nature by also encouraging more use of trails. The value of research is very limited if it isn't disseminated to and used by managers. The following section discusses the implications of the study findings and outlines recommendations that were provided to managers. Large group sizes were common at the metropolitan parks and users at all parks ranked the benefits of family bonding and spending time with friends as important. Managers and planners should consider the creation of settings specifically designed to facilitate social interaction capable of supporting the desires for social benefits. These areas should be designed as gateways to access less developed areas within a park. For example, the addition of improved trailheads and signs located in social hubs that make people aware of trail opportunities may help to increase participation in walking, and hence generate increased health benefits while at the same time encouraging greater use of less developed areas within parks that are associated with greater attainment of a range of benefits. In this study the need for improved awareness of trail opportunities was particularly evident at the metropolitan parks. At Belair, despite an extensive trail network, less than 11% of respondents reported actually using the trail system. Many respondents made comments regarding the need for improving information and orientation on trails, the ease of getting lost, and the need for improved interpretation of what the park offers and it is assumed the lack of trail use stemmed partly from concerns about safely navigating the trails and also gaining adequate benefits from walking the trails. At Jells, walking was cited by less than 9% of visitors as a main reason for visiting the park, and comments revealed that many people were unaware of the extent of the park and walking opportunities, and did not venture beyond the developed section of the park than visitors reporting their best experience in a developed area. At Wilsons Promontory, many first time visitors arrived in the developed section of the park and reported feeling disoriented and unaware of where the beach was, or what parts of the park were worth exploring. It is recommended that signs be installed in socialpetal areas (i.e., areas where people can see and interact with one another) that include interpretive information and images showing the natural features of the trails (to facilitate the important benefit *enjoy nature*), and also messages related to the HPHP program objectives (supporting the important benefits *get/keep physically fit* and *escape personal and physical pressures*).
- Focus on improving visitors' ability to escape physical pressures. Although *escape physical pressures*, was ranked as one of the top six benefit domains at all parks, attainment of the benefit was less than satisfactory. In particular, the domain item *get away from crowds* was rated very highly at each park, but attainment was less than satisfactory (below 4.0) at all parks. Attainment of the benefit, *experience tranquillity* was rated as less than satisfactory at the two metropolitan parks, while respondents from both nonurban parks rated their ability to *enjoy privacy* as less than

satisfactory. The problem was most notable at Jells, where all items associated with the domain *escape physical pressures* were rated below 4.0. This finding suggests a need for managers to focus on ways to facilitate this important benefit. Enhancement of means to experience escape from physical pressures could be achieved by improved zoning through clustering facilities (e.g., creating distinct activity hubs and sociopetal settings, leaving other areas free of development) and using natural landscape features and topography to screen facilities. Increasing vegetative plantings in campground areas to reduce noise and improve the perception of privacy should also be considered. Other ways to assist the facilitation of this benefit might be to introduce "silent walks," where visitors are encouraged to enjoy short nature walks without conversing with other people on the trails. These trails might include no obvious signs of people such as interpretive signs or rubbish bins. Marketing less popular parks, or marketing the use of parks in nonpeak season might also improve ratings on the attainment of *escape physical pressures*. It is interesting to note a large number of comments provided by Jells Park visitors revolved around people's lack of awareness of alternative park options in Victoria (Weber, 2006), so simply making people aware of quieter, less used parks, may provide people with the options to avoid crowds and experience tranquility. Initiating ranger or volunteer-led guided walks with small numbers of visitors may be another way to encourage people out of the busy areas of parks into less developed sections of a park where they are more likely to have the opportunity to experience benefits such as tranquility and escaping crowds.

- Reconsider education strategies as tools to enhance visitor experiences and achieve management objectives. Although *learning* itself was not revealed as an overly important benefit domain, it was positively linked with several important domains (e.g., *enjoy nature, family togetherness,* and *physical fitness*), and therefore its role as an intermediary benefit may be very important. Educational efforts strategically designed to inform people how to be better stewards of the environment, make them aware of participation opportunities, and provide them a forum for networking with other people interested in the environment could have far-reaching positive impacts.
- Use information about benefits to inform improve marketing campaigns. Studies have shown that enticing people outdoors into a natural environment is important (Corkery, 2007; Faber & Kuo, 2006; Kuo, 2003; Kuo & Faber Taylor, 2004; Kweon, Sullivan, & Wiley, 1998; Maller, 2004; Maller et al., 2002; Maller, Townsend, Pryor, Brown, & St. Leger, 2006). For example, Corkery (2007: 15) states "Nature should be apparent in all of the places of our daily activities rather than being something 'out there' that is the focus of the occasional excursion of special outing." Several nature-related benefits domains were important to visitors across all parks. Included were *temperature* (i.e., getting outside the house), *enjoying nature* and *escaping physical and social pressures.* It is therefore recommended that park and tourism agencies position their campaigns using the benefits we know people are seeking. Campaigns initiated by Tourism Tasmania using the concept of "Escape" and "Imagine" as marketing platforms (e.g., "Imagine an island that is one giant outdoor playground"), or the New Zealand Tourism Commission who have used the slogan "100% Pure Escape" to market their parks provide good examples of strategies that embrace the benefits visitors are seeking.
- Use the results of this study to benchmark future changes in benefit attainment. These results become meaningful only if they are used to improve management of protected areas. And, if the findings are used to guide managerial attempts to improve or create opportunities to realize specific benefits, it is critical that success in doing so be measured over time. These findings can be used as a benchmark to assess the impact of future managerial actions. For example, the state agencies that manage the parks investigated in this study are partners in the HPHP program which aims to promote the mental and physical benefits of spending time in parks. The slogan implies that the environmental health of parks results in a healthy community and that spending active recreation time in well-maintained parks, leads to greater health and fitness of both individuals and society (Parks Victoria, 2006, Sydney Parks Group, 2007). This and similar studies provide important benchmark information that can be used in

the future to demonstrate whether benefits such as *improve physical fitness* actually increase in importance following the intensive marketing campaigns and special events being conducted to encourage more active use of parks.

- Disseminate information concerning benefit attainment to managers, planners, marketers, and legislators to ensure this value-added portion of the park experience is not ignored. This study provides the agencies with empirical data to substantiate links between park visitation and an array of benefits, including both physiological and psychological health benefits. This information can be used to justify expenditures associated with parks. The use of OFM information as a budgeting tool has been common, particularly in Canada (Anderson et al., 2000). In addition, it provides guidance for managers, planners, and marketers as to the type of park, area within a park, and type of activity best able to facilitate specific benefits. However, use of the OFM framework will be limited if people are not provided with the information and afforded opportunities to understand how they can integrate such data into management of parks and other protected areas. Workshops, how-to manuals, and videotapes are just some of the methods that can be used to assist in the application of research results to management actions.
- Think beyond park boundaries to realize conservation goals. Planners and managers need to think beyond the boundaries of their own parks and use their expertise in recreation planning and natural resource management to integrate nature into the wider community. In particular, they need to understand the preferences and opinions of residents of nearby communities (see Chapter 20 of this text). In this light, some of the innovative community programs initiated or supported by various park agencies should be applauded as examples of sound direction. Those programs include school gardens, urban tree house projects, nature playgrounds, urban restoration projects, prams walks, park-based festivals, and programs that focus on people who suffer from depression. In addition, much managerially relevant information can be obtained from local park volunteer groups communities. The use of focus groups, public meetings, citizen advisory boards, and volunteer and friends groups are just some of the ways park agencies can learn from their constituents.

Summary

This chapter reported on a study conducted in four Australian parks that examined the relationship between setting preferences and benefit attainment. The benefits that were perceived to be most important to visitors at both the metropolitan and larger regional national parks included *enjoying nature, experiencing the outdoor climate, escaping personal/social pressures, escaping physical pressures,* and *learning*. These findings reflect results from previous studies conducted in similar U.S. parks and support the existence of a core group of benefits. Importantly, the study found place attachment, particularly place dependence, to play a significant role in predicting the attainment of benefits. The findings pointed to the critical importance of maintaining areas with low levels of development, as well as a need to provide infrastructure that allows social experiences, yet encourages exploration of less developed areas within a park. The outcomes visitors are receiving as a result of park experiences extend beyond the boundaries our protected areas and our thinking in terms of park management must also. OFM offers an excellent systematic tool to extend our examination of the structural reasons for participation and nonparticipation in recreation into the wider community setting, particularly communities and neighborhoods that are proximate or very near the parks and recreation areas.

In conclusion, OFM is receiving increased attention by Australian park agencies. A notable example of the approach is the HPHP campaign which has been a key driver in the repositioning of a number of major park agencies in Australia. Agencies have aligned themselves with health providers and promoted the important role parks play in providing mental and physical health benefits. Agencies are now moving beyond a marketing role and examining the underlying values people associate with parks and the benefits they gain from visiting them.

Literature Cited

Anderson, D. H., Nickerson, R., Stein, T. V., & Lee, M. E. (2000). Planning to provide community and visitor benefits. In W. C. Gartner and D. W. Lime (eds.), *Trends in outdoor recreation, leisure and tourism* (pp. 197–212). Wallingford, UK: CAB International.

Anderson, D. A., Schertz, J. M., Thompson, J. L., & Thompson, J. L. (2006). National Park Community Survey, Report Prepared for the U.S. National

Park Service. St. Paul, MN: University of Minnesota, Department of Voyageurs Forest Resources and Cooperative Ecosystem Studies Unit.

Corkery, L. (2007). The landscapes of our lives. *Adelaide's Child, 6*(9), 14–16.

Driver, B. L., Tinsley, H. E., & Manfredo, M. J. (1991). The paragraphs about leisure and recreation experience preference scales: Results from two inventories designed to assess the breadth of the perceived psychological benefits of leisure. In B. L. Driver, P. J. Brown, & G. L. Peterson (Eds.), *Benefits of leisure* (pp. 263–286). State College, PA: Venture Publishing, Inc.

Faber Taylor, A. & Kuo, F. E. (2006). Is contact with nature important for healthy child development? In C. Spencer & M. Blades (Eds.), *Children and their Environments: Learning, Using and Designing Spaces.* Cambridge, U.K.: Cambridge University Press.

Hartig, T., Kaiser, F. G., & Bowler, P. A. (2001). Psychological restoration in nature as a positive motivation for ecological behavior. *Environment and Behavior, 33*(4), 590–607.

Kaczynski, A. T. & Henderson, K. A. (2007). Environmental correlates of physical activity: a review of evidence about parks and recreation. *Leisure Sciences, 29*, 315–354.

Kuo, F. E. (2003). The role of arboriculture in a healthy social ecology: Invited review article for a Special Section. Journal of Arboriculture, 29(3), 148–155.

Kuo, F. E., & Faber Taylor, A. (2004). A potential natural treatment for Attention-Deficit/Hyperactivity Disorder: Evidence from a national study. *American Journal of Public Health, 94*(9), 1580–1586.

Kweon, B. S., Sullivan, W. C., & Wiley, A. R. (1998). Green common spaces and the social integration of inner-city older adults. *Environment and Behaviour, 30*(6), 832–858.

Maller, C. (2004). The hidden benefits of environmental education: contact with nature and children's health and wellbeing. *Echo, 43*(1), 16–22.

Maller, C., Townsend, M., Brown, P. J., & St Leger, L. (2002). Healthy Parks, Healthy People: The health benefits of contact with nature in a park context. Social and Mental Health Priority Area: occasional paper series, 1, 1–86.

Maller, C., Townsend, M., Pryor, A., Brown, P. J., & St. Leger, L. (2006). Healthy nature healthy people: 'contact with nature' as an upstream promotion intervention for populations. *Health Promotion International, 21*(1), 45–54.

Moore, R. L. & Driver, B. L. (2005). Introduction to outdoor recreation: Providing and managing natural resource based opportunities. State College, PA: Venture Publishing, Inc.

Parks Victoria. (2006). Healthy Parks, Healthy People.

Sydney Parks Group. (2007). Centennial Parklands, Melbourne, Victoria.

USDA Forest Service (1982). ROS User Guide. Washington, D.C.

Williams, D. R., & Vaske, J. (2003). The measurement of place attachment: Validity and generalizability of a psychometric approach. *Forest Science, 49*(6), 830–840.

Weber D. (2006). Healthy Parks, Healthy People: Improving our Understanding of Visitors to Jells Park. Adelaide, SA, Sustainable Environments Research Group, University of South Australia.

Footnotes

1. Note from the editor of this text: Although the study reported in this chapter purposely focused mostly on benefits, the reader is reminded (from Chapter 1) that OFM requires consideration of both beneficial and unwanted/negative outcomes. BLD
2. Information on the Healthy Parks, Healthy People program is available on the Parks Victoria website at www.parkweb.vic.gov.au/1grants.cfm

Chapter 13
Revitalizing an Inner-City Park in Detroit: A Retrospective on the Outcomes Approach to Planning

Robert W. Marrans

Learning Objectives:

1. Understand the process of using the leisure benefits concept (or Outcome-Focused Benefits) in planning for the revitalization of an urban park.
2. Understand how park planning and revitalization can be used as an instrument for community revitalization.
3. Provide a historical perspective on a major urban park from its inception to its decline and illustrate the impediments to its improvement.

Since the mid-1980s, budget cuts in Detroit have forced its recreation department to severely curtail park maintenance and recreation programming throughout the city. Among the parks and playgrounds impacted are older sites located in the inner city, most of which serve predominantly disadvantaged populations. In an attempt to demonstrate how Detroit parks might be improved when funding would become more readily available, a park revitalization project was initiated in the mid-1990s by the University of Michigan's College of Architecture and Urban Planning working in cooperation with the city's recreation department and a new city administration. A major thrust of the project was the preparation of a master plan for the revitalization of Chandler Park, the city's fourth largest park. The revitalization plan was aimed at enhancing existing park conditions and creating more recreational opportunities for residents throughout the city's east side[1]. It was also viewed as a catalyst for neighborhood revitalization in the immediate surrounding neighborhoods. Therefore, a critical element of the planning process was the involvement of neighborhood residents. At the same time, the concept of OFM, which was then called Benefits-Based Management, or BBM, as explained in Chapter 1 of this text, was introduced into the planning process.

This chapter begins with a description of Chandler Park and its surroundings from a historical perspective. It follows with a description of the planning process that evolved in the mid-1990s, including how OFM was addressed at several stages. Elements of the master plan and their anticipated benefits are then presented. Next, the events that occurred following the preparation of the master plan and the future of the park are reviewed. Finally, the chapter presents a summary of the beneficial outcomes of the plan and discusses needed next steps.

Chandler Park and Its Surroundings, Circa 1994

As noted, Chandler Park is Detroit's fourth largest park with its nearly 200 acres divided into two distinct parts. The northern part contains a golf course of approximately 110 acres and is separated from the southern part by Chandler Park Drive, a wide thoroughfare linking a major north-south street on the west with a residential area to the east. The southern part, although smaller in size, had always represented the heart of Chandler Park. It contained a mixture of open grassy areas, mature shade trees, and recreational facilities including playground equipment, horseshoe pits, a basketball court, tennis courts, athletic fields, and picnic tables and grills. Most of the equipment and facilities, despite being old and poorly maintained, were used by nearby residents, especially children and elderly men. On weekends, the picnic area was used extensively by church groups and large families. The large shade trees, forming a dense canopy around the eastern and southern edges of an interior ring road, were the park's greatest assets. To the east of the park was an unkempt area of cattail marshes, open stands of water, and low scrubby vegetation.

Despite its age and generally poor conditions, the parks department recognized its importance to east side residents. Efforts to make modest improvements were made with grass mowing in select areas, new signage,

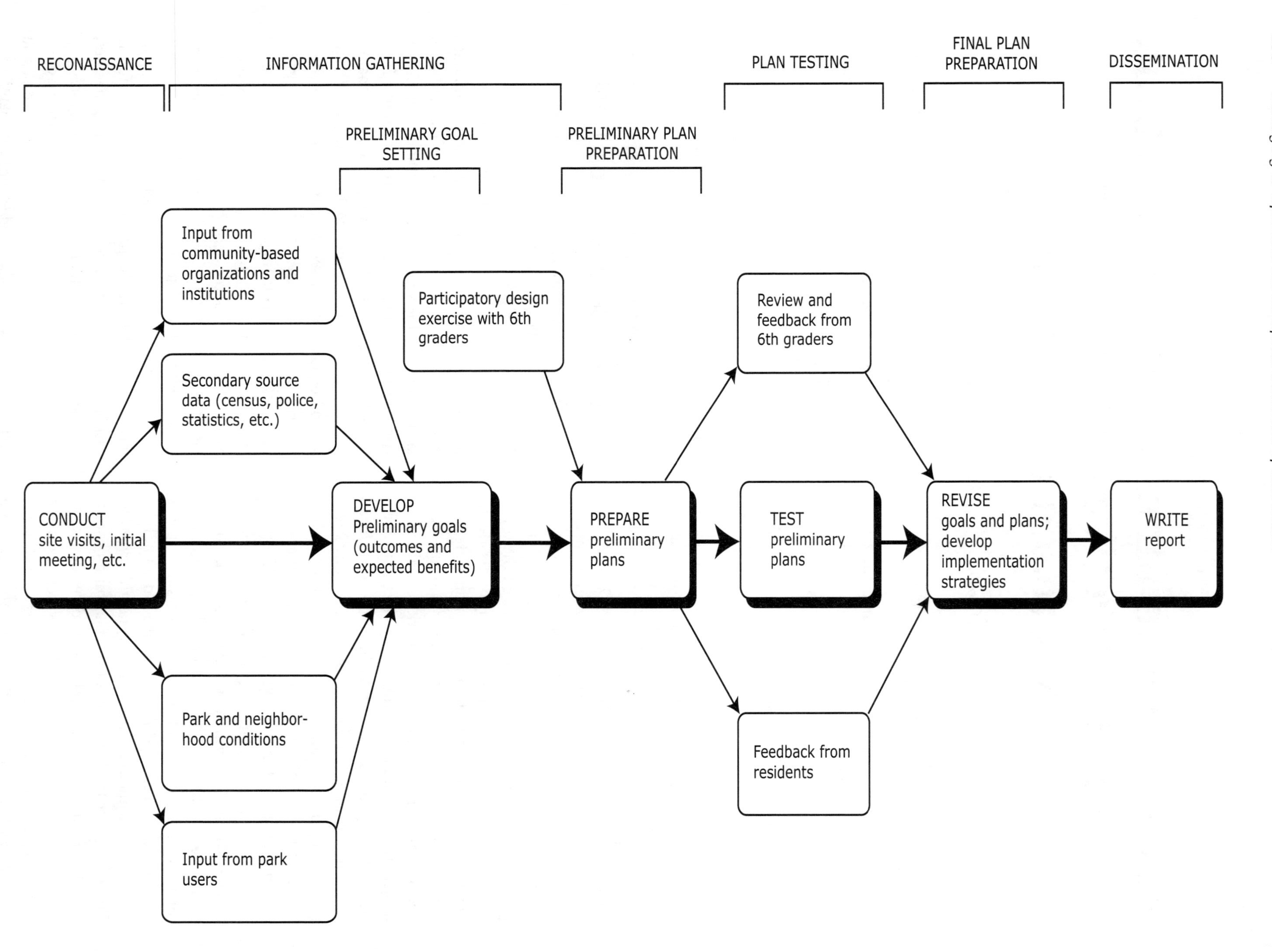

Figure 13.1 Stages in the Planning Process

and repairs to the comfort station. Nonetheless, the park remained in a state of disrepair and conveyed an atmosphere of neglect and indifference.

Chandler Park was surrounded by a combination of aging residential neighborhoods, a relatively new branch of a community college, a hospital, and a scattering of retail, industrial, and warehousing buildings. The housing stock varied from modest, well-kept, single-family homes to a partially vacant public housing complex immediately to the south. The overall area was recognized as problematic. Crime rates and poverty levels were high, and the public housing was undergoing extensive revitalization under the federally-sponsored Hope VI program. At the same time, Chandler Park and much of its immediate surroundings were within the boundaries of the city's Empowerment Zone[2].

Like many parts of Detroit, the neighborhoods around Chandler Park had lost population since the 1960s. Most of those who remained were African American with relatively low incomes and high levels of unemployment. For many of them, the park offered a sanction to a way of life that was modest at best.

The Planning Process

Because of Chandler Park's importance to residents from the city's east side, as well as those living near it, the director of Detroit's recreation department believed students and faculty from UM's College of Architecture and Urban Planning could contribute their expertise to creating a new image for the park. Initially, the UM team met to outline an approach to master planning. Developing a plan that reflected the interests of residents around the park and actively engaging them in the planning process were viewed as essential. Over a two-year period, teams of students worked on the project, which involved seven stages: reconnaissance, information gathering, preliminary goal setting, preliminary plan preparation, plan testing, final plan preparation, and dissemination. These stages are shown in the diagram in Figure 13.1 and are described below.

Reconnaissance

This initial stage involved brief visits to the park and the area surrounding it, a meeting with the city's park staff, and a meeting with the board of the nearby homeowners association. The visits included walks through the park and a driving tour of the adjacent neighborhoods. Visits were intended to acquaint the planning team with the park and its surroundings and to identify conditions which the team could examine more thoroughly and address as part of the planning process. Meetings with the parks staff informed students about the park's history and were used to discuss ideas for its future development and the need to involve numerous stakeholders in the planning process. As part of these meetings, the outcomes approach was outlined. Meetings with homeowners associations were designed to inform members of the university's charge and explain the potential benefits of the project, to hear about resident interests, and to seek their cooperation in working with the university team. The meetings also yielded a list of organizations and institutional contacts with whom the team would subsequently meet.

Information Gathering

Reconnaissance activities were essential in determining what information was needed as a basis for planning. These activities were also helpful in identifying sources of information. As Figure 13.1 shows, several informational needs were deemed important: information about the population being served by the park, information about its institutional surroundings, information about the park and conditions in the neighboring community, and information about the people who used the park.

Information About Park Users. Uses of the park during the summer and fall were determined through regularly-scheduled visits to the site by members of the planning team. During each visit, activities were observed and recorded. Information was collected about activities that were taking place, who participated, whether the activities were being carried out alone or with others, and where in the park the activities occurred. Additional information was obtained directly from users who responded to a standardized questionnaire administered to a quota sample of park users over a one-week period. The questions, which took about five minutes to answer, dealt with frequency of visits to the park; where the respondents lived; whether they drove, walked, or biked; what they liked and disliked about the park; and the benefits they received from visiting the park.

Information About the Community. Understanding the socioeconomic and demographic characteristics of the population in the neighborhood surrounding the park was considered important as a first step to understanding what kinds of people were intended to be served by the park. Data were compiled using block statistics from the 1990 census. Concurrently, meetings with various resident groups or organizations were organized to determine what different residents thought about the park, how it was being used, and their ideas about the park's future use.

Information About Institutional Surroundings. During the meetings with community-based organizations, names of key individuals at nearby schools, churches and other institutions were identified, including representatives from a nearby community college and a nearby hospital. Contacts were subsequently made to inform these representatives about the park planning project and the benefits approach, and to learn about their activities and services in the community that might take advantage of their proximity to the park.

Information about the Park and Neighborhood Conditions. An inventory of recreational facilities and natural resources in the park was made during the early months of the project. The information was used to systematically identify problems and opportunities for future development. At the same time, a windshield survey was conducted in the blocks surrounding the park. Uses and conditions of land and buildings in a twenty-block area were identified and mapped.

Preliminary Goal Setting

Information about the park and its surroundings, together with input from representatives from institutions, governmental and service agencies, community organizations, and park users were analyzed and used to formulate a preliminary statement of goals for the future of the park. These goals were subsequently modified following further meetings with community groups and in a participatory design exercise involving sixth graders from a nearby middle school (Erickson and Marans, 1999). The goals in part reflected the range of benefits of parks and open space reported by park users, the sixth graders, and others.

Preliminary Plan Preparation

Using the background information gathered during the early stages of the project and the preliminary statement of goals, teams of landscape architecture and planning students prepared physical designs showing how the park might be reconfigured by the year 2020. Because the work was carried out as part of a class assignment, students were encouraged to be creative in making their planning recommendations while also respecting the interests of the community residents and other stakeholder groups. They were also reminded to consider the potential beneficial outcomes of their proposals.

Plan Testing

Preliminary plans were reviewed by the staff of the parks department and during several meetings with community groups. Additionally, photographic displays featuring elements of the plan were used to elicit reactions from the sixth graders at the nearby middle school, approximately six months after the team's initial meeting with them. Slides showing play equipment, a water slide, basketball courts, and other key elements of the design were presented to the class, and students were asked to record their preferences in a questionnaire.

Final Plan Preparation and Dissemination

Based on feedback from the parks department staff, community groups, and the sixth graders, the original statement of goals was modified and used in preparing final plan recommendations, At the same time, the most desirable elements of the various plans that had been prepared earlier by the University of Michigan students were identified and incorporated in the final plan. During this phase of the work, programmatic ideas were also discussed, and implementation strategies for making the plan a reality were developed. The results of these activities have formed the basis for subsequent discussions about the validity of the recommendations and for further actions among the parks department, other city departments, and various residential groups.

Elements of the Master Plan

The plan for the future of Chandler Park consisted of physical components and social programs. The physical components consisted of an active recreational zone, a picnic-play zone, a passive recreational zone, and a garden-market zone. These zones and the key activities proposed in each are shown in Figures 13.2 and 13.3.

Planned Zones

Active Recreational Zone

A recreation center, a water park, and athletic fields were the main features proposed for this zone located near the western edge of the park. Other proposed

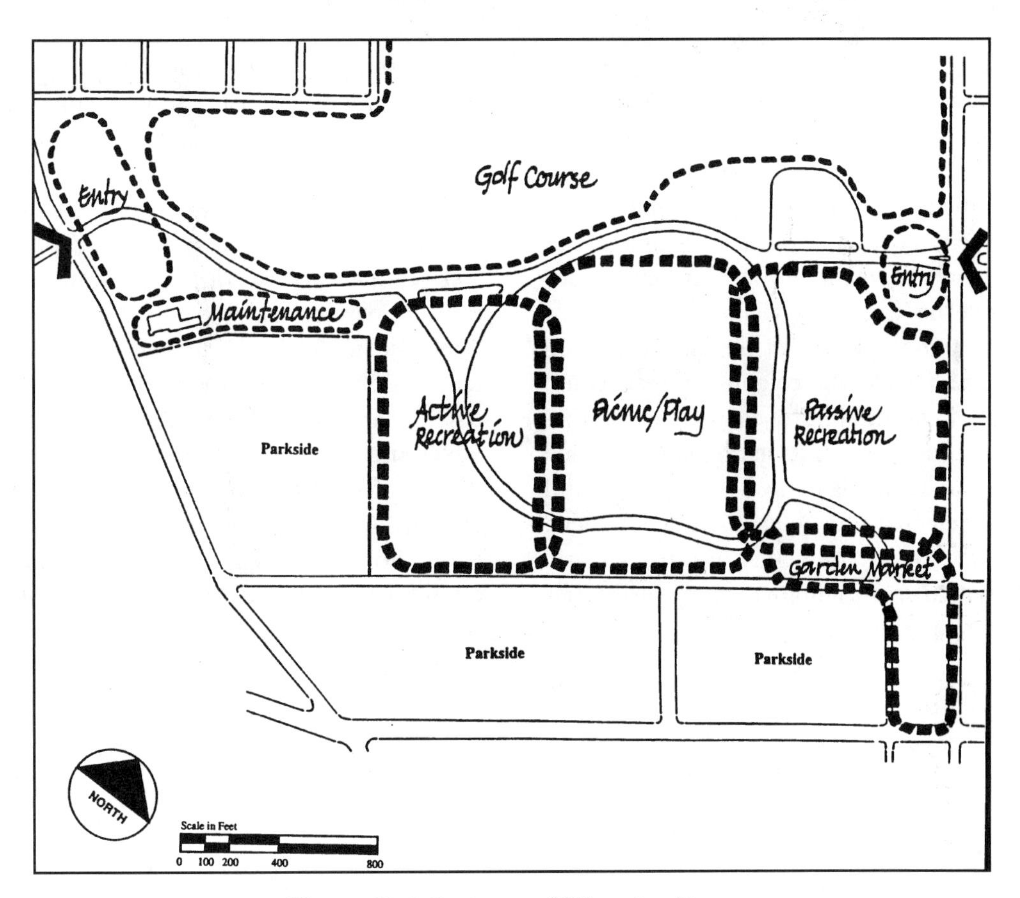

Figure 13.2 Conceptual Planning Zones

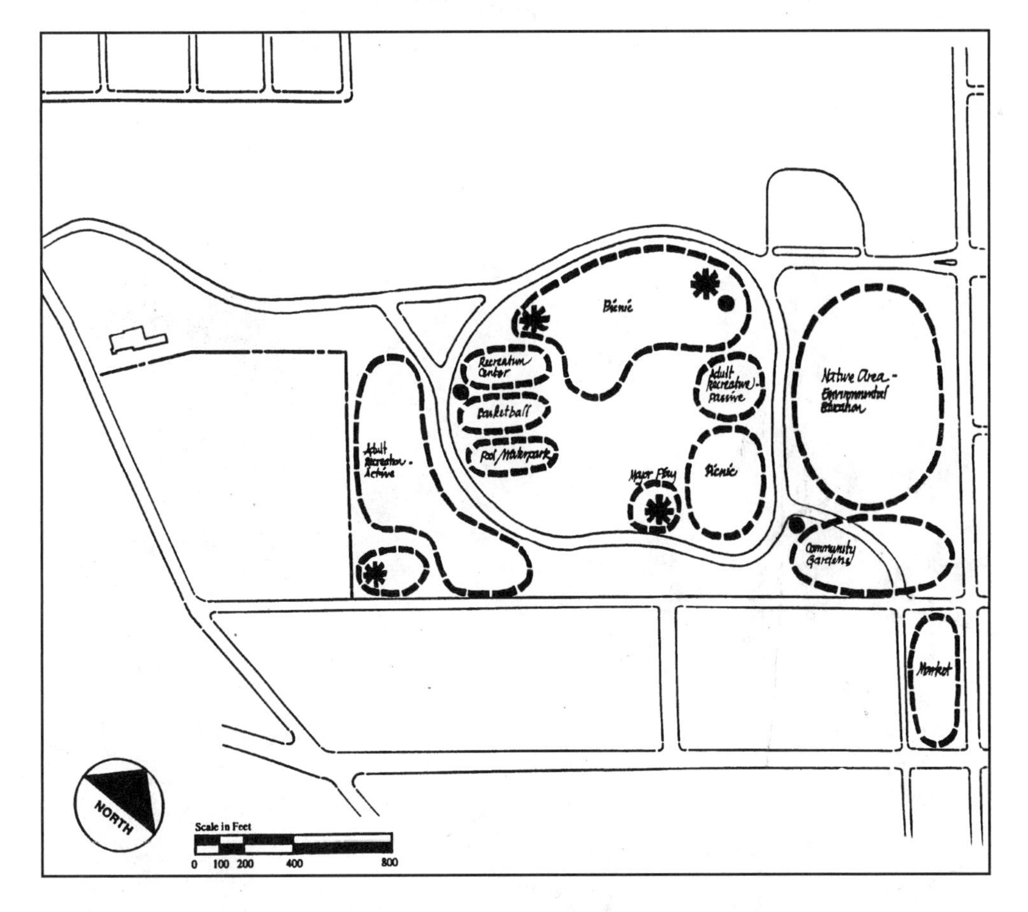

Figure 13.3 Conceptual Planning Activities

facilities included basketball and tennis courts, a small playground area, and a community garden serving the population in the nearby public housing. These facilities are shown in the illustrative site plan (Figure 13.4).

Anticipated Beneficial Outcomes. This zone was intended to provide opportunities for year-round physical activity and the accompanying health benefits for residents living in the immediate vicinity, as well as for residents living on the east side of the city. The small playground offered a place where young mothers could socialize while their young children engaged in interactive play. Similarly, the community garden was intended to be used by the elderly living in the public housing and would provide them with an intergenerational social setting. Finally, the recreation center and particularly the water park would create employment opportunities for teenagers living in the area.

Picnic/Play Zone

A large grassy area defined by shade trees on the east and west is proposed for picnicking and free play for family and group gatherings. Play apparatus would be designed for different age groups ranging from toddlers to teenagers. A proposed feature of the zone would be two amphitheaters. One would be programmed specifically for older children and would include a hard-surface area suitable for skateboarding. The other would be a larger, natural area with grassy slopes and suitable for outdoor performances.

Anticipated Beneficial Outcomes. Besides the physical health benefits associated with play, the area and play apparatus would be designed to create a sense of adventure and challenge for young people, instilling in them feelings of competence and confidence. Some settings within the zone designated for picnic shelters would hopefully instill a sense of tranquility and relaxation for users, while others would be suitable for both serious and frivolous social interactions.

Passive Recreational Zone

This zone is defined by both sides of the eastern portion of the ring-road and includes small, scattered, off-

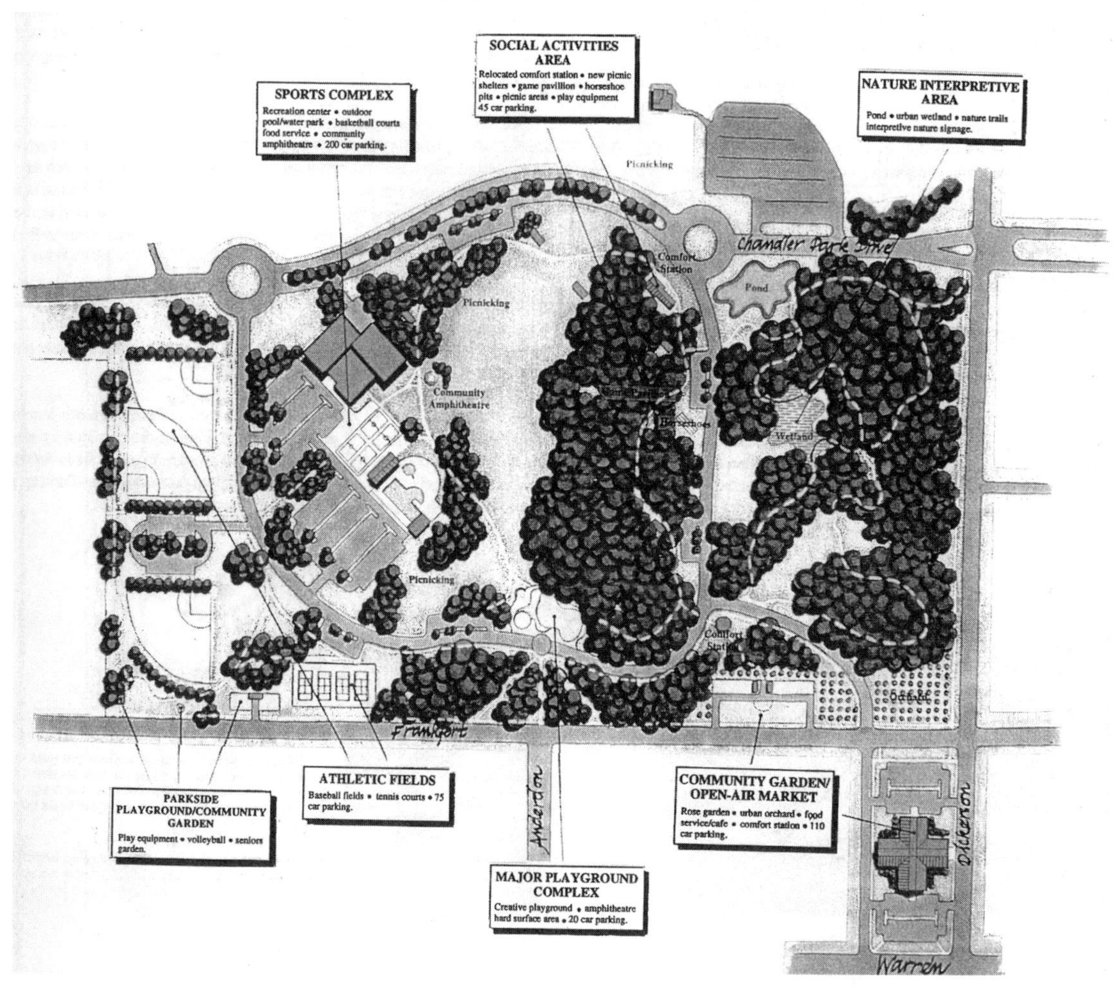

Figure 13.4 Stages in the Planning Process

street parking areas. To the west, there would be small pavilions with incorporated game tables and seating where people could congregate. In part, these facilities were included to support the location and patterns of interactions among elderly men that was occurring in the 1990s. The plan also recommended the relocation of an existing historically and architecturally significant comfort station from the western part of the park to the northern part of the zone to accommodate individuals who would visit this zone in the future. To the east of the ring-road, a natural pond was proposed adjacent to an existing marshland. A trail system including a boardwalk was planned for the area as well as an interpretive natural pavilion and signage identifying existing and newly introduced native Michigan plantings.

Anticipated Beneficial Outcomes. This zone was designed to facilitate opportunities for park visitors to socialize in a relaxed setting, exercise, and learn about the environment. During the information gathering phase, it was learned that many of the elderly men regularly met in the area, creating a strong sense of community among them. Many were retired or unemployed, and such gatherings offered a socially supportive environment. Enhancing this part of the zone with improved seating, shelter, toilet facilities, and gaming opportunities was expected to benefit users socially and culturally.

The trails and boardwalk traversing the wetlands and planted areas along with interpretive signage were intended to benefit both adults and school age children physically and educationally. Both unsupervised and supervised walks would expose users to various plantings, birds, and wildlife. Hopefully, this exposure would instill a sense of environmental stewardship and an understanding of the natural world.

Garden-Market Zone

The fourth zone, located in the southeast corner of the park features a large community garden and open-air market. The community garden would be available to both local and regional gardeners, who would have the opportunity to use their produce or sell it at the market. The plan proposes another comfort station that would be available to community gardeners and visitors as well as visitors to the passive recreational zone.

Anticipated Beneficial Outcomes. There are numerous benefits associated with the planned uses in this zone. Local residents, many of whom live in rental housing with little land, would have the opportunity to grow their own vegetables and fruits, thereby saving money and eating healthier. Produce grown could also be bartered or sold in the market. Moreover, the gardens could become an important center for meeting friends and neighbors as well as visitors form other parts of the east side. Similarly, the open-air market could become a gathering place where local residents display foods, food products, flowers, and crafts.

Planned Programs

In addition to the physical components, several programmatic proposals were offered as part of the plan. These included recreational and social programs, educational programs, and service programs.

Recreation and Social Programs

Discussions with youth and other residents in the area suggested that sports leagues and regularly scheduled classes at the recreation center would greatly increase interest in and use of Chandler Park. These programs would be defined and scheduled by resident committees working with representatives of the city's recreation department and the transportation authority. Similarly, neighborhood activities including annual festivals, cultural events, and church outings would be planned. Specific events such as senior lunch programs or pizza parties for youth were suggested to take place throughout the year.

Anticipated Beneficial Outcomes. As with the facilities proposed for the active recreation zone, recreational programming would create opportunities for year-round physical activity and the accompanying health benefits for local residents and those living elsewhere on the city's east side. Social programs would facilitate social contact among park visitors from near and far, and for many, they would foster a sense of community pride and ethnic-religious identity. Planning for events would create opportunities for greater community involvement, while participation in the programs could strengthen bonds between friends and among family members.

Educational Programs

Several programs that would take advantage of the park setting and the proposed physical changes were suggested. First, environmental education programs would be developed and offered through nearby public schools. Second, a program was proposed to train young people in designing, building, and maintaining park facilities such as trails, benches, and picnic tables. Third, training in the fundamentals of gardening and landscape maintenance would be offered. While some residents said they had gardening skills, others were less certain of their abilities and wanted to learn. The program could be established in part as a cooperative effort, enabling members to learn and to purchase equipment, planting materials, and supplies at a reduced cost. At the same time, plans would be developed to allocate garden plots and establish rules regarding access, security, hours of operation, and management. Still another proposed program would deal with job training. It was suggested that this program be developed in conjunction with the nearby community college and would include creating job skills needed in the parks and recreation profession. Finally, joint programs between the recreation department and the nearby hospital were proposed to promote the physical and mental health benefits of active living, including participation in sports.

Anticipated Beneficial Outcomes. Benefits associated with the educational programs are numerous and can appeal to individuals, to the broader community, and to the environment. For individuals, there will be opportunities to gain skills that would improve their self-esteem, sense of independence, and problem-solving abilities. Many of the skills could be marketable and thus enhance employment opportunities. Learning with others could be socially beneficial and help foster a greater sense of community among participants. Environmental education programs within the schools will not only contribute to establishing an environmental ethic and a better understanding of the interdependency of people and their surroundings, but it could have practical value in terms of maintaining quality in the park and protecting its natural environment.

Service Programs

Programs aimed at the long-term maintenance of the park and the creation of a safe and secure atmosphere for recreation were also proposed as part of the plan. Although these programs would be the responsibility of the city's recreation department, the agency could not be expected to provide quality services without active citizen involvement. It was proposed that incentives should be provided to neighborhood residents, particularly among the youth, as a way of engaging them in park maintenance. Activities such as trash pickup, lawn mowing, and caring for the athletic fields and natural areas would be encouraged.

Concerns about security and safety in the park were expressed at several stages in the planning process. As part of the programming, it was proposed that increased patrols by the police department be initiated and that consideration be given to creating a park ranger position. It was also suggested that Neighborhood Watch and safety awareness programs be established in cooperation with city officials.

Anticipated Beneficial Outcomes. The service programs could collectively foster feelings of security, higher levels of satisfaction with the community, and ultimately an enhanced quality of life (Allen, 1991; Marans and Mohai, 1991). Cooperative programs involving the recreation department and local residents that aim at maintaining the park could encourage democratic ideals, a sense of shared responsibility for the environment, and pride in ownership. At the same time, cooperative programs aimed at maintaining a safe environment could benefit the community by reducing crime and delinquency in the area.

Post-Planning Events

Although most of the recommendations for revitalizing Chandler Park were presented to Detroit's recreation department in 1996, the final planning document was not completed for another two years[3]. Besides recommendations summarized in this chapter, the report discussed priorities and resources necessary to implement the recommendations. It also offered a model for planning parks in distressed urban areas including an approach to assessing the impacts of change and measuring the extent to which outcomes have been achieved (see Figure 13.5).

During the process of documenting the recommendations, conditions changed within the larger community and in Chandler Park itself. Some of these changes were influential in setting in motion park revitalization, while other events made selected recommendations inappropriate. These changes are summarized below.

Improved Economic Conditions. When the planning process began, the economy in Detroit was bleak. Vacant commercial buildings were prevalent throughout the city, jobs had moved to the suburbs, and unemployment was high. Pessimism prevailed and the economic benefits of park revitalization were highlighted. In 1996, the announcement of Detroit's Empowerment Zone award brought a sense of optimism to the city with the promise of new job opportunities. The national economy had improved and overall crime statistics were down. At the same time, construction in nearby Parkside Homes under the Hope VI program had begun, along with new programs for seniors and

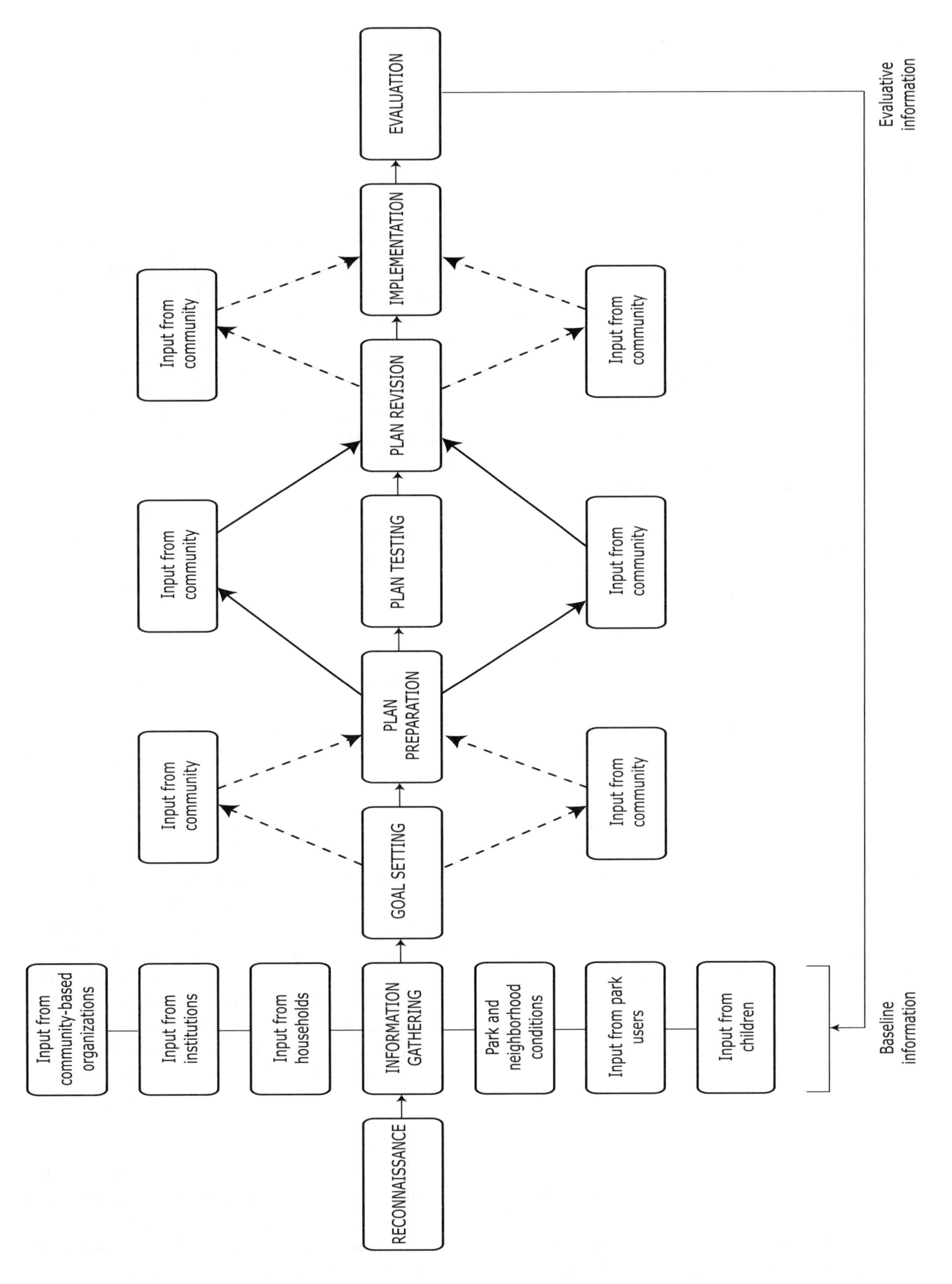

Figure 13.5 Model for Park Planning and Evaluation

youth. Some were aimed at recreation and were poised to take advantage of a revitalized Chandler Park.

Recreation Bond Millage. During the summer of 1996, voters in Detroit and the rest of Wayne County passed a referendum supporting a recreation bond millage. One component of the millage was the building of a water park in Chandler Park. While initial consideration was given to locating the water park near the site designated in the master plan, a severe storm altered Chandler Park's landscape and the recommended water park location.

Natural Disaster. In the summer of 1997, southeast Michigan experienced a number of severe storms causing extensive property damage in Detroit and its suburbs. One of them touched down in Chandler Park, destroying many of the older trees. These trees were among the park's greatest assets and contributed to its identity and serene character. The damage was extensive and forced the temporary closure of the park while crews removed the debris and damaged trees. When the park reopened, a vast clearing in the center of the park remained and offered a suitable location for the proposed water park and an associated parking lot.

Other Events. While the proposed relocation of the comfort station to a more heavily used area of the park was appropriate from a functional point of view, moving the structure was considered economically unfeasible. Instead, recreation department funds were used to renovate the building. At the same time, the decision was made to allocate funds to refurbish an older recreation center located less than a mile from Chandler Park that had been closed for several years. The renovated center reopened in 1997, giving low priority to building a new recreation building in Chandler Park. Finally, the director of the recreation department, who had initiated Chandler Park's revitalization, left Detroit to assume a comparable position out of state. His departure removed the impetus for change and diminished the likelihood of achieving the beneficial outcomes.

Chandler Park Today

Despite the passage of time, some recommendations have been implemented and a limited number of anticipated benefits described in the planning document have accrued.

In addition to programs aimed at serving the elderly and youth that were initiated during the redevelopment of the adjacent public housing, the proposed water park became a reality. Following the passage of the County's recreation bond millage in 1996, construction of the Chandler Park Family Aquatic Center began immediately. The facility has now been operational for nearly a decade. According to the senior officials at Wayne County Parks and Recreation department, the aquatic center is highly successful and attracts visitors from near and far. Furthermore, it employs nearly 100 young people, most of whom are Detroit residents and many live near the park.

In 2005, the Ray and Joan Kroc Foundation awarded a $50 million challenge grant to the Salvation Army to build a recreation center in Detroit[4]. Thirty acres at the western edge of Chandler Park have been designated as the site for the facility. Planning for the center and local fundraising efforts are currently underway. According to the website, Chandler Park was selected because it offers the greatest potential for strategic impact, with nearly 200,000 people residing within a three-mile radius of the site. The website indicates that:

> The proposed 100,000 square-foot facility is designed to provide resources that develop body, mind and spirit and will include recreation and aquatic centers, athletic fields, computer labs, performing arts training and rehearsal classrooms. It also will contain a chapel with seating for 400 that converts to an event hall with dinner seating for 250, three gymnasiums with an elevated three-lane running track, an expansive fitness center and one of the largest indoor pools in Michigan with lap lanes, slide and lazy river.

The website goes on to describe the scope of the facilities and the programs that the center will offer:

> It will contain a library with computer/media center, a game/activity area, an aerobics/dance studio, arts & crafts areas, classrooms, a senior adult lounge with computers and adjacent garden, a childcare area and counseling center..... the building and property will enrich the east side of Detroit with a much-needed facility for recreation and fitness, spiritual encouragement, social services, educational programs, job training and medical screenings......Social services will also be offered.

With the development of the recreation center in Chandler Park, there is potential to realize many of the beneficial outcomes described in the master plan. The challenge will be to raise the funds necessary to match the Kroc award, build and operate the recreation center as it is envisioned, and evaluate its impacts on users, other parts of Chandler Park, and the larger community.

FACILITIES/REC PROGRAMS	COMMUNITY	FAMILY/FRIENDS	INDIVIDUALS
New recreation center (with recreation programs), water park, improved basketball and tennis courts, horseshoe pits	Enhanced job opportunities for youth and adults; reduction in crime and delinquency	Bonding—brings family members and friends together	Physical conditioning; skill development; stress reduction; enhanced self-esteem and self-confidence, improved school grades
New/improved play areas	Enhanced community involvement and pride	Bonding—brings family members and children together	Physical exercise, development of motor skills and social skills
New/improved picnic areas		Bonding—brings family members together	
Natural areas, nature center, and environmental education program	Enhanced community pride/ satisfaction; greater support for public education	Greater family involvement in school programs	Enhanced appreciation/respect for nature; increased knowledge about the environment; increased political involvement in environmental issues; improved school grades
Community gardens, markets	More business and job opportunities for local residents; enhanced community pride/ satisfaction; greater community involvement; diversification of local economy	Brings neighbors together; cheaper food, family bonding	Greater dependency among neighbors; development of problem solving, conflict resolution

Table 13.1 Potential Benefits from New and Enhanced Recreation Facilities and Programs

Summary

This chapter discussed the process of planning for the revitalization of a large urban park including how OFM was addressed at several stages. It then described key physical improvements and programmatic elements of the plan and their anticipated benefits. These anticipated benefits are summarized in Table 13.1. The events that occurred following the preparation of the master plan and the current status of the park were then reviewed.

It has been disappointing that so little has been accomplished in Chandler Park since the idea for the plan was conceived and developed. In large part, implementation of recommendations was impeded by the city's lack of resources. Nor has there been a strong advocate for the idea of park revitalization as an instrument for community change. At the same time, the outcomes approach that was incorporated into the planning process was not always understood by participants within the city government or most community residents. Responsibility for this lack of understanding rests in part with the planners, who tended to place greater emphasis on physical improvements and new programs than on the beneficial outcomes that could accrue to individuals and the community. Furthermore, there was little follow-up after the plan was prepared. In future endeavors, a commitment will be needed by park planners to become advocates for their ideas--including clearly explaining the beneficial outcomes of their proposals. Finally, the planning process cannot be complete until the time when recommendations are implemented and their impacts are assessed. In the case of Chandler Park, motivated park officials and city resources will be required before this can occur.

Literature Cited

Allen, L. R. Benefits of Leisure Service to Community Satisfaction. (1991). In B. L. Driver, P. Brown, and G. L. Peterson (eds.), *Benefits of leisure*. (pp. 331–350). State College, PA: Venture Publishing, Inc.

Erickson, D. & Marans, R. W. (1999, Summer). Participatory Planning: Assessing Methods for Obtaining Children's Input in Park Design", *IAPS Bulletin of People-Environment Studies: Special Issue on Children, Youth and Environments* No. 13.

Marans, R. W. & P. Mohai. Leisure Resources, Recreation Activity, and the Quality of Life. 1991. In B. L. Driver, P. Brown, and G. L. Peterson (eds.), *Benefits of leisure*. (pp. 351–363). State College, PA: Venture Publishing, Inc.

Urban and Regional Planning Program, College of Architecture and Urban Planning, University of Michigan. (1998, Summer). *A Plan for the Revitalization of Chandler Park*.

Footnotes

1. The revitalization plan was supported by a grant from the Recreation Research Project of the USDA, the Forest Service's Rocky Mountain Forest and Range Experimental Station, and funding from the Corporation for National and Community Service and the Huron-Clinton Metropolitan Authority, the regional parks agency serving southeastern Michigan.
2. Detroit's Empowerment Zone was one of the first designated by the U.S. Department of Housing and Urban Development in 1996. For a discussion of the Urban Empowerment Zone Act, see http://www.ci.minneapolis.mn.us/ez/history.asp
3. Urban and Regional Planning Program, College of Architecture and Urban Planning, University of Michigan. (1998, Summer). *A Plan for the Revitalization of Chandler Park.*
4. See www.usc.salvationarmy.org/kroc

Chapter 14
Application of OFM on the McInnis Canyons National Conservation Area

Don Bruns, B. L. Driver, Brian Hopkins, and Paul Peck

Learning Objectives:

1. Better understand why, when, and how OFM was applied on the McInnis Canyons National Conservation Area.
2. Realize that when managers adopt OFM, they are committing their managerial units to shift internally (to realign recreation programs and initiatives) and externally (to engage other providers as managing partners).
3. Understand why incremental implementation of OFM is necessary.

Purposes

This chapter summarizes the first pilot-test application and implementation of Outcomes-Focused Management (OFM, which was then called Benefits-Based Management or BBM) on a wildland area. It was the McInnis Canyons National Conservation Area (MCNCA), which is managed by the Grand Junction, Colorado Field Office of the USDI Bureau of Land Management.[1] The two major purposes of the chapter are to explain why, when, and how that application and implementation happened and describe the lessons learned. Those lessons contributed to the improvements of OFM as it is described in Chapters 2, 3, and 4 of this text as did the other applications of OFM described in this text.

Legislative History and Description of the Area

Until 2000, the MCNCA was known as the Ruby Canyon/Black Ridge (RC/BR) area. On October 24, 2000 that area was designated as the Colorado Canyons National Conservation Area (CCNCA) by the U.S. Congress (P.L. 106-353). The name was again changed to the McInnis Canyons National Conservation Area (MCNCA) in the fall of 2004 by Congressional passage of P.L.108-400 in honor of former U.S. Representative Scott McInnis. That legislation added 5,200 acres in western Utah to the former CCNCA.

The eastern boundary of the MCNCA lies immediately west and is contiguous to the Colorado National Monument. The area lies near the western outskirts of the Redlands community of Grand Junction and the City of Fruita. The NCA therefore has tremendous significance for close-to-town evening and weekend recreation for residents of Colorado's largest Western Slope metropolitan community. It is described as follows in the legislation that designated it.

The McInnis Canyons NCA, located west of Grand Junction and, for the most part, south of I-70, includes 122,300 rugged acres of sandstone canyons, natural arches, spires, and alcoves carved into the Colorado Plateau along a 24-mile stretch of the Colorado River....Unique recreational opportunities abound in the area. Hiking among large concentrations of natural sandstone arches, float boating through spectacular red rock canyons on the Colorado River, exploring the world of dinosaur fossils, viewing centuries-old Native American rock art, off-highway vehicle touring to the rims of scenic plateaus and down through grand valleys, mountain bike riding on dramatic single-track trails such as the internationally renowned Kokopelli Trail, and finally, viewing diverse wildlife species that include desert bighorn sheep, bald eagles, and peregrine falcons.

The MCNCA is one of the most diverse assemblages of natural and cultural resource recreation-tourism attractions in the region. It has Colorado's largest concentration of natural stone arches at Rattlesnake Canyon; one of the state's few flat-water boating river segments; extremely rugged slick-rock and hanging canyon back-country; heritage tourism remnants of ancient cultures; a wilderness cave alcove the size of a football field; and spectacularly scenic hiking. Those diverse attractions are distributed across equally diverse settings, from an articulated in-situ dinosaur vertebrae accessible by a 15-minute walk from I-70 in a business suit, to risk-taking backcountry wilderness canyon adventure opposite the Colorado River.

Easy access to the area's outstanding recreation attractions, from both cities and I-70, enhances its significance as a regional recreation-tourism destination. It receives significant recreation use by area residents, enroute travelers, and destination visitors from more distant points of origin. That use contributes significantly to the economy of the Grand Junction area, and it varies considerably in different parts of the MCNCA (hereafter just NCA).

Why and when was OFM Applied on the NCA?

Application of OFM on the NCA was started in 1991 to guide development of the RC/BR Integrated Resource Management Plan (USDI, BLM, 1998) and was continued to guide development of the plan for the NCA which was approved in 2004. The following events converged in 1991 to cause OFM to be applied on the RC/BR area and later on the NCA.

In 1989, before *Benefits of Leisure* (Driver, Brown, & Peterson, 1991) was published, its first author arranged and coordinated a meeting of the authors and coauthors of chapters of that text to review and critique their near-final chapters. Several of the attendees (who were park and recreation administrators, managers, and planners) expressed their strong and growing need to more seriously consider the beneficial and negative outcomes of their policy and managerial decisions, but did not then know how to do so. In response, the second author of this chapter organized and coordinated a Benefits of Leisure Applications Workshop, which was held in Estes Park, Colorado, in May of 1991. That workshop was attended by 35 lead administrators, staff members, and managers of several federal, state, regional, and municipal agencies that managed public and recreation resources. It was also attended by 35 leisure scientists and educators who also wanted to see the results of leisure research applied more systematically in park and recreation policy development and management. Two early developers of the first version of the Canadian "Benefits Catalogue" (Canadian Parks/Recreation Association,1997) also attended. At that workshop:

- The early concepts of OFM were discussed and firmed up.
- The Grand Junction Field Office of the BLM had realized its need to get a better handle on growing recreational use in the RC/BR recreation area.
- The then Group Manager of the BLM's Washington Office Recreation Group attended the Estes Park Workshop, as did the lead author of this chapter, who was then Recreation Lead in the BLM's State of Colorado office. Both were interested in the relevance of OFM to the BLM, and those two attendees decided at the workshop that the RC/BR area would be a good one on which to pilot test OFM. Shortly thereafter, that BLM Recreation Group Leader transferred $40,000 dollars to Colorado BLM to help start this application of OFM.

These events led to the collaborative involvement of the first, second, and third authors of this chapter with the BLM's Grand Junction Field Office (FO). Together, they and others on that FO began applying the emerging concepts of OFM to address the recreation components of the "Ruby Canyon/Black Ridge Integrated Resource Management Plan" (USDI, BLM, 1998). Obviously, since this was its first application on a wildland area, there was little written guidance on how to apply and implement OFM when the planning efforts commenced in late 1991.

The RC/BR plan guided management of the area until 2000 when it was designated as the CCNCA by P.L. 106-353, which included a statement that directed the Secretary of the Interior to develop a "comprehensive plan for the long-range protection and management of the Conservation Area." Therefore, recreational components of the RC/BR plan were then expanded to guide OFM planning for the CCNCA, and that plan was approved on October 28, 2004, and has the title "Resource Management Plan and Record of Decision for the Colorado Canyons National Conservation Area and Black Ridge Canyons Wilderness" (USDI, BLM, 2004). No separate plan has since been developed for the NCA, so the plan for the CCNCA is being used to guide the management of that area. That plan can be reviewed on the following websites (see "Final Plan and Record of Decision" at http://www.co.blm.gov/gjra/planning.htm. For the Setting Character Prescription tables, see "Recreation Planning Tools" under "Proposed Plan" at http://www.co.blm.gov/mcncaplan/cocanprmp/cocanprmp_index.htm.

Evolution of the Planning Efforts

To appreciate the evolution and contributions of adopting OFM to guide the planning and management of the RC/BR area, it is emphasized that only the preliminary concepts about OFM (as it is now explained in Chapters 2, 3, and 4 of this text) were known in late 1991. As explained at the beginning of Chapter 3 of this text, those early concepts had not been tested by park and recreation practitioners on wildlands or in municipalities under the name of BBM or OFM by 1991. More significantly, even though parts of the OFM "puzzle," had been integrated before 1991, clear directions and *comprehensive* requirements about *how* OFM should be applied and implemented were not well understood and available then. Therefore, this first application of OFM on the wildlands of the RC/BR area was truly a *pioneering* effort.

Obviously, the planners and managers first needed to become familiar with the very early concepts about what applying and implementing OFM required. To help that process, the first and second authors of this chapter met with the managers and recreation planners of the RC/BR area to explain what was then known about OFM. That was followed by subsequent visits by the first author. After their introduction to OFM, those planners and managers began to embrace the early concepts about how OFM should be applied and implemented for several reasons. It had intuitive appeal, and perhaps most important was their former inability to answer the fundamental question raised by OFM of *why* any recreation service should be provided (see Chapter 2 of this text). Given their past orientations and organizational conditioning, their first answers were framed in terms of how those actions would advance the programs being driven by upper echelons of the BLM organization, advance special program initiatives coming down from above, meet the demands of organized activity-focused user groups, and so forth. It made sense to do those things to please those who controlled the purse strings, cultivate the support of user groups who wanted those projects, and produce enough "widgets" to get a good performance report.

As the managers and planners of the RC/BR area began to understand OFM, they realized that their answers to the "why" question had only temporary relevance and did not address what was happening to the BLM's wider constituency of visitors and affected community residents. Nor did those answers begin to address what all of those potential investments and developments were doing to the social fabric of affected communities, to their economies, and to the environment. Perhaps even more importantly, neither did those answers begin to address consequences to the character of recreation settings, conditions that distinguish the public lands from all others and affect its long-term productive capacity to positively affect people's lives. Eventually, those managers and recreation planners involved in the RC/BR effort came to understand the deficiency of activity-focused program and project-centered management, and that is when this pilot and exploratory application of OFM gained momentum.

After two years of OFM-guided planning efforts (including surveys of visitors and residents of local communities by scientists with Northern Arizona University's School of Forestry), the recreation planners developed preliminary drafts of alternative recreation management plans for the RC/BR area. In 1994, the second author of this chapter (who helped fund this pilot study when with USDA Forest Service's Rocky Mountain Research Station) recognized that the progress being made presented work a unique educational opportunity to help advance OFM. So, with the help of the planners and the first author of this chapter, a field trip to the area was organized. About 20 recreation planners, managers, and academicians from across the U.S., who were seriously interested in OFM, participated in that effort which was hosted by the area planners. They provided a close-up look at different parts of the RC/BR area and descriptions of the work they had done so far and the lessons learned and problems they had encountered so far in attempts to apply OFM in this pilot test. For example, they showed how study data was being used to explicitly target beneficial outcomes as management objectives. By doing this, they established the context for very candid and rich dialogue about OFM among the participants on that field trip.

Among other things, the dialogue stimulated during the field trip helped the area recreation planners better understand: (1) The need to think through the cause-and-effect relationships involved in implementing OFM; (2) How recreation program actions must be restructured to avoid recreation's undesirable negative outcomes and instead capture desired beneficial outcomes; (3) That deciding which outcomes to target as management objectives was not a simple task; (4) There had to be a reasonable expectation that the right combination of provider inputs (i.e., essential recreation services) and recreation setting conditions could be achieved; (5) The strategic necessity of integrating all managerial inputs within an appropriate balance of management, marketing, monitoring, and supporting administrative actions; and (6) That when considering the three components of recreation settings (i.e.,

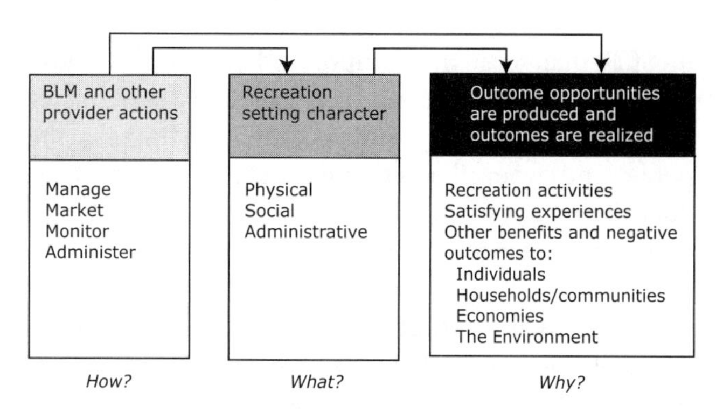

Figure 14.1 Interactions of the Components of OFM that Emerged on the RC/BR Area[2]

physical, social, and managerial--later called "administrative" by the BLM), there had to be neither too little nor too much recreation development, nor too little or too much use, nor even too little or too many services and controls. Otherwise, desired and targeted outcome opportunities would neither be produced nor attained, nor would the setting characteristics upon which outcomes that were setting-dependent be provided and maintained.

Out of the dialogue on the field trip and subsequent thought and integration by the first and third authors of this chapter, the model for applying and implementing OFM on the RC/BR area shown in Figure 14.1 took form.

Figure 14.1 shows that the RC/BR planners came to understand that they needed to try to address the indicated interactions, such as how actions of the BLM and those of their associate providers contribute directly to the production of outcome opportunities (i.e, the long arrow in Figure 14.1) and how those actions also affect setting character and thus indirectly affect the kinds of outcome opportunities produced and realized (i.e., the middle two shorter arrows in Figure 14.1). They realized that not only did they need to answer and attempt to answer the fundamental *why* question of OFM but also many other questions. Specifically, they also needed to attempt to answer several critical *what* and *how* questions. What setting characteristics made production and attainment of desired outcome opportunities possible, and how were they to be provided and maintained? What associate providers were relevant and how were they to be involved collaboratively? A big question that needed to be answered was "Is there the wherewithal to make it happen?" Or, stated differently, "Was it reasonable to expect that the BLM and its managing partners had or could acquire the capacity to deliver these necessary services and provide and maintain the essential setting character conditions identified?" The planners discovered that addressing these questions required considerably more thoughtful, in-depth analyses of customer desires, supply and demand, and a further restructuring of field operations than was required under activity-focused management.

Realizing the needs to consider the interactions shown in Figure 14.1 and to answer the questions just described and then focusing on them was innovative and guided the planners' remaining efforts on this pilot application of OFM. But, it should be recognized that while these emerging directions for OFM planning were innovative and depicted what needed to be done, it was still not well understood how all the relationships shown in Figure 14.1 were to be addressed. That issue is central to the remainder of this chapter, which evaluates the degree to which applying and implementing OFM on the RC/BR area and the meet the requirements of the OFM model described in Chapter 3 of this text, which includes the elements of Figure 14.1.

Evaluation of Applying and Implementing OFM

Evaluative Criteria

Chapter 3 of this text described a comprehensive normative model that can be used to apply and implement OFM fully. It identifies and describes in detail the *required actions/requirements* needed to accomplish that end. In that chapter, those actions are called "Steps for Implementing OFM." Those steps are organized into eight sequential phases, and each step is numbered sequentially within parentheses in the following outline of the model. The rest of this chapter will evaluate the degree to which the requirements specified in the OFM model for each step were met in the application and implementation of OFM on the NCA.

Phase 1: Preparatory Actions

- Ensure that overseeing supervisors and managers approve and support adoption of OFM (1st)
- Organize the planning team (2nd)
- Ensure that all members of the planning team understand OFM (3rd)
- Understand responsibilities and Constraints (4th)
- Consider essential collaborative management and related public involvement needs (5th)
- Identify critical issues and concerns (6th)

Phase 2: Gather, analyze, interpret, and integrate supply and demand information.

- Assess recreation preferences of the most relevant recreation participant and affected community resident markets (7th)
- Inventory or update inventories of key recreation-tourism resource attractions and services (8th)
- Analyze recreation opportunity supply by possible recreation management zones and corresponding customer market demand (9th)
- Select primary recreation-tourism markets (10th)
- Identify the most logical recreation management zones and corresponding niches within the primary market(s) (11th)

Phase 3: Develop the Management Plan

- Determine which outcomes can and should be targeted feasibly within each recreation management zone (12th)
- Develop management objectives (13th)
- Identify and prescribe the essential setting characteristics (14th)
- Define the essential recreation-tourism service environment (15th)
- Evaluate alternatives and select the preferred alternative (16th)

Phase 4: Develop an Implementation Plan

- Identify management actions to be implemented (17th)
- Identify marketing actions to be implemented (18th)
- Identify monitoring actions (19th)
- Identify supporting administrative actions (20th)
- Provide ample opportunities and time-frames for review of the proposed plan (21st)

Phase 5: Adjust Management/Implementation Plan as needed and approve Final Plan (22nd)

Phase 6: Implement Plan and Adjust Field Operations Accordingly (23rd)

Phase 7: Revise the Plan as Needed or Required by Agency Directives (24th)

Phase 8: Ensure that Performance Reports and Evaluations Document and Recognize the Sustained Production and Attainment of Targeted Outcomes as Feasible (25th)

Were the Requirements of Each Step Met?

This section refers to the current NCA plan which was completed for the Colorado Canyons NCA before its name was changed to McInnis Canyons NCA.

Preparatory Actions (Phase 1)

The six requirements of Phase 1 of the normative model are: to *ensure* that supervisors approve and support OFM; *organize* the planning team; *ensure* that all team members *understand* OFM; understand responsibilities and constraints; *consider* collaborative management and public involvement needs; and *identify* issues and concerns.

Ensure That Overseeing Supervisors and Managers Approve and Support Adoption of OFM

In the fall of 1991, the first author of this chapter met with the third author and the acting manager of the BLM's Grand Junction FO to propose that a pilot-test of OFM be conducted on the RC/BR area. Having agreed to that test, they became very supportive of OFM, along with the current manager of the BLM's Grand Junction FO. However, after the RC/BR area was designated as the CCNCA in 2000, the BLM's first manager of the CCNCA chose not to continue implementing OFM, in part, because he believed that OFM was too complex for public understanding. Therefore, the *draft* management plan mandated for the CCNCA by its enabling legislation was not developed using the OFM framework. Before the proposed management plan was finalized, the manager of the Grand Junction FO intervened, insisting that the final plan would sustain the commitment to plan and manage using OFM.

Organize the Planning Team

Plans for the RC/BR area and for the NCA were both multiple-use (also called integrated) resource management plans. Both plans were therefore developed by multidisciplinary BLM Field Office planning teams.

Ensure That all Members of the Planning Team Understand OFM

This requirement pertains both to those responsible for recreation components as well as other planning team members. If all team members do not have at least a rudimentary understanding of OFM, the concept will be marginalized. Other team members can be expected to "get grumpy" with recreation planners using a "secret language" they do not understand, and the whole planning effort can end up being at cross purposes with recreation. Range managers, for example, need to understand how OFM can help maintain traditional rural ranching lifestyles, and wildlife managers will gain from understanding how important being able to view wildlife close-up is to visitors and nearby residents alike. Fortunately, the recreation planner (the third author of this chapter and author of Chapter 18 of this text) who led the early OFM planning efforts for recreation components of the RC/BR plan picked up rapidly on the purposes, concepts, and requirements of OFM and did an excellent job applying them given the newness of OFM at that time. That enthusiasm was contagious and spread to other team members. Their curiosity led to asking what this new approach was all about. The range manager, for example, gained a new appreciation that "desired future conditions" are about more than species composition and condition, and that desired social and economic outcomes matter to permit holder families and affected communities as well as to recreation visitors.

For recreation components of the initial RC/BR planning effort, it was unfortunate that the original recreation planner for that area transferred to another BLM FO after the draft, but before the final management plan was completed and approved. The recreation planner who took his place did not fully understand OFM which made finalizing the management plan a challenge. This is understandable because implementing OFM in this early application was a dynamic process, and not all the procedures followed had been documented for the new planner. Nevertheless, the final plan was approved in March of 1998 and was OFM oriented.

The decision was made that the plan for the RC/BR area would guide management of the RC/BR area until the mandated plan for that CCNCA was approved on October 28, 2004. But after the CCNCA was created in 2000, ongoing activity-focused managerial efforts and associated day-to-day administrative issues impeded full OFM-guided implementation of it under management of the CCNCA and its first manager. Nevertheless, after OFM planning got back on track for the CCNCA, substantial efforts were taken to ensure that key members of the new planning team understood and embraced OFM. An Advisory Committee (mandated by the CCNCA legislation) was briefed by the first and third authors of this chapter on why the conceptual framework used to write the recreation components of this plan should be expanded beyond simply manage project inputs to also manage the CCNCA recreation settings to provide and facilitate the realization of beneficial outcomes and the reduction of negative outcomes. The Committee supported doing this. The first and third authors of this chapter also conducted a BLM training seminar for the first manager of the CCNCA, land use planner, recreation planner, and other team members. It was later discovered that the land use planner, having grasped OFM, had written up some initial outcome-focused recreation planning drafts from working group meeting output. Otherwise, both the training and the outcome-focused staff work had minimal impact because early planning for the CCNCA did not proceed under the OFM framework. Recreation portions of the resulting draft management plan for the CCNCA were therefore comprised of only a list of recreation program actions and projects--primarily trail and other facility construction, management controls, and a few interpretive exhibits. Setting character was not addressed, and neither were either experiential or other beneficial outcomes. It was not until the OFM framework was adopted again that these requirements of OFM were addressed.

Understand Responsibilities and Constraints

Approved plans for the RC/BR recreation area and for the NCA documented that this requirement was met, with the notable exceptions outlined above for the CCNCA planning effort. Otherwise, final plans document a clear understanding of the relevant responsibilities and constraints.

Consider Essential Collaborative Management and Related Public Involvement Needs

Both the RC/BR and the NCA planning efforts collaborated with private-sector service-providing businesses and local governments. Together, those associated providers worked with on-site recreation visitors and resident customers within contiguous or nearby communities to address their desires. Specifically, pages ii–iv of the RC/BR plan describe the membership of the ad hoc committee assembled to help develop that plan and "special work group teams" assembled to address issues relating to recreation, river management, and desired plant communities. The recreation work group team had 22 members that represented various recreation-related customer and associated provider stakeholders, as did the membership of the ad hoc committee. In addition, pages 3–2 to 3–5 of that plan identify relevant partners and their planned roles and responsibilities. Chapter 7 of that plan details specific relevant cooperative management agreements that were in place, as well as several concerned recreation interests.

The approved plan for the NCA provides even more detail about public involvement efforts involved in the development of that plan. Page 1–10 reviews those efforts, including the establishment of a federally authorized Advisory Council, project newsletters, numerous public presentations, issuing of press releases, holding public open houses, convening field trips, and "publishing" a project web site. Appendix 5 provides a ten-page description of the "Public Involvement" efforts and mentions that special "Working Groups" were set up for the four "Planning Area Zones" initially set up to consider interests in "Primary [Recreation] Activities."

Although many associated providers, or organizations which they represented, are listed in the plan, those lists did not mention many of the principal relevant associated providers upon whom the BLM and its customers depend for services (e.g., tour operators, visitor information bureaus/centers, gear rental shops, retail services, etc.) and supporting infrastructure (e.g., local governments). This omission suggests an incomplete understanding of their critical role in the provision of recreation opportunities as emphasized in the nominative model developed for guiding applications of OFM.

Identify Critical Issues and Concerns

The considerable amount of scoping and public involvement described and documented in the plans for the RC/BR area and the NCA reveal that substantial efforts were made to identify critical issues and constraints with one important exception (e.g., see section 5.2.4 of the approved plan for the NCA). In the initial phases of planning for the NCA, little scoping is evident concerning beneficial and negative outcomes. Instead, the early issues focused on recreation activities, needed facilities, and the areas most suited for particular groups' recreation activities. As elaborated in the following section, that focus fortunately changed to help guide the visitor surveys conducted and the final plan.

Gather, Analyze, Interpret, and Integrate Supply and Demand Information (Phase 2)

The five requirements of the normative model of Phase 2 are to: *assess* recreation preferences; *inventory* key recreation-tourism attractions and services; *analyze* recreation opportunity supply; *select* primary recreation-tourism markets; and *identify* RMZs and corresponding market niches.

Assess Recreation Preferences of the Most Relevant Recreation Participant and Affected Community Resident Markets

This requirement was met reasonably well for planning of the RC/BR area, but less so for the NCA (through no fault of Northern Arizona as indicated below). In each case, visitor studies were conducted by NAU, and supplemental information collected by the BLM from the planning team's public involvement efforts. The NAU studies, begun early in 1992, included both recreation participant and community studies, focus-group interviews, and an evaluation of manager-defined benefits (Stein & Lee, 1995). Researchers obtained a moderate response (68%) to a mail-back questionnaire, providing useful planning information. The initial research design divided the planning area into five study zones; but subsequent assessments demonstrated that the recreation area had at least three additional zones, each having its own distinctive market niche. These eight RMZs were identified as logical management units in the approved plan.

Another visitor survey of on-site NCA users was conducted in 2001 and 2002 by NAU's School of Forestry (Lee, Stephens, & Fuller, 2003). That study employed only five sampling zones because of the BLM requested such (page 6 of the research report states that "At BLM's request, we combined several of the zones to create five management zones to analyze and present survey results."). The study documented visitor preferences for experiences and other benefits and the perceived degree to which they were realized. The response rate to the mailed questionnaire was low (50%), but more importantly, results had only marginal utility for developing the management plan, because the final management plan was written for ten RMZs, not the five sampling zones requested by the BLM. The two additional RMZs (identified since the RC/BR plan had been completed) stemmed from more diverse customer market demand generated by NCA designation and additional area growth and development.

At the NCA manager's discretion an additional study was conducted by the US Geological Survey in 2003 that dealt "...primary with recreation-based activities in four areas: Kokopelli Loops, Rabbit Valley, Loma Boat Launch, and Devil's Canyon" (Ponds, Gillette, & Koonz (2004:1). It also profiled the users in terms of their demographics, choices of recreation activities, and management issues.

The studies completed during preparation of the NCA management plan (i.e., that by NAU and the USGS) were of on-site visitors only. In neither case were the recreation outcome and setting character preferences of local community residents studied. Nevertheless, the concerted public involvement efforts described for that management plan (see Appendix A of the approved plan) did reveal the qualitative desires of local residents and thus help ensure that OFM was addressed. Consequently, the old RC/BR recreation preference assessments and the public involvement meeting output (see Appendix A of the approved plan) was the most useful in preparing the NCA management plan. The requirement of OFM being considered here was therefore only partially met.

Attempts by the BLM recreation planners to use the results of these visitor studies demonstrated the following critical requirements that need to be attended to in the future by researchers who conduct visitor studies:

- The list of possible outcomes studied must be at least as diverse and inclusive as the RMZs for which customer preferences are being assessed. For the NCA in particular, its ten RMZs are very diverse, as are its customers.
- Ensure that assessment methods and instruments tie customer responses to a definitive, logical, and consistent response context also became very clear. It is of little help to the planners to simply find out what customers want. The planners and managers need to know how customer desires vary by RMZ, and customer preferences within each RMZ must be further related to most satisfying activities, to experience and other beneficial outcome desires, and finally to the essential recreation setting characteristics upon which production and attainment of those outcomes depends.
- Questions about setting character preferences must be asked within the context of what conditions respondents believe must be "provided and maintained" to realize their most valued experiences and other beneficial outcomes. It does little good to simply ask what settings people prefer, which they believe should be left alone, and so forth.
- Preferences for recreation and visitor services actions must also be asked within the context of those felt necessary to realize desired outcomes and maintain the setting character essential to that realization.
- The planners struggled to use assessment results that provided insufficient definition of customer preferences because of the limited range of the response formats used. For a list of possible recreation outcome and setting preferences as diverse as these for the NCA, a response format must be used that provides for clear differentiation of preferences.
- Likewise, setting character preference data that only shows relative preferences (i.e., leave as is, make more remote, or further develop) provides insufficient data for knowing what customers actually desire. Up to seven distinctly different setting descriptions (used to classify existing setting character or to prescribe desired future setting characteristics) have been identified for 13 different setting attributes. For desired outcomes targeted by management objectives which are setting-dependent, planners and managers need to know precisely which ones they need to provide and maintain.

Inventory or Update Inventories of Key Recreation-Tourism Resource Attractions and Services

This step was addressed in the approved plan for the RC/BR area under the heading "Area and Community Attractions and Services." While issues related to outfitters were addressed in the plan, no actual inventories of community attractions and provider capacity for desired and essential services were completed. Inventories instead focused on natural, cultural, and paleontological recreation attractions. The draft NCA plan also neglected addressing related community attractions and services. This was problematic because the use and enjoyment of the NCA depends significantly on both on-site and off-site services from private sector businesses associate providers (e.g., outfitters, tour operators, gear and equipment rental) and local government infrastructure support (e.g., road maintenance, emergency services). Several river boating and mountain biking outfitters are under permit from the BLM to provide on-site services to visitors who either cannot or choose not to outfit their own trips. Likewise, existing paleontology tours are authorized through the Museum of Western Colorado. The presence of the spectacular natural stone arches at Rattlesnake Canyon hint at possibilities for commercial tours, and there are other significant attractions where either tours or outfitted trips could afford greater access to those seeking to enrich their lives through recreation outings. Also, any discussion of the role of tourism industry promotional organizations (e.g., the Grand Junction Visitors and Convention Bureau, the Fruita Welcome Center) is conspicuously absent. Destination recreation-tourism markets targeted in the final plan will need adequate information about the rich diversity of outcome opportunities afforded by the NCA, and the need for appropriate promotional, visitor outreach, and other marketing actions need to be considered in light of what presently exists. The scope of these services is not limited to industry alone, for both the cities of Grand Junction and Fruita have significant visitor outreach campaigns which could benefit both prospective customers and facilitate more effective management of the area by the BLM and its collaborating partners. These likewise should have been addressed.

Few access roads to the NCA are official BLM public roads, but are instead local county roads and state highways. The role which Mesa County and the State of Colorado play in maintaining and/or developing these routes needed to be considered in assessing what kinds of implementing actions were necessary to achieve the management objectives and setting prescriptions outlined in the final plan. Some of key access routes could be left the way they are or improved, often with very different consequences for the types of recreation outcome opportunities provided. Unaddressed, those changes may well occur without any forethought.

The Affected Environment section of the approved plan for the NCA should therefore have identified the role that relevant private sector service providers and local governments would have in sustaining the qualities for which the NCA was designated by the Congress, the productive capacity and distinctive character of its recreation settings, and the ability of targeted market niches to achieve outcome opportunities targeted by management objectives.

Analyze Recreation Opportunity Supply by Possible RMZs and Corresponding Customer Market Demand

Planning for the RC/BR area addressed supply and demand as an essential prerequisite for deciding which recreation opportunities (i.e., experience and other beneficial outcome opportunities, recreation activity opportunities, the character of settings in which they occur, and available visitor services) to target in each of the plan's eight RMZs. The eight sets of recreation opportunities targeted for these RMZs were compared with other recreation opportunities available elsewhere in the relevant market areas. Analyses involved recreation areas managed by the Grand Junction FO, by other BLM Field Offices, and by other natural resource recreation-tourism providers. The planners considered outcome opportunities each RMZ could reasonably provide, to which of the markets that desire them, and both actual and potential nearby alternative venues that could satisfy this demand. These analyses were essential for deciding which recreation opportunities to target within each RMZ. Consideration of the varying size and extent of each of the most relevant markets was essential (e.g., the market for mountain biking on Kokopelli's Trail on Mack Ridge is substantially more expansive in scope than is that for dispersed camping near vehicles in Rabbit Valley). For the RC/BR plan, these considerations of supply and demand are what convinced planners that, although visitor studies considered only five sample zones, the NCA actually had eight diverse and distinctly different recreation products, and therefore eight RMZs.

The same kinds of considerations were made in preparation of the NCA management plan after OFM got back on track for that plan. This time, planners concluded that there was significant enough demand and an accompanying supply of distinctively different recreation opportunities to warrant breaking out yet two more logical RMZs, for a total of ten RMZs. In the process, planners concluded that the approved plan for the RC/BR area did not make enough hard choices in terms of limiting the set of targeted activities, experiences, and other beneficial outcomes across RMZs, as well as within each. For example, that plan targeted mountain biking in more RMZs than was either necessary or appropriate. Doing so was later recognized as a mistake because there were significant other mountain biking opportunities available on other recreation areas within the Grand Junction FO's own jurisdiction, and by other administrative units as well.

In addition, because of the change in recreation staffing, the list of outcome opportunities identified in the draft RC/BR plan was simply carried forward from the Benefits Chain of Causality worksheet drafts (see Chapter 3) to the final plan. For most RMZs, that list of outcome opportunities was too numerous to effectively guide either the BLM's management of the area, or to facilitate marketing visitors' outing choices. Among the reasons why this happened is that the most distinctive outcome opportunities were not singled out before the draft plan was finalized. A more thorough job of analyzing supply and demand would have resolved this problem.

Select Primary Recreation-Tourism Markets *and* Identify the Most Logical RMZs and Corresponding Recreation Niches within the Primary Market(s)

Regarding primary markets, the comprehensive normative model for applying and implementing OFM in Chapter 3 of the this text states "To make OFM work, it is necessary to select the *primary recreation market segments* from the many relevant markets that desire benefits from the recreation area for which the plan is being made." With that in mind, these two requirements are considered together in this section, because they are related and reflect the nonlinear and iterative nature of the required actions. They reflect the needs to first define discrete and logical recreation management units and also select the primary *relevant* markets and their segments that best correspond to each of those planning units or RMZs. That *must* be determined by the capabilities of the existing RMZs to accommodate the demands defined by the relevant market niches as well as whether it is appropriate to meet those demands given budgetary constraints, other demand on the RMZs, and feasible alterative opportunities to meet those demand more efficiently elsewhere. This *must* happen, because no one management area can simultaneously be managed to be all things to all people. However, the management plan for the NCA was written before the current guidelines for recreation planning in the BLM's *Land Use Planning Handbook* (USDI, BLM, 2005) were updated to incorporate the need to select primary recreation market segments for each RMZ. Therefore, the plan did not specifically select primary recreation-tourism markets and corresponding niches for each of its ten RMZs as is now directed by that Handbook.

Regarding the identification of logical RMZs, the normative model for applying OFM in Chapter 3 of this text states:

"Unless the area being planned and managed is quite small, it will be necessary to define and delineate physically on maps the boundaries of logical recreation management zones (RMZs) in which recreation opportunities will be provided for the primary market segment or segments [i.e., niches] to be served, and the distinctive area(s) within which the demands of market segments (i.e., relevant market niches) can be met."

It is recognized that these delineations of RMZs and the corresponding demand niches might need to be adjusted after supply and demand analyses are completed.

Both the RC/BR and the NCA plans identified "niche" as a recreation opportunity, but tended to distort to concept of niche, which is a market segment, by erroneously equating it with a place (i.e., the RMZ of subpart thereof targeted to meet that market demand). This is emphasized, because a niche is a specific segment of a recreation-tourism market and not a place on the ground. But, relevant market segment (i.e., niche) demands cannot be accommodated unless suitable and feasible places to do so exist on the planning area. Therefore, it was insufficient to identify the demanded recreation opportunities but omit identification of the specific RMZs, or subparts thereof, in which it was decided those opportunities would be provided. But it must be emphasized that when the approved management plan was written for the NCA, the BLM had not yet developed definitive guidance on how to define relevant customer markets segments (i.e., niches).

The recreational components of the draft plan were structured around only four geographically defined "planning zones" (in Figure 2-1 on page 2-2 of the draft plan) only to accommodate recreation activities. Quoting from the draft, "...to facilitate the planning process, working groups were formed based on four geographical areas in the CCNCA" (page 1-2 of the final plan), and "...each working group identified specific planning issues for each of the four planning zones within the CCNCA" (page 1-10 of the final plan).

The aforementioned intervention of the Grand Junction Field Manager into the planning process (re-instituting the OFM conceptual planning/management framework for recreation) happened while the BLM was responding to comments on the draft plan. Within an OFM context, it soon became apparent that the four planning zones (around which the draft plan was written) provided an insufficient basis for responsively differentiating between the very diverse kinds of recreation opportunities the area could provide and for responding to identified market demands for those opportunities. Therefore, those four planning areas were, in the aggregate, further subdivided into ten distinct RMZs. Those are depicted in Figure 14.2 (taken from Figure 2-11, on page 2–36 of the final NCA plan) to give readers an idea of their relative size and juxtaposition.

Although the NCA planners had re-adopted OFM, the BLM still had an obligation to its planning partners to display management directions and implementing actions for the four planning zones in the draft plan and shown on pages 2-19 to 2-30 of the approved management plan. This enabled the four working groups who had originally worked within an activity-focused framework on the draft plan to track their work. It is the only reason why portions of the final plan were still structured around the original four planning zones. These portions of the plan merely duplicate what is displayed elsewhere in the final NCA plan by the 10 final RMZs to allow tracing these actions back by those same four original draft management plan zones.

In sum, the eight RMZs originally established for the RC/BR area plan, as well as the ten established for the current NCA plan, meet most OFM requirements for identifying customer market demands, despite the problems of defining and accommodation market niches properly.

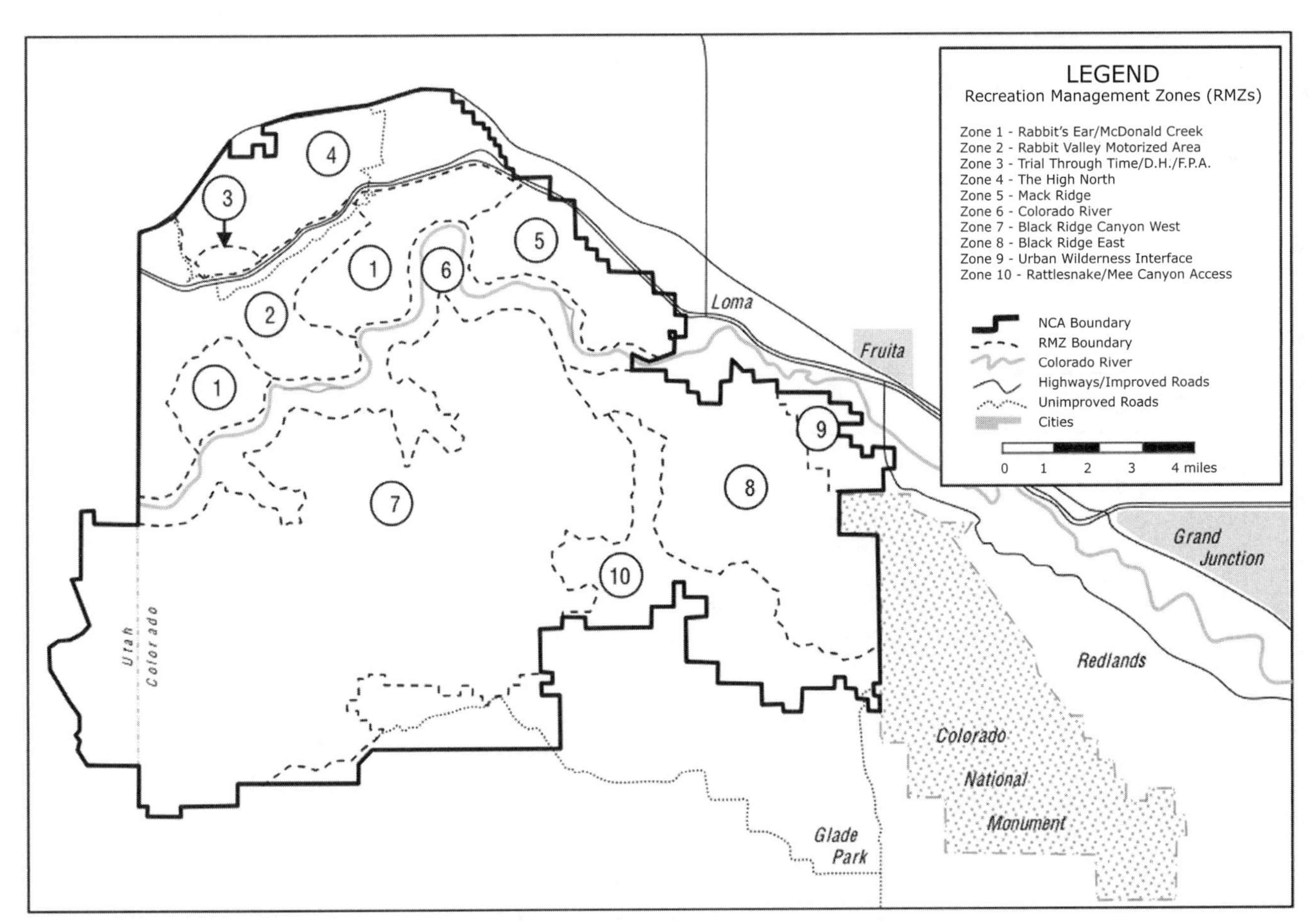

Figure 14.2 Recreation Management Zones in Final NCA Plan

<table>
<tr><th colspan="3">Rabbit Valley Motorized Area (Zone 2)</th></tr>
<tr><td>Management Objectives</td><td colspan="2">By the year 2010, manage this zone to provide opportunities for visitors to engage in Sustainable scenic, diverse motorized and mechanized play area for the Grand Valley, providing no less than 75% of responding visitors and affected community residents at least a "moderate" realization of these benefits (i.e., 3.0 on a probability scale where 1=not at all, 2=somewhat, 3=moderate, 4=total realization)</td></tr>
<tr><td colspan="3">Outcomes</td></tr>
<tr><td>Primary Activities

Motorcycle
ATV
Mountain bike
Riding
Camping</td><td>Experiences

• Enjoying frequent exercise
• Access to a range of physical challenge
• Escaping everyday responsibilities for a while
• Savoring canyon-country aesthetics
• Enjoying easy access to diverse recreation opportunities.
• Developing skills, abilities and self-confidence</td><td>Benefits

Personal:

• Improved physical fitness
• Better health maintenance
• Restored mind from unwanted stress
• Greater cultivation of outdoor-oriented lifestyle
• Improved outdoor knowledge, skills, and self-confidence
• Greater environmental awareness and sensitivity
• More well-informed and responsible visitors

Household and Community:

• Improved cultivation of aesthetic appreciation for the area and an outdoor-oriented lifestyle

Economic:

• Positive contributions to local-regional economic stability

Environmental:

• Increased resource stewardship and protection by communities</td></tr>
<tr><td colspan="3">Setting Prescriptions</td></tr>
<tr><td>Physical:

• Middle and front country with rural character along the north portion of this zone, due to proximity of the I-70 corridor; mostly natural in appearance, with a number of rustic facilities including trails, restrooms, dispersed campsites, and signage</td><td>Social:

• Group size up to 45
• Could have 30–35 encounters per day beyond encounters in staging or camping areas</td><td>Administrative:

• Brochures are available for information and opportunities
• Agency personnel are periodically available
• Rules are clearly posted and use may be temporarily restricted due to permitted events or resource concerns due to weather
• Area accommodates multiple-use including OHV</td></tr>
</table>

Figure 14.3 Management Objectives and Setting Prescriptions for RMZ No. 2

Develop the Management Plan (Phase 3)

The five requirements of the normative model of Phase 3 are to: *determine* which outcomes can and should be targeted; *develop* management objectives; *identify* and prescribe essential setting conditions; *define* the essential recreation-tourism service environment; and *evaluate* alternatives and select the one preferred.

Determine which Outcomes Can and Should Feasibly be Targeted within each RMZ, Develop Management Objectives, *and* Identify and Prescribe Essential Setting Characteristics

These three requirements are considered together because they are related. This requirement was met reasonably well for the RC/BR area plan as well as the approved NCA management plan, once it reinstituted OFM. Had that planning started under OFM guidelines, the approved plan could have built upon the initial outcome opportunities targeted in draft plan management objectives. The draft plan, however, had no such objectives; only a set of six generalized objectives for all land uses (e.g., "Preserve and protect the nationally significant area for the enjoyment of present and future generations," and "Expand education and interpretation opportunities in all areas."). The draft plan also completely neglected any mention of markets and niches. Thus all of this work in the final plan had to be done by starting not from the draft plan, but from the approved RC/BR integrated plan. The good news is that the approved RC/BR management plan, NAU's visitor studies, and a great deal of public input did provide a sufficient basis for completing this important step.

Management objectives and setting prescriptions for the Rabbit Valley motorized area, RMZ No. 2, are reproduced as Figure 14.3 (from Figure 2-12 on page 2-40 of the CCNCA plan) to illustrate the amount of detail provided to meet the two requirements now being considered. The location of that RMZ can be identified on Figure 14.2. The setting prescriptions outlined at the bottom of Figure 14.3 only summarize setting conditions that are prescribed in the final NCA plan by each of the three setting components (i.e., biophysical, social, and administrative). That summary table, however useful for comparing general differences in prescribed setting characteristics among the 10 RMZs, provides insufficient content to guide and constrain the implementing recreation actions of the BLM and its collaborating providers. It is insufficient because it does not contain the specific prescribed conditions for each of the 12 setting attributes that are essential to production and attainment of targeted experiences and other beneficial outcomes. Neither does it portray the geographic extent of each. Both elements are required if all implementing actions and facilitating outputs are to be appropriately redirected to facilitate production and attainment of targeted outcome opportunities. The final NCA management plan therefore includes both a more detailed setting classification matrix (depicting "existing" and "prescribed" recreation setting conditions to show which attributes must change and which must remain) for each RMZ as well as a corresponding set of maps (depicting the geographic extent of prescribed setting conditions for each of the three setting components comprising each RMZ: physical, social, and administrative/managerial).

Figure 14.4 is a schematic depiction of the natural resource setting prescription matrix being used to guide implementation actions for the NCA. This figure is included in this chapter to demonstrate the ease with which definitive setting prescriptions can be displayed in management plans. This matrix displays information that would otherwise be extremely difficult to convey, such as:

- Setting characteristics (along the "x" axis)
- Each of 12 setting attributes (along the "y" axis)

The matrix shown in Figure 14.4 defines the character of each of the six setting classes listed across the top of the table. It does this through the use of narrative descriptions in each cell that correspond with the 12 setting attributes listed down the table's left-hand side. As illustrated by the graphic sketch above the setting class names, setting variation ranges from primitive (on the left) to urban (on the right), which reflects the BLM's adaptation of the ROS system.

The narrative content of all cells following each of the 12 setting attributes (i.e., rows of cells) therefore defines the range of setting character variation that is possible across the six setting classes (i.e., cell columns); and the content of each cell defines setting character by class (column) and by setting attribute (row) (i.e., by intersecting columns and rows). The actual narrative definitions are not included in the cells illustrated in Figure 14.4 because the size and format of these pages does not accommodate showing them. Therefore, the following

= Existing setting description   = Targeted setting prescriptions

Setting classes   Primitive   Back Country   Middle Country   Front Country   Rural   Urban   Pristine—Transition

PHYSICAL—character of the natural landscape and built environment

a. Remoteness:						
b. Naturalness:						
c. Facilities:						

SOCIAL—character of recreation and tourism use

d. Group size (other than your own):						
e. Contacts (with other groupls):						
f. Types of encounters:						
g. Personal gear and equipment:						
h. Evidence of use:						

ADMINISTRATIVE—character of recreation-tourism provider and administrative controls

i. Visitor services:						
j. Management controls:						
k. Domestic animals:						
l. Mechanized use:						

Figure 14.4 Recreation Setting Prescription Matrix Schematic

three example sets of setting class definitions are included to illustrate the narrative definitions included in the actual matrix for the NCA plan. For example, under the "Physical" setting component, for the attribute "Remoteness," definitions for the seven setting classes appearing in Figure 14.4 are as follows (notice that remoteness is greatest for "Pristine" and least for "Urban"):

- Pristine: more than 10 miles from any road
- Transition: more than 3 miles from any road
- Back Country: more than ½ mile from any kind of road, but not as distant as 3 miles; and no road is in sight
- Middle Country: on or near four-wheel drive roads, but at least ½ mile from all improved roads, though they may be in sight
- Front Country: on or near improved country roads, but at least ½ mile from all highways
- Rural: on or near primary highways, but still within a rural area
- Urban: on or near primary highways, municipal streets, and roads within towns or cities

In the same manner, under the "Social" setting component, for the setting attribute "Group Size," definitions for the six setting classes appearing in Figure 14.4 are as follows:

- Primitive: *fewer than or equal to 3 people per group*
- Back Country: *4–6 people per group*
- Middle Country: *7–12 people per group*
- Front Country: *13–25 people per group*
- Rural: *26–50 people per group*
- Urban: *greater than 50 people per group*

Under the "Administrative" setting component, for the setting attribute "Mechanized Use," definitions for the six setting classes appearing in Figure 14.4 are as follows:

- Primitive: *none whatsoever*
- Back Country: *mountain bikes and perhaps other mechanized use, but all is nonmotorized*
- Middle Country: *four-wheel drives, all-terrain vehicles, dirt bikes, or snowmobiles in addition to nonmotorized, mechanized use*
- Front Country: *two-wheel drive vehicles predominant, but also four-wheel drives and nonmotorized mechanized use*
- Rural: *ordinary highway auto and truck traffic*
- Urban: *wide variety of street vehicles and highway traffic is ever-present*

It was in this way that these setting class definitions were used both to describe existing setting characteristics and to prescribe essential future setting characteristics for the NCA plan. As illustrated in the Figure 14.4 schematic, heavy lines were used to enclose all setting class definitions that describe existing setting character. In addition, shading was applied to all setting class definitions that prescribe each desired setting condition. A separate matrix was completed in this fashion for each RMZ.

The inclusion of these matrix setting prescriptions and accompanying maps (depicting the geographic extent of each prescription) enabled managers to better understand and explain to the public which setting attributes were to remain, which were to change and how much, and the geographic extent of each. They communicate specific guidelines required to implement approved plans by BLM managers and collaborating associated providers. Last, but not least, these paired matrix and map combinations also facilitate addressing each alternative's effects on setting character for environmental reporting. This makes possible concise and accurate quantification of limitations thereby imposed on provider services, types of allowable recreation use and user behavior, and ultimately types of outcome opportunities produced and attained.

This level of definition is required for two important reasons: (1) to ensure that all setting conditions essential to the production and attainment of targeted outcome opportunities are made explicit, and (2) to guide and constrain implementation actions accordingly. Absent this level of specificity, the final plan content would provide an insufficient framework for the necessary restructuring and design of all future provider implementation actions (i.e., management, marketing, monitoring, and administration) as needed to achieve OFM objectives. Without it, implementation planning flounders, and so does the execution of field operations. For this OFM application, these requirements have been very well met.

Approved plans for both the RC/BR area and for the NCA met these requirements well. So well, in fact, that this paired setting matrix and map format continues to be used in other applications of OFM by the BLM and for the BLM's OFM training. Pages 2-36 to 2-61 of the approved final plan presents figures for each of the NCA's ten RMZs, showing how the three requirements being considered here, and others considered later, were met. Those figures drew heavily from relevant information provided for the eight RMZs defined in the plan that was prepared earlier for the RC/BR area.

The more definitive setting prescription matrices that address all setting attributes for each of the 10 RMZs are be found in the "MCNCA Proposed RMP/EIS" (because the Field Office mistakenly omitted moving these matrices to the final plan) under the heading "Appendix 4: Planning Tools for recreation," after text that describes how OFM was applied (beginning on page A-4-9).

Define the Essential Recreation-Tourism Service Environment

As mentioned previously, the management plans for RC/BR and the NCA were written before the BLM's *Land Use Planning Handbook* was updated to incorporate OFM. Therefore, the approved management plan did not specifically attempt to meet this requirement. However, involvement of the public during preparation of the two plans did raise issues and concerns regarding the recreation-tourism-related service environment. For example, explicit attention is given in the plan to guides and outfitters and some other associated providers, but not to all relevant associated providers (see Chapter 2 of this text for why OFM requires the collaborative involvement of associated providers).

This vitally important transition step between developing the management plan and developing a separate plan which implements it still needs to be addressed for the NCA. Had the essential service environment been addressed, the implementation plan would have looked different for the NCA for several reasons:

- This section would have identified both the geographic extent of the service delivery system and all of the key associated or affecting providers within it. They are "affecting" providers because their actions will affect both setting character and outcome opportunities produced and attained. The essential service environment for the NCA includes the cities of Fruita and Grand Junction because NCA visitors depend on services provided within these communities. Without the on-site and off-site service providers, the BLM cannot successfully implement the NCA plan. Included are retail services, equipment rentals, hospitality services such as lodging and restaurants; chambers of commerce and visitor and convention bureaus), outfitters, guides, and tour operators, local government entities whose actions either change or maintain prescribed setting characteristics (e.g., local government planning and zoning offices and the Mesa County road development and maintenance offices.
- This section would have further identified mechanisms for engaging and sustaining the collaborative involvement of these associated providers as managing partners with the BLM. Following the BLM's extensive public involvement efforts, the most probable collaborative management frameworks for sustaining that cooperation (which the planning effort initiated) with these essential service and infrastructure providers could have been explored and documented, but they were not written down.
- This section also needed to identify a workable framework whereby these affecting associate partners could restructure within the OFM framework both ongoing activity-focused recreation programs and new initiatives and systems regarding trails, bicycling, and off-highway vehicle management; river management; road, trail, and other facility construction and maintenance; tourism marketing; interpretation; user ethics education; scenic byways; visual resource management; permits and fees; etc. Because this was not done, most field operations continue under the activity-focused paradigm which guided them before the plan was written and approved. The implementation framework still needs to devise a way to restructure the collaborating providers' operations in three ways to positively guide, negatively restrict, and to neutrally change what gets done.

Positively, the restructuring of all BLM and associated provider actions is still required to ensure that no essential actions are overlooked. For example, at present, the BLM has yet to identify promotional actions required to adequately inform visitors about the types of outcome opportunities being provided, the character of the different settings through which they will travel, and both the types of services being provided and where they may be obtained.

Negatively, such restructuring is required to restrict BLM programs and initiatives which are nonessential to the achievement of management objectives. For the NCA, the BLM continues to apply for and obtain external funding grants and appropriated dollars for facility development actions, which cannot be proven essential to achieving approved management plan objectives because the mechanism for subjecting and restructuring such proposals to ensure they fit the approved plan (i.e., prescribed setting conditions as well as targeted outcome opportunities) has not yet been set in place. For example, proactive, activity-focused user groups can still apply for and obtain funding for developments, operations and maintenance, and so forth. In the same way, *more neutral changes* are required to adjust the approved implementing actions to ensure that they fit the prescribed settings in which they are to occur. An implementation framework encompassing the entire essential service environment would restructure all "business as usual" field operations to ensure that all players are working towards the same ends.

For these reasons, this essential service environment section of the plan for the NCA does not yet identify an implementing framework that ensures the appropriate integration of and balance among the palette of approved implementation actions that is to follow. Implementation actions (addressed in Phase 4) were listed under recreation's most basic functional inputs: management, marketing, monitoring, and administrative support. But the late return to the OFM framework during the planning for the NCA did not afford the planners and managers the opportunity to structure and restructure these implementation actions in a way that ensures both (a) the complete integration of all relevant and necessary program inputs under each of these categories and (b) consistency and balance across these functions. Therefore for example, the marketing section does not completely address the kinds of visitor information needs necessitated by all of the facility development actions included under management. Likewise, it is not readily apparent that the NCA has yet achieved an appropriate balance in efforts being expended (i.e., actions being implemented) between its management and marketing efforts. Such balance has both intuitive and practical appeal, but the BLM's facility development tradition and its historic deficiency of effective marketing shows up in both the types and numbers of actions identified under each category. For an agency such as the BLM (whose primary recreation mission is dispersed and not facility-dependent recreation), it would make sense to expend marketing efforts promoting what is being provided (e.g., through visitor outreach, a greater on-site visitor presence, more definitive recreation-tourism promotion) that equal the agency's greater propensity for on-the-ground management project actions. Such outreach is essential to ensure that visitors end up in areas being managed for the kinds of experience and other benefit outcomes they desire and which are targeted by the NCA's approved management objectives. Although this section of the plan was not addressed in the plan for the NCA, and the ensuring implementation actions do not appear to yet be completely addressed, a good deal of work in the right direction is already being done through perceptive and skilled field operations by experienced and committed BLM park rangers.

Evaluate Alternatives and Select the Preferred Alternative

Completed plans for the RC/BR area and the NCA were comprehensively (integrated) multiple-use resource management plans rather than those solely oriented to recreation. Section 1-3 of the approved NCA management plan discusses the four alternatives considered and explains why the "Adaptive Management" alternative, rather than one of the other three alternatives, including the "Recreation Emphasis," was chosen. In sum, there was not a ranking of alternatives solely in terms of recreation, but the importance of recreation within the NCA's mix of multiple uses suggests that such a ranking would not have significantly affected which alternative was selected as the one preferred.

Develop an Implementation Plan (Phase 4)

The five requirements of the normative model for Phase 4 are to: *identify* management actions to be implemented; *identify* marketing actions to be implemented; *identify* monitoring actions; *identify* supporting administrative actions; and *provide* ample opportunities and timeframes for review of the proposed plan. At the time the NCA management plan was written, implementation actions were regarded by the BLM as essential components of a management plan. Now, however, because of subsequent amendments to the BLM's *Land Use Planning Handbook*, the actions which follow are under a separate category, separate from and prepared subsequent to the Land Use Plan itself, and are called Implementation Decisions. Those decisions do not require Land Use Plan amendments, but instead may be changed as necessary in response to monitoring feedback. And indeed they must be, for OFM requires adaptively adjusting program inputs as necessary to ensure the attainment of management objectives and setting prescriptions.

It is all too easy to underestimate the importance of this phase. OFM insists that critical actions must be taken: primary markets and niches must first be identified, next the activities and beneficial outcomes targeted for customers must be identified as management objectives, then the essential setting conditions required to produce and attain those outcome opportunities must be identified and prescribed, and finally, the framework within which essential services are to be delivered must be specified. While these actions are critically important, the perception exists that they are the most important of all because they set everything else in motion. But, that motion or momentum will be lost if necessary implementing actions are not planned carefully, specified clearly, and followed through diligently. Follow-on implementation planning is correcting these deficiencies in the final plan for this area.

<table>
<tr><th colspan="2">Rabbit Valley Motorized Area (Zone 2)</th></tr>
<tr><th colspan="2">Management and Marketing Actions</th></tr>
<tr><td>

Management Actions

Roads and Trails

- Restore closed roads that have no administrative benefit & are not included in range allotment agreements
- Modify roads and trail as needed to mitigate impacts
- Rehab nondesignated trails and trails that are closed unless there is a potential future use
- Develop multiple-use single-track trails on Harley Dome (#9 on Map)
- Relocate Trail #2 off the valley floor to the escarpment west of the main entrance (#11 on map)
- Connect Trail #4 to Trail #3 along the upper escarpment (#12 on map)
- Relocate Trail #3 to the opposite side of the drainage and connect to Trail #4 (#13 on map)
- Relocate Trail #4 and Trail #5 to on the valley floor to the dry wash that runs east-west in the same area (#15 on map)
- Designate multiple-use single track trail from stock pond west of Trail through Time, head west to state line and south to dirt road (#16 on map).
- Close dead end spurs that lateral south from the frontage road if no purpose is identified (#14 on map)
- Close and rehab route north of I-70 near Utah border (#21 on map)
- Contain parking facilities to prevent encroachment
- Harden surfaces at parking areas, trailheads, & campsites only when needed to prevent resource impacts.

</td><td>

Camping

- Construct formal campground if BLM successfully acquires the Jouflas in-holding

Other

- Develop a large area for recreational parking & events (#5 on map)
- Consider developing & designating a 2nd group-use site at the disturbed alcove location
- Develop and implement a site plan for the Rabbit Valley entrance vicinity south of I-70

Marketing Actions

- Develop comprehensive interpretive plan which includes all aspects of interpretation, education, and public outreach
- Strive to involve user groups, volunteers, and other interested public to help maintain resources through partnerships, adoption programs, special events and/or a "friends group".
- Identify partners and develop "Friends" group to assist BLM in outreach and education

</td></tr>
</table>

Figure 14.5 Management and Marketing Actions for RMZ No. 2

In the same way that the management objectives and setting prescriptions were addressed in the plan for each of the NCA's ten RMZs (as reflected by Figure 14.3), implementing actions were also specified in the approved plan for these same ten RMZs. Each will now be evaluated.

Identify Management Actions to be Implemented

A sizeable list of management actions were developed by activity-focused working groups for the draft NCA management plan. These management actions comprised the largest part of the activity-focused draft plan. When OFM was re-adopted as the final plan was being developed, NCA managers were obliged to incorporate the earlier efforts of the working groups into the approved plan. One-by-one, these actions were evaluated for consistency with OFM objectives and setting prescriptions. Those that were not consistent were omitted. Time constraints, coupled with a steep learning curve for the NCA's recreation planners, however, left little room for addressing whether all management actions essential for achieving prescribed setting conditions and management objectives had been sufficiently addressed. Those efforts resulted in summary tabulations of management actions for each RMZ. Figure 14.5 (reproduced from Figure 2-12 on page 2-41 of the approved plan) lists those required management actions for RMZ No. 2.

It was later recognized that this list of actions was insufficient to make field operations responsive to the approved plan. Aware of these shortcomings, the NCA staff is (at the time of this writing) incrementally revisiting these actions in the form of subsequent, post-RMP "Implementation Plans." This ongoing work is excellent and is now guided by the adaptive plan implementation guidance outlined in the BLM's revised *Land Use Planning Handbook*. It would be a mistake for readers to conclude that this only needed to be done because of deficiencies in the final NCA plan; this kind of adaptive implementation in fact must be done if OFM plans are to be implemented at all. And so, the BLM's ongoing implementation planning efforts for the Rabbit Valley motorized area (RMZ No. 2) also address several other RMZs on its perimeter, because visitors must travel through Rabbit Valley to get there.

A key element of OFM is that the management of recreation within each RMZ must target selected markets and niches. An erroneous statement is made in Appendix 3 of the approved plan (page A-3-5) and therefore cannot be met. It is "A broad range of outdoor recreational opportunities will continue to be provided for all segments of the public." Providers must understand that the provision of certain specific kinds of outcome opportunities for some customers precludes the provision of other outcome opportunities for others.

Identify Marketing Actions to be Implemented

Marketing actions for RMZ No. 2 are shown (along with the management actions) in Figure 14.5. That zone, Rabbit Valley, is the central staging area for visitors entering the NCA by I-70 to visit it and three adjoining RMZs. This suggests a need for more definitive information than usual about the diverse kinds of recreation opportunities that can be accessed from that particular RMZ. However, implementation actions under the marketing heading only include one action, and that is to develop an interpretive plan which is tantamount only to plan to do more planning.

It was not as though there was inadequate information to decide what kinds of visitor information and promotional outreach was needed. Both local and statewide tourism marketing efforts had already featured the NCA's superlative scenery and outdoor recreation attractions. The Rabbit Valley RMZ is also the most heavily visited zone within the entire NCA. Adjoining I-70 access ramps to the area provide access and, in effect, invite thousands of people to the area. The remaining two actions included in Figure 14.5 for marketing are supporting administrative actions (and should have been addressed under that section).

The purpose for addressing these deficiencies here is not to berate the authors of the plan or the BLM. It is to illustrate the challenge of shifting from managing independent programs (e.g., interpretation, user ethics) to managing all promotional marketing outreach as one of recreation's most basic functional inputs. So again, sensing these significant deficiencies, the current NCA manager and staff are incorporating all promotional, outreach, educational, and interpretive actions as an integrated marketing function. They are addressing the minimum actions needed to adequately inform customers about recreation opportunity availability and the varying user ethics that go with each RMZ. They are also using this entire palette of marketing actions both to ensure effective management (i.e., balancing these with the updated set of management actions, ensuring consistency, and more thorough action integration) and marketing. All of this is being achieved through ongoing implementation planning, ensuring that management message to BLM and its collaborating community providers is consistent with the marketing message to their shared customers.

Within the broader context of the entire plan, this step should have outlined a balanced and integrated set of visitor informational, promotional, educational, and interpretive actions designed to adequately inform customers about the kinds of recreation provided: targeted customer markets, primary activities and associated outcome opportunities, recreation setting character, and kinds of services provided and available. Since the BLM is not the only purveyor of this information, the marketing section needed to further identify the BLM's marketing role relative to that of tourism industry, both on- and off-site service provider businesses, and local governments. Both information content and distribution conduits should be addressed.

There are other reasons why this section of the implementation plan is deficient. As mentioned, visitors

Rabbit Valley Motorized Area (Zone 2)	
Administrative and Monitoring Actions	
Administrative Actions *Roads and Trails* • All motorized/mechanized use is limited to existing trails & roads. • Designate trail south of and running parallel to I-70 as nonmotorized (#22 on map) • Avoid locating trails near known paleo/cultural sites except where specifically intended for interpretation • Travel management signage must adhere to BLM Colorado Uniform Sign Standards • Designate & maintain all dirt roads for public access & close nondesignated roads. • Equestrian use limited to designated trails only *Other* • All dogs need to be on leash in high-use areas • Dogs under voice control elsewhere • Coordinate with Moab BLM for continuity *Permits* • See Special Recreation Permit Program in Chapter 2	*Camping* • Limited to no more than 7 consecutive nights • Portable toilets are mandatory for overnight dispersed use • All open fires must be contained in fire pan (no fires rings) • No wood cutting • Dispersed camping sites not designated unless monitoring shows unacceptable impacts. *Shooting* • No discharge of any projectile (i.e. target shooting) *Hunting* • Hunting allowed in conformance with DOW regulations *Visual Resources Management* • Class III - northern portion near I-70 corridor • Not Rated - most of southern portion **Monitoring Actions** • Assure objectives are being met and prescribed settings are being maintained • Monitor implemented actions and evaluate • A mandatory, no-fee, self-registration system would be implemented for the entire CCNCA by January 1, 2010 to contribute data on visitor use, group size, and other trends to support adaptive management of the CCNCA.

Figure 14.6 Administrative and Monitoring Actions for RMZ No. 2

must pass through this area on their way to at least three other distinct but contiguous RMZs. Unless their knowledge of the distinctly different recreation opportunities provided in each of those RMZs is to be assumed, that information must be provided at key staging areas within this RMZ. This section of the plan, however, outlines no such actions either for how it is that visitors are to receive adequate information about targeted recreation activity and outcome opportunities, prescribed setting conditions, available services, travel routes, appropriate modes of travel, or how visitors are to learn about the diverse kinds of recreation provided in each.

Here again, the planners struggled with tight time frames to get the effort back on the OFM track. That basic reality, coupled with the basic unfamiliarity of recreation planners and managers with marketing in general, only heightened the challenge. This situation underscores the need for more fully integrated marketing guidance (rather than piecemeal program guidance for interpretation, education, etc.). On the one hand, interpretation and education are deemed good things, yet promotion is worrisome because too many visitors may discover the special places and damage resources. Practical guidance is needed on how to provide the right kinds of promotional content to enable prospective visitors to learn about the kinds of recreation opportunities being provided and yet equip them to responsibly use and enjoy them. This is now happening with hands-on assistance being provided to NCA planners and managers. It is significant how OFM facilitates responsible marketing by its emphasis on promoting not only greater awareness of recreation activity opportunities, but also of associated kinds of outcome opportunities provided, the character of recreation settings wherein they occur, available services, and visitor controls that must be observed. This is a distinctly different kind of marketing (which is rightly disagreed with) than "selling" increased recreation participation for greater financial return or other reasons not related to accommodating customer preferences.

A good deal of unplanned but needful outreach has already occurred. Useful brochures have been made available that provide maps of the area and different RMZs such as Rabbit Valley, the Trail through time, Devil's Canyon, etc. They describe the natural, geographical, and cultural features of the areas; explain what types of recreation opportunities are available; explain the rules and regulations that exist for the area and subparts of it; and encourage visitors to protect and maintain the conditions of the settings on which satisfying recreation experiences depend. The "Visitor Guide" developed for the NCA and the contiguous Colorado National Monument is an excellent short guide that, among other things, very briefly explains OFM. For example, page 6 of that guide states "...from the visitor's perspective...benefits based management helps people make better recreation choices when visiting the NCA. Recreation experiences will likely be improved because visitors are matched with the appropriate zone offering their desired recreation activities, experiences and [other] benefits.[3]" Earlier on that page, the guide states "... the NCA is divided into ten different recreation, management emphasis zones. *BLM wants to help you find the zone that offers you the recreation activities, experiences and [other] benefits that you want*." The boundaries and characteristics of each zone are described in the guide.

Identify Monitoring Actions *and* Identify Supporting Administrative Actions

"Administrative Actions" and "Monitoring Actions" are specified for each of the ten RMZs of the NCA on pages 2-37 to 2-61 of the approved plan. Figure 14.6 (reproduced from Figure 2-12 on page 2-42 of the plan) shows those actions for RMZ No. 2.

Of the three actions addressed under "Monitoring" in Figure 14.6, none of them are truly monitoring. The first one outlines some of the purposes for monitoring, the second states that it will be done but does not state how (i.e., the reason for writing implementation actions), and the third is misplaced as it is an administrative action. At the time the NCA plan was written, a planning manual had not yet been written outlining essential monitoring implementation actions content. Training materials provided to the NCA staff, however, called for the identification of monitoring methods and schedules.

Monitoring content for this step suggests that the plan's authors did not understand what to do about monitoring. It only commits the BLM to monitor and evaluate. That is tantamount to evading responsibility for holding the recreation program accountable for implementing approved allocation decisions (i.e., management objectives and setting prescriptions) and for following through with planned implementation actions. Although the NCA planners were provided training on both the need to address monitoring methods and schedules, this was not completed. The current NCA staff, however, is in the process of revising the implementation section of the final NCA. In terms of standards and indicators, social monitoring indicators and standards were clearly outlined in the plan's management objectives, and environmental standards were articulated in detail in the plan's setting prescriptions. Neither of these needed to be restated here.

An initial list of administrative actions is also outlined in Figure 14.6. The administrative actions identified, inappropriately included with Figure 14.5 (i.e., with management and marketing actions) complement this list. But none of the essential collaborative management agreements and the key players with whom they must be consummated are identified. Omitted were the minimum agreements needed to engage and sustain the involvement of private sector businesses and local government as managing partners with the NCA. If the gateway recreation-tourism providers whose actions affect recreation setting character and the BLM's ability to implement the final plan design are not formally engaged, the approved plan will not be fully implemented. Necessary cooperative agreements or agreement updates with a myriad of volunteers, user groups, outside funding entities (e.g., the state trails fund), and other implementing partnerships were also not identified. The significant actions of these partners must likewise be restructured to fit the approved management plan objectives and setting prescriptions if the plan is to be successfully implemented.

Other required administrative actions are specified in other parts of the plan, including partnerships. But none of them are addressed within the context of administrative agreements required to engage all of these other providers and implementers as managing partners and achieve their mutual commitment to be guided and constrained by the plan's management objectives and setting prescriptions.

Provide Ample Opportunities and Time Frames for Review of the Proposed Plan

Section 5.4 of the approved NCA management plan documents how this requirement was well met.

Adjust Management/Implementation Plan as Needed and Approve Final Plan (Phase 5)

The Grand Junction FO land-use planner, the NCA recreation planner, and the acting NCA manager did an excellent job moving the recreation sections of the NCA plan from draft to final (approved). The first and third authors of this chapter were privileged to play a facilitative role in this process. With the decision to re-adopt OFM as the management framework for the NCA, all of the activity-focused draft plan content had to be restructured around OFM's framework (i.e., beyond the activity-focused draft's view of recreation as merely managing resources, facilities, and visitor controls). Recreation content from the draft plan consisted only of implementing actions. Setting character was not addressed, and only six generic management objectives (applicable to all land uses) were included. Therefore, planners went back to the approved RC/BR plan as a starting point, reviewed results of the NAU study, and combed though the output of numerous meetings to update the RC/BR management objectives and setting prescriptions. Accordingly, the draft management plan was further revised in response to other public review comments. The major task was to keep all of the still valid working group actions but also address key components of recreation production not addressed in that draft plan. Care was taken to ensure that when those components missing from the draft plan were added, corresponding changes to the final plan were made. Had the draft plan originally adopted the OFM framework, other affected recreation production components would have had to be addressed (e.g., if management objectives changed, those changes would have had implications for the types of setting characteristics deemed essential, and those changes in turn would have affected the types of implementation actions required).

Two significant challenges have been involved in implementing the approved plan for the NCA. First, planners and managers must ensure that all implementation actions required to achieve the plan design have been identified and addressed adequately. Second, extreme diligence is required to ensure that all actions are appropriately guided and constrained to ensure that only the minimum actions required to achieve management objectives and prescribed setting characteristics are approved. Any other actions (i.e., all programs, projects, and initiatives) are superfluous, inefficient, ineffective, and possibly even counterproductive.

Implement Plan and Adjust Field Operations Accordingly (Phase 6)

Under supervision of the current manger of the MCNCA and the manager of the BLM's Grand Junction Field Office, the plan is being implemented, consistent with Congressional appropriations.

Revise the Plan as Needed or Required by Agency Directives (Phase 7)

As noted, implementation actions in the final plan are being updated through Implementation Plan updates. This is normal and is required for adaptive implementation of OFM. As of yet, monitoring has not revealed the need for updates of the management plan itself.

Ensure that Performance Reports and Evaluations Document and Recognize the Sustained Production and Attainment of Targeted Outcomes as Feasible (Phase 8)

Especially since passage of the 1993 Government Performance and Results Act and the proliferation of articles in professional journals (notably "Public Administration Review") on performance reporting and evaluations, ever increasing attention has been and is being devoted by public agencies at all levels of government to improving their periodic reporting and evaluations of performance. Problematic from the perspective of OFM is the fact that practically all of the reports and evaluations of all public park and recreation agencies have focused, and still focus, on reporting the production of recreation program outputs (i.e., facilitating outputs as described in Chapter 2 of this text if they in fact facilitate something meaningful). Numbers and types of management actions, projects completed, programs carried out, and visitors contacted have little to do with reporting the degree to which those outputs actually do produce targeted outcome opportunities and facilitate their attainment. This remains true for required reporting related to implementation of the NCA plan.

A rather large section at the end of Chapter 3 of this text was devoted to explaining why more attention needs to be given to outcomes in performance reporting and evaluations.

Lessons Learned

It must be understood that the first attempt to apply OFM on any public wildlands was on the RC/BR area. For that reason, important lessons from that application and implementation of OFM, and later on the NCA, contributed significantly to developing and refining the normative OFM model in Chapter 3 of this text. That model not only specifies what needs to be done, but more importantly explains how to apply many of the requirements of OFM for the first time in a published document. Other applications in municipal areas and elsewhere had started and were completed before plans for the RC/BR recreation area or for the NCA were completed. They also contributed to improving the OFM model.

To help others more effectively apply and implement OFM, some of the most important lessons learned are briefly outlined below, several of which emphasize requirements of the OFM model described in Chapter 3 of this text which, as said, was improved by lessons learned from applying and implementing OFM on the NCA.

- It is absolutely necessary that supervisors, managers, and planners responsible for applying and implementing OFM understand and support it. Specifically, they must understand OFM's planning processes and application requirements and be committed to shifting field operations beyond activity-focused program and project management, *before* they begin any application. Otherwise, situations will arise as did in second generation planning efforts for the NCA.
- Logical RMZs must be delineated in terms of the types of recreation opportunities (activities and experience and other outcome opportunities) to be produced and attained in each one. When dissimilar RMZs are combined (as was done for RC/BR zones in the proposed NCA management plan), the requirements and logic of OFM is not applied, and planning processes break down. From a customer assessment perspective, assessing preferences for different markets and niches within the same RMZ yields wildly different recreation outcome desires. From a management perspective, it is not possible to provide these very different kinds of outcome opportunities within the same geographic area. Careful delineation of RMZs is therefore essential for narrowing down the palette of outcome opportunities to be targeted within each RMZ to what is reasonable achievable for well-defined, select market niches.
- Residents of local communities must be considered as customers as much as the on-site visitors, because both are recipients of the improved, maintained, and worsened conditions that result from public lands recreation use and management. The Field Office review in this chapter emphasized how difficult it is to engage affected community residents as participants in focus groups designed to assess resident preferences. It was emphasized that only when residents are aware that their quality of life is threatened will they get involved. Invitations to participate in community assessment efforts must therefore explain that OFM planning is not simply about what recreation activities to provide, but that the character of open space settings surrounding communities is also being addressed as well as resulting community effects. These realities must be creatively framed in assessment meeting notices in such a way that residents can understand why their involvement is needed. Assessment notifications should therefore address real possibilities for changes to the character of recreation settings that adjoin local communities. Providers must explain why they need to know what kinds of outcomes are desired by service providing businesses, local governments, and

the community residents thereby affected, not just recreation participants.

- Customer preference assessments, including both focus groups and more formal studies, must be oriented to logical RMZs. If results are to be useable for planning and management, all customer assessments must establish and maintain a consistently understood (by customers and providers alike) context that relates customers' preferences for experiences and other benefit outcomes to most satisfying RMZs and activities. The response context for useable customer assessments must enable different kinds of recreation participants and affected community residents to indicate what setting conditions they believe must be provided and maintained to achieve their most highly valued outcomes.
- Customer assessment response formats must provide enough definition to enable managers to exercise at least as much discretion in managing public lands recreation attractions as do visitors in deciding where to go and what to do. For mail-back visitor studies, a seven-point Likert preference scale [-3 through +3] provides managers the ability to differentiate between "somewhat, moderate, and very" desirable outcomes. By contrast, a five-point scale only provides essentially binary information, "high or low." This effort demonstrated that wherever visitor study results lack adequate definition, planners will be grateful to have access to less quantifiable, yet more definitive focus group results.
- Key local governmental officials, relevant owners of local businesses, and other associated providers must be actively involved as integral partners in the collaborative planning and management activities.
- Specific management objectives and setting condition prescriptions must be developed for each RMZ.
- All implementation actions must be both directed and constrained by OFM objectives and setting prescriptions targeted for each RMZ (the supply) and corresponding market niche (the demand). Those which only promote the advancement of recreation programs and initiatives as ends unto themselves are unnecessary. All field operations must be restructured accordingly.
- An implementation plan must be developed that identifies all essential management, monitoring, marking, and administrative actions required (i.e., of the BLM and other necessary associated recreation-tourism service and infrastructure providers) to achieve approved management objectives, setting prescriptions for targeted market niches.
- All activity-focused recreation programs, projects, initiatives, and systems must be restructured and integrated within and balanced across these most basic managing, marketing, monitoring, and administrative inputs if field operations are to be expected to embrace OFM and effectively implement OFM plans.
- Under OFM, recreation field operations may no longer proceed under the assumption that traditional activity-focused programs and projects facilitate the production and attainment of desired experiences and other benefit outcomes.
- Specific roles and responsibilities of parties responsible for implementing the plan must be clearly and consistently understood and supported by all.

Recommended Future Actions

The recommendations derived from this review are outlined below.

- A concerted effort should be made to meet all the requirements of the comprehensive normative model for applying and implementing OFM described in Chapter 3 of this text.
- The second recommendation has several parts, and each center on training. Those parts are outlined below:
    1. Train all key supervisors, managers, and recreation planners as an essential step in shifting from activity-focused project and program management to managing for outcomes.
    2. Training for supervisors and managers must be tailored to their managerial world, while training for recreation planners must contain sufficient content and detail to provide operational understanding. However, managers must have their recreation staff present to cultivate joint understanding and dialogue about what OFM means for Land Use Planning, Implementation Planning, and their application in the necessary restructuring of field operations.

  3. Integrate OFM training into community-based workshops with the private sector business service (e.g., outfitters, tour operators, convention and visitors' bureaus, chambers of commerce) and infrastructure (e.g., county and municipal governments) providers whose engagement and sustained involvement as managing partners is essential to successful plan development and implementation.
  4. Create, empower, and prepare a strike team of recreation professionals who are experienced in both doing and teaching the above to help recreation planners actually plan and apply OFM to field operations. As the old saying goes, "Telling isn't teaching, and listening isn't learning; you learn to do by doing!"
- Complete the above training and do reality checks, including in-field testing of planning applications and implementing field operations before beginning any OFM planning effort.
- Ensure that the managers, who are in charge of the relevant organizational units, motivate and empower someone having authority and influence over the above players to make this happen, because it is not automatic. Line managers are pivotal to the engagement of key private and local government service and infrastructure providing entities (upon whom they and their customers depend) as managing partners, and sustaining their continued involvement. Five essentials are involved:
  1. Managers at all relevant levels of the organization must understand and embrace restructuring (i.e., directing and constraining) all programs, initiatives, projects, and field operations to facilitate the production and attainment of targeted experience and other benefit outcomes by targeted market niches through maintenance of prescribed setting characteristics and the delivery of essential, corresponding recreation and visitor services.
  2. Expand the working definition of "customer" to include both visitor-participants as well as nonparticipating, but affected residents of gateway communities. Affected community residents often have very specific preferences for the character of public lands settings that surround their homes and communities, and these customers fall within the purview of OFM as much as onsite recreation participants.
  3. Conduct recreation preference assessments using a combination of informal interviews, focus groups, and in-depth mail-back studies. This application of OFM demonstrated that focus groups, facilitating two-way iterative communication, produced the most useful results. Informal interviews tend to be undervalued, while surveys appear to be equally overvalued. Nonetheless, only randomly-administered, statistically reliable survey results may be generalized to sample populations. No one method produces adequate results, so be sure to structure recreation participant and community resident customer preference assessments accordingly.
  4. Subject all recreation programs and project actions to the outcomes test. Implement only those needed to achieve outcomes targeted in approved management objectives and setting prescriptions, and refuse to waste staff time and funding on those that do not.
  5. Integrate recreation program actions, initiatives, and projects across all traditional activity-focused recreation programs, projects, initiatives, and systems within recreations most basic functional inputs: management, marketing, monitoring, and administrative support.
- Consummate cooperative agreements to engage, as collaborating managing partners, those principle private sector service providing business sectors (e.g., tour operators, outfitters and guides, downtown retail) and infrastructure-providing local governments (e.g., counties, municipalities) from the principal service communities whose services are essential to targeted visitor and community markets.
- Park rangers and recreation planners must understand and embrace:
  1. A commitment to stop advancing favorite programs, doing projects, and facility development merely to accommodate the desires of organized groups and interests for increased activity participation.
  2. The need to shift field operations away from primarily/merely getting projects done and *towards* managing and marketing to produce

the specific recreation opportunities targeted by management objectives, and limit field operations to only those that facilitate these ends.

3. Continuous monitoring of social indicators (by standards set by management objectives), environmental indicators (by standards set by setting prescriptions), and administrative indicators (by standards set by implementing actions), the application of results to make corresponding adjustments to implementation plans, and keeping field operations geared to achieving approved management objectives and setting prescriptions.
4. The necessity of keeping administrative actions and initiatives in a supporting role, avoiding all others' efforts to use them to skew plan implementation.

- The unfamiliarity of most resource recreation planners and managers with marketing, and their general disdain for it, requires moving beyond reliance on more traditional informational outreach and interpretive programs. Responsive OFM implementation must address "Marketing" as an integrated family of complementary promotion, information, education, and interpretive actions geared to facilitate the production and attainment of outcome opportunities targeted to select markets and niches for each RMZ. These efforts must jointly engage all of the principle purveyors of public lands recreation information, public and private.
- Give adequate attention to outcomes in periodic accomplishment reporting and personnel evaluations. Some of this may already be done in an objectively quantifiable manner right now, while others will remain more qualitative in nature.

Literature Cited

Buckley, W. (1968). *Modern systems research for the behavioral scientist.* Chicago, IL: Aldine.

Canadian Parks/Recreation Association. (1997). *The benefits catalogue.* Gloucester, ON, Canada: Canadian Parks/Recreation Association.

Driver, B., Brown, P., & Peterson, G. (Eds.). (1991). *Benefits of leisure.* State College, PA: Venture Publishing, Inc.

Driver, B. L., & Bruns, D., (1999). Concepts and Uses of the Benefits Approach to Leisure. In E. Jackson, and T. Burton (eds.), *Leisure studies: Prospects for the twenty first century,* (pp. 349–369) State College, PA: Venture Publishing, Inc.

Lee, M., Stephens, A., & Fuller, K., (2003). *Colorado Canyons National Conservation Area 2001-2003 Visitor Study: Final Report.* Arizona State University, Department of Forestry. Flagstaff, Arizona.

Ponds, P., Gillette, S., & Koontz, L. (2004). *Colorado Canyons National Conservation Area 2003 visitor user survey-Completion report.* USDI Geological Survey. Open-File Report 3 2004-1281. Washington, D.C.

Stein, T., & Lee, M. (1995). *Ruby Canyon-Black Ridge User study. Final report.* Arizona State University, Department of Forestry. Flagstaff, Arizona.

USDI Bureau of Land Management. (1998). *Ruby Canyon/Black Ridge Integrated Management Plan.* Grand Junction Resource Area. Grand Junction, CO.

USDI Bureau of Land Management. (2005). *Land Use Planning Handbook* (H-1601-1, Release 1–1693, March 11, 2005). Washington D.C.

USDI Bureau of Land Management. (2004). *Resource management plan and record of decision for the Colorado Canyons National Conservation Are and Black Ridge Canyons Wilderness.* Grand Junction Field Office. Grand Junction, CO.

Footnotes

1. This chapter draws heavily from a case study report of the application and implementation of OFM on the MCNCA which was authored by B. L. Driver, Don Bruns, and Randy Virden. That study was commissioned by the BLM's Division of Recreation and Visitor Services because of its strong and rapidly growing interest in OFM. It wanted to use the report to help others in the BLM better understand how to apply and implement OFM. The needs for and requirements of that case study convinced the editor of this text that this text was also needed for a wider audience, provide much more detail about how to implement and apply OFM than could be provided in the case study report, and have that information published in a readily available source which Venture Publishing, Inc. agreed to do. That case study report can be

found on the web at http://www.blm.gov/co/st/en/fo/mcnca/mcncaplan.html

2. By the time this chapter was written, the BLM had adopted use of the word "administrative" to describe the third component of recreation settings, and that is reflected in Figure 14.2 and other figures in this chapter. The authors of this chapter now believe that a more appropriate word is "operational' instead of "administrative" for reasons given in Chapter 3 of this text.
3. The word "other" was inserted in brackets to emphasize that OFM identifies satisfying experiences as one type of benefit of leisure, as explained in Part 1 of Appendix B of this report. Therefore, the words "experiences" *and* "benefits" erroneously implies that satisfying experiences are not benefits.

Chapter 15
Application of OFM on the Red Rock Ranger District of the Coconino National Forest

Marty Lee and Bill Stafford

Learning Objectives:

1. Understand how OFM has been applied on the Red Rock Ranger District of the USDA Forest Service and how it can be more fully implemented there.
2. Appreciate more fully how survey research can provide useful information about the preferences and opinions of dispersed-site visitors that are connected to recreation-related activities, settings, experiences, and other benefits and negative outcomes they wish to avoid in different types of biophysical, social, and managerial recreation settings.

Background and Purpose

This chapter discusses the integration of concepts of OFM into management planning for the Sedona Area of the Red Rock Ranger District of the Coconino National Forest. That District is located in north central Arizona, with the District Office being in Sedona. It is approximately 575,000 acres in size, receives over 4 million visitors per year, and contains the spectacular Red Rock Country of Sedona, the Oak Creek Canyon Recreation Area, the Palatki Ruin, the Red Cliffs Rock Art Area, the Honanki Ruin, the V Bar V Rock Art Site, and six designated wilderness areas. The District also has one of the largest outfitter-guide programs in the National Forest System with over 300,000 customers per year and over $15 million in gross business income. The Sedona Area covers nearly 160,000 acres that lie to the North, West, and South of the City of Sedona. It comprises much of the spectacularly beautiful red rock country, includes the Oak Creek Canyon Recreation area, the Munds Mountain and Red Rock/Secret Mountain Wilderness Areas (two of the most highly visited wilderness areas in Arizona), and archeological features of considerable spiritual significance to many people.

In 1987, the "Coconino National Forest Land Management Plan" was completed. In that plan, the Sedona Area was included in the Verde Valley Management Unit. This was a poor fit, because in the early 1990s, members of the local community and the staff of the Red Rock Ranger District recognized that the planned actions for the Verde Valley Management Unit were too broad to ensure proper management of the Sedona Area within that Unit. Specifically, the Sedona Area had many unique characteristics and management challenges that were not addressed in the standards and guidelines of the Verde Valley Management Unit, which was a rural area that requires less intensive management. Therefore, in 1995 the Red Rock Ranger District launched to develop a more suitable and separate plan for the Sedona Area, which was called "Amendment 12" (USDA Forest Service, 1998) to the Coconino National Forest Plan. Major issues that needed to be addressed in Amendment 12 included: conflict between residents and recreation users, land trades, trail systems, camping restrictions, road closures, area protection for places like Boynton Canyon (a Traditional Cultural Property to the Hope and Yavapai-Apache tribes), commercial tours (a $15 million a year recreation industry), and other recreation management and development. Goals, objectives, standards, and guidelines for the area were prepared for plants, wildlife, soil, air, water, scenery, prehistoric and historic archaeology, community, recreation, commercial uses, interpretation, and communication. Amendment 12 was approved in June of 1998.

Coincident with recognition of the need for Amendment 12 in the early 1990s was increased attention being given to the benefits of leisure along with growing concerns of park and recreation practitioners about how to managerially overtly target and then create opportunities for beneficial outcomes to be realized and unwanted outcomes to be reduced. For example (and in review from Chapter 1 of this text), when the *Benefits of Leisure* text (Driver, Brown, & Peterson) was published in 1991, it stimulated considerably more interest in the benefits of leisure and considerable demand to translate how information about the benefits of recreation could be used by public natural resource policy makers, recreation planners, and managers. Because of that interest, the Benefits of Leisure Applications Workshop was held in Estes Park, Colorado in May of 1991, and it was at that workshop where the preliminary basic concepts and purposes of OFM (then called Benefits-Based Management, or BBM) were developed and endorsed buy the 70 practitioners and leisure academics and scientists who attended. Concurrent efforts were being made to develop the *The Benefits of Parks and Recreation: A Catalogue* (1992) by The Parks and Recreation Federation of Ontario (now Parks and Recreation Ontario), which was improved and expanded considerably into the *The Benefits Catalogue* by the Canadian Parks and Recreation Association (1997).

In the early 1990s, the Recreation Research Project of the USDA Forest Service's Rocky Mountain Forest and Range Experiment Station started to fund or partially fund a series of pilot tests of BBM (OFM) in different locations in the U.S.[1] The primary objective of these BBM pilot projects was to bring scientists and land managers together to design and test the application and implementation of BBM on different types of amenity resources. Several of the areas studied are reported in Chapters 11, 12, and 14 of this text. More relevant here is the fact that one of those early pilot tests of BBM was on the Red Rock Ranger District.[2] The approach taken in the pilot projects was for managers and researchers to work together in designing research that would identify the settings, activities, and management actions that would facilitate realization of positive outcomes and minimize negative outcomes. A second important objective was for managers to assess the usefulness of a benefits-based approach to recreation resource management and, in this case, its application within the ecosystem management planning process.

In summary, OFM was evolving at the same time that the need for a separate plan for the Sedona Area was recognized and work on Amendment 12 proceeded. Within that historical context, this chapter summarizes the research and management decisions made in applying the benefits approach on the Sedona Area of the Red Rock Ranger District. To begin, the nature and purposes of the visitor study will be reviewed.

Sedona Red Rock Visitor Study

The first task of planning for Amendment 12 was to describe the existing condition. This included an inventory of resource and social conditions including the Sedona Red Rock Visitor Study conducted by Marty Lee and Chad Pierskalla of the Northern Arizona University School of Forestry. That study was the first attempt to seek out customer input at specific sites in the Sedona Area. The study targeted visitors to *dispersed sites* in the Area and was designed to obtain representative information about visitors' preferences and experiences that would be useful in planning and managing recreation opportunities in the Sedona Area.

Recreationists were contacted at 10 sampling locations throughout the Sedona Area during the fall 1995 and spring 1996 seasons. Sampling locations were selected in consultation with District recreation staff who wanted the information analyzed both for all users and for users of specific sites/areas. The survey of the visitors focused on the obtaining the following types of information:

- desired recreation experiences and other benefits
- activity participation
- recreation settings actually visited and preferences for setting attributes
- relative importance of the environmental amenities
- problems encountered
- perceptions of encounters
- number of and tolerated encounters
- demographic characteristics of the visitors
- trip characteristics (e.g., group size, residential status; frequency of past visits).

A combination on-site interviews and mail-back questionnaire was used to gather information. Visitors were contacted on-site by trained interviewers who gathered a minor amount of front-end information, including the participants' names and addresses for use in follow-up mailings, and distributed the questionnaires which were to be completed at the end of their visit and mailed back to Northern Arizona University in an enclosed postage-paid envelope. Many of the interviews were conducted by members of the Friends of the Forest, a very active volunteer stewardship group that works closely with the Forest Service on the Red Rock District.

Several reports on the results of the visitor study were prepared for the Ranger District for its use in planning for Amendment 12. They included a report on the relationships between setting characteristics and attainment of recreation-related experiences and other benefits. Another report was an annotated bibliography that documented the community benefits realized by residents living near the Coconino National Forest, including recreation and nonrecreation-related benefits.

Some of the results of the visitor survey are summarized here to show the reader examples of the types of information that can be gathered to help apply and implement OFM as well as to set the stage for the discussion in a later section of this chapter about how the information from the survey was used in development of Amendment 12. Additional information from the visitor survey from which the following summaries are drawn can be found in the Appendix to this chapter.

Desired Experiences and Other Benefits

Visitors to the Red Rock area desire restorative experiences such as getting away from crowds and the demands of life, experiencing quiet and solitude where they can rest mentally. Enjoying the spectacular natural scenery, and learning about the natural and cultural history of the Sedona Red Rock area were other experiences valued by the visitors. Many of the experiences studied in the visitor survey are the ones that formed the basis of the Recreation Opportunity Spectrum (ROS) system (USDA Forest Service, 1982) that was applied on the Coconino National Forest and thus the Sedona area. See Table 15.1 in the Appendix for more details.

Activities

Sightseeing, day hiking, driving for pleasure, walking, photography, looking at wildflowers, watching wildlife, meditation, vortexing, and viewing Indian ruins were activities that at least one-quarter of all Red Rock area dispersed visitors had participated in. See Table 15.2 in the Appendix for more details.

Setting Characteristics

Respondents to the survey were asked to indicate the characteristics of the recreation sites they actually visited as well as how much they preferred those characteristics. Those characteristics mirrored those which are used by the ROS system, which was applied during planning for Amendment 12. They included naturalness of the area, access to the recreation site, contacts with other people, amount and type of facilities, and amount of management or regulation. Descriptors of each were used to define what each characteristic meant. The results are shown in Table 15.3 of the Appendix, which show that at least 30% of the self-accessed visitors visited settings that were a largely undisturbed natural area, accessible by all vehicles, and where there was very little contact with other users, only a few primitive facilities such as trails and signs, and no or only a few primitive facilities such as trails and signs. At least 30% indicated that they preferred an undisturbed or largely undisturbed natural area with no evidence of humans, no motorized use is allowed and is accessible only by hiking cross-country, very little contact with other people (see six or fewer groups per day), few primitive facilities such as trails and signs, and only few visitor regulations and limited information facilities are present. There are some differences between preferences and areas actually visited, but as can be seen in Table 15.3 in the Appendix, the responses are reasonably consistent. In summary, dispersed visitors generally preferred settings that are largely undisturbed natural areas; accessible only by hiking or on mountain bikes; where there is little contact with other people; a few primitive or rustic facilities such as trails, tables, and signs; and simple information facilities.

Environmental Amenities

Visitors were asked to rate each of a list of more specific environmental conditions, here called environmental amenities, in terms of their relative importance to achieve their desired experiences. In order of relative importance the following amenities were rated as very important to moderately: clean fresh air; red rocks and cliffs, healthy vegetation; smells of nature, sounds of nature, wildlife, being able to see long distances, a hospitable climate; beautiful sunrises and sunsets; large trees; a clear blue sky, comfortable temperature; and well-preserved Indian rock art or ruins. See Table 15.4 in the Appendix for more details.

Demographics and Other Characteristics

Two-thirds of the dispersed visitors were visiting the area for the first time. The average group size was three people. Forty-one percent of the visitors came as couples, 44% in family or friendship groups, and 13% alone. Regarding demographics of the visitors, 91% were Caucasian, 68% were college graduates, 57 % reported annual household incomes of at least $50,000, 56% lived in a community of at least 75,000 people, 81% lived outside Arizona (81%), and the average age was 44 years.

When asked about specific environmental and social problems they might have encountered during their visit, visitors reported no serious problems at study sites. Minor problems focused on a lack of available information about the area, such as trails not being signed, too few information signs, and too few brochures and maps.

Amendment 12 and OFM

The management plan for the Coconino National Forest was similar to those developed for the other national forests as required by the National Forest Management Act of 1976 and which later incorporated concepts and principles of sustainable ecosystem management. As such, the recreation components of those plans primarily addressed recreation activities, facilitating outputs and facilitating settings (see Chapter 2) necessary for desired and satisfying recreation activity opportunities to be provided. In addition, the planning process did employ use of the ROS system, which focuses broadly on the types of recreation-related experiences that can be enjoyed in different settings on which specific "bundles of experiences" are dependent (see discussion of the "recreation experience/benefits gestalt" in Chapter 3). The ROS defines broad types of recreation settings that range from urban to primitive (see Chapter 9 of this text for more detail about application of the ROS system by the U.S. Forest Service). Therefore, although some specific beneficial outcomes were targeted overtly by management objectives in the plan for the Coconino National Forest, most of them can only be inferred. On the other hand, considerable concern was given in the plan to negative outcomes, especially to preventing or reducing adverse impacts to the ecosystem, visitors, and different components of local communities. Because OFM requires that all relevant beneficial and negative outcomes be targeted overly in management planning, the conclusion is reached that OMF was only partially applied in the overall plan for the Coconino National Forest.

More explicit attention to specific beneficial outcomes can be seen in Amendment 12, but the recreation components focuses primarily on activities, settings and facilitating outputs. This is understandable because:

1. The existing Coconino National Forest Plan was finalized in 1987. Although many papers had been written about the benefits of leisure by then, little if any attention had been given to the concepts, principles and requirements that now distinguish OFM (then BBM). Instead, those concepts have evolved and been refined since, starting ion the early 1990s and especially since the late 1990s. Although instructions on how to apply OMF appeared in handbooks for a few BBM training workshops by 1998 and much more recently on a Bureau of Land Management web site, the first instructions on how to apply and implement OFM on wildland areas written for publication in a readily available source are in Chapters 2 and 3 of this text.
2. Amendment 12 also started in 1995 and was approved in 1998, which was also before the now-existing requirements of OFM had been established.

For those reasons, this critique should not and does not evaluate the degree to which each of the very specific requirements of applying OFM (described in detail in Chapter 2 and 3) were met by Amendment 12. That was done in Chapter 14 (the McInnis Canyons National Conservation Area) and Chapter 18 (the Red Hill area), because they were the first two systematic applications of OFM on large wildland areas. Instead, this critique of OFM and Amendment 12 highlights some of the requirements of OFM to illustrate how concepts of OFM were woven into the decisions, goals, objectives, standards, and guidelines that now guide the management of the Sedona Area as directed by Amendment 12.

To review, OFM requires that planning start with deciding what outcomes will be targeted and that the facilitating outputs and facilitation settings needed to provide opportunities to realize the targeted outcomes will be determined by those outcomes. OFM also requires close collaboration with managerially relevant customer and associated provider stakeholders. The other requirements are specified in the comprehensive normative model for applying and implementing OFM. Some of those requirements will be referred to in the following discussion of OFM and Amendment 12 and are outlined below as seven phases, as well as the steps within the phases that indicate the actions that must be taken to fully apply and implement OFM (see Chapter 3 for more detail):

Phase 1: Preparatory actions.

- Ensure that supervisors endorse OFM.
- Organize the Planning Team.
- Understand responsibilities and constraints identify critical issues and concerns.
- Consider additional collaborative and public involvement efforts.

- Identify critical issues and concerns.
- Ensure that all members of the planning team understand OFM.

Phase 2: Gather, analyze, interpret, and integrate supply and demand information.

- Define market segments.
- Identify logical recreation management zones and special recreation niches.
- Access and interpret the preferences of your likely on- and off-site customers.

Phase 3: Develop the plan

- Determine which outcomes can and should be targeted in feasible alternatives within each management zone.
- Develop management objectives.
- Identify and prescribe the essential setting characteristics.
- Rank alternatives and select the preferred alternative.
- Define the essential recreation-tourism service environment.

Phase 4: Develop an implementation plan.

- Identify management actions to be implemented.
- Identify marketing actions to be implemented.
- Identify monitoring actions.
- Identify supporting administrative actions.
- Provide ample opportunities and time-frames for review of the proposed plan.

Phase 5: Implement the plan.

Phase 6: Revise the plan as needed or required by agency directives. (21)

Phase 7: Ensure that performance reports and evaluations document and recognize the production of targeted outcomes and their sustained attainment to the degree feasible.

The sections denote specific requirements of OFM that are related to Amendment 12.

Understanding OFM

An important requirement for applying OFM is that members of the planning team understand the concepts, principles, and requirements of OFM. This was largely impossible for planning for Amendment 12 simply because when it started in 1995, little to no information, other than by word of mouth, was available on how to implement OFM. Fortunately, however, the Recreation Staff Officer on the Red Rock Ranger District was quite familiar with the ROS system, had some knowledge of the fundamental concepts of OFM, and had given considerable thought to the benefits of recreation, having participated in a 1994 review of applying OFM on the McInnis Canyons National Conservation Area near Grand Junction, Colorado.[3]

Collaboration with Relevant Customer and Associated Provider Stakeholders

Since the 1969 Environmental Protection Act required pubic involvement on projects planned by federal agencies, great progress has been made in the movement toward a more collaborative style of management. Such collaboration is a critical requirement of OFM and does not only involve visitors to recreation areas, but also associate providers and resident customers in nearby communities (see Chapter 2). This requirement of OFM was met by the Amendment 12 planning as indicated by the comments of Ken Anderson, the District Ranger, in his transmittal letter of the plan. He wrote that the plan "...was crafted to include ideas of Forest Service resource professionals, community members, and a diverse citizenry." The planned management actions for most of the management areas defined for the Sedona Area have a major section entitled "Community" within which community-related management objectives, standards, and guidelines are specified. More significantly, Amendment 12 would not have been approved without the support of the local community simply because the Red Rock Ranger District is located in an area within which many of the residents are environmentally sensitive and proactive, as evidenced by the active "Friends of the Coconino" and other concerned groups. Close cooperation with the associated providers such as the commercial jeep tour operators, Keep Sedona Beautiful, Trails Access Resource Coalition, Sedona Noise Abatement Committee, and the City of Sedona Parks and Recreation Commission is also reflected in the plan.

Definition of Logical RMZs

OFM requires that logical RMZs be defined to accommodate specific market niches/segments to meet the preferences of probable visitors. The fact that Amendment 12 was developed separately for the Sedona Area instead of letting it remain under the overly broad managerial guidelines in the Coconino National Forest Plan for the Verde Valley Management Unit attests to concerns about meshing managerial activities with public sentiments and preferences. More specifically, the plan identifies 12 distinct management areas within the larger Sedona Area, and several of them were created in addition to what was in the original forest plan for that area. In this multiple-use and sustained ecosystem management plan, none of those 12 management areas were created to manage just for recreational uses and values. However, such uses and values were significantly important in several units such as the Oak Creek Canyon and Developed Sites management areas. Information from the visitor survey on desired benefits coupled with preferred activities, physical, social, and managerial setting conditions were used by Forest Service managers to help them define the management area boundaries, objectives, and standards for specific dispersed recreation areas.

Obtain Information on Customer Preferences and Opinions

In Chapter 3, strong emphasis was placed on the requirement of OFM to obtain reliable information on the customers' preferences, opinions, and concerns. The description of those required actions described in Phase 3 of the model for applying and implementing OFM, made it clear that that information was needed not only for the on-site visitors, but also for relevant off-site customers, especially residents of local communities. The description of the visitor survey and interpretations of its results in this chapter, including the appendix, show that serious attention was given to the preferences, opinions, and concerns of the visitors to the Sedona Area as a part of planning for Amendment 12. It also seems evident that reasonable attention was also given to the preferences, opinions, and concerns of residents of the local communities. In addition, the considerable involvement of the public in the planning process, including serious public review of the proposed plan, also attests to the fulfillment of these requirements.

Overtly Targeted Outcomes

Probably the most fundamental requirement of OFM is that specific outcomes be overtly targeted managerially in management objectives and prescribed setting conditions be defined and maintained to assure those outcomes can be attained. Many examples of such can be found in Amendment 12. A few of such are shown below with specific outcomes highlighted in bold type:

- Under Recreation Goals for Wilderness Management on page 108-1 is found "Feature opportunities for *restorative experiences and benefits*."
- In "Vision and Guiding Principles" page 206-7, these words are found "With its intriguing human history and remarkable natural environment rich with plants and wildlife, Red Rock country offers individuals and families the gifts of *discovery, inspiration, and solitude*. When wandering the Sedona/Oak Creek ecosystem, we are free to imagine, to explore and reconnect with the land. Through this landscape we can experience a *rebirth of awe and a renewal of spirit*."
- Under the "Objective" of the section on "Prehistoric and Historic Archaeology" can be found. "Allow for a *'sense of discovery'* at cultural interpretive sites (page 206-17) and an objective under "Community" is "Protect community values by *reducing the fire hazard and risk*" (page 206-19). Under "Recreation--Goals" can be found "Emphasize opportunities for individuals, families, or small groups...for *experiencing solitude, scenic beauty, and natural quiet*."
- The permitting and authorization of numerous commercial outfitter/guide tour permits provide *economic benefits* to local communities.
- Too many examples of words to quote here can be found in the numerous management objectives, goals, guidelines and/or standards that explicitly mandate actions to *protect and/or improve the basic resources,* each of which denote overtly targeted negative outcomes.

Monitoring and Marketing Plans

OFM calls for both monitoring and marketing plans. No specific mention of a monitoring plan is mentioned in Amendment 12, but the standards and guidelines stated for each use and value identified for each of the

12 management areas indicate that systematic and comprehensive monitoring is well planned for. Similarly, no mention is made of a separate marketing plan, but the Ranger District has been vigilant in providing information about the recreation opportunities on that District. Examples include the "Red Rock Country Vicinity Map" and the "Red Rock" supplement to "Recreation on Your National Forest."

Recommendations

Several recommendations for future consideration emerged from this critique of Amendment 12 and OFM. First, two significance benefits of managing the recreation resources and services of the Sedona Area were identified that were not considered in the Amendment 12 planning effort. They are:

- Sense of challenge. The sense of challenge should have been considered in the planning process, particularly as it relates to trails. In Amendment 12 decisions were made about the general location of new trails and trailheads, as well as which roads would be closed. To accommodate their stronger desire for challenge, some trail and off-road vehicle enthusiasts have continued to use routes that are not on the approved Forest Service trail system. Mountain bikers, ATV groups, and even some equestrians and hikers have voiced concerns to the District Ranger, Recreation Staff, and other employees that the Forest Service does not provide enough challenging trails and ATV roads. They blame the agency for closing many advanced skill level "social trails" and system and nonsystem roads that they want left open. They feel that managers are providing mostly one type of trail all with the same grade and width with few obstacles as well as roads for ATVs without a variety of levels of difficulty. They claim that is why the "illegal" trails and hill climbs are being found at many places. Managers are trying to accommodate these preferences by working more closely with trail and 4x4 groups to begin preparing a "Master Trail Plan" which will include challenges at all levels.
- Physical fitness. On the extreme side of the physical fitness benefit of improved health scale lies competitive training for all types of athletes engaged in mountain biking, trail running, and advanced hiking. The Red Rock District should have looked into providing more benefits for those desiring more physically challenging and longer trails. Those enthusiasts want more such trails that are not widely marketed on the maps given to the public at large. Although admittedly controversial, those customers want those trails to be lightly used so they can train without running into a lot of people. They argue that when trail locations are published on maps and opportunities do not exist to meet their preferences, they develop new trails to experience the benefits they desire.

Two final suggestions are offered for increasing awareness of OFM and its practical application in working with recreationists and community residents:

- Train field-going employees and NEPA planning personnel in the concept of BBM. A short training session about the benefits of recreation and about OFM would be useful for a variety of reasons. Field patrol personnel (e.g., law enforcement and recreation operations managers) and other District staff can use the concept of benefits to avoid conflicts when dealing with the public. An understanding of benefits would also increase the ability of the employees to find common ground with recreationists. It would enhance meaningful conversation with the public and also increase compliance with rules and regulations. For instance, we often look at recreation users in terms of the activities in which they engage such as "those mountain bikers," "those equestrians," or "those ATV folks," but in actuality "those" people are often seeking the same benefits. Defining what benefits different customers desire is a critical requirement of OFM, because OFM cannot be applied properly without that knowledge.
- Train community members and volunteers about OFM as a means of increasing commitment to and personal investment in public lands and communities. There seems to be very slow progress in getting communities and local government to invest volunteer hours and funds to help land management agencies offer opportunities to realize recreation-related benefits on public lands. The economic, public health, social well-being, and other benefits are substantial, but managers have not effectively enough articulated their need for volunteers. As emphasized in Chapter 5 of this text, there is a great need for recreation professionals to go to communities and

describe the many social benefits that accrue from outdoor recreation, including improved local economic growth and stability, physical and mental health, sense of community, enhanced environmental ethics and commitments to sustainable ecosystem management, and family cohesiveness to name only a few (see Chapter 1 for more detail about the benefits of recreation). Describing the benefits that accrue to individuals, families, communities, and the environment from management of the Red Rock area can serve as a unifying theme to encourage partnerships among land management agencies, volunteers, communities, and other recreation and tourism providers.

Conclusion

Although Amendment 12 cannot be said to have adopted all the requirements of OFM, many targeted outcomes have helped guide preparation of that plan. In addition, during the implementation of that plan, projects have been completed and many more are planned on the Sedona Area to facilitate many beneficial outcomes and reduce the magnitudes of unwanted outcomes on the visitors, the local communities, and the ecosystems involved.

The adoption of OFM is an incremental process. What was learned in planning for Amendment 12 can be built on to further advance the use of OFM by the Red Rock Ranger District and the Coconino National Forest.

Literature Cited

Canadian Parks/Recreation Association. (1997). *The benefits catalogue*. Gloucester, Ontario, Canada.

Driver, B., Brown, P., & Peterson, G. (Eds.). (1991). *Benefits of leisure*. State College, PA: Venture Publishing, Inc.

Parks and Recreation Federation of Ontario and the Ontario Ministry of Tourism and Recreation, 1992. *A catalogue of the benefits of parks and recreation*. Distribution by Canadian Parks/Recreation Association. Gloucester, Ontario.

USDA Forest Service. (1982). *ROS users guide*. Washington, D.C.

USDA Forest Service. (1987). *Coconino National Forest plan*. Washington, D.C.

Results from the Dispersed Visitor Survey

Of the 1,570 questionnaires distributed to dispersed visitors over the fall and spring sampling periods, 1,107 were returned (70%). Analysis was performed using SPSS-PC statistical software. Factor analysis was performed on the list of 35 experience and benefit items to create six benefit and experience domains. Analysis was performed using SPSS-PC statistical software.

Footnotes

1. That research was directed by the editor of this text.
2. Additional funding for the visitor survey was provided by the Southwest Region of the U.S. Forest Service.
3. He is also the coauthor of this chapter.

Appendix to Chapter 15

Theme/specific experiences comprising them	Mean*	s.d.
Spiritual Wellness	5.7	0.8
Feel stronger spiritually	5.6	
Be more creative	5.4	
Gain a sense of peace and serenity	6.1	
Think about my life and who I am	5.5	
Open up my heart and focus inward	5.4	
Experience a oneness with God, nature, and the cosmos	5.6	
Experience positive moods or emotions	6.0	
Personal Stimulation and Growth	5.7	0.9
Feel healthier	6.1	
Improve my cardiovascular condition	5.7	
Improve my skills and abilities	5.2	
Feel exhilarated	6.1	
Feel more self-confident	5.4	
Feel more independent	5.3	
Improve my overall sense of wellness	5.8	
Reduce feelings of tension and stress	6.1	
Reduce feelings of depression or anxiety	5.5	
Experience a sense of adventure	6.1	
Restorative Experiences	6.3	0.8
Get away from crowds	6.2	
Experience quiet	6.5	
Get away from the usual demands of life	6.6	
Experience solitude	5.9	
Rest mentally	6.3	
Be in a wilderness area	6.4	
Learning	5.8	1.0
Learn more about the natural history of the area	5.8	
Learn more about the cultural history of the area	5.6	
Increase my knowledge of the Native people who once lived in this area	5.6	
Learn more about nature	5.9	
Increase my understanding and awareness of the natural environment	6.1	
Strengthen Social Bonds	5.6	1.1
Spend time with my family and/or friends	6.1	
Bring my family closer together	5.2	
Feel closer to my friends	5.5	
Enjoying the Physical/Social Environment	6.0	0.8
Experience a nicer temperature	5.6	
Enjoy the natural scenery	6.9	
Be with people who share similar values	5.5	

*Desirability scale: 1=very undesirable, 2=moderately undesirable, 3=somewhat undesirable, 4=neither or not applicable, 5=somewhat desirable, 6=moderately desirable, 7=very desirable

Table 15.1 Desirability of Selected Experiential Themes and Specific Experiences

Activity	Percent
Sightseeing	84.7
Hiking (day use)	63.2
Driving for pleasure	48.9
Walking	48.1
Photography	45.2
Looking at wildflowers	33.8
Watching wildlife	33.2
Meditation	30.3
Vortexing	29.2
Viewing Indian ruins	28.1
Viewing Indian rock art	17.6
Picnicking	16.3
Nature study	14.8
Four wheel drive/All-terrain vehicle (ATV) driving	13.6
Birding	12.5
Reading for pleasure	11.9
Other miscellaneous activities	10.3
Camping near vehicle	7.3
Taking a guided tour	7.0
Mountain biking	6.9
Writing for pleasure	5.9
Swimming	4.8
Backpack camping	4.3
Rock collecting/prospecting	4.2
Partying	3.9
Sunbathing/beach activities	3.8
Wading	2.8
Jogging	2.3
Horseback riding	1.8
Road biking	1.4

Table 15.2 Percentage of Visitor Participation in Particular Activities

Setting characteristic and descriptors	Visited (percent)	Preferred (percent)
Naturalness of the Area		
An undisturbed natural area with no evidence of humans	5.8	33.7
A largely undisturbed natural area	48.3	56.5
An area that is somewhat modified but appears natural	29.4	8.1
A substantially modified area	11.9	1.6
An area where roads, buildings, and powerlines clearly dominate the landscape	4.6	0.1
Access to the Recreation Site		
No motorized use is allowed, accessible only by hiking cross-country	22.7	35.2
Accessible only by nonmotorized trails, mountain bikes, on foot	19.7	28.1
Accessible on motorized trails and primitive roads	22.7	18.4
Accessible by all vehicles	35.0	18.4
Contact with Other People		
Very little contact with other people (see 6 or fewer groups per day)	35.2	62.8
Little contact with other people (see 6-15 groups per day)	26.0	25.9
Moderate contact with other people (15+ groups per day, fewer away from roads/developed areas)	23.2	10.1
High degree of contact with other people (30+ groups per day, fewer away from roads/developed areas)	11.2	0.7
In constant contact with other people	4.4	0.5
Amount and Type of Facilities		
No facilities	20.9	18.1
A few primitive facilities such as trails and signs	59.6	53.8
A few rustic facilities provided (e.g., tables and pit toilets)	11.4	22.0
Moderate number of facilities (e.g., picnic tables, fire grates, parking)	6.3	4.6
Numerous facilities (e.g., surfaced trails, developed campground)	1.8	1.5
Amount of Management or Regulation		
No on-site visitor regulation or information facilities	39.6	27.7
A few visitor regulations, limited information facilities present	45.5	45.9
On-site regulations and controls are noticeable, simple information facilities are present	12.4	22.2
On-site regulations and controls are numerous, more complex information facilities are present	1.6	3.1
On-site regulations and controls are obvious and numerous with sophisticated information exhibits present	0.8	1.0

Table 15.3 Percentages of Visitors Actually Visiting and Preferring Specific Setting Characteristics

Site characteristic	Mean*	s.d.
Clean, fresh air	6.8	0.7
Red rocks and cliffs	6.5	0.9
Healthy vegetation	6.4	1.0
Smells of nature	6.4	1.0
Sounds of nature	6.3	1.0
Wildlife	6.2	1.0
Being able to see a long distance	6.1	1.2
A hospitable climate	6.1	1.1
A clear blue sky	6.0	1.4
A beautiful sunrise or sunset	5.9	1.3
Comfortable temperature	5.9	1.2
Large trees	5.8	1.3
Well-preserved Indian rock art or ruins	5.7	1.5
A landscape with scattered trees/open spaces	5.5	1.4
A clear and dark night sky	5.4	1.5
Well-signed trails	5.2	1.7
A stream, pond, or lake nearby	5.2	1.5
Foot trails not heavily trampled	5.2	1.4
Low humidity	5.1	1.6
Still air	5.1	1.5
Helpful and attractive information signs	5.0	1.7
A spiritual site	4.7	2.0
A traditional or inspirational meditation site	4.5	2.0
A vortex	4.4	2.0
A sense of being able to recreate "in my backyard"	4.3	1.7
A medicine wheel	3.9	1.7
Dead trees	3.7	1.7

*Importance scale: 1=very unimportant, 2=moderately unimportant, 3=somewhat unimportant, 4=neither or not applicable, 5=somewhat important, 6=moderately important, 7=very important

Table 15.4 Importance of Environmental Amenities

Chapter 16
Targeting Visitor Benefits for Minnesota State Parks

Dorothy H. Anderson

Learning Objectives:

1. Understand how Minnesota State Parks has used the Outcomes-Focused Management paradigm to plan and manage state parks.
2. Provide insights into how state park plans have been written to target and implement Outcomes-Focused Management for visitor attainment of recreation benefits.

Purpose of This Chapter

The purpose of this chapter is to briefly describe efforts at six Minnesota state parks to identify key onsite beneficial experience opportunities provided across the parks, within a park, and attained by visitors using the parks. The six parks represent the diversity of Minnesota landscapes represented in the state park system. The data gathered was a key piece of the Minnesota Department of Natural Resources Division of Parks and Recreation's (MNDNR) strategy to develop and implement an outcomes-focused approach to recreation resource management. Although each Minnesota state park is unique, they share the general setting characteristic of being located in natural or near natural environments and are managed to preserve the natural, scenic, and cultural resources of the state while providing appropriate recreational and educational opportunities for visitors. As such, many parks offer similar types of visitor experiences and other benefit opportunities. But, the types of recreation opportunities offered by different parks are not always the same nor are the specific suite of beneficial opportunities provided among the different management zones the same within an individual park. Targeting and providing beneficial opportunities for visitors demands knowledge of what is currently provided and where it is provided within a park setting. Study data reported in this chapter are intended to show similarities in benefits provided across parks and within park settings. They are also intended to demonstrate differences in the suite of beneficial opportunities that could be provided and managed across parks and within different park zones. This chapter also provides some insight into how the MNDNR attempted to use the study data to implement its strategic plan for an outcomes-focused approach to recreation resource management.

Spurred by state budget shortfalls, a growing desire to increase the visitor service focus of management, and an effort to use visitor research to guide management planning and actions, the MNDNR in 1992 entered into a cooperative agreement with the Recreation Research Project (RRP) of the USDA Forest Service's Rocky Mountain Forest and Range Research Station and the University of Minnesota, Department of Forest Resources (UMN) to conduct research on the beneficial outcomes desired and attained by visitors to six Minnesota state parks. They were Forestville/Mystery Cave, George Crosby Manitou, Interstate, Itasca, St. Croix, and Tettegouche State Parks. They represent the state's various biomes (northern conifer forests to northern hardwoods), a range of sizes (298 acres at Interstate State Park to 34,000 acres at St. Croix State Park), number of visitors (17,000 per year at George Crosby Manitou to about 500,000 per year at Itasca) and recreational opportunities (remote hiking and backpacking to rental cabins and an in-park restaurant). Research results were used to varying degrees to guide subsequent management and planning activities in the six parks. This chapter describes this research project and the application of the results. An emphasis is placed on Itasca and Tettegouche state parks because application of the research results to park planning and management activities in these two parks have been the most extensive.

Minnesota State Park System

The Minnesota state park system currently consists of 66 state parks, six state recreation areas, and eight highway waysides located throughout the state to serve its residents and visitors. Dating back to the late 1800s, the Minnesota state park system is one of the oldest state park systems in the United States. The system has a reputation for providing quality recreational opportunities in some of the Upper Midwest's most picturesque locations. As the end of the twentieth century approached, management within the system undertook several efforts to position the system to serve its clientele into the twenty-first century. At the same time, the RRP was conducting several research projects across the country to assess important and attained beneficial visitor outcomes on public lands including national forests and USDI Bureau of Land Management areas. MNDNR in partnership with the UMN sought participation in those pilot tests.

Participation in the pilot tests was sought because MNDNR management staff expressed growing interest in implementing an OFM approach in its state park system. State park managers generally believe that they offer much to visitors, communities, local economies, and the environment. They regularly witness families picnicking together, individuals overcoming physically challenging trails, people marveling at wildlife, and groups enjoying the serenity of a sunrise over a lake. These observations reinforced the MNDNR managers' beliefs that the satisfying experiences gained from participation in outdoor recreation activities are important to visitors and lead to benefits for visitors, their communities and the environment. MNDNR wanted to recognize these benefits and target benefits it could provide through state park management activities.

At the time, state park managers also were faced with increasing pressure to support funding requests for recreation programs while budgets for other public services were being reduced. In addition, increased public involvement in park planning processes was pushing state park staff to produce more accurate visitor data and information to support the recommendations contained in state park management plans. Implementation of the OFM framework (then called BBM) was viewed by MNDNR management staff as a sound strategy to better understand visitors, support budget requests, guide planning efforts, and provide a more informed perspective on management activities in individual parks.

The Minnesota Division of Parks and Recreation was selected by the RRP to participate in the pilot tests for a variety of reasons. Paramount was a commitment from the state park director and his staff to go beyond basic data collection for summary statistics and attempt to use research results to guide planning and management decisions at the central office level and in individual parks. The UMN was a willing partner in the pilot tests and the Minnesota state park system made funding available to match grant assistance received from the RRP. Minnesota state parks was also the only state park system involved in the pilot tests at the time and the RRP was eager to expand its pilot test efforts beyond federally managed lands to state protected areas such as state parks.

Minnesota State Park Visitor Study

Choosing Specific Parks

The leader of the RRP contracted with the author of this chapter at the UMN to conduct visitor research assessing the experiences and other benefits associated with participation in recreational activities within Minnesota state parks. To fulfill that contract, she worked cooperatively with MNDNR staff to select state parks for inclusion in the study. The six state parks necessary were selected because they represented the diversity found in Minnesota's state park system in terms of the range of recreation opportunities they provide, their size, geographic location in the state, and the variety of settings found within the state park system. Even though they represented the diversity of Minnesota state parks, all six of the parks chosen contain many of the same physical setting characteristics that support core recreational activity opportunities related to camping, hiking, water based activities, and picnicking. The selection of the specific parks was also influenced by the individual park manager's willingness to participate in the study and work toward application of study results. Selection of a variety of state parks representing the diversity of the state park system was also important to foster statewide support for the pilot effort among upper level management and state park managers who were not a part of the pilot project.

For all six parks, visitor use data were collected, analyzed, and presented to central and regional park management teams, state park managers, their staff, and the citizen advisory committee that works with each park.

Survey Instruments

Study data were collected with an on-site and a mail-back survey. Both the on-site and mail-back surveys were based on questionnaires used by the RRP in similar research conducted in other parts of the United States. Survey items from the other pilot tests were adapted to meet the particular settings, recreational opportunities, and management issues found in the six Minnesota state parks. Additionally, the UMN sought input for the survey design from the six park managers and their staffs. Managers offered suggestions on the specific activities, experiences and benefits, settings, conflicts, problems, and management actions likely to occur in each of the parks. Although the basic questions were the same for all six parks, separate questionnaires were prepared for each park to reflect specific differences among the parks. For example, viewing the headwaters of the Mississippi River is an activity that can only be done at Itasca State Park. Therefore, this activity only appeared as a possible activity on the Itasca State Park questionnaire. Similarly, the on-site questionnaires were tailored to each park to accommodate the fact that the number of survey zones was not the same in all six parks.

The on-site instrument was a short two-page questionnaire used to collect basic demographic profiles, trip profile, home address information, and to identify visitor interest in participating in a longer survey to gather additional data about their use, activities, and experiences in the park. The mail-back questionnaire was used to collect data across a variety of variables including visitor demographic profiles, trip profiles, visitor activities, important and experiences and benefits attained, preferred setting characteristics, problems and conflicts encountered by visitors, preferred management actions to resolve problems, importance and rating of state park services provided, and level of visitor satisfaction with services provided.

Conducting the Survey

Trained interviewers were used to conduct the on-site interviews and distribute the mail-back survey. A training/instruction manual was prepared and given to each interviewer. The manual included step-by-step procedures for implementation of the on-site survey, sample survey forms, the survey schedule, and proper public relations techniques. In addition, a training session was conducted to familiarize interviewers with the training manual and the on-site survey procedures. Additional assistance was made available to interviewers throughout the survey period by the UMN and MNDNR staff associated with the study.

A survey schedule spanning the entire survey period from Memorial Day weekend to Labor Day weekend (May 29, 1993 - September 6, 1993) was devised for each park prior to administration of the on-site questionnaire. With the exception of George Crosby Manitou Park, each park was divided into several recreation opportunity zones. The survey schedule identified the number of on-site questionnaires to be administered for each zone on each scheduled survey day. This procedure allowed particular survey zones to be targeted each day and ensured that each zone would have adequate data so that comparisons could be made within and across zones.

The on-site questionnaire was used to make the initial contact with park visitors and to distribute the mail-back questionnaire. The on-site survey was administered to visitors as they ended their visit and were leaving the park. If the visitor was leaving, had been recreating in the park, and was willing to participate in the survey, the interviewer showed the visitor a copy of the park map with recreation zones delineated on it and asked the visitor to indicate the zone where they had spent most of their time. The interviewer noted the zone on the on-site survey. If the visitor had spent the greatest amount of time in that day's target zone, the interviewer continued with the remaining on-site questions. If the visitor had spent the greatest amount of their time in a zone other than that day's target zone, they were thanked for their time and allowed to exit the park.

Once all other on-site questions were completed, respondents were asked if they would be willing to complete and return a mail-back questionnaire. Respondents who agreed to the longer survey were asked to provide a name and mailing address for follow-ups. After the respondent's mailing information was taken, the interviewer handed the visitor the longer mail-back survey along with a postage paid envelope addressed to the research team. The visitor was asked to complete and mail the survey in the envelope provided within two to four weeks of the date it was given to them. For each park, less than one percent of visitors who completed the on-site survey refused the longer mail-back questionnaire.

In keeping with Dillman's (2000) total design method, reminder post cards were mailed approximately two weeks after the on-site interview to respondents who had not returned the mail-back questionnaire. A reminder letter and a second mail-back survey were mailed to respondents who had not returned the mail-back approximately four weeks after the on-site interview. Response rates across the study parks ranged from 55 to 66 percent (Table 16.1).

State Park	On-site contacts	Surveys distributed on-site	Surveys completed and returned	
	Number	Number	Number	Percent
George Crosby Manitou	357	340	208	62
Tettegouche	815	796	508	64
St. Croix	655	643	364	57
Itasca	1088	1028	665	65
Interstate	707	625	343	55
Forestville / Mystery Cave	882	842	558	66

Table 16.1

Data Analysis

Descriptive statistics were generated for all data collected through the on-site and mail-back questionnaires. Frequencies and percentages of respondents were calculated for each variable. With the exception of the demographic, trip profile, and activities variables, mean scores and standard deviations were calculated for each variable. In addition, rank ordering was performed for each variable except the demographic, trip profile, and activities variables. OFM relies on the ability to target specific benefit opportunities in settings that are most likely to provide those opportunities. Data were analyzed by zone within a park and across all zones within a park. Analysis by survey zone was done in an effort to determine if zones provided the same or unique benefit opportunities and to determine if visitor attainment of benefits differed by zone.

General Findings

Brief descriptions of findings related to visitor activities, park setting, important experiences, and benefits attained for each park and each zone within a park will now be summarized.

George Crosby Manitou State Park

This park is a wilderness, hike-in backpack only park and is managed as one zone for recreational opportunities. It is located along Minnesota's north shore and is approximately 3,330 acres in size. The park is known for the large amount of old growth northern hardwoods and upland northern white cedar forests. It is a natural setting managed to provide opportunities for solitude. Respondents expressed a desire for opportunities to enjoy the natural scenery, enjoy the smells and sounds of nature, and get away from crowds. They preferred a setting accessible only by designated nonmotorized trails in a largely undisturbed natural area at least a mile from paved roads or areas with motorized vehicles. They expressed a desire that the area be managed so that little contact would occur with other people on trails or near their campsite. Finally, respondents want this park to be managed with rustic facilities that will protect the environment and provide for visitor safety. Respondents indicated they were at least moderately able to attain on-site benefits from the experiences they most desired. According to the respondents, better trail maintenance and information about the cultural resources and history of the park would result in greater benefit attainment.

Tettegouche State Park

This park is located along Minnesota's north shore and is near the town of Silver Bay. The park is 9,346 acres in size and dominated by rolling to steep bedrock outcroppings. Over 400,000 people visit the park annually. Like George Crosby Manitou State Park, which lies just to the north of it, Tettegouche State Park is largely forested with northern hardwoods and upland northern white cedar trees. The park is managed as two distinct zones for recreational purposes.

Zone 1 is the park's major day use and day use hiking area. It includes the 60 foot High Falls area, the mouth of the Baptism River, Palisade Head (the premier rock climbing area along Lake Superior and in the Midwest) and Shovel Point on the Lake Superior shore. Motorized use is allowed in this zone on roads. Respondents expressed a desire for opportunities to enjoy the natural scenery, enjoy the smells and sounds of nature, be with members of their own group, and get away from the usual demands of life. Overall respondents were "somewhat able" to realize these desired beneficial experiences. Although this zone allows motorized use, most of the motorized use in this zone is by visitors in cars going to and from the park office to park attractions in Zone 1. Motor use does not occur on trails. Respondents noted a preference for a setting that is accessible only by nonmotorized vehicles on designated trails in a largely undisturbed area, more than a mile from paved roads with motor use, and an area that is characterized by very little contact with other people.

Problems people reported in this zone included people being too noisy, campgrounds too full, difficulty making camping reservations, and people riding ATVs on the trails. To improve benefit attainment, the park could provide better information to visitors about the impact of visitor-caused noise on visitor experiences. Since ATV use is not allowed in this zone, enforcement of existing rules and regulations concerning motorized use on trails should improve experiences and attainment of benefits, too. Enlarging the campground to accommodate more campers, developing other campground facilities within the park or outside the park with private partners, and improving the campground reservation system would also improve benefit attainment.

Zone 2 is the park's interior backcountry area where hiking and backpacking are the predominant uses. The Superior Hiking Trail runs through this area of the park and continues on outside of the park. In addition, numerous miles of backcountry hiking trails contained wholly within the park are found in this zone. Backcountry campsites and the historic Tettegouche logging camp are also found here. The respondents' most highly desired experiences in this zone included opportunities to enjoy the natural scenery, enjoy the smells and sounds of nature, get away from the usual demands of life, be with members of their own group, enjoy a different experience than what they have at home, keep or get physically fit, feel healthier, rest mentally, experience positive moods and emotions, and reduce or release built-up tension. Respondents reported they were not at all to somewhat able to attain these experiences. These respondents preferred a setting that is accessible only by nonmotorized vehicles using designated trails, in a largely undisturbed natural area at least a mile away form paved roads and motor use and that is characterized by very little contact with other people on trails or at their campsite.

Many respondents reported problems with campsites being full, not enough screening between campsites, campsites too close together, eroded trails, trails not adequately signed, trails inadequately maintained, and inadequate information on maps depicting park facilities. Better design and maintenance of park campsites and trails in this zone would most likely result in greater attainment of benefits this zone provides. A campsite reservation system might also help to alleviate visitor problems in this zone.

St. Croix State Park

This park is the largest Minnesota state park with just slightly more than 34,000 acres. About 154,000 visitors come to this park annually. The St. Croix National Scenic Riverway (a federally protected river under the Wild and Scenic Rivers Act) forms the park's eastern boundary and its western boundary is formed by the Kettle River, which is protected under Minnesota's Wild and Scenic Rivers Act. The park is known for its unique jack pine barrens. For recreational purposes, the park is managed as three zones.

Zone 1 is the park's low use zone. Respondents who primarily used this zone expressed a desire for experience opportunities to enjoy the natural scenery, get away from the usual demands of life, be with members of their own group, enjoy the smells and sounds of nature, enjoy a different experience that what they have at home, get away from crowds, release or reduce built-up tension, experience solitude, and rest mentally. They reported an ability to somewhat benefit from the first four experiences noted while recreating in this zone, but they reported little benefit attainment related to the other experiences they desired in this zone. They preferred a setting accessible only by nonmotorized vehicles using designated trails in a largely undisturbed natural area at least a mile from paved roads and motor use, and characterized by very little contact with other people on trails.

Although the zone was characterized as low use, it covers more park area than the other two zones and contains the majority of trails and trail mileage within the park and park attractions. No restrictions exist on the number of people at one time allowed in the zone or on a specific trail. Visitors congregate at park attractions which may account for low attainment of some benefits. Regulating the number of people permitted on a specific trail at a particular time or better informing visitors of the number of people they can expect to encounter on trails and at park attractions could result in more realistic visitor expectations about park experience opportunities and other desired benefits. Respondents also reported litter and trash left by others was a minor problem in this zone. More frequent pickups of heavily used trash containers might help this problem and result in greater benefit attainment. More frequent reminders to visitors to leave campsites clean, carry out any trash they bring in, and so forth might also help alleviate this problem and result in greater benefit attainment.

Zone 2 is a high use area of the park primarily managed for horseback riding and camping. Respondents in this zone expressed desires to enjoy the natural scenery, get away from the usual demands of life, bring their family closer together, enjoy smells and sounds of nature, and be with members of their own group. They reported they were somewhat able to attain these experiences. They preferred this area be accessible by motor vehicles, be somewhat modified, near improved roads, and characterized by very little contact with other people at campsites.

Problems they saw that impacted their ability to attain benefits included making or getting reservations to camp in the area and deteriorated campsite facilities. Improving the reservation system for the horse camp and maintaining or improving the campground in this zone could result in better benefit attainment by visitors using the area.

Zone 3 is a large group camp area. Respondents who spent most of their time in this area said the most important experiences they desired were to enjoy the natural scenery, get away from the usual demands of life, be with members of their own group, enjoy the smells and sounds of nature, rest mentally, bring their family closer together, and be more attentive to their family's needs. They reported being somewhat to moderately able to attain these experiences with the exception of benefits related to their families. They preferred a setting accessible by motor vehicles in a somewhat modified area that is near or on improved roads and is characterized by very little contact with other people.

Problems they reported included poorly maintained toilet facilities and inadequate information about park facilities on park maps. Addressing these problems may or may not result in greater benefit attainment related to family bonding experiences and benefits.

Itasca State Park

This park is located in northwestern and is the flagship park of the state park system. It is approximately 30,000 acre in size and experiences more than 500,000 visitors annually. It is Minnesota's most heavily visited state park and is the only Minnesota state park to attract large numbers of national and international visitors. The headwaters of the Mississippi River are found within the park's boundaries, which is the primary reason for the park's international significance. The park is dominated by rolling hills with shallow valleys and pine forests. Besides being home to the headwaters of the Mississippi River, the park consists of old growth conifer and hardwood forests, over 100 fresh water lakes, a designated scientific and natural area, a national natural landmark, and several heritage species. Cultural features in the park include a 7,000 year old bison kill site, Woodland Indian burial mounds, multiple European exploration and pioneer settlement sites, the Douglas Lodge, and several national historic register sites. Most visitors come to the park to view the headwaters, hike, camp, drive the wilderness loop, and view the 200 year old stands of red pine.

Recreation management at Itasca occurs in four distinct zones. In our study, though, data were only analyzed for three of the zones. Zone 2 is the backcountry area of the park. In a normal year it experiences high use. In 1993, the year data were collected for this study, the summer was abnormally wet. High amounts of rainfall resulted in high numbers of mosquitoes, which reduced the number of visitors in the park's backcountry. Virtually no use was recorded in this area during the 1993 summer use period.

Zone 1 includes the park's major motorized use zone. It includes the park's major campgrounds and the "wilderness" drive motor route. Respondents report their most desired experiences in this zone include enjoying the natural scenery, getting away from the usual demands of life, enjoying the smells and sounds of nature, being with members of their own group, and bringing their family closer together. They report they are somewhat to moderately able to attain these experiences while recreating in this zone. Their preferred setting in this park is one that is accessible by motorized vehicles on designated roads in a largely undisturbed natural area with a number of onsite management regulation, controls, and information.

Problems they encountered in the zone were campgrounds that were too full. Benefit attainment might be increased with better campground management, additional campsites, or additional campgrounds.

Zone 3 is the Douglas Lodge area of the park. Respondents noted two important experiences they desired in this zone: enjoy the natural scenery of the area and enjoy the smells and sounds of nature. They reported they were somewhat able to attain these experiences while in this zone. The only problems they reported were difficulties getting reservations to stay at the Lodge, maintenance of some of the Lodge's facilities, and/or the cabins in the area. Repairing Lodge facilities may indirectly add to visitors' overall benefit attainment in this zone.

Zone 4 is the area that contains the headwaters of the Mississippi River. Respondents most desired experiences in this zone were to enjoy the natural scenery, get away from the usual demands of life, be with members of their own group, learn more about the natural history of the area, observe other people in the area, do something creative (i.e., sketch, paint, or take photographs), and bring their family closer together. Most respondents were able to attain these experience opportunities. None of the respondents reported problems in this zone.

Interstate State Park

This park is one of the smallest in the system and consists of 298 acres. Despite its size it has over 370,000 visitors annually. Its proximity to Minneapolis-St. Paul and its unique geology are major factors in its high visitation rate. The park is split into two different sections and both sections are bisected by a major state highway. Two distinct recreation management zones characterize it.

Zone 1 contains the campground, boat launch, and trail to Curtain Falls. Respondents who spent most of their time in this zone expressed a desire to enjoy the natural scenery, get away from the usual demands of life, enjoy the smells and sounds of nature, be with members of their own group, rest mentally, bring their family closer together, enjoy different experiences than they have at home, and reduce or release built-up tension. They prefer to have these experiences in a setting that is accessible by motor vehicles on designated roads in a largely undisturbed natural area that is characterized by few contacts with other people at their campsite. For the most part, respondents were somewhat to moderately able to attain these experiences in this zone.

Problems experienced in this zone included difficulty getting a reservation to camp, full campgrounds, campsites too close together, and not enough screening between campsites. Better campground maintenance and better screening between existing campsites would improve respondents benefit attainment. A redesign of this campground or an additional campground in the area might also improve benefit attainment.

Zone 2 is the main attraction of this park. This zone contains the Dalles of the St. Croix National Scenic Riverway, unique basalt rock formations, large cliffs, and hundreds of potholes carved into the rock from the last glaciers. Scenic overlooks and the pothole trail are the key recreational draws of this zone. Desired experiences in this zone included enjoying the natural scenery, getting away from the usual demands of life, enjoying the smells and sounds of nature, learning more about nature, learning more about the natural history of the area, keeping and getting physically fit, and experiencing new and different things. Respondents prefer to have these experiences in a zone that is maintained for nonmotorized trail use and that is at least a half mile from paved roads or motor use. They prefer the area to be a largely undisturbed natural area and prefer few encounters with other people on the trails. Benefit attainment was less in this zone than in zone 1.

Problems perceived in the zone included pets being allowed in the park, a degraded environment, and highly eroded trails. Better benefit attainment might be possible if pets were restricted or not allowed in the pothole area and if trails were better maintained. Because of the popularity of this area, damage to vegetation and soils along trails and around overlooks is extensive. Hardening sites and clearly marking areas where hiking and/or congregating are not allowed might help visitors attain greater benefits while recreating in the area.

Forestville/Mystery Cave State Park

This park is located in southeastern Minnesota and consists of about 2,700 acres. About 134,000 people visit the park annually. The park is located in the karst region of Minnesota, hence the existence of the cave. The cave is made up of several linear corridors and new corridors continue to be discovered and mapped. Above ground the park is characterized by steep blufflands and is at the intersection of the tallgrass prairie and the eastern hardwood forest. Remnants of a late 1800s settlement are also protected within the park's boundaries. Recreation management takes place in three different park zones.

Zone 1 is the park's major day use and camping area. The most frequently reported activity in this zone was camping. Respondents expressed a desire to enjoy the natural scenery, get away from the usual demands of life, enjoy the smells and sounds of nature, bring their family closer together, be with members of their own group, and rest mentally. They preferred a setting accessible by motor vehicle on designated roads that is somewhat modified but appears natural, and where they will have few contacts with other people. Most respondents reported they were moderately able to attain these benefits. The only problem they reported was difficulty making a campground reservation but no problems once they arrived at the campground.

Zone 2 is Mystery Cave. A guided cave tour is the most frequently reported activity in this zone. Learning more about the natural history of the area, enjoying the natural scenery and learning more about nature were the most desired experience opportunities in this zone. Respondents indicated they were moderately to totally able to attain these benefits in this zone. They reported no problems in this zone.

Zone 3 contains the park's two trout streams and most people reported fishing as their major activity in this zone. Their most desired experiences were enjoying the natural scenery, getting away from the usual demands of life, enjoying the smells and sounds of nature enjoying a different activity than what they could experience at home, resting mentally, getting away from crowds, and releasing or reducing built-up tension. They preferred a setting accessible only by designated nonmotorized trails in a largely undisturbed natural area with few contacts with other people. Respondents reported they were only somewhat to moderately able to attain these benefits. The only problem reported was trail erosion in the area. Improving trail maintenance should help visitors better attain benefits in this zone.

Incorporating Findings into Management and Planning

As noted earlier, the goal of this research was to move the MNDNR closer to an OFM approach to recreation resource management in the state parks. The intention was that the findings from the surveys would be used: a) to influence management and planning decisions for the six parks studied, b) as training material for park staffs not involved in the study parks, c) to inform the planning process for the two study parks scheduled to prepare and implement new master plans (Itasca and Tettegouche), and d) to broaden the application of an outcomes-focused approach to management in other Minnesota state parks. Partial achievement of these objectives has occurred in the ensuing years as described in the following sections.

Influence Management and Planning Decisions in the Parks Studied

Once the six park studies were completed, the research team worked with each park staff and the MNDNR's central office planners to convey key study findings. Park staff and MNDNR central office planners developed a strategy for addressing problems respondents identified as impacting benefit attainment. In some cases the park staff was aware of the problems and had developed plans for addressing the problems. The findings provided them with stronger support to request funding and/or additional seasonal staff to address the problems. For example, trail maintenance and campground maintenance were issues in a number of the zones across the six parks. Funding to bring on summer seasonal crews to address these types of problems was made available on a case by case basis and was more likely to occur when the park manager could show a connection between the problem and visitor attainment of benefits. Another example was Douglas Lodge at Itasca state park. Park staff knew the Lodge was in need of repair, the data from the study was used as part of the MNDNR's argument to the Minnesota state legislature to provide adequate funding to renovate the Lodge. Study findings helped MNDNR keep the Lodge renovation on schedule so that the Lodge was only out of commission for a season. Although not an on-site problem, campground reservations were a problem for visitors at all six study parks. The MNDNR has since revised its reservation system and reports fewer complaints with the new system.

Use Study Results as Training Material for All State Park Professional Personnel

In September of 1994, two workshop training sessions, each one lasting for one and a half days, were conducted with all professional MNDNR park staff from each of the state parks, the regional centers, and the central office. Each workshop had about 80 participants. The workshops provided participants with an overview of the six study parks and findings for each of the six parks. The purpose of the workshops was to get the park staff to think about the connections between their management of parks, settings within parks, and the condition of the settings with visitor attainment of desired experiences and other benefits. Participants were divided into groups of 7 or 8 individuals and asked to look at the data and identify what they believed were the key benefit opportunities each of the six parks provided and where within each park they thought these opportunities could be best attained. They used activity, desired experiences, benefit attainment, setting and setting preferences, perceived problems, and visitor satisfaction with current management activities to develop their list of targeted benefits. Once they completed this task, each small group presented their material. Park managers from each of the six study parks gathered the information pertinent to their park and used it as a key piece to develop a strategy for targeting benefits that would respond to visitors' most desired experiences within a zone/park, be sensitive to visitors' setting preferences, and address current problems visitors perceived in a zone/park.

Use Study Results to Aid in Developing Master Plans

Although six state parks were involved in the initial pilot test, the most extensive efforts to incorporate the research results into management and planning decisions occurred at Itasca and Tettegouche state parks. For these two parks, the workshops and workshop results became the first step in developing and targeting benefit opportunities to meet specific visitor needs and park objectives. Minnesota Statue 86A.09 requires that a master plan be prepared for units of Minnesota's outdoor recreation system. Once prepared, all state parks must update their master plan every 10-15 years. At the time of this study, Itasca and Tettegouche were scheduled to begin the planning process. For these parks, the visitor data was not only presented to the park manager and staff but also to each park's citizen advisory committee (CAC). Each park has a CAC and most CACs consist of 25-30 key stakeholders living in communities nearby or adjacent to the park. Each park has a planning team composed of two entities. The first entity is the integrated resources management team (IRM), which consists of MNDNR personnel including a state park planner from the central office, the park manager, selected park staff, and technical experts from other agencies such as FS, Minnesota Department of Transportation, Soil and Water Conservation District, and County Boards that have an interest in some aspect of the plan. The second entity is the park's citizen advisory committee (CAC). Together the IRM and CAC formulate the park's master plan. The planning process is an open public process and the resulting plan is a partnership-based plan that provides basic management direction for the park. The state park planning process is similar to other planning processes with: 1) a formal scoping session with stakeholders; 2) identification of issues, opportunities, concerns, objectives, criteria, and uncertainties; 3) analysis of the planning situation with local stakeholder knowledge included; 4) formulation of alternatives; 5) assessment of impacts; 6) evaluation and selection of plan alternative; and 7) implementation, monitoring, evaluation, and modification of the plan.

Using Study Results at Tettegouche

Tettegouche began developing its master plan at the beginning of 1994. The plan was successfully completed and approved in May 1998—nearly a four year process. The Tettegouche State Park Management Plan is the first Minnesota state park plan developed using the OFM approach to target and provide visitor benefits. As stated in the plan:

> "Benefits based management (BBM) is one way to address what human expectations can be accommodated within Tettegouche State Park on a sustainable basis. This approach identifies those benefits park resources at Tettegouche can accommodate and which are a high priority for customers. It also provides a framework to allow managers to understand how characteristics of the setting and activities in the setting help people attain desired benefits. Park management staff are working to better understand what benefits customers receive, how to maximize these benefits while preserving the park resources, and understanding what impact these benefits have on customers and their communities." (Minnesota Department of Natural Resources, Division of Parks and Recreation, 1997, pg. 9).

Throughout the planning process the authors worked with the IRM and CAC to help them better understand how they might target and provide a) benefits desired by visitors and b) benefits that would sustain the resource over time. The IRM and CAC realized that although it is necessary for the park to provide a diversity of recreation activities, park management must ensure that visitors who engage in the activities are able to attain the benefits they most desire. For example, providing a trail gives people the opportunity to hike, but if the trail is heavily used and degraded, visitors who use it may not attain benefits associated with their desired experiences of enjoying the natural scenery or reducing built-up stress. To help ensure they were targeting benefits visitors wanted to attain, they reviewed the study data and other data and documents related to park management and developed seven management objectives that would guide the planning process.

The mail-back visitor survey had a list of 49 possible experiences visitors might desire. For Tettegouche, only 35 of these experiences were desired and important to visitors at this park. Early on the planning team decided they could not address this many items individually. A hierarchical cluster analysis using Ward's (1963) method was conducted on the 35 items. The resulting clusters were considered to be the most important experience domains for visitors to the park. Each domain was unique and contained several of the individual items. Six clusters or domain groups resulted (Nickerson, 1998).

The planning team used the seven management objectives and six domain clusters to develop a matrix that showed the relationship between management objectives, experience domains, and benefit production. Benefits were labeled as direct or indirect and the label was determined by group consensus (Table 16.2). For example, if the management objective was to emphasize interpretation to promote stewardship of the park's natural and cultural resources, planning team members believed that meeting this objective would directly benefit visitors who wanted a park experience that would allow them to learn new things and would indirectly benefit visitors who wanted to enjoy different things. Six of the seven management objectives were related to two or more experience domains. One objective, maintaining infrastructure, was thought to provide indirect benefits for visitors regardless of the suite of experiences they were seeking. In other words providing park experience opportunities would be helped if park infrastructure was in good condition. The planning team believed that by implementing these objectives the park's management staff was targeting a specific set of on-site benefits that would be attained by visitors.

How well the park has done in targeting benefits and managing for specific visitor outcomes has not been measured directly. In 2002, the park worked with the UMN to develop and pilot a set of social, cultural, and biophysical indicators that were related to quality recreation experiences. The project resulted in a handbook (Lime, Anderson, & Thompson, 2004) for Minnesota state park managers and other recreation resource managers interested in OFM. Indicators and standards were developed for each zone based on visitors' desired experiences and benefits. Once developed, the Tettegouche park staff put in place a program to monitor indicators relevant to the visitor outcomes they are trying to promote. During the summer of 2007, a survey will be conducted across all Minnesota state parks that among other things will help determine how well the park is doing in targeting and providing benefit opportunities for visitors.

Using Study Results at Itasca

The Itasca State Park planning project began in 1995 with a strong commitment of public involvement that continued throughout the process. The plan was signed and took effect in December 1998. Five CAC planning committees made up of citizens and resource professionals were created to provide a mix of input. The names of these five committees were: 1) buildings, facilities and roads, 2) community and regional involvement, 3) interpretation and information, 4) recreation and visitor management, and 5) resource management planning. In addition to these committees, an Integrated Resource Management (IRM) team similar in makeup to Tettegouche's IRM was put together.

Itasca's master planning process began about a year after the process started at Tettegouche. There was keen interest in following the Tettegouche process to see how well the CAC and IRM worked together to produce a benefits-based and outcomes-focused master plan for the park. However, the master plan produced for Itasca differs in some key respects from the one developed for Tettegouche. In Tettegouche's master plan, targeted benefits are associated with overall management objectives and outcomes are discussed from a park wide

Management objectives	Experience domains					
	Get away/ stress relief	Learn new things	Enjoy different things	Family bonding	Improve physical/ mental health	Be with others/ experience excitement
Provide recreational facilities and opportunities to make park resources accessible to visitors while protecting significant resources	Direct Benefit	Indirect Benefit	Direct Benefit	Indirect Benefit	Indirect Benefit	
Focus major facility development in the recreational facilities zone. Locate and design facilities to have minimal negative effect on park natural and cultural resources.	Direct Benefit	Indirect Benefit	Direct Benefit	Indirect Benefit		Direct Benefit
When possible, develop facilities accessible by persons with disabilities.	Direct Benefit	Direct Benefit	Direct Benefit	Direct Benefit	Direct Benefit	Direct Benefit
Create a diversity of development consistent with the natural character of the backcountry zone so visitors can experience the remote park interior with minimal level of human impact	Direct Benefit		Direct Benefit		Indirect Benefit	
Emphasize interpretation to promote stewardship of the park's natural and cultural resources.		Direct Benefit	Indirect Benefit			
Provide facilities for the safe use and enjoyment of the park.	Indirect Benefit	Indirect Benefit	Direct Benefit	Indirect Benefit	Indirect Benefit	Indirect Benefit
Maintain infrastructure to protect the public investment.	Indirect Benefit	Indirect Benefit	Indirect Benefit	Indirect Benefit	Indirect Benefit	Indirect Benefit

(Source: Tettegouche State Management Plan, July 1997)

Table 16.2

Factor	Zone 1 (SNA)	Zone 2 (Backcountry)	Zone 3 (Concentrated use)
Resource management goal	Manage for sustainability of natural processes and native biodiversity	Manage for active restoration and sustainability of natural processes and native biodiversity	Manage to provide opportunities to view significant resources by maintaining them for display and use purposes
Naturalness of the area	A largely undisturbed natural area	An area that is mostly natural with some evidence of subtle modification	An area that is predominantly modified but appears to be natural. Land use activities such as mowing along roads may be present
Access to the area	By law, accessible only by pedestrians	Accessible by designated trails, roads, and waterways	Accessible by various motorized and non-motorized means using designated roads, trails, and waterways
Relationship to roads	No roads are present within the zone and roads outside the zone are visible only from the zone's borders	A limited number of roads are present within the zone and only visible from some portions of the zone	Roads are present and highly visible within the zone
Amount and type of facilities	No developed facilities except Bohall Trail, the Red Pine Trail and interpretive signage are present	Rustic facilities primarily to protect the environment and visitor safety such as trails, trail shelters, fire grates and trail signs	Facilities to accommodate users such as developed campsites, picnic tables, parking areas, resort facilities and necessary support systems
Contacts with other people	Very few or no contacts with other users	Low degree of contact with other people	Moderate to high degree of contact with other people
Evidence of other users	Very little evidence of other users	Moderate evidence of other users	Moderate to high evidence other users
Amount of visitor management and regulation	No on-site visitor management controls are preset. Regulation of activities is highly restricted by state law governing SNAs	A few on-site visitor management controls are noticeable such as trail signs and access limitations. Regulation of activities is moderately restrictive	On-site visitor management controls are readily observable. Regulation of activities is present but less restrictive than in zones 1 & 2.

(Source: Itasca State Park Management Plan, December 1998)

Table 16.3

perspective. The Itasca master plan made much greater use of the study data and identified nine key benefits to provide across the park and specifically identifies which of those benefit opportunities will be targeted for each of the park's recreation management zones. The Itasca master plan provides greater specificity than the Tettegouche plan about what visitors should expect and the benefits they should attain in a particular zone based on the activities found in the zone, experiences desired, and existing setting conditions.

For Itasca, 30 of the 49 possible experiences listed on the mail-back survey were important in providing benefits to park visitors. To pare down the number of items so that the planning team was comfortable working with them, hierarchical cluster analysis using Ward's method was used. Clustering produced nine benefit domains. The planning team used these domains to define the kinds of benefits that would be targeted and provided in each type of recreation management zone.

The Itasca master plan outlines three recreation management zone types: 1) scientific and natural areas zone, 2) backcountry zone, and 3) concentrated use zone. These three zones represent a continuum similar to the recreation opportunity spectrum (ROS) one (Table 16.3). The most restrictive zone and most natural appearing zone is the scientific and natural areas zone. The least restrictive and most developed is the concentrated use zone. Each zone is further defined by its: 1) resource management goal, 2) naturalness of the area, 3) access to the area, 4) relationship to roads, 5) amount and type of facilities, 6) contacts with other people, 7) evidence of other users, and 8) amount of visitor management and regulation. Based on these eight factors, the planning team determined which of the nine key

Target benefit	Zone 1 SNA	Zone 2 Back-country	Zone 3 Concentrated use
Enjoy nature and friends	X	X	X
Learning	X	X	X
Personal and spiritual development	X	X	X
Physical development and enjoyment	X	X	X
Relaxation and new experiences	X	X	X
Solitude and escape	X	X	
Independence, skill development, and personal achievement		X	
Family bonding		X	X
Social recognition and meeting new people			X

'X' denotes targeted benefit for a particular zone

(Source: Itasca State Park Management Plan, December 1998)

Table 16.4

benefits would be targeted and provided in each zone (Table 16.4). Five benefit opportunities were identified for all three zones. Solitude and escape are provided in the SNA and backcountry zones; family bonding in the backcountry and concentrated use zones; independence, skill development, and personal achievement in the backcountry zone; and, social recognition and meeting new people in the concentrated use zone.

Broadening the Application of OFM to All Parks in the System

The planning efforts carried out at Tettegouche and Itasca were supposed to be models for other parks and demonstrate how other park managers could develop and implement master plans that would target and provide visitor benefits. The experiences the two planning teams had preparing OFM plans targeting specific types of benefit opportunities were mixed. Both planning teams had difficulty understanding what benefits to target and how to target them. Some park managers viewed the difficulty in understanding how to target and provide benefits as "proof" that this approach does not advance park planning and management for quality visitor experiences and benefits. Other park managers saw the two plans as first attempts and were not put off by the difficulties the park planning teams had in trying to understand and implement OFM.

Park managers at Tettegouche and Itasca were enthusiastic about the possibilities of using a benefits approach and maintained that enthusiasm throughout the planning process. Today, both of these managers continue to support the outcomes-focused approach. The same cannot be said of the citizen groups involved in both planning processes. For many of the individuals who made up these groups, the level of involvement they were asked to take on in preparing these two management plans was greater and more time-consuming than past planning processes involving citizens. Their knowledge and receptiveness to new knowledge or new ways of thinking varied greatly within each CAC. Many individuals were uncomfortable with what they perceived as the abstractness of desired visitor experiences and benefits. Many expressed extreme discomfort and disbelief that park managers could target benefits and manage the biophysical resource to provide benefits important to visitors.

Some members of the IRM teams were equally disbelieving. The MNDNR central office staff who are responsible for leading the planning team also expressed some difficulty in writing OFM plans that specify the benefits the agency's management will provide to visitors. Central office staff, though, believed it was possible. But the benefits-oriented management framework was new to them; and, having no other management plans that had used this approach to refer to made them cautious in trying to apply it.

Summary and Conclusions

The two management plans represent an evolution in the MNDNR's thinking about how to manage resources for visitors and recreational use. These differences are expressed in the ways in which each team used the study data to prepare the plans. The experiences of the two park planning teams has given other park managers some comfort in knowing that there is room to interpret how benefits are specified and at what level the park provides them. The different experiences became key selling points to acceptance of the benefits approach to recreation management within the MNDNR. However, state park budgets have continued to decline along with other state budgets. This decline has meant that visitor data needed to properly prepare new state park master plans is not gathered. As a result, benefits listed as targeted benefits in park master plans prepared since 1998 tend to be broad and they do not appear to distinguish between park settings or recreation activities.

Changes in the MNDNRs central office has also led to different interpretations of benefits and OFM. The new director has shown little interest in developing management plans that target specific benefits for visitors. He has, however, continued to incorporate the identification of beneficial outcomes associated with Minnesota state parks into the system's periodic marketing and visitor satisfaction surveys. These actions demonstrate a level of commitment to identifying and considering beneficial outcomes in marketing and management decisions. Other staff changes at the central office involve the state park planning team. None of the planners working with state parks to develop master plans in the late 1990s and early 2000s when the benefits-based management approach was adopted, work in this capacity today. Some have retired, some have taken other positions within the Division of Parks and Recreation, some have taken other positions within the MNDNR, and some have taken other positions outside of the agency. It does not appear that they left behind a legacy of park planning that focused on targeting and providing visitor benefits. It seems that the newer park plans are less visionary and are less likely to acknowledge the larger role that park management plays in helping visitors to re-create themselves to meet their physical, mental, and spiritual needs.

In the summer of 2007, the MNDNR began a new effort to understand Minnesotans, their needs, and the kinds of beneficial experiences they desire while recreating in Minnesota state parks. This study also attempts to identify why Minnesotans choose state parks or do not choose state parks as a recreation destination. It also attempts to understand the constraints to recreating in state parks and how people negotiate those constraints. The MNDNR intends to use the findings from the 2007 studies to better inform its professional staff about the benefits of recreation to the people in the state and how the MNDNR can position itself to be a major provider of recreation and the benefits it provides to visitors, communities, the economy, and the environment.

Literature Cited

Dillman, D. (2000). Mail and internet surveys: The tailored design method. 2nd edition. New York, NY: John Wiley.

Lime, D., Anderson, D., and Thompson, J. (2004). Identifying and monitoring indicators of visitor experience and resource quality. St. Paul, MN: Department of Forest Resources

Minnesota Department of Natural Resources, Division of Parks and Recreation. (1997). Tettegouche State Park management plan. St. Paul, MN.

Nickerson, R. (1998). Understanding the personal onsite beneficial experiences of Minnesota state park visitors. Ph.D. thesis. Minneapolis, Minnesota: University of Minnesota Graduate School.

Ward, J. (1963). Hierarchical grouping to optimize an objective function. *Journal of the American Statistical Association, 58*, 236–244.

Chapter 17
Applying and Implementing OFM on the Gunnison Gorge National Conservation Area

Don Bruns, Karen Tucker, and John Arkins

Learning Objectives

1. Understand the need for structuring customer assessments to capture the desires of both visitors and affected community resident customers for all key components of recreation production affecting recreation outcome opportunity production and attainment.
2. To accurately target OFM objectives for selected primary customer market demand, understand the need for providers exercising at least as much discretion in analyzing that demand, and recreation-products to match it, as their customers do in choosing where to go and what to do.
3. Gain insights about how the dynamic nature of OFM requires that implementation plans remain flexible enough to allow adaptively adjusting planned actions in response to continuous monitoring feedback about how well they are achieving outcome-focused objectives outlined in management plans.
4. Appreciate the necessity of incorporating programs and systems (e.g., river running, mountain biking, four-wheeling, interpretation, permits, and fees) within recreation's most basic management, marketing, monitoring, and administrative functions as a precondition for making implementation plans and field operations truly outcome-focused.

Description of the Area

Gunnison Gorge lies a short distance northeast of the town of Montrose in west central Colorado. Its outstanding recreational characteristics were first offered legislative protection on September 23, 1972 by Public Land Order No. 5261. By designating the area as Gunnison Gorge Recreation Lands, that Secretarial Order withdrew lands for protection of scenic and geological features and public recreation values and revoked an earlier reclamation project withdrawal.

On October 21, 1999, the U.S. Congress designated 60,619 acres of public lands as the Gunnison Gorge National Conservation Area (GGNCA) under the Black Canyon National Park and Gunnison Gorge National Conservation Area Act of 1999 (Public Law 106-76). It includes the 17,784-acre Gunnison Gorge Wilderness. The area is managed by the Bureau of Land Management (BLM), Montrose Field Office. The BLM is a multiple-use land management agency, which means that recreation is one of many uses for which those public lands are to be managed (cf. *Federal Land Policy and Management Act of 1976*). NCAs are designated and managed in accordance with special Congressional provisions to permanently protect and conserve identified resource values of national interest. Among specific provisions of this legislation are the following ones enumerated in Section 7 of the enabling legislation:

(a) In General—There is established the Gunnison Gorge National Conservation Area, consisting of approximately 57,725 acres as generally depicted on the Map.

(b) Management of Conservation Area—The Secretary, acting through the Director of the Bureau of Land Management, shall manage the Conservation Area to protect the resources of the Conservation Area in accordance with (1) this Act; (2) the Federal Land Policy and Management Act of 1976 (43 U.S.C. 1701 et seq.); and (3) other applicable provisions of law.

(c) Withdrawal—Subject to valid existing rights, all Federal lands within the Conservation Area are hereby withdrawn from all forms of entry, appropriation or disposal under the public land laws; from location, entry, and patent under the mining laws; and from disposition under all laws relating to mineral and geothermal leasing, and all amendments thereto.

(d) Hunting, Trapping, and Fishing—(1) In general—The Secretary shall permit hunting, trapping, and fishing within the Conservation Area in accordance with applicable laws (including regulations) of the United States and the State of Colorado. (2) Exception—The Secretary, after consultation with the Colorado Division of Wildlife, may issue regulations designating zones where and establishing periods when no hunting or trapping shall be permitted for reasons concerning (A) public safety; (B) administration; or (C) public use and enjoyment.

(e) Use of Motorized Vehicles—In addition to the use of motorized vehicles on established roadways, the use of motorized vehicles in the Conservation Area shall be allowed to the extent the use is compatible with off-highway vehicle designations as described in the management plan in effect on the date of the enactment of this Act.

(f) Conservation Area Management Plan. (1) In general—Not later than 4 years after the date of the enactment of this Act, the Secretary shall (A) develop a comprehensive plan for the long-range protection and management of the Conservation Area; and (B) transmit the plan to (i) the Committee on Energy and Natural Resources of the Senate; and (ii) the Committee on Resources of the House of Representatives. (2) Contents of plan. The plan (A) shall describe the appropriate uses and management of the Conservation Area in accordance with this Act; (B) may incorporate appropriate decisions contained in any management or activity plan for the area completed prior to the date of the enactment of this Act; (C) may incorporate appropriate wildlife habitat management plans or other plans prepared for the land within or adjacent to the Conservation Area prior to the date of the enactment of this Act; (D) shall be prepared in close consultation with appropriate Federal, State, county, and local agencies; and (E) may use information developed prior to the date of the enactment of this Act in studies of the land within or adjacent to the Conservation Area.

Background and Context

When OFM was applied to guide planning of the recreation components of the GGNCA, it was called benefits-based management (BBM), and as explained at the beginning of Chapter1 of this text, it is identical to BBM except that the name implies managing for both beneficial and negative outcomes. The application of OFM to the GGNCA as described in this chapter principally involves the BLM and its collaborating recreation-tourism providers and volunteering partners. These collaborators include both other affecting recreation-tourism providers (i.e., local chamber and resort associations, service-providing businesses such as outfitters, and local governments who manage area access roads) and affected recreation participants, local residents, and organized user groups (i.e., OHV, environmental-wilderness, commercial, private boater associations, sporting groups such as Trout Unlimited). Other agencies also play an important role, including Delta County (transportation and other infrastructure), the Colorado Division of Wildlife (fisheries management), the Bureau of Reclamation (in-stream flows), and the National Park Service (adjoining upstream Black Canyon National Park).

The BLM has now nationally adopted the expanded conceptual framework of OFM to plan and manage visitor and resident customer demands for structured recreation opportunities (i.e., where demand for activities, experiences and other benefits, and maintenance of recreation setting character has been identified). Before that happened, the manager of the GGNCA chose to apply principles of OFM by targeting experiential and other beneficial outcomes by specific management objectives. She made that recommendation to the BLM Colorado State Director who made the final decision to go ahead.

The rationale for adopting OFM's (BBM's) expanded conceptual framework was to ensure that all key components of the recreation opportunity production process (described in Chapter 2 of this text) would be addressed in plan development and implementation. Competing user groups clearly desired different outcomes, each not available within every single RMZ. RMZs in the BLM are defined as "subunits within a SRMA [Special Recreation Management Area] managed for distinctly different recreation products...comprised of recreation opportunities, the natural resource and community settings within which they occur, and the administrative and service environment created by all affecting recreation-tourism providers, within which recreation participation occurs." The BLM defines SRMAs as units "identified in land use plans to direct recreation funding and personnel to fulfill commitments made to provide specific, structured recreation opportunities...activity, experience and [other] benefit opportunities." (Appendix C of the BLM's *Land*

Use Planning Handbook). Using OFM to diversify types of recreation opportunities provided is one of the principal applications of OFM, and the Gunnison Gorge NCA is a practical illustration of it. This has enabled managers to both diversify their recreation opportunity products and likewise diversify visitor information outreach so that prospective visitors can better match up their outcome preferences with areas being explicitly managed to meet them.

Managers also knew from experience that many of the desired outcomes (or related groups of outcomes) were setting-dependent, growing use was continuing to change setting character, and with that change was a loss of some recreation outcome opportunities. For example, increased demand for exceptional trout fishing during the annual Stone Fly hatch presented managers with the challenge of maintaining solitude within the inner gorge. At the same time, it was becoming more apparent that the NCA's diverse outcomes were of growing interest not only to recreation participants, but also to a growing population of equally diverse local residents within Montrose and other gateway communities that border the area on three sides. For example, the NCA is valued for the outcomes it provides to area households—particularly new residents who live near public lands open space. But longtime residents especially place significant value on the NCA for traditional uses such as fishing, hunting, and motorized recreation. Community leaders value significant social and economic benefits realized from the NCA by area businesses. Those who know the NCA most intimately are appropriately concerned that it be managed to maintain and improve environmental conditions, without which the production of other beneficial outcome opportunities cannot be sustained. Because the simple exercise of good traditional recreation resource stewardship was inadequate for responding to these needs and desires, the NCA manager chose to adopt OFM to manage the NCA.

The planning and managerial context in which this specific application of OFM is being applied (present tense because implementation continues) is the BLM's need for comprehensive, sustainable management. A requirement to address all components of recreation production, incorporating OFM's principles, was added to the scope of work for an outside contractor that the BLM engaged to prepare this land use plan, called a Resource Management Plan (RMP). While that management plan encompassed all resources and programs, this chapter addresses only the recreation components.

Plan Development

Recreation Use and Preference Assessments

The BLM engaged Arizona State University (ASU) to do recreation customer assessments because of its experience in working with the OFM construct and because the BLM does not have the expertise to do such studies itself. Under the auspices of both the School of Recreation and Tourism Management and the School of Community Resources and Development at Arizona State University (ASU), faculty members and graduate students worked with the BLM under an assistance agreement to identify customers and their preferences for recreation and other outcome opportunities (i.e., activities, experiences and other beneficial outcomes, recreation setting character, and different kinds of implementing actions). The ASU cooperators sampled 413 GGNCA visitors during the 2001-2002 use seasons. The study identified recreation use patterns and associated preferences for psychological experiences, other outcomes, recreation settings, and possible alternative management actions. It also generated related data on how visitors obtained information about the NCA and their economic expenditures, and demographic variables (Knopf, Andereck, & Virden, 2004).

Visitor assessments investigated outcome preferences within the context of the areas where recreation occurred and the recreation activities within which those desires were expressed (i.e., these assessments were contextually related to geographic subunits of the NCA). This was essential to ensure that the BLM and its customers were both working from the same frame of reference. The aim was to link outcome preferences to setting character preferences and also to the various management actions required to achieve them and facilitate desired outcome attainment. The intent was to further identify the essential setting conditions upon which the production and realization of desired recreation opportunities and outcomes depend. Assessments examined how the various components of recreation production are interrelated. Cause and effect relationships between resource attractions, provider actions, recreation setting character, and the resulting production and attainment of recreation and other outcome opportunities were explored.

In retrospect, study instruments for the Gunnison Gorge NCA were useful, but there were also deficiencies. First, they did not establish a response context that linked together (i.e., cause-and-effect) respondent preferences for all key components of recreation production. For example, respondents were asked to relate their setting preferences to desired experiences, but those responses should have also been tied to preferences for other desired beneficial outcomes as well. In other words, results showed visitors' setting preferences, but the "which I believe must be provided and maintained for me to realize my most desirable outcomes" part of the question was not articulated. A second study deficiency related to the kinds of outcomes for which customer preferences were assessed. Preferences for experiential and other beneficial outcomes were assessed, but none for negative outcomes. That omission ignores the underlying premise of OFM, that managers must address negative as well as positive outcomes. This is known to be the case in general, from complaints commonly heard wherever inappropriate recreation use or development leads to worsened conditions. Not unexpectedly, the NCA's customers had similar concerns.

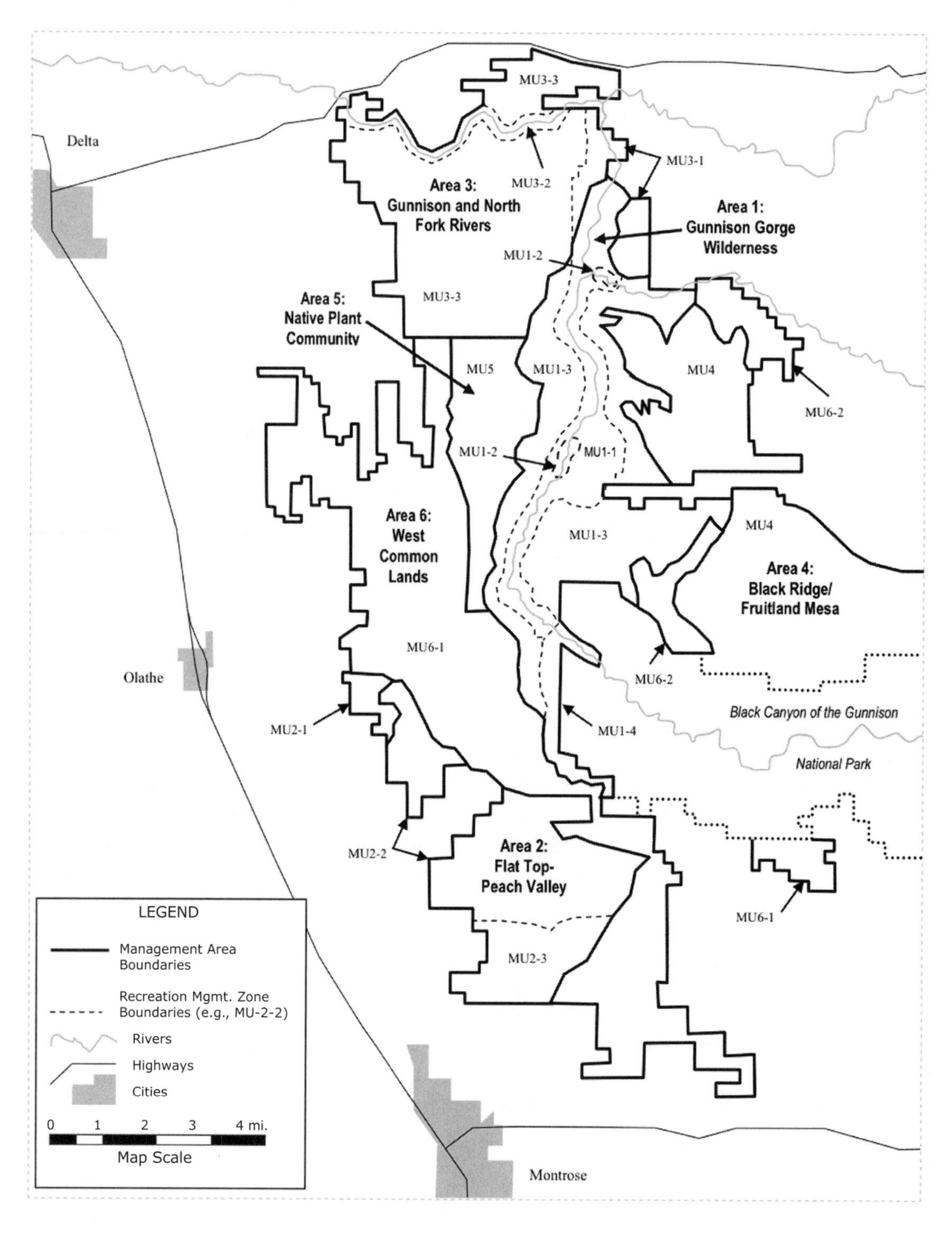

Figure 17.1 Recreation Management Area and Zones Gunnison Gorge National Conservation Area

Both beneficial and negative outcomes must be managed (see the list of identified negative outcomes in the Appendix of Chapter 3 of this text).

The study revealed that NCA visitors' recreation activity preferences varied by area, correlating strongly with recreation attractions and features (e.g., fishing and boating within the gorge, off-highway vehicle use on the rim), as was anticipated. But ASU researchers also measured visitor preferences for a set of 28 psychological experiences and 22 other additional beneficial outcomes. They concluded that particular desired experiences were, statistically, significantly more important to nonmotorized visitors within the Gunnison Gorge (Area 1) and along the lower Gunnison River (Area 3) than for motorized visitors in the Flat Top-Peach Valley area (Area 2) outside the canyon rim (see Figure 17.1). However, it is helpful to note that statistically significant differences between mean scores computed from responses to preferential questions (given adequate sample sizes) are not necessarily managerially significant in terms of their practical implications for how recreation is to be managed. To illustrate this important point, the ASU researchers developed scales to measure different experiential benefits, one of which they labeled "Experience Nature." They found that mean (i.e., average) scores for that scale were 3.9, and 3.6 respectively for users of Unit 3 (the lower Gunnison) and Unit 2 (Flat top-Peach Valley) and that those two means were statistically significantly different at a .00 probability level. While those differences may be statistically significant, the actual difference of 0.3 on the five-point response scale is managerially insignificant.

The preceding language articulates a legitimate concern about how statistical study results were interpreted, but field practitioners had other additional concerns. The five-point preference scale used by researchers yielded mean importance scores for psychological experiences ranging from the mid-fours to the mid-twos in all three areas yielding useable study results: the Inner Canyon Wilderness (Area 1), the lower Gunnison River from Smith Fork to Austin (Area 3), and Flat Top-Peach Valley (Area 2). Scores for other beneficial outcome preferences showed greater differences but only for the five most highly-valued outcomes. These results were useful for developing a responsive management plan. But it was not unexpected that visitors expressed a stronger desire for "...nature in a pristine setting," "...solitude," "...one with nature," and "...connection

Variable	Percent desiring to reduce, remove, limit, provide fewer, etc.			Percent desiring to enhance, encourage, develop, allow more, etc.		
	Inner Canyon Wilderness	Lower Gunnison	Flat Top-Peach Valley	Inner Canyon Wilderness	Lower Gunnison	Flat Top-Peach Valley
Remoteness	18	17				
Naturalness	26	20				
Development						25
Services				18		21
Contacts	16					
Control			29			17
Programs						17
Motorized	45	30	32			21
Roads						17
Facilities						25
Trails						41

Table 17.1 Preferences for Changes to Settings and Services

with nature" on the river zones than outside the canyon rim. NCA planners and managers observed that those differences could just as easily have resulted from real differences in the character of recreation attractions among those areas (i.e., along the river vs. outside the canyon rim) as from real differences among recreation participants' outcome preferences (i.e., it would not be reasonable to expect visitors to express preferences for nonexistent solitude and pristine settings outside of the canyon rim where those outcomes are not attainable). The fact that visitors expressed virtually identical preferences for outcomes such "adventure," "reduced stress," "improved physical health," and "strengthened relationships" across all three study units supported this conclusion.

In terms of outcome preferences, two things were most helpful to planners and managers in deciding which outcomes to target as management objectives. First was that the highest scores for nonexperiential benefit preferences along both river segments were those for outcomes related to nature affiliation and solitude, while outside the canyon rim they were for fitness and health, stress reduction, and challenging abilities. Secondly, greater observed within-unit differences in outcome preferences also guided planners as they searched to find the appropriate mix of outcome opportunities to target as management objectives within each RMZ (labeled as Management Units (MU) in the final NCA plan; see Figure 17.1).

Two partial and abbreviated constructs of the ROS six- to seven-class setting character classification definitions (i.e., encompassing 13 different setting attributes as applied by the BLM) were used by ASU researchers to assess customers' setting character condition preferences. While visitors routinely express different setting preferences for the three different setting components that comprise any recreation setting (i.e., physical, social, and administrative), the ASU researchers nonetheless first provided respondents with only a consolidated, abbreviated description of each of the six setting character classes. Those consolidated descriptions, however, provided managers no means for discerning differences in customer preferences for any setting's thirteen component attributes that influence outcome opportunity production and attainment, and which the BLM therefore needs to manage. Summary narrative study results from this portion of the study revealed clear preferences towards the more primitive end of the ROS, across all three study areas identified above (i.e., areas 1–3 encompassing the two river zones and the upland zone outside the canyon rim; See Figure 16.1). The NCA's existing setting characteristics exhibit much more variation than is revealed by study results showing that 86 to 68 percent of all visitors prefer either primitive or back country settings.

The study asked respondents to indicate only the direction in which each of eleven items (presented as setting attributes) should be changed (or remain the same) to enhance their experience (even though managing for outcomes requires addressing other outcomes as well as psychological experiences). A three-point response scale was presented asking respondents to indicate "Reduce, Remove, Limit, Have Fewer, Leave as is," or "Enhance, Encourage, Develop, Allow More, etc." This response format was incomplete for several reasons. Not all of the items presented as setting attributes actually were (as defined within the ROS system as adopted by the BLM). Instead, some included items were a combination of setting attributes and provider actions (i.e., "development," "programs," "roads," "facilities," and "trails"). Study results of visitors' preferences for these items showed that a majority of respondents in each of the areas thought that setting characteristics and other conditions should be left as they were. Secondly, for those desiring change, study design did not enable respondents to indicate the degree of change desired (i.e., how much?). Table 17.1 identifies the items (it would be inaccurate to call them setting attributes because not all were) for which more than 15 percent of respondents thought change should occur.

These results were useful but provided only a partial answer to the question of what kinds of setting characteristics respondents believed were essential to achieve their most highly valued outcomes. Results showing preferences for consolidated setting descriptions, rather than for each attribute, provided NCA managers no indication of which setting conditions visitors felt were most essential and should therefore provided and maintained by the BLM to achieve their most highly valued experiences and other beneficial outcomes. Furthermore, plans must target specific setting conditions for each setting attribute that is essential to the production of targeted outcome opportunities because managers cannot simply manage for the kinds of unqualified preferred setting changes which the study was designed to portray. In the end, planners were unable to write discrete setting prescriptions for each of the thirteen attributes that comprise all natural resource recreation settings.

Mgt. area	Rec. Mgt. zone	3rd: Provider service environment	2nd: Setting characteristics	1st: Recreation outcome opportunities produced and attained	
				Management objectives	
		Implementing actions	Recreation setting prescriptions	Activity opportunities	Experiences and other beneficial outcomes
Unit 3	MU 3-1	Facility development, operations, and maintenance Attractions management Visitor management Information/education Visitor services Controls/restrictions	Physical Social Administrative	Listed	Experiences Other benefits to: • Individuals • Communities • Economics • Environment

Table 17.2 Format of Recreation Sections

Planning Processes

A planning contract was awarded to Tetra Tech, who wrote a scoping report that defined desired settings and outcomes, based on assessment data provided by ASU and with the BLM's understanding of recreation participation and behavior within the NCA. Three different sets of meetings were conducted. The first set was to inform participants about the process and identify issues of concern. The second set consisted of field trips to each of the NCA's Recreation Management Areas to take a look at the issues that had been identified. The third set was to identify a range of solutions corresponding with the range of alternatives which the BLM's land use planner constructed for the entire plan (i.e., within which planning management options for each natural resource program had to fit). In all, Tetra Tech and the BLM then hosted 22 different focus group meetings and five field trips. These meetings were structured principally not to promote disclosure of participants' recreation preferences as described elsewhere in this text (cf. Krueger, 2000), but to obtain customer feedback on the various initial management alternatives the BLM had constructed. These alternatives were based on what planners and managers had learned from ASU assessments and other scoping input gathered for the plan. Within that context, participants shared perspectives, educated one another, and learned about each other's desires for the NCA's future.

Other informational meetings were held with county commissioners, chambers of commerce, and Congressional delegates as the plan developed. These ensured there were neither surprises nor inconsistencies with legislative mandates. Finally, meetings involving service clubs and ordinary citizens provided important insights from adjoining neighborhoods and communities affected by the NCA's use and future management.

As it turned out, NCA planners and managers needed both the ASU study results and the output from these several meetings to adequately define the recreation preferences of NCA visitors and affected community residents. The formal visitor study design did not fully anticipate how diverse the NCA's recreation opportunities were (i.e., not enough study zones). Be that as it may, the volume of visitors and the study budget did not enable researchers to obtain enough samples to differentiate study results within the interior of the three study areas, despite the NCA's diverse recreation attractions and opportunities. Output from the many meetings and field trips enabled the BLM to further differentiate recreation management objectives, beyond the three study/management areas to ten more specific, logical management units or RMZs (plus three additional RMZs whose boundaries coincided with the remaining three management areas) that are identified in the final plan.

The NCA's planning and management objective was "to maximize diversity of multiple uses, including human activities and opportunities, while meeting or exceeding land health standards." (as stated in the "Approved Resource Management Plan and Record of Decision," November 2004, p. 2-1). As noted, planners found some of the conclusions of the ASU research study report at odds with tabular research results. While planning time-frames did not allow the BLM to explore reasons for those differences, they were useful in that they prompted planners to take a more careful look, past the study report to tabular research results. That led them to draw different and more accurate conclusions. What BLM planners and managers found most helpful was the raw data itself. In the end, what contributed most to the utility of study results for planning and effectively managing for beneficial outcomes was the objective content displayed in tabular results, coupled with the planners' own understanding of how all of the pieces functionally fit together.

In conclusion, the adoption of the OFM's enlarged planning framework required several shifts from the traditional practice of activity-based recreation management in the way things are done. Prior to the adoption of OFM, recreation management objectives had been written primarily in terms of actions needed to accommodate identified recreation uses. Now, under OFM, management objectives had to be written in terms of recreation opportunities (i.e., for activities, experiences, and other beneficial outcomes) to be produced and corresponding outcomes to be attained. In contrast with the BLM's former activity-based recreation practice, OFM now repositions the BLM's recreation management objectives precisely to the opposite end of the recreation production process (i.e., from inputs to outputs). This now makes all implementing actions accountable to those objectives as the necessary and only means to realization of those ends. OFM now makes possible what had previously been an insurmountable challenge: finding a way to stop regarding recreation program actions as ends themselves. In addition, it now subjects the management of recreation setting character to both the production and attainment of those outcome opportunities depends. It is no longer a matter of managing settings to fulfill professional desires. Not inconsequentially, this has had the further effect of subjecting all recreation operations to achieve targeted outcomes. Thus, the need for and appropriateness of each recreation action for the NCA is now being judged on the basis of whether it contributes positively to the maintenance of prescribed recreation setting characteristics and, ultimately, to the production and attainment of the recreation opportunities and outcomes explicitly targeted by the management objectives.

Planning Results

The NCA plan recognizes six distinct management areas. These units were delineated in consideration of all resources to be managed (and not just recreation attractions), their uses, setting character, and the values ascribed to them (re: the Approved Resource Management Plan and Record of Decision for the GGNCA, 2004). The underlying premise was, and remains, that each unit will be managed to maintain its most outstanding characteristics and sustain its productive capacity for the benefit of a particular recreation-tourism market clientele of individual recreation participants, affected communities, and the environment itself. The approved management plan identifies future management direction for each of these units. For the recreation plan component, that direction specifies how each of recreation's most basic components are to be managed. Note that, while the planning process itself worked through the recreation opportunity production process from right to left (see Chapters 2 and 3 of this text), the plan itself presented those results from left to right. The idea, and in fact the essential requirement of OFM to manage for outcomes, is to ensure that all implementing actions are appropriately guided and constrained to achieve the most important things (i.e., targeted outcomes and prescribed, essential recreation setting characteristics). Table 17.2 illustrates, working from right-to-left, OFM's logic and how it is being applied to ensure that only those actions required to achieve setting prescriptions and management objectives are necessary and appropriate.

Figure 17.3, extracted from the approved management plan (Figure 2-7), shows how the final GGNCA management plan was outlined to concisely display management objectives and setting prescriptions by RMZ (i.e., within the NCA's six management areas). This figure is included here to illustrate how the BLM NCA planner and manager arranged the recreation plan content to facilitate comparisons, and to show how this content was displayed in the management plan. Thirteen different sets of recreation "products" are targeted: one set for each of the 13 different RMZs. Each of these RMZs is a logically management unit wherein

Mgt. area	RMZ	Targeted recreation activities	Recreation setting character prescriptions	Experiences and other beneficial outcome objectives
Unit 1: Gunnison Gorge Wilderness	MU1-1 Inner Gorge	Float fishing, white water rafting, camping	Primitive and back country	• Risk-taking adventure • Feeling good about solitude • Experiencing pristine nature • Closer relationship with the natural world • Stronger family relationships and friendships • Restored mind from unwanted stress • Greater appreciation of parkland mgmt. challenges • Greater community involvement • Enlarged sense of community dependence • Greater local job opportunities • Greater community stewardship • Reduced spread of invasive species • Conservation of gorge ecosystem • Greater protection of wildlife habitat • Preservation of scenery for future
	MU1-2 Smith Fork/Ute Park	Float fishing, white water rafting, camping	Back country	• Enjoying group togetherness • Having others nearby who could help if needed • Stronger relationship with family and friends • Greater access for differently skilled individuals • Increased acceptance of others different • Increased cultural history appreciation • Greater interaction with different cultures • Improved group cooperation • Increased local tourism revenue • Greater retention of distinctive natural landscape • Reduced spread of invasive species • Greater protection of historic/archaeologic sites
	MU1-3 Outer Canyon	Hiking, backpacking, horseback riding, nature study	Primitive and back country	• Enjoying exploring on your own • Testing endurance • Gaining greater self-confidence • Feeling good about isolation and solitude • Experiencing pristine nature • Enhanced awareness of nature • Greater self-reliance • Closer relationship with the natural world • Improved physical health • Increased appreciation of cultural history • Conservation of the gorge ecosystem • Preservation of scenery for the future
	MU1-4 Chukar Trailhead, Landing and Environs	Fishing, hiking, camping	Middle country and back country	• Cultivation of stewardship ethic • Enlarged sense of personal accountability • Greater awareness of this special place • Enlarged sense of community dependence • Greater appreciation of challenge of maintaining environmental quality • Improved local economic stability • Increased tourism revenue

Table 17.3 Summary of Land Use Plan Recreation Decisions

Mgt. area	RMZ	Targeted recreation activities	Recreation setting character prescriptions	Experiences and other beneficial outcome objectives
Unit 2: Flat Top-Peach Valley	MU2-1 Falcon Road OHV Play Area	Cross-country ATV, dirt bike riding, and vehicle "play"	Primitive and back country	• Developing skills • Enjoying risk-taking adventure • Enjoying family and friends, reduced stress • Greater family bonding • Enlarged sense of community dependence • Greater community involvement • Increased tourism revenue • Improved respect for private lands • Greater community stewardship
	MU2-2 Chukar Road to Elephant Skin Wash	ATV, dirt bike, and mountain bike riding	Middle country	• Enjoying easy access to natural landscapes • Developing skills • Enjoying getting needed physical exercise • Reduced stress • Increased sense of adventure • Enlarged sense of community dependence • Greater community involvement • Increased local tourism revenue • Improved respect for private lands • Greater community ownership • Increased protection of natural landscapes
	MU2-3 Flat Top and Lower Elephant Skin OHV Play Area	Cross-country four-wheel driving, ATV, and motor-cycle "play"	Primitive and back country	• Reduced stress • Improved physical health • Increased sense of adventure • Stronger personal relationships • Enlarged sense of community dependence • Greater community involvement • Improved local economic stability • Greater community stewardship
Unit 3: Gunnison and North Fork Rivers	MU3-1 Main Gunnison River Corridor	Gold medal trout fishing, flat-water boating, and wildlife viewing	Back country	• Enjoying the total aesthetic environment • Enjoying exploring on my/our own • Developing skills • Enjoying getting needed physical exercise • Strengthened family relationships and friendships • Restored mind from unwanted stress • Greater access for differently skilled individuals • Greater family bonding • Enlarged sense of community dependence • Increased local tourism revenue • Improved economic stability • Increased local jobs • Reduced spread of invasive species • Increased protection of natural landscapes • Reduced negative human impacts
	MU3-2 Lower Gunnison River Corridor	Day and multiday walk-wade and float-boat fishing, flat-water boating, camping, and picnicking	Front country	• Relishing group affiliation • Enjoying the total aesthetic environment • Developing your skills • Enjoying access to close-to-home amenities • Improved relationship with nature • Strengthened family relationships and friendships • Greater sense of adventure • Restored mind from unwanted stress • Improved physical fitness • Greater family bonding • Enlarged sense of community dependence • Increased local tourism revenue • Increased local jobs

Table 17.3 Summary of Land Use Plan Recreation Decisions (continued)

Mgt. area	RMZ	Targeted recreation activities	Recreation setting character prescriptions	Experiences and other beneficial outcome objectives
Unit 3: Gunnison and North Fork Rivers (continued)	MU3-3 Smith Mountain/ Rogers Mesa Uplands	Four-wheel driving, horseback riding, and camping	Middle country and front country	• Getting away from responsibilities for awhile • Being able to enjoy nature without having to get out into it too much • Enjoying easy access to natural landscapes • Stronger ties with family and friends • Enlarged sense of personal accountability • Greater sensitivity to the outdoors • Increased local tourism revenue • Increased local job opportunities • Reduced negative human impacts • increased awareness and protection of natural landscapes
Unit 4: Black Ridge, Fruitland Mesa		Wildlife viewing, four-wheel driving, scenic driving, and hunting	Middle country and back country	• Enjoying nature • Learning about unique species • Enjoying exploring on my own • Enhanced awareness and understanding of nature • Greater appreciation for public lands and how it is managed
Unit 5: Native Plant Community		Four-wheel driving, motorcycle and mountain bike riding, hiking, and horseback riding	Middle country	• Enjoying easy access to natural landscapes • Enjoying access through area • Enjoying the Wilderness without being in it • Improved Wilderness appreciation for nonusers • Greater understanding/commitment to sustaining area diversity • Increased sensitivity to different users • Improved cultivation of outdoor-oriented lifestyle • Greater understanding of importance of tourism to community • Demonstration of social/economic value of multiple-use recreation • Increased protection of natural landscapes • Greater protection of cultural resources • Sustaining both wilderness and motorized environments
Unit 6: West Common Lands		Scenic driving, four-wheel driving, motorcycle and mountain bike trail riding, hiking, and horseback riding	Middle country	• Enjoying easy access to natural landscapes • Enjoying access through area • Enjoying the Wilderness without being in it • Improved Wilderness appreciation for nonusers • Greater understanding/commitment to sustaining area diversity • Increased sensitivity to different users • Improved cultivation of outdoor-oriented lifestyle • Greater understanding of importance of recreation-tourism to local economy • Increased awareness of area's natural/scenic qualities • Greater protection of unique adobe landscapes • Sustaining both Wilderness and motorized environments • Greater protection of sensitive plant/animal communities

Table 17.3 Summary of Land Use Plan Recreation Decisions (continued)

the above three components of recreation production yield different but mutually compatible types of recreation and other outcome opportunities (i.e., satisfying experiences and other benefits). In other words, the entire service environment (i.e., actions of the BLM and the services of other affecting providers such as outfitters and guides, county transportation management) and the distinctive character of recreation settings are what makes the production and attainment of different recreation outcome opportunities possible. Table 17.3 is included in this chapter for those who believe that OFM is too complex and difficult to portray. Side-by-side, it shows how the essential components of OFM can be succinctly displayed to facilitate comparison of targeted recreation outcome opportunities, setting characteristics, and activities across RMZs. That ease of comparison facilitates environmental reporting for the management plan itself, makes the completed plan more useable for day-to-day management, guides the development of marketing outreach materials, etc. To save space, this table illustrates plan results only in generalized form, citing only some of the principal beneficial outcomes, prescribed setting characteristics, and most relevant activities within the 13 RMZs comprising the NCA's 6 management areas (see Figure 17.1).

It was noted earlier that recreation customer preference assessments were deficient in that they did not include the measure of degree to which any negative outcomes were concerns of visitors or other resident customers. In retrospect, it is now more apparent that management objectives likewise should have targeted negative outcomes to be avoided as well as positive beneficial outcome opportunities to be produced and attained. More specifically, these could have included those of greatest concern to both visitor and resident customers. But the managerial insight available to the BLM and its collaborating local government and service-providing business partners would most likely have surfaced other probable negative outcomes that they know must be avoided. These negative outcomes to be either eliminated or avoided should have also been included as management objectives, as is now required by OFM.

Implementation

Implementation of approved land use allocation decisions, as well as of implementing management and marketing implementation actions is ongoing within the GGNCA. Notwithstanding numerous implementation actions outlined in the approved plan, NCA managers and staff have identified a need for supplemental implementation planning to more fully restructure field operations to facilitate achieving approved management objectives and setting prescriptions. Efforts are underway to write an integrated implementation plan that will address all management, marketing, monitoring, and supporting administrative actions.

For the GGNCA, incremental implementation of OFM makes sense, for several reasons. The decision whether or not to apply OFM and manage for satisfying experiences and other beneficial outcomes was only made after considerable deliberation. When the plan was being developed, there was no formally-adopted written agency guidance, only a training syllabus and the experiences shared by recreation planners and managers who had already applied the expanded outcomes-focused conceptual framework on a couple of other Colorado BLM recreation areas. GGNCA planners and managers also learned how to begin analyzing visitor desires for beneficial outcomes and recreation setting characteristics (i.e., in addition to those for recreation activities) from the BLM's cooperating ASU researchers. So this knowledge was gained incrementally.

It was therefore challenging for NCA planners and managers to fully explain all dimensions of recreation production to collaborating partners and visitor and resident customers involved in development of the NCA management plan. Virtually everyone was still thinking in terms of activity-focused, project-centered planning models; therefore it made good sense to move immediately to the identification of planned projects and program actions. This, after all, was how all recreation planning objectives had been previously developed.

Within that former planning and management context, planned implementation actions grew not so much from what was needed to achieve recreation management objectives and setting prescriptions as they did in direct response to the kinds of actions proposed by various recreation-tourism constituents and user groups. The big question back then was: Are these actions consistent with those old "input" objectives and prescriptions? Now the question is: Are each of these actions essential for achieving management objectives and have they been tailored to fit within the prescribed setting conditions?

Revisiting those implementation decisions does not require a formal amendment of the land use plan. The reason why is that, recognizing that implementation monitoring invariably reveals a need to adaptively adjust implementing actions, BLM's planning guidance regards all management, marketing, monitoring, and supporting administrative actions as implementation decisions (rather than as land use allocation decisions). Having had a few years to begin implementing the plan, supported by fresh monitoring data, the NCA is now in an excellent position to write a follow-up Implementation Plan that fully integrates all four of the above most basic functional recreation inputs, subjecting (i.e., directing and constraining) them to the minimum necessary to achieve approved recreation management objectives and setting prescriptions.

Lessons Learned

For all the reasons listed, it made sense to expand the conceptual framework for planning and managing the NCA to shift beyond only recreation activities, to also address desired and targeted beneficial outcomes associated therewith and the essential setting characteristics required to do so. Although that decision meant more work, the NCA manager took the initiative and went forward. A three-day OFM (BBM) training course gave the NCA manager, planner, and contractor enough skills to proceed. ASU researchers already had a basic understanding of how to assess customer preferences for the principal components of recreation production (i.e., not only for recreation activities) and to explore at least some cause-and-effect relationships among them. The BLM-ASU team was able to work off the same page from the start, which helped enormously.

Advantages of Using the Expanded OFM Conceptual Framework

Specific Advantages

1. OFM-oriented surveys, focus groups, and other meeting output were extremely helpful in dividing the NCA first into management areas and then into RMZs based on visitor preferences for diverse types of outcome opportunities and the corresponding capacity of RMZs to produce them (i.e., reduced stress, improved technical skills, being with friends and family). They also helped the BLM assess its capacity to produce and maintain essential setting character conditions upon which sustained production and attainment of those outcome opportunities depend.
2. OFM principles were easily applied to existing ROS, Visual Resource Management, road and site inventories, visitor (RMIS) and other recreation and biological resource program data (grazing plans, Landscape Health Assessments, etc.) for the NCA. Critical social data from OFM-oriented surveys about visitor expectations and preferences for settings and activities provided "glue" to link our physical data with desired future condition objectives and specific physical, social, and managerial settings for each RMZ. However, setting prescriptions included in the final plan did not specify the specific classes for which each of the 13 recognized setting attributes (i.e., within ROS' three broad setting components: physical, social, and administrative) are to be managed. Nor were setting prescription maps prepared to delineate the geographic extent of each prescribed setting character class within each RMZ. These will await future plan revisions.
3. OFM was also helpful in developing educational and interpretive signs, materials, and messages targeted for specific users in various zones. In the past, our brochures attempted to cover everything for everybody and usually resulted in a lot of confusion. OFM gave the BLM a clearer understanding who its audience is, what they desire, and what kinds of information they need (e.g., area regulations, best times to come to avoid crowds, technical skills/equipment needed) to facilitate their attainment of the experiences and the individual, social, and/or environmental benefits they are seeking.
4. Knowing what kinds of physical setting conditions people desire is critical in designing recreation facilities and sites that will be appreciated and used appropriately. RMZ-specific management objectives and physical, social, and administrative setting prescriptions helped the NCA planners and manager determine where facilities should be placed, how extensive they needed to be (i.e., group picnic areas versus a dispersed campsite), and what kinds of regulations are needed to ensure visitor use is managed in ways which preserve those settings and either maintain or improve resource conditions in the zone.

5. Visitor feedback obtained through visitor studies on desired resource conditions, facilities, regulations, and their preferences related to crowding, visitor conflicts, safety issues, etc. provided critical information required to write sound justifications in BLM budget proposals for on-the-ground plan implementation projects (signing, facilities, etc.) and additional implementation planning needs. For example, funding was obtained for a critical implementation action in the NCA plan by demonstrating how the proposed project met approved OFM objectives.
6. OFM monitoring studies to assess whether the BLM is delivering the types of quality experiences and other benefits identified in a management plan are an important monitoring and management tool that was not previously available. As demonstrated by OFM instructor Brian Hopkins, levels of visitor outcome attainment can be plotted against actual use numbers to derive functional carrying capacities by RMZs. Correlating outcome attainment (through monitoring social indicators obtained by monitoring against outcome standards set by management objectives) with actual numbers (through monitoring environmental indicators obtained by monitoring against social setting prescriptions) is essential for effective capacity management. This is because capacity is defined both as the ability to contain, absorb, or receive and hold (i.e., defined by social setting prescriptions) and maximum output or producing ability (i.e., defined by experiential and other beneficial outcome-focused management objectives). This important OFM requirement will be applied to monitor commercial and private boating and walk-in fishing use in the Gunnison Gorge Wilderness, determine when a new use allocation system needs to be implemented to keep use at levels within prescribed setting prescriptions, and ensure production and attainment of targeted experience and other benefit opportunities.
7. The NCA manager works closely with local chambers of commerce, visitor and convention bureaus, tourism regions, commercial outfitters, sporting goods businesses, and other recreation support organizations and providers. Underlying principles of managing visitor services to produce opportunities for visitor and resident customers to realize desired and targeted experiential and other beneficial outcomes is now a "common" language of beneficial outcomes that is shared among all recreation-tourism constituent groups, even though they might not all express themselves in precisely the same terms. So now, instead of talking about logistics and facilities, the BLM's work with these groups always involves discussions about *why* people come to this area, *what* types of setting conditions it is within which they want to participate in their favorite activities, and *how* can the BLM and its collaborating private sector and local government providers ensure that they will have the best opportunities for continued realization of the experiences and other benefits that will continue to enrich their lives, their communities, and the environment.

Clearly Identified Customer Markets

At the time this management plan was done, the BLM had not yet recognized the importance of selecting a primary recreation-tourism market, nor selecting the most appropriate market niche or niches for each RMZ. Nor had it provided procedural guidance on how to make either of these market-related decisions. The planners and managers who chose to adopt and apply OFM had the benefit of modeling much of what they did on after the efforts of other already-completed benefits-based applications in Colorado BLM. Nonetheless, because the agency had not yet implemented this guidance, they were out front of the agency itself, and they learned as they went. It therefore fostered creativity and a sense of enthusiasm for the plan.

The relatively long and somewhat duplicative list of beneficial outcomes targeted by management objectives (Table 17.3) also reflects this need for further differentiation within target markets. All targeted outcomes may well end up being realized to one degree or another, but it is still expected that ongoing monitoring through plan implementation will reveal which of these remain most highly valued and which are customers actually able to attain. That needed differentiation will facilitate more efficient and effective management, both in terms of enabling managers to more closely focus field operations, but also in terms of marketing--helping visitors find the areas most able to satisfy their experience and other benefit desires.

Recreation Opportunity Dimension	What was done to establish and maintain a response context	What would have tightened up response context
Rec. Mgmt. Zone (RMZ)	Identified most satisfying RMZ	----
Activity Participation	Identified most satisfying activities within most satisfying RMZ	----
Experience Preferences	Identified "Importance" of experience outcomes for most satisfying RMZ	Change response metric from "most important" to "most desirable" and add both "most satisfying activity" to response context and an attainment scale
Other Benefit Preferences	Identified desirability and attainment for most satisfying activities	Add "most satisfying RMZ" to response context
Environmental (Physical Characteristics) Factors	Identified environmental concerns and problems, but provided no recreation context within which these were to be identified	Change assessment from concerns/ problems to characteristics to be provided/maintained to attain desired beneficial outcomes—all within the context of a "Physical Setting Character" preference assessment
Social (Social Characteristics) Factors	Identified social concerns and problems, but provided no recreation context within which these were to be identified	Same as above, but incorporate within the context of "Social Setting Character"
Facility Management (Administrative Setting Characteristics) Factors	Identified facility/management concerns and problems, but provided no recreation context within which these were to be identified	Same as above, but incorporate within the context of "Administrative Setting Character"
Management Controls (Administrative Setting Characteristics)	Identified controls to prevent environmental damage	Same as above, but incorporate within the context of "Administrative Setting Character"
Recreation Settings	Identified relative change desired for different setting attributes to enhance experiences	Modify response metric from relative change desired to specific setting characteristics needed...to "attain" (not "enhance") desired beneficial outcomes; and expand context to address all desired outcomes (not only experiences), within most satisfying RMZs, and for visitors' most satisfying activities.
Management Actions	Identified the importance of listed management actions and performance scores	Change the response metric from a report card to identify actions desired

Table 17.4 Improving Assessment Response Context and the Utility of Results

Definitive Study Results

Visitor preference studies completed by ASU provided essential information that helped determine which kinds of experiential and other beneficial outcomes are most important to different segments or niches within principal recreation tourism customer markets. The kinds of data needed to develop an academic graduate thesis or dissertation are not necessarily the same kinds of data required to develop an implementable recreation or land use plan. Recreation managers and researchers must therefore be careful to identify which of all study results that could be generated are most essential for management planning. The ASU study in particular generated an enormous array of data, but comparatively few of these were directly applicable to the identification of primary customer markets and niches, targeting management objectives, and deciding which setting character conditions are essential to the production and attainment of those outcome opportunities.

Since these studies were completed, the BLM's own *Land Use Planning Handbook* guidance has further tightened up the agency's recreation planning guidelines, underscoring the need for definitive customer assessments. Of all the things that matter, one of the most important is that studies make every effort to establish and maintain an assessment response context that relates to discrete, logical management units or RMZs. Particularly in areas as diverse as the GGNCA, this is extremely important, because the same visitors seek different kinds of satisfying experiences and other beneficial outcomes from different RMZs. Therefore as planners and managers explore and inquire as to what kinds of recreation opportunities are desired, every effort must be made with all customer assessment efforts to establish a definitive response context to ensure that respondents and managers are both on the same page. This requires establishing a well-defined response context that can be readily understood by all.

This need for a consistently understood assessment context involves providing respondents with definitive study parameters that both they and the managers who later attempt to interpret and apply study results will link together preferences for the different components of recreation production in the same way as did the customers. A consistently understood response context is also necessary to prevent having visitors respond idealistically, rather than in a real-world context (e.g., expressing desires for wilderness settings while four-wheel driving). Visitor preferences for desired activities and outcomes must be related to a single RMZ, preferably to the one that was most satisfying. And their preferences for consequent satisfying experiences and other beneficial outcomes must also be related to that same RMZ. To further ensure that specific setting characteristics upon which the production and attainment of those desired outcome opportunities depend are provided and maintained, all setting preference assessments must tie back to those same expressed outcome desires, then to respondents' most satisfying activities, and finally to their most satisfying RMZ. Ultimately, a failure to provide a well-defined response context that relates to what is actually being managed will make it difficult for planners to ensure that essential physical, social, and administrative setting conditions upon which customers' desired outcomes depend are prescribed, provided, and maintained. Last but not least, definitive study results are necessary to inspire managerial confidence that plan decisions are on target.

Study instrument design yielded less definition than was needed about the specific setting characteristics visitors feel must be provided and maintained to attain their most highly-valued outcomes. Although NCA managers must manage all thirteen identified setting character attributes, study results did not define visitor preferences for each. By contrast, usable assessment results require that customer assessment studies (including informal interviews, focus groups, and mail-back visitor studies) provide planners and managers enough definition to enable them to address all of the variables they have to manage. Another way of expressing this ideal is that planners and managers need to exercise at least as much discretion in managing recreation as do visitors in deciding where to go and what to do.

Much has been learned about how to make this happen since the on-site GGNCA visitor study was completed. Table 17.4 outlines ways in which a definitive assessment context was established, and ways in which it could have been tightened up. Other important lessons regarding customer preference assessments are:

- It is a mistake to assess customer preferences for beneficial outcomes only; results must also address negative outcomes visitors, affected residents, and recreation providers seek to avoid.
- The set of beneficial and negative outcomes for which customer preferences are assessed must be adequate enough to enable planners and managers to target different outcomes that reflect differences in both the productive capacity of different RMZs and the desires of the visitors and resident customers thereby affected. (It should be noted that this is not possible when assessments address either a set of outcomes that are too few in number for the numbers of RMZs involved, or outcomes that are less diverse than are preferences of the most relevant customers).
- Genuinely useful setting character preference assessments must precisely measure visitor and resident customer desires for each of the attributes already identified for setting character management (vs. other homemade setting constructs).

- Useful customer assessments must not collapse the thirteen identified setting attributes of which they are comprised. Planners need to know which of these is essential to the production and attainment of desired outcome opportunities so that all provider actions can be appropriately guided and constrained to provide and maintain them.
- Setting character preferences assessments must determine which conditions customers believe must be "provided and maintained" in order to achieve their most highly-valued outcomes. These are the conditions which influence both production and attainment of desired setting-dependent outcomes. Planners and managers must therefore know what they are to manage responsively.

Where the above conditions are not met, respondents tend to provide idealistic rather than real-world responses. When that happens, results are less than useful for planners and managers.

Comprehensive Up-Front Training

An important lesson learned was that up-front, thorough outcome-focused training is essential. That which the NCA manager and planners received prior to doing the plan was helpful, but this particular training session did not adequately address plan implementation.

PRIMARY RECREATION–TOURISM MARKET	MARKET NICHE	
Recreation Management Zone ____________		
MANAGEMENT OBJECTIVE		
Activities	Experiences	Other Benefits
PRESCRIBED SETTING CHARACTER		
Physical	Social	Administrative
Remoteness:	Group Size:	Visitor Services:
Naturalness:	Contacts:	Management Controls:
Facilities:	Types of Encounters:	Domestic Animals:
	Personal Gear and Equipment:	Individual User Fees:
	Evidence of Use:	Mechanized use:
IMPLEMENTING ACTIONS		
Management		
Marketing		
Monitoring		
Administrative Support		

Table 17.5 Summary Display of Land Use Allocation Decisions for Recreation

Of the three vitally important training dimensions (i.e., writing outcome-focused management objectives for selected market niches, prescribing essential recreation setting character conditions, and formulating appropriate implementation actions), this course only had time to address the first two—including the identification of markets and niches, explicitly stated benefits-based management objectives, and supportive setting prescriptions. Adverse weather cut this particular training short, and NCA planners felt that this "crash course" fell short of its intended goals, leaving knowledge gaps and participants grappling with how to take the OFM approach to the necessary third step of carefully designing implementing actions, giving due consideration for their implications for how on-the-ground field operations needed to change. After all, even the best OFM plan is valueless unless there is an accompanying implementation plan that ensures sustainable plan implementation.

To ensure that recreation management practice actually shifts beyond simply accommodating recreation activity participation to manage all components of recreation production, other training essentials must be addressed. Planners must know how to appropriately guide, constrain, and structure provider actions (in this case, not just those of the BLM, but those of all public-private providers upon whom the BLM and its customers depend). This involves learning how to move beyond simply managing various rivers, trails, interpretation, and other recreation programs to integrate and balance essential provider inputs around recreation's more basic management, marketing, monitoring, and supporting administrative inputs. A third and equally essential training dimension is that of showing how to redirect and constrain field operations so that the most essential actions are done, and done in the right cause-effect order. This involves making a conscious shift beyond traditional field operations and is essential for maximizing program effectiveness (i.e., to achieve management objectives and setting prescriptions) and efficiency (i.e., to curtail programs having ends no greater than their own advancement).

Both the NCA manager and planner felt that the OFM learning curve was steep. In this case, having a contractor willing to learn how to manage for outcomes was a real plus. The lesson learned here was finding a contractor who either already understands how to plan and manage for experiential and other beneficial outcomes, or one who wants to learn how.

There is also a need for follow-up field assistance. The old adage of, "Telling isn't teaching, and listening isn't learning; you learn to do by doing" certainly applies here. Both the NCA planner and manager identified a need for further on-site assistance to better understand and apply basic OFM principles. There needs to be a way to integrate the requirements of OFM within ordinary, day-to-day field operations and management as plans are developed and implemented. There needs to be a way to translate the practice of OFM to the field with on-the-ground working knowledge. One of the things that made the job easier was having a template to work from. In this case, it was a matter of being able to display the components of recreation production in a simple, straightforward manner. Figure 17.5 helps illustrate how this can work.

Tightly-Focused and Balanced Management Objectives

One of the greatest challenges to implementing OFM lies in being able to narrow the long list of desired outcomes to those that best fit both the character of each RMZ and the market niche(s) it best serves. Not everything that visitors or resident customers say they want can be provided. Of course, customer preferences for some outcomes are mutually incompatible, and these are the easiest to weed out. But it is still not managerially feasible to provide all those that are compatible. There are rarely adequate fiscal and human resources to target and actually deliver all customers' most highly valued outcome-opportunities.

There is also an urgent need to carefully examine the appropriateness of targeting the same outcomes to the same kinds of users on more than one RMZ. For outcomes that are not setting dependent, this requires lining up the right management, marketing, and supporting administrative actions. For those outcomes that are setting dependent, it also requires determining which setting characteristics are essential to produce and facilitate outcome attainment, and then further deciding how (i.e., what managerial outputs are needed) to achieve and sustain those setting characteristics.

Two factors made this need particularly challenging. The decision to squeeze an outcomes-focused application of recreation plan content into this management plan was made well after plan development was underway. In addition, planners were under tight time constraints with this time-sensitive planning effort. There was insufficient time to check and double check targeted outcomes to ensure that only those that had the best fit remained in the final palette of recreation management objectives. The good news is that the upcoming Implementation Plan and ongoing monitoring will help to refine specific targeted outcomes for each RMZ.

Chapter 3 of this text points out that, among reasons for implementing outcomes-focused plans, two are especially important: diversifying an area's recreation opportunities, and resolving identified recreation problems or issues. But there is still considerable duplication of a rather limited set of targeted outcomes among the NCA's 13 distinct RMZs. It is likely that the palette of targeted experiences and other benefit opportunities for each RMZ is not yet as tightly focused as they eventually will be when OFM is incrementally and progressively applied in plan implementation. It is anticipated that monitoring feedback will facilitate this process, both as customers' most highly-valued outcomes are more clearly revealed and as other yet missing but important outcomes come into sharper focus.

Distinguish Between Allocation and Implementation Decisions

While several implementing actions were identified in the completed management plan, managers have concluded that these inadequately outline how to best proceed most efficiently and effectively. At the time of this writing, plans are underway both to develop a more complete implementation plan. This implementation plan will also more closely structure monitoring schedules and methods for measuring the degree to which planned outcomes (identified in management objectives) and essential setting conditions (in setting prescriptions) are being achieved. The goal is to better inform, guide, and constrain implementing actions to maximize management effectiveness and promote greater managerial efficiency.

The lesson learned is that not all of the programs and projects that once comprised the BLM's recreation program—and many of which were quite naturally carried forward within the management plan—may be either unnecessary or inappropriate. The need for more in-depth training on how to transform field operations is substantial. A myriad of programs which once existed as ends unto themselves must be integrated within recreation's much more basic management, marketing, monitoring, and administrative inputs.

For providers whose recreation programs have been structured around the accommodation of a diversity of recreation activities, the challenge OFM poses is holding those programs accountable to something more than simply advancing the recreation activities around which they were built. That challenge cannot be overstated and is substantial. Within the expanded outcomes-focused conceptual framework, it is not that recreation activities no longer matter, for they do. Instead, it is that the actions geared to respond to each activity must now be held accountable to higher ends. The lesson learned is that planners and managers must work across several dimensions to make this happen. First, under OFM, actions must now accommodate only those recreation activities related to the experience and beneficial outcomes targeted for selected markets and niches. But more importantly, the focus is not on single activities, for desired outcomes often transcend multiple activities. Secondly, providers can no longer afford to structure implementing actions and field operations around single activity-focused programs or recreation management systems (e.g., river management, OHV management, wilderness management, mountain bike management, permit and fee management). To avoid piecemeal, inefficient, and counterproductive pursuit of activity-focused programs and recreation systems as ends unto themselves, implementation plans and field operations must instead be structured under recreation's most basic functional inputs including management, marketing, monitoring, and administrative support. From this point forward, no activity-focused program or initiative can be allowed to stand on its own.

One of the chief reasons that OFM is being implanted incrementally within the BLM is that not all of the detailed actions that end up being included in Land Use Plans end up getting enough scrutiny to ensure that they are in fact both necessary and appropriate to produce the outcome opportunities targeted by management objectives. Neither are they readily examined to ensure a good fit within approved setting prescriptions. This is not problematic, however, for the BLM's Land Use Planning guidance reserves as implementing actions all management, marketing, and supporting administrative actions. Thus, Land Use Plan allocation decisions need not be amended to adaptively adjust implementing actions wherever new information suggests the need to do so. In fact, to the contrary, OFM requires this kind of adaptive implementation flexibility.

Ensure that Setting Prescriptions and Implementing Actions are Adequate

What makes setting prescriptions so important is the fact that desired setting-dependent experiences and other beneficial outcome opportunities can neither be produced nor attained without them. The same holds true for implementing actions; they set everything else in motion. Both realities require knowing what specific setting characteristics and provider actions outcomes are necessary to sustain desired outcome production and attainment.

Thirteen different setting attributes that influence the production and attainment of various desired outcomes have now been identified. Some new attributes were added to those incorporated in the ROS as it is being applied by the BLM because they influence outcome opportunity production and attainment. By setting component, those attributes are as follows:

- Physical:
  - Remoteness
- Administrative:
  - Visitor Services
  - Naturalness
  - Management Controls
  - Facilities
  - Domestic Animals (new)
  - Individual User Fees (new)
- Social:
  - Group Size
  - Motorized and Mechanized Use
  - Contacts
  - Types of Encounters (new)
  - Personal Gear and Equipment (new)
  - Evidence of Use

While each of these attributes needs to be managed within an outcome-focused recreation service environment, the final NCA plan does not yet address setting character to this level of specificity. Social setting prescriptions, for example, only specify numbers of contacts with other groups; and administrative prescriptions actually listed types of actions rather than setting conditions. Some of the newly-identified setting character attributes likely need to be addressed. For example, some desired outcomes do depend on the types of personal gear and equipment encountered (e.g., radios playing in a wilderness environment). The same is true for domestic animals (e.g., some value the experience of taking pets into the back country, but dogs running off leash have also been proven to reduce close-up wildlife experiences for others). The point is that if customers' attainment of desired outcomes depends on the provision and sustainable maintenance of certain setting conditions for each of these attributes, and they do, then recreation providers must be diligent to keep them.

Challenges and Opportunities

The BLM's Recreation and Visitor Services program is one in transition from an Activity-Focused Management (AFM) to an OFM conceptual framework. This presents the agency both with significant challenges which are also turning out to be opportunities. Under the old AFM model, actions and projects were the bottom line. Under OFM, the bottom line is comprised of the value-added experiential and beneficial outcomes derived by visitor and resident customers, and maintenance of the setting characteristics upon which the sustained production of these opportunities depends. All program actions must now be both redirected and constrained by outcome-based management objectives and related setting prescriptions. This is essential for ensuring that implementing actions do indeed implement approved Land Use Allocation decisions.

As agency planning efforts make this transition, so do BLM's customers and providing partners. Although agencies have been quite comfortable writing management plans consisting of nothing other than a list of actions to be completed, not all of their constituents have been. That is because OFM insists that all key components of recreation production (i.e., outcome opportunities and setting character in addition to provider actions) be addressed, and these are the things that customers also care about. But actually doing this is more than a bit challenging. For one thing, it requires having a much greater understanding of recreation-tourism markets and of the customers within each. It means assessing their experiential and other beneficial outcome preferences as well as those for recreation activities. It also requires understanding recreation behavior well enough to link those preferences to the essential setting characteristics and visitor services upon which their production and attainment depends. Ultimately, it requires designing field operations to do more than accommodate certain recreation activities, but to facilitate targeted outcome attainment.

The GGNCA plan was one of the first in Colorado to adopt BBM's expanded conceptual framework, prior to both Bureauwide and development of Planning Handbook guidance. This created several challenges: first, learning OFM; then understanding the concepts of OFM; thirdly, applying OFM within a Land Use Planning (i.e., Resource Management Plans) planning context; and finally, communicating the principles of OFM to the public, partners and other resource specialists. The next challenges will be to implement and monitor.

Flexible and Adaptive Implementation is Essential

While the planning horizon for land use allocation plans (Resource Management Plans or RMPs, or for the BLM) such as this one have are typically long-term (e.g., 10 years or beyond), even a cursory look at the changing demographics and sociocultural shifts of the West (and particularly for Colorado) suggest that such plans may well need to be adjusted sooner rather than later. This may only require Implementation Planning adjustments. The good news is that any and all actions may be adjusted under the BLM's new Handbook guidance as necessary to keep on target. That is probably good advice for others considering how to develop OFM planning guidance. Only changes to target markets and niches, management objectives, setting prescriptions, and/or the implementation frameworks require formal land use plan (i.e., RMP) amendments. Adaptive flexibility built into current the BLM's Land Use Planning Handbook guidance, coupled with ongoing monitoring actually encourages making implementation plan adjustments as needed. Such changes promote more responsive management and greater managerial efficiency by avoiding the fiscal and human resources staffing costs of infrequent but major planning efforts, thus making needed plan adjustments as painless as possible. More importantly, this kind of flexibility is essential for keeping implementing field operations focused on approved management objectives and setting prescriptions.

The Shift from Activity- to Outcomes-Focused Management is Challenging

One of the primary challenges the GGNCA faces is truly making the shift from traditional activity-focused management to Outcome Focused Management. Even within the Gunnison Gorge RMP, a number of decisions and management actions survived the final plan, being tied only to activities such as boating, target shooting, trail development, and camping. These slipped by because all of essential elements of the shift to OFM were not equally well understood or shared by all who participated in the plan's development, public and private. All desired implementation actions were therefore not tailored to physical, social, and administrative setting prescriptions. Thus, the setting-dependent beneficial outcomes conditions targeted in approved management objectives can neither be produced nor realized without a further adjustment (i.e., redirecting or constraining) those actions. This will be necessary to ensure that only those both consistent with prescribed setting conditions and essential to the sustained production and attainment of targeted experience and beneficial outcomes are in fact implemented. In addition to the fact that no apology is needed for doing this (see above subsection), a basic tenet of OFM that field operations indeed be adjusted in response to monitoring feedback on an ongoing basis to keep plan implementation on target. The critical key will be to shift the scope and content of monitoring sufficiently to ensure that this does indeed happen, thereby ensuring that implementation actions continue to be adjusted for compatibility with targeted OFM objectives and recreation setting character prescriptions. For the NCA, that monitoring shift will need to focus on both the attainment of beneficial outcomes targeted by management objectives and the maintenance of prescribed recreation setting characteristics for each of 13 different RMZs.

In addition, some NCA implementation actions retained an inappropriate activity-focused orientation, which gave inadequate attention to the desired future conditions (i.e., prescribed physical, social, and administrative setting characteristics) and desired and targeted outcome opportunities (i.e., for which management objectives are now written). Instead, some actions remained geared on developments to accommodate nothing more than specific kinds of recreation activity participation (i.e., the old way of doing business). Unless flexibility in implementing field operations is ensured, proceeding with these kinds of projects may well move plan implementation in a direction contrary to what is provided for by the Land Use Plan.

Ensure Balance Among Implementing Recreation Actions

One of the delicate challenges in implementing OFM is balancing all implementation actions, refusing to move some ahead without others also being brought along. For example, the BLM must maneuver facility and other project development schedules to allow monitoring feedback to guide how it is done. Neither can proceed independent of the other, or it will not be possible to sustain production and attainment of the experience and other benefit opportunities targeted by management objectives, nor sustain the character of settings upon which those outcomes depend.

At the time of this writing, the BLM had unfortunately not yet conducted enough monitoring to determine the degree to which this is occurring. However, the NCA's recreation planner has identified specific instances where watchfulness is required such as where developments are needed to protect sensitive resources (e.g., cultural sites or endangered species). For example, the relatively unknown Lawhead Rock Art site has begun to show increased signs of visitation and has recently been looted. To protect this cultural site the BLM archeologist requested that the area be fenced off and that interpretive signs be installed. Yet that action would substantially change setting character along several dimensions. It would make the site more visible from the river corridor and would attract much more boater interest. While this remedy might dissuade law-abiding visitors from encroaching on the site, it would nonetheless do little to curb vandals. Moreover, it would detract the site's undeveloped natural setting character, eroding the site's remaining authentic heritage setting. This in turn would detract from the experiential sense of wonder that presently accompanies its discovery by those exploring the area. This situation begs for a deeper understanding of the interrelationship among, and the need for greater integration of, all implementing actions and their effect on both human behavior and resource stewardship.

An additional illustration helps further illustrate the need for balancing actions to facilitate the production and realization of outcome opportunities and setting prescriptions outlined in the approved management plan. The BLM continues to receive pressure from user and interest groups to develop more OHV trails, hiking trails, boat ramps, etc. It would be all too easy to simply equivocate and authorize the developments proposed. But OFM requires testing all new management actions proposals for consistency with other approved implementation management actions; balancing and integrating them with other marketing, monitoring, and administrative support actions; and continuously subjecting the entire palette of actions approved management objectives and setting prescriptions. Outside initiatives from organized users and interest groups test providers' commitments to truly get beyond the old way of doing business to implement OFM.

Incremental Plan Implementation is Essential

The GGNCA is ahead of the OFM curve within the BLM, having already completed its plan and begun plan implementation. But the transitional nature of this effort (i.e., the application was a pioneering effort, begun prior to BLM's formal adoption of OFM, development of planning manuals and handbooks, and prior to widespread training) is not unlike that to be faced by others who choose to adopt OFM. Much work remains to be done that is instructive in this regard.

The inextricable interrelatedness of recreation's most basic functional inputs (i.e., management, marketing, monitoring, and administration) also means that each action must be implemented incrementally. No provider can afford to immediately dive into management actions and leave marketing on the proverbial "back burner." These are complementary implementation tools and must be implemented in concert. Nor can providers afford to attempt monitoring outcome achievement (social indicators and standards) and setting character maintenance (environmental indicators and standards) simultaneously in all RMZs. Instead, workplace realities (e.g., limited budgets and human resources and the unrelenting need for improved program efficiency) suggest that ongoing monitoring feedback be sought within the RMZs where field operations to implement the approved plan designed are first implemented. On the GGNCA, the BLM is learning that phasing of implementation actions by RMZ and across recreation's four most basic management, marketing, monitoring, and administrative functional inputs is essential.

Traditional Notions of Monitoring Must be Reinvented

A significant remaining challenge and opportunity is that of rethinking the development of monitoring plans. In the past, these were viewed as plans separate and distinct from other implementing actions. This was a challenge for the GGNCA as well. It is inherent in the nature of OFM that planned monitoring actions be directly tiered off of the indicators and standards that already exist in the approved Land Use Allocation plans which they are to implement (properly developed, these can be directly extracted from management plans). In addition, now there is no such thing as responsible monitoring apart from its integration with all other management, marketing, and supporting administrative actions.

This means utilizing all forms of customer feedback—unsolicited feedback, informal interviews, and on-site focused interviews in particular—rather than waiting until funding capacity arrives for more global monitoring and evaluation efforts such as in-depth representative sampling. The BLM has discovered that informal visitor feedback is extremely useful for testing the validity of planned implementation actions. By inquiring about observing discrepancies between what the management plan says and the implementation actions being planned, visitors have helped the NCA's recreation planner re-evaluate the appropriateness of some planned implementation actions. In the earliest stages of plan implementation, the BLM has discovered that OFM requires exercising an unprecedented level of monitoring implementation actions themselves (i.e., administrative indicators and standards). This suggests the need for more proactively seeking more of this kind of informal customer feedback regarding outcome attainment (i.e., social indicators and standards) and closely monitoring what is happening to physical, social, and administrative setting character (i.e., environmental indicators and standards).

The NCA has also discovered that, because the BLM's recreation program is one in transition, all activity-based program advocates and actions have yet to be made accountable to OFM objectives. Both agency actions and outside activity-oriented initiatives therefore need to be watched like a hawk to make sure their initiatives do not simply advance programs and projects as ends unto themselves! Last but not least, greater effort is being required to ensure that these observations are recorded in a timely way, and that their implications are used to adjust field operations on an ongoing basis.

Implementing Field Operations Must Not be Set in Concrete

The need for suspending plan implementation until the above considerations have been carefully thought through and written into Implementation Plans in such a way that that ensures their adoption in day-to-day field operations cannot be overstated. OFM begs the direct involvement of the managers and staff who will be implementing management planning decisions in preparation of implementation plans. Although Tetra Tech and the BLM worked as a team in developing the GGNCA plan, there were several reasons it was not possible to accurately target all essential implementing actions. Cause-and-effect relationships among the three basic components of recreation production are not yet well understood. What it takes to produce targeted outcome opportunities was more dimly grasped when the plan was written than it now is. Most community-based planning partners were still working from the old activity-based paradigm wherein completed projects were ends unto themselves rather than merely means to achieving recreation's greater good. No outcomes-focused monitoring feedback was yet available at the time the plan was written to guide the development of implementation actions. These few realities underscore the need for a dynamic and flexible implementation planning document that can continue being adjusted as necessary to achieve approved management plan objectives and setting prescriptions.

The way he BLM has structured its Land Use Planning Handbook guidance separately from that for Implementation Plans is instructive in this regard. That guidance now regards Implementation Decisions (i.e., management, marketing, monitoring, and administrative support) separately from Land Use Planning Allocation Decisions themselves (i.e., primary markets, management objectives targeting outcomes desired by market niche and RMZ, prescriptions for setting characteristics essential to the production and attainment of these outcome opportunities, and implementation frameworks). This means that Recreation Planners or Managers (a) do not have to apologize for changing implementing actions in response to customer feedback, and are instead (b) actually encouraged to adaptively adjust Implementation Decisions in response to monitoring feedback. Land Use Planning Handbook content implies that (c) implementing actions are in fact going to have to change, (d) once managers begin to analyze incoming monitoring data, (e) in order to keep all management, marketing, and supporting administrative field operations geared towards the achievement of approved Land Use Planning management objectives and setting prescriptions for identified primary recreation-tourism markets and niches. Adaptive plan implementation requires periodically updating Implementation Decisions, corresponding implementation plans, and field operations as ongoing monitoring identifies necessary adjustments to these most basic management, marketing, and supporting administrative inputs. The BLM learned this from recreation staff interactions on the GGNCA and other OFM pilot applications.

Communicating OFM Essentials Internally and Externally

An additional challenge discovered through the GGNCA planning effort is that of effectively articulating the expanded conceptual framework required to manage for satisfying experiences and other beneficial outcome opportunities. The BLM has learned that how this is done varies by audience, including the general public, BLM staff specialists, collaborating business and local government partners, as well as visitors and affected resident customers. This challenge is actually an opportunity both to inform and engage others to embrace BBM principles.

At the time this plan was initiated, most of the BLM staff specialists (e.g., Range, Wildlife, Hydrology, Archeology, Engineering) had not even heard of BBM, let alone understood what it meant to manage for satisfying experiences and other benefits. The challenge has been moving mindset beyond simply getting projects done and implementing programs that accommodate increased recreation participation. Because virtually all other land management programs are focused on land and resource management and not on recreation's provision of services, many staff specialists within those programs still want the recreation staff to remain focused on managing specific activities such as controlling ATV activities or providing nonmotorized trail systems for the sole purpose of protecting resources. The challenge is therefore to communicate internally that recreation, in addition to meeting basic natural and cultural stewardship requirements, must go beyond mere resource stewardship. Because recreation's primary purpose is fundamentally different in that it exists is to produce sustainable opportunities for the attainment of satisfying experiences and other beneficial outcomes, recreation planners have been challenged to communicate that message internally.

Externally, the BLM began communicating OFM principles with other affecting providers and with organized user groups as the GGNCA plan was developed. But the NCA's planned implementation actions must yet be adjusted to outline a comprehensive marketing strategy. For the NCA, the challenge will be deciding who needs to know what; then selecting the most appropriate informational, promotional, educational, and interpretive actions for each audience; and finally identifying the best conduit for each. Last but not least, planners and managers must ensure that these communication efforts are balanced and integrated with all other implementation inputs (e.g., management, monitoring, and administrative support).

Ensuring that Administrative Actions Fit Setting Character Prescriptions

A significant challenge on the GGNCA is working with both BLM engineering staff on facility development and the construction of access roads and trails. BLM engineers have specific requirements for these facilities pertaining to road width, slope, and tread surface. But if prescribed setting characteristics are to be achieved, not all facilities can be built to the same standards. More specifically, the BLM as a whole needs to encourage adoption of a sliding scale of facility construction and maintenance standards corresponding to the six or seven different recreation setting classes. This would enable fitting needed facilities to the approved setting prescriptions of the areas wherein they are to be located. Historic road, trail, and other facility construction standards based exclusively on engineering specifications has continued to erode setting character and its capacity to produce certain desired experience and other beneficial outcome opportunities. This work must proceed both locally and within the entire BLM organization.

The same principle applies to other supporting administrative programs (e.g., comprehensive travel management; off-highway vehicle management). It also applies to numerous recreation programs as well (e.g., interpretation; accessibility programs; commercial recreation permits for outfitters; guides and tour operators; recreation partnerships). The GGNCA manager and recreation staff can address only the local context.

Summary

The GGNCA manager and planners have discovered that planning to manage under the guidelines of OFM takes considerably more time than did managing to accommodate growing recreation activity participation. It takes more time to assess outcome and setting preferences than it does to address only activity preferences. It also takes more time and effort to find out what matters to one's customers—not only to recreation participants, but affected communities, including their residents, and other affecting providers (e.g., tourism industry, local governments, service-providing businesses). Because OFM eats up much more time than was anticipated, the NCA's manager, land use planner, and recreation planner have all contributed substantial personal time to fulfill this commitment. This application of OFM demonstrated that a commitment to implement OFM requires accompanying scheduling, staffing, and funding managerial commitments from those in charge to ensure responsive application of the benefits paradigm and avoid encroaching on employee's personal lives. Those commitments must involve a willingness to adjust both work and leave schedules, budgets, and so forth. Despite having paid a personal price for their commitment to provide responsive follow-through, the authors of this chapter have come to appreciate that managing for outcomes is a virtual necessity in today's world. It certainly is on the GGNCA where today's public lands recreation-tourism constituents are very sophisticated and discriminating. They are insistent that their BLM public lands stewards exercise at least the same degree of discretion in managing recreation as they do as either recreation participants or managing partners. While BLM is an agency in transition in the adoption of BBM, the authors hope that this chapter will benefit other agencies wanting to adopt OFM. The need for all levels of any organization that chooses to implement OFM to recognize, embrace, and support their implementing managers and staffs cannot be overstated.

Literature Cited

Bureau of Land Management (2004). *Gunnison Gorge National Conservation Area—Approved Resource Management Plan and Record of Decision.* Gunnison Gorge NCA Office: Montrose.

Driver, B. L., Tinsley, H., & Manfredo, M. (1991). The paragraphs about leisure and recreation experience scales: Results from two inventories designed to assess the breadth of the perceived psychological benefits of leisure. In B. L. Driver, P. Brown, & G. Peterson (Eds.), *Benefits of leisure.* (pp. 263–286). State College, PA: Venture Publishing, Inc.

Driver, B. L. & Bruns, D. (1999). Concepts and uses of the Benefits approach to leisure. In E. Jackson & T. Burton (Eds.), *Leisure studies: Prospects for the twenty-first century.* (pp. 349–368). State College, PA: Venture Publishing, Inc.

Driver, B. L., Bruns, D., & Booth, K. (2001). Status and common misunderstandings of the net benefits approach to leisure. In *Trends 2000: Shaping the future. Contributed Papers for the 5th Outdoor Recreation & Tourism Trends Conference* (pp. 245–263). East Lansing, MI: Michigan State University, Department of Park, Recreation, and Tourism Resources.

Jordon, C. (1991). Parks and recreation: More than fun and games. In. B. L. Driver, P. Brown, and G. Peterson, (Eds.), *Benefits of leisure.* (pp. 365–368) State College, PA: Venture Publishing, Inc.

Knopf, R., Andereck, K., & Virden, R.J. (2004). *Building Connections Among Lands, People and Communities: a Case Study of Benefits-Based Management Plan Development for the Gunnison Gorge National Conservation Area.* SARR Conference Proceedings.

Krueger, R. A. and Casey, M. A. (2000). *Focus groups: A practical guide for applied research.* Thousand Oaks, CA: Sage Publications, Inc.

Moore, D. & Driver, B. L. (2005). *Introduction to outdoor recreation: Providing and managing natural resource based opportunities.* State College, PA: Venture Publishing, Inc.

USDI Bureau of Land Management. (2003). *Land Use Planning Handbook, Appendix C* (H-1601-1, Release 1 - 1693, March 11, 2005). Washington D.C.

USDI Bureau of Land Management. (2006). Information Bulletin No. 2004-072, February 27, 2004, "The BLM's Priorities for Recreation and Visitor Services Workplan 2003–2007". Washington D.C.

USDI Bureau of Land Management. (2003). *The BLM's Priorities for Recreation and Visitor Services,* BLM Workplan Fiscal years 2003–2007, May 2003. Washington D.C.

USDI Bureau of Land Management. (2004). Information Bulletin No. 2004-073, March 1, 2004, "Establishment of a Recreation and Visitor Services Advisory Team (RVSAT). Washington D.C.

USDI Bureau of Land Management. (2006). Instruction Memorandum No. 2006-060, January 10, 2006, "Incorporating Benefits-Based Management within Recreation and Visitor Services Program Policy Changes." Washington D.C.

USDI Bureau of Land Management. (2006). Instruction Memorandum No. 2007-043, January 26, 2007, "A Unified Strategy to Implement 'BLM's Priorities for Recreation and Visitor Services' Workplan" (Purple Book). Washington D.C.

Chapter 18
Outcomes-Focused Management of the BLM's Red Hill Special Recreation Management Area[1]

Brian Hopkins

Learning Objectives:

1. Better understand the importance of collaborating with local residents.
2. Understand how OFM was implemented on Red Hill.
3. Understand the contributions of this application to the refinement of OFM.

Characteristics of the Red Hill Area and the Application of OFM

This chapter reviews the use of OFM to guide the planning and management of the Red Hill Special Recreation Management Area (SRMA) area which is administered by the USDI Bureau of Land Management (BLM), and the Glenwood Springs Field Office (GSFO).

The Town of Carbondale formally recognized the Red Hill area as a community resource for its primitive (nonmotorized) recreation opportunities many years ago. In 1989, the Carbondale Board of Trustees signed a Cooperative Management Agreement with BLM. The agreement expired and was never renewed. However, interest to cooperatively preserve and manage the recreation values remained. With this in mind, a group of concerned users and neighbors formed the Red Hill Committee (now Red Hill Council). The Red Hill Council included interested citizens, adjacent landowners, the Town of Carbondale, local businesses, Aspen Glen development, Western Slope Consulting and the BLM. The partnership set out to develop recommendations that would protect Public Lands, while managing to minimize conflicts and continuing to provide for recreational use.

In 1997, the Committee worked with other local publics, to fund and complete a visitor survey (Red Hill Committee, 1998) and conducted public hearings for the purpose of identifying important values for the Red Hill area. The survey, independent of BLM, included experience, benefit, and setting questions. Their generous contribution of time and energy over an eight-month period resulted in the production of a final report.

The Red Hill SRMA is a comparatively small tract of public land that is not contiguous to other land administered by the BLM. The BLM administers approximately 3,093 surface acres. The Red Hill SRMA is located immediately north of the town of Carbondale in Garfield County, Colorado. The southern boundary of which is Colorado Route 82. That road goes from I-70 in Glenwood Springs to Aspen, with Aspen being 35 miles and Carbondale being nine miles from Glenwood Springs, respectively. Contiguous with Route 82 is the Roaring Fork River, a popular trout and rafting stream.

People have been increasingly attracted to Red Hill because of its proximity to the rapidly growing Roaring Fork Valley. Walking, hiking, running, mountain biking, and viewing wildlife tend to be the most popular activities. Recreational motorized use has always been negligible because private lands and difficult terrain restricts public access and use in the western, northern, and eastern portions of the area. General recreational use is concentrated on the south side near Carbondale because the only practical public access is where County Road 107 meets BLM lands.

Topographic elevations range from approximately 6,100 feet to 7,500 feet. Pinyon-juniper forests and sage brush shrub communities are the dominant vegetation types in this land of little precipitation and seasonal temperature extremes. The unique red sandstone formations which it is named after are formed in the Maroon Formation. Both visitors and adjacent landowners are enticed by the unique visual qualities of the landscape. "Mushroom Rock" on the south end of Red Hill is over 800 feet above the valley floor and is the most popular destination on Red Hill. From that vantage point visitors have panoramic views of Carbondale, the Roaring Fork Valley, and Mount Sopris.

It is instructive to outline how application of OFM on the Red Hill SRMA differs somewhat from the other applications of OFM to public wild lands described in this text:

1. The area is comparatively small relative to other applications of OFM to public wildlands.
2. From the very beginning, the planning and management of the area under OFM was a truly joint effort between the BLM, and the residents and local enterprises of the nearby Carbondale community. For example, the name on the implementation plan for the area shows it is a joint effort between the BLM's GSFO and the Red Hill Council (RHC). The Red Hill Council, which is the local grassroots citizen group that completed an independent visitor survey/report, provided citizen recommendations for management, assisted on the Environmental Assessment (EA), and is currently cooperatively managing the Red Hill SRMA through a Memorandum of Understanding with BLM.
3. The recreation planner who lead this application of OFM also lead early efforts to apply OFM to guide planning and management of the recreation components of the Ruby Canyon/Black Ridge area near Grand Junction, Colorado. That area, which is now named the McInnis Canyons National Conservation Area (MCNCA), was the first application of OFM to public wild lands (see Chapter 14 of this text). Experiences gained from that effort helped advance application of OFM on the Red Hill SRMA.

In addition to the aforementioned ways that applying OFM on the Red Hill SRMA differed somewhat from other application of it to public wild lands, it is also instructive to summarize the rather significant contributions of that application and the one on the MCNCA, to improving and refining OFM. Those contributions are:

1. What was learned about applying OFM on the Red Hill SRMA and especially earlier on the MCNCA contributed significantly to the development of the BLM's guidelines for planning and managing recreation resources and visitors services, which are defined in Appendix C of its *Land Use Planning Handbook* (USDI BLM, 2005).
2. In Chapter 3 of this text, a comprehensive normative model for implementing OFM is described in detail. That model has been developing incrementally as more applications of OFM are being made and as more is learned about how to improve the model. Applying OFM to guide the planning and management of the Red Hill SRMA and especially earlier on the MCNCA contributed significantly to the development of that model.
3. These contributions of BLM recreation planners who lead the early applications of OFM on the Red Hill SRMA and the MCNCA, as well as other recreation professionals in the BLM considered in Chapter 17 of this text, are recognized and appreciated by leisure professionals in several countries.

Review of OFM Application on the Red Hill SRMA

Use of the Normative Model

Most of Chapter 3 of this text was devoted to describing a normative model to guide how OFM should be applied and implemented on public wild lands. The rest of this chapter will review the degree to which the requirements of that model were applied on the Red Hill SRMA. This review will provide the reader a real-world example of how that model can be applied, which could not be done in Chapter 3. That model is comprised of six phases of planning and managerial actions required by OFM, and the first four phases have several steps that must be taken to fully implement the model. The names given to those phases and steps in Chapter 3 are outlined below. Sequential numbers are given each step in parenthesis for easy reference in the following discussion.

Phase 1: Preparatory Actions.

- Ensure that supervisors endorse, approve, and support adoption of OFM. (1)
- Organize the planning team. (2)
- Ensure that all members of the planning team understand OFM. (3)
- Understand responsibilities. (4)
- Consider essential needs for collaborative management and related public involvement. (5)
- Identify critical issues and concerns. (6)

Phase 2: Gather, analyze, interpret, and integrate supply and demand information.

- Assess recreation preferences the most relevant recreation participant and affected community resident markets. (7)
- Inventory or update inventories of key recreation-tourism resource attractions and services. (8)
- Analyze recreation opportunity supply by possible RMZs and corresponding customer market demand. (9)
- Select primary recreation-tourism market segments. (10)
- Identify the most logical RMZs and corresponding niches within the primary market. (11)

Phase 3: Develop the Management Plan.

- Determine which outcomes can and should be targeted within each management zone for feasible alternatives. (12)
- Develop management objectives. (13)
- Identify and prescribe the essential setting characteristics. (14)
- Rank alternatives and select the preferred alternative. (15)
- Define the essential recreation-tourism service environment. (16)

Phase 4: Develop an Implementation Plan.

- Identify management actions to be implemented. (17)
- Identify marketing actions to be implemented. (18)
- Identify monitoring actions. (19)
- Identify supporting administrative actions. (20)
- Provide ample opportunities and time frames for review of the proposed plan. (21)

Phase 5: Adjust management/implementation plans as needed and approve final plan. (22)

Phase 6: Implement the plan. (23)

Phase 7: Revise the plan as needed or required by agency directives. (24)

Phase 8: Ensure that performance reports and evaluations document and recognize the production and attainment of targeted outcomes as feasible. (25)

Application of the Normative Model

Phase 1

The steps of Phase 1 were accomplished relatively expeditiously in comparison to the first application of OFM on the BLM's McInnis Canyons National Conservation Area (MCNCA) near Grand Junction, Colorado because: 1) the Red Hill area is comparatively small, 2) the scope of the interested publics was narrower, and 3) most of the users are local from the Carbondale area and the Roaring Fork Valley. In addition, since this was truly a community grassroots effort, collaborative relationships were relatively easy to establish, because most relevant associated service providers were involved in the process. However, the irregular shape of the public land parcel, the many adjoining landowners, the many recreation activity demands, the many competing interests, the high political profile of the project, and the urban-interface and wildlife issues did add complexities to the project.

In reviewing the extent to which the steps of Phase 1 were performed, the actions required by each step need not be elaborated, because most, if not all, of them are implied by the requirements summarized in the above list, and additional detail is provided in Chapter 3. To be succinct, the significant Phase 1 Preparatory Actions for the Red Hill planning process are summarized here:

- The BLM recreation planner, who arrived in 1998, had prior experience and success with OFM on the MCNCA, so his supervisor was familiar with and supported use of OFM on the Red Hill SRMA (Step 1).
- An interdisciplinary multiple-use resource planning team was formed by the BLM GSFO ahead of the Environmental Assessment for the Resource Management Plan amendment. The BLM planning team was supported by an external team of citizens organized by the RHC (Step 2).
- Relevant stakeholders were already focused on recreation outcome opportunities as seen in the visitor survey questions and the public meetings. So when the conceptual framework of OFM was introduced by the recreation planner as a way to incorporate recreation outcome opportunities into a BLM planning model/process, collaboration (internally and externally) was comparatively easy to establish and maintain (Step 3).

- At the beginning of the grassroots effort, the BLM field manager assigned the recreation planner as a technical representative to the RHC. The recreation planner's role was to explain the responsibilities and constraints of both the RHC and the BLM (Step 4) and to facilitate the OFM process.
- The RHC addressed what collaborative management needs were essential by development of an MOU with users, residents, businesses, and the Town of Carbondale (Step 5).
- The RHC had held public meetings that identified critical issues and concerns. So the BLM considered the additional public involvement efforts of the RHC as adequate for the BLM's planning process (Step 6).

Phase 2

As noted earlier, what was learned through the Red Hill planning process contributed greatly to the application of OFM. The Red Hill SRMA was identified by BLM ahead of the 2005 revision of the BLM's H-1610- *Land Use Planning Handbook.* What was learned about applying OFM on the Red Hill SRMA contributed significantly to the development of the BLM's guidelines for planning and managing recreation and visitors services, which are defined in Appendix C of its *Land Use Planning Handbook* (USDI BLM, 2005). It is relevant to note that planning under OFM commenced on the Red Hill area 9 years before the BLM's Executive Leadership Team on January 6, 2006 issued the directive that all that agency's SRMAs would be planned and managed under BBM, the earlier name for OFM.

The current *Land Use Planning Handbook* states that "Each SRMA has a distinct, primary recreation-tourism market as well as a corresponding and distinguishing recreation management strategy." Furthermore, the *Land Use Planning Handbook,* and the Step 5 of the comprehensive normative model, require that logical RMZs be defined in each SRMA. As stated in the *Land Use Planning Handbook,* "Each RMZ has four defining characteristics [in that] it: (1) serves a different recreation niche within the primary recreation market; (2) produces a different set of recreation opportunities and facilitates the attainment of different experience and benefit outcomes (to individuals, households and communities, economies, and the environment); (3) has distinctive recreation setting character; and (4) requires a different set of recreation provider actions to meet the strategically-targeted primary recreation market demand.

The relative smallness of the area and the fact that most of the relevant customers lived nearby, made it relatively straightforward to analyze and interpret the preferences of the likely on-site customers and to define relevant market segments (Step 7). The BLM already had an inventory of public lands recreation-tourism resource attractions and services. The RHC determined how this attraction complemented or augmented the supply of other similar recreation opportunities within the market area to meet the community's identified recreation desires (Step 9). The primary recreation-tourism market was community-based (Step 10). One RMZ was identified when supply and demand information was analyzed by the partners (Step 11).

Phase 3

The final report of the Red Hill Project produced a series of proposed public recommendations for management of Red Hill. An information brochure was circulated and public meetings were held to further refine the recommendations. The RHC's findings, the vast local support, the concerns of residents, the residential development on nearby private lands, and the increase in use; prompted BLM to formally consider the recommendations as the proposed action in a required environmental assessment (EA) – land use plan amendment. BLM basically agreed with the proposed management strategy crafted by the RHC except for a few implementation actions that were below the scope of land use planning level decisions.

In order to avoid redundant public involvement efforts, the BLM recognized the efforts of the RHC had sufficiently fulfilled the public scoping requirements required by the National Environmental Policy Act (NEPA). Generally all partners agreed that the recreation management direction needed to shift from a "custodial" management strategy to a "structured" SRMA emphasis with specific recreation management objectives. Protection of the desired recreation setting through prescribing the essential natural resource setting characteristics required land use plan changes including:

- Visual Resource Management (VRM) classifications.
- No Surface Occupancy (NSO)/disturbance stipulations.
- Designation of mechanized travel routes.
- The "open" motorized travel area designation.

Based on the findings in the Red Hill Report and the public scoping comments, the recreation planner then facilitated a discussion with the RHC to identify the specific activities, experiences, outcomes, and recreation settings to be targeted as part of the recreation objectives in the proposed action in the EA (Steps 12 and 13). Regarding Step 14, OFM recognizes that a recreation setting has three components, each of which has attributes or characteristics that define it. They are the Biophysical, Social, and Administrative/Managerial components.

In addition to creating recreation objectives and prescribing settings, BLM also identified an implementation framework to guide subsequent implementation planning. The RHC also raised funds and completed on-the-ground archeological and biological assessments for the EA.

Following guidance provided by the NEPA, the BLM provide the public with a 30-day public comment period on a proposed action (OFM strategy) and a continuation of current management strategy (no action) (Step 15).

The environmental analysis determined that the current custodial management direction did *not:*

- Adequately address the identified issues,
- Address the publics concerns, or
- Deal with the anticipated growth in recreational use.

It was concluded that structured recreational management will help solve many of the identified problems while enhancing recreational opportunities for the community. In addition, the current management strategy didn't help maintain or achieve healthy public lands.

The BLM decided to manage for the activities of day-use walking, hiking, running, horseback riding, and mountain biking on designated routes. Other activities, such as hunting, can still take place, but BLM and/or partners will not focus funding or implementing actions for enhancement of those activities.

With the formation of specific structured management direction for Red Hill, it was felt that the Red Hill SRMA had the potential to provide outcomes to the community.

They include:

- A "close to home" area that allows for frequent access to outdoor activities.
- An area that helps maintains a sense of community pride & satisfaction.
- An area that supports the community's outdoor-oriented lifestyle.
- An area to appreciate wildlife, scenery, and natural aesthetics.
- An area that supports better mental and physical health.

Targeted Experiences	Targeted Benefits
• Escaping everyday responsibilities and other people for awhile	• Better mental and physical health through reduced tension/anxiety • Higher satisfaction with life
• Enjoying frequent access to outdoor physical activity	• Improved physical fitness/better health • Greater cultivation of an outdoor-oriented lifestyle • Heightened sense of community pride and satisfaction
• Enjoying the area's wildlife, scenery, views, and aesthetics	• Greater environmental awareness and stewardship • Greater aesthetic appreciation • Preservation of this special place • Greater understanding and respect for private property

Table 18.1 An Example Management Objective

The BLM also determined that the partners can work together to make Red Hill visitors better stewards of the land and that the following environmental outcomes can be achieved:

- Greater environmental awareness and stewardship,
- Greater understanding and respect for private property,
- Preservation of this special place, and
- Protection of cultural and biological resources.

No economic beneficial outcomes were identified. An example of an approved management objective is presented in Table 18.1

Management Objective: By the year 2005, manage this area so that 85% of visitors and community residents responding to a visitor/community survey, report at least a "moderate" realization of the targeted experiences/benefits (i.e., 3.0 on a probability scale where 1=not at all, 2= somewhat, 3= moderate, and 4= complete/total realization). The targeted experiences and benefits to which reference was just made in that management objective were defined in the approved plan as follows:

The characteristics of the recreation settings essential for visitors to realize the outcomes targeted were identified. Implementation (managerial) actions necessary to maintain and/or improve those setting conditions were developed as a part of the proposed management plan and the accompanying implementation plan. An example from that plan can be seen in Table 18.2.

Step 16 (define the relevant recreation-tourism market environment) was relatively easy to accomplish because the community focus of the project and

Red Hill SRMA Recreation Setting Condition Prescriptions	
SETTING	NARRATIVE
PHYSICAL SETTING	Retain (allow few modifications) the existing characteristic naturally appearing landscape.
SOCIAL SETTING	Visitors can expect to see, on an average day, a max. of 10–15 groups on travel routes around Mushroom Rock and +10 on the north side, slight vegetation trampling along travel routes, and infrequent evidence of other users once away from trailheads.
ADMINISTRATIVE/ MANAGERIAL SETTING	Brochures/maps give directions and help protect resources. Basic visitor controls posted with some seasonal use limitations. No fees. Mountain bike use on trails and no motorized use.

Table 18.2 Recreation Setting Condition Prescriptions

the relevant customers were from the nearby areas. It is anticipated that this will hold true in the future for the relatively small Red Hills SRMA. Therefore, Step 14 was not as relevant here as it is in applications of OFM to larger areas with a more group of customers and market demands.

Phase 4

The EA considered the overall management strategy (outcome objectives and setting prescriptions) which defined how BLM and partners will manage resources in the Red Hill SRMA and the routes to be designated for mountain bike travel. The specific on-the-ground management of: recreation use, recreation resources, and other resources is accomplished by completing and implementing a SRMA implementation plan. An Implementation Plan was developed collaboratively by the BLM and the RHC a few months after the EA was signed in 2000. The Implementation Plan identified management actions (Step 17), monitoring actions (Step 18), and administrative actions (Step 19) for all parties involved in managing the Red Hill SRMA.

No marketing actions (Step 20) were identified at the time the implementation plan was completed. However, since then, marketing issues have arisen and have been handled by looking at the effects of proposed marketing actions on community recreation-tourism market, the outcome objectives, and setting prescriptions.

A sample of how the Red Hill SRMA implementation plan was formatted is shown in Figure 16.3. The matrix format shows, specifically and simply, what implementation actions were identified to accomplish the physical setting prescription components. The partners found it easy to determine what implementations

Physical Setting Prescription	Allow a few modifications in an otherwise naturally appearing landscape. Retain the existing characteristic landscape. Maintain a few primitive trails with directional signs and erosion controls. Install interpretive sign at/near trailheads.

Designate, construct, and maintain routes open for recreational use.							
Management Actions	Priority	Where	How (Critical Steps)	When	Who	Other	Costs
Construct new Rim Trail	A	SE 1/4 of the NE 1/4 of Section 28	Cultural Analysis, Botanical Analysis, Approval of the Environmental Assessment	Spring 2000	Roaring Fork Outdoor Volunteers, Volunteers, Red Hill Council, BLM	Analyzed in amendment (EA #-CO-07 8-99-030)	$4,000
Construct wildlife and habitat improvements (i.e., guzzlers, plantings) which will be utilized to mitigate impacts to displaced wildlife	N/A	Northside	Work with the CDOW to identify projects to help mitigate conflicts. Procure funding to implement mitigation projects	Unknown	DOW, BLM, Red Hill Council, Volunteers	Analyzed in amendment (EA #-CO-07 8-99-030), Project will require EA	$1,000
Landscape the parking area at the base of Red Hill with emphasis on screening view of HW 82	C	Parking area and base of Red Hill adjacent to County Road 107 and HW 82	CDOT approvals, Town of Carbondale input, Garfield County Road and Bridge communications.	2001 or 2002	Town of Carbondale, CDOT, Red Hill Council, Volunteers	Carbondale as a beneficiary, should participate	$4,000
Develop nonmotorized connection to Highway 133 trail system and Carbondale using the tunnel under HW 82	C	Intersection of state HW 82 and state HW 133 at the base of Red Hill	CDOT, private landowner approval/easement, Town of Carbondale, engineering, procurement of funding	2001 or 2002	Town of Carbondale, Red Hill Council, Volunteers, Roaring Fork Outdoor Volunteers	Carbondale as a beneficiary, should participate	$10,000 to $100,000
Install gate/fencing at the Elk Traverse Trail	C	Elk Traverse Trail in the NE 1/4 of the SW 1/4 of section 21		2001 or 2002	Division of Wildlife, Red Hill Council, BLM, volunteers	CDOW participation is a critical element	$1,000

Table 18.3 Example of Implementation Plan Actions

actions were necessary once the recreation setting prescriptions (physical, social, and administrative) to produce the targeted outcomes were clearly defined.

The RHC and interested publics reviewed the proposed implementation plan (Step 21).

Phases 5, 6, 7, and 8

The LHC incorporated public review and comment into the final plan, making adjustments as necessary (Step 22). At the time this chapter was written, the implementation plan was successfully being implemented (Step 23). The BLM is in the process of revising (Step 24) the land use plan for the field office, which includes reviewing the Red Hill SRMA objectives, setting prescriptions, and implementation actions.

Outcomes are not considered in the reporting of work or performance at this time in the BLM, even subjectively (Step 25). To gain the needed recreation evaluation information (benefit attainment) ahead of the land use plan revision, the BLM contracted with scientists with Arizona State University to conduct an outcomes-focused visitor study and resident focus group discussions. The goal of the projects is to evaluate the degree to which the targeted beneficial outcomes are being attained, the appropriateness of the prescribed settings, and suitability of the implementation actions.

Conclusions

The Red Hill area was one of the first applications of OFM to public wildlands. It was an innovative endeavor, and much was learned in the process that helped refine and advance OFM. It is not surprising that the requirements of the comprehensive normative model were met, because what was learned from that application, and application of OFM on the MCNCA, contributed substantively to development of that model.

Literature Cited

USDI Bureau of Land Management. (2003). Land Use Planning Handbook. As amended through March 11, 2005. Washington D.C.

Red Hill Committee. 1998. Unpublished report. Red Hill Project Final Report. Carbondale, Colorado.

Chapter 19
Assessing the Benefits of the Alpine Loop Backcountry Byway in Southwestern Colorado

Randy J. Virden, Christine Vogt, and Richard C. Knopf

Learning Objectives:

1. Understand how focus groups and surveys can be utilized to understand and identify the activities, settings, experiences, and other benefits that residents of local communities and visitors desire from a backcountry byway.
2. Understand how a collaborative benefits-oriented research project can be designed to include diverse input from a variety of community-based and visitor-based stakeholders.
3. Gain insights about lessons learned from the Alpine Loop Backcountry Byway Customer Study, particularly about how research and managers interface with community stakeholders.

Purpose of This Chapter

The previous six chapters of this text described applications of OFM to guide the management of recreation resources and services. This chapter does not describe an actual application of OFM, but instead summarizes a collaborative benefits-oriented research project that was conducted in the late 1990's on Colorado's Alpine Loop Backcountry Byway. Three separate methodologies/studies were employed to collect stakeholder input that could be used be to help guide future management planning for that resource area. After presenting the overview, the lessons learned from this experience will be discussed to provide perspective and insights for future benefits-oriented research and management projects. Hopefully, the content of the chapter will help others with outcomes-oriented research needed to apply OFM properly.

Introduction

The Alpine Loop Backcountry Byway encompasses some of the most beautiful landscapes and scenery in the San Juan Mountains of Southwestern Colorado. In the 1870s, this area helped launch a colorful chapter of the West's gold and silver mining story. Today, many of those mines, mills, ghost towns, and railroads are among the cultural attractions that draw tourists into the Alpine Loop. The Alpine Loop refers to the popular two- and four-wheel drive road system that forms a National Backcountry Byway that traverses the public lands and mountain passes between the communities of Lake City, Ouray, and Silverton. These three communities form the corners of the Alpine Triangle (see Figure 19.1) and what is locally referred to as the "Jeeping capital of North America." Each of these three communities offers a unique resident and tourist experience: Lake City is a sleepy resort and ranching community on the east side of the Alpine Loop; Ouray is known for its colorful mining history, ice climbing, and famous hot springs; and Silverton is a quaint mining town with a popular narrow gauge railway that connects it with Durango.

The Alpine Loop offers visitors much more than mining history and world class four-wheeling opportunities. The resource area includes two alpine wilderness areas on adjoining National Forest lands, 14,000 foot peaks, alpine meadows, streams, and a large network of trails. The area is popular for sightseeing, four-wheeling, motorcycling, hiking, mountaineering, visiting historical sites, camping, wildlife viewing, hunting, winter sports, and fishing. The historical tie to mining (many mining claims) is responsible for the Alpine Loop being under the management control of the Bureau of Land Management (BLM) even though it includes forests, mountains, and considerable pristine backcountry acreage. When national forests were established in Colorado in the early 20th century, the complex network mining claims kept the area from leaving the pubic domain. The BLM splits the management control of the

Alpine Loop across two field offices, the Gunnison Field Office manages the eastern half of the Loop (outside of Lake City) and the San Juan Field Office (Durango) manages the western half (lands adjacent to Ouray and Silverton). The Alpine Loop is separated by two high elevation mountain passes; Cinnamon and Engineer pass both demand a high clearance, four-wheel drive vehicle to climb over the 12,000 foot passes going from east to west or vice versa.

Since 1991, interest in the beneficial and negative outcomes associated with leisure has grown considerably and has stimulated interest in OFM and Benefits-Based Management (BBM) before it (Driver et al., 1991; Allen, 1996; Driver & Bruns, 1999; Stein & Lee, 1995; Stein & Anderson, 2002; and Moore & Driver, 2005). Because of this interest, Don Bruns, the Recreation Lead with the Colorado State Office of the BLM, initiated a benefits-oriented research project on the Alpine Loop Backcountry Byway in 1995. The project was based on an earlier BBM pilot project that started in 1991. It was on the Ruby Canyon-Black Ridge Special Recreation Management Area near Grand Junction, Colorado (Stein & Lee, 1995; Bruns, Driver, Lee, Anderson, & Brown, 1994). The goal of the Alpine Loop Backcountry Byway Customer Study was to provide social science knowledge that could be used in a management plan that included specific management prescriptions for defined resource zones upon the beneficial outcomes identified and desired by visitors, residents, and collaborative partners through research. This chapter provides an overview of the benefits-oriented research project conducted in the Alpine Loop during the 1997 and 1998 summer use seasons, and what was learned from that experience.

The Research Purpose and Project Design

Acting on behalf of the of the Alpine Loop's varied community partners and through the San Juan Mountain Association, BLM worked with Arizona State University to organize this study. Key stakeholders included the BLM; local, county, and community governments; local landowners and citizens; small businesses; and other recreation-tourism service providers. The purpose of the study was to collect social science information to help guide the future management and planning of the Alpine Loop Backcountry Byway, the public lands surrounding it, and the supporting service delivery systems needed to sustain the Byway. This included obtaining public opinion from leaders and residents in the three communities (Lake City, Ouray, and Silverton) bordering the study area. Three underlying principles drove the benefits-based approach for this study: 1) a collaborative effort which encourages input from various local and regional stakeholders, 2) a focus on geographical management zones within the Alpine Loop management area, and 3) a broad assessment of the four levels of demand (assessment of desired activities, experiences, settings, and benefits) associated with recreation opportunities. Driver and Brown (1979) first articulated a hierarchy of demand for recreation based on four levels of demand for public recreation opportunities.

Toward accomplishment of the above purposes and principles, three separate data gathering methodologies were developed and employed for this research project. The first data collection method included a series of focus groups conducted with local residents, community leaders, and tourism industry providers in the surrounding communities of Lake City, Ouray, and Silverton. This phase of the research was used to identify the important issues, activities, setting preferences, and benefits from different stakeholder groups. The focus groups provided insight into the issues and questions that needed to be incorporated into a subsequent round of visitor and resident surveys. This second and most costly data collection method included an on-site and mail-back survey administered to 1,200 randomly selected visitors to the Alpine Loop in the summer of 1997. That methodology required respondents to choose their favorite zone from a map (see figure 1), which included nine geographic zones of the Alpine Loop. Since the "Alpine Loop experience" includes experiences offered by surrounding commu-

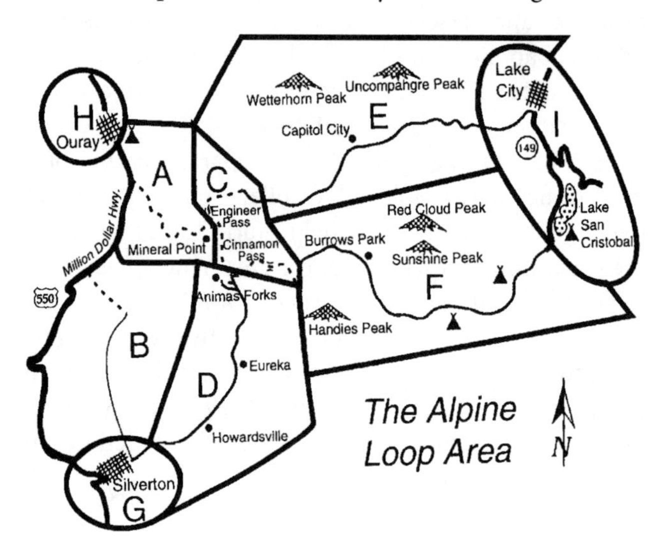

Figure 19.1 Alpine Loop Map

nities (Lake City, Ouray, and Silverton), the research team decided to include each community as a separate zone since many visitors are drawn to each of the three communities. The third study method was a mail survey administered to residents from each of the three communities to assess their preferences and attitudes toward tourism in the Alpine Loop Backcountry Byway. Finally, this paper will provide some reflections on the study results and the subsequent management actions that have occurred since the study was completed.

Each of these three studies are addressed separately in the next section of this chapter.

Community-Based Focus Groups

A series of focus groups were used to identify issues, desired recreation opportunities, and benefits of greatest concern to local communities, residents, and visitors. The purpose of the focus group process was to: 1) provide understanding and involvement from local communities concerning the importance of the Alpine Loop, 2) to involve the local communities as partners in the research and eventual planning processes, and 3) to gain insights for designing the visitor survey instruments for the subsequent survey research effort. The process included broad representation of the Lake City, Ouray, and Silverton communities, including residents, elected government officials, private sector tourism service providers, general community business enterprises, public land management agency personnel, and local recreational users of the Byway resource.

The focus groups were held in a central downtown community setting within each community and facilitated by representatives of the research team from Arizona State University. Each focus group had a facilitator and recorder (Krueger, 1994). The facilitator asked questions and involved each participant in the discussion. The recorder administered written surveys, wrote comments on flip charts, and tape-recorded the sessions. Sessions lasted from 45 minutes to 1 hour and 30 minutes. Besides the facilitator and recorder, BLM or USFS personnel were in attendance at each focus group.

While each focus group took on its own unique personality and communication focus, the participants were generally asked to share responses to the following series of questions:

1. What is your name, your profession, and/or the organization you are with? What has been your most enjoyable personal recreation experience in the Alpine Loop Area? (This question will tease out experience components.)
2. What recreational activities do you and other residents participate in while in the Alpine Loop? Next, what activities do you see tourists doing?
3. What setting features attract you and other people to the Alpine Loop area?
4. What is the importance or meaning that the Alpine Loop has in your life or the lives of others in your community?
5. What are some other places (i.e., communities, destinations) that you would like your community to be like? What are some communities/destinations that you would not like to be like?
6. Thinking about your past recreation activities and experiences within the Alpine Loop, what are the personal benefits that you personally have derived?
7. Thinking about the benefits that occur to groups like families, recreation groups or even the whole community, what are some of the social benefits that occur here because of the Alpine Loop to these groups?
8. What economic benefits may occur to individuals, local businesses, or the regional economy because of the Alpine Loop?
9. Can you identify some environmental benefits that occur because of the Alpine Loop?
10. Finally, are there any other issues or concerns you would like to share with us about the Alpine Loop area?

The focus groups were conducted in Lake City, Ouray, Silverton, and Montrose (a small community just north of Ouray) in April of 1997. The initial intention was to have two or more focus groups in each community. In Lake City, three focus groups were held including: tourism businesses and marketers, government officials, and general public. In Ouray and Silverton, there was a combined section of the three targeted groups because the total number of participants who chose to participate in the focus groups was less. The Montrose focus group was added to provide insight from regional visitors to the Alpine Loop, so some questions were altered to gain the correspondingly broader visitor perspective. A total of six focus groups were held during the period of April 10–12, 1996, ranging in size from 6 participants to 12 participants.

Key Summary Points from Each of the Six Focus Groups

It is important to remember who the participants of each of the focus groups represent (type of participants, where, when). Focus groups are more useful for gaining insight into specific issues and meanings that may be held by a group, than can be gained from more traditional surveys or questionnaires. However, it should be remembered that focus groups are not the best techniques for representing the views of a whole community or community segment–traditional surveys with random sampling do a better job of that. In short, focus groups provide part of the picture, as do the survey results that follow in the next section.

Focus Group 1: Lake City General Residents

- The beauty, setting, and recreation opportunities found in the Alpine Loop are important to the quality of life for local residents.
- Local residents participate in a variety of activities in the Alpine Loop (hiking, four-wheel driving, X-C skiing, enjoying wildflowers, snowmobiling, and visiting historical sites).
- Nature-based, nonmotorized activities (like hiking, skiing, or peak bagging) were most valued and prevalent in Lake City (compared with the other focus groups).
- The wild, scenic, accessible, and pristine character of the Alpine Loop were dominant setting features.
- Residents would like to see more visible management from the BLM (protection, interpretation, education, personnel).
- Lake City residents do not want to become commercialized like Telluride or Crested Buttes–they want to maintain there uniqueness and maintain the local quality of life.

Focus Group 2: Lake City Public/Elected Officials

- The Alpine Loop provides important social benefits related to community identity and local quality of life.
- The Alpine Loop provides an important source of recreation opportunities to the local community.
- Lake City is uniquely dependent of the Alpine Loop for its livelihood and as an important economic resource (tourism is the primary industry).
- Management issues related to the Alpine Loop are of concern—primarily related to road maintenance, law enforcement, vandalism, education, and adequate protection efforts.
- Coordinating with federal agencies, other communities, private land owners, and with zoning are key to the future of the Alpine Loop.
- It is important that the uniqueness and character of Lake City/Alpine Loop be maintained and not compromised.
- Lake City needs to engineer its future so that the social and commercial ills that plague other regional tourism destinations (e.g., Aspen, Telluride) do not occur here.

Focus Group 3: Lake City Business Owners

- The Alpine Loop is valued as both an important ecosystem and economic asset; balancing economic growth with protection of the Alpine Loop is key.
- Important features of the Alpine Loop include the scenery, "Fourteeners," accessible roads, mining history, hiking trails, wildflowers, and water features.
- Need better schools to bring year-round residents (and winter business).
- Maintenance of the roads in the Alpine Loop are very important.

Focus Group 4: Combined Ouray Group (residents, public, and business)

- The Alpine Loop is valued for a variety of recreation activities ranging from remote hiking to four-wheel driving.
- The natural character, remoteness, and scenery of the Alpine Loop area are especially important setting features.
- Ouray's identity is tied to the Alpine Loop and San Juan Mountains to the West of the Million Dollar highway.
- The visitors and tourism that is created because of the Alpine Loop and local history (e.g., mining) are very important to Ouray.
- It is an important area for the residents of Ouray to enjoy and play in.
- More signing and education is needed to influence behavior and protect the Alpine Loop area (too few signs and communication).
- Any fees in the area should be tied to better/improved management of the Alpine Loop.

- There needs to be better communication between the three counties that manage roads in the area.
- Continued efforts need to be made to stabilize the historic structures in the area.

Focus Group 5: Combined Silverton Group (residents, public, and business)

- The mining history and sites (e.g., old mines, ghost towns) contained in the Alpine Loop are very important to Silverton and Silverton's economy.
- Local identity is provided through mining heritage and scenic backcountry.
- There is a need to increase tourism revenue and encourage the use of the Alpine Loop during shoulder and winter seasons.
- More historic preservation (restoration and stabilization), education, BLM and USFS management presence needs to occur in the area.
- Any user fees need to have low administrative overhead and revenues need to go back into the area.
- A coherent (three communities and federal agencies) and collaborative management policy needs to be developed for the Alpine Loop area.
- The uneven road maintenance by the three counties is an issue in the Alpine Loop.

Focus Group 6: Montrose Visitors

- Montrose visitors also seek a broad range of recreation opportunities in the Alpine Loop (from four-wheeling to hiking).
- The majority of benefits related to the Alpine Loop are personal (e.g., fitness, stress reduction, sharing the experience) and community-based (identity for the region, recreation opportunities, brings folks together).
- The historical values of the Alpine Loop should be preserved.
- The scenic and natural features of the Alpine Loop are most important.
- Alpine Loop management has improved in recent years (e.g., restrooms, more signs, interpretive exhibits, education efforts, less litter).
- Additional management needs include greater control of OHV travel off of trail/roads, more ADA access, better maps, and more camping facilities.

While the comments and messages from each focus group had a unique flavor (see Virden, Knopf, and Vogt, 1998 for a more detailed summary of each focus group), the next summary section attempts to identify some major unifying themes that emerged across the individual focus groups.

Summary of Overall Themes that Emerged from the Focus Groups:

- The Alpine Loop is a special place valued for its scenery, geology, mining history, wildlife, vegetation, water features, and recreation opportunities.
- The Alpine Loop is used for a broad array of recreation activities by local residents, ranging from visiting historical sites to motorized recreation (e.g., Jeeping and motorcycling) to backcountry travel (e.g., hiking and mountain climbing).
- The Alpine Loop is important to the local quality of life for local residents and businesses
- The uniqueness and quality of the Alpine Loop must be protected and maintained
- The Alpine Loop provides a local/regional identity to the communities of Lake City, Ouray, and Silverton
- Local communities and businesses are dependent on the personal, social economic, and environmental benefits provided by the Alpine Loop
- A variety of suggestions were made concerning the future management of the Alpine Loop (e.g., road maintenance, fees, historical preservation, interpretation, partnerships, law enforcement, on-site personnel, education, signage).

Alpine Loop Visitor Survey

The visitor study was designed to sample Alpine Loop Back Country Byway users during the summer 1997 use season. Ultimately, the focus group process helped to identify many of the specific issues that were incorporated into the design of the survey instruments used in the visitor survey. In line with provisions of the Interagency Agreement, the study was organized to produce the following information:

1. Visitor profiles of travel behavior, group types, vehicle use, prior use history, and demographics;
2. Visitor profiles of information sources and desired information services;

3. Visitor preferences for services, facilities, activities, and experiences;
4. Visitor land management preferences;
5. Perceived benefits and experience preferences of Alpine Loop users;
6. Visitor willingness to pay for Alpine Loop Byway management services;
7. Economic impacts of Alpine Loop Byway visitors; and
8. Visitor satisfaction levels and perceptions of quality of services provided.

Given the wealth of data to be collected by the survey project, the decision was made to collect information from the Alpine Loop users in two phases. The first phase involved administration of a brief on-site survey (dedicated primarily to collecting information about visitor travel behavior, demographics, attitudes toward use fees, and home mailing addresses). The second phase involved a follow-up mail survey that allowed for more detailed assessment of visitor demographics, attitudes, and preferences. The goal, as specified in the Agreement, was to sample 1,200 visitors during the busy summer season extending from June 15 through August 30. In total, the on-site survey took somewhere between five to eight minutes to complete. The second phase involved the use of a follow-up mail survey (that allowed for more detailed assessment of visitor demographics, attitudes, and preferences). The majority of on-site surveys were administered during the busy summer season extending from June 15 through Labor Day (September 1).

On-Site Survey

An on-site interview survey was chosen as the method for identifying a random sample and for making initial contact with visitors to the Alpine Loop Backcountry Byway. The on-site visitor survey was designed to determine the following information:

1. Where the visitor traveled while in the Alpine Loop area;
2. The number of persons and type of group;
3. Which outdoor recreation activities members of the group participated in;
4. If the respondent has visited the area previously;
5. If the respondent would be willing to pay a vehicle fee to use the Alpine Loop area, and if so, what they would consider to be a fair fee; and
6. The name and mailing address of visitors who would be willing to participate in the follow-up mail survey.

The specific instrument used in data collection was an interviewer-administered on-site visitor survey. The on-site visitor survey was designed to assist in identifying a random sample of visitors that could be approached for a commitment to participate in a more in-depth mail survey. The visitor's name and address was also recorded on the on-site interview schedule for the purpose of building a sampling frame for the follow-up mail survey that is described later in this chapter. The overall target of 1,200 visitor contacts for the summer period was to be attained by collecting samples—at each of the five sample locations—on one weekday and one weekend day each week during the fourteen-week sample period.

Mail Survey

The self-administered mail survey was provided to those Alpine Loop visitors who were willing to participate in the follow-up mail survey. As with the on-site survey, the mail questionnaire instrument went through several developmental stages. Once pre-testing and the final revisions were completed, the final mail questionnaire instruments were 11 pages long and required approximately 20 minutes to complete. When implemented, the on-site survey and mail survey together will allow for the inventory and measurement of the following types of visitor-based information:

1. Visitor profiles of travel behavior, favorite zone, prior use history;
2. Visitor profiles of information sources and desired information services;
3. Visitor preferences for services, facilities, activities, and experiences;
4. Visitor land management preferences;
5. Perceived benefits (personal, social, economic, and environmental) and experience preferences of Alpine Loop users;
6. Visitor willingness to pay a vehicle fee for using the Alpine Loop;
7. Economic expenditures of Alpine Loop Byway visitors;
8. Visitor satisfaction levels and perceptions of quality of services provided; and
9. Demographic questions and two-open ended comment questions were also contained in the survey instrument.

The sampling goal for the mail survey was an extension of the previous strategy for the on-site survey. Of the total number of visitors who completed the on-site survey, 92.1% said they were willing to participate in the mail survey and provided their names and addresses. The method for administering the mail questionnaire was adapted from Dillman's Total Design Method (1978). The actual handing out of the mail survey with a pre-paid return envelope on-site (first mailing) was substituted for the initial mailing. A mailing of a reminder postcard (second mailing) was sent one week later to those original respondents who had not yet returned their surveys. Three weeks after the on-site interview, a second complete survey (third mailing) was sent to the nonrespondents.

Alpine Loop Visitor Survey Results

The response rates are reported in Table 19.1. Of the 1,450 individuals contacted on-site, 160 refused to participate in the study, 96 completed the on-site survey but declined the invitation to complete a mail questionnaire, and 74 did not meet the criteria for inclusion in the study (e.g., their group contained no one over the age of seventeen or English-speaking visitors). This resulted in a total of 1,216 completed samples for the first phase (on-site) portion of the survey (88.4% of the visitors sampled). Of the 1,216 visitors requested to participate in the second phase (mail-back), 667 returned fully completed, usable surveys—resulting in a 60.3% adjusted mail-back response rate.

For the purposes of this chapter only selected results will be presented; more in depth results can be found in the technical report. Initially, frequency tables will provide more detailed data about the favorite geographic zone, activities, and benefits most engaged in and preferred by the visitors. Highlighted below are some of the more important summary findings, organized by eleven major categories of data collected from both the on-site and mail surveys.

Favorite Zone: There was considerable diversity in response as visitors were asked to identify the geographic zone (see Figure 19.1) that added most to your satisfaction during the trip to the Alpine Loop. The zones are important as coherent management units within the resource where specific objectives and management actions can be specified. It was decided to allow each of the communities to operate as its own zone since the recreation trip often included visiting one or more of these communities. The most frequently identified zone was Zone C, the "High Mountain Pass" zone, identified by 30% of the visitors. This was not unexpected as the passes that go through this zone are popular with four wheel drive visitors and this zone has some of the most spectacular scenery along the byway. The next most frequently identified zone was the "Lake Fork" zone, identified by almost 20% of the visitors. Out of nine possible zones, the "Lake City" zone ranked third in frequency of identification. Thirteen percent of the visitors perceived that the Lake City/Lake San Cristobal community added most to their satisfaction during their visit to the Alpine Loop area. If all three of the community zones (Lake City, Ouray, and Silverton) are combined, the results indicate that 22.2% of the visitor identified a local community as one of their favorite zones.

(On the map, the Alpine Loop area is divided into nine zones, including a zone for each of the three surrounding communities. Each zone is labeled with a letter. Please identify the zone that *added most to your satisfaction* during your visit to the Alpine Loop area, by checking the appropriate box below.)

Activity Participation: The onsite survey measured all recreation in recreation participation that occurred during the trip to the Alpine Loop area. The frequency and percentage of use of activities are displayed in Table 19.3 in order of importance. A total of six activities were participated in by over half of the visitors (viewing wildflowers, driving, general sightseeing, four wheel driving, photography, hiking/walking, and watching wildlife). Other activities with significant participation include picnicking, shopping, visiting historical sites, and camping.

Completed On-sites	Refused On-sites	Refused Mailbacks	Unqualified Respondents	Total Number of On-site Contacts	On-site Response Rate
1216	160	96	74	1450	88.4%
Completed Mailbacks		Unusable Surveys (bad mail, unqualified respondents, etc.)		**Total Adjusted Mailback Response Rate**	
667		14		**60.3%**	

Table 19.1 Overall Survey Response Rates

First choice	Frequency	Valid percent
A (Mineral Creek/Point zone)	26	3.7%
B (Cement Creek zone)	17	2.5%
C (High Mountain Pass zone)	207	29.7%
D (Animas River zone)	88	12.7%
E (Henson Creek zone)	69	9.9%
F (Lake Fork zone)	135	19.4%
G (Silverton zone)	28	4.1%
H (Ouray zone)	34	4.9%
I (Lake City zone)	92	13.2%

Table 19.2 Zone Which Added Most Satisfaction During Alpine Loop Visit

Activity	Frequency	Valid percent
Viewing wildflowers	900	66.4%
Driving: General sightseeing	884	65.2%
Four wheel driving	850	62.7%
Photography	820	60.5%
Hiking/walking	702	51.8%
Watching wildlife	694	51.2%
Picnicking	584	43.1%
Shopping	573	42.3%
Visiting historical sites	555	41.0%
Camping	444	32.8%
Dining	388	28.6%
Star gazing	351	25.9%
Fishing	322	23.8%
Playing in snow	270	19.9%
Rock collecting	233	17.2%
Climbing	221	16.3%
Visiting museums	216	15.9%
Mountain climbing	182	13.5%
Nature study	179	13.2%
Backpacking	141	10.4%
Studying geology	137	10.1%
Partying	108	7.9%
Mountain biking	92	6.8%
ATV riding	86	6.4%
Motorcycling	76	5.6%
Swimming	72	5.3%
Horseback riding	53	3.9%
Other	45	3.3%
Cross-country skiing	22	1.6%
Hunting	14	1.0%
Snowshoeing	8	0.6%
Snowmobiling	6	0.4%
Kayaking	0	0%

Table 19.3 Activity Participation in Alpine Loop

Activity	Most satisfying		Second most satisfying	
	Frequency	Valid percent	Frequency	Valid percent
Four wheel driving (e.g., jeeping)	186	26.4%	87	13.1%
Hiking/walking	100	14.1%	79	11.8%
Driving: General sightseeing	96	13.6%	50	7.5%
Mountain climbing	49	7.0%	10	1.5%
Other/nonsensical	46	6.4%	35	5.3%
Camping	34	4.8%	49	7.3%
Fishing	30	4.3%	27	4.1%
Watching wildlife	24	3.4%	41	6.2%
Viewing wildflowers	24	3.4%	91	13.7%
Visiting historical sites	20	2.8%	35	5.3%
ATV riding	19	2.7%	5	0.8%
Photography	17	2.4%	58	8.7%
Climbing	11	1.5%	7	1.1%
Mountain biking	10	1.4%	9	1.3%
Motorcycling	10	1.4%	5	0.8%
Backpacking	7	1.0%	9	1.3%
Studying geology	6	0.9%	3	0.5%
Nature study	6	0.9%	9	1.3%
Cross-country skiing	4	0.6%	0	0%
Rock collecting	4	0.6%	10	1.5%
Kayaking	1	0.1%	0	0%
Horseback riding	1	0.1%	2	0.3%
Picnicking	1	0.1%	6	1.0%
Shopping	1	0.1%	7	1.1%
Visiting museums	0	0%	5	0.8%
Dining	0	0%	7	1.1%
Partying	0	0%	3	0.5%
Snow play	0	0%	3	0.5%
Snowmobiling	0	0%	1	0.2%
Swimming	0	0%	1	0.2%
Star gazing	0	0%	10	1.5%

Table 19.4 Most Satisfying and Second Most Satisfying Activities

Most Satisfying Activities: In addition to the above question about general recreation participation, each respondent was asked to choose the two activities that "contributed most to your satisfaction" in their favorite zone (Table 19.4). When these two activities are combined for their "most satisfying" zone, the favorite activities are ranked as four wheel driving (40%), hiking/walking (26%), driving/general sightseeing (21%) viewing wildflowers (17%), camping (12%), photography (11%), and watching wildlife (10%).

Satisfaction Attributes: The previous three tables addressed the importance of the resource and of activities to visitors of the Alpine Loop Backcountry Byway. To gain a better understanding of the dimensions of the visit that visitors find the most attractive, a question was developed which asked respondents the relative importance of six features that contribute to overall satisfaction in the Alpine Loop. On the whole, visitors defined their satisfaction as emerging from the natural places, the recreation activities, and companionship of the people who shared the experience. Experiences in the local communities were important contributors to satisfaction, but less so than the other three features.

Personal Benefits: Visitors to the Alpine Loop were queried as to the personal benefits that they attained from their visit to their most satisfying zone. These personal benefit items were adapted from experiences and beneficial outcomes identified in previous research (Bruns, 1995; Stein & Lee, 1995; Moore & Driver, 2005) and through consultations with BLM managers. Clear themes emerged as visitors rated their most attained personal benefits resulting from participation in their most satisfying activity and zone. The highest attained personal benefits were developing a greater connectivity with nature, reduced stress, enhanced family relationships, and strengthened relationships with companions (Table 19.6). An improved outlook on life, improved mental health, increased appreciation of the areas cultural history and improved mental health were all rated above 3.0 (good or better). While the data below reflect the overall averages across the Alpine Loop, the question was answered with in the context of the visitors' favorite zone. Consequently, it is possible to generate a zone by zone profile of personal benefits.

Satisfaction Attributes	Contributed least (1)	(2)	Contributed some (3)	(4)	Contributed most (1)	Mean	*n*
The natural places I saw (e.g., mountains, streams)	0%	0%	1.3%	13.2%	85.5%	4.84	741
The activities I did (e.g., four-wheeling, hiking)	4.0%	2.3%	10.6%	27.1%	56.0%	4.29	716
The companionship of the people in my group	6.8%	1.4%	13.5%	26.0%	52.4%	4.16	706
The opportunity to think and reflect	9.6%	9.3%	26.8%	27.2%	27.1%	3.53	711
The cultural places I saw (e.g., mines, ghost towns)	8.9%	8.3%	28.6%	29.6%	24.6%	3.53	703
The towns I visited (e.g., Lake City, Ouray, Silverton)	9.7%	12.7%	24.0%	32.2%	21.4%	3.43	718

Table 19.5 Contribution to Satisfaction while Visiting Alpine Loop

Social, Economic, and Environmental Benefits: Visitors were also asked to indicate how important it was to manage their favorite zone for each of the social, economic, and environmental benefits listed in Table 19.7. Visitors found it important to manage their most satisfying zone for a variety of social, community, economic, and environmental benefits. The greatest overall importance, however, was attached to environmental benefits— providing heightened awareness of the natural world, protection of cultural history/sites, and deeper sensitivity to local cultures. The next two most highly rated benefits were in the social category (i.e., residents, public, and business): improved family relations and providing recreation opportunities to communities. Positive contributions to local economies and greater opportunities for youth were also rated at above the moderate level of importance. As with the previous question, the social, economic, and environmental benefits can be segmented or compared across management zones. Managers can then see which benefits are relatively more or less important for each of the nine management zones.

Summary of Visitor Survey Results

The remainder of the survey questions are summarized in themed categories.

Visitor Demographics

1. Two-thirds of the visitors are from out-of-state. Visitors from Texas represent 26% of the total sample population. Nonetheless, visitors originate from throughout the nation— 44 states are represented.

Benefit	Poor	Fair	Good	Excellent	Mean
Greater connection with nature	1.0%	5.7%	30.8%	62.5%	3.55
Reduced stress	2.7%	7.8%	34.4%	55.1%	3.42
Enhanced family relationships	5.9%	6.1%	36.7%	51.2%	3.33
Strengthened relationships with my companions	4.2%	7.7%	44.6%	43.4%	3.27
Improved outlook on life	5.5%	9.8%	40.2%	44.5%	3.24
Improved mental health	4.4%	9.7%	44.1%	41.8%	3.23
Increased appreciation of area's cultural history	4.0%	17.7%	47.1%	31.2%	3.05
Improved physical health	5.7%	16.4%	47.8%	30.1%	3.02
Improved self-reliance	8.3%	20.4%	45.2%	26.1%	2.89
Increased self-confidence	7.5%	22.1%	44.9%	25.4%	2.88
Spiritual growth	12.1%	18.6%	40.5%	28.8%	2.86
Increased sense of competence	10.3%	21.0%	45.6%	23.2%	2.82
Enhanced work performance	19.8%	27.3%	36.6%	16.3%	2.49

Table 19.6 Ability to Attain Benefits of Participation in Alpine Loop

Benefit		Not at all important	Slightly important	Moderately important	Very important	Extremely important	Mean
Social & Community	Improved family bonding	9.3%	9.8%	23.1%	33.8%	24.1%	3.54
	Providing recreation to local communities	8.2%	11.4%	27.0%	34.5%	19.0%	3.45
	Greater opportunities for youth	11.1%	13.3%	30.9%	31.0%	13.7%	3.23
	Greater community involvement	18.4%	19.5%	30.4%	23.1%	8.6%	2.84
Economic	Positive contribution to local economics	10.5%	9.8%	27.2%	31.9%	20.6%	3.42
	Increased work productivity	17.7%	17.1%	31.8%	23.4%	10.1%	2.91
Environ-mental	Heightened awareness of natural world	2.6%	3.0%	10.9%	30.7%	52.7%	4.28
	Greater protection of cultural history/sites	2.9%	3.0%	14.1%	32.3%	47.6%	4.19
	A deeper sensitivity to local cultures	4.9%	9.2%	24.0%	32.6%	29.2%	3.72

Table 19.7 Importance of Benefits Provided in Alpine Loop

2. Only about 10% of the visitors are from local communities close to the Alpine Loop area, including Grand Junction, Durango, Montrose, Gunnison, Ouray, Lake City, and Silverton.
3. While there is a certain amount of diversity among the visitors, a typical visitor more often than not tends to be middle-aged, white, male, married, currently employed, and highly educated. Over two-thirds of the visitors have at least four years of post-high school education. Nearly half have annual household incomes in excess of $50,000.

Travel Behavior

1. Sixty-two percent of the visitors stated that the Alpine Loop area was one of the main reasons for their trip away from home. The remainder perceived the visit was a smaller component of a trip predominately focused on other destinations.
2. One-third of the visitors had never been to the Alpine Loop area before. Those that had visited in the past reported a mean of seventeen prior visits.
3. Approximately two-thirds of the visitors stayed overnight within the Alpine Loop area during their visit. Forty-three percent visitors reported that they stayed in local communities and 23% reported that they stayed on public lands. The average length of stay on public lands was four nights, and the mean length of stay in local communities averaged 6.5 nights.
4. Thirty-five percent stayed at least one night in Lake City, 20% stayed at least one night in Ouray, and 15% stayed at least one night in Silverton. Thirty percent of the visitors stayed in hotels, motels, or resorts, 19% in private campgrounds; and 6% in bed and breakfast establishments.
5. Nearly three-quarters of the visitors traveled through Lake City during some part of their trip. Sixty-one percent traveled through Silverton, and 41% traveled through Ouray.
6. About one-half of the visitors entered the Alpine Loop area through Lake City and exited through Lake City. Fewer visitors entered through Silverton (29%) and Ouray (16%), and exited through Silverton (33%) and Ouray (11%).
7. A significant number of visitors reported use of hiking trails during their visit, including the American Basin Trail (18%), the Uncompahgre Peak Trail (18%), the Silver Creek Trail (15%), the Cataract Gulch trail (11%), and the Matterhorn Creek Trail (10%). Eight percent of the visitors reported that they entered a formally designated wilderness area.
8. A significant number of visitors reported using four wheel drive trails beyond that of the Alpine Loop proper. California Basin (used by 12% of the visitors), Corkscrew Gulch (9%),

Nellie Creek (8%), and American Basin (8%) were among the use areas most frequently reported.

Group Types

1. The majority of visitors (61%) were with family only. Less than 3% were with a permitted, commercially-outfitted group or other form of organized group. Seven percent were alone. The remaining visitors (30%) were with friends or combination of friends and family.
2. On average, each vehicle sampled contained 2.75 individuals. Group sizes tended to be small—90% of the visitors sampled were in parties of four or less. Over 75% of the visitors were members of groups that were accommodated by a single vehicle.

Vehicle Types

1. The majority of visitors (87%) utilize a private vehicle. Eleven percent of the visitors were sampled from rental vehicles and 2% visitors enlisting the services of guided tours.
2. The majority of visitors (76%) utilized a four wheel drive vehicle. Seventeen percent utilized a two wheel drive vehicle, 3% utilized a motorcycle, 3% an ATV, and just over 1% utilized a bicycle.

Desired Experiences/Benefits

1. Visitors expressed interest in gaining a variety of psychological outcomes from their experience. Rated highest were themes related to experiencing nature, escaping crowds and stress, and being with friends or family. These core motivational forces were decidedly more important than other themes such as learning, risk taking, meeting new people, achievement, and independence.

Desired Recreational Settings

1. For a wide variety of recreation setting factors (e.g., remoteness, naturalness, facility development, number of recreational encounters, level of information services), at least 64% of the visitors felt these factors should continue to be managed to reflect the conditions experienced during their trip.
2. At the same time, there were strong indicators that many visitors would press for key changes in the setting management of their most satisfying zone. Nearly one-third of the visitors felt that their zone should be managed to restore more natural conditions, over 25% of the visitors felt that the level of road maintenance should be increased, over 20% of the visitors felt that more programs and interpretation should be provided, and over 20% felt that motorized use in the area should be more limited.

Management of the Recreation Setting

1. Of the twenty-eight possible management actions, visitors rated the following as most important in potentially contributing to their recreation satisfaction: protecting the wildlife, protecting the tundra, increasing presence of wildlife, absence of crowding, vandalism control, keeping vehicles on roads, and historical site protection.
2. In general, visitors tended to rate the performance of managers the highest for "number of four-wheel drive routes" and "availability of trails." Performance in protecting the wildlife and trail maintenance was also rated particularly high. Ratings of the performance of managers in being able to provide "absence of crowding" and "presence of wildlife" were low relative to their importance in contributing to satisfaction.
3. Seventy-two percent of the visitors felt there was no need for additional interpretation programs, interpretation facilities, or other visitor information services in the Alpine Loop area. For the minority that did want more information, the predominant interest was in more interpretive signs, trail information signs, and interpretive brochures.

Willingness to Pay

1. Three-quarters of the visitors stated that they would be willing to pay a "per vehicle" fee to use the Alpine Loop area if they knew the money would go directly to maintaining and improving the recreation opportunities in the area.
2. The median "per vehicle" fee that the visitors would consider to be fair is $5.00.
3. For those who were not willing to pay a "per vehicle" fee, the most frequently stated reasons included "too many fees/costs/taxes already," "leave the area as it is", and "should be open to all." Eleven percent of those who rejected the notion of a "per vehicle" fee were nonetheless willing to support an alternative form of fee such as an annual permit.

Trip Expenditures

1. Visitors to the Alpine Loop area, on average, reported that their group spent a total of $715.12 during their trip within 100 miles of the area.
2. The highest allocations went to lodging ($234.56). The next highest categories of expenditures were food, meals, and drink ($166.92), then shopping and gifts ($128.98).

Visitor Satisfaction

1. Ninety-five percent of the visitors reported that they were either "very" or "extremely" satisfied with their visit to the Alpine Loop area.

Community Resident and Tourist Surveys

Many natural resource recreation research or planning efforts are limited to users of a park or those activities occurring within the resource management area because of time or money constraints. The goal of the Alpine Loop study was to understand the recreation, tourism, and residential activities and impacts in gateway communities so the total impact of the natural and cultural resources of the area could be illustrated. So in addition to the on-site research efforts in the Alpine Loop, tourist and resident studies were orchestrated in three gateway communities—Silverton, Lake City, and Ouray. Our interests in tourism businesses and residential living required us to engage the local communities much more than most outdoor recreation studies and planning efforts typically require. It was believed that greater engagement of the communities would afford a more sustainable resource and tourism industry. Specifically, there was interest in vacation and recreation experiences of tourists and residents in the Alpine Loop, the gateway communities, and surrounding areas; the views of residents about the current tourism industry and future developments; the value and importance of the communities and the Alpine Loop to residents and tourists; as well as providing a more science-based profile of tourists in the area that the local chamber of commerce could use in their marketing and planning.

Methods of the Resident and Tourist Studies

Simultaneous to the on-site user surveys in Alpine Loop access areas, tourist surveys were distributed following a sampling frame designed for generalizability that asked selected businesses to involve their customers. This allowed for valid estimates of outdoor recreation and tourism activities in the Alpine Loop region for a peak season. In each of the three gateway communities their leaders assisted us in selecting and enrolling businesses to help in this effort. Each community was asked to distribute 650 surveys to tourists during the June to October peak tourism season. Four to eight businesses in each community participated, as well as the visitor center in each downtown area, in an effort to capture day and overnight tourists. Businesses included overnight accommodations, guiding businesses, and retail shops. A graduate student who lived in the area for the sampling period trained these businesses and centers and made personal contact with them each week. Over half of the 650 on-site surveys were completed by tourists and 42% to 58% of those completing an on-site survey also completed a mail-back survey where we learned much more about their stay in the area.

During the same time period, a resident study was organized in each of the gateway communities. The source of the resident list varied by community, depending on access to the most updated list of residents. In one community the water bill list was provided, another community provided the property taxes records, and the final community provided the voter registration. Only local addresses were included, therefore anyone with a seasonal home without local mailing privileges were excluded. Our response rate on the resident study ranged from 62% to 39% using a modified Dillman (1995) mail survey process with only a reminder postcard a week after the survey mailing. Additional funding would have allowed for another mailing and higher response rate.

Besides orchestrating the timing of outdoor recreation, tourism and resident studies to occur in the same season and year, the survey instruments were designed to afford comparability across the samples. Survey instruments were reviewed with resource managers and community and tourism leaders in an effort to be open and listening to their interests and planning needs.

Selected Highlights from the Lake City Studies:

- Residents' addresses were obtained from a list of registered voters in Lake City, and each resident of the community was then mailed a survey instrument. In total, 131 resident surveys were completed, yielding a 39% response rate. The tourism survey was distributed in eight Lake City businesses, as well as in the Chamber of Commerce visitor center. Of the 419 surveys distributed to tourists, 195 were returned, resulting in a 47% response rate.

- Lake City residents thought tourism should play an important role in the local economy, with 78% saying it should have a dominant role, and another 17% saying it should be equal to other industries. Local residents were also quite knowledgeable about tourism, with almost all (93%) indicating they were either moderately or very knowledgeable.

- Two-thirds of Lake City residents (67%) indicated they have been involved at least some in tourism decision making. It follows that the vast majority (86%) feel they personally benefit at least some from tourism. Over half (59%) feel they benefit quite a bit or a lot from tourism. However, less than a quarter (24%) of respondents are directly employed in the tourism industry.

- When asked what types of tourism development are acceptable in Lake City, historical/cultural attractions, outdoor recreation opportunities, parks, festivals, and museums were considered the most acceptable. Bars, hotels, and campgrounds/RV parks were rated as the least acceptable potential developments.

- Respondents were asked a series of questions to measure their attitudes toward tourism in Lake City. They were most likely to agree that residents should encourage tourism in their community and in the Alpine Loop. They also feel there are better roads and public services have improved in Lake City due to tourism. Residents disagree with statements saying they are against new tourism development or that their community should not attract new visitors.

- Most residents (86%) are either very or extremely satisfied with their past recreation visits to the Alpine Loop. None indicated they are not at all satisfied. It follows that almost all (94%) agree that the Alpine Loop means a lot to them. In addition, over half (54%) of the Lake City residents are willing to pay a "per vehicle" fee to use the Alpine Loop.

- The typical resident was approximately 54 years old, had a college degree, and earned less than $50,000 per year. Less than 10% of the respondents lived in Lake City as a child, and the median length of residency in Lake City was 11 years.

- Tourists visited Lake City for recreation experiences (30%) or for beauty/scenery (26%). Sightseeing, visiting the Alpine Loop, and photography were the most popular activities of a Lake City vacation. Nearly three-quarters of tourists (71%) planned their trips more than two months in advance; they were most likely to use past experience (62%), maps (53%), and friends or relatives (40%) for information either before or during their trip.

- Over half of the tourists had been to Lake City on a previous trip and 80% of the tourists had previously visited the region of Southwest Colorado. The largest group of tourists indicated a Lake City vacation happens every couple of years.

- A resort was the most popular accommodation type (used by 27% of the tourists). The average length of a Lake City stay was 7 days and 8 nights and the average party size was 5 persons.

The average expenditure in the Lake City area was $794.

- Tourists were most likely from Texas, followed by Oklahoma and Denver. They were high income earners with 49% of the sample earning between $50,000 and $100,000 with another 21% earning $100,000 or higher.

Selected Highlights from the Ouray Studies:

- Residents' addresses were obtained from a water bill list of Ouray customers, and 249 residents of the community were mailed a survey instrument. One hundred and fifty residents responded for a 62% response rate. The tourism survey was distributed in eight Ouray businesses, as well as in the Chamber of Commerce visitor center. A total of 322 surveys were distributed and 136 were returned for a 42% response rate.

- Ouray residents thought tourism should play an important role in the local economy, with 54% saying it should have a dominant role, and another 38% saying it should be equal to other industries. Local residents were also quite knowledgeable about tourism, with almost all (86%) indicating they were either moderately or very knowledgeable.

- Close to two-thirds of Ouray residents (60%) indicated they have been involved at least some in tourism decision making. It follows that the vast majority (70%) feel they personally benefit at least some from tourism. Only 20% of the resident sample was directly employed in the tourism industry.

- When asked what types of tourism development are acceptable in Ouray, historical/cultural attractions and outdoor recreation opportunities were considered the most acceptable. Bars and motels or hotels were rated as the least acceptable potential developments.

- Respondents were asked a series of questions to measure their attitudes toward tourism in Ouray. They were most likely to agree that residents should encourage tourism in their community and in the Alpine Loop. They also feel public services have improved in Ouray due to tourism. Residents disagree with statements saying they are against new tourism development or that their community should not attract new visitors.

- Most residents (82%) were either very or extremely satisfied with their past recreation visits to the Alpine Loop. Only a few residents indicated they are not at all satisfied with their Alpine Loop experience. It follows that almost all (93%) agreed that the Alpine Loop means a lot to them. In addition, over half (52%) of the Ouray residents are willing to pay a "per vehicle" fee to use the Alpine Loop.

- The typical resident was approximately 56 years old, had a college degree, and earned less than $50,000 per year. Less than 20% of the respondents lived in Ouray as a child, and the median length of residency in Ouray was 21 years.

- Tourists visited Ouray for the beauty/scenery of the area. Sightseeing and photography were the most popular activities of an Ouray vacation. Three-five percent of tourists planned their trips more than two months in advance; they were most likely to use past experience (53%), maps (55%), and friends or relatives (32%) for information.

- Over half of the tourists had been to Ouray on a previous trip and 64% of the tourists had previously visited the region of Southwest Colorado. The largest group of tourists indicated an Ouray vacation happens once every couple of years.

- Hotels and motels were the most popular accommodation type (55% of the overnight market). The average length of an Ouray stay was 3 days and 3 nights and the average party size was 3 persons. On average, this vacation in Ouray costs $478.

- Tourists were most likely from Texas, Denver, and other Colorado communities. They were high income earners with 49% of the sample earning between $50,000 and $100,000 with another 18% earning $100,000 or more.

Selected Highlights from the Silverton Studies:

- Residents' addresses were obtained from a property tax list for Silverton, and each resident of the community was then mailed a survey instrument. In total, 113 resident surveys were completed, yielding a 62% response rate. The tourism survey was distributed in four Silverton businesses, as well as in the Chamber of Commerce visitor center. Of the 332 surveys distributed to tourists, 192 were returned, resulting in a 58% response rate.

- Silverton residents tended to think tourism should play an important role in the local economy, with 44% saying it should have a dominant role, and another 50% saying it should be equal to other industries. Local residents were also quite knowledgeable about tourism, with almost all (91%) indicating they were either moderately or very knowledgeable.

- Two-thirds of Silverton residents (66%) indicated they have been involved at least some in tourism decision making. It follows that the vast majority (79%) feel they personally benefit at least some from tourism. Over half (58%) feel they benefit quite a bit or a lot from tourism. Less than half (39%) of respondents are directly employed in the tourism industry.

- When asked what types of tourism development are acceptable in Silverton, community parks and second homes were the top choices in terms of acceptability. Other favorable development options included retail stores and museums. Festivals were the lowest rated development option by residents.

- Respondents were asked a series of questions to measure their attitudes toward tourism in Silverton. They were most likely to agree that residents should encourage tourism in their community and in the Alpine Loop. They also feel roads and public services have improved in Silverton due to tourism. Residents disagree with statements saying they are against new tourism development or that their community should not attract new visitors.

- Most residents (83%) are either very or extremely satisfied with their past recreation visits to the Alpine Loop. Only 2% of the residents rated satisfaction at very low levels. It follows that almost all (94%) agree that the Alpine Loop means a lot to them, however the majority was not willing to support a fee to use or visit the Alpine Loop area. For the 31% of residents who would support a fee, the mean was $3.89.

- The typical resident was approximately 49 years old, the largest education group was a college degree, and earned less than $50,000 per year. Less than 20% of the respondents lived in Silverton as a child, and the median length of residency in Silverton was 19 years.

- Tourists visited Silverton for beauty/scenery (21%) or the railroad (16%). Sightseeing, visiting the museums, and photography were the most popular activities of a Silverton vacation. The most common planning horizons for a Silverton trip was between 3 weeks and 3 months prior; they were most likely to use maps (58%), their own past experiences (49%), and friends or relatives (31%) for information before or during the trip.

- Over half (52%) of the tourists had been to Silverton on a previous trip and 60% of the tourists had previously visited the region of Southwest Colorado. The largest group of tourists indicated a Silverton vacation happens once every couple of years.

- A resort was the most popular accommodation type (reported by 42% of respondents). The average length of a Silverton stay was 4 days and 3 nights and the average party size was 3 persons. Tourists spent, on average, $336 per travel party in the Silverton area.

- Tourists were most likely from Texas, followed by Denver and other Colorado communities. They were high income earners with 46% of the sample earning between $50,000 and $100,000 with another 17% earning $100,000 or more.

Implications and Recommendations

This section presents implications from the study and provides recommendations for developing a collaborative planning process which addresses the future management of the Alpine Loop. The study implications are presented in three themed areas. The first section addresses implications for recreation resource management, a second section addresses implications for information and marketing, and the third section focuses on monitoring/evaluation implications. The fourth and final section in this chapter makes recommendations concerning a future strategy (an overall process and more specific considerations) for cooperative planning and management of the Alpine Loop area. An assumption underlying these implications and recommendations is that the present study is an initial step in a longer collaborative planning process for the Alpine Loop.

Management Implications

- In general, the visitors seem to be suggesting that the current course of management within the Alpine Loop area is quite acceptable. Ninety-five percent of the visitors report their visit as either "very" or "extremely" satisfying. The majority of visitors expressed that "current" conditions of a wide range of environmental variables such as remoteness, naturalness, development, interpretive services, management controls, road maintenance, and facility maintenance were acceptable. Such strong affirmations of current management conditions would not have emerged if major concerns existed about the existing management of the Alpine Loop resource.

- Through a variety of indicators, it becomes clear that management attention needs to focus on processes for enhancing and restoring natural conditions of the area. Exposure to the natural environment has been identified by the study as the most dominant contributor to visitor satisfaction. At the same time, it has been identified as the single opportunity that the visitors are most concerned about losing. Managing the environment to reduce damaged tundra, to keep vehicles on existing roads, and to maximize encounters with wildlife must be important elements of the quest to restore natural conditions of the Alpine Loop area.

- Management should proceed with caution in establishing new initiatives for the addition of support facilities. There was not a strong call for the addition or enhancement of facilities, and such holds potential for counteracting a shift toward more natural conditions within the resource. Of particular note, the vast majority of visitors felt the existing levels of information and interpretive services were adequate for their needs.

- The availability of maneuverable access roads throughout and near the byway is important to the visitors, but further research is needed on what the precise character of such access roads should be. While over 25% of the visitors feel that the level of road maintenance should be increased in their most satisfying portion of the area, 10% of the visitors felt the opposite. The data should be further explored to define whether perception of needed change is linked to specific portions of road networks within the resource. Until such analysis is accomplished, existing road maintenance standards should remain intact.

- From a visitor support perspective, managers would be justified in instituting a "per vehicle use" fee under the condition that receipts would be used directly to improve management of the Alpine Loop resource. In general, it appears a palatable use fee would be $5.00 per vehicle.

- Natural resource policymakers need to consider the contributions of local communities in developing management plans for the Alpine Loop resource. Over 20% of the visitors stated that local communities "contributed most" to their satisfaction, and 22% of the visitors identified a local community when asked to specify a zone of the Alpine Loop that "contributed most to their satisfaction." Moreover, visitor groups, on average, spent over $700 on lodging, food, shopping, and other services in the local communities. These facts speak to the necessity of natural resource managers to engage in collaborative planning with local communities in the quest to simultaneously maximize the visitor experience and protect the natural environment.

Information and Marketing Implications

The results of this study can be applied to public information functions, product (place or experience) marketing, as well as communication and interpretation functions. Moreover, the findings of this study can be utilized to consider: who are the recipient, audiences, or target markets; what are the most appropriate communication channels or placement of messages; and what is the value of information (content of messages) to the visitor? Most importantly, information and marketing should be viewed as a method of positioning the Alpine Loop area in customer's minds. Positioning traditionally includes: imaging the place or experience in customer's minds, communicating the benefits of visiting the area, and setting the place and experience apart from competitor's or possible substitutes.

The recipient or audience of any information or marketing campaigns should be directed at target markets. Some of the key segmentation variables include: prior experience levels (first-time visitors versus repeat visitors), geographic home location, family status, and income levels. These variables can be useful in contacting potential visitors to the Alpine Loop area, including the three communities. Specific considerations related to the audience or target markets:

- Consider analyzing the segments of visitors that are attracted to the three difference communities surrounding the Alpine Loop.
- Consider further analysis to identify zone (i.e., nine study zones) and/or visitor activity (e.g., sightseers, off-highway vehicle use, backcountry travelers) segmentation that is occurring.

Communication channels are dominated by personally sourced information according to the findings of the study. Two of the top three information sources included prior experience and word-of-mouth, findings which are very prevalent in destination marketing. The top information source was a map of the area. Four additional information sources which received between 10% and 20% coverage by Alpine Loop visitors were: travel books and guides, local visitor center or Chamber, local businesses, and public land agency contact or brochure. All four of these information sources are traditional distribution places for outdoor recreation and tourism information and appear to have a strong presence and role in the local area. A final information channel that yielded less than 10% of the respondents is poised to make increased usage in the future—the Internet. Specific considerations related to information sources include:

- A point to keep in mind is that individuals plan some aspects of their trips at home and need to be knowledgeable of information distributors to be able to make contacts.
- Making existing information on the Alpine Loop and the communities accessible on the Internet. New information products and content should also be considered for electronic formats (e.g., reservations, up-to-date weather and road conditions).

Messages to capture the attention of interested and less interested potential visitors are very much needed and central to effective information and marketing programs. The results of the study suggest the following messages because either the majority or large segments considered these features or benefits of the Alpine Loop to be central to their experience:

- A first message consideration is activities. The most popular recreational activities (over 50% of respondents) in the Alpine Loop were wildflower viewing, four-wheel driving, general sightseeing, photography, hiking/walking, watching wildlife, and visiting historical sites.
- Top motivations for the Alpine Loop trip include: enjoying scenery, being close to nature, getting away from crowds, being with family and friends, tranquility, solitude, and escaping responsibilities. The elements of the experience that contributed the most to satisfaction include the natural place, activities, and companionship. Reflection time, cultural places, and communities contributed at a lower level to overall satisfaction.
- Respondents also included strong attachment to the Alpine Loop and expressed these feelings with the following content "means a lot to me," "holds strong memories," "no other place can compare," and "thinking a lot about coming to this area."
- Finally, benefits should be considered viable content. The top-rated benefits to the Alpine Loop experience were heightened awareness of the natural world, greater protection of culture history and sites, and a deeper sensitivity to local cultures; all these messages align with environmental benefits. Additional nonenvironmental benefits that might also be considered in messages are connection to nature, reduced stress, and enhanced family relationships.

Finally, these highlighted information and marketing implications should be considered in a positioning statement. The Alpine Loop appears to be a one-of-a-kind natural, scenic area that is unlike others. Benefits of visiting the area stem primarily from environmental appreciation and consciousness. Very aesthetic words and pictures should be incorporated into information and marketing pieces to ensure potential visitors with no prior experience to the Alpine Loop can actually see the images and experiences by processing information and marketing products. These information and marketing ideas are best presented and directed in a regional marketing plan. The supporters of the Alpine Loop area, including all three communities, should seriously consider a comprehensive regional marketing plan that includes cooperative promotional strategies. This does not preclude the development of community specific marketing strategies (each community has its own unique character and "tourist experience"). Moreover, a regional marketing plan would allow all partners (communities, tourism industry, land management agencies) to have a regional perspective and to be in a better position to understand and market all of the diverse opportunities available in the Alpine Loop area.

Monitoring Implications

Ongoing monitoring efforts in the Alpine Loop will be an important part of any future planning and management effort. The current visitor study can be considered an attempt to monitor social science conditions in the Alpine Loop as well as the preferences of Alpine Loop visitors. Future monitoring of the area will also need to consider natural resource (e.g., tundra, wildlife, vegetation), road/trail/facility, cultural resource, mining, grazing, and water quality conditions of the Alpine Loop. All of these systems or parts of the Alpine Loop affect the visitor experience as well as the integrity of the resource itself. It would be most efficient if future monitoring could be integrated with other ongoing resource monitoring programs that exist in the Alpine Loop. For example, grazing, mining, mining reclamation, water quality, road maintenance, and historical preservation monitoring programs already exist in the Alpine Loop area. The recommendations below will primarily focus on social science monitoring and other related monitoring programs in so far that they directly impact the visitor experience or visitor impacts to the Alpine Loop area.

Five key issue areas are presented below as a structure for conceptualizing the social science monitoring implications component. The first area relates to the absence of ongoing visitation or travel (road or backcountry) information about the magnitude of total use in the Alpine Loop area. Relatedly, there is little seasonal or geographical sensitive visitation (e.g., number of visitors, vehicles, party size) information. As a result, it is very difficult to estimate the magnitude of visitation (or economic impact) attributed to the area. This deficiency also makes tracking trends (season to season increases or decreases) difficult and unreliable. Specific recommendations related to the creation of a visitation baseline include:

- The development of a traffic counter methodology to measure and monitor vehicle and visitor volume on an annual or semi-annual basis.
- The development of a similar methodology to track seasonal use patterns (e.g., winter, spring, summer, fall).

The second area of importance for future monitoring builds directly on the data collected in the present study, a visitor demand profile. The purpose of collecting data to provide a summary of visitor demand to better understand visitor needs, preferences, and behavior for management and planning purposes. Such data would be useful to all the Alpine Loop partners and cost sharing may be appropriate across public and private sector organizations. The frequency of collecting such data would depend on planning, marketing, and management needs; perhaps once every 3 to 5 years. As with the present study, both an on-site and mail survey methodology would be appropriate. Specific recommendations related to the assessment of visitor demand include:

- Monitoring the desired activities, experiences, settings, benefits, and management actions of visitors (preferences).
- Monitoring the actual activities participated in, expenditures, information sources utilized, and past experience of visitors (behavior).
- Monitoring the travel patterns (zone travel, entering, and leaving point), communities visited and accommodations utilized (travel patterns).

The third area addresses the monitoring of service quality. The concept of service quality monitoring is relatively new to public land agencies, but more common in the tourism and other service industries. The purpose of collecting such data would be to provide assessment of the quality of the recreation/ tourism product to identify where improvements in service quality might occur. Such data would also be useful to all the Alpine Loop partners and cost sharing may be appropriate across public and private sector organizations. Such monitoring could be completed in tandem with the visitor demand monitoring described above. Specific recommendations related to the monitoring of service quality include:

- Monitoring overall experience satisfaction and satisfaction with specific service functions like friendliness, courtesy, staff availability, security, and information availability.
- Monitoring of tangible facility, trail, road, parking, and sign conditions and quality. The appropriateness, availability, and appearance of these components would be useful to managers in determining where to focus future efforts.
- Monitoring the personal, social, environmental, and economic benefits realized by visitors to the Alpine Loop.
- Monitoring the perception of depreciative behavior and visitor conflicts among all visitors.

The fourth area for future monitoring addresses a variety of other resource management areas that are related to experience quality or visitor impacts. In some cases, ongoing resource uses have both positive and negative impacts (e.g., mining and historical mining structure preservation) on the visitor experience. Recreation and tourism also cause certain physical impacts that harm or deteriorate the physical resource. Specific recommendations related to resource interaction include:

- Monitoring the visual/scenic impacts of grazing and mining on the recreation experience.
- Monitoring the visual, aesthetic, and natural conditions of the Alpine Loop in the eyes of visitors to the area.
- Monitoring of historical mining structures for safety and vandalism.
- Monitoring the new "unofficial" roads and trails that develop, especially on the tundra and near riparian areas.
- Monitoring the water quality in streams, rivers, and lakes for public health and aesthetic purposes.

A fifth and final area to consider is the future monitoring that focuses on local communities, residents, and businesses. The economic and social health benefits to the local communities are important to the viability and sustainability of the entire Alpine Loop system. Specific recommendations related to key indicators in the local communities include:

- An assessment of resident attitudes and preferences toward the management and use of the Alpine loop area and its contribution to local quality of life.
- An assessment of resident attitudes toward tourism (e.g., community resident surveys) and the type of tourism that is both appropriate and desired.
- Monitoring of economic indicators in the local tourism economy to follow economic trends and health within and across the regional economy.

Recommended Strategy for Applying Study Results to Management of the Area

The purpose of this section is to chart a strategy for continuing the collaborative, community-based planning model that was initiated with this study. That strategy is built upon recommendations expressed by local residents, government officials, business owners, federal land management personnel, and other Alpine Loop stakeholders at public hearings within the communities of Lake City, Ouray, and Silverton on April 2 and 3, 1997. The strategy includes a process for further analysis of the study data in a way that will produce informed management decisions that will benefit both local communities and visitors to the resource.

Based upon inputs from key stakeholders of the Alpine Loop resource, the following are key elements of the recommended strategy for applying study results to future management:

- The strategy must recognize that local community governments, elected officials, merchants, and residents are key providers of recreation opportunities for Alpine Loop visitors. Thus, when it comes to developing a plan which will ultimately impact upon the visitors and these key providers, all parties should become engaged as equal partners with federal land management agencies in charting the Alpine Loop's future. Local community stakeholders clearly embraced the proposed shifting of the management paradigm—from the historical model of one being directed by the BLM and other federal agencies to a full-fledged community-based collaborative venture. Under the collaborative model, all stakeholders seek to define a management plan that balances visitor and local stakeholder desires for various recreation experiences and services to ensure that one set of stakeholders—either visitors or local constituencies—is not being served at the other's expense.

- The primary focus of the collaborative, community-based management strategy is to define the nature of the recreation products to be offered within the Alpine Loop area, and the features of the recreation settings that are necessary to create them. This study was designed to enable that process. Much insight about the needs of the communities and the needs of the visitors can be gained from the analyses presented in this report. However, the true value of the data will emerge as studies are made of the differentiating sub-sets of visitors who carry differing recreational interests, differing management needs, differing community support needs, differing impacts on the environment, and indeed differing economic contributions to local communities. The strategy for developing a management plan, therefore, must include a process for determining what forms of data analysis would be useful in order to help stakeholders determine what kinds of recreation products and services should be emphasized in the management of the Alpine Loop area. Under the collaborative, community-based management model, these determinations are to be made not by the researchers or by federal land management agencies. Rather, they are to be determined by a coalition representing all stakeholders in the resource. Thus, an immediate requirement for creating a collaborative, community-based management venture is to create a steering committee comprised of representatives of stakeholders from each of the three local communities within the Alpine Loop area, local governments, and the federal government. The purpose of this steering committee is to make decisions about what forms of data analysis would be helpful in making determination about appropriate recreation use for the Alpine Loop area, and needed land management and community support services. Based upon recommendations received at the April 2 and 3 public hearings, this committee should be comprised of three individuals from each community and a representative from each BLM Resource Area and Forest Service District with stewardship responsibilities for the Alpine Loop area. Under this scenario, each community would be responsible for nominating or electing the three individuals to represent the interests of the local business community, local (nonbusiness) interests, and local governments.

- The steering committee should be assembled immediately, and should participate in a full day workshop to determine what forms of data analysis would most critically enable the collaborative planning effort. The workshop should be facilitated by one or more authors of this report (the Arizona State University research team)— or any research team with credentials in survey and focus group methodology, and with credentials in applying survey and focus group research to issues in outdoor recreation and tourism management. Through the April 2 and 3 public hearing process, a menu of possible analyses can be constructed. While this menu is neither comprehensive nor complete, it is illustrative of the interests that have already been expressed by Alpine Loop stakeholders:

  a) *Profiling visitors with greatest contributions to local economies.*The intent is to determine the activities, experiences, benefits, and community support services desired by those who would contribute the most to local communities from an economic perspective. Knowing this information, coupled with information on the sources of information used in making travel decisions, would enable local merchants to target their advertising toward populations with the greatest potential for positive economic impact.

  b) *Determining the managerial and community impacts of user fees.* While the potential imposition of user fees is a controversial issue, directives from Congress make the consideration of use fees on resources such as the Alpine Loop a reality. Use fees also represent an opportunity for generating needed revenues for the ultimate implementation of a collaborative, community-based management plan. The intent of this analysis is to determine which populations of visitors would be lost under the imposition of a use fee program, and the kinds of economic impacts that would occur under different scales of fee structures by impeding demand for the resource. Analyses could be run to determine the ideal pricing structure for a fee program, given the sometimes competing goals of generating management revenue and maximizing both recreation opportunities for visitors and economic cash flow for local communities.

c) *Assessment of community tourism support service needs.* To maximize the draw, retention, and repeat visitation of visitors to a community, one needs data on the interests and support needs of existing visitors to that community. The intent of this analysis is to segment the Alpine Loop visitor population into populations who currently spend time in each community as part of their Alpine Loop experience. Interests of visitors who predominately spend time in the Ouray community, for example, can be analyzed and contrasted with interests of those who predominately spend time in Silverton or Lake City. An assessment can be made of what recreation and tourism support services are important in each community, and what services might be lacking. The 1997 general tourist studies conducted within each of the three communities (conducted separately from this Alpine Loop visitor study) hold tremendous potential for enhancing the power of this data for gathering insight about needed tourism support services at the community level.

d) *Comparing and contrasting desired recreation experiences across management zones.* Appendix V presents the fundamental variables of this study on a zone-by-zone basis. While the information is useful, there is inherently no framework for systematically integrating the information so it becomes clear how visitors view the different zones in unique ways and how they view the different zones in homogeneous (or substitutable) ways. The intent of this analysis is to determine if, from the perspective of visitors, segmentation of Alpine Loop resource into the nine different zones is truly significant managerially, and if so, what the priorities for management should be in each zone.

e) *Linking desired activities, experiences, and settings to benefits produced.* There is a movement within federal land management agencies to quantify the benefits produced by various land use alternatives, and to evaluate the worth of each alternative in the context of the benefits that are produced under that alternative. This movement is commonly referred to as the BBM approach to land use planning. The intent of this analysis is to create linkages between variables in the study in a way that shows managers how different land use practices result in different recreation products or benefits to the visitors and to the surrounding communities (Virden and Knopf, 1989). Specifically, relationships will be examined between (i) recreation products (i.e., activities, experiences, and benefits), (ii) characteristics of the recreation setting that will produce them (i.e., physical, social and managerial setting attributes), and (iii) perceptions of the various management actions needed to achieve the desired products. With such analyses completed, it will become clear exactly what the ultimate products will be for any proposed kind of management intervention.

f) *Detailed assessment of attitudes toward specific management actions or land use issues.* The intent of this analysis is to explore the data base for richer perspective on the attitudes of visitors toward management practices identified as of particular concern to the visitors, or of potential controversy to stakeholders. For example, the character of road maintenance appears to be of paramount importance to both visitors and community stakeholders. Further analysis of the data would yield information on how the definition of ideal road conditions varies with other descriptive characteristics of the visitor (i.e., travel patterns, activities engaged in, experiences sought). Then, scenarios on the ability of different read conditions to attract differing visitor populations (and the affiliated recreation products including economic contributions to local communities) could be constructed. Specific issues to be analyzed in such detail would be determined by the steering committee.

g) *Assessment of effective marketing strategies.* The intent of this analysis is to define linkages among study variables that would assist stakeholders in defining effective strategies for advertising, promoting and marketing the Alpine Loop area in general, local communities as particular tourism destinations, or specific businesses with specific products. Going beyond the marketing implications already articulated in this report, detailed analyses would reveal the particular promotional elements that would be effective in targeting a diverse range of consumers to an identified product (the resource in general, or a community or business— e.g., four-wheel driving—in particular). The analysis would also identify the most successful modes for targeting specific market segments. Here again, the 1997 general tourist studies conducted within each of the three communities (conducted separately from this Alpine Loop visitor study) hold tremendous potential for enhancing the efforts to design effective promotional campaigns for various stakeholders.

- The goal of the collaborative, community-based management planning process is to craft a management plan that (i) reflects insights of this study and the further analyses such as those enumerated above, and (ii) maximizes returns to both visitors and local communities. The strategy must recognize that this can only be accomplished with outside facilitation. There are at least four reasons that external facilitation is necessary, all of which were expressed during at least one of the April 2 and 3 public hearings. First, a carefully chosen external agent, can be devoid of being biased in favor of the interests of any one particular stakeholder. Second, historical practices have built a legacy of distrust on the part of some community stakeholders as to the motives of federal land management agencies. External facilitation will provide a means for communication among all parties and amelioration of this concern. Third, for individuals not familiar with the translation of survey data into management practice, the task can be formidable. Expert assistance in demonstrating how data analyses can be used to effectively design meaningful futures for communities is essential. Fourth, the process of managing collaborative planning processes is complex indeed. Building an environment of mutual respect and tolerance of diverse perspective is challenging, and requires the skills of professionals trained in community-based planning. The process of generating and consolidating issues and ideas and then moving several communities and land management agencies through a consensus building process takes experience, conceptual skills, and networking capacities.

- The external consultant should create a governance structure for managing the collaborative planning process that was not in existence prior to the preparation of this study. Existing advisory mechanisms such as the Alpine Recreation Task Force and the Southwest Resource Advisory Council may be perceived by community stakeholders as ineffective in galvanizing a broad distribution of stakeholder interests. The steering committee assembled for purposes of diagnosing additional data needs to drive the collaborative planning effort may be charged with the responsibility for representing stakeholder interests throughout the whole of the planning process. The external facilitator, then, provides counsel to this committee regarding specific strategies for reaching stakeholder consensus on the provisions of a management plan.

The final strategy, after consensus is reached on the collaborative, community-based plan, is to create a cooperative management agreement wherein all identified stakeholders formally consent to the enactment of specific management actions each will take to implement the plan. Such a decree not only formalizes endorsement by all key stakeholders, but also identifies what parties are legally responsible for each element of the action plan.

Closing Thoughts: A Perspective on Lessons Learned

Perhaps the most important lesson learned from this study is the manner is the multisector approach to defining the problem, and the methodologies for gaining perspective. The study was designed in full partnership with local residents, the business community, and the multiple sets of governmental service providers holding an interest in the future of the Alpine Loop. At the onset of this study, all stakeholders involved were informed of the new benefits-based paradigm for assessing the issues, desired benefits, and future management directions of the Alpine Loop area. The paradigm called for the formation of collaborative, community-based research project that would provide the necessary data for constructing a collaborative, community-based long range management plan. The power of the paradigm became manifested as community-based focus groups not only generated raw material for the visitor survey, but also set the stage for public discussion of the multiple array of benefits that emerge from the Alpine Loop that serve the interests of different stakeholders.

If the benefits paradigm for Alpine Loop planning is to come to its full potential in the Alpine Loop area, the ultimate unfolding of management implications from the data must be determined through a collaborative, community-based process. The data base has served well in articulating the collections of recreation activities, recreation experiences, environmental settings, and management actions that can serve different stakeholders. The data base was enhanced by incorporating measures important to a diverse range of stakeholders. At the same time, the data can only help to define what this diversity might be. Having established this, the community again must be engaged to determine the what mix of activities, experiences, settings, and management actions would best serve the various constituencies— and to develop a set of performance indicators around which future monitoring and assessment programs could be built.

This never-ending process of community engagement, followed by objective scientific analysis, followed by another cycle of community engagement must continue in perpetuity to maximize the flow of benefits from our public lands. The recreating public, the business sector, the public lands, and the communities that embrace them will be the ultimate beneficiaries.

Literature Cited

Allen, L. (1996). Benefits-Based Management of Recreation Services. *Parks and Recreation,* 31: 64–76.

Bruns, D. (1995). New paradigms for outdoor recreation and tourism management in government. In J. L. Thompson, D. W. Lime, B. Gartner and W. M. Sames (Compilers), *Proceedings of the Fourth International Outdoor Recreation and Tourism Trends Symposium and the 1995 National Recreation Resources Planning Conference.* (pp. 425–430). St. Paul, MN: University of Minnesota Press.

Bruns, D., Driver, B. L., Lee, M. E., Anderson, D. H., & Brown, D. H. (1994). Pilot Tests for Implementing Benefits-based Management. Paper presented at *The Fifth International Symposium on Society and Natural Resource Management.* Fort Collins, CO.

Driver, B. L. (1990). Focusing Research on the Benefits of Leisure: Special Issue Introduction. *Journal of Leisure Research, 22*: 93–98.

Driver, B. L. & Brown, P. J. (1978). The opportunity spectrum concept in outdoor recreation supply inventories: A rational. Pages 24–31 in *Proceedings of the integrated renewable resources inventories workshop.* Gen. Tech. Rep. RM-GTR-55. Ft. Collins, CO: U.S. Department of Agriculture, Forest Service, Rocky Mountain Forest and Range Experiment Station.

Driver, B. L. & Bruns, D. (1998). Needs for and underlying concepts and uses of the benefits approach to leisure. In T. Burton and E. Jackson (Eds.), *Leisure studies at the millennium.* (pp. 349–368). State College, PA: Venture Publishing, Inc.

Driver, B. L. & Knopf, R. C. (1976). Personality, outdoor recreation, and expected consequences. *Environment and Behavior, 9*(2): 169–193.

Krueger, R. A. (1994). *Focus groups: A practical guide for applied research.* Newbury Park, CA: Sage Publications.

Moore, R. L. & Driver, B. L. (2005). *Introduction to outdoor recreation: Providing and managing natural resource based opportunities.* State College, PA: Venture Publishing, Inc.

Stein, T. V. & Lee, M. E. (1995). Managing Recreation Resources for Positive Outcomes: An Application of Benefits-based Management. *Journal of Parks and Recreation Administration, 13*(3): 52–70.

Stein, T. V. & Lee, M. E. (1995). Ruby Canyon–Black Ridge User Study. A technical report prepared for the Bureau of Land Management (BLM C950-AZ-006). School of Forestry, Northern Arizona University. Flagstaff, AZ.

Stein, T. V., Anderson, D. H., & Thompson, D. (1999). Identifying and managing for community benefits in Minnesota State Parks. *Journal of Park and Recreation Administration, 17*(4): 1–19.

Stein, T. V. & Anderson, D. H. (2002). Combining Benefits-based Management with Ecosystem Management for Landscape Planning: Leech Lake Watershed, Minnesota. *Landscape and Urban Planning, 60*: 151–161.

Virden, R. J. & Knopf, R.C. (1989). Activities, experiences, and environmental settings: A case study of recreation opportunity spectrum relationships. *Leisure Sciences, 11*: 159–176.

Virden, R. J., Knopf, R. C., & Vogt, C. (1998). Final Report of the Alpine Loop Backcountry Byway Customer Study. A report submitted in partial fulfillment of a cooperative agreement with the San Juan Mountain Association and the Bureau of Land Management, Department of Recreation Management and Tourism, Arizona State University. Tempe, AZ.

Virden, R. J., Vogt, C., Larkin, K., & Knopf, R. C. (1999). A Geographic Segmentation of Nature-Based Tourists to the Alpine Loop. A refereed abstract accepted for the NRPA 1999 Symposium on Leisure Research, Nashville, TN.

Chapter 20
OFM and Local Community Benefits

Dorothy H. Anderson, Mae A. Davenport, Jessica E. Leahy, and Taylor V. Stein

Learning Objectives:

1. Appreciate the complexities of identifying and using OFM to provide opportunities for community benefits.
2. Understand the significance of trust and place attachment to realization of community benefits.

Introduction

Public land managing agencies such as the USDA Forest Service, USDI Bureau of Land Management, USDI National Park Service, USDI Fish & Wildlife Service, and the U.S. Army Corps of Engineers, manage lands to provide benefits to people and society. As defined by Driver, Brown, and Peterson (1991), benefits are advantageous changes or improvements in a condition (a gain) to individuals, groups, society, or even another entity such as an endangered species. Said more simply, benefits add value to people's lives. Later to facilitate operationalizing OFM (earlier called benefits-based management) two additional types of benefits of leisure were recognized that included the prevention of a unwanted condition and the realization of a satisfying recreation experience (see Chapter 1 of this text for elaboration) Thus, the OFM framework is designed to facilitate the production and delivery of all types of benefits of leisure to customers, as well as minimize negative impacts or outcomes. As documented in this text, support for OFM is growing, which means that support for the fundamental requirements of OFM is growing also. One of those requirements is that attention must be given to all the customers who benefit from the provision of leisure services by public park and recreation agencies. As emphasized in Chapter 2 of this text, those customers not only include the on-site visitors, but also the customers who reside in nearby communities and even the more remote customers who value the protection of public park and recreation resources and willingly pay their tax dollars to support such. Nevertheless, too little attention has been given in the past (and even today) by public park and recreation administrators, managers, and planners to local resident customers and in particular to the production of recreation-related benefits to local communities.

This chapter describes several studies designed to identify benefits accruing to communities and attained by community residents resulting from public lands management. They are organized in the chronological order in which they were conducted to show the progression of what was learned about implementing OFM at the community level.

Applying OFM to lands contiguous to or near public lands is difficult for a number of reasons: 1) in most cases, public land managers have no legislative authority to manage lands outside the boundaries of the lands they administer, 2) public land managers often do not have data specific to outcomes desired by residents living in nearby communities, 3) people living in towns and communities near public lands may be unaware of public land managers' desires to target and provide specific beneficial outcomes for people residing in these areas, 4) people living in these towns and communities may not trust public land managers to perform their roles in ways that benefit local towns and communities, 5) local residents may not believe that public land managers understand the meanings they attach to an area and therefore do not believe public land managers can provide them with the kinds of outcomes they desire, and 6) in some areas, meanings attached to special places are contested and conflicts may emerge as new communities develop or existing communities grow and their residents diversify.

What Are Community Benefits?

In this chapter, community benefits are defined as benefits resulting from public land management that accrue to residents living in communities nearby or adjacent to public lands. These benefits are associated with the social, biophysical, and economic attributes of a community and should enhance a community's social, natural, and economic capital. Community benefits add value to communities and to the lives of the people living in them. Further, community residents need not recreate on nearby public lands to attain all of the benefit opportunities provided by public land management. However, residents who engage in recreational activities may attain a greater diversity of benefits provided by public land management than residents who do not engage in recreational activities on nearby or adjacent public lands. Lastly, considerable research has shown that just the presence of local amenities are among the top five factors that contribute most to peoples' perceived quality of, or satisfaction with, their lives as well as being a significant consideration in where people choose to live (Campbell, 1981; Marans & Mohai, 1991; Allen, 1991).

For over 15 years, the authors of this chapter have conducted studies to identify community benefits, local community members' perceptions of benefits attained by them as individuals and by their communities as a result of public land management, and constraints to attaining benefits. Those studies point to a number of interesting findings: 1) residents living in communities nearby or adjacent to public lands can clearly articulate the individual and community benefits they desire from public land management, 2) benefit opportunities that public land managers believe they provide are oftentimes not attained by local communities, 3) recreation benefit opportunities desired by local communities differ from those desired by nonlocal visitors, 4) agency understanding and appreciation of local community members attachment to nearby public lands is a key to benefit attainment by residents living in local communities, and 5) agency-community trust relationship is a key to community attainment of benefits related to social, economic, and natural capital of local communities. The remainder of this chapter reviews the studies that have been made and highlights the need to include place attachment and inculcate more trust between the managers and residents, and better facilitate how OFM can be implemented to influence benefit attainment at the local community level. Four studies are presented, and each is treated as a separate case study example. For each case, a general description of the study area and land managing agency is given, followed by a brief description of the study methods and selected key findings, and ends with a brief discussion about the ways in which the study findings have been or are being used by communities and the land managing agency to target and provide community benefits.

The Case Studies

Case 1: Identifying Community Benefits: Minnesota State Parks, Minnesota

Early attempts by the authors to identify and target community benefits of public land management were conducted in 1995 and 1996 with the Minnesota Department of Natural Resources' Division of Parks and Recreation (DPR). Identifying and providing for on-site visitor benefits had been the focus of efforts by the authors for these parks in 1993 and followed the lead of other agencies such as the USDI Bureau of Land Management for targeting benefit opportunities for visitors to BLM lands (see Chapters 14, 17, and 18 of this text). However, too little research that focused directly on community benefits related to management of public lands for outdoor recreation had been done.

In the mid-1990s the DPR developed a new strategic plan to guide management of Minnesota's state park system. The plan called for DPR to adopt a BBM approach to outdoor recreation planning and management. That approach meant that DPR would engage local communities and citizen groups not only in identifying the kinds of visitor benefits it should target and manage within a park's boundaries, but also the kinds of community benefits it should target and assist local communities in providing. Two state parks were selected for this research, Tettegouche and Itasca. Those two parks were selected because the DPR was in the process of rewriting the comprehensive management plans for each. Those parks are also two of Minnesota's premier state parks and attract state, national, and international visitors. As such, the DPR had a strong interest in maintaining the quality of these parks, the experience and benefit opportunities they provide for visitors, and the benefits they provide for local communities.

Data Collection and Analysis Methods: In response to the DPR's efforts to change their outdoor recreation planning process to include production of targeted benefits for communities near or adjacent to state parks, residents in communities adjacent to Tettegouche and Itasca State Parks in Minnesota were invited to participate in one of several focus group sessions. The sessions were conducted by the authors of this chapter in the winter of 1995. For each park, the citizen advisory committees, which consist of 25–30 key stakeholders living in communities nearby or adjacent to each park, and park staff were invited to attend one of two sessions held for each park. Each session lasted two hours and for each session, participants were asked to respond to each of the following questions: 1) what benefits do you believe your community receives from the state park, 2) what do you believe are the most important community benefits, and, 3) what can state park managers do to help your community realize these benefits? Participants were also asked to provide names and addresses of other people living in the community whom they considered to be key stakeholders in the community and who have thought about the relationship of their community to the park of concern. The information obtained from the focus group sessions was used to develop a questionnaire about community benefits and state park management. In the summer of 1995, the questionnaire was mailed to members of the citizen advisory committees and the names of people they had provided. A total of 194 surveys were mailed out and 133 (or 69%) were returned.

Selected Findings: Among other things, the questionnaire asked respondent to identify how much state park management contributes to each of 24 possible benefits their communities could attain as a result of their proximity to either Itasca or Tettegouche state parks (Stein, Anderson, & Thompson, 1999). Respondents were also asked to look at the 24 benefits and rank order their top seven. Six of the top seven benefits were the same for both parks (Table 1). Only one of the top benefits identified for both parks was related to economic benefits. The other six benefits were related to keeping or enhancing the communities' social and natural capital.

Using the Findings: These findings were presented to the DPR planning team and the citizen advisory committee (CAC) for each park at one of the park's planning meeting. The outcome of each park meeting was that DPR and each park's CAC would use the data to identify and target specific managerial actions for each of the top seven benefits listed for a particular park and for any other benefits identified by residents living near a particular park that the planning team and CAC believed were important to target and provide.

Writing OFM objectives for providing community benefit opportunities proved to be difficult for both DPR and each park's CAC. Although the DPR and the CAC could agree on important benefits to provide for visitors and ways to monitor whether those benefits were being attained by visitors, they could not reach agreement on how to provide or measure community benefits. The final management plan for Tettegouche State Park was approved in 1998, and the Lake Itasca plan

Benefit opportunities rank ordered by state park		Relationship of benefit opportunity to community social, natural, and economic capital		
		Social	Natural	Economic
Itasca State Park	A chance to attract tourism dollars to the community			X
	A place to preserve/conserve various natural and unique ecosystems		X	
	A chance to experience unique outdoor recreation opportunities	X	X	
	A natural setting in which community can take pride	X	X	
	A greater understanding of your natural environment	X	X	
	A feeling that your community is a special place to live	X		
	A sense of security that the natural environment will not be lost	X	X	
Tettegouche State Park	A chance to experience unique outdoor recreation opportunities	X	X	
	A place to preserve/conserve various natural and unique ecosystems		X	
	A sense of security that the natural environment will not be lost	X	X	
	A chance for local people to maintain an outdoor-oriented lifestyle	X	X	
	A chance to attract tourism dollars to the community			X
	A feeling that your community is a special place to live	X		
	A natural setting in which community can take pride	X	X	

Table 20.1 Most Important Benefit Opportunities State Parks Provide for Nearby/Adjacent Communities

was approved in 1999. Both plans fell short of specifying community-related outcomes or providing a means to measure attainment of community benefits. Instead, both management plans relied on general statements about the necessity of keeping community benefits in mind while managing the resources of those parks.

The DPR's planning team and the CAC's inability to reach agreement might have been related to the CAC's assessment of how well each park's management staff worked with the local communities. One of the questions each CAC responded to during the focus group sessions was "What can (name of park) park employees do to help communities realize the benefits you listed?" Most of the actions CAC members listed suggest that park staff may not understand the communities and their needs as well as they should. In addition, comments such as "provide services to community members," "(park) employees should spend money locally," "do your job well, the community will notice," "organize and give credit to the volunteers, they are the community," "inform communities about what you're doing to improve and maintain the park, and why you're doing it," "participate in local activities," "remind park employees of where they work and its significance. It's a special place to work—attitude adjustment," "parks need better ways to clue in the community and local business about the park and what it offers for them," and "park needs to think of more than outside visitors" suggest that CAC may not believe the park staff understands their needs and their attachment to the area well enough to target and provide specific community benefits.

As mentioned in Chapter 2 of this text and as shown in this case study, community members understand that adjacent natural areas impact their communities and these impacts can be beneficial as well as detrimental. Researchers and natural resource managers are still attempting to understand how to best integrate these community benefits and detriments into specific management plans. As mentioned, community members believe recreation resource managers and their staff need to have a close, working relationship with communities to fully understand of the impacts of their management of a contiguous or nearby public recreation area on those communities. Although community surveys help inform managers of a community's needs, this case study showed that informal discussion, involvement in community activities, and regular meetings with community stakeholders about the state park of concern and its impact on the community can serve well to also identify the variety of benefits a nearby public recreation area can provide to a community. Since many of the community benefits identified in this study focused on community members' values and attitudes (e.g., pride, understanding, and sense of security), increased interaction of local managers with the community might also serve as the "facilitating strategy" to help produce those benefits and avoidance of negative benefits as required by OFM.

Case 2: Understanding Resource Meanings: Niobrara National Scenic River, Nebraska

The Niobrara National Scenic River (NIOB) is located in northern Nebraska in the Sand Hills region of the state. The river was designated as a federal scenic river in 1991. While some local community members lobbied for designation, many others fought the designation unsuccessfully. Once designated, the USDI National Park Service (NPS) developed a General Management Plan (GMP) and an Environmental Impact Statement (EIS), which were approved. However, before the plan could be successfully implemented it was contested in the courts and the NPS was ordered to prepare a new GMP and EIS (Federal Register: May 22, 2000 (Volume 65, Number 99) Page 32121-32122). At about this same time, a new superintendent was assigned to the NIOB, and one of his responsibilities was to prepare the new GMP and EIS. One of the stipulations of the court order was that new visitor data be gathered for the new plan. During the summer of 2000, the Midwest Regional Office of the NPS contacted the authors of this chapter and asked that we gather visitor data that could be used to identify visitors' use patterns, characteristics, perceptions of management, and desired experiences and on-site benefits. These data would be used in preparing the GMP using the Visitor Experience Resource Protection (VERP) planning framework to identify, target, and manage for visitor desired experience and benefit opportunities (USDI National Park Service, 1997). Visitor data were gathered over the summer seasons of 2001 and 2002. During the 2001 summer season, conversations were held with many local residents and the Niobrara River Council, a local group of stakeholders working with the NIOB staff as an advisory group in the GMP process. Many of them expressed concern that the NPS and NIOB staffs were not meeting the needs of local community member. Community benefits related to NIOB management were specifically targeted per the court order, which required that one of the specific issues to be addressed was to look at the "extent and manner in which partnerships can and will be employed to achieve management objectives" [Federal Register: May 22, 2000 (Volume 65, Number 99) Page 32121-32122]. Engaging local community members at this time would be difficult, though, because the working relationship between NPS, the Council, and the greater community was often contentious. Some local citizens viewed NPS as an intruder who did not understand or appreciate them. At the same time, many local citizens feared that the Council would not represent the needs and desires of the broader community in its advisory role, but would instead act as individuals pushing their own personal agendas.

Furthermore, informal conversations with local people during the 2001 field season revealed that many local residents did not believe the NPS planning process was transparent, nor did they believe that NPS was accountable to local people and local concerns. Informal conversations also revealed that many local people did not see benefits accruing to them or to their communities as a result of the Niobrara River's designation and management as a national scenic river. While select local residents had clearly reaped economic benefits through the burgeoning tourism service industry (e.g., canoe rentals, campgrounds, hotels), many residents questioned the economic, social, and biophysical outcomes of increased visitation, escalating infrastructure demands, and tightening land use regulations on their river communities altogether. Residents' level of distrust for the agency and/or their belief that agency "outsiders" could not target and provide community benefits without understanding community members' histories and attachments to the river and river corridor appeared to interfere with their ability to achieve community benefits. These sentiments also served as barriers to building strong community-agency relationships and partnerships in river management.

Developing a shared vision for management of public lands is critical to benefit attainment, and that shared vision must include local residents. While public land managing agencies believe they play a role in rural community development and sustainability, many see that role narrowly and focus on economic benefits and services the community provides for tourists on their way to visiting public lands. Understanding both historical and contemporary connections communities have with nearby or adjacent public lands and the meanings these lands hold for them is critical to OFM for community benefits. Many public land managers do not see the role they can play in local communities in providing noneconomic benefits related to health, social equity, cultural history, and maintenance of natural areas outside a park or river corridor's boundaries. Inability to see this role can result in misunderstandings between the agency and local communities and in missed opportunities for the agency to meet its long-term goals of providing benefits to people and society. To some extent, misunderstandings and missed opportunities had developed between NIOB management and landowners in the river corridor. The new superintendent was aware of local residents' feelings about the establishment of the Niobrara as a scenic river and aware that many residents did not think NPS understood or appreciated local people's connections to the river and the river corridor. The superintendent was also very interested in changing the relationship between the agency and local communities to a more positive one. The authors worked with the superintendent and his staff to develop an interview guide designed to identify local residents' connections to the river, their perceptions of the river, and their visions for the future of the river.

Data Collection and Analysis Methods: Capturing a broad range of local residents' perspectives was integral to understanding the nature of the human-environmental connection on the Niobrara River. Since the Niobrara River community is not a homogenous group, seeking out diversity in perspectives was essential to the study. The "network" or referral-chain-participant-selection technique was used to capture a range of perspectives. An original set of community leaders or key informants was identified from observations and interactions in the 2001 summer field season. These individuals were asked to provide names of other community members who were invested in the future of the Niobrara River. Specifically, participants were asked, "Are there others that you think I should talk to about their perspectives on the Niobrara River?" "Who else has a similar perspective?" and "Who might have a very different perspective?"

A total of 28 community members were contacted over a period of three months during the 2002 summer field season. Of those initially contacted, 25 agreed to participate in the study. Initial contacts were made by phone or in person. Study participants included residents working in agriculture and forest industries, recreation services, city and county government, and other local businesses. Sixteen of those interviewed were male and nine were female. The average age of interviewees was 55. The authors conducted formal interviews with these 25 individuals following the interview guide protocol that had been developed with input from the NIOB management staff. Each interview was tape recorded and transcribed. Interviews lasted from 25 minutes to 2 hours.

Analysis of the interview data consisted of organization and interpretation based on Strauss and Corbin's (1990) analysis procedures in grounded theory. The qualitative analysis software NUD*IST was used in the initial stages of data organization to enumerate text units and remove words or phrases that would jeopardize a participant's anonymity. Data were organized in categories and sub-categories. Each interview was individually analyzed and themes were recorded. Coding procedures followed. In coding, specific topics embedded in participant perspectives were given a representative name and then grouped into broad categories. Since the strength of qualitative assessment and underlying goals of the study are depth and breadth of meaning, the various words, categories, and themes were not quantified. The trustworthiness of the study was judged using the four criteria of credibility, transferability, dependability, and confirmability (Lincoln & Guba, 1985).

Selected Findings: From data collection, organization, and interpretation, common themes and patterns within those themes emerged (Davenport & Anderson, 2005). Figure 20.1 summarizes the meanings participants ascribed to the river, specifically the four major themes and related subthemes. The figure also shows the interconnections between themes and subthemes. The four major meanings identified by interviewees relate to the role of the river and river corridor in: a) defining local people's identity as individuals and as a community—*identity*, b) sustaining local people and their communities economically—*sustenance*, c) providing recreational benefits for local people—*tonic*, and d) protecting natural areas within and outside the federally designated river corridor—*nature*.

A critical message to take away from these findings is that by offering them a venue to share their stories, local community members articulated quite eloquently their place meanings and relationships which provides a richer and more sophisticated understanding of emotional attachments to public lands and the community benefits (and drawbacks) of public lands management. Many place meanings were interconnected. For example, with respect to the river as sustenance one participant asserted that "Water is a great play medium. It's a source of irrigation. It's a source of entertainment." All three of these attributes overlap significantly and encompass both personal- and community-based meanings. The river as tonic embodies notions of freedom, solitude, and enjoyment. As one participant summarized, "To put it into three words, it's good for the mind, body, and soul." Some meanings expressed by participants were highly symbolic and central to their personal, family, and/or community identity: "For the people that live here it's their home and their livelihood." For others the notions of independence and self-sustainability came through: "The people that live out here, that settled this place, were a very independent-

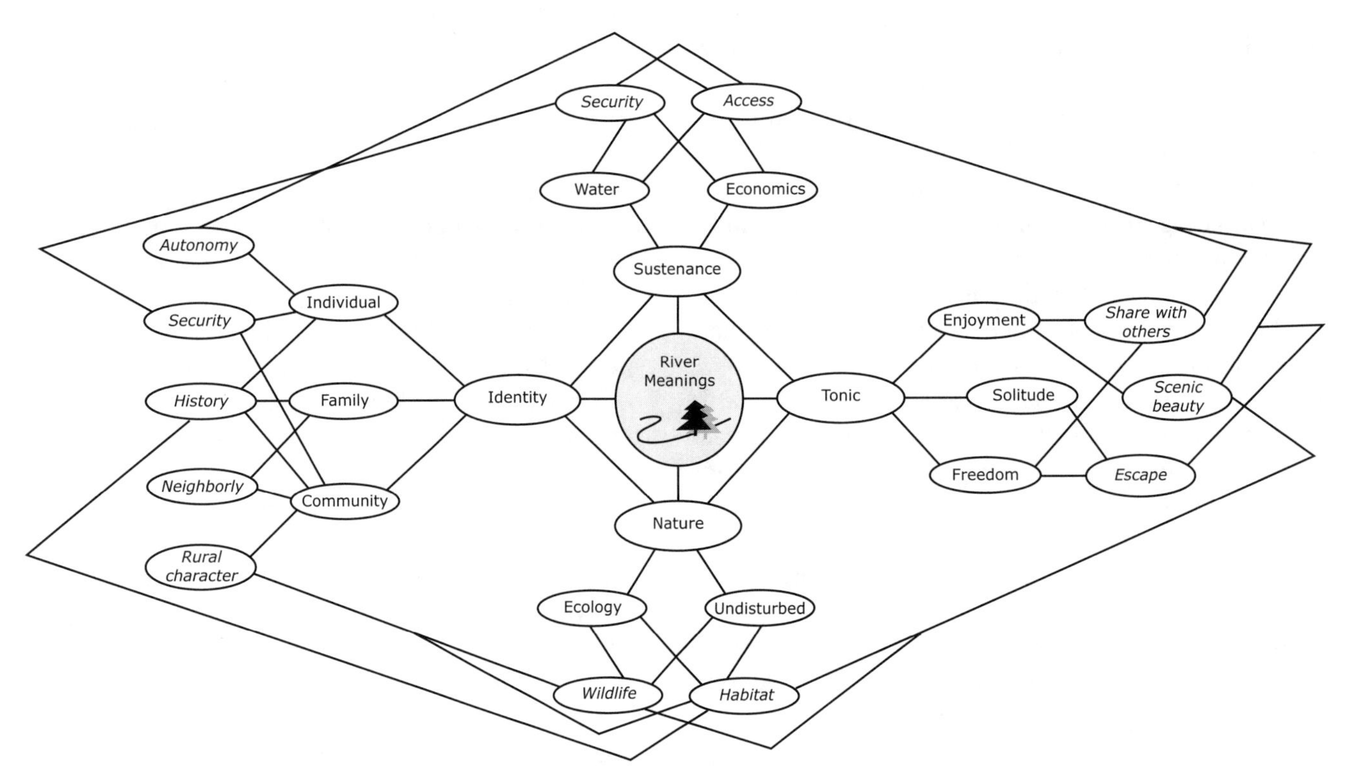

***Figure 20.1** Web of meanings and interconnectedness of meanings associated with the Niobrara National Scenic River, Nebraska (Source: Davenport & Anderson, 2005)*

minded lot of people and still are. It's not an easy deal to be a rancher in the Sand Hills. It's tough and you've got to be an independent-minded person. They feel like they know what they're doing and they've been doing it for years. They're the best stewards of the land. They live there." The river's ecological uniqueness and undisturbed nature was not lost on residents either: "The beauty...the lack of development along the river. It's extremely pristine...and that's something most everybody around here values." Another participant offered that "I like the idea that it is an oasis in the middle of the Great Plains that attracts and/or nurtures lots of species that wouldn't really exist here if it weren't for the river. The birds, the neotropical migrants...the plants that are here...the animals that are here, that wouldn't be here otherwise. ...It's just wonderful." Finally, one respondent noted that, "This is literally the ecological center of the North American continent, where east meets west and north meets south. Can't say that about any other place in the United States."

Another key message to take away is that public land managers who do not know how local residents or communities connect with their environment, will struggle to manage using OFM to target and provide desired community benefit opportunities. Establishing a community vision for a publicly protected area can help managers anticipate potential beneficial and negative outcomes of resource management and planning. In turn, positive outcomes can be enhanced and negative outcomes can be avoided or reduced. At its most fundamental level, a community member's connection to the Niobrara River is a matter of time and space. Respondents were quick to establish their spatial and temporal connection to the River by describing their family's historical connection to the river and the river corridor. Given that most managers will not have the temporal or spatial connections to the public lands they administer that local community members have, systematically documenting these connections through interviews, surveys, focus groups, or visioning workshops will fill in those gaps—informing decision making and serving as community relations training tools for new management staff.

Using the Findings: One of the most important products that came out of this study was a booklet—*A River of Meanings: Developing a Community-based Vision for the Management of the Niobrara National Scenic River* (Davenport, 2003) which was written for residents living in the river corridor. Information in the booklet was presented to local people at a community meeting. The booklet uses the words of the residents to describe what the river means to them and their way of life. The booklet was distributed to local people and NIOB staff free of charge; copies were also placed in local community centers and libraries. Finally, a digital copy was provided to libraries so that all community members would have access to information it contained. Many residents expressed appreciation that their words and feelings about the river had been captured and that it gave them a sense of legitimacy when they talked with agency staff about river management. Residents and NIOB staff have found the booklet useful in starting conversations about the kinds of community benefit opportunities community members and agency staff can work together to develop and provide and that will meet shared management objectives for the river and its corridor.

Although the community member interviews were valuable to community members and to NIOB staff in preparing the new GMP, staff thought that many of the issues community members identified cast NIOB staff in an unfavorable light. This feeling among staff was especially true for issues related to community-agency trust. During the interviews some participants brought up feelings of distrust for the agency. Distrust seemed to be connected to their feelings about the way the federal government had acquired the land, their perceptions of the NPS competence, and their perceptions that their individual rights and freedoms had been trampled in acquiring, developing, and managing the River. NIOB staff thought the study findings would have been more valuable to them and their work with the communities if staff had also been interviewed. They believed their input concerning decisions they have made with respect to developing and managing the NIOB resource would play a bigger role in continued development and maintenance of a shared vision for the Niobrara Scenic River. While the study was aimed at developing a community vision for the Niobrara River, the authors agree that understanding park staff, their role as managers of the resource, and their connections to the NIOB is also important. A shared vision depends on understanding all parties concerned with the long-term sustainability of the river and the communities that surround it.

Case 3: Community-Agency Trust, Place Attachment, and Benefits—Kaskaskia River Watershed, Illinois

The U.S. Army Corps of Engineers (USACE) has been incrementally adopting the OFM approach for providing benefits to people and society (see Chapter 7 of this text). As an agency with responsibility for managing public lands, "The Army Corps of Engineers is the steward of the lands and waters at Corps water resources projects. Its Natural Resource Management Mission is to manage and conserve those natural resources, consistent with ecosystem management principles, while providing quality public outdoor recreation experiences to serve the needs of present and future generations" (Engineer Regulation 1130-2-550, Chapter 2, Paragraph 2-2.a.(1), dated 15 November 1996). Principally, the USACE's natural resource management mission is to manage for recreation, flood control, water quality, fish and game habitat, and dredging to provide benefits to visitors, communities, the economy, and the environment (http://www.vtn.iwr.usace.army.mil/pdfs/recreation.pdf). Although charged to provide these types of benefits, specific community benefits are not always known and therefore impossible for USACE to target and provide.

In the spring of 2002, the USACE asked the authors to provide assistance in identifying and understanding community benefit opportunities and community benefit attainment for three USACE projects in the Kaskaskia River watershed in central Illinois—Lake Shelbyville, Carlyle Lake, and the Navigation Project. The Kaskaskia River Watershed was chosen as a study site because of its large, diverse geographic area, interesting social history, and evidence of collective action related to natural resources management. USACE was interested in using the results of the study to develop a web-based tool kit for its managers so that the agency would have a consistent way to apply OFM (then called BBM) for communities in close proximity to USACE project sites.

The Kaskaskia watershed is distinctive in many ways. Through its two lake projects and river navigation project, USACE provides access to public lands and resources that are in limited supply in Illinois where nearly 90% of the land is in private ownership. Within the Kaskaskia River Watershed, about 80% of the land is agricultural and the remaining 20% is in residential, public land, or other land uses (Illinois Department of Natural Resources, 2001). "Measured by almost any standard—ecological, recreational, and economical—it is a crucial natural resource for a great swathe of Mid-Illinois," concluded an Illinois Department of Natural Resources assessment (Illinois Department of Natural Resources, 2001, p. 1). A brief description of the three USACE projects follows.

Lake Shelbyville is the northern-most reservoir in the watershed. It was the second of the three USACE projects completed in the watershed. It is located approximately 222 miles upstream from the mouth of the Kaskaskia River. The dam creating the lake was finished in 1970. Land was taken from private ownership by the federal government via eminent domain. At this lake, the USACE owns the lands around the lake, up to the 100-year flood estimate point. Managers estimate that over 20% of the Lake Shelbyville visitors come from the Chicago metro area (U.S. Army Corps of Engineers, 2001).

Carlyle Lake is located 115 river miles south or downstream of Lake Shelbyville. It was the first USACE project built in the watershed. The dam creating this lake was finished in 1967. The USACE acquired the land for the lake impoundment using eminent domain. However, unlike Lake Shelbyville, the USACE purchased the right to flood adjacent private land instead of purchasing the land outright. It is a comparatively larger lake than Lake Shelbyville and considerable recreational use of Carlyle Lake and the surrounding lands is made by St. Louis metro area (50 miles away) urban visitors (U.S. Army Corps of Engineers, 2001; Carlyle Lake Planning Committee, n.d.).

Kaskaskia River Navigation Project extends from the lock and dam at the mouth of the Kaskaskia River to the town of Fayetteville (approximately river mile 36). The lower portion of the Kaskaskia River was modified to be 275 feet wide and 9 feet deep to allow commercial barge traffic on the river. The lock and dam's first year of operation was in 1973. The navigation project reduced the number of river miles from 52 miles to 36 miles, and in the process created many oxbows along the river (U.S. Army Corps of Engineers, 2001). Compared to the two lake projects, limited private land was acquired from private landowners to build this project.

Results of our previous research on community benefits with Minnesota's DPR and with the NPS Niobrara National Scenic River showed that place attachment and a community's level of trust in an agency strongly influence the perceptions of residents of local communities about the attainment of personal and community benefits from the management of nearby public land. Place attachment and trust also influence the building of social capital within communities and between community residents and the public land managing agency. Social capital is important because the greater a community's social capital, the more likely it is that benefits will accrue to the community. Communities with high amounts of social capital tend to be more connected, more trusting of one another, and have a greater number of networks and groups that exist to improve their communities and enhance the well-being of those who live in the communities than communities with low levels of social capital (Putnam, 2000). These earlier studies also suggested that agency perception of local residents and communities influences how agency personnel select and implement strategies to target and provide community benefits. Finally, these earlier studies illustrated the important role that public land managing agencies play in creating and using social capital to produce benefits for local communities located near or adjacent to public lands.

To understand how OFM could be applied to improve and enhance delivery of community benefits for the three USACE projects in the watershed, the role of trust in community-agency relationships and the community members' attachment to the area were explored. In the USACE study, informal conversations with community leaders and groups suggested that these community leaders and groups had a good working relationship with USACE managers of the three project sites and could articulate how they benefited from these relationships and how they could be improved. USACE expressed interest in improving on the good working relationships that existed. Both USACE and community leaders were willing to share their views about what worked and did not work that affected providing and delivering community benefits.

The Kaskaskia River Watershed study was conducted in two main stages using both qualitative and quantitative research methods. The first stage of the study was designed to: 1) describe components of social capital involving USACE and local communities in the watershed, 2) identify meanings of trust present within community stakeholders toward USACE and the variables that influence trust, and 3) describe the impacts in the form of community benefits, social capital development, and its use on natural resource management and local communities. In other words, in the first stage of the study the authors wanted to understand the relationship between trust and perception of personal and community benefit attainment. Since the authors could find no empirical studies linking trust to community benefit attainment, a qualitative study design was chosen for the first stage. In this stage the authors focused their efforts on: a) understanding the trust relationship between community members and USACE staff, specifically the dimensions of trust that appear to be important to perception of community benefits provided by USACE, and b) identifying the specific personal and community benefits provided through agency management of the projects and attained by residents and their communities. Data from the first stage was used to inform the second stage of the study. The second stage was designed to measure importance and attainment of personal and community benefits, place attachment, and community-agency trust. The second stage used a mailback questionnaire sent to a random sample of community residents living within 15 miles of each of the three USACE projects. Each stage, stage results, and implementation of results are described below.

Stage 1

Data Collection and Analysis Methods: A qualitative approach was chosen for this initial, exploratory research stage about the relationship of trust to individual and community benefit perceptions and attainment in the Kaskaskia River Watershed. The specific research framework used was the social structural symbolic interactionism framework. The authors viewed trust or lack of trust as a social problem that is influenced by the attributes an individual or group (e.g., community residents) associates with an entity (e.g., agency), and/or the interactions a community member(s) might have with a representative of the public land managing agency (e.g., staff person). The social structural symbolic interactionism approach is often used in this type of research because each individual and community of interest can be a unique, socially constructed object or a situation, which is subject to common structural constraints. In the case of the Kaskaskia River Watershed study, the authors wanted to collect data that would shed light on residents' meanings, symbols, interpretations, and interactions with USACE staff at each of the three project sites. The same type of data was gathered from USACE staff to shed light on their interactions with community members living in communities adjacent to or nearby one of the three project sites.

Data was gathered using a semi-structured interview format. This format allowed the use of a standard set of interview questions for all participants and it yields rich and in-depth data. Interview questions were primarily open-ended and interviews were conducted with USACE staff and key community stakeholders associated with each project site. An interview guide was developed for each group. The interview guide for USACE staff contained questions centered on four main topic areas: 1) community and place connections, 2) interviewee's relationship with the community, 3) the community-agency relationship, 3) perspectives on agency decision-making and management, and 4) vision for the future. The interview guide for community residents was similar and centered on five major topics: 1) community and place connections, 2) the interviewee's

Question content area	Interview question
Agency management and decision making	• What information and knowledge do you think go into management decisions? • Whose (or what) values are reflected in management decisions? • How have management decisions affected the community?
Perceptions about ways to increase community benefits in the future	• What are some ways in which the Corps can improve its relationship with you? • What are some ways in which the Corps can improve its relationship with the community? • What are some ways in which the Corps can improve its management of [Lake Shelbyville, Carlyle Lake, or the Navigation Project]?
Relationship of trust to benefits	• Suppose the Corps followed your suggestions, how would this influence your overall trust in the Corps? • What would it take for you to trust the agency to manage [Lake Shelbyville, Carlyle Lake, or the Navigation Project]? OR What would it take for your trust in the Corps to be maintained?

Table 20.2 Community members' perspectives on benefits from agency's management and decision making

relationship with the agency, 3) the community-agency relationship, 4) perspectives on the agency's decision-making and management, and 5) vision for the future (Table 2).

Community members selected for interviews were intentionally selected for their broad range of knowledge about USACE in the Kaskaskia River Watershed. They were not selected to be representative of the larger population, but were selected to provide a diversity of the potential perspectives that exist among the watershed's key community stakeholders. USACE agency personnel selected included site managers, rangers, interpreters, and other field and office staff. USACE employees at the three project sites helped the authors identify community members to interview.

Using the initial set of names provided by USACE employees, a network sampling approach was used to identify additional community member participants. Many of the community members USACE initially recommended were Kaskaskia Watershed Association (KWA) members. The KWA works with the USACE and serves as a citizen's advisory group to USACE for management of the watershed and the three project sites. The KWA is the principal resource-based citizen organization in the watershed. It was formed in 2000 as an umbrella organization to unite the many interests and groups (e.g., Lower Kaskaskia Stakeholders, Upper Kaskaskia Local Planning Council, Original Kaskaskia Area Wilderness, Okaw River Basin Coalition, Lower Okaw River Basin Coalition, Carlyle Lake Association) within the watershed. The KWA has about 23 members, and each member represents an entity with a stake in the management of the watershed. USACE works closely with the KWA to make collaborative management decisions to benefit local communities and their members. Study participants who were part of KWA were encouraged at the end of their interview to recommend other community members who were not involved in the KWA but who are key watershed stakeholders because of their strong connections to the watershed and their concern about its management. USACE personnel also identified watershed communities and community leaders (city or village mayors, clerks, and councilmen/aldermen) from those communities whom they believed were important to interview.

A total of 32 community members and 10 USACE employees were contacted for interviews. Forty-one interviews were completed; only one person contacted was unable to participate. During summer 2003 formal interviews were conducted with the 41 individuals who agreed to an interview. The interviews followed the protocol laid out in the interview guide. Each interview was tape recorded and transcribed. Interviews lasted anywhere from 25 minutes to 2 hours. Interviewees included residents working in agriculture industries, recreation services, city and county government, environmental organizations, and other local businesses throughout the watershed (Table 20.3). About equal numbers of USACE employees were interviewed from each project site; 13, 7, and 11 key community stakeholders from Lake Shelbyville, Carlyle Lake, and the Navigation Project respectively, were interviewed (Table 20.4).

Participants	Number interviewed	Percent interviewed
U.S. Army Corps of Engineers	24	10
Recreation/tourism (business)	12	5
Agriculture	12	5
Residential	12	5
Local government	12	5
Recreation (participation)	10	4
Industry	10	4
Environmental	7	3

Table 20.3 Summary of Participant Stakeholder Interest Areas

Location	Community member		Agency personnel	
	Number	Percent	Number	Percent
Lake Shelbyville	13	42	4	40
Carlyle Lake	7	23	3	30
Navigation Project	11	36	3	30

Table 20.4 Number and Percent of Participants by Watershed Location and Group

Nine of the interviewees were female (five community residents and four agency personnel). The average age of community interviewees was 56; agency personnel interviewed averaged 52 years of age.

Analysis of the interview data primarily involved coding the data. Coding largely followed procedures recommended by Creswell (1998). Following coding, data were organized in categories and sub-categories to identify themes, patterns, and relationships concerning social capital in the Kaskaskia River Watershed. As noted earlier, the strength of qualitative assessment and the underlying goals of the study are depth and breadth; therefore, words, categories, and themes were not quantified. The trustworthiness of the study was judged using the four criteria of credibility, transferability, dependability, and confirmability (Lincoln & Guba, 1985).

Selected Findings: Overall findings from stage 1 suggested that the Kaskaskia River Watershed is an area that has been developing social capital related to water resources management for a number of years. A connected network of water resources management players has developed and extends between and within the KWA, other citizen watershed groups, local governments, local communities, other natural resource agencies, and within USACE (Figure 20.2). Interviewees talked about individuals, various organizations, and USACE as: "banding together," "having constructive meetings," "being involved," "looking for partnerships," "working together," and "rising to a level that the Corps would respect us as a sounding board." These connections occurred because of the intertwined relationship and exchanges that have developed between residents, communities, watershed associations, other entities, and USACE. Both community members and USACE personnel described the intertwined reliance not in terms of obligations to one another but in terms of mutual benefit or gain. As one community member noted: "It's almost a symbiotic relationship. The Upper Kaskaskia planning group need (Lake Manager) and they need the planning group." Although the community and USACE respondents saw themselves generally working for the

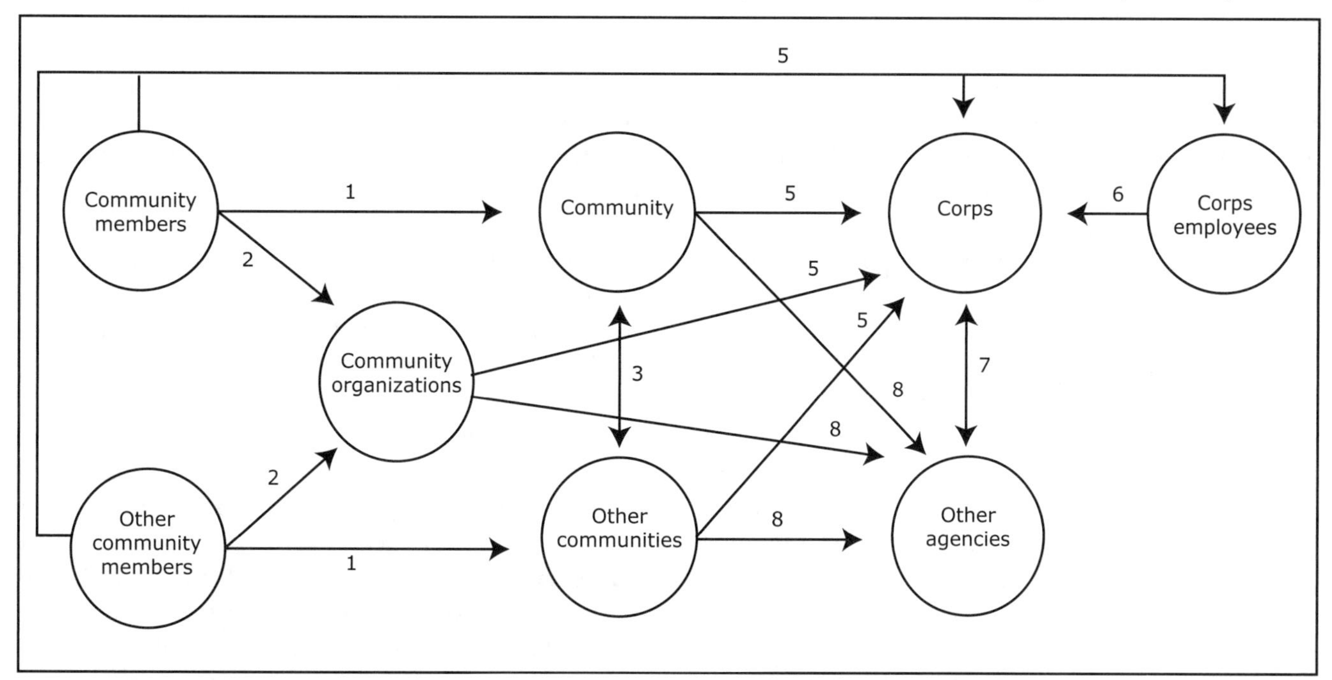

Figure 20.2 Social Networks in the Kaskaskia River Watershed (Source: Leahy 2005)

good of all in the watershed, some noted that at times some groups, organizations, or even USACE seemed to "have a 'what's in it for me' attitude instead of 'what's good for the community' attitude." Finally, USACE personnel were sometimes viewed as not working under common rules, which resulted in some respondents not trusting USACE to manage the three projects in ways that would benefit local communities.

Community-agency trust: Trust in USACE by community members was complex and multidimensional (Leahy, 2005). Even though USACE and the communities exhibited a history of working with one another to build social capital that would result in benefits to both groups, low trust or distrust in the agency to manage the watershed was expressed a number of times by interviewees. Key findings of the studied showed that:

Trust and distrust were related to an individual's general trust in government and all of its agents.

Trust seemed to be related to social or generalized trust: "Well I'd like to think that it's important that you can feel like as human beings you can trust each other so I would have to think it (trust in USACE) would have to very important."

Trust was defined in terms of moral competency. As one community participant noted: "They're very conscientious...about how what they do affects the whole community." Another community participant offered: "They want to do the right thing and do things that benefit the area and the region...they're usually decent people trying to do the right thing."

Trust was defined in terms of technical competency. For example, one participant said: "The people running the lake as far as I'm concerned are experts, they know what they're doing." Another offered that he trusted USACE "Because the meetings I've attended, and someone's asked a question, like 'how'd you come up with that?' they always have the answer. It's not just, 'well because we feel like it' or 'I'm not really sure why' or 'this is what we thought would be good.' There's always some research or numbers for why they're doing this."

Trust and distrust was reflected by comments community participants had about shared values and interests. When community members thought USACE had the same priorities they had and would benefit community members, then participants trusted USACE management. Distrust resulted when a participant thought USACE's values differed from the participant's values.

Trust and distrust were associated with respondents' perception of the fairness of the procedures USACE uses to make decisions. Decisions viewed as fair resulted in participants saying they trusted the agency whereas decisions viewed as unfair resulted in participants saying they did not trust the agency.

Factors that appeared to influence or moderate trust included a) community members' history in the area and USACE's legacy in the area, b) passage of time, c) information available from USACE about USACE plans and decisions, d) community members dependence on USACE for water resources particularly related to economic dependence, e) informal interactions, f) media accounts of USACE management, g) transparency of USACE decisions, h) USACE personnel turnover, and i) consistency of USACE decisions.

All of these factors appear to play a role in USACE's abilities to create and use social capital to provide beneficial opportunities for local communities. When levels of trust were perceived to be high between USACE and community members or an organization, then community members were more likely to engage in collaborative actions with USACE that result in benefits to a community and its members. For example, at Lake Shelbyville, the two most commonly mentioned collaborations between USACE and the community that resulted in a number of benefits to local communities was community members involvement in the improvement of the regional sewer system and the planning and development of a bike trail that would loop around the entire lake. The two actions are partly related. The sewer project involved community leaders from communities around Lake Shelbyville, several USACE employees, and the regional bike trail committee. Within the watershed, the towns of Sullivan, Shelbyville, and Findlay developed a regional sewer system plan that surrounds all but the northwest portion of Lake Shelbyville. USACE got involved in the project because it wanted its many campground water and toilet facilities to hook into the system rather than maintain private sewer systems in each campground. The bike trail committee saw an opportunity to use the same right of way as the sewer system. Using the same right of way for the trail meant that local communities would not have to acquire land or easements on private lands to construct the bike trail. Another benefit of the bike trail is the benefits its use would provide to local residents and its ability to attract and tourism dollars to the communities. These types of opportunities to collaborate and provide personal and community benefits to residents living in nearby towns came about because of the levels of trust local residents have in USACE especially trust expressed in terms of shared values the agency has with local communities, moral and technical competency of the agency to manage the resource for the benefit of local people and their communities, and community members perceptions that the agency operated in a fair and equitable manner.

Community benefits: Perception of benefits and benefit attainment were related to shared values and interests. Shared values enabled local community members to trust USACE, because they believed that USACE actions would benefit them or otherwise be aligned with their values and preferences. The USACE was involved with local community members and watershed associations in all aspects of social capital creation and maintenance. It was an active participant in exchanges, had numerous social network connections with the local communities and organizations, was generally perceived to be considerate of the local community goals, and had achieved some measure of success when it came to building trusting relationships in the watershed. The USACE accomplished this through their projects, public involvement, participation in community organizations and meetings, and support of local watershed associations. Based on the USACE's actions and involvement with local communities, the communities viewed the USACE as providing many benefit opportunities that community members were able to attain.

Benefits to individuals, communities, and economies were also associated with social capital use and creation by community members. When local community members discussed their examples of social capital use and development, they concomitantly described community benefits that result from their cooperative and collaborative efforts (Figure 20.3). These included personal, social, and economic benefits. Personal benefits were widespread and included personal recreation opportunities, nature appreciation, health benefits, quality of life, and enjoyment from involvement in activities that built social capital. Within this category of enjoyment from involvement in civic engagement activities were feelings of personal efficacy; empowerment; pride in oneself, pride in the group, and pride in results; learning benefits; and socialization benefits. Social benefits included community recreation opportunities; infrastructure development such as sewers, roads, buildings, grain loading facilities, and other structures; and building a sense of community. The sense of community benefit was comprised of benefits originating from creating a cohesive social group, solidifying social connections and networks, and improving understanding between the many water resources management players in the watershed including the USACE. Finally, economic benefits were largely related to economic development through industry (maintaining lock and dam operations for barge traffic), residential (creating more demand and users for city water and sewer), and tourism (increasing the recreation season through flood control).

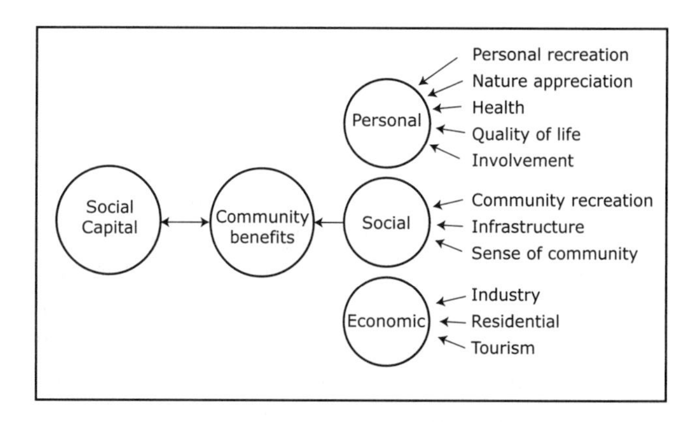

Figure 20.3 Community benefits related to social capital in the Kaskaskia River Watershed, Illinois (Source: Leahy, 2005)

Using the Findings: Results from stage 1 of this study were presented to USACE managers and the KWA at their yearly summit meeting during winter 2003. KWA and other community leaders and USACE staff in attendance committed to using findings of the study to strengthen their partnerships and commitments to target and provide benefits for nearby and adjacent communities. Additional meetings with USACE staff were held in spring 2003 to develop and carry out stage 2 of the study. Stage 2 of the study built on stage 1 findings and would take a broader look at community members' relationship with the USACE and community benefit attainment. Both USACE and community leaders wanted a community survey conducted to elicit responses covering a number of different areas including community members' perceptions of benefits USACE management provides to them and their communities, as well as community members' perceptions of the relationship existing between the communities and the USACE.

Stage 2

Data Collection and Analysis Methods: The second stage of the study was the development of a survey instrument to elicit responses on items related to a wide range of variables including community benefits, place attachment, and community-agency trust. A total of 32 items made up the community benefits pool of items (Table 20.5). The items were developed from data gathered from interviews conducted in the Kaskaskia River Watershed, from other study sites[1] not in the watershed, and from the literature. Both importance and attainment were measured for each community benefit item. Twenty-seven items made up the place attachment item pool (Table 20.6). These items came from the literature and interviews conducted at other sites primarily the Niobrara National Scenic River, Nebraska. The place attachment items were grouped into six different meanings categories (i.e., nature and natural processes, general attachment, family legacy, community character, self-identify, experience achievement, and economic stability). For each place attachment item, respondents were asked to indicate how much they agreed or disagreed with the item. A total of 28 items were used to measure trust (Table 20.7). Findings from stage 1 of this study and the literature were used as input for developing scale items for the six dimensions of trust (i.e., overall trust in government, general trust in others, technical competency, moral competency, shared values, and procedural justice) identified in the community interviews. For each trust item respondents were asked to indicate how much they agreed or disagreed with it.

Survey Sampling International (SSI) generated and provided us with a random sample of community member names and addresses. Names and addresses were compiled from tax records, phone books, and other sources to create a complete list of community residents living in the study area. In total SSI provided a random stratified sample of approximately 1,600 names and addresses of people living within 15 miles of Lake Shelbyville, Carlyle Lake, or the Navigation Project. The 15-mile limit was based on the USACE's knowledge and experience managing the study sites and on two summers of field work identifying communities that considered Lake Shelbyville, Carlyle Lake, or

Item primarily related to:	Community benefit
Natural capital	Knowing conserved natural resources exists for future generations Improved soil, water, and air quality A sense of security that the natural environment will not be lost A natural setting in which your community takes great pride A greater concern for the natural environment among residents A greater retention of distinctive natural landscape features A place to conserve various natural & unique ecosystems
Economic capital	Increased job opportunities within my community Providing jobs through farming operations Providing jobs through river navigation (barging) Attracting tourism dollars to my community Having a more stable economy within my community Having a more stable economy for the surrounding region Gaining financially by using natural resources
Social capital	Providing a good quality of life A higher quality of life Feeling that your community is a special place to live Opportunities for exercise that improves local people's health Living in a healthy environment A chance for local people to maintain an outdoor oriented lifestyle A feeling of community pride A greater ability to preserve small town feeling of your community Better maintenance of community infrastructure Increased knowledge about the area's cultural resources Heightened sense of community satisfaction Opportunities for residents to grow spiritually Improved care for community aesthetics More community involvement in recreation Having a better sense of my place within my community A stronger sense of family bonds within the community A stronger sense of community togetherness or cohesion Greater retention of community's distinctive architecture

Table 20.5 Community benefit items related to social, natural, and economic capital

the Navigation Project to be a part of them. Each study site represented one strata of the sample. To ensure enough responses so that comparisons could be made between study sites, an equal number of names and addresses was requested for each stratum.

Office of Management and Budget (OMB) approval was sought and given to administer the questionnaire. In April 2005, questionnaires were mailed to 533 Lake Shelbyville residents, 533 Carlyle Lake residents and 533 residents living adjacent to or nearby the Navigation Project. A modified Dillman (2000) technique was used to administer the survey. In the Lake Shelbyville sample, a total of 213 completed and useable questionnaires were returned; 65 questionnaires were returned because of insufficient addresses, forwarding orders that had expired, deceased participants, or because a respondent declined to participate. The overall response rate was 45.51% (213/468). In the Carlyle Lake sample, a total of 233 completed and useable questionnaires were returned; 41 questionnaires were returned for one of the reasons stated above; the overall response rate was 45% (223/492). For the Navigation Project, 201 completed and useable questionnaires were returned; 25 questionnaires were returned for reasons noted above. The overall response rate was 39.57% (201/508). Nonresponse bias check was conducted using the extrapolation method of successive waves (Armstrong & Overton, 1977). Comparisons of first and last wave respondents on gender, education, income, and age showed no differences in the Lake Shelbyville and Navigation Project samples. Carlyle lake respondents differed on education with first wave responders indicating more college than last wave responders.

Selected Findings: A complete discussion of the study results for each project site is not possible in this chapter. However, readers interested in the specific findings for each site can obtain copies of the technical reports from the authors. General descriptions of

Place attachment meaning categories	Place attachment item
Community character	This lake has helped put my community on the map This lake contributes to the character of my community My community's history is strongly tied to this lake
Nature and natural processes	This lake is important in providing habitat for wildlife This lake is important in protecting water quality This lake is important in protecting the landscape from development
General attachment	I am very attached to this lake This lake means a lot to me This lake is very special to me No other place can compare to this lake
Family legacy	This lake is a special place for my family Many important family memories are tied to this lake I feel a sense of pride in my heritage when I am there
Self-identity	I feel that I can really be myself at this lake When I am there others see me the way I want them to see me I feel this lake is part of me I identify strongly with this lake Visiting this lake say a lot about who I am Few people know this lake like I do
Economic stability	My community's economy depends on this lake Illinois' economy depends on this lake My family's income or livelihood depend on this lake
Experience/achievement	This lake is the best for what I like to do Doing what I do at this lake is more important to me than doing it in any other place I get more satisfaction out of visiting this lake than any other I wouldn't substitute any other area for doing the types of things I do at this lake The things I do at this lake I would not enjoy doing just as much at a similar site[2]

Table 20.6 Scale items used to measure place attachment

Trust dimensions	Trust items
Social	If I have a problem, there is always someone to help me Most people can be trusted People are interested in others welfare as well as their own[2] Most of the time you don't have to be alert because people will not take advantage of you[2] You don't need to be too careful when dealing with people[2]
Government	I am not generally skeptical of any government agency[2] I can trust the federal government to do what is right most of the time I feel connected to the US government The US government is effective in solving problems The federal government efficiently spends money
Moral competence	Corps employees are honest Corps employees are sensitive to the local economic impacts of tourism and recreation Corps employees are not self-serving in decision making Corps employees are sensitive to the local economic impacts of farming Corps managers really care what happens to me
Technical competence	Corps employees are well trained Corps employees are knowledgeable about technical matters I have confidence in Corps employees to manage this lake well Corps employees explain things clearly
Shared values	The Corps has similar goals to mine The Corps supports my views The Corps shares my values The Corps thinks like me The Corps is like me
Procedural justice	The planning process of the Corps is fair Corps management decisions reflect public input Citizens have a voice in Corps projects

Table 20.7 Items used to measure community-agency trust relationship

findings related to the three major areas of interest are presented for the project sites.

Place attachment: Residents living in communities near or adjacent to all three project sites attached similar meanings to the sites. The most important meanings they attached to a site were related to nature and natural processes, followed by community character and family legacy. For Lake Shelbyville and Navigation Project communities, items related to economic stability had the least meaning for them.

Community-agency trust: For all three project sites most respondents indicated that they generally trust people, but they do not trust government. For the most part community respondents believe the USACE employees at each of the three project sites are morally and technically competent. However, most respondents associated with each project site do not believe that the USACE employees share their values or that the processes the USACE uses to make decisions are fair.

Community benefits: Community respondents associated with the Lake Shelbyville and Carlyle Lake sites rated more than half of the benefits listed as important or most important while respondents living near the navigation project rated only about a third of the 32 benefits listed as important (Table 20.8). When respondents were asked to indicate their ability to attain these benefits, economic benefits seemed to be the most difficult to attain given their importance to the communities.

Using the Findings: In the summer of 2006 the authors conducted three workshops with the USACE staff and community leaders from each project site and from the KWA. The purpose of the workshops was to convey study result, create a positive working environment for community and agency attendees, and begin the process of developing a strategy for delivery community benefits. The strategy was called for in the USACE business plan for each project. The agenda for each workshop was to present detailed study findings, break into small work groups, and brainstorm possible ways to use the data to enhance current benefit production and attainment and to develop new ideas to create community benefits, share small group efforts, and select the

Project	Community benefits rated most important to important	Rank ordered by most important to important	Rank ordered by ability to attain the benefit	Difference between importance and attainment rank
Lake Shelbyville	Living in a healthy environment	1	1	0
	Attracting tourism dollars to my community	2	10	-8
	Increased job opportunities within my community	3	8	-5
	Knowing conserved natural resources exists for future generations	4	30	-26
	Having a more stable economy within my community	5	19	-14
	Having a more stable economy for the surrounding region	6	19	-13
	A higher quality of life	7	11	-4
	Providing a good quality of life	8	4	4
	A sense of security that the natural environment will not be lost	9	12	-3
	Improved soil, water, and air quality	10	16	-6
	A natural setting in which your community takes great pride	11	3	8
	Feeling that your community is a special place to live	12	6	6
	A greater concern for the natural environment among residents	13	14	-1
	A place to conserve various natural & unique ecosystems	14	15	-1
	A greater retention of distinctive natural landscape features	15	9	6
	Opportunities for exercise that improves local people's health	16	5	11
	A feeling of community pride	17	7	10
	A chance for local people to maintain an outdoor oriented lifestyle	18	2	16
	A greater ability to preserve small town feeling of your community	19	13	6
Carlyle Lake	Living in a healthy environment	1	2	-1
	Increased job opportunities within my community	2	19	-17
	Attracting tourism dollars to my community	3	9	-6
	Knowing conserved natural resources exists for future generations	4	7	-3
	Having a more stable economy within my community	5	20	-15
	A sense of security that the natural environment will not be lost	6	8	-2
	Providing a good quality of life	7	11	-4
	A higher quality of life	8	4	4
	Having a more stable economy for the surrounding region	9	14	-5
	Feeling that your community is a special place to live	10	6	4
	Improved soil, water, and air quality	11	17	-6
	Opportunities for exercise that improves local people's health	12	5	7
	A natural setting in which your community takes great pride	13	3	10
	A chance for local people to maintain an outdoor oriented lifestyle	14	1	13
	A greater concern for the natural environment among residents	15	10	5
	A feeling of community pride	16	12	4
	A place to conserve various natural & unique ecosystems	17	14	3
	A greater retention of distinctive natural landscape features	18	13	5
Navigation Project	Living in a healthy environment	1	1	0
	Improved soil, water, and air quality	2	4	-2
	A higher quality of life	3	5	-2
	Knowing conserved natural resources exists for future generations	4	9	-5
	Increased job opportunities within my community	5	22	-17
	A sense of security that the natural environment will not be lost	6	7	-1
	A place to conserve various natural and unique ecosystems	7	9	-2
	Having a more stable economy for the surrounding region	8	14	-6
	A chance for local people to maintain an outdoor oriented lifestyle	9	2	7
	Providing a good quality of life	10	2	8
	A greater concern for the natural environment among residents	11	8	3

Table 20.8 Community Benefits Rank Ordered by Importance and Attainment by USACE Project

most promising ideas for which to develop and implement a strategy.

Many of the most promising ideas generated focused on economic benefits that would be realized through greater promotion of tourism and recreation opportunities in the local communities and at each project site. From the findings it was clear that economic benefits were important and were seldom realized or at least not realized to the degree that communities would like. Some of the ideas talked about the need for more tourism and recreation related infrastructure such as hotels/motels, bed and breakfasts establishments, local eating establishments, campgrounds, and trails. Other ideas included ways to use the recreation backdrop of the project sites to carefully grow the area by encouraging new businesses and industry that would not detract from the rural character and feel of the communities. Community leaders in the Carlyle Lake area were especially concerned with new developments currently springing up near their communities and the Lake that essentially were bedroom communities for St. Louis, Missouri. They did not want to see their communities become an extension of urban sprawl development from St. Louis.

To help develop a way to target and deliver the kinds of benefits community members and the USACE identified as most important, USACE and the KWA contracted with the University of Illinois (UI) Extension Service to work with local community members to develop a strategic plan. The University of Illinois lies just north of Lake Shelbyville in Champaign-Urbana, Illinois and its extension agents have a long history of working with local groups in the watershed. The authors have been asked to work with the University of Illinois to interpret data and review the proposed strategy for incorporating study findings in a plan to develop opportunities for community benefits that increase the social, natural, and economic capital that already exists in the watershed.

Case 4: Community-Agency Trust, Community Benefits and Place Attachment—Voyageurs National Park, Minnesota

Voyageurs National Park (VNP) was authorized in 1971 and established in 1975 to preserve, for the inspiration and enjoyment of present and future generations, the outstanding scenery, geological conditions, and waterway system which constituted a part of the historic route of the Voyageurs. The National Park Service (NPS) is the managing authority for VNP. The park is located approximately 12 miles east of International Falls, Minnesota, and extends 60 miles eastward along the United States—Canadian border. With 218,054 acres of forested woodlands, water, shoreline, and islands, VNP is a scenic land and water environment of exceptional natural and cultural resources, scenic beauty, and recreational potential. The majority of the park's acreage consists of Rainy Lake in the northern part of the park and Kabetogama Lake and Namakan Lake in the southern part of the park. The Kabetogama Peninsula separates the Rainy Lake from the two large lakes that make up the southern portion of the park.

Even before the area that is now VNP was authorized and established, the history of this area had been one of challenge and disappointment (Gray, 2003). Challenges to creating the VNP included defining it as a national park versus a national recreation area; determining what lands, waters, and bays would be a part of the park; as well as determining whether wilderness would be a useful designator to parklands, and if so, what parklands would be classified as wilderness. Later there was the disappointment that the economic boon predicted for the communities surrounding VNP has yet to occur. In part because of the challenges and disappointments, local support for the park and the relationship of the park to its local neighbors have been problematic. In fact, local groups once approached the U.S. Congress in an attempt to de-authorize the park. The effort failed, but feelings between local individuals and park administrators continue to be strained.

In winter 2005, the NPS Midwest Regional Director and VNP's acting superintendent asked the authors to work with the region and VNP to better understand community needs and desires with respect to the management of VNP. In particular the director and acting superintendent were interested in changing the relationship between the park and surrounding communities from one of distrust, sabotage, and anger to one of trust that would result in partnerships between VNP and local groups to provide benefits that would meet a wide variety of community needs. NPS was particularly interested in a community survey to examine trust between community members and park staff. Two other NPS units in the region (Pictured Rocks National Lakeshore, Michigan; Ozark National Scenic Riverway, Missouri) had been a part of the community-agency trust interview studies. Findings from the interviews conducted at these two units were used in the development of the survey instrument to examine the relationships between trust, place attachment, and community benefits.

The VNP park staff wanted to use the survey instrument with local community members because staff saw it as a way of opening dialogue between the park and local communities. The dialogue would help both sides understand one another better and develop a shared vision for managing the park in ways that would benefit local communities. VNP park staff believed that the survey would not be successful (i.e., response rate would be extremely low) if community leaders were not a part of the decision-making process to use it. In fact, park staff would not gather data using the survey unless community leaders endorsed its use. The new superintendent decided to hold a meeting with local leaders (county commissioners, mayors, business leaders, and local planning officials) and park staff. The purpose of the meeting was to introduce the community to VNP's new acting superintendent and to gain community support to conduct a community survey examining community-agency trust, community residents' attachment to the area, and community members' perception of the important community benefits the park provided and community attainment of those benefits. The author was invited to the meeting to talk about the research the authors had conducted over the past few years in these areas and provide examples of how this research was being used by other communities to improve community-agency relationships and community benefit attainment.

To make it convenient for as many community leaders as possible to attend, two community-park staff meetings were held in spring 2005. One meeting was held at VNP headquarters in International Falls, Minnesota, which is located on Rainy River. The other meeting was held in Orr, Minnesota, which is along the park's southern area. A comment made by a county commissioner at the International Falls meeting was that this was the first time in 10 years that community leaders had been in the park's offices. This comment was not an exaggeration. Under the previous superintendent, community leaders did not feel welcome or a part of park decision making.

After talking about the community-agency studies conducted on other public lands, community leaders and park staff were interested in pursuing similar research. Many community leaders in the International Falls area were skeptical about a number of questions in the survey. Before they agreed to endorse it, they wanted an opportunity to review and edit items in the survey with other community leaders not in attendance. They also wanted the opportunity to suggest additional questions, reword items, and/or delete items they did not like. A one-week review period was agreed upon, but it was pointed out that changing the wording of scale items and/or deleting scale items would change the intent of the survey. It was suggested that they review the survey based on the objectives of the survey that they not change or delete scale items. They agreed. At the end of the review period, another meeting took place to talk about the survey.

Community leaders representing the northern and southern communities strongly endorsed the survey. They gave several reasons for their strong endorsement. Among them were: 1) this was the first time the park had formally "studied" them and what they thought was important about the park and park management; 2) they wanted the community-park relationship to improve and thought that what they would learn from the survey could move them toward improving the relationship; 3) many leaders noted that the existing relationship was hurting the communities economically; 4) they were curious to see how they compared to other communities with whom the authors had worked; and 5) many leaders saw the survey as a way to get the harsh feelings many community residents had for the park out in the open and in the public arena. One city planning official thought this survey would give a voice to the grieving many community residents felt when the land was taken from them and their families via eminent domain to become parkland.

Data Collection and Analysis Methods: Once the survey was vetted with the community members and park staff, OMB approval was sought. The survey questions used in this study were virtually identical as those used in the Kaskaskia Watershed study. Minor edits were made to items in Tables 20.5, 20.6, and 20.7 to remove mention of 'the Corps' and replace it with "the park." Once OMB approval was granted, local community leaders sent flyers to all residents encouraging them to complete the survey if they received it. The flyer was printed on color paper and was sent in the same envelope with each resident's monthly utility bill. During fall of 2005 and at least a week after the flyers were received, surveys were sent to a representative sample of people randomly selected from the population of community residents living in communities adjacent to or in close proximity to VNP.

The names and addresses of the study sample were provided by Survey Sampling International (SSI) using tax records, phone books, auto registrations, credit card information, and other sources to create a complete list of community residents living in the study area. A total of 1,150 names were obtained, of which 996 (or 87%) were deliverable. The sample of 996 names provided by SSI was divided into two strata of approximately 500 names each. The first strata included 506 individuals living in communities closes to the northern part of the park. The first strata included International Falls, Minnesota. The second strata included 490 individuals living in VNP gateway communities in close proximity to the southern portion of the park. These strata were developed because of the belief that International Falls and communities near it would be most familiar with the Rainy Lake portion of the park, while residents living in other gateway communities south of International Falls would be more familiar with the Kabetogama Lake area of the park. Community leaders and park staff agreed that compared to people living in the communities closest to the southern part of the park, people living in northern communities close to the park differed in their history with the park and their feelings toward park management. A modified Dillman (2000) technique was used to administer the survey.

After reminder mailings, 610 usable surveys were returned: 313 participants from the International Falls and other northern communities strata and 297 participants from the southern communities strata. The overall response rate was 61.2 percent. The response rate for each strata was 61.8 percent from the northern strata and 60.6 percent from the southern strata. Based on the high return rates, no nonresponse bias check was performed.

Selected Findings: As with the USACE study, a complete discussion of the study results for the park is not possible in this chapter. However, readers interested in the specific findings for the park overall and for the northern and southern sections of the park can obtain copies of the technical report from the authors. General descriptions of findings related to the three major areas of interest are presented for the project sites.

Place attachment: Individual study participants see VNP as a place: a) that means a lot to them individually and to which they are very attached, b) that protects the natural environment, water quality, and wildlife in the area, c) where management should balance environmental and economic concerns, d) that is special to them and their families, e) that is a place where they can be themselves, and f) that is one of the best places to engage in their favorite recreational activities, and where engagement in those activities allows them to have experiences that result in personal benefits, especially benefits related to being with family and enjoying the natural environment.

Community-agency trust: Community respondents agreed that they: a) are generally trusting of other people, b) have little trust in 'big' government, c) trust NPS somewhat at the national level, and c) trust VNP staff about the same as they trust the NPS. They also note that their level of trust overtime in VNP has worsened.

Community respondents generally: a) believe the VNP staff is technically competent, honest, and give prompt responses to community members questions and concerns, b) are satisfied with and trust VNP management of most recreational resources and uses, c) are not as trusting of VNP management of selected recreational activities or resources where those activities might occur (e.g., they do not trust VNP management of houseboats, snowmobile trails, and motorized use as they are of other uses in the park), d) are split on their belief that they have much influence in making their communities better places to live, and e) are split on whether VNP staff care about them or are sensitive to economic impacts related to recreation and tourism that affect them.

Community respondents generally: a) do not believe the NPS is an innovative agency, b) do not believe VNP shares their values, thinks like them, or that the decision making processes the park uses are fair, and c) are not likely to be involved in active civic engagement actions related to the park. Most community respondents would be encouraged to become more involved with VNP if they believed that: a) local involvement mattered and park staff listened to their concerns, b) communications (i.e., written) with the park improved, c) the park was involved in an issue or concern of great importance to them, d) management and management tactics around decision making in the park changed, and e) community politics toward the park changed.

Community benefits: Importance of economic benefits dominated the most important benefits communities want to realize from the existence of the park (Table 9). However, economic benefits more so than other types of benefits were least likely to be attained. From a community perspective study participants see VNP as a place: a) that contributes to the character of their communities, b) provides opportunities for their community to attain benefits related to maintaining the natural environment as well as their outdoor oriented lifestyle, c) that could better provide economic opportunities for local communities and the region, d) where management of water quality, natural and cultural resources, recreation opportunities, and park concessions and businesses benefit their communities, and e) where educational and interpretive programs are provided that add value to the lives of the people living in nearby communities.

Using the Findings: In spring of 2006, the authors presented the park and community leaders with draft copies of the study findings. During the time the sur-

	Community benefits rated most important to important	Rank ordered by most important to important	Rank ordered by ability to attain the benefit	Difference between importance and attainment rank
Voyageurs Nathional Park	Living in a healthy environment	1	5	-4
	Having a more stable economy for the surrounding region	2	21	-19
	Having a more stable economy within my community	3	24	-21
	Increased job opportunities within my community	4	28	-24
	Attracting tourism dollars to my community	5	8	-3
	Improved soil, water, and air quality	6	16	-10
	A chance for local people to maintain an outdoor oriented lifestyle	7	7	0
	Knowing conserved natural resources exists for future generations	8	1	7
	Providing a good quality of life	9	11	-2
	A sense of security that the natural environment will not be lost	10	2	8
	A higher quality of life	11	14	-3

Table 20.9 Community Benefits Rank Ordered by Importance and Attainment for VNP

vey was being conducted, the Midwest Regional Office named the acting superintendent as the new superintendent for VNP. The choice was popular with park staff and community leaders. Both saw the new superintendent as someone who wanted to make a positive difference in the park's relationship with local communities and saw the survey as a first step in communicating and sharing visions for the future of the area with one another. Once the draft of the survey research was received, VNP staff invited the authors to formally present the study findings to community groups and park staff. An invitation was accepted and in spring 2006 a meeting took place at community locations in International Falls and Orr, Minnesota to present and talk about preliminary findings. These meetings went well with lots of ideas and sharing about the results and how to use them to improve community-agency trust and to target and provide desired community benefit opportunities. Based on written and verbal comments provided at the meetings, the final draft technical report was written and sent to park staff and key community leaders in early summer 2006.

At the same time the report was prepared, the VNP was preparing an update to its business plan. They wanted the business plan to reflect what had been learned from the survey. They met with community leaders to decide how best to use the survey results so that community members would see the park's effort to improve communications as sincere. It was decided that seven workshops would be held at seven different locations around and in the park. The workshops were held in mid- to late-summer of 2006. Workshop dates and times were advertised in the local papers and flyers were put out at public places inviting people to attend. Workshops were held during the day and in the evening to encourage as much attendance as possible. The workshops were well-attended and community residents were enthusiastic and happy to be a part of deciding their community's future with the park.

Each workshop had the same agenda: present study findings, discuss findings, and brainstorm ways to implement findings, identify sources of funding (local, regional, state grant monies, etc.) and potential partnerships to implement selected findings, apply for funding and develop partnerships, and implement findings. As part of the workshop presentation materials the authors prepared six large wall posters (4'x5') to graphically display key findings related to each of the major themes in the survey (place attachment, trust, and community benefits). The posters were displayed during each workshop session and were a useful way for people to quickly see and understand survey findings. During every workshop at least one person commented that the park, by taking the time to "study community members," had taken an important step toward changing local people's views about the park's willingness to work with them and to be transparent and accountable in the park's decision making.

One of the outcomes of the workshops was the establishment of the Voyageurs National Park Communities Partnership. This partnership is continuing to dialogue with the park staff to stimulate open communication and collectively work on a vision for the region. The partners see an ongoing collaboration that builds on success and works towards a prosperous and sustainable regional economy based on the assets of its people and places. Another outcome was the reinvigoration of the Friends of Voyageurs National Park group. Members of this group were present at most of the workshops and were instrumental in facilitating discussion between park staff and community members. Two other successful outcomes were successful grant applications to the Arrowhead Regional Development Commission (a northern Minnesota group) for assistance with developing a comprehensive plan for communities adjacent to Kabetogama Lake in the southern part of the VNP and for economic assistance to build trail connections from park communities to park trails and regional trails in the area.

Conclusions and Recommendations

Managing public lands to provide community benefits cannot be successful without a clear understanding about how the land managing agency and the local communities it serves interact with each other. An agency's lack of understanding of the connections local people have to a resource and their level of trust in the agency to manage the resource in ways that sustain those connections can effectively block attainment of community benefits. In the studies covered in this chapter, it is assumed that the goal of community-agency interaction is to foster engaged communities that are sustainable economically, ecologically, socially, and culturally. Although not explicitly stated, OFM is an attempt to target and provide benefit opportunities that result in sustainable communities. Communicating, marketing, and promoting the opportunities and existing benefits a park or any natural area provides to local communities is a key strategy in OFM. Sending out press releases, developing community "open house" days, becoming involved in regional tourism plans, and developing educational programs for youth can all be considered "facilitating outputs" (under the expanded OFP and OFM model) that directly lead to the outcomes community members desire. Although they are not beneficial in and of themselves, they result in the multitude of economic, social, and individual benefits communities' desire from natural areas. Based on findings of the case studies presented, the following section is suggested for agencies managing using the OFM framework.

Focus on Social Capital Development as Part of Outcomes Focused Management

"Parks, recreation, and leisure service professionals have an opportunity to make conscious choices about making a difference in our communities by promoting the development of social capital" (DeGraaf & Jordan, 2003: 5). Public land managing agencies should consider incorporating a greater social capital focus into their management, public involvement, and communication efforts with local communities. In the Kaskaskia River Watershed and at Voyageurs National Park, agency personnel have already begun to do this and have begun to see some success in working with community leaders on projects that will benefit them and the communities they serve. Agency personnel should be encouraged to continue these efforts. Increasing awareness of the role of social capital in the successful implementation of OFM can help guide future efforts between agency personnel and community leaders. For natural resources management, in general, incorporating a social capital focus would involve continuing to develop collaborative management opportunities, including attending and hosting public meetings, resource-based organization meetings, volunteer opportunities, and site visits. The activities of these collaborative management meetings could include "adopting best management practices, issue assessment, cost sharing, education, monitoring, issue identification, issue prioritization, goal setting, and developing a common vision" (Lubell et al., 2001: 150).

Viewing public involvement as an opportunity to build social capital, better understand the connections local people feel toward the area in which they live, and identify benefits important to the long-term sustainability of the community may change the social environment of these sometimes hostile, unproductive, or unattended meetings. The social capital focus could also encourage agency personnel to concentrate on the processes within the meetings, thereby reaping some of the benefits from procedural justice. Our research shows that even when community members and agency staff appear to have good working relationships with one another, community members do not believe that the processes the agency uses are transparent or fair and therefore difficult to hold the agency accountable for its actions.

Communication with community members, such as environmental education, outreach, public presentations, and classroom visits, could be enhanced with a social capital focus. The Minnesota DPR, USACE, and

NPS all indicated an interest in developing a stronger outcomes-focused communication message that would highlight the personal, social, economic, and environmental benefits of the projects they undertake. A social capital focus could highlight more strongly those benefits accruing from social capital use like pride and sense of community. Ideally, the result would promote outward-looking perspectives and a conceptualization of the agency projects as community resources that benefit the entire community.

Use Dimensions of Trust as a Trust Building Guide

Results from these studies suggest that many possibilities are available for public land managing agencies to develop and foster trust with local community members. The many meanings of trust suggest areas the agencies can focus on to establish their trustworthiness. For people who associate an agency with the larger federal government, the agency might focus on face-to-face interactions with local community members. If people who associate an agency with their overall general trust, the agency could work to build a sense of community and increase overall trust within these local communities by assisting with community events. For people who rely on shared interests and values between themselves and an agency, the agency is in a more difficult position. If an agency's interests are clearly expressed and understood by community members, then some community members might embrace agency interests but others might still reject those interests. Agencies might be better served by focusing on the procedural justice dimension. Developing a fair decision-making process so that the interests of the public are considered in planning and management activities is critical.

Agency competencies related to moral and technical competence are important ways to garner community trust. Across all of the agencies we worked with, most community members gave the agency high marks on both of these trust dimensions. However, room for improvement exists. For people concerned about the moral competency of an agency's employees, the agency might try to create incentives for local personnel to meet and interact with local community members over a significant amount of time. These interactions would allow community members to meet and assess the integrity of local agency personnel.

Agencies can also focus education and outreach efforts on communicating what the agency provides to the local communities in the way of economic and non-economic benefits. These efforts would make it easier for local community members to see how an agency works for the local community's benefits instead of its own personal benefit. Finally, the technical competence of agency personnel, like their academic education and specialized training, can be highlighted in news reports, class presentations, and other communication efforts.

Literature Cited

Allen, L. (1991). Benefits of leisure services to community satisfaction. In B. Driver, P. Brown, and G. Peterson (Eds.), *Benefits of leisure* (pp. 331-350). State College, PA: Venture Publishing, Inc.

Campbell, A. (1981). *The sense of well-being in America: Recent patterns and trends.* New York, NY: McGraw Hill.

Carlyle Lake Planning Committee. (n.d.). Carlyle Lake Watershed Plan. Carlyle, IL: Carlyle Lake Planning Committee.

Davenport, M. A. (2003). A river of meanings: Developing a community based vision for the Niobrara National Scenic River. St. Paul, MN: Department of Forest Resources.

Davenport, M. & Anderson, D. (2005). Getting from sense of place to place-based management: An interpretive investigation of place meanings and perceptions of landscape change. *Society and Natural Resources, 18*(7), 625–641.

Driver, B. L., Brown, P., & Peterson, G. (Eds.) (1991). *Benefits of leisure.* State College, PA: Venture Publishing, Inc.

Illinois Department of Natural Resources. (2001). The Kaskaskia River Basin: An inventory of the region's resources. Springfield: Illinois Department of Natural Resources.

Leahy, J. (2005). U.S. Army Corps of Engineers and Kaskaskia River Watershed community relationships: Social capital, trust, and benefits. Ph.D. dissertation, Minneapolis, MN: University of Minnesota Graduate School.

Lincoln, Y., & Guba, E. (1985). Naturalistic inquiry. Beverly Hills, CA: Sage Publications.

Putnam, R. D. (2000). *Bowling alone: The collapse and revival of American community.* New York, NY: Simon & Schuster.

Marans, R. & Mohai, P. (1991). Leisure resources, recreation activity, and the quality of life. In B. L. Driver, P. Brown, & G. Peterson (Eds.), Benefits of leisure. (pp. 351–363). State College, PA: Venture Publishing, Inc.

Stein, T., Anderson, D., & Thompson, D. (1999). Identifying and managing for community benefits in Minnesota state parks. *Journal of Park and Recreation Administration, 17*(4), 1–19.

Strauss, A. & Corbin, J. (1990). *Basics of qualitative research.* Newbury Park: Sage Publications.

U.S. Army Corps of Engineers. (2001). Corps program results: Recreation. Retrieved May, 2006 from : http://www.corpsresults.us/recreation/

USDI National Park Service (1997). VERP: A summary of the visitor experience and resource protection (VERP) framework. Department of Interior: Denver Service Center.

Footnotes

1. It should be noted that the stage 1 interviews to understand community-agency trust were part of a larger study the authors conducted on community-agency trust that involved multiple sites and multiple agencies. USDA Forest Service sites included Hiawatha National Forest in Michigan, Midewin National Tallgrass Prairie in Illinois, and Mark Twain National Forest in Missouri. USDI National Park Service sites included Pictured Rocks National Lakeshore in Michigan and Ozark National Scenic Riverway in Missouri. USDI Fish & Wildlife Service included one site: the Sherburne National Wildlife Refuge in Minnesota. Community-agency interviews were conducted at all of these sites during spring, summer, and fall of 2001 and 2002. Data from these studies, along with the data from the Kaskaskia watershed sites was used to supplement development of trust scales for the six trust dimensions identified.

Chapter 21
Assessing Local Economic Impacts of Recreation and Tourism

Daniel J. Stynes

Learning Objectives:

1. Understand the basic concepts and methods for estimating local economic impacts of recreation and tourism activities.
2. Demonstrate the application of the National Park Service's Money Generation Model to estimate local employment and income effects of visitor spending at Grand Canyon National Park.

Introduction

There are a number of economic consequences of recreation and tourism activities. Costs are incurred by participants and providers of the recreation opportunities, and there are also externalities imposed on others such as the added costs for infrastructure, services provided by local government units, congestion, and other costs imposed on local residents. Similarly, there is a wide range of benefits to participants, providers and local communities (Driver et al., 1991).

A widely touted outcome of recreation and tourism is the contribution to local economies. Spending by visitors and recreation providers generates income and jobs for local communities. Local residents receive this income in the form of wages and salaries, businesses in profits and rents, and local governments in taxes and fees. Recreation and tourism activities support major industries including those providing accommodations and amusements, as well as firms that manufacture, repair and sell boats, RVs, and sporting goods.

Given the political importance of employment and economic development, it is not surprising that recreation and tourism providers have increasingly used local economic impacts as a justification for programs. Most states regularly estimate the economic significance of their tourism industries to state and local economies (Travel Industry of America, 2006). Many communities, recreation industries and individual firms/providers have also estimated their contributions to jobs and income in an area (Fleming and Toepper 1990).

The intent of most recreation and tourism economic impact studies is not to measure outcomes of specific actions. Tourism studies typically measure the importance of tourism to a local, state, or national economy through aggregate measures of spending and jobs. These economic "outcomes" result from many distinct actions of public and private providers and are therefore not readily traced to any particular decision. Similarly, recreation industries like boating, camping, downhill skiing, or hunting and fishing measure the jobs and income associated with a particular recreation activity, not the impacts of any particular decision. These studies serve to quantify the importance or contribution of recreation and tourism to an economy and are used primarily for public relations purposes rather than to evaluate alternatives.

There are a number of ways that economic impact analysis is used to evaluate specific actions. Estimates of local economic impacts are frequently included in feasibility studies for new recreation or tourism facilities. Hotels, marinas, and other businesses use such information to obtain favorable treatment from local planning authorities, which in some cases includes local tax breaks. Local economic impacts are one of the factors that public agencies consider in evaluating alternative policy and development choices (Switzer, 1996). Tourism promotional programs are frequently justified on the basis of their success in attracting more visitors and generating additional sales and income for the area. Economic impact studies are frequently conducted in support of festivals and special events (Getz, 1994; Crompton, et al., 2001).

Tracing Economic Effects

Outcomes of particular actions are best measured by tracing the underlying cause-effect relationships. For example, the opening of a new campground attracts additional visitors who spend money in the local area. Businesses receiving this revenue, in turn, hire employees, pay out wages and salaries, and purchase goods and services from other businesses. These employees spend their wages and salaries in the area, inducing additional economic activity. Local businesses sell goods and services to the campground, paying wages to their employees and in turn purchasing materials from other firms in the area. The process described here is captured formally within an input-output model of an area's economy.

Input-output models estimate direct and secondary effects by tracing flows of money within a region's economy (Miernyk, 1965; Richardson, 1979). The models can estimate impacts of opening or closing an auto plant or of changes in hotel or restaurant sales resulting from increased tourism. Direct effects of recreation and tourism spending are the sales, jobs and income in firms selling goods and services directly to visitors (i.e., hotels, restaurants, amusements, and retail shops). These firms, in turn, purchase goods and services from other businesses in the region, creating what are termed "indirect effects." Employees of firms that are directly or indirectly affected by visitor spending spend their wages and salaries in local businesses creating "induced effects". Secondary effects are the sum of indirect and induced effects.

An advantage that regional economic analysis has over other kinds of outcomes of recreation activity is the presence of a simple, tangible measure of flow (dollars), and a straightforward process for generating the outcomes. Flows of money within a region's economy are traced from firm to firm, and sales are converted to jobs and income based on a production function for each industry. The system of economic accounts maintained by federal and state governments provides the data for estimating input-output models.

To take advantage of these economic models in evaluating recreation programs or actions, one must first translate the action or decision being evaluated into changes in the levels and types of recreation activity. Changes in recreation activity are then translated into changes in spending in the area. The usual approach is to multiply the changes in visits by visitor spending averages that have been estimated in a visitor survey. Finally, the estimates of spending changes become inputs to a regional economic model to determine changes in economic activity resulting from this spending. The model can further trace impacts through direct and secondary effects and also convert spending to the associated jobs, income and value added[1] in the local economy. The process is illustrated in Figure 21.1.

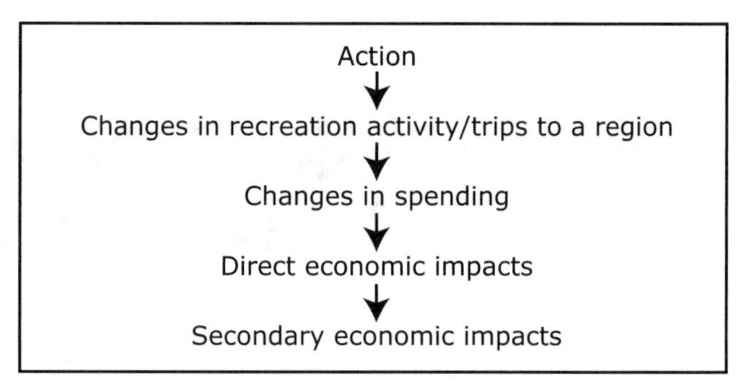

Figure 21.1 Process for estimating economic impacts

This process is fairly standard for virtually any recreation or tourism activity. Depending on the intended purpose and use of the analysis, a study may stop at any of the steps in Figure 21.1. Outcomes may be summarized in terms of changes in recreation use, changes in spending, based on just the direct effects, or covering overall employment and income including secondary effects.

The direct effects are generally the most useful impact measures[2]. Direct effects are fairly straightforward to estimate and are the most directly tied to the action being evaluated. Spending figures can be misleading as spending in different sectors of the economy has distinct employment and income effects. For example, only the retail margins on retail purchases generally impact the local economy, as most goods purchased by visitors are not locally made. So sales figures tend to exaggerate the local impacts of factory outlet malls and other kinds of retail establishments relative to, for example, hotels and restaurants.

Service sectors are more labor intensive than manufacturing sectors, but in most cases pay lower wages. The choice of an impact measure is therefore important when comparing alternatives that involve different industries. Compared to manufacturing, tourism generates more jobs, but typically at lower wages. Extending impact measures to include secondary effects increases the estimates of the impacts, but at the cost of additional assumptions and complexity. Secondary effects can become far-removed from the initial action being evaluated and depend considerably on the size of the impact region.

There are a number of important decisions that underlie an impact estimate. A region must be specified to define the scope of spending and economic activity to be included. For example, the impacts of camping on the national economy will be much different from the impacts on a local community. Impact results also depend on which kinds of spending is included in the analysis. A camping study may be restricted to spending of campers on trips to the local area, or it may also cover purchases of recreational vehicles and camping equipment, or expenses associated with public and private campground operations. Impacts are larger if secondary effects are included. Since impact studies differ widely in their scope and methods, these choices must be clearly understood when evaluating or comparing impact study results. Unfortunately, many of these details often become lost when impact results are conveyed in the mass media.

Economic Impact or Significance

As with most evaluation research, impacts should usually be assessed in a "with-versus-without" context. That is, what is the change in spending or jobs in the region *with the action* versus what they would be *without* it? A with-versus-without analysis requires the analyst to control for other factors that could have caused the change and also to account for substitutions that may diminish or enhance the effect. For example, if evaluating impacts of a promotional program, one must isolate the changes in visitors or spending due to the program from those resulting from other causes such as changes in prices, weather, quality and quantity of substitutes, economic conditions, etc.

Many tourism promotion evaluations use before-after designs that do not establish clear causal linkages between the promotional program and the measured effects. Instead, they compare measures of visits or spending before the promotional program with corresponding measures after the program. If travel activity increases, it is all attributed to the promotional program. Decreases are frequently blamed on the weather, the economy or other factors. Sorting out impacts with versus without the promotional program requires research designs that control for factors that could be causing a change in visits or spending patterns (Woodside, 1990).

When assessing impacts of recreation facilities or special events, regional economists typically exclude spending by local residents. The argument is that in the absence of these facilities or programs, local residents would have spent their money on something else in the local area[3]. There would therefore be no net gain to the local economy from their spending. The focus in tourism impact studies is therefore on visitors from outside the local region, whose spending represents "new money" to the area.

When evaluating impacts of a particular facility or attraction, some additional sorting out of substitutions is in order. For example, a new hotel may not yield a large net increase in visitors or spending if it simply displaces visitors at other nearby hotels. If visitors to a particular attraction or event are in the area for other reasons (visiting relatives or on business), not all of their spending can be considered a net increase for the area.

Many recreation and tourism studies measure the impacts of all visitors, covering all visitor spending in the area. To distinguish these from studies that sort out with-versus-without effects, some refer to these as measures of economic significance or importance rather than impact. Economic significance applies to most industry studies, which assess the overall economic contribution of particular activities or industries, like hunting and fishing, boating, snowmobiling, or downhill skiing. Such studies frequently measure the overall size of the industry, including what participants spend on trips as well as purchases of durable goods like boats, snowmobiles, RVs, or sporting goods.

Special events pose particular problems for estimating impacts, including distinguishing local visitors from nonlocals and identifying what Crompton (2006) terms "time switchers" and "casuals." Time switchers have substituted a trip during the special event for one they may have made at another time. Casuals are in the area for other reasons, perhaps visiting relatives. Input-output models will typically overstate the impacts of short-term events as a spike in spending because a short period usually does not yield increases in employment or income comparable to the same spending spread more evenly over the year. If increases in visitors for a special event fill otherwise excess capacity in hotels and restaurants, it may not produce additional jobs or income. Spending accruing to outside vendors and local volunteer organizations at such events also requires special treatment.

Impacts of What?

While the vast majority of recreation and tourism studies focus on spending of participants on trips, some studies also include other kinds of expenditures. Many recreation activities involve the use of durable goods such as boats, recreational vehicles, snowmobiles, bicycles, and a variety of sporting goods including camping, fishing and hunting equipment, golf clubs, downhill skis, etc. Industries aligned with particular recreation activities often estimate the sales and jobs associated with equipment purchases.

Other studies have included operational expenditures of government organizations, and impacts associated with construction of facilities and infrastructure.

Estimates of local economic impacts of national parks include both visitor spending and national park payrolls (Stynes, 2006). In this case, park entry fees and other spending accruing to the National Park Service are excluded from the visitor spending impacts to avoid double counting. Operations and visitor trip spending have long-term effects as these yield an annual flow of dollars into the economy for the life of a project. Construction impacts can be substantial, but involve short-term effects.

Some studies have also attempted to quantify volunteer time and in-kind contributions. While this type of information may supplement an economic impact analysis, only actual monetary transactions should generally be included in the formal economic impact analysis.

It is especially important to recognize that economic impact analysis is a regional analysis. A study may assess the impacts of a national park on a particular gateway community, one or more counties around the park, or the impacts on a state or national economy. These distinct definitions of the region will yield very different results. The region defines which spending should be included and the geographic scope of the impacts.

The MGM2 Model

The "Money Generation Model" (MGM2) used by the National Park Service illustrates the procedures for estimating economic impacts resulting from changes in the number or types of visitors to an area (Stynes et al., 2002). MGM2 is a spreadsheet-based model for estimating economic impacts of changes in recreation or tourism activity in a region. There are three basic inputs to the model:

1. The change in the number of visitors or visitor days in a region due to a proposed action. The MGM2 model breaks visitors/trips into distinct types based on different spending patterns. For example, spending by visitors on day trips will be different than those on overnight trips. Moreover, expenses will also vary based on lodging types (hotels, campgrounds, stays in seasonal homes or with friends or relatives), transportation modes (auto, air, bus, etc.), and trip purposes (business or leisure).
2. Spending profiles for each visitor segment. A spending profile gives the average amount spent on a per trip or per day basis within a set of spending categories (e.g., lodging, restaurant meals, groceries, gas, local transportation, amusements and entertainment, and souvenirs). The spending categories are defined to facilitate the matching of visitor spending to particular economic sectors.
3. A set of economic ratios and multipliers for the region. MGM2 employs distinct multipliers for the primary tourism-related industry sectors. Economic ratios convert spending to the associated income and jobs, while multipliers estimate the secondary effects as the visitor spending flows through the local economy. Multipliers simplify the estimation of impacts, compared to making use of a complete input-output model for the region. Multipliers and economic ratios built into the MGM2 model are derived from IMPLAN models. The IMPLAN system has been widely used to estimate impacts of recreation and tourism activity.

The MGM2 model estimates total visitor spending by multiplying the number of visitor trips or days by the spending averages. Spending in each category is then bridged to the relevant economic sectors and applied to a set of multipliers for the area. This general approach can be applied to virtually any change in the number or types of visitors to a region, or in their spending patterns. It can also be applied to evaluate structural changes in the local economy. The most common applications are:

1. Estimating impacts of current levels of tourism or park visits (Travel Industry Association of America, 2005).
2. Estimating impacts of a particular industry or activity, e.g., hunting and fishing, boating, snowmobiling. (USDI, 2002).
3. Evaluating impacts of special events (Crompton et al., 2001).
4. Estimating impacts of external shocks, such as terrorism, wars, or fuel prices. (Bonham, Edmonds, & Mak, 2006).
5. Estimating impacts of a particular facility, such as a new marina, hotel, campground, museum, or visitor center (Mahoney and Stynes, 2006).
6. Estimating impacts of a change in policy, management or marketing programs (Schwer et al., 2000).

The first two types of applications tend to measure economic significance rather than impacts, while the last four focus more clearly on evaluating economic outcomes of particular actions. While the same general approach applies to all of these, the impact assessment problems demand special attention in separating out

Spending category	Segment						
	Day trip	In-park hotel	In-park camp	Back-country	Outside park hotel	Outside park camp	River runners
Hotel/Motel	0	125.34	0	0	102.51	0	6.38
Camping fees	0	0	16.24	3.09	0	18.5	0.25
Guide fees	2.9	13.69	2.21	0	3.33	0.83	393.36
Restaurants/Bars	22.84	82.97	15.58	10.18	52.46	18.3	3.49
Groceries/Take out	4.37	10.66	12.89	4.41	9.83	12.54	0.85
Gas and oil	13.52	7.76	10.59	10.35	14.62	12.89	1.68
Other transp. expenses	22.93	20.24	2.4	0.32	30.87	3.64	3.17
Amusements/Recreation	15.87	39.72	8.55	4.19	21.61	14.61	1.46
All other purchases	31.16	36.52	29.16	10.51	36.11	15.22	1.49
Donations	0.37	1.27	0.06	0.09	0.87	0.42	0.04
Total	113.96	338.17	97.68	43.14	272.21	96.95	412.18
Party nights (000's)	357	190	119	88	641	138	72.4
Percent of nights	22%	12%	7%	5%	40%	9%	5%

Table 21.1 Spending averages for Grand Canyon visitors by segment

local visitor spending and controlling for a variety of potential substitutions.

Applying the Model to Grand Canyon National Park

Procedures for estimating economic impacts of recreation and tourism can be illustrated using Grand Canyon National Park as an example. Impacts of Grand Canyon visitor spending on the surrounding region were estimated for 2003 using the National Park Service (NPS) Money Generation Model (Stynes and Sun, 2005). Input data for the model included a visitor survey (Littlejohn and Hollenhorst, 2004a and 2004b), park use statistics, and multipliers from an input-output model of the local economy (Coconino county, Arizona). Park concession receipts were used to validate estimates of spending from the visitor survey.

The park reported 4.125 million recreation visits in 2003. As the NPS counts entries to the park, visitors who enter the park more than once during a stay in the area are counted multiple times. Many park visitors stay overnight outside the park and are counted each day they enter the park. After adjusting for park re-entries, the park hosted 2.66 million visitors to the area in 2003. To estimate visitor spending, these trips were divided into seven distinct visitor segments[4]:

- Day trips: visitors from outside the region, who do not stay overnight in the area. This segment includes pass-through travelers, who may be staying overnight outside the local area. Visitors staying with friends/relatives or at an owned seasonal home in the area are also treated as day trips for the purpose of estimating spending.
- In-Park Hotel: visitors staying in hotels, cabins, or lodges inside the park.
- In-Park Camp: visitors staying in developed campgrounds inside the park.
- Backcountry campers: visitors staying overnight in backcountry sites.
- Outside-Park Motel: visitor staying in hotels, motels, cabins, rented condos or B&B's outside the park within the local region.
- Outside-Park Camp: visitors staying in private or other public campgrounds outside the park within the local region.
- River runners: visitors taking commercial or private rafting trips through the canyon.

Spending averages for the first six segments were estimated from visitor surveys at the north and south rims[5]. A random sample of 1,000 visitors were contacted at entrance stations between June 22–28, 2003. The distribution of visitors across the seven segments and their spending patterns were estimated from 735 completed surveys. Visitors staying overnight inside the park were estimated from park overnight stay data, and the number of river runners was estimated directly from river permits.

Average spending per party per day ranges from $43 for backcountry visitors to $338 per night for visitors staying in park lodges (Table 21.1). Campers spend about $97 per party per night. Expenses of river runners were constructed based on concessionaire receipts and the average number of nights on the river. It should

Spending category	Segment							
	Day trip	In-park hotel	In-park camp	Back-country	Outside park hotel	Outside park camp	River runners	Total
Hotel/Motel	0.00	23.88	0.00	0.00	65.68	0.00	0.46	90.02
Camping fees	0.00	0.00	1.93	0.27	0.00	2.55	0.02	4.77
Restaurants & bars	8.15	15.81	1.85	0.89	33.61	2.53	0.25	63.09
Groceries/ Take-out	1.56	2.03	1.53	0.39	6.30	1.73	0.06	13.60
Gas & oil	4.82	1.48	1.26	0.91	9.37	1.78	0.12	19.74
Other transp. expenses	8.18	3.86	0.29	0.03	19.78	0.50	0.23	32.86
Amusements/Recreation	6.83	10.42	1.29	0.38	16.54	2.19	28.59	66.23
Souvenirs/other expenses	11.12	6.96	3.47	0.92	23.14	2.10	0.11	47.81
Total	40.67	64.42	11.61	3.78	174.42	13.39	29.85	338.13
Percent of spending	12%	19%	3%	1%	52%	4%	9%	100%

Table 21.2 Total spending by Grand Canyon NP visitors in 2003

be noted that since spending outside the local region is not included, the spending totals do not include airfares and other en route expenses incurred more than 100 miles from the park[6].

Total spending is estimated by multiplying the number of party nights by each segment times the average spending per night. Total visitor spending was estimated at $338 million in 2003 (Table 21.2). Visitors staying in hotels/motels outside the park accounted for 52% of the spending. The greatest spending was for lodging, restaurant meals, amusements (including guide fees), and souvenirs.

Local economic impacts of the $338 million in spending are estimated by applying the spending in each category by a set of sector-specific economic ratios and multipliers representing the economy of the local region.

Impacts can be divided between direct and secondary effects. Direct effects occur in firms that are directly selling goods and services to visitors, e.g., hotels, restaurants, amusements, gas stations, and retail stores. Direct employment and income effects can be estimated quite easily by applying ratios of employment and income to sales for each industry (Table 21.3). These ratios can be estimated by dividing total jobs or wages and salaries in a particular industry by total sales in a given year. If these data are not readily available, the ratios for a typical firm in the area will suffice.

Using the hotel sector to illustrate, there were 20.54 jobs per million sales in Coconino county, Arizona, in 2001. Forty-four percent of hotel sales went to wages and salaries (including payroll benefits), and 71% of sales represented value added by the hotel sector. The remaining 29% of revenue is used by hotels to purchase goods and services.

The number of direct hotel jobs supported by Grand Canyon NP visitor spending is computed by multiplying the $90 million in hotel spending by 20.54 jobs per million sales. Similarly, direct income and value added for the hotel sector are calculated at $39.3 million in personal income and $63.7 million in value added by the hotel sector.

Secondary effects are considerably more complicated, but when armed with multipliers for the region, they can be easily computed. The total effects multipliers in Table 21.3 for Coconino county are taken from an input-output model of the economy estimated with IMPLAN and using 2001 economic data. Similar multipliers may be purchased for particular regions and sectors from MIG, Inc. based on IMPLAN models (MIG, Inc. 1999) or the Bureau of Economic Analysis based on their RIMS II model (USDC, 1997). MGM2 includes built in "generic" multipliers for regions of varying size and economic development.

An input-output model traces flows of spending within the region. For example, the $90 million in hotel sales/revenue is divided between the value added components (wages and salaries, profits and rents, and indirect business taxes) and other inputs to the hotel's production function. Hotel spending on wages and salaries and purchases of other goods and services is circulated within the local economy to estimate the secondary effects of visitor lodging expenditures.

There are two primary types of secondary effects. Indirect effects result from the hotel's purchases of goods and services from backward-linked industries, while induced effects result from hotel employee's spending of their incomes in the region. The 44% of hotel revenue that goes to wages and salaries starts the induced effects, while the 29% used by the hotel to purchase goods and services begins the rounds of indirect

Sector	Direct effects			Total effects multipliers			
	Jobs/ $MM sales	Income/ sales	Value added/ sales	Sales Type II	Jobs/ $MM sales	Income/ sales	Value added/ sales
Hotels and motels, including casino hotels	20.54	0.44	0.71	1.42	26.89	0.58	0.95
Other accommodations	7.50	0.13	0.31	1.53	15.49	0.30	0.62
Food services and drinking places	28.00	0.40	0.46	1.46	34.86	0.55	0.71
Other amusement, gambling, and recreation industries	24.15	0.37	0.62	1.45	31.31	0.52	0.87
Automotive repair and maintenance	10.66	0.16	0.37	1.38	16.34	0.29	0.58
Transit and ground passenger transportation	31.38	0.50	0.57	1.52	39.67	0.69	0.86
Sporting and athletic goods manufacturing	6.53	0.20	0.27	1.37	11.84	0.33	0.47
Retail Trade	22.19	0.46	0.60	1.51	30.18	0.64	0.90
Wholesale trade	12.17	0.37	0.65	1.40	18.60	0.51	0.88

Table 21.3 Multipliers for the local region

effects. The input-output model traces this spending through several rounds to compute effects that may be three or four steps removed from the initial hotel purchase. Total effects multipliers sum up the aggregation of these effects.

Returning to the example, total sales generated by the $90 million in hotel sales is computed by multiplying the sales multiplier (1.42) for the area by $90 million. Total jobs, income, and value added, including secondary effects, may be computed in a similar fashion. The size of the secondary effects may be obtained by subtracting the direct effects from total effects. For example, secondary employment effects per million dollars in hotel sales is about six jobs (26.89 -20.54).

Making these calculations for each of the spending categories in Table 21.2 yields the total impacts on the local economy (Table 21.4). Direct effects are reported for the key tourism-related sectors, while secondary effects are reported in the aggregate[7]. Notice that total direct sales of $293.9 million is less than total visitor spending ($338 million). This is because most goods purchased by visitors at retail are not made in the local area, so only the retail margin (and a portion of wholesale margin) is counted as direct sales, while the cost of goods sold at retail is assigned to imports and leaks immediately out of the local economy. The retail trade sector includes the jobs and income associated with gas stations, grocery stores, and other retail establishments in the region.

The impacts represent the anticipated losses to the local economy if the park were closed and none of these visits to the region occurred. Even if the park were closed, some of the trips represented by park visits may still be made to the region, but most would not. Some visitors would substitute with visits to nearby parks or tourist attractions such as Lake Meade, Lake Powell, or National Forest recreation sites. Others may be in the area anyway to visit relatives or on business trips. A true with-versus-without analysis would adjust the impact estimates to take into account these substitute sites and activities.

Three out of four South Rim visitors and two-thirds of North Rim visitors indicated the primary purpose of their trip was to visit Grand Canyon. For these visitors all spending was attributed to the park, assuming that in the absence of the park these trips would not be made. For visitors in the area for other reasons, only one night of spending was counted. The assumption is that visitors extended their stay by one night in order to visit Grand Canyon.

There are additional economic impacts from construction and park operations that have not been included here. In 2006, the park itself employed over 500 people with a payroll for fiscal year 2006 of $21.8 million in wages and salaries and $5.8 million in payroll benefits. Spending by park employees of their income

Sector/spending category	Sales $millions	Jobs	Personal income $millions	Value added $millions
Motel, hotel cabin, or B&B	90.0	1,849	39.3	63.7
Camping fees	4.8	36	0.6	1.5
Restaurants and bars	63.1	1,766	25.5	28.7
Admissions and fees	66.2	1,599	24.4	40.9
Other transportation expenses	32.9	350	5.4	12.3
Retail Trade	31.7	704	14.7	19.2
Wholesale Trade	4.1	50	1.5	2.7
Total Direct Effects	293.9	6,354	111.4	169.0
Secondary Effects	128.2	1,983	43.9	73.9
Total Effects	422.1	8,337	155.3	242.9

Table 21.4 Economic impacts of visitor spending

in the region supported another 200 jobs in the area[8] (Stynes 2006).

Steps for Estimating Economic Impacts of Recreation Visitors

The procedures for estimating regional economic outcomes of recreation activity can be summarized by the following steps:

1. Define the action to be evaluated and the study region.
2. Translate the action into a net change in the number and kinds of visitors or trips to an area (typically for a single year).
3. Identify subgroups of visitors with distinct spending patterns.
4. Estimate a spending profile for each subgroup and the percentage of visitors/trips from each subgroup.
5. Estimate the overall changes in spending broken down by major spending categories, usually by multiplying per visitor or per trip spending averages by the expected change in trips.
6. Obtain economic multipliers for the local region.
7. Apply multipliers to spending estimates in order to estimate impacts.

Note that the second step is often the most difficult part of the analysis. When evaluating past actions, the analysis must measure changes in visits and isolate those changes attributable to the action being evaluated by taking into account potential substitutions, and in some cases, trip intentions. When projecting likely impacts in the future of present or planned actions, future use must be forecasted under a set of plausible assumptions.

The Grand Canyon example is typical in that the primary input data comes from different sources. Visitor estimates come from secondary sources of visitor counts or a demand/forecasting model. Spending averages generally are estimated from visitor surveys, while economic ratios and multipliers are derived from secondary economic data and input-output models. When combining these data for an impact assessment, it is important that the data be consistent and in comparable units. For example, if visits are in person trips, while spending is on a party per day basis, the figures must be converted to common units, usually based on party size and length of stay information. Margining of retail purchases and adjustments of multipliers to the same year as the spending figures are also required to properly apply multipliers.

Summary and Conclusions

We have illustrated how local economic impacts of Grand Canyon National Park can be estimated. More precisely, we have estimated the economic impacts of park visitor spending in 2003 on the economy of Coconino County, Arizona. These economic outcomes are the result of many decisions, starting with the establishment of the park in 1919, to more recent decisions about transportation systems, concessions in the park, and the actions of private businesses in developing lodging facilities, restaurants, retail shops and other attractions in the region.

If the analysis has fully sorted out visits to the region and spending that would not have occurred if the park were closed, the reported impacts represent the expected losses in jobs and income to the region in the absence of the park. However, in most cases, closing the park or converting it to another use is not a realistic scenario. For a true with-versus-without analysis, we would need to more precisely specify the alternatives. Economic effects would be quite different if the park were sold to commercial interests compared to being left idle or converted to some other public purpose.

Impacts of current levels of visitor use and spending illustrate the contributions of the park to the local economy. Economic analysis provides tangible measures of the linkages between the park and economic activity in the region. The park uses this information in support of management and policy decisions and to help foster support and cooperation among local constituencies. Local businesses and tourism organizations, in turn, can use the information to quantify the importance of park visitors to their operations and to evaluate how changes in park policy or management may affect them.

The same methods illustrated above to estimate impacts of all visitor spending can be applied to estimate impacts of more specific management, policy, or marketing actions. For example:

- Closing a park campground or expanding one
- Reducing or expanding river running opportunities
- Reducing or expanding spending opportunities inside or outside the park
- Policies related to air over flights of the park
- Special events in the park
- Changing transportation systems or tour options
- Special promotional programs or marketing strategies

Each of these scenarios must be translated first into changes in the number and types of visitors to the park, or changes in their lengths of stay or spending patterns. Changes in spending and associated impacts can then be estimated using the MGM2 model. In all cases, the appropriate impact measure is to identify the changes with-versus-without the proposed action, taking into account substitutions that might occur.

As a spreadsheet application, the MGM2 model facilitates the simulation of alternative scenarios by modifying the number of visitors, the percentage of visitors from each segment, the assumed spending patterns, or local economic multipliers. Using the model, impact estimates can be updated over time by replacing visit count figures, spending averages or multipliers.

Economic impacts are one of the more quantifiable outcomes of recreation and tourism activity. Armed with reasonable estimates of the number and types of visitors and their spending patterns, it is fairly easy to generate estimates of their impacts on local economies.

However, caution is recommended when evaluating economic impact reports. Estimates can vary widely depending on decisions about which spending to include, the scope of the local region, and whether or not secondary effects are covered. Many studies have exaggerated impacts due to inflated visitor counts or misuse of multipliers (Archer, 1984). There is also some upward bias inherent in the use of input-output models, as they assume there are no constraints to production and the models do not fully capture substitutions that may result from price changes (Dwyer et al., 2006). Economic impact studies also tend to focus on benefits to the economy and often do not address economic, social, or environmental costs (Fleming and Toepper, 1990).

In spite of the political importance of jobs and economic development, it should be noted that economic impacts are not the primary justification for many recreation programs. While tourism is generally advanced as an economic development option, recreation programs are more often designed primarily to provide benefits to local residents and visitors. The mission of the National Park Service is to preserve and protect natural and cultural resources and to provide for the enjoyment of the same for present and future generations. The NPS attempts to carry this out without imposing high costs on visitors.

Local public recreation programs also usually strive to minimize the costs to participants, rather than to stimulate their spending. Using economic impacts to justify museums, nature centers, nature preserves and local recreation programs can distract people from the real purposes of these programs. In these cases, economic impact analyses capture some of the secondary economic effects of these programs and shed light on the benefits to nearby commercial interests.

Finally, it should be noted that regional economic impacts are basically a zero sum situation. The gain to a destination region from attracting visitors and spending is a loss of income and jobs to the originating regions. Gains to the boating industry from increases in boat sales and activity are offset by corresponding losses in other industries. In this sense, economic impact analyses shed light on who gains and who loses, rather than measuring an overall change in economic welfare.

Literature Cited

Archer, B. H. (1984). Economic impact: Misleading multiplier. *Annals of Tourism Research, 11*(3): 517- 518.

Bonham, C., Edmonds, C., & Mak, J. (2006). The impact of 9/11 and other terrible global events on tourism in the United States and Hawaii. *Journal of Travel Research,* 45(1): 99–110.

Crompton, J. L., Lee, S. & Shuster, T.J.. (2001). A guide for undertaking economic impact studies: The springfest example. *Journal of Travel Research, 40*: 79–87.

Crompton, J. L. (2006). Economic impact studies: Instruments for political shenanigans? *Journal of Travel Research, 45*(1): 67–82.

Driver, B. L, Brown, P. J., & Peterson, G. L. (1991). *Benefits of leisure.* State College, PA: Venture Publishing, Inc.

Dwyer, L., Forsyth, P., & Spurr, R. (2006). Assessing the economic impacts of events: A computable general equilibrium approach. *Journal of Travel Research, 45*(1): 59–66.

Fleming, W. R. & Toepper., L. (1990). Economic impact studies: The positive and negative impacts to tourism development. *Journal of Travel Research, 29*: 35–42.

Frechtling, D. C. (2000). The tourism satellite account: foundations, progress and issues. *Tourism management* 20: 163–170.

Frechtling, D. C. (2006). An assessment of visitor expenditure methods and models. *Journal of Travel Research, 45*(1): 26–35.

Getz, D. (1994). Event tourism: Evaluating the impacts In *Travel, tourism, and hospitality research, second edition.* J.R.B. Ritchie and C.R. Goeldner (Eds.), New York: John Wiley and Sons, Inc.

Littlejohn, M. & Hollenhorst, S. (2004a). *Grand Canyon National Park north rim visitor study: Summer 2003.* Visitor Services Project report #143. Moscow, ID: National Park Service and University of Idaho.

Littlejohn, M. & Hollenhorst, S. (2004b). *Grand Canyon National Park south rim visitor study: Summer 2003.* Visitor Services Project report #144. Moscow, ID: National Park Service and University of Idaho.

Mahoney, E. & Stynes, D. J. (2006). Economic impacts of boater spending: Proposed Harpeth Shoals marina. East Lansing, MI; Recreation Marine Research Center, Michigan State University.

Miernyk, W. H. (1965). *The elements of input-output analysis.* New York: Random House.

MIG, Inc. (1999). *IMPLAN Pro, 2.0. User's Guide, Analysis Guide, Data Guide.* Stillwater, MN: Minnesota IMPLAN Group Inc.

Richardson, H. W. (1979). *Regional economics.* Urbana, IL: University of Illinois Press.

Schwer, R. K., Gazel, R., & Daneshvary, R. (2000). Air tour impacts: The Grand Canyon case. *Annals of Tourism Research, 27*(3):611–623.

Stynes, D. J., Propst, D. B., Chang, W. H., & Sun, Y. (2000). Estimating regional economic impacts of park visitor spending: Money Generation Model Version 2 (MGM2). East Lansing, MI: Department of Park, Recreation and Tourism Resources, Michigan State University.

Stynes, D. J. (2005). Economic significance of recreational uses of National Parks and other public lands. *Social Science Research Review, 5*(1). National Park Service Social Science Monograph Series.

Stynes, D. J. & Sun, Y. (2005) *Economic Impacts of Grand Canyon National Park Visitor Spending on the Local Economy, 2003.* Report to National Park Service.

Stynes, D. J. (2007). *National Park Visitor Spending and Payroll Impacts, 2006.* Report to National Park Service.

Switzer, R. R. (1996, Spring). Why assess the economic impacts of National Parks? *Park Science*: 26-27.

Travel Industry Association of America. (2005). *Impact of travel and tourism on the U.S. and state economies, 2005 Edition.* Washington D.C. Travel Indusry Association of America.

U.S. Dept. of Commerce, Bureau of Economic Analysis. (1997). *Regional multipliers: A user handbook for regional input-output modeling system (RIMS II),* third edition. Washington, D.C.; U.S. Gov't Printing Office.

U.S. Dept. of the Interior, Fish and Wildlife Service and U.S. Dept. of Commerce, Census Bureau. (2002). 2001 National Survey of Hunting, Fishing and Wildlife-Associated Recreation.

Footnotes

1. Value added is the preferred measure of the contribution of an industry to a state or local economy. Value added includes wages and salaries, profits and rents, sales taxes and other indirect business taxes. Alternatively, value added may be defined as total sales minus the cost of all nonlabor inputs to production. The intent of value added is to avoid double counting in the system of economic accounts, by assigning to a restaurant, for example, only what it adds to goods and services purchased from other firms.
2. Many tourism studies stop at estimating spending or its direct effects on tourism-related industries. Tourism satellite accounting methods (Frechtling, 2000) often focus on direct effects.
3. If the closing of recreation facilities in an area causes local residents to travel outside of the region, their expenditures will represent a loss to the local economy and can be legitimately included in an impact analysis.
4. Generally one should also include a local visitor segment and exclude their spending when estimating impacts. Based on the visitor survey at Grand Canyon, the number of local visitors was deemed to be insignificant.
5. Since river runners were not surveyed, their expenses were estimated based on concession receipts, adding one night of lodging and other expenses to cover an extra day in the area before or after the trip through the canyon.
6. Impacts beyond the local region can be substantial. For example, Schwer et al. (2000) estimated that sales impacts on Clark county, Nevada from visitors taking air-tours from Las Vegas to Grand Canyon were more than $200 million. Grand Canyon attracts many international visitors, who spend considerable amounts elsewhere in the United States during their trip.
7. If a complete input-output model is used, the secondary effects may be traced to individual sectors.

8. Park admission fees are not included in the visitor spending estimates to avoid double counting . Since only a portion of the operating budget of the park is covered by park admission fees, a more complete picture of the local economic effects of spending by the park is obtained by estimating the impacts of the park payroll and operations separately from visitor spending.

Chapter 22
NRPA's Health Initiatives

Kathy Spangler and Ellen O'Sullivan

Learning Objectives:

1. Be able to trace the development of the focus on health benefits from the formation of the park and recreation profession to current benefits based applications.
2. Understand the components and outcomes of NRPA's initial health benefit initiatives such as Hearts N' Parks and Step Up to Health.
3. Understand the role and nature of the 7Ps defined as components of the benefits based health initiatives developed through NRPA.
4. Understand the NRPA partnership model with specific applications for health and well-being.

Informed citizens are aware of the tremendous benefits associated with all people maintaining good mental and physical health. They also know that the social costs of health care continue to increase rapidly and constitute a large and growing percentage of the budgets of all industrialized nations. Increasingly, research has demonstrated that participation in various forms of recreation can contribute to mental and physical health while keeping healthcare costs lower than they would be otherwise. In addition, recreation can contribute even more to health and livability goals, which is the topic of this chapter. Specifically, this chapter reports on the nature and contributions of several health initiatives of the National Recreation and Park Association (NRPA).

Health: An Important Basis for the Evolution of the Benefits Movement in Parks and Recreation

Health as a core element of the Benefits Movement actually surfaced at the turn of the last century when early pioneers of the Park and Recreation Movement responded to "the" critical issues of the day and, in so doing, defined a century-long social service agenda for parks and recreation. The early efforts contributing to health outcomes largely centered on restoring or maintaining the health of people throughout society and led these luminaries to create innovations that impacted social behavior and advanced efforts to foster more livable community environments. Their professional stewardship formed the basis of the emerging parks and recreation movement and ignited a benefits-based focus on health as essential to ensuring a quality of life for individuals, communities, and the physical environment. These efforts to secure a healthy social and physical environment for all people were central to the development of the field during its first one hundred years.

The professional family tree in parks and recreation is laden with outstanding individuals whose enormous contributions to society took a variety of forms. The public accolades bestowed upon this relatively small group of individuals include membership in the National Basketball Hall of Fame, a recipient of the Nobel Peace Prize, and a presidential appointment as the first Sanitary Commissioner of the United States. While the important contributions made by Jane Addams, Frederick Law Olmsted, and Luther Gulick took on different forms, there were two common threads interwoven among their efforts. Of the common threads amplifying their individual and collective contributions was a shared concern for the overall health of individuals, neighborhoods, communities, and society as a whole. A second shared value uniting the efforts of these park and recreation pioneers was the foresight that health was contingent upon an ecological model that included open space, physical activity, and civic engagement to create a healthy and livable community.

While each of these three individuals are fairly well-known for their early contributions to physical education, landscape architecture, and the settlement house movements which formed the basis for park and recreation services in the United States during those early years, what is less well-known about these individuals is the origins and interests in health shared by each of them:

- While Frederick Law Olmsted is well-known as the lead developer of New York City's Central Park and a forefather of landscape architecture, it is less widely known that Olmsted served as Executive Secretary of the U.S. Sanitary Commission, a precursor to the Red Cross in Washington D.C. where he was responsible for tending to the sick and wounded during the Civil War. The health and quality of life benefits he envisioned for Central Park carried over into this directly related health endeavor. (Source: http://www.fredericklawolmsted.com/Lifeframe.htm)
- Jane Addams is likely best known as one of the founders of Chicago's Hull House in 1889. What was intended as a place to take care of children and nurse the sick evolved into a complete community recreation center with art gallery, gymnasium, swimming pool, coffee house, art studio, and music group among some of the offerings within its walls. Addams clearly recognized the underlying causes of poor health for individuals and also identified community building as central contributor to the overall well-being of urban America. A lesser know fact about Addams is that prior to founding Hull House, she studied medicine which she had to forego due to her own health conditions.
- While Luther Gulick is not the originator of basketball, it was on the basis of his urging that this now widely popular sport was developed. While working in the late 1890s at a YMCA in Springfield, MA he became concerned about the lack of physical activity for the participants during the winter months and assigned one of his physical education instructors, James Naismith, with the task of creating an indoor game. That's exactly what Naismith did as he created basketball as a game that would address Gulick's recognition of the need for vigorous physical activity during the winter months for young men. Gulik was a physican by formal training and a lesser-known contribution is that Gulick is widely attributed as the architect of the symbol for the YMCA (Young Men's Christian Association) holistic approach to health and well-being which included a triangle representing spirit, mind, and body.

Defining Moments: The First Hundred Years

The first one hundred years of the public parks and recreation movement saw growth and development to address emerging societal issues of the times. Public policies were enacted to authorize various means for the preservation of open space and provided public funding for recreation. For example, early in the 20th century, bond issues passed to build Chicago, Illinois community centers and to establish a Playground Commission in Los Angeles, California. The ensuing years brought about the establishment of the national and state park systems and witnessed the Great Depression which stimulated government funded labor projects such as the WPA and Civilian Conservation Corps.

The post-World War II years could be referred to as the boom years for parks and recreation as the benefits supporting the health and well-being of individuals, communities, and the environment expanded significantly. To care for the healthy development of the largest generation in American history, communities invested public funds and established professionally managed park and recreation departments to expand youth and family recreation activities, sport leagues, and outdoor camp programs. As the profession advanced, the associations representing early disciplines merged to form the National Recreation and Park Association (NRPA) in 1965. At the same time, the policies and practices of the federal government gave rise to federal funding through the National Trails Acts, Land and Water Conservation Funding, and the Bureau of Outdoor Recreation which had a profound effect, through its grants, on the development of the park and recreation infrastructure nationwide.

Shift Toward Benefits

In the period following the work of Addams, Olmsted, Gulick, and others to contribute to the overall health and well-being of people and the communities in which they resided, the parks and recreation movement changed significantly. Initially the result of the efforts of well-meaning citizens and a few professionals, the expanding parks and recreation movement transitioned into a movement comprised of more professionals and fewer citizens. The benefits-based strategies employed by these pioneers also shifted from addressing overall community issues to organizing professionally administered public agencies to meet the specific interests of smaller groups of individuals.

Arguably, the watershed moment that exacerbated this shift from community service to a market driven focus and away from the social imperative of overall health and well-being was the 1978 passage of California's Proposition 13. This proposition resulted in a cap on property tax rates statewide and caused substantial cuts to government services deemed "nonessential." This tax roll back legislation spread across all fifty states forcing local governments to abolish public services supported by property tax revenues or make wholesale changes to sustain them. Through a decade of severe budget cuts, the park and recreation movement struggled to adopt a new marketing approach consisting of charging fees for program activities, events, and facility admissions in an effort to maintain modest service levels.

At end of the 1890s, when parks and recreation was forming as a means to address important community issues, the beginning of the 1980s found the field surviving on the basis of offering what people were willing to pay for. It was this survival mode that led to a great philosophical shift within the movement. Courses on social work in college and university curricula were replaced with courses on marketing and promotion. The great vision of the early pioneers had been altered by a profession struggling to innovate for survival and a citizenry that had lost its sense of stewardship for what parks and recreation contributed to community life.

Benefits Revival

During the 1980's, the emphasis on generating revenue was a challenge for public parks and recreation agencies. Increasingly, the revenue generation emphasis influenced management decisions focused on individual preferences where citizens had a willingness to pay for direct services. As departments became more adept at revenue generation and citizens became more tolerant of incremental fees for service, appropriations to support the ongoing operations and services of public parks diminished. This shift to a market driven environment in public parks and recreation was fueled by the growth in the broad spectrum of leisure industries creating both a lure of private sector employment and the adoption of business-like practices in the public sector.

The Benefits Movement started at a time when the profession was searching for direction and leadership to align the traditional services it was founded upon with increasing pressure to implement business metrics and public demand for customer services from the public sector expanded. Several forces converged in the 1990s that prompted wider attention on the benefits of leisure. One significant factor was publication of the text *Benefits of Leisure* (Driver, Brown, & Peterson, 1991)[1]. It described what was known scientifically about the different benefits of leisure and what additional research needed to be done by relevant disciplines. The chapters were written by well-known leisure scientists from several countries. That text then became the stimulus for development of *The Benefits of Parks and Recreation: A Catalogue* (1992) by The Parks and Recreation Federation of Ontario (now Parks and Recreation Ontario). That catalogue was improved and expanded considerably into the *The Benefits Catalogue* by the Canadian Parks and Recreation Association (1997)[2]. For several reasons, it has had tremendous influence on promoting the benefits movement in the U. S. and Canada. By cataloging the results of research on the benefits of leisure into the four categories of social, physical, economic, and environmental benefits, it documented the wide scope of those benefits. It fully referenced the many studies done and interpreted the results in a language that was clear and understandable to all interested parties, not just scientists. Most significantly, it made people realize that much more was known scientifically about the benefits of leisure than they previously realized, and it made them aware of the great contributions of leisure to human welfare. The Canadian Parks and Recreation Association is now revising their 1997 catalogue.

In 1995, Geof Godbey and Alan Graefe of The Pennsylvania State University were commissioned by the NRPA through a grant from the National Recreation Foundation to conduct research on the public perception of the benefits received from local park and recreation systems. This NRPA publication, *The Benefits of Parks and Recreation*[3] served to identify how local park and recreation systems impact quality of life indicators across the benefit categories identified in *The Benefits Catalogue*. The NRPA Pacific Northwest Regional Council can be credited among the early adopters of the benefits framework by collaborating with their Canadian counterparts, providing leadership training and developing public visibility tools to communicate the benefits to community stakeholders.

During the 1995 NRPA National Congress on Parks and Recreation in San Antonio, Texas, NRPA hosted a landmark meeting with Canadian leaders of the benefits movement to discuss a unified vision for the benefits movement. This meeting set the stage for NRPA to develop resources that would assist park and recreation professionals implement a benefits-based agenda. The American Park and Recreation Society under the leadership of President David Clark secured funding from NRPA to develop *The Benefits Movement-Putting the Pieces Together*[4]. Ellen O'Sullivan of Southern Connecticut State University was awarded the contract to write the resource guide which was used as the curriculum for over one hundred training events between 1996 and 1998. This resource guide served as a practical tool kit to train practitioners how to translate the science into practice by shifting from a "delivery system" approach to an "outcomes" approach. It also offered practical examples of how practitioners could use the research presented in *The Benefits Catalogue* to improve communication with stakeholders and decision makers.

At the same time, NRPA developed a slogan around the benefits movement, entitled *Parks and Recreation...The Benefits are Endless!* NRPA trademarked this slogan with The ADvisors Marketing Group, a small promotional company who developed an extensive promotional product line. NRPA partnered with state associations to offer these promotional products to local agencies until NRPA concluded its relationship with Advisors Marketing in 2001.

Two additional studies were commissioned through NRPA and funded by grants from the National Recreation Foundation during 1996 to fuel the benefits movements. First, Larry Allen of Clemson University was contracted to conduct a demonstration project on benefits based programming. This study evaluated how benefits-based recreation programming could impact quality of life indicators.

NRPA also contracted with John Crompton of Texas A&M University in a study to determine the economic benefits of special events conducted by park and recreation agencies. Between 1996–1998, NRPA lead a multipronged approach to advance the benefits movement through research, professional development, and public awareness. State affiliates and local agencies were keen to adopt the programming and public visibility elements of the movement, but much of the outcomes framework failed to be adopted at administration and planning levels. This period also ignited debate regarding what vision the benefits movement should strive for and what investments NRPA or others should make to develop new resources. Without a comprehensive vision for the movement from the national organization, debate among stakeholders supporting various components of the agenda ultimately segregated rather than aggregated the comprehensive potential of the movement. Although NRPA commissioned a task to develop a strategic plan in 2000, a clear and concise strategy for the national organization was never formally adopted.

As a follow-up to the original *The Benefits Movement–Putting the Pieces Together,* NRPA published a second benefits resource in 1999 entitled *Setting a Course for Change*[5]. That publication focused on practice to policy approaches whereas the first text emphasized science to practice strategies. The publication highlighted successful examples from state and local agencies and became the basis for another round of training programs targeting administrative practices.

NRPA also published two additional books by John Crompton entitled *Measuring Economic Impact of Visitors to Sports Events and Special Events*[6] and *The Impact of Open Space on Property Values and the Property Tax Base*[7]. These publications offered early quantitative analysis of the economic impact of parks and recreation at the community scale and became effective management tools for public policy development and budget justification.

Building capacity to address the health benefits of parks and recreation was of primary interest and a number of unprecedented opportunities fueled the expansion of benefits based health efforts through NRPA. As one of ten national organizations to be awarded a cooperative agreement from the Centers for Disease Control and Prevention to promote the 1996 Surgeon General Report on Physical Inactivity, NRPA initiated a benefits-based communications campaign entitled *Active Living/Healthy Lifestyles.* This campaign illuminated the health benefits associated with active participation at parks and in recreation programming and launched a focused agenda for NRPA that encompassed the benefits-based elements.

Having already partnered with the National Heart, Lung, and Blood Institute (NHLBI) of the National Institutes of Health on a park-focused media campaign for youth, NRPA was invited to collaborate with NHLBI in the development of a heart health initiative entitled Hearts N' Parks. This became the first NRPA benefits-based national program for health promotion. Ellen O'Sullivan served as the pilot project's principle investigator while on sabbatical from Southern Connecticut State University. During 1998 through 2000, NRPA conducted two pilot studies in twelve North Carolina communities and in Arlington County, Virginia.

NRPA's Health Initiative Close Up: Hearts N' Parks

Brief History

Hearts N' Parks was initially a slogan created by staff at the National Heart, Lung, and Blood Institute (NHLBI). The slogan resonated strongly with that group because it incorporated its focus upon heart health while providing a springboard to collaborate more intentionally with the world of parks and recreation, a long time aim of the agency. The slogan soon took on a life of its own under NRPA leadership in the form of a pilot project in North Carolina called, *Hearts N' Parks Y2K*.

Hearts N' Parks Y2K was piloted during the summer of 1999 at 33 sites in 12 North Carolina communities involving more than 2,000 participants. An evaluation showed that participants retained information about heart-healthy behaviors and intended to eat healthier. By the conclusion of that pilot project, children reported learning new physical activities and improving their performance in others; seniors reported feeling healthier and experiencing less pain in their daily lives.

The success of this project was followed closely by a second pilot project in Arlington County, VA Department of Department of Parks, Recreation, and Community Resources. The pilot projects led to the creation of a three-year project implemented in park and recreation departments throughout the country. This expansion to 11 states throughout the country in the fall of 2001 brought 50 new Magnet Center sites into the program. At that time the Magnet Center sites made a three-year commitment to implementing heart healthy activities that emphasize the 5 Ps of Hearts N' Parks (People, Programs, Partners, Public Visibility, and Performance Measures).

Importance of the Hearts N' Parks' Goals

Hearts N' Parks was a national, community-based program supported by the NHLBI of the National Institutes of Health and the NRPA. The intent of this innovative program was to reduce the growing trend of obesity and the risk of coronary heart disease in the U.S. by encouraging Americans of all ages to aim for a healthy weight, follow a heart-healthy eating plan, and engage in regular physical activity.

The goals and activities associated with Hearts N' Parks were especially critical given the health picture within the United States at this time, which included:

- Heart disease was the leading cause of death in the United States with being overweight and obesity increasing one's risk of developing heart disease.
- The proportion of overweight children and adolescents, as well as obese adults in the United States, had more than doubled over the past two decades.
- Adopting heart-healthy behaviors including following a healthy eating plan and participating in regular physical activity, helped individuals achieve or maintain a healthy weight, reducing the risk factors associated with preventing cardiovascular disease and/or reducing its severity in those with existing disease.

Key Aspects of the Program

Hearts N' Parks incorporated science-based information about lifestyle choices for reducing an individual's risk of heart disease and skills for incorporating heart health into the regular activities offered by park and recreation departments. The program also provided tools for measuring the impact of these activities. Among the key elements inherent within this collaboration between the National Heart, Lung, and Blood Institute and the NRPA included the following:

- Hearts N' Parks focused on nutrition and fitness activities, stress reduction, and family activities that could be incorporated into existing park and recreation programs as well as targeting youth, teens, adults, and senior citizens.
- Training of recreation and park departments and staff from community partners received training.
- Consumer-oriented materials communicating heart-healthy messages related to weight management, physical activity, high blood pressure, cholesterol, and heart disease were provided for the departments. Materials targeted to specific populations, such as African Americans and Hispanics, were also made available.
- Evaluation materials that measured the program's impact were included and provided an important element of the project.
- Public recognition of parks and recreation as providers of health-related outcomes.

- Development of partnerships at both national and community levels were supported.

The North Carolina Pilot Phase

The *Hearts N' Parks Y2K* program was an exemplary example of the power of partnerships as it was the result of a partnership between the NHLBI of the National Institutes of Health and the NRPA. NRPA engaged the Southern Connecticut State University's sabbatical leave program to assist with program design, training, and measurements and North Carolina State University to launch the first phase of the pilot project.

The purpose of the pilot project was two-fold. The overall intent was to increase the number of children and adults who engaged in regular, moderate-intensity physical activity and adopted a heart healthier eating plan. The second and equally critical focus of the project was to demonstrate the positive impact that community park and recreation departments had upon the adoption of such healthy behaviors. While many public park and recreation departments had long thought they were delivering such benefits, this was a critical juncture for the field to actually demonstrate and document the intended outcomes of their efforts.

North Carolina was selected as the location for the pilot site due to its high level of cardiovascular disease and the large number of strong departments within the State that had been supported over the years by North Carolina State University and its extension services program.

Participating sites consisted of large municipalities, urban and rural county departments, as well a medium-sized suburban and rural communities throughout the state and included the following communities and counties: Albemarle, Fletcher, Garner, Greenville, Hickory, Madison—Mayodan, Mecklenburg County, Raleigh, Roanoke Rapids, Smithfield, Wilson, and Winston-Salem.

The departments in the State of North Carolina who chose to take this leap are to be heralded for their willingness to volunteer to participate in this pilot and particularly for the short turnaround time they were given. Volunteer agencies were sought in January, trained in March, and delivered statistically significant results by the end of August within the same calendar year.

Departments were asked to identify two existing programs, one that focused on children and one on adults, and incorporate heart healthy information and activity into these two programs. The departments administered pre- and posttests to determine the role that park and recreation activities played in acquiring information, changing attitudes, and influencing behaviors. The information, handouts, and pre- and posttests were based upon the Child and Adolescent Trial for Cardiovascular Health Study (CATCH)[8]. A follow-up study on CATCH was announced in the *Archives of Pediatric and Adolescent Medicine* on July 14, 1999. These findings reported that children who learned heart-healthy behaviors in grades 3 through 5 from the CATCH program continued to practice these behaviors for several years. CATCH materials were distributed to all of the North Carolina communities participating in *Hearts N' Parks.*

Types of Evaluation

Three types of efforts were undertaken to evaluate the program. An outcome evaluation was conducted by NRPA as it collected data from participants at the 12 sites, at the beginning of the program (pretest) and after completion of the program (posttest). An evaluation of the process was examined in two ways. After completion of the program, telephone interviews were conducted with site personnel associated with the pilot project and then a roundtable discussion with site personnel meeting jointly was held at the state's annual conference in November.

Report Summary

All sites elected to conduct the adult portion of the program with senior citizens. The size of the programs ranged from 9 participants in Smithfield to more than 1,000 in Mecklenburg County. Most programs had between 20 and 40 participants.

Before the start of the project at the 12 sites, pre- and posttest surveys were distributed at training sessions. Two types of tests were available, one for youth programs and one for adult programs. Each of the sites independently decided which type of program it would conduct. Instructions on how to administer the tests were given verbally and in written form to site personnel by NRPA. One copy of each type of test packet was given to the sites, depending on which of the programs they were planning to conduct. Sites were responsible for making copies of the tests and returning them for analysis.

In general, the participant data showed improvements at posttest. Overall, youth scores significantly improved for knowledge of healthy eating and intention to eat healthy in the future. Overall, adult scores significantly improved for healthy eating habits. Although some scores did not show statistically significant improvement, there was some improvement in most other variables. Improvement was seen in all posttests that were administered.

Based on the results of the analysis of the participant data, several recommendations were made to improve administration and results in the future.

Age-appropriateness was an issue for the youth tests. The youth programs had participants ranging in age from 4 to 17, and the youth tests were clearly designed for younger children. The adult tests were more appropriate for mature adults or senior citizens. An additional set of materials meant for older children or adolescents was added to the program.

The size of the program was deemed very important for this project. Small sites (fewer than 30 participants) were likely to do a good job but didn't necessarily see improvements in their test scores due to smaller sample sizes. Very large sites, on the other hand, often lacked the time or resources to adequately monitor test administration.

Based on the data analysis and examination of the data quality, programs with approximately 40 participants fared best.

Telephone Interviews

Telephone interviews were conducted with recreation directors, coordinators, supervisors, and program assistants from each community. The length of the interviews varied, but the usual duration was approximately 10 minutes. The specific intent of these interviews was to assess the value of the materials, training, and support provided by the NHLBI and NRPA before program implementation, as well as to learn about what other types of support were received by the sites. Information was also gathered about what support or information the sites needed but did not receive. This input was used to provide additional information for the development and design of the roundtable discussion conducted in November 1999, as well as to improve future program implementation.

Interviews were conducted using a semi-structured interview that asked what parts of the planning process provided by the NHLBI and NRPA were helpful or not helpful in implementing the program. Interviewees were also asked about what types of support were provided to the program outside of training and orientation by the NHLBI or NRPA and what types of support they needed that they did not receive from any source. In addition, the respondents were asked whether they would repeat the program next year or recommend the program to colleagues based on their experiences this year with the *Hearts N' Parks* program.

Responses for each question in the interview were compiled and synthesized. The following is a summary of the key findings from the interviews. The ideas presented in this section are generally based on responses from several interviewees. The findings were not quantitative in nature and should be interpreted accordingly.

The training sessions, materials, and support were very well-received and well-liked by the respondents. Respondents indicated that they would like to implement the program again next year and would highly recommend it to colleagues; some respondents were continuing with the program in their fall and after-school programs.

Issues of concern to the respondents were obtaining financial support and donations, obtaining and developing media support, and recruiting partners to be involved in and support the program. Several respondents said they had some financial support but would have like additional support, such as healthy food donations. Only a few respondents mentioned having any type of media attention. One person suggested that speakers related to the *Hearts N' Parks* program from the national or state level might be helpful in drawing media attention.

Roundtable Summary

In November 1999, a roundtable discussion was conducted with staff members from several sites that participated in the *Hearts N' Parks Y2K* program. The discussion took place in conjunction with the annual North Carolina Recreation and Park Society conference in Charlotte, North Carolina. Participation in the discussion was voluntary and was open to any representatives of the sites. Roundtable participants filled various roles, ranging from program director to camp assistant. Two representatives from a local hospital who participated in the project were also part of the discussion.

These findings were based upon responses from discussion participants are not quantitative in nature and should be interpreted accordingly. Based on their experiences, participants in the discussion confirmed previous research that they would participate in the program again. Many said *Hearts N' Parks* was a valuable and positive program that provided good information. All participants said they would recommend the *Hearts N' Parks* program to colleagues at other parks or agencies based on their experiences. Respondents felt that they were doing something beneficial and important for the community at large and that *Hearts N' Parks* was a good and effective program with excellent materials.

Overall, the program was very successful but discussion participants indicated that it made for a busy time. There were very few insurmountable problems, and most participants expressed interest and concern regarding the maintenance of the program over time. Overall, participants valued the support and training provided by the NHLBI and NRPA. Throughout the discussion, several ideas for ways that NHLBI and NRPA could help recreation and park programs in the future emerged.

General consensus from the group included the following:

- All agreed that the "status" of being part of a national program with prestigious lead agencies was helpful in accomplishing the desired activities. Keeping the national status would be important to secure support for future years and to expand the program to additional states.
- Data analysis support was deemed invaluable. Even preliminary evaluation data provided desirable information and had been helpful in garnering the support of others and proving the value of the programs.
- More materials and other resources would be invaluable. Across the board, participants believed that being provided with more templates would be a strategic support because templates allowed them to generate more activities with minimal effort on the planning stage and move more quickly to implementation.
- Marketing advice and support lent both credibility and needed expertise. The top-down approach (i.e., through an NHLBI news release), was an effective means that helped during the first summer. Additional information on how to involve businesses and the community as partners were cited as being useful, as would more involvement from the NHLBI or NRPA in enlisting media attention for community programs.

Conclusions

Without question, the pilot of *Hearts N' Parks Y2K* was a success. It met its goals of improving heart-healthy knowledge and behavior among participants during the course of the program; implementing a process for conducting and evaluating the program; and providing professional development for site personnel. Since *Hearts N' Parks* was a pilot project, several areas were identified that could be improved for the future and were noted throughout the report. Moreover, this pilot project showed the capacity of NRPA to develop benefits based initiatives of social importance that built relevance for the role of parks and recreation locally and NRPA nationally.

Second Pilot Round

Arlington County, VA, located in the Washington, DC metropolitan area, was a fitting choice to help initiate the second pilot site for *Hearts N' Parks*. Each year, the Arlington County Department of Parks, Recreation, and Community Resources offered a wide variety of services and activities for youth and adults, including recent immigrants and people with special needs so it expanded the reach of this effort.

A kickoff event for this pilot was held on July 18, 2000 by the Arlington County Department of Parks, Recreation, and Community Resources as a way to celebrate the outcomes of the pilot project in North Carolina and launch the second year of *Hearts N' Parks*. A special launch event was held, featuring U.S. Surgeon General David Satcher, NHLBI Director Claude Lenfant, NRPA President-Elect Alice Conkey, and Olympic Figure Skating Champion Michael Weiss. The daylong program was timed to coincide with July is Recreation and Parks Month, an annual celebration of the NRPA.

Throughout the day, the Thomas Jefferson Community Center in Arlington was the scene of a number of activities promoting heart-healthy eating and physical activity, including:

- Healthy cooking demonstration and classes conducted by the Fresh Fields grocery chain
- Tennis demonstration conducted by the U.S. Tennis Association
- Volleyball demonstration led by the George Washington University and Georgetown University women's volleyball coaches
- Jumping-rope demonstration
- Blood pressure screening by Arlington Hospital
- Boxing demonstration by the Arlington Boxing Club
- Gymnasium activities and demonstrations, including cycling, seated exercises, pickle ball, volleyball, and strength training
- Clinic on race-walking
- Sidewalk heart-art activity

Highlights of the Arlington County, VA launch were aired on Channel 31, *County Line*, which generated much interest from the local community.

Hearts N' Parks Magnet Center Field Study

NRPA convened a group of key organizational leaders, partners, and members in January 2001 to inform and ratify a new concept that could be used to develop national initiatives across a variety of social issues of importance to the organization. This was NRPA's first "thought leader summit" and the focus centered on a new "magnet center" strategy developed by Kathy Spangler of NRPA and Ellen O'Sullivan of Southern Connecticut State University to strengthen the impact potential of the NRPA Benefits Movement on relevant social issues such as health. The strategy identified and designated "early adopter" departments that were interested in partnering with NRPA to build benefits-based practices that would demonstrate impact on key social issues. This benefits-based concept focused on issue relevance, commitment to improve practice, and leadership to advance the field. Additionally, the magnet center concept concentrated on geographic proximity to advance new practice models surrounding magnet centers by serving as best practice examples on a regional and national scale. The goal was to effectively field test new strategies in a variety of departments across the country so that new practice standards could be easily replicated by others. The framework of the magnet center model included using science-based approaches to add value to existing services and improve professional practices so that desired outcomes can be achieved.

Following the successful pilot projects, and beginning in the fall of 2001, Hearts N' Parks was expanded to include 56 new magnet center sites in 11 states throughout the country. The states selected to participate in the Hearts N' Parks Magnet Center Field Study were among those with the highest risk for cardiovascular disease, demographic diversity, and park and recreation agency interest and capability. The states were Arizona, Florida, Georgia, Illinois, Indiana/Ohio (combined states), Maryland, Michigan, Missouri, New Mexico, and Nevada. The Marine Corps served as an additional "state agency" with six bases designated as Hearts N' Parks sites.

Hearts N' Parks magnet centers included the following locations:

- Arizona—Glendale, Phoenix, Sierra Vista
- Florida—Largo, Lee County, Oldsmar, Tallahassee, Tamarac
- Georgia—Athens, Roswell, Savannah
- Illinois—Decatur, Homewood, Rockford, Urbana
- Indiana—Bloomington, Fort Wayne, Gary, Indianapolis, Lafayette, South Bend
- Maryland—Baltimore, Howard County, Montgomery County, Prince George's County, Queen Anne's County
- Michigan—Adrian, Meridian Township, Monroe, Muskegon
- Missouri—Jefferson City, Kansas City, Poplar Bluff, Rolla, Springfield, St. Louis County
- Nevada—Henderson, Las Vegas, Reno
- New Mexico—Albuquerque, Las Cruces, Rio Rancho, Roswell
- Ohio—Bowling Green, Elyria, Greene County

Magnet Centers were also located in the following Marine Corps bases: Kaneohe Bay, Hawaii; Camp Pendleton, California; Beaufort, South Carolina; and Cherry Point and Camp LeJeune, North Carolina.

The magnet center sites agreed to a 3-year commitment to the Hearts N' Parks Field Study and were asked to fulfill specific responsibilities. These responsibilities included the following:

- Attend annual trainings for Hearts N' Parks.
- Administer the pre-test and posttest measures to participants.
- Enter performance measure data, as well as information about personnel and facilities into an Internet database, in order to obtain a report.
- Evaluate the program's sustainability and growth annually by tracking specific markers related to the 5Ps of Hearts N' Parks.
- Report progress annually.
- Utilize an extranet to communicate to other sites.
- Serve as ambassadors/trainers for other sites interested in Hearts N' Parks.
- Expand heart-healthy programming efforts each consecutive year.

2002 Hearts N' Parks Results

Results for 2002 Hearts N' Parks were based upon written questionnaires administered by Hearts N' Parks program staff in sites across the country to more than 1200 children, adolescents, and adults

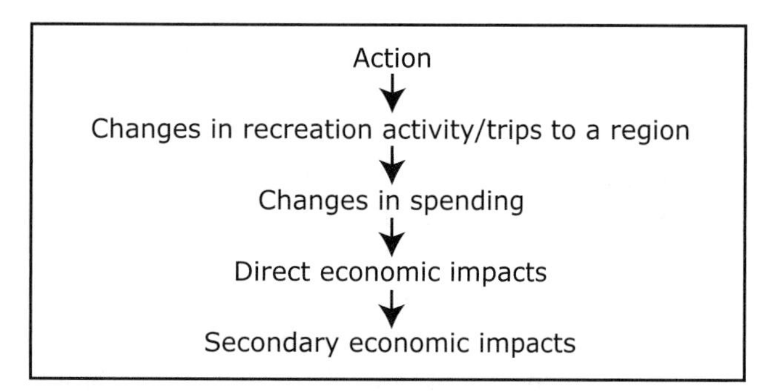

Figure 22.1

on their knowledge, behavior, and attitudes regarding heart-healthy eating and physical activity before and after participating in a program in 2002.

The Report of 2002 Magnet Center Performance Data included information on 68 programs varying in size and duration. Data was collected by 36 Hearts N' Parks sites during their first year as magnet centers. The majority of programs for children or adolescents were summer camps or after-school activities being held for 7 to 11 weeks. The adult programs averaged 12 weeks and predominantly included senior citizens and women.

The performance report compared the scores of pre-test and posttest questionnaires completed by 2,800 participants from 48 Hearts N' Parks magnet centers across the country. NHLBI outlined the following elements as results of the 2002 Hearts N' Parks project:

- Children, adolescents, and adults reported adopting healthier behaviors including choosing heart-healthy foods more often after participating in a Hearts N' Parks program.
- Adults said they boosted their level of regular physical activity after being in the Hearts N' Parks program.

Highlights of the performance report included:

- Children's scores improved significantly in all areas: heart-healthy eating knowledge (8% increase in correct answers), behavior (14% increase), and intention (19% increase).
- Children's scores in physical activity attitude increased. They reported that they "learned" or "would like to play again" an average of five activities while they "got better at" approximately seven activities.
- Adolescents' scores improved significantly in heart-healthy eating behavior (20% increase), intention (15% increase), and in overweight/obesity knowledge (7% increase).
- Adult participants significantly improved their scores in all areas of knowledge, attitude, and behavior studied. They increased their knowledge of heart-healthy nutrition with a 9% increase in correct answers. Scores increased by 6% to 7% in knowledge of overweight/obesity risks, physical activity, causes of high blood pressure, and ways to control cholesterol levels. Posttest scores derived from self-reports also suggested healthier attitudes toward overweight/obesity, heart-healthy eating habits, and physical activity, and improvements in how frequently participants chose healthy foods.
- Adult participants reported adding, on average, 2 hours of moderate physical activity per week (from 8 hours to 10 hours), such as bicycling, walking, and golfing, after participating in Hearts N' Parks. In addition, they reduced the time spent in sedentary activities by an average of 8 hours per week (from 41 hours to 33 hours).
- Posttest scores of participants over 60 years old showed greater improvement overall than younger adults. Seniors' pre-test knowledge scores were lower than younger adults' scores, but posttest knowledge scores were comparable. Seniors also significantly increased time spent weekly in physical activity on average from slightly fewer than 6 hours to more than 8.5 hours, and significantly lowered the amount of time each week in sedentary tasks by 10 hours (down to 20 hours).

Hearts N' Parks 2003

The impact of Hearts N' Parks expanded significantly during 2003 as the number of participants more than doubled (up from 1200 in 2002), as did the number of programs (142 programs in 2003, compared to 68 in 2002). The magnet centers also significantly increased participation by adolescents, adult males, and Hispanics, groups that traditionally were less likely to participate in recreation programs previously conducted by magnet centers.

Performance results for 2003 included:

- Children learned to identify healthy foods and reported being more willing to choose healthier foods over less healthy foods. On average, posttest scores from 1,735 children increased 26% for heart-healthy eating knowledge; 15% for heart-healthy eating intention. Children also increased their interest in various forms of physical activity.

- Hearts N' Parks programs for adolescents expanded in 2003. Data from nearly 370 teens (up from 93 teens in 2002) indicate significant improvements in heart-healthy eating knowledge and attitude, and overweight/obesity knowledge and attitude.
- Adult participants significantly improved their knowledge of heart-healthy eating, overweight and obesity health risks, proper ways to engage in regular physical activity, causes of high blood pressure, and ways to control blood cholesterol levels. They also improved their heart-healthy eating behavior and attitude toward heart-healthy eating, overweight and obesity, and physical activity.
- http://www.nhlbi.nih.gov/new/press/03-07-03.htm

Hearts N' Parks Year 2004

The final year of the three-year program was an extension of the initial two years. Staff and partners from magnet centers attended a training which focused more specifically upon success stories from previous years as well as a nutrition education component. Forty-three magnet centers collected data for analysis in this final year of the project. The sites averaged four programs per site with the participation numbers ranging from 4 to 76 individuals. Data was collected from 177 programs with 168 of the programs providing valid data for analysis. A total of 3,772 participants participated in Hearts N' Parks programming and approximately 3,573 of them completed both the pre- and posttests that served as the basis for data analysis.

Hearts N' Parks was once successful again in 2004 as improvements were demonstrated from pre- to posttests in all indicators of heart-healthy eating knowledge, self-reported attitude, behavior, and physical activity. Some of the results from the 2004 programming included:

- Significant improvement by children in all areas of heart-healthy eating including knowledge, intention, and self-reported behavior.
- Scores in attitude towards physical activity among children also increased significantly, with children reporting that they learned a wide range of new activities during the programs (an average of five new activities per child).
- Of the 33 adolescent programs with pre- and posttest data significant improvement was demonstrated in all seven tested areas with most notable improvements in physical activity levels, heart-healthy eating behavior, and heart-healthy eating attitude.
- Both adolescent boys and girls improved equally in all the test categories, with boys scoring higher than girls for the categories related to overweight and obesity attitude, heart-healthy eating behavior, and heart-healthy eating intention.
- Adult program participants increased score in all five knowledge categories, heart-healthy nutrition, overweight and obesity risks, proper physical activity, causes of high blood pressure, and controlling high blood cholesterol.
- Posttest scores for adults demonstrated a significant increase in how frequently adults reported making healthy food choices and increased time reported in moderate physical activity.

Overall Findings of the Hearts N' Parks Project

In the Report of the Magnet Center Performance Data of Hearts N' Parks issued by the NHLBI, an analysis of the 2002, 2003, and 2004 data was provided to detect differences across the three-year period and to identify the overall effects of the Hearts N' Parks project.

In the conclusion section of this report, it is stated that "the results of the three full years of Hearts N' Parks demonstrated the ability of community-based organizations such as park and recreation departments to positively impact heart-healthy knowledge and, potentially behavior changes among residents of all ages" (http://www.nrpa.org/content/default.aspx?documentId=2683)[9]. The report details the increase in the number of participants growing from 1,919 in 2002 to 3,772 in 2004, as well as the number of programs increasing from 68 in the first year of the project and reaching 177 by the third year. Other findings based on the overall results of the Hearts N' Parks project included the following:

- Across the three years of the program, children showed improvement in every section of the pre- and posttest questionnaires with the exception of the two measurement tools related to physical activity that cannot be analyzed for pre- and posttest changes.
- Across the years, scores for adolescents improved in almost all sections.
- All adult scores improved from pre- to posttest in all three years of the program.

Transition Time

The Hearts N' Parks Magnet Center Field Study demonstrated the effectiveness of parks and recreation as a leader to mobilize communities for health by in incorporating evidence-based information and interventions into existing services. NRPA and NHLBI discussed strategies to build greater momentum with the Hearts N' Parks initiative, but ultimately agreed to develop independent resources to advance their common agenda. The collaboration between NRPA and NHLBI provided a mutually beneficial opportunity for each organization. For NRPA, the scientific credibility of NHLBI was unmatched in any previous relationship and provided the necessary documentation of health benefits associated with parks and recreation to the field as an essential resource for health promotion. For NHLBI, the access and opportunity to conduct a field study at the community scale was unprecedented on the scale afforded the agency through the collaboration with NRPA. The 56 magnet center agencies proved that public park and recreation agencies had a capacity and capability to impact health behaviors.

NHLBI subsequently developed *We Can!* ("Ways to Enhance Children's Activity & Nutrition"), a national program designed for families and communities to help children achieve a healthy weight. The program focus includes *three* important behaviors: *improved* food choices, *increased* physical activity, and *reduced* screen time.

Some of the innovations associated with this new effort include the collaboration of NHLBI with some of its counterparts within the National Institutes of Health including the National Institute of Diabetes and Digestive and Kidney Diseases, National Institute of Child Health and Human Development, and the National Cancer Institute. Fourteen Intensive Community Sites were selected from across the country to implement and evaluate the *We Can!* program in June 2005. These fourteen sites included a variety of community outreach organizations such as some park and recreation departments, state and local health departments, community health coalitions, and hospital settings.

Step Up to Health

The interest generated from the Hearts N' Parks magnet center was greater than expected with nearly 1,500 communities expressing interest to participate in the magnet center initiative by the end of the three-year field study. Because it was a research-based initiative, Hearts N' Parks resources primarily focused on the 56 magnet centers. To respond to the interest generated during Hearts N' Parks, NRPA focused on expanding its benefits-based health agenda throughout the nation. Step Up to Health (SUTH) was developed to leverage the lessons learned from Hearts N' Parks magnet centers and to coincide with the United States Department Health and Human Services Steps to a Healthier US for which NRPA was a recognized partner. To mount a nationwide effort, NRPA sought grant funding from the Centers for Disease Control and Prevention. Although the proposal was recommended for acceptance, funding was not available. Undaunted, NRPA submitted the grant proposal to the National Football League Youth

Spending category	Segment						
	Day trip	In-park hotel	In-park camp	Back-country	Outside park hotel	Outside park camp	River runners
Hotel/Motel	0	125.34	0	0	102.51	0	6.38
Camping fees	0	0	16.24	3.09	0	18.5	0.25
Guide fees	2.9	13.69	2.21	0	3.33	0.83	393.36
Restaurants/Bars	22.84	82.97	15.58	10.18	52.46	18.3	3.49
Groceries/Take out	4.37	10.66	12.89	4.41	9.83	12.54	0.85
Gas and oil	13.52	7.76	10.59	10.35	14.62	12.89	1.68
Other transp. expenses	22.93	20.24	2.4	0.32	30.87	3.64	3.17
Amusements/Recreation	15.87	39.72	8.55	4.19	21.61	14.61	1.46
All other purchases	31.16	36.52	29.16	10.51	36.11	15.22	1.49
Donations	0.37	1.27	0.06	0.09	0.87	0.42	0.04
Total	113.96	338.17	97.68	43.14	272.21	96.95	412.18
Party nights (000's)	357	190	119	88	641	138	72.4
Percent of nights	22%	12%	7%	5%	40%	9%	5%

Figure 22.2

Football Fund which had expressed an interest to fund community health promotion efforts. The NFL Youth Football Fund awarded NRPA a $150,000 grant to develop the Step Up to Health curriculum and to conduct 18 Step Up to Health Summits during 2005.

The benefits-based curriculum for Step Up to Health built upon the Hearts N' Parks initiative, but also included new elements such as the Community Guide for Promoting Physical Activity[10] and the latest public health recommendations from the Centers for Disease Control and Prevention. Additionally, the community mobilization framework was expanded to add two additional assets that were identified through the Hearts N' Parks field study including physical environments managed by parks and recreation agencies (places) and their ability to institute procedural changes (policies).

Once the curriculum was completed, NRPA identified sites to host the 18 one-day summit events with special consideration being given to NFL team markets, Hearts N' Parks magnet centers and state affiliate organizations involved in state level health promotion efforts. NRPA hired a public health professional to assist in conducting the Step Up to Health Summit Tour.

The first SUTH Summit was conducted in Houston, Texas with over 100 attendees representing public health, medical, academic, private and nonprofit organizations, public officials, and park and recreation professionals. The premise of the Step Up to Health Summit curriculum included strategies to:

- Inform stakeholders about public health concerns regarding obesity, physical inactivity and poor nutrition.
- Expose stakeholders to national recommendations for local action to address these health concerns.
- Engage stakeholders to mobilize a grassroots effort to advance healthy and livable communities in partnership with parks and recreation.

The Centers for Disease Control and Prevention became an active partner in the execution of the SUTH Summits providing technical resources, promotional outreach and material support to participating agencies. This partnership included the critically acclaimed VERB® Multi Media Campaign. CDC customized existing television, radio, print, and internet media to include NRPA and the benefits of parks and recreation. This customized access to professionally developed and tested media executions provided participating agencies with a credible science partner for their local efforts and provided the parks and recreation profession unique national exposure through NRPA.

The early success of the Step Up to Health Summits fueled interest in hosting additional events beyond the 18 originally scheduled, so NRPA submitted a second grant proposal to the NFL Youth Football Fund to conduct an additional 18 summits through the spring of 2006. A total of 32 Step Up to Health Summits were conducted through the NFL grant reaching 2,205 individuals and engaging 811 communities.

Executive Summary

Pre-Summit Survey-National Overview

There were 702 respondents to the pre-summit survey which is just half of summit participants (52%). This survey was designed to determine what level of readiness park and recreation agencies had to address emerging health promotion issues.

Spring summits mainly reached small to mid-range communities. Of the 702 respondents, 209 have populations between 25,000–75,000. A close second is a population size between 75,000– 200,000 (165 respondents). 53% of all respondents are within these two population ranges and the majority of responses are suburban when describing their community setting.

An overwhelming majority of respondents described their current position as program development, supervision, and coordination (70%). Only one quarter (24%) of respondents were agency directors.

When asked about staffing policies and practices related to health promotion, respondents were split between basic and advanced. 42% claimed that only a few staff focus on healthy lifestyles through their work and 39% believe their agency is taking a leadership role to coordinate healthy lifestyle opportunities throughout the community.

A significant majority (76%) of current program participants enjoy open enrollment to sports, physical, and healthy-related activity programs and facilities provided by respondents.

A majority of respondents (72%) use a traditional fee-based structure for lifestyle programming (i.e., fitness classes, sports leagues, etc.). Only 16% offer programming with physical activity and nutrition as a central focus and 12% designed and evaluated their programming in order to enhance the health and well-being of the community. This is a large area for improvement. Only 12% cited purposeful when designing and evaluating their programs. This suggests that more directed and strategies are needed to develop health programming.

Facility usage for health tended to be at a basic level. 61% of those reporting had facilities that are available to all age groups in the community interested in pursuing a healthy lifestyle. A much smaller percentage (16%) reported reaching out to other service providers to expand the reach of their services. Almost a quarter (24%) of respondents has a master plan that identified health as an important community goal.

Almost half (45%) of respondents believed their users receive health benefits from their programs and services. 38% of respondents believed their community decision makers recognize the role of parks and recreation around health and livability issues, while only 17% of respondents believed the community seeks their leadership around health and livability issues. 38% of communities believed the decision makers recognize them for the job they do.

Fifty percent of respondents offer programming without the support of partners. A third cited having community partners to support their healthy lifestyle efforts and 18% belong to a community coalition that focuses on health and wellness.

Minimal evaluation processes are occurring in the park and recreation agencies who responded to the survey. An overwhelming majority of respondents (81%) evaluate programs based upon registration and attendance figures through participant satisfaction surveys. Only 9% of respondents conduct an annual needs assessment around health and livability issues and implement program evaluations, and 10% of respondents recognized the importance of demonstrating results.

When looking at health-focused agency policies and procedures, 39% of respondents operate at a basic level by promoting health through risk management procedures. 37% believe health and well-being have a central place in their agency's mission, and 25% are at an advanced level in which their agency has policies and procedures that are consistent with a community-wide commitment to health and livability.

A majority (62%) of respondents believe their role is as a community leader to address healthy lifestyle issues. They provide access to facilities and programming. 24% support community services with space for events and meetings and 15% believe their agency supports community programs and services reaching populations with mental health issues, rehabilitation needs, and health disparities.

Post-Summit Evaluation

The majority of respondents (76%) increased their knowledge of America's health crisis either "to a great extent" or "somewhat." This confirmed the original assumption of the general knowledge of park and recreation around overweight/obesity and health issues. Similarly, 85% of respondents understood the role of parks and recreation to address the health crisis. It's encouraging that these percentages are similar since knowledge is a baseline fundamental and their ability to act upon it is essential for (change/leadership) to occur.

Readiness to improve job-related activities to promote health as a result of the summit was rated 'to a great extent' by 58%, and 'somewhat' by 35%. Only 7% of respondents reported feeling unprepared to make improvements around health.

At the conclusion of the Step Up to Health 32 City Summit Tour, it was decided that the training materials could be provided through an online format to allow NRPA the opportunity to develop new health-focused resources for the field. Step Up to Health Online premiered in October 2006.

The one critical gap in the transition from Hearts N' Parks to Step Up to Health was the capacity to conduct an outcome evaluation on the merits of the initiative. To address this, NRPA focused on demonstrating the progress and leadership contribution of participating park and recreation agencies to advance health outcomes. Utilizing the 7 Ps as a framework, over 100 community examples have been posted on the NRPA website (www.nrpa.org/health) to illustrate the compelling role that parks and recreation plays to support healthy lifestyles and livable communities.

Advancing Leisure Sciences and Health

To advance the health benefits associated with parks and recreation, NRPA has also contributed to the advancement of the leisure sciences by funding or facilitating a number of research projects to reinforce the health benefits of parks and recreation. Projects ranging from active aging to health partnerships have contributed to the expansion of awareness among the public health community that leisure science contributes to the overarching knowledge needed to promote physical activity and other more broadly construed health benefits such as mental health, emotional health, environmental health, and social well-being. NRPA served as a sponsor of a landmark scientific conference in October 2006 at the Cooper Institute in Dallas, Texas, which brought together lead researchers from both public health and leisure sciences to develop a collaborative framework to promote physical activity for health outcomes. The results of this conference were published as a supplement to the Journal of Physical Activity and Health in 2007.

The issue of measurement as it relates to health has been a challenge for the field. NRPA has funded the development of instruments to assess park and recreation environments and existing programs to better document and demonstrate the capacity benefits of what parks and recreation contribute to public health goals. Unique management practice resources such as assessment resources and community-based programs will continue to be developed under the umbrella of the NRPA Step Up to Health Agenda.

The journey from Hearts N' Parks to Step Up to Health encompassed 15 years, multiple programs and partnerships, and professional engagement. The NRPA efforts in health have been among the most sustainable of any strategic agenda the organization has undertaken largely because of the stewardship of professionals at both the academic and practitioner levels who saw the value of reconnecting current day practices with the longstanding health benefits associated with park use and recreation participation. This effort has largely been focused on the contributions that the field of parks and recreation has on socially relevant issues such as health. In so many ways, the health benefits effort mounted by NRPA has brought out the best of what parks and recreation do to enhance the quality of life for all people.

Current NRPA Models

NRPA Partnership Model

NRPA's contributions to the benefits movement include an expanded understanding of the capacity-building strategies developed through the NRPA partnership agenda. The health initiatives outlined in this chapter provided significant momentum to the advancement of strategic partnerships developed by the NRPA. The myriad strategic alliances and community-based programs promoting health developed since 1991 exposed the national organization to new possibilities through partnerships. The response from the member agencies to emerging national initiatives offered through NRPA partnerships reinforced the value members placed on NRPA leadership in this regard.

As the Hearts N' Parks initiative was being pilot tested and the NRPA "Benefits are Endless" campaign was at its height, another significant decision was made to formalize a commitment to develop partnerships on behalf of the field by launching a national partnerships department in 1998. This nascent effort, which was initially staffed by one person, has grown to be a vital resource for the organization with eight full-time staff administering external relationships that support the field to expand the potential to deliver benefit-based outcomes at the community level.

The initial partnership protocol that was developed in 1998 continues to serve as the cornerstone for advancing the benefits of parks and recreation:

- NRPA pursues partnerships to advance health throughout the lifespan, youth development, environmental stewardship, and quality sports agendas.
- These partnerships will enhance services to more effectively communicate, facilitate and publicly advocate the benefits of parks and recreation while supporting the resource needs of the organization, affiliates, and local agencies.
- These partnerships endeavor to accentuate the role that the multi-faceted parks and recreation profession has in securing a quality of life for an increasingly aging, culturally diverse, and technologically advanced society.

Since 1998, numerous partnerships have assisted in the development of strategic models for developing successful partnerships and effectively implementing benefits- based initiatives at a grassroots level nationwide. The NRPA Partnership Strategy Model is built upon the notion that NRPA is a national organization of local concerns and initiatives that build relevance at the local level are necessary to advance strategic goals nationally.

Research and Evaluation

Lacking specific capacity to mount a research agenda, NRPA has strengthened its position among various stakeholder groups by engaging the academic community and supporting multidisciplinary research efforts to advance strategic agendas such as health.

Science-Based Initiatives

A commitment to partnership initiatives that are science based provides NRPA increased credibility and member agencies greater confidence regarding the substance of each initiative NRPA offers. It also defines a commitment to outcome evaluation and measurement.

Public Visibility

The nonprofit sector is too often the beneficiary of media attention and the public sector is often overlooked

Spending category	Segment							
	Day trip	In-park hotel	In-park camp	Back-country	Outside park hotel	Outside park camp	River runners	Total
Hotel/Motel	0.00	23.88	0.00	0.00	65.68	0.00	0.46	90.02
Camping fees	0.00	0.00	1.93	0.27	0.00	2.55	0.02	4.77
Restaurants & bars	8.15	15.81	1.85	0.89	33.61	2.53	0.25	63.09
Groceries/ Take-out	1.56	2.03	1.53	0.39	6.30	1.73	0.06	13.60
Gas & oil	4.82	1.48	1.26	0.91	9.37	1.78	0.12	19.74
Other transp. expenses	8.18	3.86	0.29	0.03	19.78	0.50	0.23	32.86
Amusements/Recreation	6.83	10.42	1.29	0.38	16.54	2.19	28.59	66.23
Souvenirs/other expenses	11.12	6.96	3.47	0.92	23.14	2.10	0.11	47.81
Total	40.67	64.42	11.61	3.78	174.42	13.39	29.85	338.13
Percent of spending	12%	19%	3%	1%	52%	4%	9%	100%

Figure 22.3

when social issues are addressed. The public sector is often not allowed or has limited resources to promote their "good works" to the community. NRPA has focused on the development of partnerships that provide increased public visibility for the benefits of parks and recreation. For example, when NRPA assisted *Sports Illustrated* with their 50th anniversary, instead of taking a fee, NRPA chose to accept $5 million in paid advertising in the magazine. A series of eight advertisements were created to increase public awareness of parks and recreation as essential to health through the *Healthy Lifestyles. Livable Communities. It Starts In Parks!* campaign.

Advocacy

Public sector institutions are challenged to develop advocacy efforts that influence public policy. NRPA seeks partnerships that have the potential to influence advocacy at local, state, and national levels. The longstanding NRPA partnership with the United States Tennis Association (USTA) has developed over time to include program support to local communities, facility grants for new tennis court construction, media tools and coverage, and grassroots advocacy. The 800,000 members of the USTA care about the health of their sport and with over 70% of all tennis being played on public courts, they have invested in a comprehensive advocacy strategy that will support local, state, and federal funding efforts because they consider their sport to promote lifetime health.

The sustainability of public parks and recreation is enhanced when external organizations support and contribute to developing research, mounting science-based initiatives, expanding public visibility, and advancing advocacy efforts around socially relevant issues such as health. This is the benefits in action through a partnership lens and NRPA has been recognized nationally by the American Society of Association Executives and National Association for Fitness and Health among others for its innovative model for partnering.

Grassroots Implementation Methodology

The development of a comprehensive strategy to implement successful grassroots initiatives through parks and recreation has evolved since the launch of the NRPA partnership department. Based upon the national partnership model and the 7 P's of community mobilization, NRPA has developed a grassroots implementation methodology to achieve greater effectiveness, relevance, and efficiency. The methodology is predicated on delivering benefits to and through parks and recreation agencies that impact socially relevant issues such as health promotion, youth development, active aging, inclusion, and quality sports.

The overarching goal of the methodology is to increase participation, including both the number of communities participating in NRPA partner projects and the number of citizens involved in local initiatives.

Activate

Individuals and institutions need to consciously commit to be involved. The strategies used to initiate participation is based in relationship building approaches to share in addressing emerging issues collectively.

Designate

When asked how NRPA could expand the Hearts N' Parks Magnet Center Project following the three-year field study, communities expressed interest in retaining the exclusivity of their "designation" as a magnet cen-

Sector	Direct effects			Total effects multipliers			
	Jobs/ $MM sales	Income/ sales	Value added/ sales	Sales Type II	Jobs/ $MM sales	Income/ sales	Value added/ sales
Hotels and motels, including casino hotels	20.54	0.44	0.71	1.42	26.89	0.58	0.95
Other accommodations	7.50	0.13	0.31	1.53	15.49	0.30	0.62
Food services and drinking places	28.00	0.40	0.46	1.46	34.86	0.55	0.71
Other amusement, gambling, and recreation industries	24.15	0.37	0.62	1.45	31.31	0.52	0.87
Automotive repair and maintenance	10.66	0.16	0.37	1.38	16.34	0.29	0.58
Transit and ground passenger transportation	31.38	0.50	0.57	1.52	39.67	0.69	0.86
Sporting and athletic goods manufacturing	6.53	0.20	0.27	1.37	11.84	0.33	0.47
Retail Trade	22.19	0.46	0.60	1.51	30.18	0.64	0.90
Wholesale trade	12.17	0.37	0.65	1.40	18.60	0.51	0.88

Figure 22.4

ter. This desire to be uniquely designated by national partners is an incentive for participation by grassroots organizations in a national movement.

Engage

Once activated and designated as a participant, grassroots initiatives will falter with ongoing engagement. *Communication* is a essential factor in securing the benefits desired at both individual and organizational levels.

Recognize

Simply put, NRPA has learned that it has succeeded when it makes member agencies "heroes in their own towns." Bringing a national spotlight to local efforts not only boosts the credibility of the local organization, but expands the trust and respect a national organization can receive. NRPA successfully illuminated itself by shining the spotlight on 50 communities that were recognized as the Sports Illustrated 50th Anniversary Sportstown in their state during 2004. When Sports Illustrated and NRPA arrived in each community to present a commemorative road sign the 50 recognized communities illuminated the benefits of parks and recreation with unexpected celebration. The year-long celebration took Sports Illustrated and NRPA on a journey that elevated the pride of a profession and illustrated the diverse benefits what a community commitment to parks and recreation can bring.

Renew

NRPA has smartly hedged against the development of independent partnerships for the advancement of its mission driven agendas. This agenda-building approach requires constant evaluation to document and demonstrate progress, as well as a renewed commitment by all parties to stay focused on the desired outcome. All too often initiatives are developed and not sustained. Through the renewal process, NRPA uses incentives, recognition and unique designations to renew the enthusiasm of partners at both the national and local levels. For example, with a grant obtained through the National Recreation Foundation, NRPA found a unique way to renew Step Up to Heath Communities for the third year of the initiative. Participating communities were asked to provide a summary of their community example of excellence for the previous year and in exchange, NRPA showcased communities based upon the comprehensiveness of their efforts. Basic examples were showcased on the NRPA website, intermediate examples were showcased in a written publication distributed to public officials nationwide, and advanced examples were showcased at a national health and livability summit. Renewal efforts can provide documentation of progress toward goals and support assessing strengths and weaknesses in the ongoing process to support improvement with appropriate resources.

The Benefits Movement has profoundly impacted the work of the NRPA through its national partnership functions and has advanced organizational capacity and recognition. This has benefited the work of the field through resources that add value, improve practice, and advance the field.

Current NRPA Models

The 7Ps of Community Mobilization

As a result of the pilot projects associated with Hearts N' Parks, a Community Mobilization Guide was developed by the NHLBI and the NRPA. The guide provided all the necessary tools for implementing Hearts N' Parks and was designed to help local community park, and recreation agencies promote heart-healthy lifestyle and changes such as increased physical activity and heart-healthy eating among children and adults. These tools included background information and materials, techniques for creating and delivering heart-healthy activities to participants, tools and strategies for reaching targeted groups, forming partnerships, working with the media, and assessment tools to measure program performance.

The guide was organized around 5Ps identified by Spangler and O'Sullivan as they worked with the North Carolina departments participating in Hearts N' Parks Y2K. These are five critical elements that serve as a framework around which a community could mobilize its heart-healthy efforts. The original 5Ps consisted of people, programs, public visibility, partners, and performance indicators. The lessons learned in the ensuing years of NRPA's health initiatives and efforts led to the expansion of original 5 Ps to include two additional, critical elements: places and spaces and policies and practices.

The 7Ps formed the basis for the Step Up to Health project, the major health-focused initiative of NRPA at this time. Each of the 7Ps are overviewed in the online training for Step Up to Health with explanations for each element as well as suggestions for implementations and examples of community activities associated with the various elements.

- 1st P = People
- 2nd P = Programs
- 3rd P = Public Visibility
- 4th P = Partnerships
- 5th P = Performance Measures
- 6th P = Places and Spaces
- 7th P = Policies and Practices

Sector/spending category	Sales $millions	Jobs	Personal income $millions	Value added $millions
Motel, hotel cabin, or B&B	90.0	1,849	39.3	63.7
Camping fees	4.8	36	0.6	1.5
Restaurants and bars	63.1	1,766	25.5	28.7
Admissions and fees	66.2	1,599	24.4	40.9
Other transportation expenses	32.9	350	5.4	12.3
Retail Trade	31.7	704	14.7	19.2
Wholesale Trade	4.1	50	1.5	2.7
Total Direct Effects	293.9	6,354	111.4	169.0
Secondary Effects	128.2	1,983	43.9	73.9
Total Effects	422.1	8,337	155.3	242.9

Figure 22.5

1st P: People

It always has been and always will be about people. The benefits of parks and recreation are delivered for and by people, and as such, people serve as the foundation for all efforts, activities, and outcomes associated with our profession. Harnessing the interest, energy, and intellectual capacity of individuals is fundamental to any community change effort. Health, with its complex interconnections among individual behavior, group influence, and environmental factors, qualifies as such an effort. It is critical that the "people" elements within community mobilization appear first in the process due to the following factors:

- The leisure needs and interests of people are fundamental to the existence of parks, open space, and recreation.
- Involvement and acceptance by people is a requirement of any successful effort to address complex social.

People, as referred to in this context, consist of both individuals and various groups of individuals. The construct for "people" can be further segmented into two additional different groups: internal and external. The involvement of individuals and groups of individuals from both sub-groups are essential to an agency's mobilization efforts and future success.

Those sub-segments identified as "internal" refer to individuals or groups of individuals who are employed or associated in some more formalized manner with the organization. The following illustrate some of those "internal" people: decision makers, which, depending upon your organization could include members of a governing board; city or county administrators; staff, including full-time, part-time, seasonal, and volunteers; and any other advisory groups or quasi-partners within your agency. Depending upon the circumstances or approach, current and former participants of your programs and services may also be considered part of the internal makeup of your "people" element.

External groups within the "people" category are those people who have no official relationships or no recognized involvement with your agency and can include: media, community partners, the general public, the business community, neighborhood groups, and community-based organizations. Nonparticipants or people who are unaware that they are utilizing your facilities or spaces could be included within this category as well.

Any one or several of these individuals or groups of individuals within the "people" element may serve as the impetus for your department's involvement with a health focus. However, the long-term outcome of a community's success for mobilization of health resources will need to incorporate all of these groups.

Participants

Once an agency decides to move forward with a health emphasis, the sub-group referred to as "participants" can be further segmented for the purposes of targeting outcome goals and developing programs. The term participants can reference a variety of classifications inlcuding:

- Primary participants are people who are regularly involved with your programs, facilities, or services.
- Secondary participants, people who are not registered or active in your program, but come in close contact with individuals that do participate (parents are a good example).
- Potential participants, people who are aware of your services but don't actively utilize or benefit from them.
- Independent participants, individuals who are likely using your parks or facilities on their own without a direct or formal involvement with the department.
- At-risk or underserved individuals.
- Nonparticipants or individuals unaware and/or unengaged in department sponsored programs, services, or facilities.

1st P: People—Community Examples

The following list highlights successful approaches used by various community departments as they implemented this 1st P:

Jefferson City, MO: The City Survivor Challenge program targeted public employees and focused on heart-healthy eating and physical activity. It not only involved city staff in heart healthy behavior, but served as a way to raise awareness of the role of parks and recreation among city decision makers, recreation staff, and city employees. A group of 21 city employees was divided into three teams with a leader for each team. During the initial meeting, each participant received an activity log to record physical activities. Teams met weekly to weigh-in, turn in activity logs, and receive materials on healthy eating and the benefits of physical activity. Every four weeks, the teams challenged each other to a game or contest. The first challenge was an obstacle course relay, the second was a volleyball match, and the third was a floor hockey game. On the last day of the program, certificates were given to the individual and team that logged the most physical activity minutes. All participants received a gift bag filled with healthy snacks.

Florida Disabled Outdoors Association (FDOA): The FDOA offered a Recreation Activity Program for Adults with Disabilities for residents in Leon, Wakulla, and Gadsden counties in Florida. The program is designed to stimulate and educate persons with disabilities on the opportunities available in sports, recreation, and leisure. FDOA has formed a partnership with the Department of Health and its Brain and Spinal Cord Injury Program. The initial project focused on the development of a database of accessible recreation and leisure resources. A new accessible field is being built in Tallahassee through the efforts of FDOA and Miracle League, enabling people with disabilities to engage in baseball, power soccer, and a variety of other accessible sports.

2nd P: Programs and Services

If people are the essential reason why parks and recreation exists, then programs and services most certainly are at the heart of public sector delivery systems. They are the framework and conduit for parks and recreation departments to provide activity or activity and programming for the purpose of addressing important individual and societal issues.

Programs and services serve as the most direct way for park and recreation agencies to connect with people and to deliver information, activities, and other services. The myriad of community-based programs and services are coordinated to reach more individuals, groups, neighborhoods, and service providers and enrich existing program services to intentionally impact an expressed community need such as increasing physical activity levels among youth and adults.

It is this "added value" approach to increasing capacity by addressing social change that forms the basis for altering and expanding upon this critical 2nd P: programs and services. In most instances, existing programs and services can serve as impetus for promoting health within a community. The basis of success among the Hearts N' Parks magnet centers was the use of existing programs and services to increase the knowledge and awareness of participants regarding heart-healthy behaviors. Programs that were originally health related (e.g., aerobic classes, senior stretch classes) as well as programs that were seemingly unrelated to health outcomes (e.g., summer playgrounds, community-wide events) were successfully enriched by program managers committed to infuse new activities and information approaches to their existing programs.

Other program/service strategies include offering new programs, lending resources and support to other providers or potential providers and/or specifically targeting underserved populations or at-risk health groups.

2nd P: Programs and Services—Community Examples

The following list highlights successful approaches used by various community departments as they implemented this 2nd P:

Saint Paul, MN Parks and Recreation: Saint Paul has partnered with the Saint Paul School District to utilize a Carol M. White PEP grant in the amount of $464,126. Their involvement in the PEP grant includes an assessment for physical skills and nutrition knowledge. Additionally, Saint Paul Parks and Recreation has partnered with NRPA, the Säjai Foundation, and the University of Minnesota to measure the impact of an after school physical activity and nutrition curriculum on K-6 grade students at five sites within the community.

Indy Parks, Indianapolis, IN: Youth vs. Staff = Fun was a youth versus staff "3 on 3" basketball and dodgeball tournament. Most of the staff had not participated in sports for some time, but managed to pull together and even win some of the games. The four-week program was held on Friday nights and a couple of added positives was the keeping kids occupied and off the streets as well as serving participants fresh fruit each evening. The department's report on the program included a reference to a rumor that the park manager organizing the tourney lost ten pounds by the end of the program.

3rd P: Public Visibility

While public park and recreation departments are often successful at garnering public visibility for large scale community events, they are not as successful in highlighting the role that their programs, practices, places, and spaces play in regards to important individual and societal issues. Step Up to Health and its many offshoot activities provides a platform for such visibility.

Gaining public visibility for the importance of health and well-being and the role played by parks and recreation is critical to social change strategies. Most park and recreation agencies have a core constituency of participants and advocates. Often, even these well-informed stakeholders don't fully understand the scope of services or the goals of a public park and recreation department.

Making sure that core constituents and the public at-large understand what a public park and recreation department is constituted to achieve requires a commitment to generate public visibility. Social service providers often invest the majority of resources in the delivery of services and fail to generate the kind of buzz needed to sustain the effort over time.

Public Visibility can consist of a number of different levels including:

- Defining the health issues currently facing our society
- Building awareness as to the importance of heart-healthy behavior and overall health
- Explaining the role to be played by parks and recreation related to issues
- Providing a context that explains and demonstrates how services support the important health issues
- Inviting additional and expanded participation among various sectors of the community

Effective use of the messages identified among the various levels can be linked to where various individuals or groups of people are related to the message. For instance, if an individual is not particularly aware of the serious health issues facing the United States, then they are less likely to appreciate the vital role parks and recreation may play in addressing this issue.

Three Major Alternatives

Three of the major alternatives available to departments within the critical element of public visibility relate to becoming newsworthy, engaging more of the public, and securing outside resources. Most organizations view themselves as "good news" stories that are worthy of media coverage. In this instance, the health crisis in America may be the social issue that your agency is addressing, but in reality, the health crisis is the news story. Playing a role in this crisis and becoming an expert on the issue is more likely to result in your gaining visibility. Programs that create results or have an impact are even more newsworthy since they document and demonstrate a positive result or impact.

The second alternative involves engaging the public as a way of ensuring social change. Social change is predicated on grassroots adoption and participation. A single program or event may influence behavior, but building a network of reinforcement across unique programs and service providers has a better chance of succeeding. Engaging the public as participants, thought leaders, and advocates can influence a system-wide effort to address a social issue such as health, obesity, and cardiovascular disease.

An additional public visibility outcome relates to outside support for your efforts. Park and recreation agencies are adept at securing sponsorships to support a variety of community facilities, programs and services. These relationships have augmented the resources needed to balance diminishing tax support for operational needs. Reductions in public funding for park and recreation services have challenged the profession to seek alternative resources and an emerging trend is toward mission driven partnerships.

3rd P: Public Visibility—Community Examples

The following list highlights successful approaches used by various community departments as they implemented this 2nd P:

Columbus, GA: The park and recreation department has retooled one of its passenger vans and turned it into a mobile "Step Up to Health" program. While the van is outfitted with equipment that can be used to engage in heart-healthy behavior, it serves as an ongoing reminder to members of the community that it is indeed time to "Step Up to Health."

Sarasota County, FL, Parks and Recreation: Sarasota reaped a great deal from the Centers for Disease Control's public visibility campaign, VERB. VERB was directed towards preteens with its catchphrase "verb—it's what you do." This department adopted the VERB Scorecard and has successfully utilized this PR campaign for multiple years. Information on the VERB summer scorecard program was distributed to area elementary and middle schools. Additionally, they started partnering with the Department of Health (DOH) to integrate multiple programs. DOH will provide trail signage, limited funding, and promotions to SCPR. SCPR will in turn register participants, track participant's progress, and maintain the database.

4th P: Partnerships

Partnerships bring together the varying assets of individual organizations in pursuit of a mutually beneficial relationship for the purpose of achieving goals. The goals of the individual organizations within a partnership may not be one and the same, but the overall philosophy and approach should be complementary.

Park and recreation departments generally pursue sponsorships for specific events, programs, or facilities, but are less apt to enter into true partnerships. Sponsorship agreements generally involve an exchange of benefits to the parties involved rather than a contribution to overall mission of both organizations. A beverage vendor donating drinks to a road race is more likely to be a sponsorship, while a hospital, community park, and recreation department jointly building a fitness center would be an example of a partnership.

Partnerships are formed for mutual benefits and the assets that each organization brings to the partnership may be tangible, intangible, or a combination of both. The intangible benefits are often equally or even more important aspects of partnerships. A local hospital desiring to position itself as a health promotion center enters into a partnership with a park and recreation department to provide outreach programs and services in local parks and facilities. Tangible benefits for the hospital are physical spaces to offer such programs outside of a medical setting while tangible benefits for the park and recreation may include increased visibility or participation.

While sponsorships often bring a specific resource to an organization to address a current need, partnerships make an overall contribution to the long-term success of the organization and its progress towards reaching important goals. The progress towards reaching important goals or societal change expands the traditional range of partnerships to include communication, coordination, and collaboration.

Achieving overall health in a community requires the communication of information among community providers and the general public, so communication is a key aspect of partnerships. Coordination, especially in an era with a focus upon participation numbers or revenue generated, is almost a requirement to ensure that all members of the community are provided with physical recreation and related health benefits. The importance of true collaboration cannot be overlooked in this critical P of partnership, since true and lasting change requires the input and involvement of all stakeholders.

Uniquely, the park and recreation movement has the capacity to lead community initiatives that convene stakeholder voices, engage disparate service providers, and advance a community-focused agenda that results in an enhanced quality of life for all people. As a public sector agency, there is a balancing act between revenue generating services to offset expenses and the role of community steward. Increasingly, park and recreation agencies are rediscovering their mission-driven responsibility, and also that alternative resources can be acquired to accomplish great things through a partnership strategy.

4th P: Partnerships—Community Examples

The following list highlights successful approaches used by various community departments as they implemented this 4th P:

Kirkland, WA: Community Summit Success: Kirkland (WA) Parks and Community Services has made significant progress in their Step Up to Health efforts. A community-wide summit held in February 2004 brought 80 participants, including 20 seniors, 10 youths, and representatives from both private and public companies and agencies attended the summit.

The goal of the summit was to educate the public on health trends and issues, both nationally and locally, and to develop a community plan for making a cultural change to inspire our community to be more physically active. The morning consisted of educational sessions while the afternoon breakout sessions, facilitated by Meeting Works, were designed for participants to "roll up their sleeves" and provide input and ideas on how to get our community more physically active.

Ohio Parks and Recreation Association (OPRA): OPRA led the charge to create a statewide coalition to support and promote healthy lifestyles, the Ohio Coalition for Physical Activity. Major stakeholders participating in the Coalition include Healthy Ohioans (Ohio Department of Health), and local chapters of the American Cancer Society and American Heart Association. OPRA currently serves on a number of statewide coalitions focused on health and wellness. OPRA serves on the following boards, coalitions, alliances, task forces:

- Governor's Advisory Council for Physical Fitness and Health
- Healthy Ohioans Statewide Task Force
- Ohio Cardiovascular Alliance
- Ohio Diabetes Alliance
- Ohio Action for Healthy Kids

5th P: Performance Measures

Public service providers have been challenged to identify outcomes and impact measures associated with their use of resources. The field of parks and recreation has traditionally measured outputs; those metrics associated with number of participants and cost-benefit ratios. While these measures do provide information, they fail to demonstrate the numerous ways park and recreation services influence the lives and overall well-being of individuals, communities, and society.

There are aspects of outcomes and impact measures that can be identified and demonstrated at both the individual and community levels. Outcome demonstration at the individual level involves focusing upon one participant at a time. While that individual may be participating as a member of a group, the results of his or her involvement needs to be examined for each person. This generally involves some measurement of the individual's starting point by identifying the preprogramming levels of knowledge, attitude, or behavior. The pre- and posttests associated with the Hearts N' Parks project were designed and delivered to secure exactly these types of individual changes.

Community-wide outcome measures are a second area where performance measures can be incorporated. These indicators can be both easier and more difficult to assess. Some of the data is already available, as it is mandated for collection by school or public health departments. The data can sometimes be difficult to access and that's where partnerships can become helpful. A secondary challenge relates to the multitude of forces that may or may not be influencing changes within a community, making it difficult to pinpoint the role that certain park and recreation programs or services made in positive change within the community. The efforts and results associated with park and recreation departments involved in *21st Century School* projects can serve as a model for such measurements.

Measuring outcomes does not demand a team of researchers being added to your staff. It does, however, require a shift in program and service intention, as well as additional focus on the part of staff delivering the programs and services being measured. Staff must be made aware of the potential contribution that they can make to individual health and livability. This awareness needs to be followed up with programming that is designed with the intention for health and livability built into existing activities, and then plans to measure the starting and ending impact upon participants need to be made.

Planning for and measuring outcomes had slow adoption rates among park and recreation agencies, but the trend is beginning to change. Much of the confusion is with the level of rigor required to actually document and demonstrate outcomes. Certainly, it takes attention in planning and a concerted commitment to utilize validated evaluation measures. What it doesn't require is scientific research or population wide studies. Start with one program or one population. Decide what impact is desired and determine how it can be measured. Turning the focus from documenting the process of delivery to seeking information that demonstrates the impact on the target audience is essential.

5th P: Performance Measure—Community Examples

The following example highlights successful approaches used by various community departments as they implemented this 5th P:

Westerville, OH, Parks and Recreation: FitQuest is a free fitness-based initiative including a children's component that and allows kids to track their daily fruit and vegetable consumption, water intake, physical activity, and screen time. Fitness assessments were provided to FitQuest program participants. FitQuest 2005 Successes include:

- 1,430+ registered participants
- Average weight loss equals 4.2 pounds
- Body fat decreased by 3.9%
- Resting heart rate decreased by 3% while resting systolic blood pressure decreased 9% and diastolic remained the same
- Local muscular endurance increased 8% for upper body and 16% for abdominals

Spaces

The most unheralded and unique value of parks and recreation systems are the places and spaces that create the essence of neighborhood and community livability. Identifying what differentiates the market position of public parks and recreation from all the other community service providers, public, nonprofit, or commercial relates to this unique asset that often undervalued. Park and recreation agencies represent the largest public asset for health and livability and, yet, leveraging this unique value to substantiate the role, responsibility, and value of public sector park and recreation systems has only recently been recognized.

Understanding how and why these public assets contribute to the sustainability of "community quality of life" and how they foster individual, family, and community life is fast becoming a priority. The five million dollar NRPA campaign entitled "Healthy Lifestyles, Livable Communities. It Starts In Parks!" differentiates the unique value proposition of parks as a requisite asset for attractive communities. *The Proximate Principle* by John Crompton of Texas A&M University[11] was published by NRPA and outlines the economic value of property values in relative proximity to public parks. The National Institute of Health and NRPA sponsored Hearts 'N Parks Field Study and recognized by the Cooper Institute for its gold standard to reduce obesity illuminated the unique capacity of parks and recreation to leverage its places, spaces, and programmatic resources to improve a societal condition, community by community, on a national scale.

While it may seem as if places and spaces to be physically active are located everywhere, the reality, as well as the perception of that reality, might not be the case. Not all places and spaces are designed with active recreation as a desired outcome and in some cases, these places and spaces are not operated in such a way to encourage or allow participation by all members of a community. Some of these places and spaces may not be safe to use, accessible by the entire community, or welcoming to people or perceived as such.

The overall desired, long-term outcome is increased participation among all members of the community in self-directed, lifelong active recreation pursuits within park spaces, trails, and recreation program settings that are well-designed, maintained, safe, accessible, and welcoming. Such efforts and documentation of these efforts can form the basis for establishing parks and recreation's role as an essential component of individual and community health.

6th P: Places and Spaces—Community Examples

The following example highlights successful approaches used by various community departments as they implemented this 6th P: Places and Spaces:

Rockville, MD, Community Walking Program: The Rockville Park & Recreation Department "Step Up to Health" community-wide walking program. Fourteen walking paths were designed around local schools, parks, neighborhoods, and businesses so residents can take advantage of fitness at their doorstep. The routes are 1 and 2 miles in length and are easy to follow with printed maps available online and at various city facilities. Residents are encouraged to keep track of their steps using a pedometer, and submit total steps each month to be counted as part of the city-wide Walk Rockville program. Participants also will be eligible for awards for the most steps walked. Neighborhood coordinators have been recruited to help coordinate walking groups within their respective neighborhoods and act as the point of contact to get information about the program out to neighbors.

Policies and Practices

Public policies and practices associated with park and recreation systems have traditionally focused on optimal management practices that impact operational effectiveness and efficiencies including issues such as risk reduction and overuse. Increasingly, public park and recreation systems and government in general have embraced inherent risks associated with serving the diverse segments of society. Facilities ranging from dog parks and BMX tracks to climbing walls and adventure water parks have proliferated since the early 1990s and policies have been developed to address the inherent risks associated with specialized activities.

As parks and recreation expands an emphasis on the health and wellness, the focus of policies and practices include a myriad of ways parks and recreation influence health behavior and environmental access within communities. Already, workforce policies, concession practices, and sponsorship criteria have come under greater scrutiny. If parks and recreation systems are to claim a mission to "enhance the quality of life of all people" then the field must be willing to transcend policies and practices that support management practice and embrace policies and practices that impact community life. The range of these practices is extensive and can include sunblock and shade structures for lifeguards to healthy snacks served at after-school programs. Promoting your agency as a health-focused institution, but executing a concession contract that doesn't require adequate choice for consumers to be healthy is not consistent. Saying a department is environmentally focused, but not instituting recycling practices is reflective of a system practicing one thing and saying their mission is another.

Small changes in practices and policies can begin to align an organization's operational requirements with a mission. Prudent public policy isn't always reflected in public ordinance, but in the management philosophy and operational intent of the park and recreation system.

Policies and practices begin at the highest level of intent and operation of the organization and can include the following:

- Broadest Overview of Agency Purpose—Vision and Mission
- General Directions—Major Policies
- Specific Directions—Minor Policies
- Operations—Rules and Regulations
- Day to Day Behavior—Practices

In the ensuing years, public park and recreation organizations will adopt or modify a substantial number of policies that support enhancing the quality of life for individuals and the community. It is essential that through major policies we "talk the talk" and that through the implementation of rules and regulations that we "walk the walk." These policies can range from relatively smaller initiatives such as regulations for vending machines to larger initiatives such as community workforce wellness.

7th P: Policies and Practices—Community Examples

The following examples highlight successful approaches used by various community departments as they implemented this 7th P: Policies and Practices:

Georgia Recreation and Park Association: GRPA adopted a health resolution regarding vending/concession foods and beverages. They've begun a 13-site pilot on Health Good Choices with GA Division of Public Health, Initiative on Nutrition and physical activity. Sites will be looking at different strategies to introduce healthier choices and educating the public. GRPA is also partnering with the Georgia Department of Human Resources, Chronic Disease section and Georgia Coalition for Physical Activity and Nutrition.

County of San Diego, CA, Department of Parks and Recreation: SDDPR Director signed the Vending Machines Content Policy, which specifies that 100% of the food and beverages sold in vending machines in youth-oriented facilities meet California School Nutrition Standards. All other vending machines are required to have 50% healthy choices. The policy served as a model for other local agencies and for the creation of a similar county-wide policy approved by the Board of Supervisors. SDDPR has also adopted the San Diego Nutrition Network's Meeting Well Policy which states that all meetings and events where food will be served, water and/or 100% fruit or vegetable juice, and fruits and/or vegetables will be available. In addition, there will be time for physical activity breaks.

Interrelatedness of the 7Ps

The 7 Ps of Step Up to Health and the other NRPA health initiatives were developed to serve as a framework for empowering departments to embark upon the process in an area they felt most comfortable or prepared. It is not the intent that departments should view or utilize the 7 Ps in isolation from one another. In fact, it is virtually impossible to do so.

The "Chicago Moves Day," an annual celebration focused upon getting city residents up and moving represents the inter-relatedness of the 7Ps as follows:

- It focused on internal staff as a specific effort was made to encourage city employees to participate in the Mayors Fitness Council Challenge, a six-week active lifestyle program to help Chicagoans make a commitment to getting active and forming a new healthy habit.
- It included a variety of partnerships including the Illinois Governor's Office offering a walk as part of the State's Walk Across Illinois program.
- The celebration brought program opportunities to residents The Chicago Park District and Bally Total Fitness are taking the lead by providing a multitude of resources to promote, educate and motivate all participants as Bally Total Fitness offered free access to all of its health club locations for six weeks and The Chicago Park district offered one free week of fitness classes and access to their 42 fitness centers.

A County-Wide Activity Resource, an endeavor of the *Wausau and Marathon County (WI) Parks, Recreation & Forestry Department* designed to assist families in more easily finding active recreation opportunities for youth and adults. This resource includes contact information for all sports and active recreation associations, maps to trails and parks, sports camps, and agencies that offer health and fitness programs for the public is another solid example of the inter-relatedness of the 7Ps. Evidence of inter-relatedness includes the following:

- This endeavor did not happen without the involvement and support of partners including HEAL (Healthy Eating, Active Living Coalition of Marathon County), Aging and Disability Resource Center, Aspirus Hospital, CARE Foundation, Marathon County Health Department, Marshfield Clinic, University Hospital Family Practice Clinic, Wausau School District, D.C. Everest School District, and the Newman Catholic School District. The extent and success of the partnerships led to the project being funded by a grant from Wisconsin Partnership Fund. The total grant fund is $450,000, of which approximately $20,000 will go to help defray the costs of producing the resource guide and will also be used to plan an incentive-based activity challenge for families called the Active Family Challenge.
- Performance measures and indicators round out the Ps framework of this endeavor by measuring the increased number of children who walk or ride their bikes to school through Safe Routes to Schools; conducting nine School Health Index studies at area elementary schools following up on an earlier study of 2nd, 4th, 6th and 8th graders to review their current body mass index numbers and blood glucose levels as compared with those numbers measured two years ago.
- Naturally, public visibility is just naturally attracted to this type of effort. The daily newspaper has covered their efforts as well as the local CBS affiliate TV station and in a weekly alternative paper. Wausau and Marathon County Parks, Recreation and Forestry are currently working with the daily paper to track two families through the Active Family Challenge!

Springfield-Greene (MO) County Park Board demonstrates not only the inter-relatedness of the 7Ps, but the extent to which this framework can extend the values and benefits of parks and recreation through an entire community. The following is an excerpt from their Vision 20/20 Plan.

A. Neighborhood Access Policy

GOAL — Working with the neighborhood associations, modify the Vision 20/20 Plan to ensure that at least four major neighborhoods have the facilities necessary to support regular and convenient physical activity and easy access to nutritious foods.

STEPS —

- Potential partners: Ozarks Transportation Organization, Ozark Greenways, City Planning, Vision 20/20 Board, University of Missouri Extension Office, Master Gardeners
- Research city policy regarding sidewalks by December 31, 2006.

- Working with neighborhood associations, assess sidewalk needs in the Springfield city limits by December 31, 2007.
- Prepare report on sidewalk needs and present to City of Springfield by December 31, 2008.
- Working with Vision 20/20 board, modify transportation plan to mandate progressive completion of sidewalk connections within neighborhoods by December 31, 2009.
- Research community gardens/co-ops that have been successful in other communities by December 31, 2006.
- Prepare a report on the steps needed to successfully implement a community garden by December 31, 2007.
- Working with Vision 20/20 board and Master Gardeners, modify plan to include the implementation of at least four community gardens by December 31, 2010.

B. School Policy

GOAL — Achieve active participation of Hearts 'N Parks Coalition members on Springfield Public Schools (SPS) Wellness Committee to improve variety of nutritious meals and snacks available by December 31, 2010.

STEPS —

- Potential partners: Springfield Public Schools
- Obtain (or research and prepare) a report analyzing current *scientific data on childhood obesity* and changing dietary intake of youth ages 5-17 over the past two decades by December 31, 2006.

C. Work Policy

GOAL — Encourage at least 5% of employers in the Springfield to implement a wellness policy and/or program for employees by December 31, 2010.

STEPS —

- Potential partners: Springfield Chamber of Commerce, Springfield's Best
- Research low-cost, effective strategies that can be used by small businesses (less than 30 employees) to improve the health of employees. Prepare a report/presentation that can be given to small businesses by June 30, 2006.
- Survey at least 30% of small business in Springfield for interest in report by December 31, 2007.
- Present the report to at least 20% of small businesses in Springfield by December 31, 2008.
- At least 5% of small businesses in Springfield will sign implement a wellness policy and/or program by December 31, 2010.
- Work with Ozark Greenways and city utilities to increase Bike to Work Week participation to:
- 150 participants or 2,600 driving miles saved by May 2006;
- 200 participants or 2,800 driving miles saved by May 2007;
- 250 participants or 3,000 driving miles saved by May 2008;
- 300 participants or 3,200 driving miles saved by May 2009; and
- 350 participants or 3,400 driving miles saved by May 2010.

Conclusion

As the first decade of the 21st century stretches toward the next, America is challenged to tackle the consequences of issues such as global warming, energy dependence, and sedentary lifestyles. The increasing demand for limited natural resources and the burdens associated with the obesity epidemic have become a rally point for communities, states, and national organizations to view public health and the built environment holistically. The social, physical, environmental, and economic benefits of public parks and recreation will continue to impact the social imperatives identified under the umbrella of healthy lifestyles and livable communities. The role of the National Recreation and Park Association is aligned well for leadership in advancing the benefits-based strategies that engage citizen stewardship, improve professional practice and advance the relevant work of the field.

Literature Cited

Driver, B., Brown, P., & Peterson, G. (1991). *Benefits of leisure.* State College, PA. Venture Publishing, Inc.

Parks and Recreation Federation of Ontario. (1992). *The benefits of parks and recreation: A catalogue.* Ottowa, ON: Ontario Ministry of Tourism and Recreation.

Godbey, G. and Graefe, A. (1992). *Benefits of Parks and Recreation.* Ashburn, VA. National Recreation and Park Association.

O'Sullivan, E. (1996). *The benefits movement: Putting the pieces together.* Ashburn, VA. National Recreation and Park Association.

O'Sullivan, E. (1999). *Setting a course for change.* Ashburn, VA. National Recreation and Park Association.

Crompton, J. (1999). *Measuring Economic Impact of Visitors to Sports Events and Special Events.* Ashburn, VA. National Recreation and Park Association.

Crompton, J. (2000). *The Impact of Parks and Open Space on Property Values and the Property Tax Base.* Ashburn, VA. National Recreation and Park Association.

Luepker, R. V., Perry, C. L., McKinlay, S. M., Nader, P. R., Parcel, G. S., Stone, E. J., Webber, L. S., Elder, J. P., Feldman, H. A., Johnson, C. C., Kelder, S. H., & Wu, M. (1996). Outcomes of a field trial to improve children's dietary patterns and physical activity. The Child and Adolescent Trial for Cardiovascular Health (CATCH). *Journal of the American Medical Association, 275,* 768–776.

National Heart, Lung and Blood Institute. (2001). *Hearts N' Parks: Community Mobilization Guide.* Bethesda, MD: National Institutes of Health.

Crompton, J. (2002). *The proximate principle.* Ashburn, VA. National Recreation and Park Association.

Chapter 23
Developing Recreation Opportunities that Promote Youth Development

Teresa W. Tucker and Lawrence R. Allen

Learning Objectives:

1. Understand how recreation and leisure experiences are a critical vehicle for youth development.
2. Understand basic principles, goals, and programming tenets of youth development.
3. Recognize the connection between youth development programming and outcome-focused programming (OFP).

Introduction

This chapter explores the relationship between OFP and youth development. In Chapter 4, the implementation of OFM for municipal parks and recreation agencies was outlined with an emphasis on the development of OFP.[1] OFP focuses on the process of developing intentional and purposeful programs within municipal parks and recreation agencies. It should be mentioned here that the editor of this text and the coauthor of this chapter have heard that some professional associates have problems with using the word "programming" of opportunities to realize particular benefits of leisure. They do, because they fear it will limit free choice and spontaneity and thereby constrain those two fundament dimensions of leisure behavior. But, it must be understood that the word "programming" is not used here in an authoritative manner, but only to reflect that many recreation programs are created and structured to accomplish predefined objectives (e.g., dance lessons are programmed to transmit dancing skills, nature interpretation programs are structured to enhance learning about nature, etc.) Furthermore, no such programs should be implemented by a public park and recreation agency without the approval of, and close collaboration with, the relevant constituents.

The steps for implementing OFP in municipalities were outlined in Chapter 4 of this text as follows:

- Step 1: Identify Target Issues and Outcomes
- Step 2: Develop Programs to Specifically Address Outcomes
- Step 3: Measure Program Goals and Outcomes
- Step 4: Realize Impacts and Communicate Successes

Typically programs developed within the recreation and leisure service profession, particularly in municipal parks and recreation agencies, target specific age groups and/or demographics. In fact, the need to develop programming for youth was a driving force behind the development of the recreation and leisure service profession in the United States. Programming for youth continues to be a major area of focus for the majority of park and recreation agencies. Since the early 1990s, "youth development" has been the buzzword not only among recreation and leisure service professionals but public school educators and administrators as well. Youth development is "a process which prepares young people to meet the challenges of adolescence and adulthood through a coordinated, progressive series of activities and experiences which help them to become *socially, morally, emotionally, physically, and cognitively competent* "(National Collaboration for Youth, 1998).

This chapter will briefly examine the evolution of the recreation and leisure service profession as it pertains to youth, and it will delve more fully into the specific aspects of youth development. Furthermore, the major thrust of this chapter will focus on the role of recreation and leisure on youth development while paying particular attention to the relationship to OFP.

Recreation and Youth Development: Brief History

To fully understand the relationship between youth development and the recreation and leisure service profession, it is important to gain a historical perspective. The intent of this section is to provide a brief synopsis of the influences, ideas, and events that have led to the current state of youth development, especially in the area of programming, within the recreation and leisure service profession.

The birth of the recreation and leisure service profession in the United States dates back to the Industrial Revolution in the 19th century. With the onset of the Industrial Revolution masses of people migrated from the countryside to work in the cities, consequently bringing about horrendous working and living conditions for both children and adults (Kraus, 1998). Around the turn of the century, with the advent of child labor laws and public education, children were no longer working long hours in the factories, thus allowing them more free time. Reformers such as Jane Addams, Joseph Lee, and Luther Halsey Gulick became greatly concerned about the living conditions of the poor, including the discretionary time experiences of the youth (Kraus, 1998). They, along with others, wanted to ensure that children were not only staying out of trouble in their free time but also that they were participating in enriching and wholesome recreation and leisure. Eventually these pioneer reformers would form the American Playground Association, with the purposes of providing youth opportunities for development through organized recreation, preventing delinquency, and indoctrinating youth, particularly immigrant children, into the socially acceptable American way of life (Kraus, 1998). The American Playground Association was one of several agencies that evolved into today's National Recreation and Park Association (Kraus, 1998).

Along with the creation of the American Playground Association, other organizations, such as the YMCA, Boy & Girl Scouts, American Camp Association (ACA), Campfire, etc. were also formed around the beginning of the 20th century to address and meet the recreational and social needs of children and youth (Kraus, 1998). These organizations, both voluntary and professional, viewed purposive recreation and leisure experiences as a vehicle to build character and to enrich the lives of children and youth. Basically, from 1890–1916, issues and concerns about the development and quality of life for children and youth became the central driving force behind the emergence of recreation and leisure services as a profession (Henderson, Bialescheki, Hemingway, Hodges, Kivel, & Sessoms, 2001). This focus continued up to and included the era immediately preceding World War II. There was a concentrated effort on the part of recreation and leisure service agencies and departments to keep young people out of trouble, to prevent antisocial behavior, and to devise constructive ways to occupy their free time (Henderson et al., 2001).

Following the end of World War II, the focus of recreation and leisure programs and services changed. The developmental and preventative role of these services was replaced by more of an orientation to diversionary activities and activities engaged in for the sheer fun and enjoyment of the participants (Kraus, 1998). Not that the human and social development focus was totally lost, but it certainly was not emphasized as it had been during the late 19th and early 20th centuries. Times were good, prosperity abounded, and children and adults were experiencing the good life.

Circumstances changed during the latter part of the 20th century. The world was shifting. Family structure was being challenged, community support systems were waning, the small school atmosphere was being lost, and mass media was exposing us all to lifestyles and behaviors that were rarely talked about or seen in open forums (Eccles & Gootman, 2002). Generally, the world became much more dynamic and complex. During the 1980s, policymakers, educators, recreation professionals, among others, became increasingly concerned about how young people would be able to meet the challenges of this rapidly changing and more complex world. As stated in the National Research Council's project on youth development, "The future well-being of the country depends on raising a generation of skilled, competent, and responsible adults" (Eccles & Gootman, 2002, p. 2). Thus, a conceptual framework for community programs evolved under the heading of positive youth development. This framework also embraced the role of recreation and leisure experiences in promoting positive youth development. In the next section, the basic tenets of youth development are explained.

Youth Development

As stated, American society was rapidly changing in the latter part of the 20th century, and continues to do so today. Factors such as both parents working outside the home, increased exposure to violence and drugs through the media, the disappearance of the "neighborhood," increased rates of crime and poverty, etc. contributed to a decline of the social and moral community network for youth (Eccles & Gootman, 2002). The concept of positive youth development emerged as society became increasingly concerned about youth being capable to successfully navigate the path and expectations of becoming moral and productive citizens.

During this time, programs were evolving that looked at youth through a lens that suggested all youth had assets, regardless of the problems or behaviors they brought with them. One organization, the Search Institute, proposed the concept of developmental assets that should be cultivated in youth in order to facilitate their transition into adulthood. These assets (initially 40) were in the domains of physical, intellectual, emotional, and social development (Hamilton & Hamilton, 2004). At one point, the YMCA had these assets listed on the back of the T-shirts worn by participants in their youth sports program.

Additionally during this time period, extensive research on the issue of resiliency for "at-risk" youth contributed greatly to the advancement of positive youth development. Researchers and communities began to realize that youth needed programs and services that went beyond intervention, prevention, and elimination of problems and focused more on the acquisition of "skills, knowledge, and a variety of other personal and social assets to function well in today's society" (Eccles & Gootman, 2002).

Many researchers started to identify and clarify some overarching principles that are critical for positive youth development to take place. Some of the principles that have evolved include the following:

- All youth need support, opportunities and encouragement.
- All youth have assets and skills that can and need to be developed.
- Focus on strengths rather than deficits.
- Every young person has the potential for successful, healthy development.
- Engage young people as participants, not merely recipients (Hamilton & Hamilton, 2004).

Another perspective on these youth development principles would be to apply the ABCD acronym:

- Agency—acting or exerting influence and power in a given situation; the developing person's active involvement in shaping the process of development, i.e., youth voice, participation, empowerment (Hamilton & Hamilton, 2004)
- Belonging—developing meaningful relationships with peers & adults
- Competence—developing new abilities and being appreciated for one's talents
- Diversity/cultural competence—breaking down barriers and realizing youth had more in common with people they once considered "different" (Mitra, Sanders, Movit, & Perkins et al., 2007)

Although these principles tend to be thought of in isolation from one another, the most effective means of ensuring positive youth development occurs when there exists a "synergy" or simultaneous interconnectedness of all of these principles (Mitra et al., 2007).

A key phrase evolved out of the work and research of the late 20th century and early 21st century: "problem free, fully prepared, and fully engaged" (Pittman, 2000). Clearly, being free from problems is important for youth, but it is not sufficient for a successful transition through adolescence and into adulthood. They also need to be fully prepared to take on the responsibilities associated with adulthood. They need to learn new skills and possess new knowledge that allows them to be productive, satisfied and happy adults. Further, being a contributing member of society suggests that they must be fully engaged with their local affairs and communities (Villarruel, Perkins, Borden, Keith, 2003). This suggests an expanded base of knowledge and skills as well as the development of an attitude of citizenship and "giving back." Again, these are experiences and assets that may need to be taught to these young citizens.

As the concept of youth development continued to evolved, it became clear that,

> "All adolescents, in all economic and social circumstances, need generous amounts of help, instruction, discipline, support, and caring as they make their way from childhood through adolescence and into adulthood. Such assistance comes from many sources: solid families, good schools, supportive and safe neighborhoods, and a surrounding culture that emphasizes constructive lives and respective relationships." (Eccles & Gootman, 2002, p. 19).

The focus has now shifted from the individual to a more community perspective and involves all youth, not just those considered "at-risk."

The bringing together of the individual, family, school, neighborhood, community, and youth professionals to support, facilitate, and provide youth with positive experiences and opportunities is the foundation of community youth development.

> "Community youth development is defined as purposely creating environments that provide constructive, affirmative, and encouraging relationships that are sustained over time with adults and peers, while concurrently providing an array of opportunities that enable youth to build their competencies and become engaged

> as partners in their own development as well as the development of their communities" (Villarruel et al., 2003, p. 6).

With community youth development, youth do not merely have a voice but are considered partners throughout the process.

In establishing the goals of youth development, it is important to consider that positive youth development is more about the process and progress than it is about attaining a definitive, measurable goal (Hamilton & Hamilton, 2004). However, the establishment of goals is an integral part of the program planning process. Since goals and methods for youth development are closely intertwined, the goals listed below are broad enough that they can provide a framework to guide action and programming (Hamilton & Hamilton, 2004).

Developmental Goals of Youth Development—Six "C"s

- Competence—academic, social, emotional, physical, vocational; knowledge and skills that enable a person to function more effectively to understand and act on the environment (intentions and adaptability)
- Confidence—identity development; assuredness a person needs to act effectively; demonstrate and build competence and character in challenging situations
- Connections—building relationships; social relations with adults, peers, and younger children
- Character—positive values, integrity; what makes a person intend to do what is just, right, and good
- Caring and Compassion
- Contribution—social responsibility; service to others; make a difference

Based on these goals and the principles of youth development, programs that contribute to positive youth development should contain the following characteristics:

- Engage youth in the program development
- Define clear focus and direction
- Encourage positive adult relationships
- Create reflective learning opportunities-experiences that engage them to think of who they are!
- Give opportunities to build skills and competencies—especially as they get older
- Provide a variety of experiences and activities that address multiple interests and learning styles

There is a great deal more to youth development than is presented in this chapter. This section was designed to provide some basic tenets of youth development with programming implications. In this next section, the role and significance of recreation and leisure to youth development will be explored.

Power of Recreation and Leisure Contexts for Youth Development

Due to the influence of the Puritan work ethic in this country, people often assume that recreation and leisure are frivolous, secondary, and expendable. However, the power of recreation and leisure contexts for youth development cannot be underestimated. For the last 100 years or so, recreation and leisure services have provided a significant social service. Since the turn of the 20th century, recreation and leisure services have centered on being concerned about the quality of life, as well as attempting to address the social and educational needs of all people, but especially children and youth (Henderson et al., 2001).

Recreation is an important aspect of human development. Research has shown that recreation and leisure provide a significant context for youth to develop and form their identity, and there are thus considered positive development assets (Henderson et al., 2001). Recreation and leisure are also a means for youth to actively engage with their environment, which is paramount for positive youth development. The perpetual challenge for professionals in the recreation and leisure profession and other youth development professions is to create engaging and enriching environments that foster the goals of youth development (Hamilton & Hamilton, 2004).

In line with the significance of healthy relationships and developing competencies through challenging activities to facilitate youth development, recreation and leisure can assist youth with their development of essential life skills and in the provision of supportive environments for their transition into adulthood (Henderson et al., 2001).

> "Recreation promotes healthy growth with joy, enthusiasm, and a sense of intense commitment and pleasure that reinforces learning and involvement. And society benefits when children and youth have experiences that promote their physical health, social competence, emotional

well-being, and intellectual growth" (Kraus, 1998, p. 139).

Youth development and recreation seem to go hand-in-hand on many levels. The next section will delve more fully into the relationship between OFP and youth development.

OFP and Positive Youth Development

The evolution of positive youth development as a conceptual framework for programming has brought about shifts at the management and programmatic level within park and recreation departments. Initially, with regards to youth programming, the mission of parks and recreation departments was somewhat limited in that it focused on keeping kids safe, off the streets, and out of trouble through fun activities. Most purposive programming targeted youth who were considered "at-risk." Nowadays, however, park and recreation departments are taking a more comprehensive approach to youth programming by implementing programs that build individual and community assets, reduce risky behaviors, and promote resiliency (Witt & Compton, 2002).

Park and recreation departments, as well as other recreation and leisure agencies that are invested in youth development are going well beyond diversionary programming to recognize the importance of purposive programming. Positive youth development does not just happen because of good programming but because the programming is intentional in addressing the goals and principles of youth development. OFP provides a purposeful programming approach that can be utilized for all recreation and leisure programs and services, thereby promoting positive youth development.

Listed here are several examples of how parks and recreation departments and other agencies serving youth have embraced both OFP and community youth development:

> The Youth Master Plan, in Claremont, California, under their parks and recreation department, is an example of this shift to the development of community youth development. Developed in 1995 and under revision in 2006–2007, the Youth Master Plan is considering "incorporating a whole youth developmental framework that features a focus on the family, school and neighborhood quality of life to assist Claremont in strategically planning for supportive services through an evidenced based measurement tool" (http://www.ympupdate.com/).

On the website of the parks and recreation department of Hampton, Virginia, there is information about the Young Planners. Since 1997, the Young Planners program includes teens in city planning. Two teens serve in a part-time capacity "overseeing the youth component of the city's comprehensive plan." A unique aspect of this program is that these youth have an official voice in city government. These Young Planners focus on the issues of youth space, transportation, employment, and caring relationships. They also "conduct research, interviews, surveys, etc., and then deliver the results to relevant city agencies (the school board, department of transportation, parks/recreation, and so forth)" (http://www.pps.org/tcb/youth_planners.htm).

The parks and recreation department of Austin, Texas offers The Neighborhood Teen Program. As stated on their website,

> "Although the basis for this program is recreational by nature, the Neighborhood Teen Program addresses the issues affecting teens, their community, and their environment with understanding and sensitivity. The program is designed to keep the teens off the streets and in a structured environment where they can learn to become contributing members of the Austin community by discouraging gang participation and substance abuse while emphasizing school and recreation. The overall goal of NTP is to aid and enhance the quality of life for the teens of Austin by providing relevant, diversified, educational, and recreational programs and services within a safe and positive learning environment" (http://www.ci.austin.tx.us/parks/ntp.htm).

Another illustration of this shift has occurred with the Girl Scouts of the USA. In 2003, under the leadership of its CEO and National Board, the mission of the GSUSA was revised to state, "Girl Scouting builds girls of courage, confidence, and character, who make the world a better place." GSUSA's mission reflects principles of positive youth development. The values of empowerment and girl-centric are still at the forefront for GSUSA. Nothing makes that more apparent than the creation of their new personal growth/leadership program. The key concepts of this model include:

- Discover—knowing oneself
- Connect—reaching out to others
- Take Action—making a difference in the world

The CEO stated, "Everything we do as a Girl Scout organization needs to connect to leadership...and how we make a difference in the world through the work we do." (Girl Scouts of the USA, n.d.).

Furthermore, youth are becoming more actively engaged in the planning and initiation of programs at park and recreation departments with the support from professionals and other adults, as opposed to programs being planned and implemented entirely by professional leaders (Hamilton & Hamilton, 2004). The role of recreation and leisure staff is shifting from being the "leader" or "director" to being a facilitator and/or mentors for youth who are running the programs.

For example, the park and recreation department of Raleigh, North Carolina, offers a number of teen programs such as the Teen Youth Council, Alternative Spring Break, and Domino Day that "provide opportunities for youth to create, plan, and implement programs, and to design and develop projects and special events that will be of benefit to their peers, the community, and to themselves as individuals." Specifically the Raleigh Youth Council is teen-driven and designed with an emphasis on civic engagement, leadership opportunities, community service, recreation, and fundraising. "The Raleigh Youth Council creates a forum where teens can freely express their ideas and opinions and serve as advocates for teens in Wake County" (http://www.raleigh-nc.org/portal/server.pt/gateway/PTARGS_0_0_306_204_0_43/http;/pt03/dig_web_content/dept/public/Dept-AboutUs-ParksnRec.html). This department emulates key aspects of community youth development.

The evaluation process for programs has also been affected by this shift in parks and recreation departments that embraces youth development. Prior to this shift, the evaluation process focused primarily on attendance, service quality, and satisfaction measures. Now, however, the focus has become evaluating outcomes such as increased protective factors or developmental assets, or reductions in risk behaviors (Witt & Compton, 2002, p. 32; Hamilton & Hamilton, 2004).

The challenge for recreation and leisure departments and organizations is to gather evidence that articulates the social value and outcomes of organized recreation. It is not merely enough to gather evidence but make this evidence known to the policymakers, community stakeholders, participants, staff, and general public so that they all are aware of how recreation can contribute to the betterment of society. The concept described in the shift in the recreation and leisure profession aligns with OFP.

As mentioned at the beginning of this chapter, Chapter 4 describes the steps of implementing OFP. They are repeated here to guide the following discussion of the congruency between the steps of OFP and positive youth development.

- Step 1: Identify Target Issues and Outcomes
- Step 2: Develop Programs to Specifically Address Outcomes
- Step 3: Measure Program Goals and Outcomes
- Step 4: Realize Impacts and Communicate Successes

Step 1: Identify Target Issues and Outcomes

Identifying target issues and outcomes is essential for creating effective youth development programs through recreation. Target issues that have significance on the part of key stakeholders are essential for continued public support. There are many key issues relating to youth, including substance abuse, violence, crime, lack of citizenship, etc. Specific outcomes addressing these target issues can then be developed using recreation experiences as the medium for accomplishing these outcomes. By identifying these outcomes, youth development programs become intentional and structured so as to enhance the capacity of individuals as they look to the future (Hamilton & Hamilton, 2004). Intentionality is a key phrase in establishing outcome-focused programs. It suggests that youth development and recreation programmers move beyond the obvious outcomes related to recreation experiences such as skills development to the building of specific attitudes, skills, values, and knowledge (Edginton, Kowalski, & Randall, 2005) related to the target issues being addressed through the recreation experience.

Important features of this type of programming (Hamilton & Hamilton, 2004) suggest that the programs should:

- Be clearly focused with specific outcomes defined.
- Be youth centered.
- Have an embedded curriculum. This refers to the intentional development of skills attitudes, dispositions and aptitudes beyond the obvious direct skills development of the experience.
- Engage caring community partners that can reinforce and support the skills, dispositions, and attitudes being developed through the programs and experiences.

- Involve cycles of planning, practice, and performance that enable youth to make small steps toward reaching future goals.

Step 2: Develop Programs to Specifically Address Outcomes

As stated earlier in Chapter 4, the provision and development of programs is the cornerstone of what parks and recreation departments, along with other youth-focused recreation agencies, do. Within the framework of OFP it is important to grasp the following:

- Recreation Programming Fundamental Guidelines
- Outcome-Based Programming Concepts
- Program Identification and Activity Analysis
- Program Structure and Daily Outcome Objectives
- Processing the Recreation Experience
- Monitoring of Programs

It cannot be understated that when utilizing an OFP approach to programming the concepts of accomplishment, encouragement, high expectations, recognition, and a support system are to be incorporated into every recreation experience.

Specific to the promotion of positive youth development, the following guidelines should serve as the foundation for youth development programming (Edginton, Kowalski, & Randall, 2005):

- experiences within a physically and psychologically safe environment
- structure that is developmentally appropriate
- opportunities for adolescents to experience supportive adult relationships
- opportunities to learn how to form close, durable, and positive human relationships
- opportunities to feel a sense of belonging and have meaningful involvement in family, school, and community
- opportunities to develop a sense of individualism, identity, and self-definition
- opportunities for skill building, mastery, and creative expression
- opportunities to develop confidence in one's abilities to master one's environment (sense of personal self-efficacy)
- opportunities to make a contribution to one's community and to develop a sense of mattering and self-worth.
- opportunities to develop a sense of independence, autonomy, and control
- strong links between families, schools, and broader community resources in decision making; opportunities for leadership and involvement in community

Although every youth development program might not contain every one of these guidelines, the incorporation and inclusion of as many of these as possible greatly impacts a program's ability to promote positive youth development. Under OFP, the development of programs to address outcomes complements established programming guidelines for positive youth development. In order to ascertain the impact of a youth development program, the next step is to measure and evaluate the goals and outcomes of that specific program.

Step 3: Measure Program Goals and Outcomes

For youth development as well as for OFP, it is not just important to provide and develop programs targeting specific outcomes; there must be a systematic process for evaluating whether a program is actually addressing its designated outcomes. In alignment with OFP, evaluation for youth development programs is essential. According to the Committee on Community-Level Program for Youth established by the Board on Children, Youth, & Families and the Committee on Adolescent Health and Development (2002), evaluation in youth development can:

- inform program design, selection, and modification
- assist organizations in making informed decisions about which programs to fund
- guide staff in clarifying objectives
- improve design and delivery of programs

Furthermore, based on their extensive research in the field of youth development, the Committee recommended that "all community programs for youth should undergo evaluation-possibly multiple evaluations-to improve design and implementation, to create accountability, and to access outcomes and impacts. For any given evaluation, the scope and rigor should be appropriately calibrated to the attributes of the program, the available resources, and the goals of the evaluation" (Eccles & Gootman, 2002, p. 16).

For example, the American Camp Association has written a series of publications based on their research about the impact of the organized camp experience on outcomes of youth development. As stated on their website, "The value of the camp experience in the positive development of our young people has been a focus of ACA research for the past several years. The information collected from over 100 camps and thousands of campers has become the foundation for two new resources. These resources, Creating Positive Youth Outcomes and the Youth Camp Outcomes Questionnaires, help camps focus on how to reach desired outcomes and offer tools to help measure outcome levels." These outcomes include:

- Friendship Skills (i.e., make friends and maintain relationships)
- Independence (i.e., rely less on adults and other people for solving problems and for their day-to-day activities)
- Teamwork (i.e., become more effective when working in groups of their peers)
- Family Citizenship (i.e., encourage attributes important to being a member of a family)
- Perceived Competence (i.e., believe that they can be successful in the things they do)
- Interest in Exploration (i.e., be more curious, inquisitive, eager to learn new things)
- Responsibility (i.e., learn to be accountable for their own actions and mistakes)

Not only have they extensively researched and evaluated the camp experience as it relates to youth development, but they have used this research to develop tools for camps to evaluate their own programs.

Again, the Youth Master Plan of Claremont, CA, through its Evaluation Plan Process, provides another example of the presence of a comprehensive evaluation model for youth development. In partnership with Evaluation Consultants, the city has been developing and implementing both qualitative and quantitative measurement tools to measure quality of life within a community-based model. This effort will provide "outcome based models that will inform governing bodies on youth and family strengths and areas where continued supportive services are needed to ensure optimal community development, planned program growth and direction along with ensuring public safety for the present and future will influence the evaluative component design." (http://www.ympupdate.com/)

Evaluating outcomes is an integral part of positive youth development. However, the power of the evaluation process crystallizes when the results of this process are shared with others.

Step 4: Realize Impacts and Communicate Successes

To reiterate from Chapter 4, realizing the impacts of recreation programs and communicating successes to include a wide variety of audiences is an important final step in the implementation of outcome-focused management and programming as well as positive youth development. Publications by the American Camp Association such as *Inspirations,* which features research relating to the Developmental Supports and Opportunities of Youths' Experiences at Camp, and *Innovations,* which relates to the Program Improvement Project (PIP), are just two examples. The Girl Scouts of the United States, on both a council and national level, in their annual reports publish the results of how positive youth development outcomes are being met and addressed through their programs. Many parks and recreation departments are now developing annual reports and other publications that clearly document the changes in participants' attitudes, behaviors, or skills as a result of their involvement with recreation experiences. These reports are much more meaningful than merely listing the number and types of programs and the number of participants.

In conclusion, OFP in municipal parks and recreation departments and other youth-focused recreation and leisure service organizations have embraced a youth development conceptual framework and its principles, thereby perpetuating, encouraging, and enhancing positive youth development within communities. Although recreation plays a significant role in positive youth development, collaboration with other organizations, stakeholders, community agencies, schools, etc. is essential. Positive youth development is not a recreation issue, an agency issue, or a school issue; it is a community and nationwide issue.

> "Even with the best staff and best funding, no one single program can necessarily serve all young people or incorporate all of the features of positive developmental settings. The complexities of adolescent development & the increasing diversity of the country make the heterogeneity of young people in communities both a norm and a challenge. Therefore, effective programs must be flexible enough to adapt to this diversity among the young people they serve and the communities in which they operate." (Eccles & Gootman, 2002, p. 11)

Literature Cited

American Camp Association. (2007). ACA Youth Development Outcomes Research. Retrieved May 27, 2007 from http://www.acacamps.org/research/youthoutcomes.php

Austin, TX Park & Recreation Dept. (n.d.) Neighborhood Teen Program. Retrieved June 10, 2007 from http://www.ci.austin.tx.us/parks/ntp.htm

Claremont, CA Parks & Recreation Dept. (2006). Youth Master Plan. Retrieved June 10, 2007 from http://www.ympupdate.com/

Eccles, J. & Gootman, J. A. (Eds.). (2002). Community programs to promote youth development. National Academy Press: Washington, D.C.

Edginton, C. R., Kowalski, C. L., & Randall, S. W. (2005). *Youth work: Emerging perspectives in youth development.* Sagamore Publishing: Champaign, IL.

Girl Scouts of the USA. (2006). Core Business Strategy: Gap Teams. Retrieved Nov. 30, 2006, from http://www.girlscouts.org/strategy/gap_team.asp

Hamilton, S. F., & Hamilton, M. A. (Eds.). (2004). *The youth development handbook: Coming of age in American communities.* Thousand Oaks, CA: Sage Publications, Inc.

Hampton, VA Parks & Recreation Dept. (n.d.) Youth Planners. Retrieved June 10, 2007 from http://www.pps.org/tcb/youth_planners.htm

Henderson, K. A., Bialescheki, M. D., Hemingway, J. L., Hodges, J. S., Kivel, B. D., & Sessoms, H. D. (2001). *Introduction to recreation and leisure services.* (8th ed). State College, PA: Venture Publishing, Inc.

Kraus, R. (1998). Recreation & leisure in modern society. (5th ed.). Jones and Bartlett Publishers, Inc.: Boston, MA.

Mitra, D. L., Sanders, F. C., Movit, M. M., & Perkins, D. F. (2007, April) *Examining ways in which youth conferences can spell out gains in community development and engagement.* Paper presented at the annual conference of the American Educational Research Association, Chicago, IL.

Pittman, K. J. (2000, March). Grantmaker strategies for assessing the quality of unevaluated programs and the impact of unevaluated grantmaking. (Speech presented at Evaluations of Youth Programs symposium at the Biennial Meeting of the Society for Research on Adolescsnce, Chicago).

Raleigh, NC Parks & Recreation Dept. (n.d.) Teen Programs. Retrieved June 10, 2007 from http://www.raleigh-nc.org/portal/server.pt/gateway/PTARGS_0_0_306_209_0_43/http;/pt03/DIG_Web_Content/category/Leisure/Activities/Teen_Program/Cat-Index.html

Villarruel, F. A., Perkins, D. F., Borden, L. M., & Keith, J. G. (Eds.). (2003). *Community youth development: Programs, policies, and practices.* Thousand Oaks, CA: Sage Publications, Inc.

Witt, P. A., & Crompton, J. L. (2002). Best practices in youth development in public park and recreation settings. Ashburn, VA: National Recreation and Park Association.

Footnotes

1. In Chapter 1 of this text, the Outcomes-Focused Paragon (the umbrella paradigm which includes OFM) was also referred to as OFP.

Chapter 24
Application of EFM and OFM to Fisheries and Wildlife Management

David C. Fulton, Michael J. Manfredo, and Dorothy H. Anderson

Learning Objectives

1. Understand the history of research in experienced-focused and outcomes-focused management related to fisheries and wildlife management.
2. Appreciate why the barriers to implementing EFM/OFM are different in fish and wildlife management agencies than in other agency contexts.
3. Understand strategies for integrating OFM into existing management efforts within fish and wildlife management agencies

Purpose of the Chapter

The purpose of this chapter is to examine attempts at implementing experience-based and outcomes-focused management in the context of wildlife management. The particular focus of the chapter is on efforts directed at wildlife-based recreation, but we argue that OFM is an appropriate framework for wildlife management in general and not just the management of wildlife-based recreation. To this end, we examine how an outcomes-focused approach can be used as a broader planning framework to manage wildlife, fisheries and related resources for recreational and nonrecreational outcomes.

Introduction

In this chapter we briefly summarize the breadth of literature from the Experienced-Focused Management tradition that has been directed at managing wildlife-based recreation--hunting, fishing and wildlife viewing. In addition we will examine the extent to which EFM and OFM ideas have been adopted by fish and wildlife management agencies, and potential barriers to OFM adoption by these agencies. Finally, we explore the use of OFM as a general framework for fisheries and wildlife management.

As described in earlier chapters, the motivations and experiences desired by people from interacting with amenity resources is at the foundation of the production process for OFM. By the 1970s, the developers of Experienced-Based Management (Driver and Brown 1975; Brown et al., 1977) and other researchers (Potter et al., 1973; Hendee, 1974) were calling for management recognition that effective wildlife-based recreation management required action to address the multiple "satisfactions" and desired "experiences." In fact, research projects directed at understanding hunter and angler motivations represent some of the pioneering work conducted in the development of EFM (Brown et al., 1977; Driver and Knopf, 1975). Driver (1985) provided a cogent articulation of the need for wildlife management agencies to understand what they produce in terms of desired hunting experience opportunities and other outcomes for society and environment—a clear precursor to today's OFM specific to wildlife management.

Despite the intense focus and numerous EFM and "multiple-satisfactions" studies directed at fisheries and wildlife recreation, the state fish and wildlife agencies and the U.S. Fish and Wildlife Service (USFWS)—the agencies with lead responsibility for fish and wildlife management—have not embraced EFM or OFM. Compared to the USDA Forest Service, National Park Service, and state park programs, the wildlife agencies have seemed particularly reluctant to move towards OFM. In fact, despite more than 20 years of discussion most wildlife agencies appear somewhat reluctant to recognize "that the products of wildlife management are opportunities for use that depend on more than just the presence of wild animals" (Driver, 1985).

The History of Experienced Focus Studies of Wildlife-Based Recreation

Hunting

In 1974, Hendee and others argued that wildlife managers would be wise to recognize that hunters were not just seeking to harvest game but were, in fact, pursuing a variety of "satisfactions" or experiences from hunting. Early studies conducted in Colorado clearly demonstrated that deer hunters (Brown, Hautaluoma, & McPhail, 1977; Hautaluoma & Brown, 1978)) and elk hunters (Hautaluoma, Brown and Battle, 1982) could be meaningfully segmented by the experience opportunities they desired. Numerous similar studies have been conducted in several states during the past three decades for deer, moose, waterfowl, and small game hunters (e.g., Decker, Brown, and Gutierrez, 1980; Vaske, Fedler, and Graefe, 1986; Decker and Connelly, 1989; Hammitt, McDonald, and Patterson, 1990; Hazel, Langenau and Levine, 1990; Gigliotti, 2000; Hayslette, Armstrong, and Mirarchi, 2001; Fulton and Hundertmark, 2004; Schroeder, Fulton and Lawrence, 2006) but the use of EFM as a guiding framework to define and then manage for what is produced by wildlife agencies, as yet, has not been realized to any large extent.

Management of deer and elk in Colorado is an illustrative example. Although solid foundational research was accomplished in the 1970s, EFM as a guiding framework was not adopted by the Colorado Division of Wildlife (CDOW). In the early 1990s, CDOW was facing intense public concern with decreasing quality of deer hunting opportunities, urban populations of deer, overabundance of elk, and the rise of chronic wasting disease. An established EFM/OFM framework would have greatly assisted agency decision making and planning in the face of this challenging management environment. Instead decision making was reactive and dramatic changes in deer hunting season structure were made that had negative impacts on satisfaction and participation (Fulton & Manfredo, 2004).

Throughout the 1990s, researchers at Colorado State University (CSU) worked intensely with managers to encourage adoption of an OFM approach for managing deer and elk. Although CDOW embraced efforts to use social science research to inform and address management issues, the idea of a broader EFM planning and decision-framework as defined in to guide agency decision making as defined in Chapter 3 was not adopted by lead administrators. In the late 1990s, researchers at CSU worked closely with CDOW staff to develop and implement the initial steps of an EFM/OFM process to assess demand for elk hunting opportunities (Fix, Pierce, and Manfredo, 2001; Manfredo, Fix, Teel, Smeltzer, and Kahn, 2004). The findings from these studies aided the Colorado Division of Wildlife in updating its big-game hunting regulatory process, so EFM information has proven useful and has been incorporated into decision making at CDOW. However, despite its clear value in this process, it remains unclear whether EFM will be formally adopted to guide future management within CDOW (Manfredo et al., 2004).

Fishing

Research and application of EFM ideas to the management of fisheries has followed a similar history as EFM of hunting. Beginning in the 1970s (Driver and Knopf, 1976; Driver and Cooksey, 1977) management agencies were providing funds to researchers to identify the preferred experiences and psychological outcomes among anglers. By the mid-1980s research focused on identifying angling motivations and preferred site and management conditions was occurring in a variety of states (Ditton, 1985; Chipman and Helfrich, 1988; Falk, Graefe, and Ditton, 1989). Some states even appeared to be on the verge of adopting an EFM approach to guide classification of angling opportunities (Driver, 1985; Driver et al., 1984). But as with hunting, the lack of a commitment by lead administrators to support and promote application of EFM has apparently stymied large-scale implementation of the concepts within the fisheries management agencies.

Nevertheless, research essential to identifying the demand for different types of fishing opportunities has continued to be funded by an array of state management agencies through the present time (e.g., Anderson, Phillips, and Krehbiel, 1990; Holland and Ditton, 1992; Spencer, 1993; Siemer and Brown, 1994; Gigliotti, 1996; Fisher, 1997; Forbes, Gill, Schramm and Bray, 1998; Connelly, Knuth and Brown, 2001; Hunt and Ditton, 2001; Vlaming and Fulton, 2002; Schroeder, Fulton, Currie, and Goeman, 2006). Likewise, general social science research concerning fisheries management continues to be funded by state agencies, but as noted by Ditton (2004) it appears that this social science information is not routinely used in agency decision making. We appear to be stuck at a perpetual crossroads concerning the use of "human dimensions" research in fisheries management in general, and the adoption of EFM/OFM in particular. Agency decision makers seem to agree that it is needed, but the embrace of full-scale implementation has not occurred. Ditton (2004) suggests this sticking point might be occurring because fisheries managers are largely composed of trained biologists who are uncomfortable with social science research about user preferences and motivations.

Wildlife Viewing

Throughout most of the 20th Century, wildlife management agencies were but passive managers of wildlife viewing activities. Beginning in the 1970s, increasing attention was focused on the activity by the public and agencies. The National Survey on Hunting, Fishing, and Wildlife-Associated Recreation charted a steady increase in the activity through the 1970s and 1980s (1975, 1980, 1985, 1991). The first study to collect EFM information specifically on wildlife viewers, however, was Manfredo and Larson (1993). Since that time, several studies in North America and Europe have been conducted to understand the motivations and desired experiences of wildlife viewers (McFarlane, 1994; Scott, Baker and Kim, 1996; Cole and Scott, 1999; Hvenegaard, 2002; Scott and Thigpen, 2003; Scott et al., 2005).

Despite the relatively late start in conducting research to understand wildlife viewing experiences, the EFM/OFM approach gained considerable momentum for state and federal agencies for planning and managing wildlife viewing opportunities. Manfredo (2002) developed a handbook that provided a detailed description of the necessary research and management steps for applying EFM to wildlife viewing. A series of management workshops, organized and conducted with this handbook as a primary resource, targeted both agency decision-makers and managers and were well-received. Perhaps the lack of established management programs for wildlife viewing provides an opportunity to facilitate the adoption of EFM/OFM as a guiding framework (Pierce and Manfredo, 1997). However, as with hunting and fishing, formal adoption of the EFM/OFM for wildlife viewing has not occurred among any state agencies responsible for wildlife management.

Barriers to Implementation in Fish and Wildlife Management Agencies

Despite the considerable research attention focused on gathering information about the range of wildlife-based recreation experience opportunities desired by users, no fish and wildlife agencies have committed to an EFM or OFM type management framework. To some observers the lack of impetus to embrace frameworks committed to improving recreational experiences might be surprising. After all, the protection of wildlife for recreational use served as the primary impetus for creating wildlife management agencies, and license revenue and sales taxes collected from hunters and anglers has been the primary funding mechanism of state wildlife agencies in the North American Model. Why then, have fish and wildlife agencies not focused on producing recreational experiences?

Unlike national and state parks and forests, fish and wildlife management agencies have primarily focused on managing wildlife populations and their habitats, with recreational and other social uses seen as secondary to the primary mission of these agencies. The mission of the U.S. Fish and Wildlife Service is working with others to conserve, protect, and enhance fish and wildlife and their habitats for the continuing benefit of the American people. Staff expertise in the USFWS is almost exclusively focused on conserving, protecting, and enhancing wildlife and their habitats, and not on understanding and providing for human benefits.

Fish and wildlife agencies were created at a time of crises when game and fish populations had collapsed due to unregulated commercial use of the resources and poor land management that had devastated habitats. From this perspective, consumptive use of wildlife was viewed as an activity that must be tightly controlled. Instead of focusing on the broad array of motivations and desires of recreational hunters and anglers, management agencies focused on how to capture revenue to ensure management directed at protecting or building fish and game populations. Throughout the 20th century, fish and wildlife management agencies relied almost exclusively on professionals trained in the ecological sciences. Professional training in fish and wildlife management has emphasized the scientific management of wildlife populations and their habitat as resources, or supplies, that provide for recreational activities and are impacted by human recreational use. Provision of recreational activities is an important part of the mission of fish and wildlife agencies (e.g., National Wildlife

Refuge System Improvement Act of 1997 P.L. 105-57), but most fish and wildlife management agencies have not emphasized programs with professional staff directed at managing for recreational experiences. Although the agencies are providing hunting, fishing, and viewing opportunities, they generally do not define themselves as being engaged in recreation management.

Despite the previously reviewed research on experienced-based management of hunting, fishing, and wildlife viewing, the management models of hunting and fishing embraced by fish and wildlife management agencies largely do not consider experiential and motivational factors beyond harvest success (Enck et al., 2006). Thus, fish and wildlife agencies have not focused on managing for recreational outcomes per se, but rather the focus has been on managing populations of fish and wildlife. The assumption behind these management models is that large, healthy populations (or supplies) of fish and wildlife and access to these supplies will ensure quality recreation and continued participation in wildlife-based-recreation activities (Manfredo, 2002; Roggenbuck, 2000). Leopold, in his Conservation Esthetic (1966), suggested that outdoor recreation was the human reaction to or experience of nature and not the resource itself. He argued that the management of outdoor recreation was more than the provision of supplies or facilities, but one of managing for the human experience of nature. In practice, however, wildlife management has almost exclusively focused on the outcomes of wildlife populations and their habitats and not the experiences of people.

How Do We Overcome the Barriers?

Given the history and momentum of fisheries and wildlife management, fish and wildlife agencies seem much less likely than other recreation-oriented agencies to embrace a recreational model of management such OFM. We suggest two strategies for encouraging adoption of the OFM perspective among fish and wildlife management agencies. The first strategy is to encourage the adoption of OFM as a generalized management and planning process for agency decision making and not as a recreation management process. The second strategy is to provide professional training in OFM at mid-career wildlife professionals who will soon take on leadership roles in their respective agencies.

The leadership and most professional staff within fish and wildlife agencies have not been trained in recreation management, and most of them really do not perceive agency management activities as "recreation management." For this reason, they are highly unlikely to adopt the tenets of OFM if it is presented as a model of recreation management. OFM researchers and planners are more likely to have a meaningful impact on agency decision making if the OFM model is presented as a generalized model for agency decision making and planning. OFM can be quite readily integrated with planning and decision-making processes being used to by fish and wildlife agencies to manage fish and wildlife resources. For example, OFM as it as outlined in Chapter 2 and 3 appears to be very compatible with Adaptive Management, which is arguably the most influential model of decision making and planning currently embraced by fish and wildlife agencies (Walters, 1986; Lee, 1993; Williams, Szaro and Shapiro, 2007). Adaptive management is defined by the National Research Council (2004) as:

> ...flexible decision making that can be adjusted in the face of uncertainties as outcomes from management actions and other events become better understood. Careful monitoring of these outcomes both advances scientific understanding and helps adjust policies or operations as part of an iterative learning process. It is not a "trial and error" process, but rather emphasizes learning while doing. Adaptive management does not represent an end in itself, but rather a means to more effective decisions and enhanced benefits. Its true measure is in how well it helps meet environmental, social, and economic goals, increases scientific knowledge, and reduces tensions among stakeholders.

As defined by Williams et al. (2007), the operational steps for implementing adaptive management can easily accommodate the tenets of OFM (Table 24.1).

Recent critiques of Adaptive Management from within the wildlife profession (Enck et al., 2006; Riley et al., 2003) suggest the adaptive management process can be improved by ensuring that outcomes and objectives identified in the process are relevant to resource users and other stakeholders. These critiques of Adaptive Management, however, do not provide clear direction on how to manage for socially relevant outcomes. OFM provides a clearly defined process for doing so and could provide an important contribution in making Adaptive Management processes in fisheries and wildlife management more socially relevant. More generally, OFM can provide an important context for directing fisheries wildlife management to focus on identifying what it is

Set-up phase

Step 1 - Stakeholder involvement
Ensure stakeholder commitment to adaptively manage the enterprise for its duration

Step 2 - Objectives
Identify clear, measurable, and agreed-upon management objectives to guide decision making and evaluate management effectiveness over time

Step 3 - Management actions
Identify a set of potential management actions for decision making

Step 4 - Models
Identify models that characterize different ideas (hypotheses) about how the system works

Step 5 - Monitoring plans
Design and implement a monitoring plan to track resource status and other key resource attributes

Iterative phase

Step 6 - Decision making
Select management actions based on management objectives, resource conditions, and enhanced understanding

Step 7 - Follow-up monitoring
Use monitoring to track system responses to management actions

Step 8 - Assessment
Improve understanding of resource dynamics by comparing predicted vs. observed change in resource status

Step 9 - Iteration
Cycle back to Step 6 and, less frequently, to Step 1

Table 24.1 Adaptive Management Operational Steps (From Williams, Szaro, & Shapiro, 2007)

that fish and wildlife management agencies are trying to produce (Driver, 1985).

To illustrate how OFM researchers can work with wildlife managers to integrate EFM and OFM ideas and information into wildlife conservation planning, we present a case study at Sherburne National Wildlife Refuge. Researchers at the Minnesota Cooperative Fish & Wildlife Research Unit and the University of Minnesota worked closely with refuge personnel and region planning staff to collect and incorporate EBM and OFM information into the Sherburne NWR's Comprehensive Conservation Plan. This effort was conducted as part of a larger planning process and not as "recreation management plan" per se.

Essentially all of the managers and biologists in state and federal fish and wildlife agencies are professional fisheries or wildlife biologists. While academic programs and professional societies are requiring more social science training, most of the leaders and decision makers, while aware of human dimensions, have very limited training or expertise in the social aspects of recreation management or social aspects natural resources management in general. If OFM is to be embraced by the current and next generation of decision makers in fish and wildlife agencies, mid-career education and training efforts are essential. Without in-depth knowledge of OFM principles, these decision makers will not commit their agencies to make planning processes and management decisions based on OFM. Such training efforts must be of sufficient depth and breadth so that the OFM process and its advantages can be fully appreciated. Most of these professionals in fish and wildlife agencies will not have a working knowledge of recreation management or the social sciences, so the training efforts are particularly challenging and will likely be greeted with skepticism by many. To illustrate what such a training effort entails, we present a case study of a training program that was developed by Manfredo and his colleagues directed at encouraging EFM and OFM for wildlife viewing within state and federal agencies (Manfredo, 2002).

Overcoming the Barriers: Two Case Studies

Applying EFM and OFM to Comprehensive Conservation Planning in National Wildlife Refuges: A Study of Sherburne NWR

Background

The National Wildlife Refuge System administered by the U.S. Fish and Wildlife Service consists of more than 540 federal properties encompassing more than 93 million acres. Until 1997, this vast system did not have an "organic act" defining the mission or goals of the Refuge System as a whole. Unlike other federal lands, there also was no mandate for long-term planning on the refuges. The National Wildlife Refuge System Improvement Act of 1997 (P.L. 105-57) provided organic language and direction for the Refuge System and required each U.S. Fish and Wildlife Service National Wildlife Refuge to develop a Comprehensive Conservation Plan by 2012.

The CCP is a 15-year plan that outlines a management vision for each refuge, guides management decisions, and delineates goals, objectives, and strategies. The plan must also encompass recreational and public uses focusing on the following six wildlife recreational uses: wildlife observation, photography, education, interpretation, fishing, and hunting.

With the passage of the Refuge Improvement Act, USFWS refuge managers and regional refuge planning staff faced the daunting task of assembling plans for each Refuge. Planning staff from Region 3 USFWS expressed a desire to incorporate relevant social science information concerning visitors and local communities into the Comprehensive Conservation Plans within the region. The staff, however, also expressed concern that most of the professional planning staff in the USFWS were not trained in social planning processes or recreational management.

To facilitate identification of research needs in the CCP process, the Minnesota Cooperative Fish and Wildlife Research Unit, the Cooperative Park Studies Program, and the Department of Forest Resources held a workshop for USFWS professionals in February 2000 at the University of Minnesota Campus. One product of the workshop was a summary of emerging priority issues related to managing USFWS lands for recreational

Experience	Importance[1]				Attainment[2]				
	N	Mean	SD	R[3]	N	Mean	SD	R[3]	RD[4]
Experience nature	402	6.13	1.40	1	299	3.33	0.75	4	-3
See wildlife	421	6.07	1.38	2	315	2.97	0.88	20	-18
View scenic beauty	406	6.00	1.37	3	308	3.35	0.77	2	1
Enjoy smells and sounds of nature	406	5.94	1.37	4	299	3.34	0.77	3	1
Get away from the usual demands of life	402	5.65	1.6	5	269	3.29	0.81	5	0
Release tension, relieve stress	389	5.53	1.6	6	251	3.24	0.76	7	-1
Learn more about nature	388	5.48	1.50	7	263	2.76	0.82	27	-20
Enjoy a place that is special to me	399	5.43	1.6	8	250	3.22	0.80	8	0
Do something with my family	390	5.40	1.77	9	228	3.39	0.91	1	8
Get away from crowds of people	393	5.31	1.8	10	229	3.16	0.87	12	-2
Be with other people who enjoy same things I do	390	5.04	1.75	11	203	3.21	0.87	10	1
Experience excitement	385	5.04	1.60	12	226	3.02	0.84	18	-6
Experience new and different things	379	5.02	1.52	13	211	2.67	0.85	29	-16
Participate in activities that I otherwise wouldn't be able	377	4.98	1.6	14	172	3.12	0.86	15	-1
Think about personal and/or spiritual values	392	4.95	1.8	15	202	3.09	0.84	16	-1
Maintain physical fitness	388	4.94	1.7	16	193	2.85	0.86	23	-7
Help others (e.g., my children) develop values and ethics	380	4.90	1.9	17	173	2.84	0.94	25	-8
Be with friends	386	4.87	1.70	18	170	3.18	0.93	11	7
Get away from the noise back home	392	4.85	1.8	19	191	3.25	0.79	6	13
Experience solitude	387	4.84	1.8	20	198	2.97	0.89	19	1
Learn about the natural history of area	377	4.81	1.52	21	182	2.51	0.88	32	-11
Develop skills and abilities	390	4.78	1.75	22	197	2.83	0.69	26	-4
Be on my own	382	4.62	1.87	23	165	3.15	0.89	13	10
Feel a sense of pride in my heritage	383	4.61	1.8	24	148	2.86	0.80	22	2
Do something creative such as take photographs	385	4.52	1.6	25	158	2.59	1.08	30	-5
Use my equipment	383	4.49	1.79	26	159	3.12	0.87	14	12
Help others develop their skills	386	4.47	1.7	27	151	2.68	0.91	28	-1
Gain greater sense of independence or autonomy	367	4.38	1.71	28	123	2.93	0.79	21	7
Talk to new and varied people	380	4.32	1.64	29	136	2.55	0.97	31	-2
Do things my own way	377	4.31	1.70	30	133	3.08	0.84	17	13
Gain sense of self-confidence	372	4.29	1.69	31	130	2.84	0.81	24	7
Get away from family for a while	379	3.46	1.8	32	74	3.22	0.85	9	23

Source: Mail-back questionnaire, question 9.

[1] Responses based on a seven-point scale from 1 (very unimportant) to 7 (very important).
[2] Responses based on a four-point scale from 1 (did not attain) to 4 (totally attained).
[3] Rank order determined by mean value.
[4] Rank difference between importance and attainment means.

Table 24.2 Importance of experiences and attainment of those experiences by visitors at Sherburne National Wildlife Refuge

opportunities related to fish and wildlife (Fulton, Nelson, Anderson, & Lime, 2000). One of the priority issues identified at the workshop was the need to match refuge services and opportunities visitor motivations and expectations. As a result of the workshop, Sherburne NWR was selected as a place to conduct a visitor use study, where the study results would be directly applicable to the CCP process.

Sherburne NWR was established in 1965 to protect and restore the habitats for migratory birds and other wildlife in the St. Francis River Valley of central Minnesota. Federal Migratory Bird Hunting Stamp funds were used to purchase the land. Sherburne is 30,665 acres in size, consists mainly of oak savanna, prairie, and wetland habitat, and is situated in the east central region of Minnesota, approximately fifty miles northwest of the Minneapolis-St. Paul metropolitan area. The Refuge sits in a transition zone between two major ecosystems (deciduous hardwood forest and tallgrass prairie). Numerous recreational opportunities are available including observing wildlife, hiking on trails, hunting, boating, fishing, and participating in educational programs.

EFM Research at Sherburne NWR

The Comprehensive Conservation Planning process for Sherburne NWR was initiated in November 2000. This planning process was not an OFM process as described in Chapter 3, but was a generic comprehensive planning process sharing several similarities to the OFM planning process. Of key importance was the early inclusion of stakeholders. The process followed 8 basic steps described by the USFWS planning policy, including:

- Preplanning: Planning the Plan
- Initiate Public Involvement and Scoping
- Review Vision Statement and Goals and Determine Significant Issues
- Develop and Analyze Alternatives
- Prepare Draft Plan and NEPA Document
- Prepare and Adopt Final Plan
- Implement Plan, Monitor, and Evaluate
- Review and Revise Plan

Social science researchers affiliated with the U.S. Geological Survey and the University of Minnesota

Components	All respondents		Hunters		Nonhunters	
	N	Mean[1]	N	Mean[1]	N	Mean[1]
Providing habitat for wildlife	438	6.38	175	6.39	263	6.38
Ensuring the natural and undeveloped land will exist for future generations	431	6.30	169	6.24	262	6.34
Maintaining natural and undeveloped lands	435	6.18	172	6.04	263	6.27
Maintaining unique habitat	435	6.14	173	5.98	262	6.25
Maintaining diversity of native plants and animals	432	6.14	171	5.94	261	6.28
Experience a serene and healthy environment	431	6.06	170	5.94	261	6.14
Providing opportunities to view wildlife	435	6.04	173	5.94	262	6.11
Maintaining scenic beauty	433	6.02	172	5.91	261	6.09
Improving ecosystem health	429	6.00	172	5.91	258	6.13
Helping clean the air	430	6.00	171	5.92	259	6.04
Providing a place where all people are welcome	431	5.82	173	5.77	258	5.84
Providing educational and interpretive opportunities to learn about the natural area	430	5.80	169	5.59	261	5.93
Restoring the native landscape	430	5.65	172	5.30	258	5.88
Storing and purifying water	428	5.53	170	5.23	258	5.63
Providing a place for family and friends to come together	433	5.53	171	5.58	262	5.49
Being able to see my tax dollars being put to use	433	5.34	171	5.57	262	5.19
Providing diverse recreation opportunities	431	5.29	171	5.40	260	5.23
Providing flood control	426	5.28	170	5.23	256	5.32
Providing opportunities for photography	433	5.17	171	5.06	262	5.24
Preserving a part of our history	428	5.76	170	5.72	258	5.79
Providing hunting opportunities	434	4.74	174	6.19	260	3.78
Aiding the region's overall economy	428	4.69	169	4.79	259	4.62

Source: Mail-back questionnaire.

[1] Responses based on a seven-point scale from 1 (very unimportant) to 7 (very important).

Table 24.3 Importance of landscape and community components to visitors at Sherburne National Wildlife Refuge

were included as technical experts in the planning process and participated throughout process. As part of the CCP process, we designed and implemented a visitor survey to gather data on:

- visitor activities and experiences while visiting the Refuge;
- attainment of experiences;
- attachment to the Refuge;
- importance of benefits provided by the Refuge;
- perceptions of crowding at the Refuge;
- perceptions of visitor-caused problems and management actions to resolve problems;
- participation in environmental actions; and
- sociodemographic characteristics of visitors.

Although the overall CCP planning process was not a refined OFM process as described in Chapter 3, the information we collected was closely guided by previous work on EFM and OFM efforts (Payton, Fulton, Anderson, and Dougherty, 2003; Payton, Fulton, and Anderson, 2002). Our efforts focused on information that would allow Phase 2 of an OFM planning effort—the gathering and analyzing of supply and demand information to allow definition of market segments and preferences of visitors and local community members. A summary of the desired experiences and attainment of those experiences for visitors at Sherburne NWR was a key aspect of this information (Table 24.2), as were visitor ratings of importance of the social and environmental benefits or outcomes provided by the Refuge (Table 24.3).

This information was closely reviewed and incorporated into the Comprehensive Conservation Plan for Sherburne NWR (USFWS, 2005). The CCP has been finalized and two broad goals are identified that provide an important opportunity for more thoroughly implementing OFM within the management of the Refuge in the future. These goals are:

- Goal 5: Visitors enjoy wildlife-dependent opportunities that further an appreciation of Refuge wildlife and habitats (USFWS 2005).
- Goal 6: Visitors and local citizens demonstrate a strong conservation ethic that leads to support of the Refuge, conservation of the surrounding landscape, and global environmental awareness.

Each of these goals within the CCP identifies a strategy of conducting more research with visitors and community members to develop "step-down" plans for achieving these goals. Strategies under Goal 5 further specify the management of six recreational activities (hunting, fishing, wildlife observation, wildlife photography, environmental education, and interpretation) at the Refuge to achieve high quality experiences for visitors. While OFM is yet to be implemented at the Refuge, the CCP provides a framework for doing so and lead Refuge staff are supportive and promote the idea of OFM for accomplishing these two goals. We have worked closely with Refuge staff during the past year to continue research and planning efforts focused on managing for outcomes of recreational visitors as well as broader community outcomes. As the Refuge moves forward with developing step-down plans to address goals 5 and 6 of the CCP, it is clear that the tenets of OFM will strongly influence these plans. For visitor management, the Refuge has clearly moved beyond a simple philosophy of activity provision toward focusing on the outcomes of the recreational experiences of visitors. Perhaps more exciting, the Refuge is clearly interested in interacting with the local community and managing the Refuge to achieved desired community outcomes.

Lessons

While Sherburne NWR has yet to fully embrace OFM, to our knowledge Sherburne NWR is the first refuge in the National Wildlife Refuge System to move so far towards the tenets of OFM. In reviewing the case, we identified a few keys reasons why OFM has found a foothold at the Refuge. First, is the fact that several key USFWS personnel involved with the planning efforts at Sherburne NWR were favorably disposed to the ideas of OFM. One of the planners within the USFWS Region 3 Office had extensive academic training and experience in the U.S. Forest Service with the ideas of EFM. This individual proved insightful and influential in encouraging other Regional staff and Refuge staff to understand and embrace the ideas of OFM. The lead biologist at the Refuge also had extensive graduate level training in recreation management with a focus on EFM and OFM ideas. Her credibility with other biological staff, including the Refuge manager, and her own interest in OFM ensured that CCP planning efforts would include an OFM perspective for visitors and the community.

Second, we were persistent and patient in trying to encourage the adoption of OFM ideas within the process. The CCP process was going to occur with or without our participation. The process itself largely focused on the biophysical features of the Refuge and was not a "recreation planning" process. Our OFM ideas did not take center stage in the process, but we continued to participate and encourage an OFM perspective for planning and management to address visitor and community issues. The adoption of OFM has not occurred quickly, but we have continued to work closely with Regional and Refuge staff, on and off, for a 7-year period. We have volunteered time and effort and have looked for ways in which we can help Refuge staff. Because agencies such as the USFWS do not have a corps of recreation planners, much less a core staff focused on OFM, their adoption of OFM tenets will be slow and will require continued effort and involvement from those of use interested in OFM. These agencies will continue to primarily focus planning efforts on wildlife populations and their habitats, as was done during the Sherburne CCP process. We must adapt our interest in OFM to match these planning efforts and not expect to replace them with an OFM-focused planning process directed at recreation or community management.

Third, we made considerable effort in educating and training USFWS personnel about the ideas of EFM/OFM. With assistance from USGS, we worked closely with Regional staff to develop and host a training workshop with invited speakers focused on EFM/OFM and related ideas (Fulton et al., 2000). We made numerous presentations to planning staff and stakeholders in the CCP process about EFM/OFM. Without this background information, we do not believe EFM/OFM information would have been incorporated in the CCP process at Sherburne NWR. Although several other Refuges have collected information from the public during CCP planning efforts, these studies have not collected detailed information relevant to EFM/OFM. Because USFWS and other fish and wildlife agency personnel are largely trained in fisheries or wildlife ecology, concerted training efforts targeting agency planners and managers are important if we expect adoption of EFM/OFM with these agencies.

Wildlife Viewing: An Effort at Training Managers in Experienced-Based Management

Manfredo (2002) provides an example of the depth of training that might be required to encourage adoption of an EFM/OFM perspective among wildlife managers. Recognizing that developing professional planning and management tools for the rapidly growing wildlife viewing activity was essential, Manfredo (2002) developed a thorough management handbook for wildlife viewing based on the tenets of EBM. This text was intended to describe EFM/OFM approach, demonstrate how EFM/OFM provide direction for the many facets of the management planning process, and describe how biological management tools can be integrated with an EFM/OFM approach. The text provides a thorough review of the outcomes basis for management action and the process for identifying the experiences and outcomes that direct management output. Various chapters address issues such as organizing a planning process, developing a stakeholder involvement process, developing standards, choosing actions, economic considerations, and communication and marketing strategies (Manfredo, 2002).

The management handbook alone was a valuable resource that certainly informed some wildlife managers about EFM/OFM. The core authors of the text, however, also provided several in-depth training and education workshops throughout the country in 2002 through 2004. These workshops assured that a few hundred wildlife managers from federal, state, and local agencies as well as nongovernmental organizations were exposed to the ideas of EFM/OFM and how to implement them within the context of wildlife management. Such training is essential because most of the managers working to implement wildlife-based recreation programs within fish and wildlife agencies do not have extensive training in recreation management. As indicated in previous chapters of this text, encouraging adoption of EFM/OFM among agencies and entities who define their mission to be recreation provision is challenging. As noted by Manfredo (2002) encouraging the adoption of EFM/OFM among wildlife managers and decision makers who do not have a clear mission or philosophy of providing a service to people might require a dramatic shift in management philosophy or even personal paradigms of natural resources management. The initial step is describing this philosophy and articulating how it can be integrated into the established philosophy of wildlife and habitat protection.

While it is uncertain whether or not OFM efforts were initiated by state and federal agencies based on these workshops, it is clear that many of the managers attending the workshops embraced the ideas and are now poised with the knowledge and ability to advocate for and implement OFM programs focused on wildlife viewing within their agencies. Given that few managers had such knowledge prior to the workshops, this advancement in knowledge and education is a clear success. Ideas from the workshop will undoubtedly influence the planning and management efforts of these managers even if their agencies do not fully embrace OFM. While Driver and Bruns (Chapter 3) make it clear that success of OFM implementation is dependent upon support from agency leadership, such support in fish and wildlife agencies is likely to come incrementally as more and more professional staff become aware of and are trained in OFM. These staff will also have to develop strategies for incorporating OFM into existing agency decision-making frameworks such as adaptive management.

Future Directions

Fish and wildlife management agencies are principally focused on the management of fish and wildlife populations and their habitats. For this reason, professionals within these agencies are almost exclusively trained in the biophysical sciences. Few wildlife and fisheries managers have extensive training in recreation management or the social sciences. The management philosophy of these agencies and their primary disciplines (fisheries and wildlife ecology) are focused on a resource protection orientation with human service given secondary consideration. These orientations and philosophies are not likely to change in the near future. If OFM is to be adopted within these agencies, those of us encouraging its use need to adapt it to match the current orientations of the agencies. Converting the professionals within these agencies from a focus on wildlife protection to recreation service is an unlikely scenario. However, if OFM is presented as a system to address desired visitor and social community outcomes within the context of adaptive management or other similar management frameworks currently embraced by fish and wildlife agencies, then successful use of OFM principles can be obtained. Achieving this success will require patience and a concerted effort of OFM researchers and practitioners to work with and train managers and decision-makers within fish and wildlife agencies.

References

Anderson, D. A., Phillips, C., & Krehbiel, T. C. (1990). Wyoming angler attitudes and preferences: application of strategic choice modeling. University of Wyoming, Lararmie.

Brown, P. J., Hautaluoma, J. E., & McPhail, S. M. (1977). Colorado deer hunting experiences. *Transactions of the North American Wildlife and Natural Resources Conference, 42*, 216–225.

Chipman, B. D. & Helfrich, L. A. (1988). Recreational specialization and motivations of Virginia river anglers. *North American Journal of fisheries Management, 8*: 390–398.

Cole, J. S. & Scott, D. (1999). Segmenting partipants in wildlife watching: a comparison of casual wildlife watchers and serious birders. *Human Dimensions of Wildlife, 4*(4): 44–61.

Connelly, N. A., Knuth B. A., & Brown, T. L. (2001). An angler typology based on angler fishing preferences. *Transactions of the American Fisheries Society*, 130: 130–137.

Decker, D. J. & Connelly, N. A. (1989). Motivations for deer hunting: implications for antlerless deer harvest as a management tool. *Wildlife Society Bulletin, 17*, 455–463.

Decker, D. J., Brown, T. L., & Gutierrez, R. J. (1980). Further insights into the multiple-satisfactions approach for hunter management. *Wildlife Society Bulletin, 8*(4), 323–337.

Ditton, R. B. (1985). Understanding the diversity among recreational fishermen. In R. Stroud, (Ed.), *World angling resources and challenges.* (pp. 223–231) International Game Fish Association, Fort Lauderdale, FL.

Driver, B. L. (1985). Specifying what is produced by management of wildlife by public agencies. *Leisure Sciences, 7*, 281–295.

Driver, B. L. & Brown, P. J. (1975). The social and psychological determinants of recreational choice with implications for recreation resource planning. In *Assessing demand for outdoor recreation* (pp. 63–88). National Academy of Sciences.

Driver, B. L. & Cooksey, R. W. (1977). Preferred psychological outcomes of recreational fishing. In R. A. Branhard and T. D. Roelofs (Eds.), *Catch-and-release fishing as a management tool: A national sport fishing symposium.* (pp. 27–39). Humboldt State University, Arcata, CA.

Driver, B. L. & Knopf, R. C. (1976). Temporary escape: One product of sport fisheries management. *Fisheries, 1*(2), 21–29.

Driver, B. L., Phillips, C., Bergersen, E. P., & Harris, C. C. (1984). Using angler preference data in defining types of sport fisheries to manage. Transactions of the North American Wildlife and Natural Resources Conference, 49: 82–90.

Enck, J. W., Decker, D. J., Riley, S. J., Organ, J. F., Carpenter, L. H. & Siemer, W. F. (2006). Integrating ecological and human dimensions in adaptive management of wildlife-related impacts. *Wildlife Society Bulletin, 34*, 698–705.

Falk, J. M., Graefe, A. R., & Ditton, R. B. (1989). Patterns of participation and motivation among saltwater tournament anglers. *Fisheries, 10*(4): 10–17.

Fisher, M. R. (1997). Segmentation of the angler population by catch preference, participation, and experience: a management-oriented application of recreation specialization. *North American Journal of Fisheries Management, 17*: 1–10.

Fix, P. J., Pierce, C. L., & Manfredo, M. J. (2001). Estimating demand for deer and elk hunting in Colorado. Project report for the Colorado Division of Wildlife—Report Number 42. Human Dimensions in Natural Resources Unit, Colorado State University, Fort Collins.

Fulton, D. C. & Hundertmark, K. 2004. Assessing the impact of a selective harvest system on moose hunters. *Human Dimensions of Wildlife, 9*(1): 1–16.

Fulton, D. C. & Manfredo, M. J. (2004). Effects of regulatory changes on deer hunters' satisfaction and perceptions of constraints to hunting. *Human Dimensions of Wildlife 9 (1)*: 35-56.

Fulton, D. C., Nelson, K. C., Anderson, D. H., & Lime D. W., (Eds.), (2000). *Human Dimensions of Natural Resource Management: Emerging Issues and Practical Applications.* University of Minnesota, St. Paul.

Gigliotti, L. M. (1996). A good fishing spot. *South Dakota Conservation Digest, 63*(2): 2–5.;

Gigliotti, L. M. (2000). A classification scheme to better understand satisfaction of Black Hills deer hunters: The role of harvest success. *Human Dimensions of Wildlife, 5*(1), 32–51.

Hammitt, W. E., McDonald, C. D. & Patterson, M. E. (1990). Determinants of multiple satisfaction for deer hunting. *Wildlife Society Bulletin, 18*(3), 331–337.

Hautaluoma, J. & Brown, P. J. (1979). Attributes of the deer hunting experience: A cluster-analytic study. *Journal of Leisure Research, 10*(4), 271–287.

Hautaluoma, J. E., Brown, P. J. & Battle, N. L. (1982). Elk hunter consumer satisfaction patterns. *Forest and River Recreation: Research Update.* (Misc. Pub. 18). St. Paul: University of Minnesota Agricultural Experience Station.

Hayslette, S. E., Armstrong, J. B. & Mirarchi, R. E. (2001). Mourning dove hunting in Alabama: Motivations, satisfactions, and sociocultural influences. *Human Dimensions of Wildlife, 6*, 81–95.

Hazel, K. L., Langenau, Jr., E. E. & Levine, R. L. (1990). Dimensions of hunting satisfaction: Multiple-satisfactions of wild turkey hunting. *Leisure Sciences, 12*, 383–393.

Hendee, J. C. (1974). A multiple-satisfaction approach to game management. *Wildlife Society Bulletin, 2*(3), 104–113.

Hendee, J. C. & Schoenfeld, C. (Eds). (1973). Human dimensions in wildlife programs. Washington, D.C.: Wildlife Management Institute.

Holland, S. M. & Ditton, R. B. (1992). Fishing trip satisfaction: a typology of anglers. *North American Journal of Fisheries Management, 12*: 28–33.

Hunt, K. M. & Ditton, R. B. (2001). Perceived benefits of recreational fishing to Hispanic-American and Anglo anglers. *Human Dimensions of Wildlife, 6*, 49–66.

Hvenegaard, G. T. (2002). Birder specialization differences in conservation involvement, demographics, and motivations. *Human Dimension of Wildlife, 7*: 21–36.

Lee, K. N. (1993). *Compass and gyroscope: Integrating science and politics for the environment.* Island Press, Washington, D.C.

Leopold, A. (1966). *A Sand County almanac with essays on conservation from Round River.* Ballantine Books, New York.

Manfredo, M. (Ed.). (2002). *Wildlife viewing: A management handbook.* Corvallis, OR: Oregon State University Press.

Manfredo, M. J. & Larson, R. A. (1993). Managing for wildlife viewing recreation experiences: An application in Colorado. *Wildlife Society Bulletin 21*, 226–236.

Manfredo, M. J., Fix, P. J., Teel, T. L., Smeltzer, J., & Kahn, R. (2004). Assessing demand for big-game hunting opportunities: applying the multiple-satisfaction concept. *Wildlife Society Bulletin, 32*, 1147–1155.

McFarlane, B. L. (1994). Specialization and motivations of birdwatchers. *Wildlife Society Bulletin, 22*, 361–370.

Payton, M., Fulton, D. C., Anderson, d. H., & Dougherty, E. M. 2002. Sherburne NWR visitor use study. Minnesota. Minnesota Cooperative Fish & Wildlife Research Unit. Report to U.S. Fish and Wildlife Service. University of Minnesota, St. Paul.

Payton, M., Fulton, D. C., & Anderson, D. H. (2005). Influence of place attachment and trust on civic action: a study at Sherburne National Wildlife Refuge. *Society and Natural Resources, 18*, 511–528.

Pierce, C. L. & Manfredo, M. J. (1997). A profile of North American wildlife agencies' viewing programs. *Human Dimensions of Wildlife, 2*(3), 27–41.

Potter, D. R., Hendee, J. C., & Clark, R. N. (1973). Hunting satisfaction: game, guns, or nature? *Transactions of the North American Wildlife and Natural Resources Conference, 38*, 71–84.

Riley, S. R., Siemer, W. F., Decker, D. J., Carpenter, L. H., Organ, J. F., & Berchielli, L. T. (2003). Adaptive impact management: an integrative approach to wildlife management. *Human Dimensions of Wildlife, 8*, 81–95.

Roggenbuck, J. W. (2000). Facilitating high-quality visitor experiences at national wildlife refuges (Pp. 11–29). In D. C. Fulton, K. C. Nelson, D. H. Anderson, and D. W. Lime (Eds.), *Human dimensions of natural resource management: Emerging issues and practical applications.* University of Minnesota, St. Paul.

Schroeder, S. A., Fulton, D. C., Currie, L., & Goeman, T. (2006). He said, she said: Gender and angling specialization, motivations, ethics and behaviors. *Human Dimensions of Wildlife, 11,* 301–315.

Schroeder, S. A., Fulton, D. C., & Lawrence, J. S. (2006). Managing for preferred hunting experiences: a typology of Minnesota waterfowl hunters. *Wildlife Society Bulletin, 34,* 380–388.

Scott, D. & Thigpen, J. (2003). Understanding the birder as tourist: Segmenting visitors to the Texas Hummer/Bird Celebration. *Human Dimensions of Wildlife, 8*, 199–218.

Scott, D., Ditton, R. B., Eubanks, T. L., & Stoll, J. R. (2005). Measuring specialization among birders: utility of a self-classification measure. *Human Dimensions of Wildlife, 10*, 65–74.

Scott, D., Baker, S. M. & Kim, C. (1996). Motivation and commitment among participants in the Great Texas Birding Classic. *Human Dimensions of Wildlife, 4,* 50–67.

Siemer, W. F. & Brown, T. L. (1994). Motivations and satisfactions of Lake Ontario boating salmonid anglers. *Journal of Great Lakes Research, 20*: 457–470.

Spencer, P. D. (1993). Factors influencing satisfaction of anglers on Lake Miltona, Minnesota. *North American Journal of Fisheries Management, 13*: 201–209.

U.S. Department of Interior, Fish and Wildlife Service, and the U.S. Department of Commerce, Bureau of Census (2002). 2001 National survey of fishing, hunting and wildife associated recreation. Washington, D.C.: U.S. Government Printing Office. USFWS 1975, 1980, 1985, 1991.

U.S. Fish and Wildlife Service. (2005). Sherburne National Wildlife Refuge Comprehensive Conservation Plan.

Vaske, J. J., Fedler, A. J. & Graefe, A. R. (1986). Multiple determinants of satisfaction from a specific waterfowl hunting trip. *Leisure Sciences, 8*(2), 149-166.

Vlaming, J. & Fulton, D. C. (2003). Trout angling in southeast Minnesota: a study of trout anglers. Report submitted to Minnesota Department of Natural Resources.

Walters, C. J. (1986). *Adaptive management of renewable resources.* Caldwell, NJ: Blackburn Press.

Williams, B. K., Szaro, R. C. & Shapiro, C. D. (2007). *Adaptive management: The U.S. Department of the Interior Technical Guide Adaptive Management Working Group,* U.S. Department of the Interior, Washinton, D.C.

Chapter 25
An Evolving OFM and the Future

Perry J. Brown

The era of government and business in which we now find ourselves is one of a focus on outcomes and assessment of performance. Whether it is business, medicine, education, urban services, or natural resources, we want to know what we get from public and private investments and how people's lives might be made better through these investments. As explained in Chapter 1, 2, and 3 of this text, recreation scientists, managers, and planners have been preparing for this emphasis on outcomes for the last few decades. But, what are the challenges for OFM in the future? This chapter addresses a few of them after a brief review of the evolution of OFM.

Three Stages of Progress toward OFM

The first stage of the evolution of OFM occurred in the late 1960s and early 1970s. In 1968, Driver and Tocher (1970)[1] introduced us to a new way to look at recreation through a behavioral lens. They defined recreation as a type of human experience based on intrinsically rewarding voluntary engagements during nonobligated time. That definition was a radical departure from the prevailing sociological, historical, and philosophical perspectives about leisure and especially from the notion of recreation as just an activity, and it put emphasis on the outcomes of participation in activities. That paper was the beginning of a truly behavioral approach to outdoor recreation planning and management and helped lead leisure scientists to focus attention on recreation experiences and the recreation opportunities that facilitate such experiences. Then, Driver and Brown (1975) introduced both production and behavioral process explanations of recreation demand and engagement. Behaviorally, that paper introduced the concept of a hierarchy of recreation demands (described in Chapter 2 of this text) which emphasized purposeful demands not only for recreation activities, but also for outcomes defined as satisfying experiences and other benefits. Chapter 3 describes seminal works by many authors that promoted this behavioral interpretation of leisure behavior and describes recreation planning and management models that integrated that knowledge.

Much of the thought about leisure behavior in the 1970s and early 1980s concentrated on recreation experiences and their relevance to management. This led to the second stage of the evolution of OFM, during the 1980s, which reflected a shift toward experience-focused management (or EFM, as explained in detail in Chapter 2). To wit, a rapidly growing number of planners and managers began to understand and accept that recreationists purposefully seek (i.e., demand) satisfying experiences and that experience-focused planning and management can and should be practiced overtly. They recognized that they provide recreation experience opportunities and information about them and it is recreationists that actually produce satisfying experiences and related beneficial outcomes. Put simply, practitioners began to recognize that it is desired experiences that should drive how they manage recreation activity opportunities and attributes of settings to produce desired recreation experience opportunities. With those realizations, it was during the 1980s that the managerial paradigm shifted dramatically toward the experiential components of OFM.

The third and current stage of the evolution of OFM began in the mid- to late-1980s and reflected a focus on all of the benefits of recreation and not just the experiential benefits. Two significant outcomes of this attention were publication of *Benefits of Leisure* (Driver, Brown, and Peterson, 1991) and *The Benefits Catalogue* (Canadian Parks/Recreation Association, 1992).[2] Those two works documented and substantively expanded understanding of the science-based knowledge about the wide variety and pervasiveness of the benefits of leisure and gave the emerging OFM needed scientific credibility. Thereby, OFM was able to incorporate knowledge about all the benefits of leisure and not just knowledge about the experiential benefits on which EFM was based. Thus, from the late 1960s to the early 1990s, we had moved from an activity-focused paradigm, to an experience-focused paradigm, to OFM which incorporates and integrates activities, settings, experiences and other benefits as well as unwanted outcomes. As such, OFM articulates a robust paradigm built on concepts of behavioral and production processes that focuses on the end states that people and societies achieve through the production of recreation opportunities and from engagement in recreation, tourism, and other leisure pursuits. As OFM evolved, its name was changed several times and the label "OFM" is used in this text for the reasons given at the beginning of Chapter 1.

OFM Today

This text represents a culmination of work by many people who have researched, developed, and applied OFM in a variety of wildland and urban settings in four countries. The text exposes many avenues for future research, experimentation, and practical application from which we might learn how to be better stewards of recreation resources and better providers of recreation opportunities for people so their lives might be enhanced. It provides a rationale for investment in recreation and gives insight into how recreation policies might be adapted and changed to meet the needs of people, communities, states and provinces, and the nation.

Most fundamentally, OFM insists that it is desired and expected outcomes that should drive decisions about the planning and management for recreation resources, programs, and services. The ultimate demand is for benefits from recreation (and avoidance of disbenefits). If we know the outcomes we want to achieve, both individually and socially, we can provide opportunities for people to engage in recreation activities that have a high probability of delivering these outcomes. If we know, we can decide how we are going to deploy our resources of land, labor, and capital to provide opportunities that facilitate satisfying experiences and lead to the other benefits or outcomes that are desired. Alternatively, if we do not know what outcomes we desire to achieve, why would we invest in recreation? Would we simply want to take the chance that we might get something good? Or, might we want only what the manager wants or what one group of vocal users might want? The OFM model leads us along a path of listening to relevant voices (such as customer stakeholders), investigating what might be possible, making choices about what will be offered, being explicit about why it is offered, and then providing opportunities and information that allow people to produce the experiences they desire, as well as realize other benefits and avoid negative outcomes.

An Unfolding Future for OFM

One of the significant changes to affect recreation management and policy is the decidedly urban nature of the human population. This is not only true in the U.S., where over 80 percent of the population lives in urban places, but also it is true for the world, where over 50 percent of the population is urban. This places new responsibilities on municipal park and recreation departments and on wildland recreation providers as well. In addition, connections to the land, when they exist, are often quite different for these urban populations than they were for agrarian societies.

The proportion of people engaged in hunting and fishing is declining, the proportion of people in the U.S. visiting national parks is declining, sedentary leisure activities are ascending, and the challenging complexities of urban and ecological relations and the human dependency on healthy and clean environments are being recognized. Those who are engaged in identifying the outcomes of recreation have the responsibility to tease out how urban people define recreation resources (both at home and afar), what they perceive are the best uses and values of these resources, and what are acceptable and unacceptable means of managing these resources. Recreation practitioners will be called upon to participate in conservation education activities, advising educators about recreation and its value and helping them devise means for learning about these resources and their importance to people. They also will be challenged to work on issues of poverty, human health, and environmental degradation and identify how recreation might mitigate problems, especially in urban environments where so many people live. Others will be enmeshed in advising policy makers about the importance of these resources and how they might be managed. Overall, they will find themselves using the paradigm of OFM to characterize and justify what needs to be done and what they do in a world filled with urbanites.

The burgeoning urbanization of the world suggests an approach to OFM that is not readily inherent in the management perspectives that have dominated recreation management in the past. Drawing on the synthesis perspectives of anthropology and geography, social issues of indigenous rights and values, poverty, governance, and social justice will need to be more fully explored. This will lead to consideration of the relationship between recreation and phenomena such as human-wildlife conflicts, ecotourism, illegal harvesting and trade, co-management, recreation and human health, and the effects of recreation on the development of culture and human spirit. These issues likely are to be prominent in our future and will represent a new focus, a new theoretical underpinning, and a new set of inquires for OFM managers and researchers. The book, *Nature and the Human Spirit* (Driver et al., 1996) provides a glimpse into this emerging world, and OFM has the potential for helping us manage that glimpse.

Over the last 40 years many voices have been legitimized in public resource decision-making processes, and future recreation scientists and policymakers will need to attend to similar voices. From what was an elite/authoritarian system of decision making about the management and use of natural and municipal recreation resources, a far more pluralistic and democratic system has been forged, bringing a much more diverse set of ideas and actors into the arena, including many ethnic and local voices (Brown, 1995). This calls for recreation scientists and practitioners to continue to move past mere public input to develop means for active participation by the various interests to truly collaborative planning and management required by OFM.

Local voices in particular have been increasing our attention to issues of community and collaboration. They have done this because recreation is very much a local resource issue—things that people do and cherish daily and on vacation. As we have moved toward a more participatory democracy, especially at the local level, recreation scientists and practitioners have been called upon to develop effective means of local participation and to develop means of regional, national, and sometimes international participation in the face of strong local participation. They have been called upon to examine the various collaborative schemes that have been developing and to help determine when they are and when they are not effective. As we consider appropriate arrangements for governance of recreation, both urban and wildland, a rich field of inquiry is before us.

Along with urbanization and the enfranchisement of many people, economic development still remains an important issue for our time. Global, national, and regional competition drives much of our lives and many areas are scrambling to devise ways to better their economic position. Because OFM requires consideration of economic benefits and costs, it presents a model for recreation and tourism within an economic context for both rural and urban settings. In sum, by its focus on outcomes, many of which might be economic, OFM provides a model for considering economic futures and what one does in making recreation and tourism investments to reach those futures.

As with all life, we often become surprised at the way events unfold and we can seize opportunities if we are attentive. Warming of the earth is challenging our countries, societies, and resource management in ways not experienced before, and recreation and tourism are not immune from it. For current and future OFM practitioners, there will be plenty to investigate and understand. For example, many of our parks and protected areas are islands in the midst of buildings and roads or even larger landscapes that include towns and cities, multiple-use forests and grasslands, the headwaters of rivers, municipal watersheds, and other critical spaces. These protected areas will experience changes in plant and animal composition, hydrologic regimes, and pressures for alterative uses just as will the surrounding lands. While these changes are occurring, human populations surrounding them will be involved in dealing with air and water pollution, traffic congestion, rising temperatures, wildfire,s invasive species, attacks from bugs and pathogens, and urbanization. They will want to be involved and they will be perplexed about what is happening to these special places, especially the special recreation places that they know and value. Those working within an OFM framework are likely to be in the middle of helping societies understand how environments are changing and adapting to climate change that is occurring on a scale that has not been observed in modern times. They will be involved in identifying appropriate and acceptable responses to these changes and the many policies that will evolve so that we will be able to receive positive outcomes from recreation in changed environments, whether at home or in the backcountry.

Water and energy development will present particular challenges for the future of recreation in both municipal and wildland areas. Governments will press for changes in resource management as they confront changes in policy for water and energy use. That water and energy developers will need to consume more and more land to extract resources will be exacerbated by growing human populations and by climate change. We are currently seeing some of the effects of such developments regarding energy and water in several regions of the U.S. For example, exceptionally rapid energy developments are occurring in the Rocky Mountain states, where large landscapes are undergoing dramatic change and stimulating concern by increasingly vocal local residents about loss of previous amenities. Problems related to water shortages in the southwest and southeast are affecting local political decisions including those related to recreation and related amenities such as swimming pools and lawn watering. Understanding what is happening and how people and their governments are reacting to these types of changes will be a growing challenge. Understanding how we might mitigate some of the negative effects of change will be a challenge for recreation professionals and one should expect that the OFM framework, with its focus on outcomes, will help structure and enhance the rationality of those debates and discussions and the reasonableness and acceptability of the ensuing decisions.

To these big picture changes that are emerging and logically will continue to influence what we do in the future, we must acknowledge that there are many advantages of OFM that need to be more widely recognized and understood. For example, how might more managers be encouraged to adopt an OFM perspective? How might policymakers and legislators be encouraged to use such a framework in making investment decisions? What are the important values underlying the many benefits that we perceive from recreation and how are these values changing? What are the outcomes most important at various geographic scales and governance jurisdictions? What are the linkages between activities, settings, experiences, and specific benefits to both individuals and societies?

The foregoing are just a few of the issues and questions before us. We have been working to answer them, but we still lack firm answers. So, as we tackle big picture items of change in the world, we also need to tackle these more specific issues that are ongoing.

Conclusion

The chapters of this text have led us through an explanation of why OFM is needed, what it is, a description of how to apply and implement it, and lessons learned from many past and ongoing applications. We have seen how OFM has been applied in policy development and as a guide for planning and managing recreation resources, programs, and services and in related areas such as wildlife management, youth development, and health initiatives. Most importantly, this text presents the implementation piece which has been lacking in a readily available source. Hopefully, the text will be used to move recreation programming forward so that we truly do "optimize the beneficial outcomes of recreation" and thereby enhance the human condition as the world in which we live undergoes dramatic social and environmental change.

We have reached a time when full implementation of OFM is possible and desirable. It is time that we recognize that desired outcomes can and should drive our decisions about the recreation investments and opportunities that we offer people. The OFM paradigm is the result of an evolution following a radical shift from the activities approach to recreation, to an approach that focuses on people and their potential to create benefits for themselves and the society in which they live.

Literature Cited

Brown, P. J. (1995). Forestry Yesterday and Tomorrow: Institutional Assumptions and Responses. XIX William P. Thompson Memorial Lecture. Flagstaff, AZ: Northern Arizona University.

Canadian Parks/Recreation Association. (1997). *The Benefits Catalogue.* Gloucester, ON, Canada: Canadian Parks/Recreation Association.

Driver, B. L. & Brown, P. J. (1975). A Social-Psychological Definition of Recreation Demand, with Implications for Recreation Resource Planning. Appendix A in *Assessing Demand for Outdoor Recreation.* Washington, D.C.: National Academy of Sciences.

Driver, B. L., Brown, P. J., & Peterson, G. L. (1991). *Benefits of leisure.* State College, PA: Venture Publishing, Inc.

Driver, B. L., Dustin, D., Baltic, T., Elsner, G., Peterson, G. L. (1996). *Nature and the human spirit: Toward an expanded land management ethic.* State College, PA: Venture Publishing.

Driver, B. L. and Tocher, S. R. (1970). Toward a Behavioral Interpretation of Recreation Engagements, with Implications for Planning. B. L. Driver, (Ed.). Elements of Outdoor Recreation Planning. Ann Arbor, MI: University Microfilms.

Footnotes

1. First published in 1968 by University Microfilms International before it was republished in 1970 by the University of Michigan Press.
2. A considerably enlarged version of *The Benefits Catalogue* was published in 1997 by the Canadian Parks/Recreation Association.

Other Books by Venture Publishing, Inc.

21st Century Leisure: Current Issues, Second Edition
by Valeria J. Freysinger and John R. Kelly
The A•B•Cs of Behavior Change: Skills for Working With Behavior Problems in Nursing Homes
by Margaret D. Cohn, Michael A. Smyer, and Ann L. Horgas
Activity Experiences and Programming within Long-Term Care
by Ted Tedrick and Elaine R. Green
The Activity Gourmet
by Peggy Powers
Advanced Concepts for Geriatric Nursing Assistants
by Carolyn A. McDonald
Adventure Programming
edited by John C. Miles and Simon Priest
Assessment: The Cornerstone of Activity Programs
by Ruth Perschbacher
Behavior Modification in Therapeutic Recreation: An Introductory Manual
by John Datillo and William D. Murphy
Benefits of Leisure
edited by B.L. Driver, Perry J. Brown, and George L. Peterson
Benefits of Recreation Research Update
by Judy M. Sefton and W. Kerry Mummery
Beyond Baskets and Beads: Activities for Older Adults with Functional Impairments
by Mary Hart, Karen Primm, and Kathy Cranisky
Beyond Bingo: Innovative Programs for the New Senior
by Sal Arrigo, Jr., Ann Lewis, and Hank Mattimore
Beyond Bingo 2: More Innovative Programs for the New Senior
by Sal Arrigo, Jr.
Boredom Busters: Themed Special Events to Dazzle and Delight Your Group
by Annette C. Moore
Both Gains and Gaps: Feminist Perspectives on Women's Leisure
by Karla Henderson, M. Deborah Bialeschki, Susan M. Shaw, and Valeria J. Freysinger
Brain Fitness
by Suzanne Fitzsimmons
Client Assessment in Therapeutic Recreation Services
by Norma J. Stumbo
Client Outcomes in Therapeutic Recreation Services
by Norma J. Stumbo
Conceptual Foundations for Therapeutic Recreation
edited by David R. Austin, John Dattilo, and Bryan P. McCormick
Constraints to Leisure
edited by Edgar L. Jackson
Dementia Care Programming: An Identity-Focused Approach
by Rosemary Dunne
Dimensions of Choice: Qualitative Approaches to Parks, Recreation, Tourism, Sport, and Leisure Research, Second Edition
by Karla A. Henderson
Diversity and the Recreation Profession: Organizational Perspectives (Revised Edition)
edited by Maria T. Allison and Ingrid E. Schneider
Effective Management in Therapeutic Recreation Service, Second Edition
by Marcia Jean Carter and Gerald S. O'Morrow
Evaluating Leisure Services: Making Enlightened Decisions, Second Edition
by Karla A. Henderson and M. Deborah Bialeschki
Everything from A to Y: The Zest Is up to You! Older Adult Activities for Every Day of the Year
by Nancy R. Cheshire and Martha L. Kenney
The Evolution of Leisure: Historical and Philosophical Perspectives
by Thomas Goodale and Geoffrey Godbey
Experience Marketing: Strategies for the New Millennium
by Ellen L. O'Sullivan and Kathy J. Spangler
Facilitation Techniques in Therapeutic Recreation
by John Dattilo
File o' Fun: A Recreation Planner for Games & Activities, Third Edition
by Jane Harris Ericson and Diane Ruth Albright
Functional Interdisciplinary-Transdisciplinary Therapy (FITT) Manual
by Deborah M. Schott, Judy D. Burdett, Beverly J. Cook, Karren S. Ford, and Kathleen M. Orban
The Game and Play Leader's Handbook: Facilitating Fun and Positive Interaction, Revised Edition
by Bill Michaelis and John M. O'Connell
The Game Finder—A Leader's Guide to Great Activities
by Annette C. Moore
Getting People Involved in Life and Activities: Effective Motivating Techniques
by Jeanne Adams

Great Special Events and Activities
by Annie Morton, Angie Prosser, and Sue Spangler
Group Games & Activity Leadership
by Kenneth J. Bulik
Growing With Care: Using Greenery, Gardens, and Nature With Aging and Special Populations
by Betsy Kreidler
Hands On! Children's Activities for Fairs, Festivals, and Special Events
by Karen L. Ramey
Health Promotion for Mind, Body, and Spirit
by Suzanne Fitzsimmons and Linda L. Buettner
In Search of the Starfish: Creating a Caring Environment
by Mary Hart, Karen Primm, and Kathy Cranisky
Inclusion: Including People With Disabilities in Parks and Recreation Opportunities
by Lynn Anderson and Carla Brown Kress
Inclusive Leisure Services: Responding to the Rights of People with Disabilities, Second Edition
by John Dattilo
Innovations: A Recreation Therapy Approach to Restorative Programs
by Dawn R. De Vries and Julie M. Lake
Internships in Recreation and Leisure Services: A Practical Guide for Students, Fourth Edition
by Edward E. Seagle, Jr. and Ralph W. Smith
Interpretation of Cultural and Natural Resources, Second Edition
by Douglas M. Knudson, Ted T. Cable, and Larry Beck
Intervention Activities for At-Risk Youth
by Norma J. Stumbo
Introduction to Outdoor Recreation: Providing and Managing Resource Based Opportunities
by Roger L. Moore and B.L. Driver
Introduction to Recreation and Leisure Services, Eighth Edition
by Karla A. Henderson, M. Deborah Bialeschki, John L. Hemingway, Jan S. Hodges, Beth D. Kivel, and H. Douglas Sessoms
Introduction to Therapeutic Recreation: U.S. and Canadian Perspectives
by Kenneth Mobily and Lisa Ostiguy
Introduction to Writing Goals and Objectives: A Manual for Recreation Therapy Students and Entry-Level Professionals
by Suzanne Melcher
Leadership and Administration of Outdoor Pursuits, Third Edition
by James Blanchard, Michael Strong, and Phyllis Ford
Leadership in Leisure Services: Making a Difference, Third Edition
by Debra J. Jordan
Leisure and Leisure Services in the 21st Century: Toward Mid Century
by Geoffrey Godbey
The Leisure Diagnostic Battery Computer Software (CD)
by Peter A. Witt, Gary Ellis, and Mark A. Widmer
Leisure Education I: A Manual of Activities and Resources, Second Edition
by Norma J. Stumbo
Leisure Education II: More Activities and Resources, Second Edition
by Norma J. Stumbo
Leisure Education III: More Goal-Oriented Activities
by Norma J. Stumbo
Leisure Education IV: Activities for Individuals with Substance Addictions
by Norma J. Stumbo
Leisure Education Program Planning: A Systematic Approach, Third Edition
by John Dattilo
Leisure for Canadians
edited by Ron McCarville and Kelly MacKay
Leisure Education Specific Programs
by John Dattilo
Leisure Studies: Prospects for the Twenty-First Century
edited by Edgar L. Jackson and Thomas L. Burton
Leisure in Your Life: New Perspectives
by Geoffrey Godbey
The Lifestory Re-Play Circle: A Manual of Activities and Techniques
by Rosilyn Wilder
Making a Difference in Academic Life: A Handbook for Park, Recreation, and Tourism Educators and Graduate Students
edited by Dan Dustin and Tom Goodale
Marketing in Leisure and Tourism: Reaching New Heights
by Patricia Click Janes
The Melody Lingers On: A Complete Music Activities Program for Older Adults
by Bill Messenger
Models of Change in Municipal Parks and Recreation: A Book of Innovative Case Studies
edited by Mark E. Havitz
More Than a Game: A New Focus on Senior Activity Services
by Brenda Corbett
The Multiple Values of Wilderness
by H. Ken Cordell, John C. Bergstrom, and J.M. Bowker

Nature and the Human Spirit: Toward an Expanded Land Management Ethic
edited by B.L. Driver, Daniel Dustin, Tony Baltic, Gary Elsner, and George Peterson
The Organizational Basis of Leisure Participation: A Motivational Exploration
by Robert A. Stebbins
Outdoor Recreation for 21st Century America
by H. Ken Cordell
Outdoor Recreation Management: Theory and Application, Third Edition
by Alan Jubenville and Ben Twight
Parks for Life: Moving the Goal Posts, Changing the Rules, and Expanding the Field
by Will LaPage
The Pivotal Role of Leisure Education: Finding Personal Fulfillment in This Century
edited by Elie Cohen-Gewerc and Robert A. Stebbins
Planning and Organizing Group Activities in Social Recreation
by John V. Valentine
Planning Parks for People, Second Edition
by John Hultsman, Richard L. Cottrell, and Wendy Z. Hultsman
The Process of Recreation Programming Theory and Technique, Third Edition
by Patricia Farrell and Herberta M. Lundegren
Programming for Parks, Recreation, and Leisure Services: A Servant Leadership Approach, Second Edition
by Debra J. Jordan, Donald G. DeGraaf, and Kathy H. DeGraaf
Protocols for Recreation Therapy Programs
edited by Jill Kelland, along with the Recreation Therapy Staff at Alberta Hospital Edmonton
Puttin' on the Skits: Plays for Adults in Managed Care
by Jean Vetter
Quality Management: Applications for Therapeutic Recreation
edited by Bob Riley
A Recovery Workbook: The Road Back from Substance Abuse
by April K. Neal and Michael J. Taleff
Recreation and Leisure: Issues in an Era of Change, Third Edition
edited by Thomas Goodale and Peter A. Witt
Recreation and Youth Development
by Peter A. Witt and Linda L. Caldwell
Recreation Economic Decisions: Comparing Benefits and Costs, Second Edition
by John B. Loomis and Richard G. Walsh
Recreation for Older Adults: Individual and Group Activities
by Judith A. Elliott and Jerold E. Elliott
Recreation Program Planning Manual for Older Adults
by Karen Kindrachuk
Recreation Programming and Activities for Older Adults
by Jerold E. Elliott and Judith A. Sorg-Elliott
Reference Manual for Writing Rehabilitation Therapy Treatment Plans
by Penny Hogberg and Mary Johnson
Research in Therapeutic Recreation: Concepts and Methods
edited by Marjorie J. Malkin and Christine Z. Howe
Service Living: Building Community through Public Parks and Recreation
by Doug Wellman, Dan Dustin, Karla Henderson, and Roger Moore
Simple Expressions: Creative and Therapeutic Arts for the Elderly in Long-Term Care Facilities
by Vicki Parsons
A Social History of Leisure Since 1600
by Gary Cross
A Social Psychology of Leisure
by Roger C. Mannell and Douglas A. Kleiber
Special Events and Festivals: How to Organize, Plan, and Implement
by Angie Prosser and Ashli Rutledge
Stretch Your Mind and Body: Tai Chi as an Adaptive Activity
by Duane A. Crider and William R. Klinger
Survey Research and Analysis: Applications in Parks, Recreation, and Human Dimensions
by Jerry Vaske
Taking the Initiative: Activities to Enhance Effectiveness and Promote Fun
by J. P. Witman
Therapeutic Activity Intervention with the Elderly: Foundations and Practices
by Barbara A. Hawkins, Marti E. May, and Nancy Brattain Rogers
Therapeutic Recreation and the Nature of Disabilities
by Kenneth E. Mobily and Richard D. MacNeil
Therapeutic Recreation: Cases and Exercises, Second Edition
by Barbara C. Wilhite and M. Jean Keller
Therapeutic Recreation in Health Promotion and Rehabilitation
by John Shank and Catherine Coyle
Therapeutic Recreation in the Nursing Home
by Linda Buettner and Shelley L. Martin
Therapeutic Recreation Programming: Theory and Practice
by Charles Sylvester, Judith E. Voelkl, and Gary D. Ellis

Therapeutic Recreation Protocol for Treatment of Substance Addictions
by Rozanne W. Faulkner

The Therapeutic Recreation Stress Management Primer
by Cynthia Mascott

The Therapeutic Value of Creative Writing
by Paul M. Spicer

Tourism and Society: A Guide to Problems and Issues
by Robert W. Wyllie

Traditions: Improving Quality of Life in Caregiving
by Janelle Sellick

Trivia by the Dozen: Encouraging Interaction and Reminiscence in Managed Care
by Jean Vetter

Venture Publishing, Inc.
1999 Cato Avenue
State College, PA 16801
Phone: 814-234-4561
Fax: 814-234-1651